INTRODUCTION

AND ISSUES

To The Wandering Islands
and
Jody

4TH EDITION

INTRODUCTION TO
TOURISM
DIMENSIONS, AND ISSUES

Colin Michael Hall

Hospitality
Press

Copyright © Pearson Education Australia Pty Limited 2003

Pearson Education Australia
Unit 4, Level 2
14 Aquatic Drive
Frenchs Forest NSW 2086

www.pearsoned.com.au

First published 1991
Second edition 1995
Reprinted 1995, 1996 (twice) 1997, 1998
Third edition 1998
Fourth edition 2003

Publisher: Cath Godfrey
Senior Project Editor: Kathryn Fairfax
Editorial Coordinator: Marji Backer
Copy Editor: Ross Gilham
Proofreader: Tom Flanagan
Indexer: Gary Cousins
Cover and internal design by R.T.J. Klinkhamer
Cover photograph courtesy of Australian Tourist Commission
Typeset by Midland Typesetters, Maryborough, Vic.
Printed in Malaysia
1 2 3 4 5 07 06 05 04 03

National Library of Australia
Cataloguing-in-Publication data

Hall, Colin Michael, 1961–.
Introduction to tourism: dimensions, and issues

4th ed.
Includes index.
ISBN 1 86250 523 3.

1. Tourism – Australia. 2. Tourism – New Zealand. I. Title.

338. 479194047

An imprint of Pearson Education Australia.

CONTENTS

1 THE SCOPE OF TOURISM STUDIES   *1*

2 HISTORICAL DIMENSIONS OF TOURISM   *37*

LIST OF FIGURES

LIST OF TABLES

INTRODUCTION TO TOURISM

LIST OF COLOUR PLATES

TOURISM INSIGHTS ON THE WEB

CONTRIBUTORS

Jane Ali-Knight, School of Marketing, Curtin Business School, Perth, Western Australia

Thomas G. Bauer, Department of Hotel & Tourism Management, Hong Kong Polytechnic, Hong Kong

Christine Beddoe, ECPAT (End Child Prostitution, Pornography and Trafficking) Australia/Childwise, South Melbourne, Victoria

Brock Cambourne, CRC for Sustainable Tourism, University of Canberra, Australian Capital Territory

Neil Carr, School of Tourism and Leisure Management, University of Queensland, Ipswich, Queensland

Glen Croy, Department of Tourism, School of Business, University of Otago, Dunedin, New Zealand

Ross Gregory, International Marketing Manager, West Australian Tourism Commission, Perth, Western Australia

Bernadette McMenamin, National Director, ECPAT (End Child Prostitution, Pornography and Trafficking) Australia/Childwise, South Melbourne, Victoria

Richard Mitchell, Tourism, La Trobe University, Bundoora, Victoria

Jenny Nichol, Consultant, Perth, Western Australia

Mark Priddle, University of Canberra, Australian Capital Territory

Brent Ritchie, Tourism, University of Brighton, Brighton, England

Sue Russell, Impact Consultants, Dunedin, New Zealand

Kristy Rusher, Department of Tourism, School of Business, University of Otago, Dunedin, New Zealand

Reid Walker, Department of Tourism, School of Business, University of Otago, Dunedin, New Zealand

Heather Zeppel, Tourism Program, School of Business, James Cook University, Cairns, Queensland

PREFACE

This fourth edition of *Introduction to Tourism* represents a continued expansion and revision of the contents of the previous editions. The book has been substantially revised in terms of the events, developments, and literature of recent years, although some material as always has had to be left out for the sake of brevity. This new edition was just about to go into press when the events of the September 11 and the collapse of Ansett Australia happened. Fortunately, I have been able to include reference to some of the impacts of these events on tourism in Australia. However, the full implications of these momentous events will only really be able to be addressed while this is being read. I therefore encourage the reader to further examine these issues with the advantage of hindsight.

Some of the relevant Internet addresses for tourism resources are also provided. However, please note that website addresses do change over time—if in doubt then use your search engine. One of the advantages of referring to relevant websites is that it should become easier for students to access the most recent statistical and policy information of relevant tourism organisations. Nevertheless, readers should be aware that the provision of research information by tourism organisations on the Internet is somewhat sketchy, although it has undoubtedly improved in recent years, with some organisations—such as the Australian Tourist Commission, Department of Industry, Tourism and Resources, and the various state and territory tourism organisations—proving very worthwhile, while others provide little more than tourism promotional material.

As noted in the preface to the first edition, the rapid growth of tourism and tourism research makes it extremely difficult to cover all aspects of tourism development. However, *Introduction to Tourism* does attempt to draw together many of the contemporary issues and themes in Australian tourism in a manner which is hopefully understandable and useful to students of tourism, hospitality, leisure, recreation, geography, environmental studies, and resource management at a number of levels. One of the aspects of the book which may prove of interest to readers, particularly at the introductory undergraduate level, is the extent to which there are 'old' references in the text, that is, as one student said to me, 'before I started high school!' The reason is simple, I think it is important that we remain aware of some of the significant studies which have influenced our way of thinking about tourism research as well as also realising that, in many cases, there is 'nothing new under the sun' in terms of some of the key issues and debates which surround Australian tourism and the field of tourism studies in general. The field of tourism studies is often much more 'mature' than we are told!

Being an Australian currently living in New Zealand (Australia's seventh state—after all Dunedin is closer to Sydney than Perth) who has the opportunity to travel regularly to Australia each year for pleasure travel, Visiting Friends and Relations (VFR), and research, also provides for an interesting perspective on some of the issues which face Australian tourism. It is hoped that this sense of 'passionate detachment' provides a viewpoint which is both considered as well as challenging at times for the reader. I have found it remarkable that some issues—such as coordination, labourforce concerns, the perceived impacts of tourism, boosterism, and the use of events, never seem to go away. Other areas, such as the development of food and wine tourism, seem to grow in their importance. Yet some issues, such as the interrelationship of industry and government, or the associated issue of tourism research and scholarship in Australia and its relationship to government and industry funding, hardly ever seems to be addressed.

I am most grateful to my students and various colleagues over the years for the opportunity to test material from the book in the form of lectures, external teaching materials, tutorials, seminars, discussions, diatribes and polemics, and to be able to receive their comments and criticisms. In particular I would like to thank Carmen Aitken, Sue Beeton, Stephen Boyd, Dimitrios Buhalis, Bill Bramwell, Dick Butler, Brock Cambourne, Neil Carr, Cate Clark, Chris Cooper, Nicola Costley, Dave Crag, Jenny Craik, David Duval, Ross Dowling, Ian Dutton, Mel Elliott, Thor Flognfeldt, Derek Hall, Sandra Haywood, Cass Higham, Tom Hinch, John Jenkins, Brian King, Bernard Lane, Neil Leiper, Alan Lew, Jim Macbeth, Niki Macionis, Simon McArthur, Richard Mitchell, Dieter Müller, Stephen Page, John Pigram, Chris Ryan, Isabelle Sebastian, John Selwood, Dallen Timothy, Lesley Tipping, Geoff Wall, Jim Walmsley, Betty Weiler, Josette Wells, Allan Williams, and Heather Zeppel, who have all contributed in various ways to some of the ideas contained within, although the interpretation of their thoughts is, of course, my own.

In this particular volume a number of colleagues have contributed material for the book and the website for which I am extremely grateful. I would also like to acknowledge the coauthorship of Glen Croy and Reid Walker for sections of Chapter 4 from recent research that we have been undertaking. The formative contribution of the Universities of Canberra, South Australia, and Tasmania, and Southern Cross University to my attitudes towards tourism education and research in Australia must also be acknowledged, and, in particular, I must acknowledge Don McNicol former Vice Chancellor of the University of Tasmania who was especially encouraging.

I would like to thank Ron Harper, who supported this project initially, and all at Pearson Education Australia for their continued help and support particularly when the manuscript for the fourth edition was unfortunately delayed. The assistance of Mel Elliott in producing the final manuscript is also gratefully acknowledged as is the assistance of all colleagues in the Department of Tourism at the University of Otago. Gavin Bryars, Jeff Buckley, Nick Cave, Bruce Cockburn, Elvis Costello, Stephen Cummings, Ebba Fosberg, Indigo Girls, This Mortal Coil, The Sundays, Ed Kuepper, Neil and Tim Finn, David Sylvian and Sarah McLachlan also helped ensure that the book was completed. Jody provided much appreciated moral support which, as usual, cannot be adequately repaid though I will try. Finally, I would like to thank all my friends in various parts of Australia, New Zealand, and the rest of this ever-smaller world for their continued support; and acknowledge the interest of those colleagues who recommend this book and those that read it.

March 2002

LIST OF ABBREVIATIONS

AHA	Australian Hotels Association
ANTA	Australian National Travel Association
APEC	Asia–Pacific Economic Cooperation
ASCOT	Australian Standing Committee on Tourism
ATC	Australian Tourism Commission
ATIA	Australian Tourism Industry Association
ATSIC	Aboriginal and Torres Strait Islander Commission
BIE	Bureau of Industry Economics
BTR	Bureau of Tourism Research
CER	Closer Economic Relations
CONCOM	Council of Nature Conservation Ministers
CVTC	Country Victoria Tourism Council
DASETT	Department of the Arts, Sport, Entertainment, Tourism and Territories
DIMA	Department of Immigration and Multicultural Affairs
DIST	Department of Industry, Science and Tourism
DITR	Department of Industry, Tourism and Resources
DOT	Department of Tourism
DSRT	Department of Sport, Recreation and Tourism
DTM	Domestic Tourism Monitor
ECPAT	End Child Prostitution, Pornography and Trafficking
ESD	Ecologically Sustainable Development
IAC	Industries Assistance Commission
IC	Industries Commission
IVS	International Visitor Survey
MICE	Meetings, Incentives, Conventions and Exhibitions
NCDC	National Capital Development Committee
NPPAC	National Parks and Primitive Areas Council
NTITC	National Tourism Industry Training Committee
NTP	National Tourism Plan
NTTC	Northern Territory Tourism Commission
NVS	National Visitor Survey
NZTB	New Zealand Tourism Board
ONT	Office of National Tourism
QTTC	Queensland Tourist and Travel Corporation
SATC	South Australian Tourism Commission

SWOT	Strengths, Weaknesses, Opportunities and Threats
TCA	Tourism Council Australia
TFC	Tourism Forecasting Council
TMC	Tourism Ministers' Council
TNSW	Tourism New South Wales
TQ	Tourism Queensland
TSA	Tourism Satellite Account
TTA	Tourism Training Australia
TTF	Tourism Task Force
VFR	Visiting Friends or Relatives
VTC	Victorian Tourism Commission
WATC	West Australian Tourism Commission
WCED	World Commission of Environment and Development
WCS	World Conservation Strategy
WTO	World Tourism Organization
WTTC	World Travel and Tourism Council

THE SCOPE
OF TOURISM
STUDIES

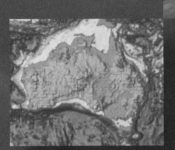

1

Twenty-five to thirty years ago, even, the idea that Australia's hospitality and tourism industries would occupy the role they do in the Australian way of life and the Australian economy and the hopes that we have for the future of our country, would have been completely undreamt of. Indeed, the idea of Australians being specialists at hospitality and recreation is something that somehow or other people twenty-five to thirty years ago didn't imagine (The Prime Minister, John Howard, Address at the Tourism Council Australia Lunch, Regent Hotel, Sydney, 29 August 1997).

Tourism is impervious to recession, natural disaster, war and politics (Moynahan 1985, p. 266).

TOURISM is now widely regarded as one of the cornerstones of the Australian economy. Since the early 1980s there has been an enormous expansion in the number of international visitors coming to Australia and an increased recognition of the significance of tourism for improvement in the balance of payments. Tourism is also seen as one of the key mechanisms for economic development and for the generation of employment. However, there has also been disquiet at the rapid pace at which tourism has grown in many destination areas. Concerns have been expressed at the environmental impacts of tourism, particularly in coastal areas, and the potential social effects of tourism. The emergence of tourism as an item of importance on the political agenda, particularly in the aftermath of the terrorist attacks on New York and Washington DC and their effects on the international aviation and tourism industries, has meant that increasing numbers of people are looking for an informed debate on tourism issues.

TOURISM INSIGHT

DEPARTMENT OF INDUSTRY, TOURISM AND RESOURCES (DITR) TOURISM PROFILE, FEBRUARY 2002

- Tourism directly accounted for 4.5% of expenditure of gross domestic product (GDP) in 1997/98.

- In 1997/98, tourism was directly responsible for employing 512 900 people, or 6% of total employment.

- In 1997/98, international tourists to Australia consumed $12.8 billion worth of goods and services. This represents 11.2% of total export earnings.

- In 2001 there were 4.8 million international visitors to Australia.

- In 2000/01 Australian residents spent a total of 292 million nights away from home and took 153 million day trips, resulting in $5.1 billion being spent on domestic tourism.

DITR (2002a)

The purpose of this book is to provide a critical introduction to tourism in an Australian context. However, it is impossible for any text to cover adequately all aspects of such a dynamic industry as tourism. Rather, the book utilises a thematic presentation which, while giving students an appreciation of the tourism industry, also illustrates the central concerns that surround tourism development and management in Australia.

Each chapter discusses a component of tourism and the issues that have emerged in tourism development within the framework of sustainable tourism. In this manner it is intended that the reader will be made aware of the current state of tourism and will also be in a position to assess potential future options and directions critically. However, before analysing the various components of tourism we will discuss some of the key concepts in the tourism field.

THE FIELD OF TOURISM STUDIES

There are few human activities which can simultaneously attract academic attention from economists, geographers, environmental scientists, psychologists, sociologists, and political and management researchers. Tourism is one (Bull 1991, p. xiii).

Tourism studies, 'like its customers who do not recognize geographical boundaries, does not recognize disciplinary demarcations' (Jafari & Ritchie 1981, p. 22).

The study of tourism is a multifaceted area of research and scholarship (Mowforth & Munt 1998; Meethan 2001). Tribe (1997, p. 638), for example, described tourism analysis as interdisciplinary, multidisciplinary, and 'conscious of its youthfulness'. The predominant attitude among many tourism researchers was perhaps best summed up by Bodewes (1981, p. 37), who argued that 'tourism is usually viewed as an application of established disciplines, because it does not possess sufficient doctrine to be classified as a full-fledged academic discipline'. Tribe (1997) even suggested that the search for tourism as a discipline should be abandoned, and that the diversity of the field should be celebrated. Therefore, students often undertake courses on the economics of tourism, the marketing of tourism, or the geography of tourism, which reflect such a disciplinary approach. However, the growth of bodies such as the International Academy for the Study of Tourism and the Tourism and Travel Research Association, and the proliferation of numerous academic journals, both general in their scope, (for example, *Annals of Tourism Research, Journal of Travel Research, Tourism Management* and *Current Issues in Tourism*), and more specific (for example, the *Journal of Sustainable Tourism, Journal of Travel and Tourism Marketing, Tourism Geographies, Tourism Economics* and *Journal of Ecotourism*) suggest that tourism is becoming recognised as a legitimate area of study in its own right (Ryan 1997), and that it possesses many of the characteristics of a discipline. These include:

- a well established presence in universities and colleges, including the appointment of professorial positions;
- formal institutional structures of academic associations and university departments; and
- avenues for academic publication, in terms of books and journals.

Indeed, as Johnston (1991, p. 2) has observed:

> It is the advancement of knowledge—through the conduct of fundamental research and the publication of its original findings—which identifies an academic discipline; the nature of its teaching follows from the nature of its research.

Nevertheless, Meethan (2001, p. 2) urged a cautionary note when he suggested: 'Yet for all the evident expansion of journals, books and conferences specifically devoted to tourism, at a general analytical level it remains under-theorised, eclectic and disparate'.

For much of the 1980s and 1990s Australian tourism research generally lagged behind that of the rest of the world. As Hall and Jenkins (1989, p. 122) reported in a review of one of the first Australian tourism research conferences: 'despite the economic significance of the industry and its potential environmental and social ramifications, Australian tourism . . . may be broadly characterised as sparse and fragmented'. However, the rapid development of tertiary tourism courses since 1989, and government recognition of research as a source of competitive advantage, have meant that greater attention is now being given to tourism research than ever before (Faulkner et al. 1994) even if the value of academic research is not always readily acknowledged by the tourism industry (Ryan 2001).

Tourism, leisure and recreation

One of the main themes in tourism research is the relationship of tourism to recreation and leisure studies (Ryan 1991; Williams 1998; Pigram & Jenkins 1999; Hall & Page 2002). For instance, Bodewes (1981) saw tourism as a phenomenon of recreation, and D.G. Pearce (1987, p. 1) noted the 'growing recognition that tourism constitutes one end of a broad leisure spectrum'. Williams (1998, p. 4) has wisely commented that 'in approaching the study of tourism . . . we need to understand that the relationships between leisure, recreation and tourism are much closer than the disparate manner in which they are treated in textbooks might suggest'. Historically, research in outdoor recreation has developed independently of tourism research. As Crompton and Richardson noted (1986, p. 38): 'Traditionally, tourism has been regarded as a commercial economic phenomenon rooted in the private domain. In contrast, recreation and parks has been viewed as a social and resource concern rooted in the public domain.' Outdoor recreation studies have tended to focus on public-sector (that is, community and land management agencies) concerns, such as wilderness management, social carrying capacity, and non-market valuation of recreation experiences. In contrast, tourism has tended to have a more 'applied orientation' which concentrates on traditional private-sector (that is, tourism industry) concerns, such as the economic impacts of travel expenditures, travel patterns and tourist demands, and advertising and marketing (Harris, McLaughlin & Ham 1987). Nevertheless, although the division between public and private activities might have held relatively true from the end of the post-war period through to the early 1980s, in recent years the division between public and private sector activities has been substantially eroded in Western countries including Australia (Hall & Jenkins 1995).

The distinction between tourism and recreation can therefore be regarded as one of degree. Tourism primarily relates to leisure and business travel activities which centre around visitors to a particular destination, and which typically involve an infusion of new money from the visitor into the regional economy. According to Helber (1988, p. 20): 'In this sense, tourism can be viewed as a primary industry which, through visitor spending, increases job opportunities and tax revenues, and enhances the community's overall economic base'. On the other hand, recreation refers to leisure activities which are undertaken by the residents of an immediate region, and their spending patterns involve 'a recycling of money within the community associated with day, overnight and extended-stay recreation trips' (Helber 1988, pp. 20–1).

Natural settings and outdoor recreation opportunities are clearly a major component of tourism (Cater & Lowman 1994; Ceballos-Lacuarain 1996; Lindberg & McKercher 1997), perhaps especially so in Australia where much of the international appeal is based on images of such attractions as the Great Barrier Reef, Kakadu National Park, Uluru (Ayers Rock), the Blue Mountains, the rainforests of Eastern Australia and the 'outback'. Indeed, outdoor recreation and tourist resources should be seen as complementary leisure experiences (Fedler 1987; Williams 1998; Pigram & Jenkins 1999; Hall & Page 2002). Nevertheless, whereas authors such as Pigram (1985, p. 184) have taken the view that 'tourism is carried on within an essentially recreational framework', others, such as Murphy (1985) have conceptualised recreation as one component of tourism. However, the demarcation line between recreation and tourism is rapidly becoming 'fuzzy and overlap is now the norm' (Crompton & Richardson 1986, p. 38). As Pigram (1985, p. 184) argued:

> Little success has been afforded to those attempting to differentiate between recreation and tourism and such distinctions appear founded on the assumption that outdoor recreation appeals to the rugged, self-reliant element in the population, whereas tourism caters more overtly for those seeking diversion without too much discomfort.

According to Moore et al. (1995, p. 74) there are common strands in the 'relationships between the various motivating factors applicable to both leisure and tourism; and as Leiper (1990a) argued, tourism represents a valued category of leisure, in which there is a degree of commonality between the factors motivating both tourist and recreational activities and many of the needs, such as relaxation, can equally be fulfilled in a recreational or tourism context. Although there is some merit in Leiper's approach, grouping leisure into one amorphous category assumes that there are no undifferentiated attributes that distinguish tourism from leisure (Hall & Page 2002). As Pigram and Jenkins (1999, p. 19) have confirmed, 'the term recreation demand is generally equated with an individual(s) preferences or desires, whether or not the individual has the economic and other resources necessary for their satisfaction'. In addition, many of the theoretical concepts in leisure and recreation studies are readily utilised by tourism researchers in their own studies (Ryan 1991; Williams 1998; Hall & Page 2002). Some of the various dimensions of the relationships among leisure, recreation and tourism are noted in Figure 1.1.

Tourism can therefore be interpreted as but one of a range of choices or styles of recreation expressed either through travel or a temporary short-term change of residence. Tourism is thus one dimension of temporary mobility and circulation (Bell & Ward 2000; Urry 2000; Williams & Hall 2000). Definitions of tourism are examined below. However, the merging of aspects of leisure, recreation and tourism research, along with the study of migration (Williams & Hall 2000; Williams et al. 2000; Hall & Williams 2002), circulation and mobility (Urry 2000), has had a profound influence on the manner in which tourism studies are perceived as an area of academic interest. Indeed, it is only recently that temporary movements away from home—such as tourism, but also including activities such as travel for work or education, or travel for health reasons, or even going overseas after finishing university—have begun to catch the awareness of demographers and those interested in

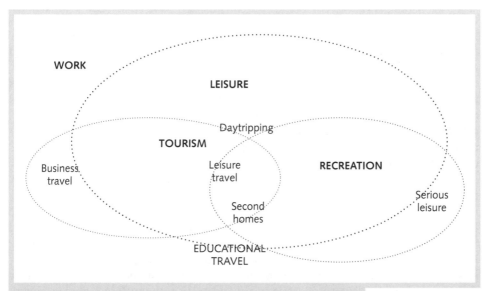

Figure 1.1 Relationships between leisure, recreation, and tourism

migration (Bell & Ward 2000; Bell 2001). Yet such an approach is significant because it recognises tourism as just one form of temporary mobility in a world in which mobility of people is becoming increasingly the norm.

In contrast to a multidisciplinary approach to tourism which combines elements of different disciplines such as economics, geography, and marketing (to name just a few of the potential contributory areas), Australian writers such as Leiper (1979, 1981) and Stear (1981) have argued for the creation of a new discipline of tourism studies. Indeed, Leiper (1981, p. 32) went so far as to claim that a multidisciplinary base is an impediment to tourism education, and argued that 'while different disciplines will always have specialized contributions to make to the study of tourism, a need exists for a different approach to form the central ground'. Leiper thus believed that an interdisciplinary approach is required for the study of tourism. An interdisciplinary approach integrates concepts and ideas from different disciplines or fields within the one approach. Similarly, Jafari (1977, p. 8) believed the interdisciplinary approach to be 'more expedient, productive and meaningful'. Such concerns are not solely academic, because an understanding of the underlying approaches and consequent methods used by researchers and analysts is crucial to the modern-day tourism industry.

According to Jafari and Ritchie (1981, p. 29), 'In contrast to most disciplines where teaching and research are intimately related, tourism education and tourism research appear to have developed, and be developing, largely independent of each other'. Although they were writing of the North American situation, their observations generally apply equally well to Australia where tourism research in the private and government sectors has lagged substantially behind the rapid development of tourism in the tertiary education sector (Faulkner et al. 1994). Unless students have the opportunity to benefit from current developments in tourism research and have the results of such research passed onto them, the development of an innovative, responsive and aware tourism industry will be in doubt. As Jafari and Ritchie (1981, p. 29) noted: 'Those institutions which recognize this fact and move to correct it will attract the best professors and the best students. Those that do not will be perpetually viewed as second class vocational diploma mills'.

In the 1970s, Buck (1978) identified two major emphases in tourism studies—the business development emphasis and the impacts–externalities emphasis—and noted that there was a need to unite these two streams into a theoretical synthesis. Thirty years later such a split still exists although, arguably, the split now involves not only the fields of business and impact studies but also cultural studies and social theory, which have shown a strong interest in tourism and travel (Crouch 1999a, 1999b; Meethan 2001), although the language and approaches of these social disciplines are often unintelligible and irrelevant to those in the business tradition or those undertaking applied research (Hall & Page 2002).

Within Australia, and overseas, the economic, environmental, social, and political significance of the tourism industry requires due recognition from government, industry, and researchers alike. In addition, it must be demonstrated that there is no room for academic prejudice against industrial issues. Although the phrase 'tourism is an industry', has almost acquired the status of religious dogma among industry representatives and some academics (Leiper 1983, p. 279), it is nevertheless vital that students of tourism critically examine tourism issues. It is hoped that the present book will go some way towards presenting the different perceptions of tourism studies in a manner that is relevant to the development of tourism.

DEFINITIONS OF KEY CONCEPTS
IN TOURISM STUDIES

An understanding of the various definitions of tourism is very important at both a practical and a theoretical level. At a practical level it enables us to gain a better understanding of the myriad sources of tourism data and information, and at a theoretical level it illustrates the broad dimensions and character of tourism and the degree of legitimacy that tourism studies has achieved. Burkart and Medlik (1981) traced the historical development of the term 'tourism', and noted the endeavours of researchers to differentiate between the concept and the technical definitions of tourism. In the view of Burkat and Medlik (1981, p. 41), the concept of tourism refers to the 'broad notional framework, which identifies the essential characteristics, and which distinguishes tourism from the similar, often related, but different phenomena'. In contrast, technical definitions have evolved through time as researchers have modified and developed appropriate measures for statistical, legislative and operational reasons, implying that there might be various technical definitions to meet particular purposes (Hall & Page 2002).

The many perceptions of what constitutes tourism are reflected in the multitude of definitions of tourism. Leiper's (1979) classification of definitions of tourism as 'economic', 'technical' or 'holistic' went some way towards clarifying the nature of the concept. However, as S. Smith (1988) correctly observed, Leiper's goal of a single, comprehensive and widely accepted definition of tourism appears beyond hope of realisation. Nevertheless, students of tourism would be wise to heed S. Smith's remark that 'practitioners must learn to accept the myriad of definitions and to understand and respect the reasons for those differences' (1988, p. 180).

The Australian House of Representatives Select Committee on Tourism (1987, p. 3) observed that the problem of definition is 'not just a statistical problem, but one which reflected the high degree of fragmentation that exists in the industry and the diversity of the prime interests of the components of the industry'. Similarly, S. Smith (1988, p. 181) noted that:

> . . . there are many different legitimate definitions of tourism that serve many different, legitimate needs; that existing definitions are inadequate as definitions of tourism as an industry; and that the lack of an adequate industrial definition has had regrettable consequences for tourism.

One of the most frustrating things for a student undertaking a tourism course is that almost every text provides a different definition of tourism. This is not necessarily because authors are trying to be difficult and confuse the student, although some students might suspect that this is indeed the case! Rather, each author is trying to be specific about exactly where his or her text fits into the broad spectrum of tourism studies and is trying to delimit the boundaries of the book.

The above approach is fundamental to any subject. Each discipline and area of scholarship and research has, as one of its first tasks, the identification of the things that comprise the foci of study. In tourism studies we are faced with four interrelated concepts—tourism, tourist, tourism industry, and tourism resources—which provide the basis, in one form or another, for the subject that we study. By defining terms we give meaning to what we are doing. Moreover, we are able to give each term a specific, technical basis that can be used to help communicate more effectively and to improve the quality of our research and management. Table 1.1 provides several examples of different definitions of tourism from a number of leading texts.

Definitions of tourism tend to share a range of common elements:
- tourism is the temporary, short-term travel of non-residents along transit routes to and from a destination;
- it can have a wide variety of impacts on the destination, the transit route and the source point of tourists;
- it can influence the character of the tourist; and
- it is primarily for leisure or recreation, although business is also important.

TABLE 1.1 Definitions of tourism

Tourism denotes the temporary, short-term movement of people to destinations outside the places where they normally live and work and their activities during the stay at these destinations. Much of this movement is international in character and much of it is a leisure activity (Burkart and Medlik 1974, p. v).

Tourism is a study of man away from his usual habitat, of the industry which responds to his needs, and of the impacts that both he and the industry have on the host socio-cultural, economic, and physical environments (Jafari 1977, p. 6).

Tourism is a phenomenon variably distributed in space (and time), and it can thus be approached from a variety of geographical branches. The locations of markets and destinations, and the flow of people, capital, goods and ideas are at the core of tourism. It influences the form, use and protection of the landscape (Britton 1979, p. 282).

Any person residing within a country, irrespective of nationality, travelling to a place within this country other than his usual place of residence for a period of not less than 24 hours or one night for a purpose other than the exercise of a remunerated activity in the place visited. The motives for such travel may be (1) leisure (recreation, holidays, health, studies, religion, sports); (2) business, family, mission, meeting (World Tourism Organization 1981, p. 89).

Tourism is an open system of five elements interacting with broader environments, the elements being a dynamic human element, tourists; three geographical elements: generating region, transit route and destination region; and an economic element, the tourist industry. The five are arranged in functional and spatial connection, interacting with physical, technological, social, cultural, economic and physical factors. The dynamic element comprises persons undertaking travel which is to some extent leisure-based and which involves a temporary stay away from home of at least one night (Leiper 1981, p. 74).

. . . the sum of . . . the travel of non-residents (tourists, including excursionists) to destination areas, as long as their sojourn does not become a permanent residence. It is a combination of recreation and business (Murphy 1985, p. 9).

Tourism is essentially about people and places, the places one group of people leave, visit and pass through, the other groups who make their trip possible and those they encounter along the way. In a more technical sense, tourism may be thought of as the relationships and phenomena arising out of the journeys and temporary stays of people travelling primarily for leisure or recreational purposes (Pearce 1987, p. 1).

Tourism can be defined as an economic and social activity based on the enjoyment of experiences of visitors—gained by their interaction with a natural and host environment (Tourism South Australia 1989b, p. 2).

The broad range of tourism definitions available in the literature illustrates that tourism has both physical and social (or psychological) components which relate to issues of mobility. Tourism is a commercial phenomenon of industrial society which involves a person, either individually or in a group, travelling from place to place (the physical component of tourism). Such travel often includes journeying from one psychological state to another (the re-creating component of tourism). Tourism studies is therefore the examination of these phenomena, the associated physical, political, economic, social and technological structures and relationships that make the phenomena possible, and the impacts of the phenomena on the sociocultural, physical and economic environments.

TOURISM INSIGHT

TOURISM AND TEMPORARY MOBILITY

Mobility is one of the central concepts in understanding an increasingly glob-alised world. Mobility takes many different forms, including the movement involved in trade, investment, and knowledge. Human mobility includes tourism and migration, as well as the movement of refugees. Indeed, Bauman (1998), in his discussion of the human consequences of globalisation, juxtaposed the tourist and the vagabond as the two extreme character types of contemporary mobility, and as a metaphor for the new, emergent, stratification of global society. In an observation which is of relevance to the contemporary debate surrounding refugee and migrant intakes in Australia, Bauman noted that entry visas are being progressively phased out all over the world as part of the deregulation of desired human mobility and the encouragement of future growth in inter-national tourism (Hall 2001a, b). 'But not passport control. The latter is still needed—perhaps more than ever before—to sort out the confusion which the abolition of visas might have created: to set apart those for whose convenience and whose ease of travel the visas have been abolished, from those who should have stayed put—not meant to travel in the first place' (Bauman 1998, p. 87).

The tourists travel because they want to. The vagabonds travel because they have no choice. 'The tourists move because they find the world within their (global) reach irresistibly attractive—the vagabonds move because they find the world within their (local) reach unbearably inhospitable . . . What is acclaimed today as 'globalization' is geared to the tourists' dreams and desires . . . Vagabonds are travellers refused the right to turn into tourists' (Bauman, 1998, pp. 92–3).

This juxtaposition of tourist and vagabond is an interesting metaphorical device, but it also oversimplifies what is, in effect, a continuum of human mobility which extends from those with the wealth to travel and to select home and holiday dwellings (temporary and multiple as these might be) to those who are forced into mobility.

As Williams and Hall (2002) have noted, discrete literatures have devel-oped around tourism and migration, with the inevitable consequence that they have developed along separate lines, even though they share a common interest in many forms of temporary mobility and circulation. This has led to chaotic conceptualisation whereby both forms of mobility have been abstracted from complex social realities, with little attention to the sophisticated conceptualisation that this should entail. Bell and Ward (2000, p. 89) have observed that analysis of temporary mobility has been made difficult by its multidimensional nature, by the poor quality of the available secondary data, and by a weak theoretical framework. In part, this is due to the blurring of production and consumption in the motivations and behaviour of temporarily mobile individuals, an issue that both migration and tourism theories have failed to address adequately (Williams & Hall 2002).

The heart of the conceptualisation problem lies in differentiating temporary mobility from tourism. An extremely useful contribution came from Bell and Ward (2000, p. 88) who observed: 'Tourism represents one form of circulation, or temporary population movement. Temporary movements and permanent migration, in turn, form part of the same continuum of population mobility in time and space.' Bell and Ward focused on the essential characteristics of temporary mobility and permanent migration. Permanent migrants have no intention of returning. Their movement involves a lasting relocation and a single transition, and their arrival in a destination has only minor seasonality. In contrast, temporary migrants plan to return home or move elsewhere, have varying duration of stay, and are usually involved in repeat movements. Their arrival tends to have a strong seasonal distribution. Another difference is that the place of 'usual residence' is a central feature of permanent migration but not of temporary migration. Moreover, the growth of temporary mobility is related to changes in family and household circumstances due to various factors, including the increased rate of marital breakdown and changing work patterns, so that increasing numbers of temporary migrants occupy a 'network of places' rather than a usual residence (Taylor & Bell 1996). 'Networks of places' invariably generate circulation flows. The super rich with homes dotted around Australia and the world provide the most spectacular examples of such circulation, but the term also applies to the children of separated parents. Such children habitually spend some of their school vacations with one parent or the other. The term also applies to the owners of second homes on the peripheries of Australia's major cities. For example, the southern coast of New South Wales is a common second location for people from Canberra and Sydney, as are Augusta and Margaret River for people from Perth.

In an attempt to improve the conceptualisation of mobility, Bell and Ward sought to locate the different types in a two-dimensional representation of space and time. A substantially modified expression of this model is shown in Figure 1.2. This is most effective at the two poles. 'Permanent' moves are measured in years and occur at different scales, for different purposes. At the other extreme is mobility which does not involve overnight stays, such as shopping and commuting to work, school or university (though this can be weekly or at longer intervals). In between these two types, the different forms of temporary mobility tend to be blurred in terms of scale and time, despite the suggestion in Figure 1.2 that there is a clear hierarchy. Therefore, temporary mobility is best viewed as 'a sequence of intersecting and overlapping layers, of varying intensity and spatial extent, each representing a different form of mobility behaviour' (Bell & Ward 2000, p. 93). Attempts to produce a definition based on motivations is no more successful because, as Bell and Ward have observed, both temporary and permanent mobility can be for reasons of consumption or production, or for a combination of these. Furthermore, the balance between these can shift over time. Emphasising the need to avoid undue oversimplification, they argued that individuals can hold a variety of these motivations in any time period, as well as over the course of their lives.

Tourism fits comfortably into this review of temporary mobility, with tourism being located towards the centre of the time and space continuum. In reality, however, tourism can be of varying duration, individual trips can be motivated by a combination of tourism and economic goals, and these goals can change over time. For example, a move to a location initially for a preferred working environment might subsequently lead to a decision to retire at the new location for similar lifestyle reasons, which incorporate an element of tourist behaviour. Indeed, the initial decision to move somewhere to improve lifestyle or to purchase a second home in a particular location might well have been influenced by initial holiday behaviour.

Nevertheless, such a breakdown of different forms of temporary mobility highlights the importance of appreciating that hard definitional divides cannot be placed between different forms of temporary mobility. One form of mobility can go on to influence later behaviour.

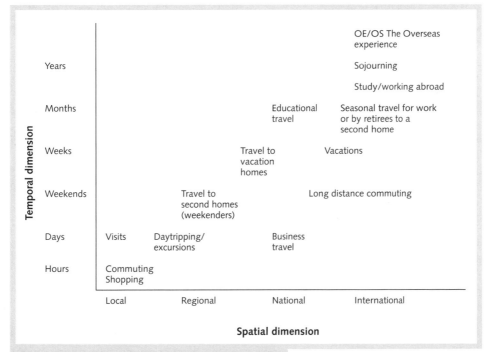

Figure 1.2 Temporary mobility in space and time

Definitions of *tourist* and *tourism*

One of the first Australian definitions of tourism was in the interim report of the House of Representatives Select Committee on Tourism (1977, p. 6) which defined tourists as 'all short term visitors into an area for any purpose—other than to commute to work'. However, the final report of the committee found the above definition to be quite unsatisfactory for its purposes, and chose to define tourists as 'persons who travel more than 40 kilometres from their normal place of residence for any reason other than to commute to a normal place of work' (1978, p. 4).

The Australian Government Committee Inquiry into Tourism (1987a, 1987b) chose to use the definition utilised by the Australian Bureau of Industry Economics (BIE) in a 1984 study of tourist expenditure in Australia. According to the BIE report, tourism includes 'all overnight and certain day trips undertaken by Australian residents and all visits to Australia by overseas residents of less than twelve months duration.' Under this economic orientation to tourism, a tourist was defined (Australian Government Committee Inquiry into Tourism 1987a, p. 11) as either:

- a person who undertakes travel, for any reason, involving a stay away from his or her usual place of residence for at least one night; or
- a person who undertakes a pleasure trip involving a stay away from home for at least four hours during daylight, and involving a round distance of at least 50 km; however, for trips to national parks, state and forest reserves, museums, historical parks, animal parks or other man-made attractions, the distance limitation does not apply.

Similarly, the Country Victoria Tourism Council (CVTC) (1997, p. 3) stated that: 'Tourists are generally defined as those people who decide to travel away from home for purposes other than employment or schooling', and noted that this definition 'is often expanded to differentiate day trip visitors (who return home at the end of the day' and tourists (who stay away overnight)'. The council then went on to note that tourism is made up of both tangible and intangible elements. According to the CVTC (1997, p. 3), tangible elements include:

- *transport* (trains, aeroplanes, coaches, taxis, trains, cars, horse-drawn carts);
- *accommodation* (hotels, motels, bed and breakfast establishments, backpacker hostels, caravan parks, camping grounds);
- *food and beverage* (restaurants, take-away outlets; hotels and pubs; picnic and barbecue facilities); and
- *shopping* (souvenirs, clothing, arts and crafts, jewellery, postcards).
  Intangible elements include:
- *education* (informative);
- *culture* (developing an understanding of other cultures);
- *adventure* (excitement, learning new skills, sports, activities or challenges);
- *romance* (a chance to meet others or relax with family and loved ones);
- *escape* (an opportunity to try new things);
- *identity/status* (to be treated well, receive good service, meet interesting and knowledgeable people); and
- *dreams* (to feel special; to live a different lifestyle).

Australian and other national definitions of tourism have been strongly influenced by international definitions of tourism from such organisations as the United Nations (UN 1994) and the World Tourism Organization (WTO) (WTO 1981; see also

French et al. 1995). In order to improve statistical collection and improve understanding of tourism, the UN (1994) and the WTO (1991) have recommended differentiating between visitors, tourists and excursionists. The WTO has recommended that an international tourist be defined as: 'a visitor who travels to a country other than that in which he/she has his/her usual residence for at least one night but not more than one year, and whose main purpose of visit is other than the exercise of an activity remunerated from within the country visited'; and that an international excursionist (for example, a cruise-ship visitor) be defined as '[a] visitor residing in a country who travels the same day to a country other than which he/she has his/her usual environment for less than 24 hours without spending the night in the country visited and whose main purpose of visit is other than the exercise of an activity remunerated from within the country visited'(1991). Similar definitions have also been developed for domestic tourists, with a domestic tourists having a time limit of 'not more than six months' (WTO 1991; UN 1994).

It is of interest that the inclusion of a same-day travel 'excursionist' category makes the division between recreation and tourism even more arbitrary, and there is increasing international agreement that 'tourism' refers to all activities of visitors, including both overnight and same-day visitors (UN 1995, p. 5). Given improvements in transport technology (see Chapter 2), same-day travel is becoming increasingly important in some countries, with the UN observing that 'day visits are important to consumers and to many providers, especially tourist attractions, transport operators and caterers' (1994, p. 9). Although there is little comprehensive research on same-day travel in Australia, it is apparent that the impact of the day-trip market is substantial. For example, the Western Australian Tourism Commission (WATC) (1997e) estimated that in 1996 more than ten million pleasure-oriented day trips were undertaken in Western Australia with a total expenditure of just under $200 million. The definition of 'day trip' used by the WATC (1997e, p. 1) was 'a trip taken mainly for pleasure which lasts for at least 4 hours and involves a round trip distance of at least 50 km. For trips to national parks, state forests, reserves, museums and other man-made attractions the distance limitation does not apply'.

An additional difficulty in attempting to understand the scope of domestic tourism and the division between tourism and recreation is the significance of second home tourism in some parts of Australia. In these cases, travel is to a vacation or holiday property.

Given the vast array of definitions, many students will sympathise with the sentiments of Williams and Shaw who observed that 'the definition of tourism is a particularly arid pursuit' (1988a, p. 2). Nevertheless, they went on to note:

> . . . the definition of tourism industry is crucially important. In most countries tourism is 'statistically invisible' and, usually, only the most obvious sectors or those exclusively devoted to tourists are enumerated in official tourism data. Inevitably, this tends to be the accommodation sector and, perhaps, cafés and restaurants. Yet the tourism industry is far larger than this. Tourists also spend money directly on recreational facilities, tourist attractions, shops and local services. In turn, these have indirect effects on agriculture, wholesaling and manufacturing, while secondary rounds of spending of tourism create induced linkages in the economy.

One of the major problems that many students have in approaching tourism is the confusion among the terms 'tourist', 'tourism', and 'tourism industry'. This difficulty is a product of the definitions of the terms, and the uses for which these definitions were designed. According to S. Smith (1988, p. 181), the shortcomings of the majority of definitions is that they 'do not adequately reflect the fact that tourism is an industry', and instead indicate a failure to 'conform to existing standards and conventions used in other fields'.

Defining *tourism industry*

To many people the notion of 'tourism' is inseparable from that of 'the tourism industry' (Jafari & Ritchie 1981, p. 16). This approach was adopted in Hollander, Threlfall and Tucker's study of energy and the Australian tourism industry. In their view, the tourism industry was understood 'to encompass all activities which supply, directly or indirectly, goods or services purchased by tourists' (1982, p. 2). Similarly, the landmark Australian Government Committee of Inquiry into Tourism (1987a, p. 11) described the tourism industry as 'not one discrete entity but a collection of inter-industry goods and services which constitute the travel experience', and noted that 'the definition can vary according to whether it includes industries which wholly, primarily, partially or incidentally provide goods and services to the tourist'. However, defining the 'tourism industry' is extremely difficult. As Lickorish and Jenkins (1997, p. 1) observed: 'The problem in describing tourism as an "industry" is that it does not have the usual production function, nor does it have an output which can physically be measured, unlike agriculture (tonnes of wheat) or beverages (litres of whisky)'. This situation has been well identified by the Department of Industry, Tourism and Resources (DITR) (2002g, p. 1):

> The lack of identification of tourism as an industry in the official statistics results from the nature of tourism and of how industries are identified. The Australian and New Zealand Standard Industrial Classification (ANZSIC) is the official classification of Australian (and New Zealand) industries. The ANZSIC defines industries in terms of groups of businesses which produce a similar product. This is a supply side based definition. However, tourism is a demand side activity, defined in terms of the consumption of a particular type of consumer (viz. a visitor). This consumption may involve any type of product supplied by any type of business, i.e. it may involve supply by any industry.

As illustrated in the previous section, S. Smith (1988) provided a dramatic departure from the common approach to definitions of tourism which have tended to define tourism in terms of who is a tourist. In an attempt to gain comparability with other industrial definitions, Smith focused on the development of a supply-side definition of tourism which paid particular attention to the commodities which tourism produces. Therefore, from a supply-side perspective, the tourism industry can be defined as 'the aggregate of all businesses that directly provide goods or services to facilitate business, pleasure, and leisure activities away from the home environment' (Smith, S. 1988, p. 183).

Three key features emerge from an examination of the above definition. First, the tourism industry is essentially regarded as a service industry. Second, the inclusion of business, pleasure, and leisure activities emphasises 'the nature of the goods a traveller requires to make the trip more successful, easier, or enjoyable' (Smith, S. 1988, p. 183). Third, the definition includes the notion of a 'home environment', which refers to the arbitrary delineation of a distance threshold or period of overnight stay. These three elements of the definition combine to conceptualise and measure tourism in a manner which is consistent with that of other industries.

Smith's approach was similar to that of the House of Representatives Select Committee on Tourism (1978, p. 4) which suggested 'that the tourist industry is made up of those enterprises whose economic future is dependent upon fulfilling the requirements of the traveller'. As the committee noted, the travel and tourism industry can be broadly conceived as representing the sum of those commercial and industrial activities which produce goods and services which are wholly or mainly consumed by travellers. Several areas can therefore be distinguished as being a part of the tourism industry under the 'supply-side' approach (after Australian Government Committee of Inquiry into Tourism 1987, p. 11):

- international and domestic operators and carriers;
- accommodation operators;
- restaurants, clubs and other catering establishments;
- tour operators, wholesalers and travel agents;
- attraction/entertainment facility operators;
- national parks;
- manufacturers of souvenirs;
- specialist information suppliers;
- specialist convention and meeting centre operators; and
- specialist retailers, such as souvenir shops.

Such a perspective has also been an important driver in the development of Tourism Satellite Accounts (see Chapter 8).

When we refer to the tourism industry in the present book we will therefore be discussing it primarily in terms of the supply-side concept of tourism and the segments of that industry which are listed above.

Tourism systems

As noted in the previous section, the tourism industry consists of many interrelated parts. It is an industry with many components—hospitality, marketing, government regulation, transport, and service—to name but a few. And, as we have seen, tourism studies can be examined from a wide variety of academic perspectives. However, it is clear that impacts in one part of the tourism industry have significant implications for other sectors. For example, the opening up of a new transport route to a previously neglected destination has substantial implications for the development of tourism at that destination. Conversely, as in the case of the 1989 Australian air pilots' dispute, the opposite can occur. As Mill and Morrison (1985, p. xix) observed: 'The system is like a spider's web—touch one part of it and reverberations will be felt throughout'.

According to Mill and Morrison (1985) and many other writers (Leiper 1989; Laws 1991; Page 1995; Hall 2000a; Holden 2000; Buhalis & Laws 2001), tourism can best be conceived of as an interrelated system. A system is an assemblage or interrelated combination of things or elements forming a unitary whole. Several different types of systems models have been utilised in tourism studies. At a geographical level, three basic elements can be identified (D.G. Pearce 1987; Leiper 1989), as illustrated in Figure 1.3. These basic elements are:

- *generating region*—the source region of the tourist and the place where the journey begins and ends;
- *transit region or route*—the region through which the tourist must travel to reach his or her destination; and

• *destination region*—the region which the tourist chooses to visit and where the most obvious consequences of the system occur.

The basic tourism system model is useful for identifying the flow of tourists from the generating region to the destination region. Of course there might be more than one destination and therefore a whole pattern of destination regions and transit route regions can be built up. Moreover, another interesting dimension of the basic tourism system model is that, arguably, at each stage of the system the tourist will be in a different psychological state. Travel 'involves people moving from one environment through a range of other environments to a destination site and then home via a return trip . . . people not only act in their present setting, they also plan for subsequent settings. People prepare to arrive in another setting to carry out preplanned behaviors' (Fridgen 1984, p. 24). Tourist travel within the basic geographical tourist system can therefore be regarded as consisting of five stages:

• travel decision making and anticipation;
• travel to a tourism destination or attraction;
• the on-site or at destination experience;
• return travel; and
• recollection of the experience and influence on future decision making.

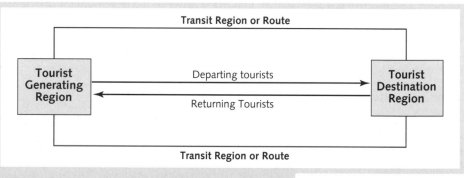

Figure 1.3 Geographical elements of a tourist system

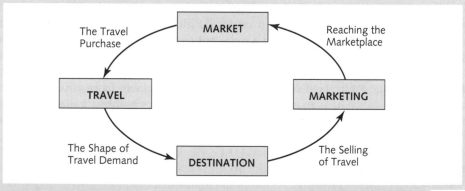

Figure 1.4 Mill and Morrison's tourism system
Source: Mill, R.C. and Morrison, A.M., (1985) *The Tourist System: An Introductory Text,* Prentice Hall International, p. 2.

This has significant implications for tourism marketing and promotion, and for a better understanding of tourist behaviour.

A more commercially oriented tourism system is that provided by Mill and Morrison (1985) (Figure 1.4), who argued that the system consists of four parts: market, travel, destination, and marketing. The market segment highlights the decision of the individual to travel or become a tourist. The second segment of the model describes and analyses the where, when, and how of the individual tourist's travel behaviour. The third segment of the model consists of the study of the destination mix—the attractions and services that are used by the tourist. The fourth component of the model highlights the importance of marketing in encouraging people to travel. As Mill and Morrison (1985, p. xx) observed: 'The development of a marketing plan, the selection of an appropriate marketing mix and the choice of a distribution channel will spell success or failure for the destination's attempt to encourage tourist travel'.

Alternatives to the models of the tourism system provided by Mill and Morrison (1985) and Leiper (1989), are models which emphasise the supply-and-demand dimensions of tourism (Murphy 1983, 1985) and which focus on the importance of the tourist experience. As Murphy (1985, p. 10) noted: 'the travel experience is this industry's product, but unlike other industries it is the consumer who travels and not the product'. Such an observation also highlights the intangible dimension of much tourism service product (such as hotel accommodation, or a place in a tour group), and the highly perishable nature of tourism services (in that they cannot be carried in inventory, but are consumed in production).

THE TOURISM MARKET SYSTEM

The model of tourism utilised in this text is that of the tourism market system (Figure 1.5). The model has been developed from the work of Murphy (1985) and Hall and McArthur (1993, 1996). The model attempts to integrate the behavioural and sociocultural context of tourism with the demand and supply of the tourism experience.

The focal point of the model is the tourism experience—the experiences that the tourist has while he or she is travelling. However, the desired experiences or travel outcomes differ from person to person and from culture to culture. Therefore, one of the key components of the tourism market system is the sociocultural context in which the travel occurs—this might be restricted to within a culture or might involve the meeting of cultures. Nevertheless, an individual who participates in the tourist encounter will be constrained by the values and ideas of his or her own culture. The tourist experience itself is culturally bound by the society from which the traveller has come. For example, the majority of Australians are likely to see the tourist experience in terms of a Eurocentric cultural system. In short, it is difficult to see beyond the boundaries of our own experiences. We can learn to appreciate, and perhaps even adopt, certain cultural values and mores of other societies, but it is difficult (or perhaps impossible) to transcend our own views of the world.

Demand factors

Demand is comprised of the motivations, perceptions, previous experiences and expectations of the tourist. Although the motivations of the tourist will be further

THE SCOPE OF TOURISM STUDIES

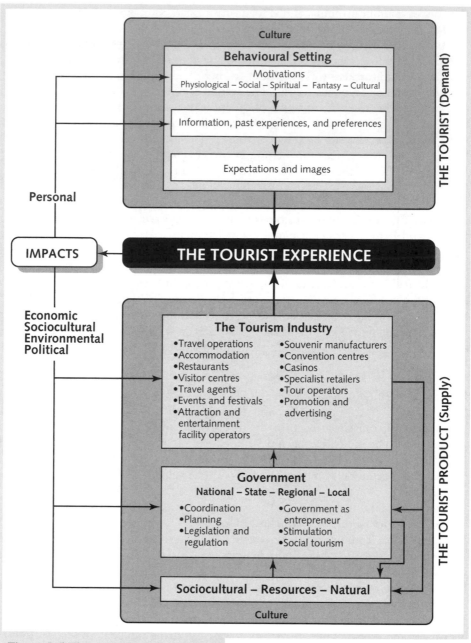

Figure 1.5 The tourism market system

examined in Chapter 3, it is perhaps worthwhile at this point to note some of the basic desires of the traveller.

The motivations of the tourist arise from a variety of sociocultural factors. Many tourist motivations have arisen from the demands made on the individual by modern industrial society. As Krippendorf (1986a, p. 131) argued, people 'do not feel at ease where they are, where they work and where they live. They need to escape the burdens of their normal life'. From this perspective a holiday is 'a temporary refuge from the burdens imposed by the everyday work, home and leisure scene' (Krippendorf 1987, p. xv). However, although escape is a significant travel factor, more positive motivations exist, including the attraction of visiting family or friends. In addition, it should also be noted that stage in life and travel histories, as well as the availability of financial resources, are also powerful influences on demand.

Motivators

The need to seek refuge or escape has been reflected in five basic travel motivations: physiological, cultural, social, spiritual, and fantasy. Each of these is considered below.

PHYSIOLOGICAL MOTIVATORS

Physiological motivators include the need for relaxation and improved health. For example, cruise travel has long been associated with rest and relaxation, and spa tourism is also increasing in importance (Goodrich 1994).

CULTURAL MOTIVATORS

Cultural motivations refer to the desire to observe and learn about other societies and their customs, both formally and informally. For example, study tours are increasing in popularity, and many travellers appear to be desiring more 'authentic' tourism experiences in which they meet 'real' local people.

SOCIAL MOTIVATORS

Social motivators include visiting friends and relatives (the extremely important VFR market segment), business and conference travel, and the prestige and status of travel ('keeping up with the Joneses').

SPIRITUAL MOTIVATORS

Pilgrimage, religion, and spiritual quest have long been part of tourism. The idea that travel can provide insights into the human condition or can change lives remains strong today. Christians travel to Jerusalem or Rome, and Muslims to Mecca, in order to satisfy religious motivations. However, it is important to note that pilgrimage can also be secular (Delaney 1990). For example, overseas travel by university students after finishing their degrees is often regarded as part of 'maturing' and 'seeing the world'.

FANTASY MOTIVATORS

One of the most critical elements of the modern travel experience is that of fantasy. As Dann (1976, p. 22) has observed, the tourist builds up a picture of the world 'that marks an escape from present reality, an environment for acting out psychic needs, and the playing of certain roles which cannot be fulfilled at home, and it is this which forms part and parcel of tourist motivation'. Dann (1977) also identified two different types of fantasy motivators: (i) *anomie*, in which there is a desire to escape the monotony of everyday life; and (ii) *ego-enhancement*, in which there is an attempt to fulfil psychological desires such as romance or sexual adventures while on holidays.

Tourism motivations are not the same for an individual throughout his or her life. Motivations change according to past life experiences and current stage in life. In addition, motivations vary because of tourism promotion campaigns which create

THE SCOPE OF TOURISM STUDIES

certain perceptions of potential tourist destinations, holidays, and travel options. The role of perceptions in the tourism market will be addressed next.

Information, past experiences, and preferences

The perceptions of the traveller are produced by three different elements: past experiences, preferences, and information. Each of these is discussed below.

PAST EXPERIENCES

The choice of destinations is affected by past holiday experiences and their relative success or failure. For example, if an individual had a bad experience with one hotel in a hotel chain he or she will be less likely to stay with another hotel in that chain, even though it is located in a different destination and has different management and staff.

PREFERENCES

Preferences refer to individual priorities, and often reflect the individual's personality as he or she searches for the satisfaction of particular desires or needs (Murphy 1985).

INFORMATION

One of the most crucial factors in the development of individual tourist perceptions is the information that he or she receives. Information comes from a variety of sources, one of the most obvious being formal sources of tourism information such as the travel pages in newspapers and magazines, tourism promotion, travel brochures, guidebooks, tourist websites and travel agents. However, information can also come from informal sources such as novels, movies, television, and radio, and friends, family, and work associates. Indeed, informal sources of information can be much more influential in determining destination images than formal sources such as the advertising campaigns of tourism organisations (Altheide 1997).

Expectations and images

Motivations and perceptions combine to construct each individual's image of tourist destinations and the associated series of expectations regarding the experience at the destination. The tourist image created is of the utmost importance because the appeal of tourist attractions arises largely from the image conjured up, partly from direct or related experience, and partly from external sources and influences (Hunt 1975; Fodness & Murray, 1999). Mental images are the basis of the evaluation and selection of an individual's choice of a destination. As Goodall (1988, p. 3) observed:

> Each individual, given their personal likes and dislikes, has a preferential image of their ideal holiday. This conditions their expectations, setting an aspiration level or evaluative image, against which actual holiday opportunities are compared.

According to Murphy (1985, p. 11):

> This image may be defined as the sum of beliefs, ideas and impressions that a person has regarding a destination. It is a personal composite view of a destination's tourism potential, and where prices are comparable it is often the decisive factor in a tourist's selection process.

However, because each individual has a unique mix of motivations, preferences, experiences and information, the images and understanding of a product or place are not necessarily the same for each visitor.

Clearly, image plays a central role in the tourism industry. It can even be argued that tourism is an industry built on the selling of image and fantasy rather than reality (Gold & Ward 1994; Bramwell & Rawding 1996). However, in the promotion of images, potential major problems can arise. For example, what if the local people do not like the image that is being created to promote their community to tourists (Kearns & Philo 1993)? In the long term, an even greater problem for tourism development is the disparity between image and reality from the perspective of the tourist (Lew 1989). If there is a significant divergence, will the tourist have a satisfactory experience that will ensure a return visit or the recommendation of the destination to friends? As Blanton (1981, p. 121) has noted:

> . . . tourist behaviour is often the product of heightened expectations, deflated hopes, exaggerated fears, or frustrated plans. Travellers have special needs and concerns, and the neglect of seemingly small details can sometimes lead to serious consequences.

Image has played a major role in tourism development in Australia. For example, the terms 'Gold Coast' and 'Sunshine Coast', now the official administrative names for these areas of Queensland, were originally marketing slogans used to promote a positive image of the regions to tourists. Image has even become important for such things as car number plates, which in themselves have become a cheap form of advertising to reinforce state image. For example, New South Wales is the 'premier state' with Sydney promoting its 'Olympic city' status, Victoria has used the phrase 'garden state', and South Australia has been promoted as the 'festival state'. Perhaps the most rapid attempt to change image was in Western Australia in the 1970s and 1980s when the state government attempted to change the image from a 'wildflower state', to a 'state of excitement', and then to 'the home of the America's Cup', only to be replaced yet again when the cup was lost.

Supply factors

Much tourism research and writing, particularly at the commercial and government agency level, has been on the subject of demand for the tourism product— for example, the many studies of the characteristics of consumers and market segments. However, there is an increasing recognition that if tourism development is to be long-term and sustainable, attention must also be given to the supply side of tourism, and to the nature of the destination in particular (Ashworth 1992; Bramwell 1994; Ding & Pigram 1995; Goodhead & Johnson 1996; Hinch 1996; Blowers 1997; Page & Thorn 1997; Hall & Lew 1998; Williams & Shaw 1998; Hall & Page 2002). The tourist product should not be seen only as the immediate commercial package which the customer purchases. Rather, the tourist product is an amalgam of factors, including physical resources, people, infrastructure, materials, goods and services, which, taken together, provide the tourist experience within specific destination areas. Nevertheless, as Pigram and Jenkins (1999, p. 57) recognised in the case of outdoor recreation:

> In a perfect world, demand for outdoor recreation activities would be matched by an ample supply of attractive and accessible recreation resources . . . In reality, interaction between demand and supply factors is qualified by spatial, social/institutional/political, psychological, economic and personal impediments.

The three main components of the supply side of tourism are resources, government, and the tourism industry.

Tourism resources

The capacity of any destination, be it a nation or region, to deliver a tourist product is dependent on the composition and nature of its tourism resources. Tourism resources can be classified as 'natural' (for example, the Great Barrier Reef or the Australian Alps), 'built' (for example, Parliament House in Canberra or the Opera House in Sydney), or 'sociocultural' (for example, the Adelaide Festival or the Australian Football League Grand Final in Melbourne) (Jafari & Ritchie 1981).

An alternative economic conception of resources was provided by Bull (1991), who categorised resources as being 'scarce' or 'free' in nature (Table 1.2). However, what actually constitutes a tourism resource depends on the motivations, desires and interests of the consumer and the changing social context within which those motivations occur. A tourism resource becomes a resource only if it is seen as having utility value, and different cultures and nationalities can have different perceptions of the tourism value of the same object. For example, to the majority of Australians and New Zealanders sheep are part of the landscape and are not seen as a tourist attraction in themselves. However, for Japanese visitors to Australia and New Zealand, the opportunity to see sheep is highly valued. As Lucas (1964, p. 409) observed: 'All resources are defined by human perception . . . The importance of resource perception is particularly obvious for recreational, scenic and amenity resources because of the internal, personal and subjective way such resources are used.' Similarly, Pigram and Jenkins (1999, p. 59) argued that the 'identification and valuation of elements of the environment as recreation resources will depend upon a number of factors (e.g. economics, social attitudes and perceptions, political perspectives and technology)'. As a result, Pigram and Jenkins (1999) recognised that outdoor recreation and tourism resources can encompass a wide range of settings associated with space, topography and climatic characteristics. This expands upon Hart's (1966) notion of the 'recreation resource base', which referred to the natural values of the countryside or landscape. This notion was clarified by Clawson and Knetsch (1966, p. 7) in these terms:

> There is nothing in the physical landscape or features of any particular piece of land or body of water that makes it a recreation resource; it is the combination of the natural qualities and the ability and desire of man to use them that makes a resource out of what might otherwise be a more or less meaningless combination of rocks, soil and trees.

TABLE 1.2 Economic categorisation of tourism resources

Category	Resource
Scarce	
Labour	labour and enterprise including public goodwill
Capital	public provision (for example, access and infrastructure including airports, roads and sewage)
	private provision (for example, accommodation facilities)
Land	especially its attributes such as scenery and activity base (for example, alpine areas, beaches, lakes)
Free	
'Natural'	climate, culture, traditions, and 'way of life'

Source: after Bull (1991, p. 6).

However, such resources are not static, since new trends or cultural appraisals can lead to new notions of the environment as a recreational resource. A tourist resource is therefore that component of the environment (physical or social) which either attracts the tourist and/or provides the infrastructure necessary for the tourist experience. From this notion of tourism resources we can see that if a destination or operation wishes to attract more tourists, two things need to be provided: (i) quality attractions to induce people to visit; and (ii) services to make them feel comfortable and welcome. Therefore, the setting, range, quality and promotion of attractions and facilities contribute significantly to the image and appeal of a tourist attraction (Goodall & Ashworth 1988; Long & Nuckolls 1994).

Murphy (1985) identified three characteristics of the resource base of tourism. First, a combination of human and physical resources on which to base a tourism industry is required; for example, a national park. Second, the physical resource might be seasonal in nature, often because of climatic factors, and this has substantial implications for the acceptance of tourism in the host community, and the ability of tourism to develop. Patmore (1983, p. 70) argued that 'one of the most unyielding of constraints is that imposed by climate, most obviously where outdoor activities are concerned. The rhythms of the seasons affect both the hours of daylight available and the extent to which temperatures are conducive to participant comfort outdoors.' Some destinations (for example, beach, mountain, skiing, hunting, or fishing destinations) are especially seasonal because of the nature of the resource. This is reflected in the seasonality of recreational activity which inevitably leads to peaks in popular seasons and a lull in less favourable conditions. In contrast, urban destinations have more continuous operation throughout the year because they depend upon a more diversified demand and less on seasonal resources (WTO 1984, p. 43). Third, tourism can be characterised as a search for the 'four Ss'—sun, sand, surf, and sex. (A somewhat controversial fifth 'S' has been added to this list by Matthews (1978)—servility.)

Peters (1969) noted that the optimum situation for any destination is to offer 'an asset so outstanding and unique that the tourist industry can largely depend on, and be promoted by, this feature' (in Murphy 1985, p. 13). This situation is extremely difficult to achieve. One solution has been to create attractions that distinguish one destination from another destination. In Australia some of the best examples of this are to be found in the construction of giant pineapples, avocados, bananas, cattle, rams, and prawns. However, although such attractions have a novelty or 'kitsch' value for a short time, the long-term viability and attractiveness of such a solution is questionable, especially as the construction and the novelty factor become dated.

Various countries and regions have a comparative advantage in the resources which they are able to offer tourists (for example, high-quality sandy beaches or ski fields). However, tourism resources are extremely heterogeneous in nature and are not necessarily fixed in space or time. As we will see in the following chapter, as consumer preferences change, so does the perceived utility of particular tourism resources. Marketing strategies, government policy and cost structures all contribute to the popularity and viability of particular resources.

Government

To turn resources into tourist attractions requires the investment of capital. Capital is wealth employed in, or available for, the production of more wealth. Capital investment might come from the private sector or the public sector, or both.

As Chapter 5 illustrates, government has a number of functions in tourism. Most significantly, government provides the regulatory framework within which the private sector operates. The degree of government involvement in tourism depends on the political systems of various nations (Hall 1994a, 2000a; Hall & Jenkins 1995). Historically, government in Australia has had a major entrepreneurial function in tourism although, in recent years, demands for smaller government have led to direct government involvement in tourism being scaled back to being primarily responsible for destination promotion. However, government plays a major indirect role in tourism development through the provision of infrastructure, through ensuring that negative environmental impacts are minimised, and through legislation and regulation in areas as diverse as industrial relations, building codes, and licensing. In addition, government plays a major role in imaging and branding destinations.

Tourism infrastructure, including the provision of public utilities, road links, sewage systems, and water supplies, is usually the domain of government—particularly local government. In the case of larger developments, government might require the commercial developer to contribute to the establishment costs of infrastructure. Alternatively, government might construct infrastructure to attract private developers to potential tourist destinations.

The tourism industry

In Figure 1.5 (page 18), the tourism industry was regarded as synonymous with private-sector involvement in tourism (although it should be noted that government also plays a major role in the direct provision of tourism product). The tourism industry includes: (i) those sectors which become part of the product at the destination (for example, facilities and attractions); (ii) those sectors which enable the tourist to travel to and from the destination (for example, travel agents, airlines, bus companies, rental car companies, and tour operators); and (iii) the human component of the tourism industry (in the form of an educated and trained labour force, an appropriate union structure, and the development of positive service attitudes).

Facilities and attractions include such items as accommodation (hotels and motels), convention and conference centres, theme parks, national and state parks, retail stores, events and festivals, casinos, tourist information centres, and interpretation centres.

Accommodation is one of the most critical components of the demand side of the tourism system and, perhaps more than any other component, influences the sort of tourism industry which a destination develops (Young 1973). This is because accommodation both determines, and is determined by, the nature of demand from visitors. Tourism-related accommodation includes not only high-profile hotels and resorts, but also backpacker and youth hostels, camping and caravan parks, private homes, rental homes, villas, farm stays, and second homes. The last of these is an especially underappreciated, although very significant, component of the available accommodation stock in many rural regions (Jaakson 1986; Williams & Hall 2000). Clearly, the character of the accommodation has a major influence on the types of tourists who are attracted to the host region, the length of stay, and the economic flow-on of tourism to the local community in the form of employment and income.

The tourist product for each destination is related to the image that each destination wishes to convey to the consumer, and to the capital and resources available at the destination. Clearly, the success of the tourist product is related to the cohesion and quality of the product in the marketplace. Murphy (1985, p. 16) identified four phases in the matching of the product with the demands of the consumer:

- the development of a tourist product and promotion of a tourist image by a tour wholesaler;
- the selling of individual holidays by travel agents;
- the arrangement of accommodation and/or the provision of supplementary information on the tourist destination; and (it is to be hoped)
- a satisfied customer.

However, Murphy's phases were only partly correct, even at the time they were written. The advent of new communications technology in particular has meant that many consumers now organise their own accommodation and holiday activities directly, and the intermediary is now often the Internet, rather than a travel agent. Nevertheless, destinations and producers still need to create awareness of the tourism product in the consumer's mind.

The tourist experience

The central element in the tourism market system is the tourist experience. The tourist experience dictates not only why people travel but also why they continue to do so. However, we must be aware that the tourism experience is constantly changing, and that the relationship of consumer to product is a two-way relationship (hence all the arrows in the tourism market system model in Figure 1.5!). Thus travel affects the motivations, preferences and expectations of the tourist, and, conversely, the tourist affects the make up of the product. This, in turn, affects future consumers. It is therefore imperative that the tourist experience and the tourism industry are sustainable, and that they do not damage the capacity of the physical, social and economic environment to absorb tourism.

SUSTAINING THE TOURISM SYSTEM

In the development of a tourist attraction, the creation of a distinct, original and satisfying package should be a primary objective. Product differentiation is the basis of successful marketing and promotion of tourist attractions. However, one of the other central components of ensuring the viability of the tourism product is the support of the local community. Without community support there can be no hospitality and, potentially, no resources, tourism industry, or tourism—regardless of how they are defined. As P.E. Murphy (1981, p. 100) commented: 'In the business world of tourism it is numbers and market research which has dominated while the causes and effects have often been ignored'.

Undoubtedly there has been an increased recognition of the importance of a wider understanding of the impacts of tourism in less-developed countries, particularly in the areas of cross-cultural communication, the impacts of tourism, and the relationship between host and guest (Harrison 1992, 2001; Mowforth & Munt 1998). Attention is now being given to the effects of tourism in Western industrialised nations such as Australia, most notably through minimisation of the negative impacts of tourism and the establishment of long-term approaches towards tourism development.

Tourism and sustainable development

Sustainable development is positive socioeconomic change that does not undermine the ecological and social systems upon which communities and society are dependent. Its successful implementation requires integrated policy, planning, and social learning processes; its political viability depends on the full support of the people it affects through their governments, their social institutions and their private activities (Rees 1989, p. 13 in Gunn 1994, p. 85).

'Tourism development' is one of the most commonly used, but least understood, expressions in the tourism lexicon (Hall 1994a; Hunter 1995). Development means different things to different people. '*Development* is one of the more slippery terms in our tongue. It suggests an evolutionary process; it has positive connotations; in at least some of its meanings it suggests an *unfolding from within*' (Friedmann 1980, p. 4). Tourism South Australia (1989b, p. 2) defined 'development' as 'the setting aside of . . . resources for particular sustainable human uses. In the case of tourism, it is to enhance visitors' experience of these resources in order to derive economic, social and environmental benefits' for individuals, governments, operators, and communities.

Much of the ambiguity over the use of the term 'development' arises because it refers to both a process and a state, with the state of development being derived from the economic, social, political, and cultural processes which have caused it (D.G. Pearce 1989). Friedmann (1980, p. 4) has observed that development:

> . . . is always of something, a human being, a society, a nation, a skill . . . It is often associated with words such as *under* or *over* or *balanced*: too little, too much, or just right . . . which suggests that development has a structure, and that the speaker has some idea about how this structure *ought* to be developed. We also tend to think of development as a process of change or as a complex of such processes which is in some degree lawful or at least sufficiently regular so that we can make intelligent statements about it.

D.G. Pearce (1989, pp. 7–10), drawing on the work of Mabogunje (1980), has identified five different ways in which the concept of development is used:
- economic growth;
- modernisation;
- distributive justice;
- socioeconomic transformation; and
- spatial reorganisation.

D.G. Pearce (1989) noted that 'development' is a dynamic concept, interpretations of which have changed over time. However, development is usually defined in terms of economic growth 'and is frequently assumed to be an economic condition' (Smith 1977, p. 203). In many countries development is measured in such terms as per capita income, gross national product, or per capita wealth, although such statistical measures do not indicate the distribution of income or wealth within a given region. Nevertheless, a purely economic approach to development does not give any appreciation of the environmental and social implications of development or an empirical measure of the quality of life, and 'any development indicator based on monetary value of production is subject to both technical and conceptual shortcomings' (Smith 1977, p. 203).

Economic data alone do not give any appreciation of the productive utilisation of resources—for example, whether or not the resources are renewable. A purely economic approach does not record the environmental and social costs that might be associated with economic production (D.G. Pearce 1989). As Redclift (1987, p. 16) argued:

> From an environmental standpoint . . . GNP [gross national product] is a particularly inadequate guide to development since it treats sustainable and unsustainable production alike and compounds the error by including the costs of unsustainable economic activity on the credit side, while largely ignoring processes of recycling and energy conversion which do not lead to the production of goods and marketable services.

The concept of sustainability came to public attention with the publication of the World Conservation Strategy (WCS) in March, 1980. The WCS was prepared by the International Union for Conservation of Nature and Natural Resources (IUCN) with the advice, cooperation, and financial assistance of the United Nations Environment Education Program (UNEEP), the World Wildlife Fund (WWF), the Food and Agricultural Organization (FAO) of the United Nations, and the United Nations Educational, Scientific and Cultural Organization (UNESCO). The WCS 'launched sustainability onto the global stage, bringing the cautious but sometimes negative thinking of the conservationist together with the positive but sometimes heedless world of the developer' (Bramwell & Lane 1993, p. 1). The WCS is not an international treaty, but a strategy for the conservation of the earth's living resources in the face of major international environmental problems such as deforestation, desertification, ecosystem degradation and destruction, extinction of species and loss of genetic diversity, loss of cropland, pollution, and soil erosion. The international significance of the WCS was illustrated by the fact that more than 450 government agencies from over 100 countries participated in preparing the document.

The WCS defined conservation as 'the management of human use of the biosphere so that it may yield the greatest sustainable benefit to present generations while maintaining its potential to meet the needs and aspirations of future generations' (IUCN 1980, s.1.6). The WCS has three specific objectives (IUCN 1980, s.1.7):

- to maintain essential ecological processes and life-support systems (such as soil regeneration and protection, the recycling of nutrients and the cleansing of waters), on which human survival and development depend;
- to preserve genetic diversity (the range of genetic material found in the world's organisms), on which depend the breeding programmes necessary for the protection and improvement of cultivated plants and domesticated animals, as well as much scientific advance, technical innovation and the security of the many industries that use living resources; [and]
- to ensure the sustainable utilization of species and ecosystems (notably fish and other wildlife, forest and grazing lands), which support millions of rural communities as well as major industries.

The notion of sustainable development espoused in the WCS emphasises the relationship between economic development and the conservation and sustenance of natural resources. The idea of sustainable development requires a broader view of development and the natural environment than has hitherto been the case in Western society. 'The term "sustainable development" suggests that the lessons of ecology can, and should, be applied to economic processes' (Redclift 1987, p. 33). Therefore, sustainable development stresses that economic development is dependent upon the continued well-being of the physical and social environment on which it is based (Dasmann 1985; Barbier 1987; Brookfield 1988; Butler 1991; Hall & Lew 1998).

The report of the World Commission on Environment and Development (1987), commonly known as the 'Brundtland Report', provided further impetus to the concept and practice of sustainable development. Five basic principles of sustainability were identified in the report (Bramwell & Lane 1993, p. 2):
- the idea of holistic planning and strategy making;
- the importance of preserving essential ecological processes;
- the need to protect both human heritage and biodiversity;
- the need to develop in such a way that productivity can be sustained over the long term for future generations; and
- the need to achieve a better balance of fairness and opportunity between nations.

In Australia the principles behind the WCS led to the establishment of national and state conservation strategies which were designed to help achieve the goals of the WCS at national, regional, and local levels. In response to the Brundtland Report, and to domestic and international concerns regarding the state of the environment, the Commonwealth government initiated a series of Ecologically Sustainable Development Working Groups in 1990 to 'provide advice on future policy directions and focus on measures which will encourage the integration of environmental considerations into decision-making processes' (1991, p. iii). The principle of sustainable development has become a highly contentious issue in Australian politics, particularly in debates over mining in national parks (for example, uranium mining in Kakadu National Park), the condition of the rural environment (for example, pastoralism in arid Australia), and logging in National Estate areas (for example, logging in the forests of south-eastern New South Wales). However, controversy over tourism development in Australia indicates that the concept of sustainable development has direct application to the Australian tourism industry (DITR 2002h).

Krippendorf (1982) contrasted 'hard' or 'mass' tourism strategies with 'soft' or 'appropriate' tourism strategies, the latter bearing many of the hallmarks of sustainable tourism (see Table 1.3). Krippendorf (1982, pp. 147–8) also argued that a 'careful' tourism policy was necessary because of:
- the special vulnerability of the rural environment;
- the irreversibility of certain processes;
- the special importance of the environment as the raw material; that is, the basis of tourism and its economic driving force;
- the lack of evidence and uncertainty in measurement of damage to the environment; and
- the sensibilities of the local population and its claim to independence.

Similarly, Kariel (1989) indicated that mass forms of tourism development can have such impacts as urban sprawl, a negative effect on the aesthetic values of the natural landscape, and a decline in the level of local ownership. Given the dangers of unrestricted tourism development, D.G. Pearce (1989, p. 292) argued that 'tourist development in the future must be better planned, more professionally managed and set in a broader context of development'. A number of problems surrounding the nature of tourism require an appropriate policy and planning response if tourism is to achieve sustainable, long-term growth. According to Butler (1990a, p. 40), these include:
- ignorance of the dimensions, nature, and power of tourism;
- lack of ability to determine the level of sustainable development (that is, capacity);
- lack of ability to manage tourism and control development;
- lack of appreciation that tourism is an industry that does cause impacts, and that these cannot be easily reversed;

- lack of appreciation that tourism is dynamic, and causes change as well as responding to change; and
- lack of agreement over levels of development, over control, and over the direction of tourism.

TABLE 1.3 Hard versus soft tourism

Hard tourism	Soft tourism
A. General concepts	
Inconsiderate	Considerate
Offensive	Defensive
Aggressive	Cautious
Fast/impetuous	Slow/thoughtful
Long strides	Short steps
Unchecked	Controlled
Unregulated	Regulated
Maximal	Optimal
Excessive	Moderate
Short-term	Long-term
Particular interest	General interest
Outside control	Self-determination
Least resistance	Greatest resistance
Sector-based	Entirety-based
Price-conscious	Value-conscious
Quantitative	Qualitative
Growth	Development
B. Tourism development strategies	
Development without planning	Planning before development
Project-thinking	Concept-thinking
Each community plans for itself	Centralised planning for larger areas
Indiscriminate development	Concentrate development on particular areas
Haphazard and scattered building	Conserve land, build in concentration, keep open spaces
Exploit especially valuable landscapes	Conserve especially valuable landscapes (reserves)
Create new building stock. Build new bedspaces	Improve use of existing building stock. Exploit existing bedspaces
Build for indefinite demand	Fix limits on expansion
Develop tourism in all areas	Develop tourism only in suitable areas and where local population available
Tourism development left to outside concerns	Opportunity for decision making and participation by local population
Utilise all available labour (also outsiders)	Development planning according to indigenous labour potential
Consider only economic advantages	Weigh up all economic, ecological, and social advantages (costs/benefits)
Regard farming population only as landowners and tourist labour	Preserve and encourage agriculture
Leave social costs to be paid by society	Leave costs to be paid by perpetrators

(continues)

TABLE 1.3 Hard versus soft tourism *(continued)*

Hard tourism	Soft tourism
Favour private transport	Encourage public transport
Provide facilities for maximum demand	Provide facilities for average demand
Remove natural obstacles	Preserve natural obstacles
International style urban architecture	Local architecture (building design and materials)
General automation of tourist resorts	Selective technical development, encouragement of non-technical tourism forms

C. Policy frameworks

Retain concentration of holiday departures	Stagger holidays
Admit tourism personnel without certificate of ability	Improve education of those responsible in tourism
Spread 'stereotype' holidays on offer	Prepare travellers
Hard selling	'Heart selling'
Regard tourism as an economic panacea	Seek new options within, and alternatives to, tourism

D. Tourist attitudes

Mass tourism	Travel alone, with friends or family
Little time	Plenty of time
Rapid means of transport	Appropriate (or even slow) means of transport
Fixed itinerary	Spontaneous decisions
Outside-inspired	Self-inspired
Imported lifestyle	Native lifestyle
'Sights'	Experiences
Comfortable and passive	Strenuous and active
Little or no intellectual preparation	Previous research on destination country
Unable to speak the language	Learning to speak the language
Feeling of superiority	Willingness to learn
Shopping	Bringing presents
Souvenirs	Memories, diaries, new perspectives
Snaps and postcards	Photography, drawing, painting
Curiousity	Tact
Loud	Quiet

Source: reprinted from Krippendorf, 'Towards new Tourism Policies: The Importance of Environmental and Sociological Factors' (1982) *Tourism Management,* vol. 3, no. 3, pp. 145–6, with permission from Elsevier Science.

Sustainable tourism development is a major issue for tourism (Hall & Lew 1998). For example, in response to demands for greater environmental responsibility the Australian Tourism Industry Association (ATIA)—the former national tourism industry body—drew up a code of environmental ethics (1990d), the draft of which stated that: 'Members of the industry . . . must recognise their responsibility to both the human community and the wider environment. That responsibility is primarily maintaining the capability of the land and resources they utilise' (ATIA 1989a, p. 2). Similarly, the Ecologically Sustainable Development Working Group on Tourism stated that the four principles of ecologically sustainable development (ESD) identified by the group could be directly applied to tourism (1991, p. xxi):

Improvement in material and non-material well-being

An ecologically sustainable tourism industry will be one which considers carefully the quality of experiences offered, as well as simply numerical outcomes, such as numbers of visitors. A difficulty in this respect is finding appropriate measures of quality.

Intergenerational and intragenerational equity

An ecologically sustainable tourism industry would not diminish the range of educational, recreational and environmental activities available to present or future generations, in accordance with the principle of intergenerational equity. Species diversity and ecosystem integrity cannot be replaced or substituted, and it is therefore inappropriate to design tourism developments which threaten these values. Further, tourism ventures should deal cautiously with risk, and proposals involving high levels of environmental risk should not proceed.

Within the tourism industry some social equity problems can be avoided by expanding the opportunities for, and use of community participation in decision-making processes.

The protection of biological diversity and the maintenance of ecological processes and systems

Tourism development should occur in such a way which maintains biodiversity and supports the maintenance of ecological processes. Any tourism development should be of such a kind or scale that allows the ecosystem to continue providing the full range of functions, thus maintaining the capacity to adapt to any subsequent environmental changes.

The global dimension

Global aspects of ESD include issues of trade and of international obligations, including global environmental issues such as climate change. An ecologically sustainable tourism industry ought not to contribute towards unsustainable activities in other countries.

Source: Ecologically Sustainable Development Working Group on Tourism, *Final Report—Tourism*, (1991), AGPS, Canberra, p. xxi. Copyright Commonwealth of Australia. Reproduced by permission.

However, although the Working Group's report represented a substantial contribution to the sustainable tourism debate in Australia, and provided impetus to Commonwealth policy in this area, it must be noted that the group's activities were focused on *ecologically* sustainable development rather than a concept of sustainable development which also incorporated *social* dimensions of development processes. As Dutton and Hall (1989) argued, the concept of sustainable development can offer a basis for maintaining the long-term growth of the Australian tourism industry, but it is only achievable if attention is also given to the social context within which development occurs. Similarly, as Brookfield (1991, p. 42) commented that although environmental sustainability refers to environmental regeneration and the maintenance of biodiversity, it must also 'be measured by progress along a vector made up of attributes that include improvement in income and its distribution, in health, in education, freedoms, and access to resources'. McKercher also noted difficulties with the application of the concept of sustainability and argued (1993b, p. 131) that sustainability:

> . . . is being used by both industry and the conservation movement to legitimize and justify their existing activities and policies although, in many instances, they are mutually exclusive. Rather than acting as a catalyst for change, sustainability may serve to entrench and legitimize extant policies and actions, thus exacerbating rather than resolving conservation/development conflicts.

Tourism in Australia is at a critical point in its development. Can Australia continue to host the number of tourists it has been attracting without damaging the very resources which attract them? (DITR 2002h) Given the current dependence of some parts of Australia on tourism, can Australia afford not to maintain the number? After the strong growth of the 1980s and early 1990s, particularly in inbound tourism, tourism growth decreased substantially as a result of financial difficulties in key Asian markets such as Malaysia, South Korea and Thailand in the second half of 1997 and most of 1998 (Hall & Page 1999). The Olympics produced a recovery in inbound tourism, but the terrorist attacks in New York and Washington on 11 September 2001, and the collapse of Ansett Australia, an airline owned by Air New Zealand, delivered new blows against inbound tourism. Arrivals in 2001 decreased by 2.6% (4 816 800) from 2000. This was the first calendar year decrease in arrivals since the Asian economic crisis in 1998 (Australian Tourist Commission 2002a). The Australian tourism industry and Australian governments face a crucial decision. How do they ensure that tourism development in Australia is maintained at a level which ensures long-term, stable growth? (DITR 2002h) The answer lies in the application of the ideas behind sustainable development of tourism.

A sustainable approach to tourism is concerned with the appropriate development of the economic, social and physical resources of a region in a manner which conserves the social and physical environment and which promotes the long-term goals of the community (Dutton & Hall 1989; Cronin 1990; de Kadt 1990; Spiegler 1990; Bramwell & Lane 1993; Wight 1993). The approach contains several essential components.

1 Tourism development cannot be measured solely in economic terms. Social and environmental development are interdependent with, and equally important as, economic development.
2 Tourism development must ensure the maintenance and conservation of ecological processes and the physical environment.
3 Tourism development must ensure the maintenance of social processes and the social environment.
4 Tourism development requires full public participation and community involvement. Indeed, the most appropriate form of tourism development for some communities might well be no tourism development.
5 Tourism development must ensure the conservation of the uniqueness and integrity of the destination on both a local and a national scale.
6 Tourism is but one of a range of mechanisms that might be appropriate for the economic development of particular regions.

The above approach to tourism development is regarded as fundamental to the future of tourism in Australia. There are many reasons for people selecting particular travel destinations, including climate, distance, costs, and the character of the destination. However, probably one of the most compelling motivations for travel is the desire to experience new and unique environments. As Helber (1988, p. 20) observed:

> We are intrigued and fascinated by unusual and scenic natural environments and the different lifestyles and characteristics of people outside our communities. It is these differences that motivate large numbers of people to travel to both domestic and international destinations. A very basic strategy then, in tourism development, is to retain and preserve these aspects which make our community or region uniquely different from all others.

Tourism inevitably brings change to local communities. However, as we shall see throughout this book, change can be both positive and negative. From the viewpoint of the destination, it is essential to ensure that communities can absorb significant increases in visitors and the resulting development pressures, without adversely affecting the social and physical environment. From the standpoint of the consumer, and the industry which serves the consumer, it is similarly essential that adverse changes which contribute to the loss of the special attributes and original appeal of the destination do not occur. In all cases it is important that tourism is seen as a means to an end, not as an end in itself.

To many readers, the approach espoused by this book to tourism development in Australia might sound very 'green' and inappropriate. Unfortunately, much of the meaning of conservation has become lost in the environmental debates which have raged in Australia over the past twenty years and, to some, 'conservation' has become a dirty word. Nevertheless, as Helber (1988, p. 20) has pointed out, conservation can be a highly effective tool for:

• the retention of those special attributes which establish the tourism appeal of a particular destination; and
• gaining support for tourism through the preservation of the social and cultural values of local people.

That is, conservation and development can be highly compatible.

This book sees conservation as such a tool in maintaining Australia's competitive advantage and, along with the other components of a sustainable approach to tourism development outlined above, as an essential mechanism to ensure the survival of a healthy tourism industry in the twenty-first century.

Building on the concepts outlined above, the following chapters examine the various components of tourism and their relationship to the development of a sustainable approach to tourism. Chapter 2 provides a historical account of tourism and the social and technological conditions which have contributed to tourism growth. Chapter 3 outlines the nature of the international and domestic tourism markets and the factors which encourage people to travel. Chapter 4 looks at various aspects of destination image and branding. Chapters 5 and 6 discuss the roles of government at federal, state, and local levels. Chapter 7 examines the various sectors of the tourism industry, the nature of the labour market and, most significantly, the difficulties of attaining a coordinated approach towards tourism development among the various elements of the tourism industry.

Tourism cannot be sustained unless the effects of tourism on destinations or regions are well understood. Therefore Chapter 8 examines the economic framework of tourism in Australia, and Chapters 9 and 10 analyse the social and environmental impacts of tourism respectively. Chapter 11 identifies the role of planning in achieving sustainable tourism development, with emphasis on the potential of community-based planning to ameliorate the negative impacts of tourism development. Chapters 12 and 13 survey some of the opportunities for the development of new forms of tourism product, and the relationship of particular market segments and types of tourism development to long-term growth, with Chapter 12 concentrating on the rural environment and Chapter 13 dealing with the urban environment. Given the imperative of sustainable development and the need for government, the private sector, and the wider community to understand the nature of tourism better, the final chapter (Chapter 14) examines the future of tourism and the issues that must be addressed if the Australian tourism industry is to become sustainable.

CHAPTER SUMMARY

This chapter has provided a brief introduction to the field of tourism studies and the relationship of tourism research to leisure and recreation studies. Attention has focused on the definitions of key concepts such as 'tourism', 'tourism industry', and 'tourism resources'.

The chapter has provided an outline of the framework of the book and the significance of the concept of sustainable development to tourism in Australia. Six components of a sustainable approach to tourism development were identified and their relationship to conservation stressed. However, it is essential to recognise that sustainable development is not just a 'green' reaction to the negative impacts of tourism but a strategy for long-term economic, social and environmental development that is appropriate to Australia's present situation and future needs. It is argued that long-term development of the Australian tourism industry cannot be achieved unless it is recognised that tourism is dependent upon the wise use and sustenance of the physical and social resources that provide the basis for the experience sought by tourists.

It is hoped that the remainder of this book and the ideas and reactions it generates in students will go some way towards achieving that goal.

SUGGESTIONS FOR FURTHER READING

The majority of introductory textbooks on tourism, leisure and recreation contain sections on definitions of key terms and concepts. Broad overviews of tourism supply and demand issues, including the issue of definition and its implications for statistics are to be found in Hall and Page (2002).

Readers requiring an Australian perspective on the cognate fields of leisure and recreation should consult Chapter 1, 'Monitoring the spectator society: An overview of research and policy issues', in Mercer (1994). Lynch and Veal (1996) is also useful in this respect. Useful contributions on the nature of the growth of tourism studies and academic–industry relationships are to be found in Ryan (1997, 2001).

Readers who wish to study the nature of the tourism phenomenon and the difficulty of definition in greater depth should see Leiper (1979, 1983, 1989, 1990a, 1995).

An 'industry' or supply-side definition of tourism is provided in S. Smith (1988), and his 1989 text, *Tourism Analysis: A Handbook*. A rejoinder to Smith's (1988, 1991, 1993) supply-side view has been written by Leiper (1990b, 1993).

Chapter 1 of Bull (1991) provides a valuable discussion of the nature of tourism resources. It is envisaged that the current healthy debate on the nature of tourism as industrial activity and/or social activity, and the debate over the meaning and implementation of sustainable development principles, will be maintained for many years to come!

On the relationship between tourism and sustainable development, readers should note the contributions of Butler (1990a, 1991, 1992), Pigram (1990), Inskeep (1991), Smith and Eadington (1992), Bramwell & Lane (1993), Wight (1993), Hunter (1995), Mowforth and Munt (1998), and Hall (2000a), as well as the various chapters in books edited by France (1997), Stabler (1997), and Hall and Lew (1998).

INTERNET SITES

- The website of the World Tourism Organization provides pages on the current statistics, publications, members and meetings of the WTO. The site also contains the global code of ethics for tourism and details of other WTO campaigns regarding sustainable tourism.
    www.world-tourism.org

- The website of the World Travel and Tourism Council is the home site for the major global private-sector tourism organisation. The site provides information on recent press releases, road shows, and markets, as well as economic research and policy statements.
    www.wttc.org

- Pacific Asia Travel Association (PATA) is the leading tourism organisation of the Asia–Pacific region. Its site provides much information on current activities, members, and events, and also contains a number of links to destinations, airlines, and affiliated sponsors.
    www.pata.org

- The Cooperative Research Centre (CRC) for Sustainable Tourism—funded jointly by government, industry, and universities—is one of the main umbrellas for tourism research in Australia.
    www.crctourism.com.au

- Also see Tourism Insights—the photoessay on Australian tourism by Thomas Bauer.
    www.prenhall.com/hall_au

FOR DISCUSSION AND REVIEW

This section has been prepared to assist students in discussing and reviewing some of the key concepts and questions that emerge in the study of tourism.

Key concepts

Key concepts discussed in this chapter were:
tourism studies, recreation, leisure, multidisciplinary approach, interdisciplinary approach, defining tourism, tourism industry, tourism system, tourism resource, sustainable development, tourism development.

Questions for review and discussion

1 Is it possible to distinguish tourism from recreational activity?
2 What are the various approaches to the study of tourism? Which one do you think is the most important?
3 What are the differences between the concepts of 'tourism' and 'tourism industry'?
4 What is a tourism system?
5 What are the key components of the demand and supply sides of tourism and which are the more significant?
6 What do you think will happen if supply and demand are not balanced in the tourism market system?
7 What constitutes a tourism resource?
8 What were the three objectives of the World Conservation Strategy and how can they be applied to tourism?
9 What factors need to be considered if tourism is to be made sustainable?
10 Why is the idea of sustainable tourism so important?
11 How has the tourism industry responded to the concept of sustainable development?

HISTORICAL DIMENSIONS OF TOURISM

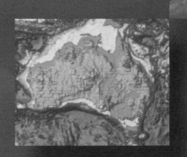

2

The typical course of development has the following pattern. Painters search out untouched and unusual places to paint. Step by step the place develops as a so-called artist colony. Soon a cluster of poets follows, kindred to the painters: then cinema people, gourmets, and the jeunesse dorée. *The place becomes fashionable and the entrepreneur takes notes. The fisherman's cottage, the shelter-huts become converted into boarding houses and hotels come on the scene. Meanwhile the painters have fled and sought out another periphery—periphery as related to space, and metaphorically, as 'forgotten' places and landscapes. Only the painters with a commercial inclination who like to do well in business remain: they capitalize on the good name of the former painters' corner and on the gullibility of tourists. More and more townsmen choose this place, now* en vogue *and advertised in the newspapers. Subsequently the gourmets, and all those who seek real recreation, stay away. At last the tour agencies come with their package rate travelling parties: now, the indulged public avoids such places. At the same time, in other places the same cycle occurs again; more and more places come into fashion, change their type, turn into everybody's tourist haunt (Christaller 1963, p. 103).*

D ESPITE the appeal to many people of Henry Ford's statement that 'history is more or less bunk', it is important to note that the factors that have influenced the past development of tourism still play a major role in its growth and character. Significant lessons can be learnt for the long-term viability of tourist attractions by examining the manner in which destinations have won or lost favour with tourists in the light of changes in popular appeal, fashion, cost and accessibility. Examinations of the history of tourism in a region or a nation are not just 'ivory tower' studies. Rather, they can provide dramatic insights into present tourism management problems at a destination, the motivations of tourists, and the mechanisms by which the attractiveness of a tourist destination can be extended (Butler 1980; Butler & Wall 1985).

A direct link between the changing nature of the travel market and the development of a tourist destination was provided by the work of Butler (1980). Butler's model hypothesised that tourist destination areas pass through various stages of development (Figure 2.1). Butler's notion that tourism destinations evolve through a variety of stages as they pass through a development or marketing cycle was not new. Similar patterns of tourist development had long been identified by a number of researchers (Christaller 1963; Plog 1973; Stansfield 1978; Hovinen 1981, 1982; Clary 1984; Murphy 1985). However, the majority of research on the evolution of tourist destinations has tended to see the importance of such cycles in terms of the

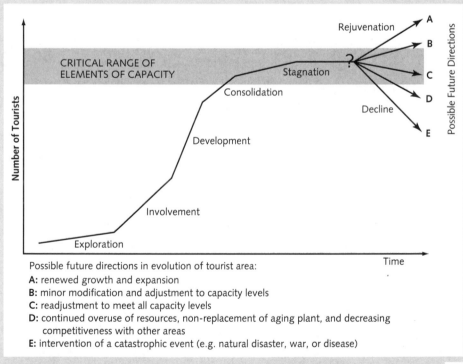

Possible future directions in evolution of tourist area:
A: renewed growth and expansion
B: minor modification and adjustment to capacity levels
C: readjustment to meet all capacity levels
D: continued overuse of resources, non-replacement of aging plant, and decreasing competitiveness with other areas
E: intervention of a catastrophic event (e.g. natural disaster, war, or disease)

Figure 2.1 Hyphothetical stages in the evolution of a tourist area
Source: reprinted from Butler, R. 'The Concept of a Tourist Area Cycle of Evalution: Implications for Management of Resources', *The Canadian Geographer*, vol. 24, no. 1, 1980, pp. 7, 11.

changing nature of the tourism market and the motivations of the traveller, rather than the economic, social and physical impacts of those changes on the destination. Indeed, one of the most significant aspects of Butler's model was that it emphasised the synergistic relationship between the marketplace (demand) and the destination (supply) in that changes in one have effects on the other. However, Mowforth and Munt (1998, p. 85) have argued that the Butler model failed 'to explain the relationship between the different elements of the industry (tourist, service provider, and local populace at its simplest) and the wider context of development processes'. And Graber (1997) has argued that identification of the forces behind the life cycle and the key actors responsible is not yet available.

Despite such criticism, Butler's (1980) concept of a tourist area cycle of evolution remains one of the most widely recognised frameworks for understanding tourism development. The life-cycle model has been applied in a number of environments and settings representing the development of a destination through time and space (Cooper & Jackson 1989; Cooper 1990, 1992, 1994; Ioannides 1992). Because of its relative simplicity, the concept of a destination product life cycle has emerged as a significant concept for strategic destination marketing and planning, and it underpins much of our understanding of urban tourism development. Butler's concept provides a wide appreciation of the marketing dimension of tourism and its link to the evolution and decay of tourist destinations. In particular, Butler noted the environmental, physical and social factors which limit a destination's capacity to absorb tourists and their associated facilities and institutions, and the damage that can be caused if those capacities are exceeded.

Butler's model traces the development of a tourist destination through a number of stages. According to Butler (1980, p. 8), during the *development phase* of a tourist destination:

> . . . local involvement and control of development will decline rapidly. Some locally provided facilities will have disappeared, being superseded by larger, more elaborate, and more up-to-date facilities provided by external organisations, particularly for visitor accommodation. Natural and cultural attractions will be developed and marketed specifically, and these original attractions will be supplemented by man-made imported facilities. Changes in the physical environment of the area will be noticeable, and it can be expected that not all of them will be welcomed or approved by all of the local population.

The changing nature of the tourism market, the tourists' motivations, and the satisfaction of their wants and desires by the tourism industry obviously raises significant questions about the manner in which host communities and destinations undergo the process of tourism development. Some of the key concerns are the inevitability of decline and the processes by which attractiveness, and hence competitiveness, can be sustained.

This chapter provides a brief overview of some of the main factors and trends in the development of Australian tourism. The ability of individuals to participate in touristic activities is a function of social circumstance and the level of transport technology. As indicated in the first chapter, tourism is intimately related to recreation, and therefore much emphasis is given in the present chapter to the implications of changing leisure patterns for the development of tourism, particularly at the domestic level. Considerable attention is given to the changing social and technological context of tourism and leisure behaviours, including social attitudes, and the embodiment of these social and technological changes in government regulations. As the following pages

According to Cooper and Jackson (1989) the two most substantial managerial benefits of the life-cycle concept are its use as a descriptive guide for strategic decision making and its capacity as a forecasting tool. As a descriptive guide the life-cycle idea implies that in the early stages of product development the focus is on building market share whereas in the later stages the focus will be on maintaining that share. However, the utility of the destination life-cycle concept as a forecasting tool relies heavily on the identification of those forces that influence the flow of tourists to a specific destination, and the time period under examination. As Haywood (1986) recognised, most models work well in their early stages but then fail in their prediction of the later stages of the model. Haywood (1986) along with other commentators (for example, Cooper 1992, 1994; Ioannides 1992) noted that there is a variety of different-shaped curves of supply and demand, with the shape of the curve depending on both supply-side and demand-side factors. Indeed, Haywood (1986, p. 154) went so far as to argue that the life-cycle approach, 'represents the supply side view of the diffusion model', by which consumers adopt new product.

According to Haywood (1986) there are six operational decisions when using the destination life-cycle concept:
• unit of analysis;
• relevant market;
• pattern and stages of the tourist area life cycle;
• identification of the area's shape in the life cycle;
• determination of the unit of measurement; and
• determination of the relevant time unit.

Using Haywood's insights as a basis for undertaking research on the life cycle, Graber (1997) undertook an analysis of the destination life cycles of 43 European cities using the variables of growth data for domestic and international tourism, first-time visitor percentage, length of stay, guest-mix distribution, and number of competitors. Only a small number of the variables tested proved to be significant correlates of the life cycle. According to Graber (1997, p. 69): 'A diminishing rate of first-time visitors is obvious for cities passing through later stages of the cycle'. The implications of these results are significant for destinations because monitoring of the variables might provide a more strategic approach to understanding patterns of tourism development, particularly with respect to destination marketing and planning (Getz 1992).

will demonstrate, the evolution of tourism in Australia is associated with the development of transport technology, changing fashion, growth in available leisure time, and an increase in disposable incomes for the vast majority of the Australian population.

THE UNWILLING TRAVELLERS

On the morning of the 13 May 1787, the First Fleet, under the command of Captain Arthur Phillip, set sail from Plymouth in England with 736 convicts to establish the Colony of New South Wales. The passengers and convicts on the First Fleet can perhaps be described as 'unwilling tourists'. Yet it was these people who paved the way for the creation of the Australian nation.

The first European settlers were the result of a Georgian social experiment on a grand scale—the creation of a penal settlement in the South Pacific for a supposed 'criminal' class (R. Hughes 1987). The Colony of New South Wales was a means to rid Britain of as many of its 'criminal' elements as possible and, it was hoped, by sending them so far away to prevent them from returning. The first settlers faced a grim existence in, what was to European eyes, a barren, inhospitable environment. They lacked the knowledge and many of the tools that were required to come to terms with their new land (Powell 1977). The majority of British people in the eighteenth century had probably never travelled more than ten kilometres beyond their villages. Therefore, the voyage to Australia could be likened to the experience of landing on another planet.

One of the key logistical problems of the early days of settlement was the vast distance between Australia and the rest of what the settlers regarded as the 'civilised world'. The many months required for travel to Australia meant that for many years Australia was just too far away to be considered as a destination for international travellers. The only people to come were those who came for business or those who came because they had no choice.

The 'tyranny of distance' (Blainey 1983), which has provided such a metaphor for Australian society, existed not only in the international context but also in the domestic situation. For the early domestic travellers transport was slow, tiresome, and often unreliable. Moreover, the harshness of life meant that time had to be spent ensuring the survival of the colony, rather than on travel for pleasure. Nevertheless, as J. Horne noted, 'Tourism in Australia is closely connected with European exploration as well as a means of seeing how western intellectual thought has interpreted the local environment' (1991, p. 85).

For the first arrivals, there were undoubtedly few formalised leisure and recreational activities. However, following the arrival of large numbers of free settlers after the turn of the nineteenth century, the social and physical condition of the colony began to improve. It is impossible to account for tourist activity in early New South Wales in modern-day terms. Travelling 40 or 50 kilometres in a day, which might satisfy some modern definitions of tourism, was often impossible on a land transport system that was poorly developed. Furthermore, the colony was, for all intents and purposes, a British outpost in the South Pacific. The cultural mores and social values, and consequently its leisure activities, were that of England, and it was to be many years before a distinctively Australian element emerged in leisure and travel. However, as the nineteenth century wore on, and the number and distribution of settlers expanded, the first signs of the commercialisation of leisure and travel began to appear.

Perhaps the first domestic Australian tourists, broadly defined, were the farmers and squatters in the outlying districts who travelled to the towns and villages for supplies and relaxation. The popularity of alcohol is an extremely common theme in early writings on Australians and their leisure activities. 'All visitors to the Australian colonies, and in particular those who toured the country towns, were appalled, or impressed, by the drinking capacity of Australian working men, who seemed to have no other pleasure than to seek relief or release in intoxication' (Crowley 1980a, p. 26).

Commentaries on Australian life were published in Britain from the beginning of the nineteenth century to attract settlers or to serve as guide books, and were extremely important to the commencement of tourism to Australia. In a century when technological innovations and wider schooling meant that a greater proportion of the middle classes could read than ever before, books on the Australian colonies served to raise awareness and interest in one of the Empire's most far flung stations. Therefore, tourism and immigration were closely related, as tourism provided an encouragement to immigrate. For example, the Immigration and Tourist Bureau of New South Wales was under the New South Wales Premier's Department until 1919, when the immigration function was transferred to the Commonwealth government (J. Horne, 1991).

Australia was often pictured to the British audience as a rural Arcadia in which the fruits of the soil could be easily won. Commentaries were couched in descriptions that were understandable, if inaccurate, to the reader's European experience. For example, in the early 1840s the Hunter River district in New South Wales was described in quite glowing touristic terms as 'the Rhine of New South Wales' by the first editor of *The Hunter River Gazette* (Crowley 1980a, p. 17). Such romantic imagery was extremely important in attracting both tourists and immigrants to Australia, and still influences perceptions of the Australian landscape to this day (Hall 1992a).

Australia was advertised in Britain as 'a land of promise for the adventurous—a home of peace and independence for the industrious—an El Dorado and an Arcadia combined' (Sidney 1852, in Powell 1976, p. 21). As Curr (1824, pp. 11–12) observed:

> For after all, in our Australian paradise, our highest aim is to exhibit on a small scale something like the beauties which rise up at every step in the land to which we have bade adieu, well content if we can here and there produce a corn-field surrounded by a post and rail fence, or a meadow of English grasses clear of stumps.

Significantly, the paradise of which Curr wrote was the re-creation of the pre-enclosure and pre-industrial revolution English countryside of the early eighteenth century (Proudfoot 1986). Indeed, Curr (1824, p. 34), while appreciating the natural beauty of some sections of Van Diemen's Land (Tasmania), firmly believed that without its transformation into a rural landscape moral decline would surely ensue:

> Strange that where nature loves to trace
> As if for gods a dwelling-place;
> There man, enamoured of distress,
> Should mar it into wilderness!

This is a sentiment which is clearly at odds with the present-day needs of nature-based tourism in Tasmania and the high value placed on wilderness as a tourist attraction!

The creation of a 'New Britannia in another world' (Wentworth 1873) was 'an expression of English social aspiration that men had no desire to see fulfilled in England itself, and an elegy to the way of life that had passed away before an age of industry and machines' (Lansbury 1970, p. 122). Nevertheless, the dream of a 'new Britannia' played an important role in altering attitudes towards 'the bush' and the

Australian environment in general. The changed nature of rural Britain forced settlers to readjust their attitude to the Australian landscape. As Powell (1972, p. 6) noted:

> The despoliation of the British countryside and the shame and horror of industrialisation slowly changed the image of Botany Bay from a small and distant cesspool of depravity to a veritable Arcady in which a Golden Age of rural prosperity and individual dignity might be recaptured.

Victorian attitudes towards tourism, leisure, and recreation were somewhat paradoxical. Although certain leisure activities were seen as being immoral, recreation *per se*, and hence travel for recreational purposes, was regarded as essential to escaping the supposed negative effects of city living on spiritual and physical health. For example, when the North Shore Steam Ferry Service, linking Sydney City with the then rural North Shore, commenced operation in early 1842, it was argued that 'Health, pleasure, convenience, and economy, will all be promoted by this useful arrangement' and would provide 'a new and delightful resource' for 'healthful recreation' (*The Sydney Herald*, 10 March 1842). The establishment of commercial steam ferry operations in Sydney also led to the development of other domestic travel businesses. For example, the lessees of Sir Joseph Banks Hotel used the ferries to bring customers to the Botany Bay Zoo (Crowley 1980a).

The Australian experience of Victorian attitudes towards leisure and recreation runs directly parallel to British developments. For example, the steamboat rides to the North Shore and Botany Bay can be regarded as the antipodean equivalent of the ferrying of city-weary Londoners to the coastal resorts of Southend and Margate (Walton 1983; Corbin 1995). However, the use of steamboats for commercial recreation was only one aspect of the impact of technological innovations on the growth of mass travel and tourism. On land, perhaps the most significant event for making travel accessible to all classes of society was the coming of the railway, and with it, the development of mass tourism.

The onset of rail was to lead to a revolution in tourism and recreational activities. Before the arrival of rail, recreational travel was restricted to the immediate areas surrounding centres of population. With the arrival of the railways it became possible to open up the hinterland to the domestic traveller. In addition, improvements in shipping technology were to witness the arrival of the first overseas tourists to Australia and New Zealand.

THE DEVELOPMENT OF MASS TOURISM

Mass tourism is generally acknowledged to have commenced on the 5 July 1841, when the first conducted excursion train of Thomas Cook left Leicester station in northern Britain. Since that time tourism has developed from being the almost exclusive domain of the aristocracy to become an experience that is enjoyed by tens of millions of people worldwide.

As secretary of the Leicester Temperance Society, Cook wanted to enable the British working man to travel and wanted to steer him away from the perils of alcohol. To Cook, 'travel for the millions' was not just rhetoric but a firm personal belief. To this end, Cook started to run tours as a commercial business in 1845 with a tour from Leicester to Liverpool, then the gateway to North America and North

Wales. This seemingly inauspicious event in fact heralded the beginning of the era of relatively cheap travel for the emerging middle classes. Cook marketed the qualities of the destination to his prospective customers, persuaded four railway companies to provide reduced prices for his tour, examined the quality of the accommodation and restaurants that would be available to the tour members, and even arranged side tours to Caernavon and Snowdon (Swinglehurst 1982). The age of mass tourism had begun.

British international tourism beyond the traditional European destinations developed hand-in-hand with the growth of the British Empire. By 1872 Thomas Cook was able to advertise to his readers in *The Excursionist* an opportunity to embark on a world tour which, by 'the extraordinary facilities now offered by the steamboat arrangements of the Pacific, the Indian, and the Red Seas, and the firm footing that Mr. Cook's tourist arrangements had secured in the East', was able to include 'glimpses of our own Colonies of New Zealand and Australia' (*Cooks' Excursionist and Tourist Advertiser*, 24 June 1872, p. 9).

The inclusion of Sydney and Melbourne on the Cook itinerary marked the beginning of packaged international tourist travel to the Australian and New Zealand colonies. The inclusion of Australia in the travel destinations of wealthy Europeans and North Americans was further strengthened by the opening of Thomas Cook's first Australian offices in Melbourne at the time of the Centenary of the Governor Phillip's landing at Botany Bay. Such was the importance of the Melbourne office that it was initially superintended by Frank Cook, Thomas Cook's son (Swinglehurst 1982). The Cook initiative brought Australia within an international travel network which, although closely allied with the British Empire, also allowed information about the attractions of Australia to be disseminated throughout Europe and North America through the pages of *The Excursionist* and other travelogues. In particular, the establishment of the Indian branch of Cook's offices, just prior to the opening up of the business in Australia, laid the foundations for tourist opportunities between India and southern Australia's more temperate climes. For example, one of the first attempts at attracting international tourists to Australia began with the unsuccessful attempts of the Tasmanian government in the late nineteenth century to persuade members of the British Raj to travel to Tasmania during the Indian summer, rather than journey to the foothills of the Himalayas (Mosley 1963).

Thomas Cook's significant role in the development of international tourism to Australia continued in the 1880s and 1890s. In 1889 the company published a book of advice to travellers to Australia and New Zealand (Thomas Cook & Son 1889). In addition, Cook sold tickets for Australian transport concerns, such as the Victorian Railways Commission, in Europe, Asia, Africa, and America. As Swinglehurst noted, 'wherever railways were established the Cook's Tour followed' (1982, p. 164).

An indication of the development of travel to Australia was demonstrated by the visit of the prominent English biographer and historian, James Froude, to Australia and New Zealand in 1885. Froude was 'probably the most famous intellectual to come to Britain's southern colonies in the second half of the nineteenth century' (Blainey 1985, p. v) and his writings of the time he spent in Australia were to prove extremely influential to the way the 'Mother Country' came to see Australia. Indeed, Blainey (1985, p. ix) stated that he knew 'no travel book of the nineteenth century which paints our part of the world with such brilliant prose'. In the late nineteenth century, travel books were the major source of information on potential tourist destinations. The potential significance of Froude's ability to establish a positive image of Australia can be seen in his description of Port Jackson (1985, originally 1886, p. 79):

> Port Jackson, the harbour proper . . . is the largest and grandest in the world. A passage about a mile wide has been cut by the ocean between the walls of sandstone cliffs which stretch along the south-west Australian shores. The two headlands stand out as gigantic piers, and the tide from without, and the freshwater flood from within, have formed an inlet shaped like a starfish, with a great central basin, and long arms and estuaries which pierce the land in all directions, and wind like veins between lofty sandstone banks. The rock is grey or red. Worn by the rains and tides of a thousand human generations, it projects in overhanging shelves or breaks off into the water and lies there in fallen masses.

The Australasian colonial governments were clearly aiming to impress Froude. In an early example of tourism marketing, the Victorian Railways laid on a special train to enable him to travel to the goldfields of Bendigo and Ballarat. As Froude noted: 'Travelling in Australia was made an inexpensive process to us—we had free passes over all the lines in Victoria, and free passes were sent us from New South Wales on the mere report that we were going thither' (1985, originally 1886, p. 77). It is of interest that Froude writes of Ercildoune in Victoria where 'two young English lords on their travels were paying a visit' and 'had been up the country kangaroo-shooting', indicating the travels of the British élite to the colonies. However, the social activities of the Australian colonies were clearly seen as an extension of those in Britain and failed to impress Froude. For example, he noted that in Victorian society: 'Party followed party, and it was English life over again: nothing strange, nothing exotic, nothing new or original, save perhaps in greater animation of spirits' (1985, originally 1886, p. 34).

The importance of transport developments for the establishment of tourism

The evolution of tourism in Australasia is inseparably linked to development in transport technology. For obvious reasons of geography, the first travellers to Australia arrived by ship. As well as enabling travel to Australia, water transport assumed early importance in Australia's history. For reasons of ease of transport new settlements were established along or near rivers. Although many of the river boats which provided the travel links between country towns have now disappeared, the economic importance of inshore passenger services has now come full circle. As Andrews (1983, p. 43) recorded: 'riverside towns such as Echuca and Mildura have now discovered that their paddle steamer heritage is worth tourist dollars'.

The gold rushes of the 1850s were a watershed in the promotion of travel to Australia. The gold rushes sparked a dramatic increase in interest in Australia and the promise of gold lured thousands to the colonies. Moreover, the increase in traffic to Australia made the route viable for the use of steamships, with substantial improvement in the time it took to reach Australia from Britain. For example, when the P&O Company's Royal Mail carrier SS *Chusan* arrived in Sydney on 3 August 1852, via the Cape of Good Hope and Melbourne, the 'time for conveying letters to and from Australia by sailing vessels was 275 days, and by steam via the Cape of Good Hope 135 days' (Crowley 1980a, p. 224).

In Australia, work on the first railway line (Sydney–Parramatta) commenced in 1850 and heralded a revolution in transportation and mass recreational travel. For example, at the opening of the Williamstown to Geelong Railway on 25 June

1857, *The Argus* commented: 'There is another feature in the opening of this line which must not be lost sight of, and that is the increased facility for amusement and excursions it will afford to residents both in Geelong and Melbourne'. Similarly, when rail access became available to Brighton Beach from Melbourne in December 1861, it was regarded as providing 'a means of healthful recreation to thousands and tens of thousands of the citizens of Melbourne' (*The Age*, 21 December 1861).

The 1850s were also marked by the introduction of one of the institutions of Australian travel in the second half of the nineteenth century—the horse-driven coaches of Cobb and Co. The services of Cobb and Co. commenced with a Melbourne–Port Melbourne run in 1853, and used American coaches especially designed for rough roads. The coach service was extended to the Victorian goldfields in January 1854. However, it eventually declined due to the growing influence of the railways, particularly in outlying areas. Nevertheless, it was not until August 1924 that the last Cobb and Co. run operated on the Yeulba–Surat route in Queensland.

The gold which attracted so many settlers and visitors to Australia also served to improve the physical and social condition of the urban centres, with considerable attractions for residents and visitors. As Crowley (1980a, pp. 313–14) commented:

> By the mid-1850s Sydney was a bustling town, emporium and seaport, and it offered a wide variety of amusements and diversions . . . There were walks in the parks and gardens in fine weather, and visits to museums in wintry weather. The theatre was well patronised all year round, and coaching services fanned out in all directions from the central business area.

Major exhibitions

Another measure of the material progress of the Australian colonies can be found in the hosting of major exhibitions which promoted both domestic and imported produce. In addition to promoting produce, these exhibitions were used in the same way as the 1988 Brisbane Expo or the 2000 Summer Olympics in Sydney—to attract the interest of national and international visitors. For example, the 1879 international exhibition supplement of *The Sydney Morning Herald* (17 September 1879) argued that: 'There is no place in the world that present[s] greater facilities for enjoying a holiday than Sydney; there is no place where such facilities are more availed of'. The first exhibition to be held in Australia was opened in Melbourne on 17 October 1854 by Sir Charles Hotham, the Governor of Victoria. It lasted for nearly two months and consisted of items intended for the Paris exhibition of 1855. The first intercolonial exhibition was held in Melbourne from 24 October 1866 to 23 February 1867, and attracted more than 270 000 visitors. Similarly, the intercolonial exhibition of 1870 attracted more than 184 000 people (Crowley 1980a). However, the success of these exhibitions pales in comparison with the Centennial Intercolonial Agricultural Exhibition of 1888–89 which attracted nearly two million visitors (Crowley 1980b).

Social and technological development

The economic development of the Australian colonies went hand-in-hand with major social developments. In a departure from the work conditions of industrial Britain, most Australian urban trades and occupations adopted the principle of 'eight hours labour, eight hours recreation, eight hours rest' in the late 1850s. Leisure was seen in a positive light by mid-Victorian era opinion makers. As *The Adelaide Observer* (5 January 1856) commented: 'as recreation is a necessity of our existence, the man who devises a means of healthful, rational, moral amusement is a benefactor of society'. In particular, the railway made new destinations accessible and helped to establish travel as a permanent part of Australian popular culture. Therefore, it was no understatement when *The Sydney Morning Herald* (29 May 1869) described the opening of the railway line between Sydney and Goulburn in 1869 as 'a great social revolution'. This perspective is reinforced when we recognise that the railway provided the basis for the now familiar Christmas holiday rush away from the cities: 'Cheap trains convey numbers of excursionists away from the city . . . at the very time when a flight from dusty streets and glaring pavements to the sea-side is most appreciable' (Kerr 1872, in Crowley 1980a, p. 600). Similarly, in Adelaide, the new found accessibility to holiday destinations was eagerly taken up by the residents. According to Heathcote (1975, p. 80), 26 trains a day were taking passengers to Glenelg at weekends by 1880, and it was claimed that more than one million passengers were making the trip per year by the early 1880s.

The railway lines were also important to the establishment of Australia's first national parks which were set aside for the recreational activity of the city-dweller, rather than for the protection of fauna and flora as we know national parks today. The first national parks in New South Wales, South Australia, and Western Australia were all the result of the need for scenic and recreational amenities (Hall 1989a, 1992a). As *The Sydney Morning Herald* (3 October 1888) expressed on the completion of the railway to Kiama: 'Nor can it be doubted that in the course of time the attractiveness of the National Park, to which this line and branch give ready access, will create a large and profitable excursion traffic'. Indeed, the *Official Guide to the National Park* noted 'The Railway Commissioners, ever ready to study the convenience of the travelling public, after consultation with the Trustees, run a service suitable to the large and growing traffic between the metropolis and the railway stations adjacent to the holiday resort' (Elwell 1893, p. 19).

Despite the importance of the railway in opening up Australia to travellers, it must be noted that the rail systems were separate colonial entities and a truly national rail system was not to come into existence until well into the twentieth century. For example, the rail link between Sydney and Brisbane was not completed until May 1889, and, even then, passengers had to change trains at the border because the railway lines were built with different gauges.

By the end of the nineteenth century, tourism and leisure activities were not just the regime of the wealthy. The development of the railway had seen travel become a possibility for the majority of the Australian population. While the railways had led to the development of domestic travel, the steamship and the opening of the Suez Canal in November 1869 had made the voyage to Australia faster and shorter, and had brought Australasia within closer reach of the European world.

The twentieth century was to see further technological advances, particularly with the development of the motor car and the aeroplane, which were to make travel even more accessible. However, many of the patterns of present-day tourism in Australia were established during the nineteenth century. Urban attractions such as museums, art galleries, exhibitions, and parks, were as significant to the people of the Victorian era as they are today. For example, Sydney's Hyde Park was as important a centre of leisure activities in the 1850s as it is today. In addition, the popularity of several locations as travel destinations, such as the Blue Mountains, were also well established by the end of the nineteenth century although, as the next section will illustrate, changing fashions and social values have greatly altered the patterns of leisure behaviour.

The development of spas and resorts

One of the central features of tourism and popular culture in Australia and New Zealand is the attraction of sun, sand and surf (Davidson 1996). Yet few Australians realise that it was not until November 1903 that it became legal to swim at one of Sydney's premier natural tourist attractions, Manly Beach, during the day. Indeed, it was not until 1935 that the Hobart City Council amended a local government Act which prohibited 'bathing or washing in any public water or river or near any road or land under the control of the council' (Wells 1982, p. 22). Such examples illustrate the changing nature of attitudes to what is considered fashionable, healthy, and moral in Australian society. Nevertheless, the fashions of British and European high society in the nineteenth century did play an important part in the development of spas and resorts in Australia. For example, in 1840, Port Melbourne, then called Sandridge, was advertised as Brighton-on-the-Sands: 'clean, white and shelly with tea tree and wildflowers and birds . . . the fashionable resort of Melbourne society' (Wilbraham Liardet 1840, in Wells 1982, pp. 127–8).

The first true Australian coastal resorts were established in the late nineteenth century at places such as Sandgate and Cleveland in Queensland, Glenelg in South Australia, Brighton, Portsea, and Sorrento on Victoria's Port Phillip Bay, and at Lorne along the Victorian southern coast. However, initially they were not places for swimming—Victorian morality saw to that. Following British fashion they became places to 'take the sea air and waters' as a cure for all manner of ailments. It was only around the turn of the twentieth century that bathing became possible, and then only with the utmost privacy and prudery, and certainly not in mixed company. As Archbishop Kelly commented in 1911 (*The Sun*, Sydney, 14 August 1911):

> I think promiscuous surf-bathing is offensive in general to propriety, and a particular feature of that offensiveness is the attraction it has for idle onlookers . . . There is no border-line between vice and virtue. Our worst passions are but the abuse of our good ones. And I believe that the promiscuous intermingling of sexes in surf-bathing makes for the deterioration of our standard of morality . . . Woe betide Australia if she is going to encourage immodesty in her women.

A further example of the transfer of English moral standards to Australian beaches can be seen in the adoption of the use of bathing machines. The Australian version of the bathing machine, with its specially constructed grated enclosures to keep out sharks, proved very popular at the turn of the twentieth century—not only because of the privacy they offered but also because they were regarded as a status symbol. Bathing boxes—small private huts on the beachfront in which one could change in privacy—were also extremely popular. Few bathing boxes have survived to the present day. However, bathing boxes still remain on Port Phillip Bay, jealously guarded by their owners and by the Brighton Bathing Box Association, and they remain tourist attractions to this day.

In an effort to emulate British seaside resorts such as Brighton, Margate, and Southend, several coastal areas built baths, jetties, piers, and pavilions. Such constructions were regarded as necessary to provide refined recreation for the people, and to assist in the taking in of the 'ozone'. Several of Australia's premier beaches, such as

Bondi and Manly (Sydney), Glenelg (Adelaide), and Cottesloe (Perth), which had begun their lives as picnic spots, found themselves the target of promoters who wanted to recreate Blackpool in the antipodes. However, like many of their British counterparts, Australia's baths and piers have all but disappeared through storm and neglect, with the pier and rotunda at St Kilda (Melbourne) being perhaps the last of its kind in the country (Wells 1982).

In the late 1800s, Tweed Heads in northern New South Wales, and the Queensland towns of Coolangatta and Southport, grew rapidly as the lowering of the hours in the working week meant that many workers spent a day at the beach on weekends. The growth of such areas was also associated with increased holiday time, particularly over the Christmas period, and with the building of railways which provided cheap transport for the workers. In addition, the popularity of places such as Noosa and the present-day Gold Coast was already becoming established, with the construction of guest houses to serve the recreational and holiday needs of the more leisured classes (Vader & Lang 1980; Cato 1982).

The previous section noted the importance of the railways in the development of tourism in Australia. However, the growth of tourism was not restricted to the travel opportunities which the railways made available. The colonial railway departments also served as entrepreneurs in the development of tourist opportunities. For example, some of the first tourist bureaux in Australia were originally sponsored by railway departments, including Victoria's, which commenced operations in 1888, having been established for the International Melbourne Exhibition of that year (Piesse 1966; Department of Tourism and Recreation 1975).

The development of a railway system also provided opportunities for the establishment of inland tourism destinations. As in New Zealand and North America, many railways travelled through scenic countryside to the health spas that were to prove attractive to the metropolitan market (Rockel 1986). One of the first examples of this in Australia was the rail link between Sydney and the Blue Mountains. From the mid-nineteenth century, Katoomba and the Jenolan Caves area were major tourist attractions and featured on the itinerary of many domestic and overseas visitors (Smith 1984; J. Horne 1991; Hall 1993a). The Blue Mountains area was popular for its spectacular scenery and the supposed health-giving properties of its mild climate (Stanbury 1988). Katoomba became a model tourist-town with a number of large hotels being established for the sightseeing trade of the late 1880s. By the turn of the century the Jenolan Caves were receiving three or four thousand tourists each year. However, as the twentieth century progressed the picturesque and romantic vistas which led to the initial development of the region gradually became replaced by a tamed landscape in which nature was 'improved'.

Katoomba came out of the depression as a hardened, pseudo-sophisticated, flashy town. As Burke (1988, pp. 114–15) has reported: 'The employment projects . . . had produced a gauche, pebbled archway above the thousand-stepped Giant Stairway . . . *The Echo*, exclaimed "the Three Sisters, always spectacular and awe inspiring, have become doubly so under flood-lighting conditions"'.

As tourism developed in the Blue Mountains, the hotels of the Katoomba region increasingly catered for the mass market, and tourism subsequently declined. Furthermore, the popularity of the railways and the tourist destinations that depended on them was threatened by further advances in transport technology in the form of the car and the plane.

Hill stations are generally associated with India and other outposts of the British Empire in Asia such as Malaya (Crosette 1999; Douglas & Douglas 2000). Hill stations, occasionally referred to as 'sanatoria', were 'specialised highland outposts of colonial settlement . . . insular little worlds that symbolised European power and exclusiveness' (Aiken 1994, p. vii). Just as significantly, they were resorts located at an altitude in which the ruling élite could find some respite from the summer heat on the plains below. However, the hill stations soon developed characteristics of tourism resorts: 'specialised social places the Europeans frequented for fun and relaxation . . . or for mere dalliance' (Aiken 1994, p. 2). Arguably, Australia also had its share of 'hill stations' which developed in the hinterland of several of the colonial capital cities in the nineteenth century. Examples of areas in which hill station resorts were developed include the Blue Mountains in New South Wales, Mount Macedon and the Dandenong Ranges in Victoria, the Mount Lofty Ranges in South Australia, Mount Tamborine in Queensland, Kelmscott and Darlington in the Darling Ranges near Perth in Western Australia, and Mount Field in Tasmania, which was promoted as a summer resort to India as well as the domestic market.

TOURISM BETWEEN THE WARS

The growth of mass transport with the advent of the family car and well-developed shipping and rail systems meant that once remote beaches and attractions came within easy reach. For example, in the Whitsunday Islands in northern Queensland, 'tourism enterprises gradually evolved from the market opportunities provided by local recreational activity and coastal steamship operations' (Barr 1990a, p. 28). Similarly, Surfer's Paradise, first called Meyer's Ferry and then Elston, owes its success to a commercial agreement between the Surfer's Paradise Hotel (from which the town received its name) and the Victorian and New South Wales railways for the accommodation and transport of Victorian tourists (Wells 1982). The original development of the Gold Coast and Sunshine Coast as tourist resorts was quite different from what it is today. For example, Surfers Paradise was devoid of the high-rise buildings that now characterise the coastal strip. Visitors stayed in boarding houses or refined guest houses, and many camped. However, the 'development ethos' which characterises the Gold Coast had already become well entrenched, as reflected in a Queensland government tourist pamphlet of 1917 which stated: 'The municipal councillors of Coolangatta have made "Progress" their watchword, and high and dry areas where once were swamps, seats and shelters, graded roads and easy access to good views are numbered among their good works' (Fitzgerald 1984, p. 459).

In contrast to the growth of coastal resorts was the development of the bush-walking movement. Although relatively small in number, the establishment of bushwalking clubs in the interwar years, such as the Sydney Bushwalkers led by prominent conservationists and walkers Myles Dunphy and Paddy Pallin, helped pave the way for the popularity of bushwalking and other outdoor activities and the modern conservation movement (Hall 1992a). For example, in 1932, members of various walking clubs helped form the National Parks and Primitive Areas Council (NPPAC) in New South Wales. Indeed, these days the bushwalkers would probably be termed 'ecotourists' (Hall 1997d).

Upon its creation, the NPPAC focused on the preservation of two 'primitive' (wilderness) areas—the Blue Mountains and the Snowy–Indi area—areas around which conservation issues linger to the present day. Among the objectives of the NPPAC was the advocacy of 'the protection of existing tracks, paths and trails in use, particularly those having scenic and historical interests and values' (Dunphy 1963, pp. 7–8 in Bardwell 1979, p. 17). The use of tourism as an economic justification for the preservation of the natural environment, an issue which is still controversial today (see Chapter 10), was a major tactic of the NPPAC in attempting to persuade the New South Wales government to set national parks aside for wilderness recreation.

An example of the connection between tourism and preservation was the NPPAC's campaign for the preservation of the Blue Mountains area. The NPPAC's Greater Blue Mountains National Park Scheme probably represented the first major attempt of an Australian conservation group to mobilise mass support for the preservation of wilderness, and anticipates the more recent conservation battles over the Great Barrier Reef, Tasmanian wilderness areas, Kakadu, and the tropical rainforests of North Queensland. On 24 August 1934 the NPPAC paid for a four-page supplement, complete with maps and photographs, to be included in the *Katoomba Daily*. The supplement was highlighted by Myles Dunphy's proposal for a Blue Mountains National Park with 'primitive areas'(NPPAC 1934, p. 1):

> The Blue Mountains of Australia are justly famous for their grand scenery of stupendous canyons and gorges, mountain parks and plateaux up to 4,400 feet altitude, uncounted thousands of ferny, forested dells and gauzy waterfalls, diversified forest and river beauty, much aloof wilderness and towns and tourist resorts replete with every convenience for the comfort and entertainment of both Australian and overseas visitors.

One of the few surviving examples of the original tourist accommodation at Noosa.

Although New Zealand had established a national tourism organisation—the Department of Tourism and Health Resorts—in 1901 (Pearce 1992), the Australian national government did not begin to encourage overseas visitors in earnest until the interwar period. One of the key factors in the Commonwealth government's actions was the perceived economic benefits from tourism at a time of economic difficulties and restructuring; a theme which echoes through to the present day. As Norval (1936, p. 132) observed:

> It is only since the economic crisis of 1929 that tourist traffic as a factor in international trade has begun to receive the serious considerations of governments, who have begun to see in the current of their nationals visiting foreign countries an instrument by which the national interests may be promoted, either by stimulating exports thither or by mobilizing foreign claims due to them on such countries.

In 1929 the Australian National Travel Association (ANTA), the forerunner of the present-day Australian Tourism Industry Association (ATIA) and Australian Tourist Commission (ATC), was established. ANTA was inaugurated by the Commonwealth as a national, non-profit organisation under the *Companies Act 1928* of Victoria. Although regarded by Norval (1936, p. 273) as 'purely a publicity organisation', the 'main objects' of ANTA bear substantial similarities to several aspects of current government policies with respect to tourism development and promotion and the development of quality standards, improved industry coordination, and regional economic development (Table 2.1). ANTA promoted international tourism to Australia through such measures as the opening of offices in London and San Francisco in 1930, with the result that, in 1935, approximately 23 000 visitors came to Australia, mainly due to the promotional efforts of ANTA (Piesse 1966; Department of Tourism and Recreation 1975).

TABLE 2.1 The main objectives of the Australian National Travel Association (1929)

(a) To advertise Australia overseas and to disseminate information concerning the Commonwealth with the view of attracting thereto tourists, investors and investor-settlers.

(b) To encourage, promote, develop and stimulate inter-state travel in Australia.

(c) To endeavour to improve the standard of hotel and guest-house accommodation throughout Australia, particularly in rural areas, and generally to endeavour to create better conditions for visitors and tourists, including transportation facilities to enable both groups of persons and individuals to gain more readily an insight into the producing areas and the life of rural Australia.

(d) To endeavour to establish a closer co-ordination between the various transport bodies and entities in Australia, including in particular the Commonwealth and State Railway Departments and the Tourist Bureaux.

(e) To take such steps by personal and written appeals, public meetings, or otherwise, as may from time to time be deemed expedient, for the purpose of procuring contributions to the funds of the Association in the shape of donations, annual subscriptions, or otherwise, to which end an endeavour will be made to educate Australians to a better realization of the benefits to be derived by carrying out the above-mentioned policy of the Association.

Source: Constitution of the Australian National Travel Association (in Norval 1936, p. 273).

It is testimony to the pace of technological development that regular airline services between Australia and overseas commenced only seventy years ago when the first airmail service between Australia and Britain was inaugurated by the Duke of Gloucester on 10 December 1934. The service provided the stimulus for the formation of Qantas Empire Airways with capital from Qantas (Australia) and Imperial Airways (United Kingdom) and the operation of the Brisbane–Singapore sector of the Australia–UK route. This period also saw the registration of Australian National Airways (ANA) (the forerunner of Ansett Airlines) as a company on 14 May 1936. By 1937 it had a network of airlines from Cairns to Perth with a connection to Launceston (Crowley 1973a). However, the intervention of war in Europe and the Pacific prevented the immediate further development of the Australian tourism industry.

THE POSTWAR LEISURE BOOM

The period after the Second World War witnessed an unparalleled development in leisure services for the Australian population. A new period of prosperity following the depression of the 1930s and the war years meant that people had greater disposable incomes and more leisure time in which to enjoy their prosperity, particularly as three weeks of annual holidays became standard. One of the greatest impacts was the growth in personal mobility through car ownership. For instance, there were fewer than 200 motor vehicles per 1000 head of population in 1950, but 248 in 1957 (Crowley 1973b, p. 348). The increase in personal mobility also had a substantial impact on the nature of tourist destinations. The central role of guest houses in resorts went into decline, as motels, specifically designed for the needs of the mobile traveller, became more prominent.

Another significant factor in the development of the modern Australian tourism industry was the enormous amount of postwar migration from Europe to Australia. Apart from providing both the manpower and a market upon which much of the postwar growth could be based, migrants brought with them cultural attitudes and practices that were to see Australia develop a more cosmopolitan society. In addition, the newly strengthened relationship between Australia and the migrants' former homelands, particularly Greece and Italy, encouraged the development of new air routes and, hence, further growth in Australia's participation in the international tourist market.

Also in the postwar period, Qantas started to assert its central position in the development of Australia's tourist industry. Qantas was nationalised on 1 July 1947, when the Australian government acquired all of the shares in Qantas Empire Airways. In stark contrast to present-day attitudes, government ownership was seen as the best mechanism to provide the necessary capital for expansion of the airline to enable it to compete in the international market (Drakeford 1949, pp. 1926–8).

The postwar reconstruction period also saw the Commonwealth government become heavily involved in the domestic aviation industry. Trans-Australia Airlines was established in September 1946, after the Labor government had been compelled by the High Court to abandon its proposal of the previous year to nationalise all private interstate airlines. In the private sphere, ANA was taken over by Ansett Transport Industries in August 1957. The growth of commercial domestic airline routes had a tremendous impact on the tourism industry, particularly in Queensland and Tasmania, as destinations came within easier reach of holidaymakers from the source areas of Melbourne and Sydney.

The growing importance of international tourism to Australia was demonstrated by the inauguration of a Qantas round-the-world service in January 1958. The practical significance of this for the tourism industry was noted by the Premier of Victoria, Mr Bolte, who upon the opening of direct overseas air links 'expressed the hope that, with the assistance of Qantas, thousands more tourists would be attracted to Australia' (*The Age*, 15 January 1958). In 1958 Australia was visited by about 60 000 international tourists, of whom approximately 47 000 came from British Commonwealth countries. The economic impact of international tourism on the economy at the time was negligible, 'contributing only seven-tenths of 1 per cent of the national income. The fact is that Australia has not yet begun to use international tourism as an economic tool' (Clement 1961, p. 193). However, despite the growing awareness of the economic potential of tourism, the traditionally conservative cultural mores of much of Australian society were to lag behind the more cosmopolitan requirements of many tourists and visitors.

The 1960s

> Australia stands on the threshold of great opportunity in the field of international tourism. Concurrently, it faces challenges in providing for an expanding travel movement of Australians at home and for the travel needs of a greatly increased flow of overseas visitors. It is now at a critical point where, to meet these challenges, it should make decisions, establish policies, and plan for the development of its travel industry, destination areas and travel facilities (Harris, Kerr, Forster & Co., Stanton Robbins & Co. 1966, p. 3).

The 1960s saw the development of many of the attractions, government structures and promotion strategies which characterise present-day tourism in Australia. For instance, events have been used as mechanisms to promote host cities as tourist destinations since the 1956 Melbourne Olympics. Such a strategy was clearly uppermost in the minds of the organisers of the 1962 Perth Commonwealth Games who believed that the games would allow Perth to break into the international spotlight (*The West Australian*, 22 November 1962). Although sporting events were extremely significant in raising the international awareness of Australia as a tourist destination, the growing cosmopolitan nature of the nation was also being expressed in arts festivals. One of Australia's premier arts events and cultural tourist attractions, the Adelaide Festival of Arts, was first held in March 1960. However, it was apparent that the 'City of Churches' was unwilling to adjust its conservative regulations to assist in the promotion of the event, as complaints were made about the closing of hotels on Sundays and the six o'clock closing time on weekdays (Kavass 1960).

These conservative attitudes to the issue of trading and licensing hours still exist in Australia to this day. In addition, substantial controversy surrounds the development of casinos throughout Australia because of their traditional association with organised crime and prostitution. For example, the establishment of Australia's first casino, at Wrest Point in Hobart, was strongly opposed by many people, including the local churches. Nevertheless, with the establishment of casinos in other states, the development of casinos has been justified in terms of supporting local tourism industries and ensuring their long-term survival. As R.S.J. Valentine, President of the Hobart Chamber of Commerce, commented on the casino vote in the Tasmanian Parliament in December 1968, '[E]ach member of the House of Assembly, regardless of party, who votes against the proposal may hammer an individual link in a ball and chain and nobble the tourist industry' (*The Mercury*, 29 October 1968).

Perhaps the single-most important feature of Australian tourism during the 1960s was the report on Australia's travel and tourism industry undertaken by the American consultants Harris, Kerr, Forster and Company and Stanton Robbins and Company (1966). The report had far-reaching implications for the future growth of Australian tourism, as it helped to shape the roles of the state and federal governments in the tourism industry. The most important recommendation concerned the establishment by the Commonwealth of a statutory authority, later to become the Australian Tourist Commission (ATC), which was to be responsible for overall industry coordination and the international marketing of Australia. The report stressed the need for a coordinated approach to tourism planning and marketing through the development of master plans, a substantial tourism research capacity, and the 'determination of roles of the Commonwealth Government and State and Territory Governments in relation to each other and to the activities of the many business organizations and individuals engaged in the various segments of the industry' (1966, p. 3) (see Chapter 5).

Unfortunately, many of the far-sighted recommendations of the report were never acted upon or have only recently received appropriate recognition. For example, the report emphasised the need for the development of an appropriate education and research base as a critical element in achieving long-term tourism growth in Australia. The report also highlighted the need for planning to replace the *ad hoc* approach of government at all levels towards tourism development and noted: 'Travel and tourism in Australia have developed from pressures created by expanding needs of the movement of people rather than by planning and direction' (Harris, Kerr, Forster & Co., Stanton Robbins & Co. 1966, p. 65). In addition, the report stressed the need for government and industry to recognise the role of Aboriginal peoples and national parks in tourism, through the establishment of more national parks and reserves and the need to conserve the values of traditional Aboriginal culture.

Heritage and tourism

Much of the discussion that has gone on in Australia about tourism has assumed that there isn't really very much reason for anyone to come to Australia, or at least nothing for which we ourselves can take credit. The Reef and the Rock, of course, and the beaches, and a concept of the bush in which jolly swagmen hump their portable barbies so that tourists can toss prawns on to them. But, overwhelmingly, Australia's appeal is taken to be Nature rather than Culture (D. Horne 1991, p. 1).

Apart from the potential of history to teach us a number of lessons about tourism development in Australia, history is now also an attraction in its own right. One of the best indications that Australia has come of age as a nation is the attention that Australians now pay to their own heritage (see Chapter 13). Only forty years ago historic buildings in the inner cities were frequently being demolished to make way for offices and new shopping developments. Although demolition still occurs, state and national heritage listing, and a general concern for the environment, have led to greater protection of Australia's heritage, in part because of its attractions for tourists.

One of the primary motivations for heritage protection has been the recognition by government and industry alike that heritage pays (Hall & McArthur 1993). Many tourists want to see Australia's history, the things that make Australia unique, not just the international-style modernist architecture that is the same the world over. As D. Horne (1991, p. 1) commented with respect to Cairns in the early 1990s:

> They have ripped out segments of the old Cairns and put up (usually) standard-style hotels owned by foreigners. The fragile and distinctive character of Cairns has gone. When people stay at Cairns now, they may remember their excursions to the Reef or up the coast or into the mountains. But why would they remember Cairns?

For this reason, preservation of the colonial architectural heritage of Sydney's historic Rocks area should be regarded as a tourism product just as much as it is a matter of concern for the members of the local community who wish to save their living space. Similarly, areas such as Katoomba and the Blue Mountains are increasingly capitalising on their unique landscape assets, rather than allowing inappropriate development which is unsympathetic to the natural and cultural heritage of the region, and, in the same way, Tasmania is focusing on its heritage in its promotion and marketing.

A concern for heritage can also be witnessed in rural areas. For example, sections of the historic Ghan railway (owned by the Central Australian Railway) which commenced on 19 January 1878 and closed in 1980, have been refurbished as a tourist attraction. The Ghan now offers tourist income to the communities along the old railway and an authentic experience to international and domestic tourists alike. As Wood (1982, p. 58) reported:

> To travel by road, down from Alice Springs to Marree, along the now closed line, is quite another experience. For me it was a childlike journey through a vibrant land populated by ghosts, an almost continuous stream of new feelings, awe inspiring sights and extraordinary personal revelations.

Indeed, with the proposed completion of the Adelaide–Darwin train line, the tourism significance of railways is making something of a comeback.

A further aspect of the development of tourism is that it has assisted Australians in appreciating their environment and national identity as never before. Tourism has helped Australia's search for a social meaning in its environment. As D. Horne has observed, 'As the Swiss found national identity in the Alps, Australians have found identity in the red granite of Ayers Rock' (1984, p. 3). Similarly, Fiske et al. (1987, p. 129) noted that:

> . . . the eternal present in which the ancient land and Aboriginal cultures are seen to exist becomes an instant history for the white European tourists, replacing the very different and less 'natural' European history that they have dissociated themselves from. The search for national identity necessarily involves a search for history.

THE INFORMATIONAL SOCIETY

Castells (1996, p. 27) has noted that '. . . the ability to use (and to some extent to produce) information technologies has become a fundamental tool of development. It is the historical equivalent to electrification during the industrialization stage'.

The growth of the Internet is just one component in 'a technological revolution of historic proportions' (Castells 1996, p. 15) that is fundamentally changing Australian economy and society. Depending on their perspective, different authors use different names for this transition. From a technological perspective, Negroponte (1995) commented on the 'transition from atoms to bits', by which he meant that the production, distribution and consumption of physical products (atoms) are becoming relatively less important than the production, distribution and consumption of digitised information (bits), which can be transmitted in computer networks at the speed of light.

The term 'globalisation' is often used to refer to the increasing interdependence of national economies, and the social process by 'which the constraints of geography on social and cultural arrangements recede and in which people become increasingly aware that they are receding' (Waters 1995, p. 3). Castells (1996) talked about the emergence of an 'informational society'—that is, a society which is dependent upon, and structured by, information and communication flows. He recognised that the informational society is also a 'network society', in that 'our societies are fundamentally made of flows exchanged through networks of organizations and institutions' (Castells 1996, p. 29).

Whatever term is used to describe this new society, there seems to be a consensus that the changes under way in modern society are radical and fundamental. Innovations in telecommunications are an important element in this transition, although they have not triggered it. They are, as Capello and Gillespie (1994, p. 168) have argued, 'only necessary but not sufficient conditions for these dynamics'. However, Castells (1996, p. 15) has acknowledged the 'extraordinary social change represented by new information technologies. In an obvious historical parallel the steam engine did not create the industrial society by itself. But without the steam engine there would not have been an industrial society'. And, reflecting on what was discussed earlier in this chapter, we might also observe that without the steam engine there would have been no mass tourism.

According to Castells (1996), two basic features of the current technological revolution are especially important: (i) its process orientation; and (ii) the role of information as the basic raw material. With respect to the first, Castells (1996, p. 16) noted that: 'Because it is process oriented (as was the industrial revolution) its effects are pervasive, and cut across all spheres of human activity'. With respect to the second, Castells (1996, p. 15) observed that: 'Its fundamental raw material, as well as its principal outcome, is information . . . In this the information technology revolution is distinctive from preceding technological revolutions. While information and knowledge were always essential elements in any process of scientific discovery and technical change, this is the first time in history in which the new knowledge applies primarily to generation of knowledge and information processing.

However, economic and industrial change typically does not result from telecommunication infrastructure directly. Rather, it comes from organisational changes in businesses in reaction to advances in telecommunication. Therefore, the 'organizational variable is regarded as a fundamental and crucial "bridge" to capture the linkages between technological changes and their spatial dynamics' (Capello & Gillespie 1994, p. 168). To utilise an advanced telecommunication infrastructure such as the Internet to its full potential, businesses have to adjust their organisational structures to fit the new requirements and opportunities (Marshall & Richardson, 1996). As Castells (1996, p. 19) has observed: 'Overall, and as a general trend, multidirectional networks are substituting for vertical bureaucracies as the most efficient, archetypical form of the new system, on the basis of flexible, affordable, and increasingly powerful information/communication technologies'. This emergence of firm networks was well under way even before the Internet became a business tool (Bergman et al., 1991). However, the Internet has helped speed up this development. Just as the pattern of industrialisation during the Industrial Revolution determined the economic fate of countries and regions, the manner in which companies utilise telecommunications technologies and integrate them into their business operations will, along with an array of other factors, set the framework for economic prosperity in the future (Maier & Kaufmann 1997).

Three main factors can be identified as contributing to the growth of tourism in Australia:
- the development of transport technology that reduces travelling time;
- changes in attitudes to tourism and leisure activities and their social, economic, and political dimensions; and
- improvements in economic conditions and increases in personal disposable income that can be used for travel and leisure purposes.

From the perspective of these factors, the evolution of tourism in Australia can be regarded as the result of interplay among the social, political, economic and technological forces operating on and within Australian society (Figure 2.2). Therefore, considerable attention needs to be paid to the potential for social and technological forces to influence the establishment and likely success of a sustainable approach to tourism development. In recent years a range of technological innovations has emerged with substantial implications for tourism development in Australia. For example, developments in communications technology, such as the Internet, have had tremendous impacts not

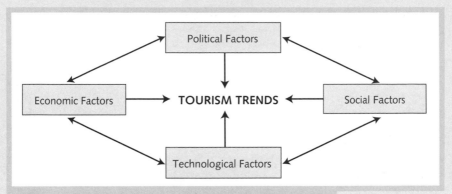

Figure 2.2 Factors in the determination of tourism trends
Source: Hall (1994b, p. 2).

only on how tourists purchase tourism products and gain knowledge about tourism destinations, but also on the nature of economic and industrial development and Australian identity.

It is also apparent that government has had a major role in tourism development through its promotion of tourism, establishment of infrastructure (particularly transport), the development of regulatory frameworks for tourism development. Mosley's observation in his landmark Tasmanian study that, 'Government participation in tourist promotion, prompted partly by economic difficulties, has led to the provision of facilities and services at a higher level than could probably have been achieved by voluntary and commercial effort alone' (1963, précis), holds true to the present day. Despite the fact that the role of direct government involvement in tourism development is increasingly questioned in what is now essentially seen as a private enterprise activity, public demands for social and environmental responsibility in tourism development might well produce a reorientation, rather than a reduction, in the role of government.

The major geographic factor in the development of Australian tourism has been that of distance. The size of the Australian continent, the distance between major urban centres, and the distance from overseas tourist generating regions have all restricted the growth of tourism. Domestic tourism has traditionally been restricted to destinations near cities, especially coastal destinations (Department of Tourism and Recreation Cities Commission 1975). The rapid development of Western Australia, northern Queensland, and Tasmania as significant tourist destinations in recent years has occurred only because developments in transport technology reduced the relative isolation of those areas. However, as Blainey (1983, p. 342) observed:

> Australia will continue to be seen as isolated. All isolation is relative. To a traveller who has flown 13 000 miles to reach Australia, even an additional 500 miles from Sydney to Melbourne can seem an intolerable burden. The most important reason why Sydney in the years 1955–1980 was able to challenge Melbourne as the financial hub, and to become the base for so many of the American and Japanese

companies in finance and banking, was simply its slight advantage in proximity to East Asia and North America and its possession of the main international airport. Sydney's advantage was a few ticks of the clock but that was a big advantage.

Despite technological advances, the concept of distance, which exists in the mind as well as in space, still poses significant problems for present-day travellers. In international terms Australasia will continue to be relatively isolated from the tourist-generating regions of Europe and North America. Therefore, Australia will need to harness features such as its unique natural and cultural attractions, and its relative safety, if it is to enhance its appeal as a destination. The significance of this strategy should be readily apparent given the manner in which tourist areas tend to evolve. As Plog (1974, p. 16) observed: 'Destination areas carry with them the potential seeds of their own destruction, as they allow themselves to become more commercialized and lose their qualities which originally attracted tourists'.

Given the rapid growth in Japanese, Taiwanese and Korean travel to Australia in recent years, the immediate future of inbound tourism appears to lie in South-East Asia and the Pacific Rim (Hall 1994b, 1997b; Hall & Page 2000). The reaction of some Australians to this new travel market has been mixed, and the development of Australian tourism is closely related to the social context.

Until the Second World War the dominant perspective in Australia was that of an Anglo-Saxon society, an outpost of European civilisation and the British Empire in the South Pacific. Nevertheless, as recent controversies over multiculturalism and the creation of an Australian republic have highlighted, Australia is now a racially mixed culture, forging a new national identity. However, old attitudes die hard. Xenophobic reactions to Mediterranean and Slavic peoples in the late 1940s and 1950s and South-East Asian peoples in the 1980s have reflected the various stages of migration to Australia, even though such migration contributes substantially to Australia's economic and social development, and to tourism in particular (Jackson 1990; King 1994; Nguyen & King 2001). Australians now face a new 'invasion' of overseas visitors much larger in number than that of the greatest periods of migration. The enormous number of international tourists, especially from Asia, presents a new challenge to the perceptions and values of Australian society. Moreover, more Australian residents are travelling overseas than ever before. Relatively little research has been conducted on the social impacts of tourism in Australia but, in the long term, the ability of Australian society to absorb tourists will determine the future viability of the tourism industry.

In recognition of the growth in inbound and outbound tourism we can note the emergence of a new trend (or force) in Australian tourism, that of globalisation and mobility. As a result of technological changes Australia is closer to the rest of the world than ever before. 'Time–space compression' means that relative travel times and costs have been reduced, and that Australia's relationship with the rest of the world, in communications terms at least, is almost instantaneous. In addition, more than ever, Australia is part of a global economy in which economic changes far from Australian shores can have dramatic impacts on the viability of tourism in this country. The world is changing, not only in relation to traditional ideas of what constitutes tourism but also with respect to work and labour markets, second homes, and education. It is in this changing historical context that we investigate tourism in Australia.

SUGGESTIONS FOR FURTHER READING

For an extremely readable and informative discussion of the history of tourism see Feifer (1985). The excellent book by Towner (1996) is also a valuable reference tool. A special 1985 issue of *Annals of Tourism Research*, vol. 2, no. 3, examined the evolution of tourism and contains a valuable introductory paper by Butler and Wall which provides an overview of the field. Much of the research on the historical development of tourist destinations has examined the application of life-cycle concepts to the evolution of tourist areas. On this topic see Butler (1980) and Haywood (1986) in particular. Richardson (1999) provides a very general introduction to some aspects of Australian tourism history.

Tourism-related histories have been written on several Australian locations. On the Gold Coast see Jones (1986) and Vader & Lang (1980). On the Blue Mountains and Katoomba see Smith (1984) and Stanbury (1988), especially Chapter 7 by Anne Burke entitled 'Awesome cliffs, fairy dells and lovers silhouetted in the sunset— a recreation history of the Blue Mountains, 1870–1939'. Readers should also consult Anne Burke's unpublished 1981 honours thesis, *Images of popular leisure in the Blue Mountains*. An interesting account of tourism in the Whitsundays is to be found in Barr (1989, 1990a, 1990b), and a detailed history of tourism development at Noosa and the Cooloola area is contained in Cato (1989). The PhD thesis by Mosley (1964) provides excellent coverage of the development of touristic activities in Tasmania from settlement to the early 1960s in a manner unmatched by other Australian research. For a detailed discussion of the history of national parks and wilderness conservation in Australia and its relationship to tourism see Hall (1992a). An excellent collection of readings on various aspects of Australian travel history and travel in Australian culture is to be found in *Travellers, Journeys, Tourists*, the tenth edition of *Australian Cultural History* (Horne & Walker 1991). Two useful articles on the place of the beach in Australian society and its role in tourism are Abel (1994) and Davidson (1996). The recent book by Booth (2001) is also extremely valuable.

INTERNET SITES

- Australian History Links
  www.dropbears.com/l/links/history.htm

- Rail Australia
  www.railaustralia.com.au

- Also see Tourism Insights at
  www.prenhall.com/hall_au

Key concepts

Key concepts discussed in this chapter were:
transport technology, social attitudes, spa tourism, fashion, available leisure time, disposable income, 'tyranny of distance', mass tourism, heritage.

Questions for review and discussion

1 Describe how the 'tyranny of distance' has affected the development of tourism both to and within Australia.
2 Why did the inclusion of Australia on the itinerary for Cook's tours prove to be a turning point for travel to Australia?
3 Why was the railway such a critical factor in the development of tourist and resort destinations?
4 Why was the period after the Second World War marked by a boom in leisure and tourism?
5 What are the main factors that can be identified as contributing to the growth of tourism in Australia?
6 According to the discussion paper prepared for Australia's 10 year plan for tourism (DITR 2002h, p. 79):

'The projected growth of tourism in Australia (both domestic and inbound) will place increasing demands on the existing tourism infrastructure and on energy and resource consumption. Adequate planning and innovative strategies will be needed to ensure tourism is able to grow sustainably, within the environmental and social carrying capacity of tourism destinations and meet international expectations'

Does history give us any insights as to the indications of tourism growth?

WHY DO WE TRAVEL? TOURIST MOTIVATIONS AND MARKETS

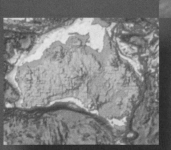

3

Regardless of where you are going there is a certain art of travelling. Whether you intend leaving our shores or exploring other parts of Australia, every journey creates a feeling of anticipation. It is a break from the regular daily routine. An opportunity to let both the mind and the body relax and savour the experiences of different attitudes and cultures (Travelstrength 1988, p. 2).

. . . I imagine—but I was always weak on psychology—that what prompts most people to travel is simply the infernal monotony of things. Live in the same place long enough, among the same people, pursuing the same daily round of work and play, and there must come an uncontrollable longing for change, a longing to get out of that place, away, the farther the better, from those people—anywhere, anywhere, so long as it is somewhere else. Men want a holiday from business, women want a rest from housekeeping; but that is not what they chiefly want—they want a change, they want to see something different, different streets, different faces (Murdoch 1939, p. 713).

As the previous chapter demonstrated, although there remain certain common themes in the history of tourism development, tourism is an incredibly dynamic industry. Destinations rise and fall in popularity and all markets change over time. The changing attractiveness of destinations and their ability to draw tourists are related to both the supply and demand components of the tourism market system. Indeed, as the model of the life cycle of a tourist area (Figure 2.1, page 38) illustrated, the two are inextricably related.

A tourist market can be described as a defined group of consumers for a particular tourist product or range of tourist products (Holloway & Plant 1992). How the market is defined is of great importance in determining the industry (supply side) response to consumers' perceived motivations, expectations and needs, and the long-term relationship between the supply and demand sides of the tourism development process. Tourism consumers are not homogeneous. Therefore, in order to understand the consumer better, the tourism market can be divided into a number of segments which share a set of common purchasing and behavioural characteristics. The characteristics of travellers can be measured objectively in terms of demographic, geographic, and socioeconomic factors and past travel behaviours, whereas motivations, expectations, likelihood of travel and preferred experiences can be inferred. Both objective and inferred measures of tourist characteristics can, in turn, be examined from general and situation-specific perspectives (see Figure 3.1). This process is known as market segmentation. Segments are usually identified along three main sets of characteristics: geographic, demographic, and psychographic, and combinations thereof.

Geographic segmentation

Geographic segmentation refers to the origin or source area of visitors to a destination. Such segmentation allows tourism marketers and planners to identify the 'catchment region' of both existing and planned tourism products. In the case of international visitors to Australia for example, such segmentation indicates the growing importance of the Asia–Pacific region as a tourist-generating region for Australia over the past decade (Hall 1994b). Much of the readily available data on inbound tourism into Australia are presented in the form of geographic segmentation based on country of origin. Geographic segmentation can also reveal that different countries hold different images of a place. For example, Tourism New South Wales (TNSW 1997e, p. 1) undertook research on the image of Sydney which confirmed that the city is perceived differently by its main markets.

> . . . potential visitors from the UK believed Sydney's major attractions were, in order of importance, its clean, modern fresh look, outdoor lifestyle, blue skies, beaches, nature, friendly and relaxed people and its food and wine. On the other hand potential visitors from Asia, other than Japan, believed Sydney was special for shopping, eating out, family activities, wildlife and icons such as the Sydney Opera House.

Demographic segmentation

Tourist markets can be segmented according to such variables as age, sex, occupation, level of income, ethnic association, religion, level of education, and class. For example, an ethnic festival which celebrates the culture of a particular ethnic group will probably be an attraction to the members of that ethnic group. Similarly,

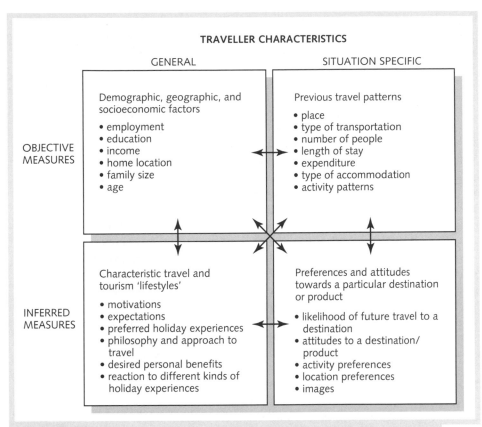

TRAVELLER CHARACTERISTICS

	GENERAL	SITUATION SPECIFIC
OBJECTIVE MEASURES	Demographic, geographic, and socioeconomic factors • employment • education • income • home location • family size • age	Previous travel patterns • place • type of transportation • number of people • length of stay • expenditure • type of accommodation • activity patterns
INFERRED MEASURES	Characteristic travel and tourism 'lifestyles' • motivations • expectations • preferred holiday experiences • philosophy and approach to travel • desired personal benefits • reaction to different kinds of holiday experiences	Preferences and attitudes towards a particular destination or product • likelihood of future travel to a destination • attitudes to a destination/product • activity preferences • location preferences • images

Figure 3.1 Classification scheme for tourism and travel data variables
Source: adapted from Bryant, B.E. & Morrison, A.J. (1980) 'Travel market segmentation of market strategies', *Journal of Travel Research*, Winter, p. 3.

TOURISM INSIGHT

TOURISM AND MIGRATION

Despite its potential significance, relatively little research has been undertaken on the links between tourism and migration (Williams & Hall 2000; Hall & Williams 2002). However, recent research on Visiting Friends and Relations (VFR) tourism has brought to light a likely connection between immigration and a subsequent increase in VFR tourism. Jackson (1990) reported that the movement of immigrants increased the numbers of VFR coming to visit by their presence and by the fact they could provide accommodation and support for the visitors. The movement is especially evident after the initial immigration of people. There is also movement in the other direction as immigrants travel to their country of birth to visit friends and family, a view supported by the work of King (1994), Yuan et al. (1995), and Nguyen & King (2002). Significantly, the influences of such transnational relationships can last several generations as the second and third generations of immigrants might well return to their 'home' country or region to trace their roots and ancestry.

According to King (1994), ethnic VFR tourism will increase in countries that have received large immigrant groups in the last two decades and in countries where it is easy to enter and leave. For example, China has established a tourism bureau which specifically targets the foreign Chinese population in order to attract them as visitors (King 1994). This development has implications for countries such as Australia which has a population with an ancestor base scattered throughout the world. King (1994) believes VFR tourism is an increasing force in 'ethnic' tourism which he defines as 'the search for "exotic" cultures and travel which is motivated by purposes of ethnic reunion'.

The migration patterns of people leaving their countries of residence to reside in another country provides an increased motivation for VFR travel, although it should be noted that this type of tourism does not necessarily involve visitors staying with friends and/or family. For example, a study by King and Gamage (1994) analysed the travel patterns to Sri Lanka of expatriate Sri Lankan residents living in Australia. Their analysis showed a decline in return travel over time, and therefore only first-generation residents were studied. The authors found that a majority of respondents had travelled back to Sri Lanka or were intending to do so. VFR was the main motivation for travelling back to Sri Lanka, with others citing holiday motivations and a mixture of VFR, holiday, and business.

Dwyer et al. (1993) investigated the links between settler arrivals and subsequent tourism to Australia. Through correlation analyses they found that visiting relatives (VR) tourists from South-East Asia, and holiday visitor and business visitor movements from Asia and the Middle East, were all strongly associated with settler arrivals from these regions. In contrast there did not appear to be an association between immigrants and VR tourists from Europe in the 1980s, although moderate VR movements did appear to be associated with large numbers of immigrants from Yugoslavia, Greece and Italy who arrived in the postwar economic boom. However, the authors noted that the lack of a relationship between European immigrants and VR could be due to the distance between Europe and Australia. As Jackson (1990) noted, VFR tourists are more likely to travel short distances, making Asian VFR more likely. Furthermore, the fact that the majority of European immigration took place in the 1950s, 1960s, and early 1970s could indicate that time since departure may account for the decline in visits by friends and family. This assessment is supported by the work of Jackson (1990), who found that increased length of time since immigration results in lower VFR travel.

On a global scale the role of return visitation is integral to the migration process and is an important element in the creation of transnational identities. Return visitation is also important in the maintenance of multiple senses of place often witnessed in migrant communities or in 'new' migrant countries where the issues of 'who we are' and 'where do we belong' become matters of much debate. In this sense return visitation, which can also be understood as VFR tourism or even ethnic tourism, can be likened to a form of secular pilgrimage and an important component of cultural renewal in establishing personal and collective identities (for example, see Baldassar 1995, 1997, 1998, in her work on Italian migrants in Perth, Western Australia). This can even extend to the purchase of retirement or second homes in the country of emigration (Hall & Williams 2002).

Although the data are often hard to obtain, Dwyer et al. (1995) made a number of suggestions regarding possible mechanisms through which the relationship between tourism and immigration could operate. These suggestions have found support in more recent research (Hall & Williams 2002). The suggested mechanisms are:

- *demonstration effect:* tourists, not intending to migrate, like the place and decide to immigrate;
- *information-gathering effect:* intending migrants visit to see for themselves whether they are likely to want to emigrate;
- *special category tourists/immigrants:* tourists might be in Australia for a special purpose (for example, education) and might be keen to immigrate afterwards; or older people might visit Australia and seek to come on extended visits in the future;
- *illegal immigrants:* tourism, short-term education, and work visas offer opportunities to enter the country and overstay; and
- *tourism as a substitute for immigration:* rather than immigrating permanently people make extended visits as tourists, including the purchase of second homes.

As Rodriguez (2001, in Hall & Willams 2002) observed: 'The challenges posed by a temporary or permanent change of residence can only be understood in terms of individual and family decision making, the mechanisms that facilitate their stay in the destination and the broader socio-economic structures which influence their decision'. Tourism is a major part of this phenomenon, whether as a source of employment or of information.

China has a substantial amount of VFR tourism because of the importance of maintaining relationships with the 'home' village. Such travel will still occur after several generations.

demographic analysis of international visitors might reveal factors related to the growth and development of the visiting friends and relatives (VFR) market and recent immigration to Australia (Jackson 1990; Cooper 2002; Nguyen & King 2002).

Psychographic segmentation

Markets can be identified in terms of motivations, images, expectations, and reasons for travel. For example, some cultural tourism events, such as art exhibitions and festivals, are deliberately structured so as to appeal to 'up-scale' market segments which seek exclusiveness, prestige, and status (Zeppel & Hall 1992). Bull (1991) also noted that tourists can be segmented by purpose of travel, and although such a segmentation is extremely useful, it is essentially a component of psychographic segmentation.

Regardless of which way the tourist market is segmented, an attractive market for a destination or tourist product is one in which:

- the market segment is of sufficient size to make the tourism product (or products) viable;
- the market segment has potential for growth;
- the market segment is not 'taken' or 'owned' by existing tourist destinations or products; and
- the market segment has a relatively unsatisfied interest or motivation that the destination or product can satisfy.

The above segmentation types (demographic, geographic, and psychographic) are used in this chapter to provide a framework for the analysis of the tourism market. This chapter discusses the changing international tourism market (both inbound and outbound) and the Australian domestic market. Some aspects of tourist motivations are related to the psychographic segmentation of travel markets. It is noted that domestic tourism, although not as glamorous as international travel, still accounts for the majority of tourist visitation within Australia (although the proportion is slowly decreasing as international visitation increases). The chapter concludes with an examination of forecasts of the growth of tourist visitation.

WHY DO PEOPLE TRAVEL?

Tourist motivations are an integral part of the tourist experience. In examining tourist motivations we are seeking to answer the question: 'Why is it that people leave their homes to visit other areas?' (Pearce 1987, p. 21). However, it is difficult to say with certainty that there is a definitive relationship between individual motivation and the selection of a destination because 'tourists are not mere numerical abstractions, but complex individual personalities, having a variety of complex motivations' (Bosselman 1978, p. 98). Furthermore, as noted in Chapter 1 (see Figure 1.5, page 18), consumers undertake a complex decision-making process in selecting holiday destinations and products. This process involves their needs and desires, motivations, preferences, expectations, images, perceptions, and evaluations of alternative holidays, before they make a final decision to select a particular product (Goodall 1988).

The complexity of travel motivations has been highlighted by Krippendorf (1987), who identified a number of popular interpretations of why people travel. According to Krippendorf travel is concerned with numerous motivations, including:

- recuperation and regeneration;
- compensation and social integration;
- escape;
- communication;
- broadening the mind;
- freedom and self-determination;
- self-realisation; and
- happiness.

The above list of motives is long and might even contain somewhat contradictory elements. Motivations are also dependent on other factors such as the traveller's social status, stage in personal life cycle, family relationships, education, and upbringing. Nevertheless, as Krippendorf (1987, p. 28) stated, the contradictions 'reveal the true nature of tourism—a scintillating and multifaceted part of human and social reality . . . We must not forget that the traveller . . . is a mixture of many characteristics that cannot be simply assigned into this category or that one'.

Wanderlust and sunlust

One of the first, and most quoted, statements on tourist motivation is that of Gray (1970). According to Gray, the two basic reasons for pleasure travel were 'wanderlust' and 'sunlust'. Gray (1970, p. 57) described wanderlust as:

> . . . that basic trait in human nature which causes some individuals to want to leave things with which they are familiar and to go and see at first hand different exciting cultures and places . . . The desire to travel may not be a permanent one, merely a desire to exchange temporarily the known workaday things of home for something which is exotic.

Sunlust depends on the existence elsewhere of different or better amenities for a specific purpose than are available locally.

The significance of these two concepts relates to the nature of the destination sought by the tourist and its associated facilities (Table 3.1). As Burkart and Medlik (1981, p. 58) suggested:

> A journey to a resort in a foreign country motivated by sunlust contains an element of satisfaction of wanderlust; conversely a tourist seeking to satisfy his wanderlust also expects some of the amenities of a resort holiday. But the distinction, even though one of degree, expresses realistically the flows of modern tourism.

TABLE 3.1 The attributes of sunlust and wanderlust travel

Sunlust	*Wanderlust*
Resort orientation	Broader accommodation spectrum
Single country/destination visited	Probably multicountry and multidestination travel
Travellers seek domestic amenities and accommodation	Travellers seek foreign cultural experiences
Natural attractions important especially climate	Interest in built and cultural attractions; climate less important
Travel a minor consideration after arrival at destination	Further travel a significant ingredient throughout visit
Either relaxing and restful or very active	Neither restful nor sportive; ostensibly educational
Relatively more domestic travel	Relatively more international travel

Source: adapted from Gray (1970).

According to Pearce (1987, p. 22), one expression of sunlust is, literally, a 'hunt for the sun' as typified by the large tourist flows to the Caribbean from North America or travel to the Mediterranean by northern Europeans. Examples of sunlust tourism in Australia include travel to the Gold Coast and Cairns in Queensland or to the alpine skifields in New South Wales and Victoria during the ski season. Wanderlust travel follows less popular routes and avoids the haunts of the sunlust-motivated tourists. It bears some of the hallmarks of 'backpacker' tourism and 'alternative' tourism. Examples of wanderlust tourism destinations in Australia include the wilderness area of south-west Tasmania and the Shark Bay area of Western Australia. However, one of the ironies of wanderlust travel is that the explorers of destinations often become the precursors of mass tourists who follow as destinations become increasingly popular and economically dependent on tourists.

Plog (1990) suggested a continuum of tourists—from allocentric to psychocentric. This basically described a range of behaviours from those who seek new destinations (allocentric) to those who seek organised mass tourism (psychocentric). Australians doing their 'OS' (overseas trip) or New Zealanders doing their 'OE' (overseas experience) can be placed within Plog's allocentric categorisation—with some qualification. OS and OE participants do travel great distances, but for many their destination is Britain, which has cultural similarities, a virtually identical language, and a supportive community in terms of a good number of expatriates and the likelihood of friends and relatives (Mason 2002) (see below). Indeed, in many cases people who go to the UK for their 'OE' often spend as much time socialising with other Australians and New Zealanders as they would do at home.

Push and pull factors: escapism and fantasy

According to Pearce (1987, p. 22): 'Wanderlust may be thought of essentially as a "push" factor whereas sunlust is largely a response to "pull" factors elsewhere'. Although development studies and promotional efforts in destination areas have continued to concentrate on the 'pull' factors with respect to the product they offer, recent motivational research has tended to emphasise the 'push' factor—that is, the need to break from routine and to 'get away from it all'. As Krippendorf (1987, p. xiii) noted:

> A restless activity has taken hold of the once so sedentary human society. Most people in the industrialised countries have been seized by a feverish desire to move. Every opportunity is used to get away from the workday routine as long as possible. Shorter trips during the week and on weekends, longer journeys during the holidays. The fondest wish for old age is a new place to which to retire. Anything to get away from home! Away from here at any cost!

Similarly, Leiper (1984, p. 249) has pointed out that 'all leisure involves a temporary escape of some kind'. However:

> . . . tourism is unique in that it involves a real physical escape reflected in travelling to one or more destination regions where the leisure experiences transpire . . . A holiday trip allows changes that are multi-dimensional: place, pace, faces, lifestyles, behaviour and attitude. It allows a person temporary withdrawal from many of the environments affecting day to day existence.

Leiper (1984) argued that tourism enhances leisure opportunities, particularly for rest and relaxation. However, of particular interest is the idea that one of the prime motivations for the tourist experience is the desire for escape and fantasy.

The role of escapism was central to the work of Dann (1976). According to Dann, fantasy motivators form an important element of travel demand and illustrate its individualistic nature. He observed (1976, p. 22) that:

> . . . holidays are essentially experiences in fantasy . . . A certain picture is built up of a world that marks an escape from present reality, an environment for acting out psychic needs, and the playing of certain roles cannot be fulfilled at home, and it is this which forms part and parcel of tourist motivation.

Dann identified two types of fantasy: (i) the 'anomic', in which the average city dweller desires to transcend the monotony of everyday life; and (ii) 'ego-enhancement', which provides psychological boosts through such activities as gambling holidays or sexual adventures—real or imagined.

One of the most cited studies of tourist motivation has been that of Crompton (1979a). Crompton (1979a, p. 145) noted that:

> . . . the essence of "break from routine" was, in most cases, either locating in a different place, or changing the dominant social context from the work [environment], usually to that of the family group, or doing both of these things.

Having established a 'break from routine' as the basic motivation for tourist travel, Crompton suggested that it was possible to identify more specific directive motives which serve to 'guide the tourist toward the selection of a particular type of vacation or destination in preference to all the alternatives of which the tourist is aware. In most decisions more than one motive is operative' (1979a, p. 145). Crompton also argued that the different motives of his respondents could be conceptualised as being 'located along a cultural–socio-psychological disequilibrium continuum'. The socio-psychological motives were often not expressed explicitly by the respondents but Crompton (1979a) identified seven central travel motives.
- escape from a perceived mundane environment;
- exploration and evaluation of self;
- relaxation;
- prestige;
- regression (less constrained behaviour);
- enhancement of kinship relationships; and
- facilitation of social interaction.

Crompton's seven factors broadly correspond to Dann's (1977) identification of the basic motivations as being a reaction to anomie (1, 6, 7), ego-enhancement (4), and fantasy (4, 5). Two primary cultural motives were expressed by Crompton's respondents—novelty and education—although Crompton did suggest that these motives could be more perceived than real. They also appear to be closely associated with some of the sociopsychological motives. For example, the search for novelty might well be complemented by the escape from a perceived mundane environment. Similar ideas have been expressed by Leiper (1984). Leiper distinguished between recreational leisure (which restores) and creative leisure (which produces something new). He saw the three functions of recreation as being:
- rest (providing recovery from physical or mental fatigue);
- relaxation (recovery from tension); and
- entertainment (recovery from boredom).

It should be noted that these three functions broadly correspond to Crompton's sociopsychological motives, whereas creativity covers aspects of the cultural motives.

Ryan and Hall (2001) have utilised the idea of liminality in relation to sex tourism to describe how a tourist engages in a temporary escape from the world of work, but later returns to it. Through travel away from the home environment, the tourist enters a liminal space in which normal behaviours and mores can be suspended because the tourist has a degree of 'separateness' from both home and the destination—thus allowing behaviours to be ritually 'inverted' (Turner 1969, 1974, 1982). Similarly, Graburn (1983a) considered that a substantial part of tourism activity constitutes forms of ritual. He viewed the play of tourists as a re-creation in which there is a ritual expression of deeply held values about health, freedom, nature, and self-improvement. As with Turner, Graburn suggested that, during leisure tourism activity, life is experienced as out of time and place. Tourists can therefore live as liminal people caught between the worlds of their own home and the temporary holiday home, but not in the homes and worlds of their hosts (Ryan et al. 1998). Indeed, as Ryan and Hall (2001) observed, sometimes their holiday homes are artificial homes, architecturally designed to encourage life by the side of the swimming pool, to gaze upon other tourists and cosseted so that daily tasks of making beds and washing dishes are no longer required. Holidays are therefore the marginal periods that possess the latent potential to change people's lives. Sometimes the change is substantial. For example, Wickens (1994, p. 821) attributed the label 'Shirley Valentine' (after the film and play of the same name) to a group of hedonistic tourists in Greece, and presented one such tourist as describing herself in these terms:

> You are here to please yourself. As far as I can, I leave my everyday life behind. When I'm in England, I'm fitting into an appointed role of somebody's wife, somebody's secretary. Here, you can relax, and rub off some of the sharp corners. You are not restricted. Greeks are very tolerant of us. If you give yourself a chance, you can find out things about yourself that you did not know before. I am less age-conscious here. I like sex but not with my husband. I come to Greece for a bit of fun.

The changes that occur to people might not be as dramatic as in the case above but, arguably, a substantial proportion of tourism does imply the search for something more than people experience in their everyday lives. In some cases this may be pleasure, as in the case of leisure holidays; in other instances it may be searching for 'home'.

Arguably the search for 'home' or a sense of belonging is one of the hallmarks of the modern condition in which an increasingly globalised world is marked by increased circulation, mobility, and rapidly accelerating rates of exchange, movement and communications across space and time. As Schiller et al. (1992, p. 11) observed, the constant and various flows of:

> . . . goods and activities have embedded within them relationships between people. These social relations take on meaning within the flow and fabric of daily life, as linkages between different societies are maintained, renewed, and reconstituted in the context of families, of institutions, of economic investments, business, and finance and of political organisations and structures including nation states.

To some commentators, such multilocational relationships have profound implications for our sense of identity. According to Harvey (1996, p. 246): 'The foreboding generated out of the sense of social space imploding in on us . . . translates into a crisis of identity. Who we are and what/space do we belong'.

Several authors (Williams & Kaltenborn 1999; Urry 2000; Williams & Hall 2000; Hall & Williams 2002) have argued that research on community, home, leisure, migration, and tourism, are infused and 'encumbered' by outdated assumptions of a geographically rooted subject often marked by traditional notions of a single, permanent residence. They have argued that the movement of peoples, rather than being seen as an integral aspect of social life, should be regarded as 'a special and temporary phenomenon . . . examined under the heading of migration, refugee studies, and tourism' (Halstrup & Olwig 1997, p. 6). Williams and Kaltenborn (1999) went on to claim that with circulation and movement becoming more the rule than the exception: 'an important geographic dimension of leisure practices is to understand how people in differing cultural contexts use leisure and travel to establish identity, give meaning to their lives, and connect with place' (1999, p. 215).

Going 'OS'

One of the most significant, but underresearched, aspects of the travel behaviour of Australians and New Zealanders is the phenomenon known in Australia as the 'OS' ('overseas') and in New Zealand as the 'OE' ('overseas experience'). These usually occur after finishing studies at school, TAFE, or university, and after a year or so of earning money to fund the travel. The OS and OE are examples of travel behaviour somewhere between tourism and migration, given that many people stay away for more than a year and therefore break the bounds of most technical definitions of tourism (see Chapter 1). Despite the length of time away from home, the OS or OE exhibits features common to tourism experiences. One of the major factors similar to other tourism experiences is the intention to return to the starting point of the journey. Therefore, the OS or OE does not seem to fit within traditional definitions of migration (Bell & Ward 2000; Williams & Hall 2000, 2002). However, it does share some characteristics of migration, in that working during the OS or OE is usually viewed as a key component of the experience, and one of the motivational factors in the activity (Mason 2001).

Cultural motivations are recognised as an important factor in the OS or OE. For some this is related to a desire to visit the lands of their forebears in the United Kingdom, southern Europe or, more recently, Asia (King 1994; Kang & Page 2000; Nguyen & King 2001). Countries such as Ireland and Scotland, which experienced

The opportunity to visit the 'must see' sites and icons of Europe becomes an important part of the 'OS' travel experience.

huge migrations to Australia in the nineteenth and early twentieth centuries, actively encourage and promote visits by Australians to 'discover' their Irish and Scottish heritage. Indeed, Chaddee and Cutler (1996) indicated that the desire to experience other cultures was the primary travel motivation of New Zealand students intending to take part in overseas travel. In their study of nearly 400 New Zealand university students, 59% of those surveyed indicated that they intended to travel to Europe, whereas 25% intended to travel to Asia (Chaddee & Cutler 1996). Moreover, those who intended going to Europe planned to stay away longer than those going to other areas. Chaddee and Cutler also indicated that a very high proportion of respondents (87%) had previously travelled overseas and that 90% intended to take part in an OE. Hence, previous experience of travel was also a significant factor influencing motivations and future travel and work plans (Mason 2002). However, Chaddee and Cutler (1996) found that the idea of supporting the OE by working while abroad was a motivating factor for only 8% of respondents, whereas almost two-thirds (65%) indicated that their OE would be funded from savings. They also found that 25% intended staying in backpacker hostels. The importance of family ties was indicated by 35% of respondents who indicated that they intended to stay with friends and relatives, whereas 32% intended to stay in hotels and motels. However, it should be noted that this was a survey of intentions rather than actual travel behaviour, and that financial restrictions might have limited the actual number of nights eventually spent in hotel and motel accommodation. Nevertheless, the results of Chaddee and Cutler's research have provided some support for the study of Bywater (1993) who contended that there is a growing trend away from hostel/backpacker accommodation to more expensive hotels and motels among student travellers.

According to Chadee and Cutler (1996) and Mason (2002) another important reason for going on an OS or OE is the desire to take part in some form of adventure. However, as Mason (2002) has noted, in using the ideas of Cohen (1974), participants who try to become part of the culture in which they are staying cannot be classified as 'drifters'. Rather, it is quite likely that OS or OE participants regard themselves as 'explorers' (Cohen 1974) wishing to make the most of their experience by immersing themselves in the local society, despite never fully becoming part of it. Mason has argued, in a similar fashion to Ryan and Hall (2001) above, that the desire of OS and OE participants for adventure is part of the process of stepping outside the bounds of 'normal' society. Mason has related this intention (to have experiences not obtainable at home) to the concept of a 'rite of passage'. Turner and Turner (1978) have argued that the notion of 'rite of passage' is relevant not only to social processes in 'tribal' societies, but also to religious and secular pilgrimages (Delaney 1990). The relationship between pilgrimage and travel is widely acknowledged in the tourism literature. Pilgrimage is 'an intrinsically processual social practice that has as its core journeying' (Morinis 1992, p. 2). The liminal component of pilgrimage was also acknowledged by Morinis who argued that pilgrimages are exceptional practices taking place outside habitual social realms. As Mason (2002) observed: 'these arguments suggest that it is possible to view the OE as a both a rite of passage and as a form of pilgrimage'.

According to Graburn (1983a, pp. 12–13) the type of tourism that involves a rite of passage: 'Often consists of prolonged absences, often arduous which are a kind of self testing wherein the individuals prove to themselves that they can make the life changes'. The idea of overseas travel as a form of pilgrimage and a rite of passage can be found in Mason's (2002) report of Jamieson's (1996) finding that OE participants regarded the experience as a suspension of the usual home environment activities. Jamieson's study of what people actually did on their OE confirmed that the behaviour of most participants was markedly different from that at home. Therefore, according to Mason (2002), the journey is not just a movement in space from the familiar to the unfamiliar, but is also a spiritual ascent. As Turner and Turner (1978, p. 3) stated:

> The pilgrim undergoes a number of transformations, in which previous orderings of thought and behaviour are subject to revision and criticism and unprecedented modes of ordering relations between ideas and people become possible and desirable.

A pilgrimage involves stepping outside normal boundaries, leaving one's ordinary daily life behind, and departing on a journey to the 'centre out there' (Turner 1973, 1974). Turner (1978) also suggested that pilgrimage allows a confrontation of identities—between the one left behind and the new one created during the journey. Indeed, many people who are going on an OS often say that they are looking to 'grow up', 'find themselves', or 'find the world'. A pilgrimage can be viewed as part of a rite of passage, and Jamieson claimed that the OE constitutes the separation stage of a rite of passage for many. Therefore, it is possible to regard the OE in the context of a ritual expression, as suggested by Graburn (1983), and thus to regard it as a part of a pilgrimage.

TOURISM INSIGHT

ANZAC DAY AND SECULAR PILGRIMAGE

Anzac Day, 25 April, is probably Australia's most important national commemoration. The acronym 'ANZAC' stands for Australian and New Zealand Army Corps, and Anzac Day marks the anniversary of the first major military action fought by Australian and New Zealand forces during the First World War. On 25 April 1915 a combined Allied force landed on the Gallipoli Peninsula in Turkey, in an attempt to defeat Turkey and provide improved access for Russian forces to hasten the end of the war. Unfortunately, the operation was poorly planned and executed, with the Turkish forces being far more capable than the British commanders had expected. The Allied forces occupied Turkish soil from 25 April 1915 to 20 December 1915. Of the 50 000 Australians who fought at Gallipoli, 8709 were killed and 18 235 were wounded, with the majority of deaths and injuries occurring at what is now known as Anzac Cove on the western side of the Gallipoli Peninsula. The Turkish forces also suffered huge losses with an estimated 86 000 being killed (Winter 1994).

The idea a 'blood sacrifice' was a necessary rite of passage (or initiation ceremony) in the birth of a nation was common in the late Victorian and Edwardian period (Phillips 1999). In Australia, 25 April was officially named Anzac Day in 1916. During the 1920s, Anzac Day became established as a national day of commemoration for the 60 000 Australians who died during the First

World War. With symbolic links to the dawn landing at Gallipoli, a dawn 'stand-to' ceremony became a common form of Australia's Anzac Day remembrance during the 1920s with the first official dawn service being held at the Sydney Cenotaph in 1927. By 1927 all six Australian states observed some form of public holiday on Anzac Day. By the mid-1930s all the rituals associated with Anzac Day in present-day Australia—dawn vigils, marches, memorial services, reunions, sly 'two-up' games—were firmly established as part of the culture of the day (Andrews 1993; Phillips 1999). The use of the word 'Anzac' is strictly controlled by government, further enshrining the Anzac myth and the sacredness of Anzac Day (NZ History Net 2000).

In 1915, Australia was a new nation, fewer than fourteen years old, and the creation of the ANZAC was the first time that Australians from all the former colonies had came together to form an Australian army, having previously fought as individual colonial forces during the Boer and Crimean wars.

In Australia, Anzac Day is recognised as one of the most important days of nationhood and national identity with the spirit of Anzac being central to Australians' self-image. This was not because of a military victory but because of the manner in which the Australian and New Zealand troops performed on the battlefield and supported each other in what has become known as the spirit of 'mateship'—a spirit celebrated particularly in relation to the myth of the bush or 'outback' (McGregor 1966; Hall 1985). For example, at the 2000 Anzac Day service at Gallipoli the Australian Prime Minister told the largely youthful crowd at the 85th commemorative dawn service:

> We come . . . to observe not only a dawn, but a dusk . . . Soon the story of Anzac will pass gently from memory into history. Soon its record, once written on pages wet with tears, will be ours alone to guard, ours to cherish, ours to live. It is a remarkable legacy . . . History may choose to chronicle the Battle of Lone Pine as an unsuccessful military feint . . . but to us, it will always be about young Australians, exactly like those with us here today (Grattan 2000, p. 1).

The bush myth and the entwined myths and images of larrikinism, mateship, and hardship were represented in Peter Weir's internationally acclaimed movie 'Gallipoli', released in 1981 (Gammage 1984). These images have continued to be portrayed and reinforced in the film character 'Crocodile Dundee', which has confirmed the strength of the myth of the bush in the Australian national psyche. Such strong images of popular culture have also ensured a permanent position of the Anzac spirit within Australia's national identity (Back 1995).

It is also the source of the popular mythical conception of a 'typical' Australian—a tall, lean, sun-tanned, slow-talking character with 'a chip on his shoulder', who hates authority, is loyal to his mates, stands up for the underdog, and believes that a man is as good as the next, if not a damned sight better. He is a seminal pioneering figure, and no doubt this is how many Australians like to think of themselves (McGregor 1966, pp. 18–19).

Travel to Anzac Day commemorations is important for both domestic and international travel operators. In domestic terms, attendances are increasing at Anzac Day services and parades. For example, in Sydney, Anzac Day in 2000 'began with an unprecedented pilgrimage in wet, cold darkness as more than 10 000 people made their way to the Cenotaph in Martin Place, which marks the site of the city's main World War I recruiting office' (Hill 2000, p. 1). Later 150 000 people lined the streets of Sydney to watch more than 20 000 marchers.

In terms of international travel, Anzac Day is also significant. For example, it was reported that between 10 000 and 15 000 people heard the Australian Prime Minister address the dawn service at Gallipoli in 2000 (Grattan 2000; Hill 2000). Similarly, from a New Zealand perspective, the 75th anniversary of the Gallipoli landings in 1990 (coinciding with the 150th anniversary of the signing of the Treaty of Waitangi) attracted immense interest at Gallipoli. The official delegation was led by the Governor-General and included a Gallipoli veteran. The delegation, together with a host of Australian and New Zealand tourists, attended an emotional Anzac Day dawn service. Since that time many New Zealanders have made a pilgrimage to Gallipoli for Anzac Day, with nearly 3000 Australians and New Zealanders being present in 1997 (NZ History Net 2000).

The notion of pilgrimage is utilised by the travel industry in promoting travel to Turkey by Australians and New Zealanders, especially at the time of the Anzac Day commemoration. For example, ICTurkey (2001) has noted that its Anzac tourism package is 'included with other pilgrimages', claiming that 'ICTurkey's passengers paid the lowest for the best Anzac Pilgrimage'. Several other tour companies, such as ANZAC House, Down Under Travel Agency and First 48 Tours, also specialise in catering to younger Australians travelling in Europe, often as backpackers. The secular pilgrimage to Anzac Cove has even been enmeshed with religious pilgrimage. For example, ICTurkey (2001) included its Anzac pilgrimage with a range of other Jewish and Christian pilgrimages to Turkey, and Harvest Pilgrimages (2000, p. 38), official tour operator for the 'Great Jubilee' claimed to 'pay tribute and pray for these souls of the heroes of those tragic months of 1915' in its guided tour to Gallipoli. Similarly, the Royal British Legion (2001) has operated visits to Commonwealth war cemeteries through its 'Pilgrimage Department', and Australian government departments have also run pilgrimages to visit war graves (Reid 1995).

The attendance at the annual dawn service and related national services is now so great that both the Australian Embassy in Turkey and the Australian Commonwealth Department of Veterans' Affairs have warned of traffic congestion in the area and heavy demands on accommodation. Indeed, many Australian backpackers sleep in their sleeping bags on the beach (Grattan 2000), and thousands of travellers, mainly Australians and New Zealanders, travel to Çanakkale by tour buses and public vehicular ferries to take part in the dawn service at Anzac Cove. In keeping with other forms of pilgrimage, attendance at the services carries a degree of hardship—although clearly not as great as that experienced by the original Anzacs. According to the Commonwealth Department of Veterans' Affairs (2001):

The dawn service is held at 0530. Visitors arriving for the dawn service should carry a torch and follow the instructions of officials. As the morning can be cold extra clothing might also be appreciated. The day is long and some food and drink can help keep the spirits going. Those arriving the night before are advised to keep to the main congregation areas and to be aware of their personal safety as the area is undeveloped. There are no facilities such as fresh water and toilets.

As a result of increasing numbers of international visitors attending the Anzac memorial sites, and the demand on Anzac Day in particular, the Australian and New Zealand governments have financially contributed to the upgrading of facilities at Anzac Cove—including a new commemorative site, designed to accommodate the ever-expanding crowds as Gallipoli (Grattan 2000).

The exact number of Australian and New Zealand visitors to Gallipoli is difficult to ascertain because of the lack of accurate Turkish regional tourism statistics. Nevertheless, Australian and New Zealand travel to Turkey is substantial, and is encouraged by all governments involved. According to the Turkish Ministry of Tourism (1999) 18 667 Australians stayed in officially registered accommodation establishments in 1998. Significantly, Australian and New Zealand arrivals to Turkey increase substantially in April, and at a higher rate than other market segments, reflecting the significance of the Anzac Day commemoration (Hall 2002a). Anecdotal evidence also suggests that Gallipoli has now become a major year-long attraction for Australian and New Zealand tourists, and an Australian guide book on the Gallipoli battlefield has now entered a second edition after several reprints (Taylor & Cupper 1997).

Although Anzac commemorative services do have religious overtones, the Anzac pilgrimage is not a religious pilgrimage. Nor is it the pilgrimage of a migrant returning to the ancestral home in search of cultural identity. Rather, Anzac is a secular pilgrimage of national identity in which the myths of nationhood are paramount. For the majority of countries around the world, secular pilgrimages to the birthplaces of nationhood are usually within their own territories. Australia is unusual in that one of its key national birthplaces is on the barren and forbidding shores of Turkey. The significance of Gallipoli as a site for pilgrimage travel has increased over the years while the number of survivors of the Gallipoli campaign has dwindled. Such travellers are locating identity in a pilgrimage to the symbolic birthplace of an important set of national myths. The travel, and the myths it reproduces, are officially encouraged by the Australian government through support for official services, maintenance of war graves, and the development of official commemorative sites. The travel and myths are also backed by the tourism industry, which is well positioned to support and encourage pilgrimage to Gallipoli.

Australian Embassy to Turkey: **www.embaustralia.org.tr/anzac/anzacdayatgallipoli.htm**
Commonwealth Department of Veterans Affairs 'Visit Gallipoli': **www.anzacsite.gov.au**

Table 3.2 indicates many of the motivational factors discussed above, within the context of the motivational headings utilised in the model of the tourism market system presented in Chapter 1.

Many of the motivational factors discussed above were brought together by Iso-Ahola (1980, 1982, 1983), who proposed a theoretical model for motivation in which the escaping element is complemented or compounded by a seeking component (see also Pearce 1987, p. 23). One set of motivational forces derives from an individual's desire to escape his or her personal environment (for example, personal troubles, problems, difficulties, and failures) and/or the interpersonal environment (for example, co-workers, family members, friends, and neighbours) (see Figure 3.2). Another set of forces derives from the desire to obtain certain psychological or intrinsic rewards, either personal or interpersonal, by travelling to a different environment. In general, Iso-Ahola's examples of personal rewards (for example, rest and relaxation, ego-enhancement, and learning about other cultures) and interpersonal rewards

TABLE 3.2 Motivations of the tourist

Motivational Category	Motivations
Physical motivations	refreshment of body and mind for health purposes for participation in sports contact with an outdoor way of life
Cultural motivations	curiousity about foreign countries, people, culture, and places interests in art, music, architecture, and folklore interest in cultural heritage and historical places experiencing specific cultural events
Social motivations	visiting relatives and friends meeting new people seeking new friendships and relationships seeking new and different experiences travelling for travel's sake prestige and status fashion (for example, 'keeping up with the Joneses') pursuit of hobbies continuation of education or learning seeking of business contacts and professional goals conferences and meetings
Spiritual motivations	visiting places and people for religious reasons travelling as part of a pilgrimage travelling to 'find oneself' contact with nature
Fantasy	personal excitement of travelling 'anomic'—escaping from one's own permanent social environment (for example, desire for a change) 'ego-enhancement'—sensual indulgence (both real and imagined)

Source: adapted from Mathieson and Wall (1982); Pearce (1982); Mill and Morrisson (1985); Murphy (1985); Goodall and Ashworth (1988); McIntosh and Goeldner (1990); Weiler and Hall (1992).

(essentially greater social interaction) correspond closely with Crompton's specific motivational forces noted above. According to Iso-Ahola (1983, p. 260), the model can be used for practical considerations 'because a person's reasons (the relative importance of the two forces and their dimensions) for travel may significantly influence his selection of the tourist group with whom he wishes to travel'. Furthermore, 'the model emphasizes the dialectical character of tourism motivation and demonstrates that it is futile to attempt to categorically separate reasons from benefits, because reasons (e.g. exploring new places) can be benefits and benefits (e.g. escape from routine) can be reasons for tourism behavior' (1980, p. 260).

The central point of Iso-Ahola's work is that tourism provides an outlet for simultaneously avoiding something and seeking something. Recognition that elements of both sets of forces—the relative importance of which differs from case to case—can be satisfied at the same time, is extremely useful in clarifying some of the issues in motivational research. Iso-Ahola has also suggested that, in terms of dominant motives, it is theoretically possible to locate any tourist or group in a different cell at a given time. However, it should be noted that individuals within a group might be in different cells, and that any given individual can change from one cell to another during the course of a trip or from one trip to another.

This last point is particularly important because motivations—along with attitudes, images, and levels of satisfaction—change depending on what stage of a trip a visitor is on. Individual visitor motivations, attitudes, behaviours, and expectations do not remain constant. They change over the life cycle of an individual, are affected by prior experiences, and are impacted by media, word-of-mouth opinions, and other information sources. Much market analysis focuses on the implications of these

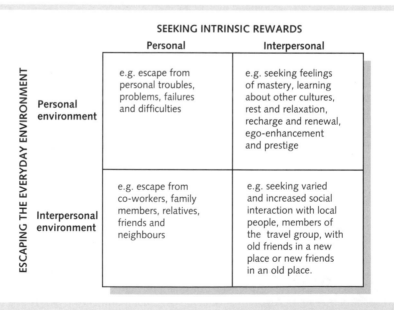

Figure 3.2 A social psychological model of tourism motivation
Source: After Iso-Ahola, S.E. (1983) 'Towards a social psychology of recreational travel', *Leisure Studies*, vol. 2, pp. 45–56, Taylor & Francis Ltd, **www.tandf.co.uk/journals**.

changes for target marketing and positioning, and on their effects on subsequent visitation to tourism attractions and destinations. An understanding of the psychological changes that occur during the stages of the travel experience is thus important for gaining a better understanding of the tourism experience, and for effective marketing of tourism. The components of the basic model of a tourism system (Figure 1.3) therefore represent not only different stages in space and time, but also different psychological states. As Fridgen (1984, p. 24) has observed, tourism:

> . . . involves people moving from one environment through a range of other environments to a destination site and then home via a return trip . . . people not only act in their present setting, they also plan for subsequent settings. People prepare to arrive in another setting to carry out preplanned behaviors.

From this perspective travel should be recognised as having five distinct stages: (i) decision making and anticipation; (ii) travel to a tourism destination or attraction; (iii) the on-site experience; (iv) return travel; and (v) recollection of the experience (Table 3.3). It is important to note that each of these five stages has different psychological characteristics, with implications for how tourism organisations and businesses establish a relationship with the customer. For example, the Forestry Commission of Tasmania used the five-stage model to formulate an information strategy for visitors to Tasmanian forests. This strategy identified four components of the visitor information strategy—motivation, strategic, enhancement, and reinforcement/extension. Existing services and products were then identified and allocated to these stages (Hall & McArthur 1996). Similarly, a nature-based tourism organisation in New Zealand gave videos and books to clients as a way of reinforcing the visitor experience, thereby seeking to improve positive word-of-mouth recommendation and return visitation (Hall et al. 1993).

Another interesting application of the staged model of the visitor experience is in wine and food tourism. A positive service encounter at the wine cellar, for example, can then lead to later purchases of the product when the tourist returns home. In those instances, every time the consumer opens a bottle of wine, the nature of the experience at the wine cellar is reinforced by the opportunity to discuss the experience with friends and family (because the wine serves as a prompt), and by the taste and the smell of the wine (because smell and taste can be very evocative senses). These experiences act as reinforcements of the relationship between the supplier and the customer (Mitchell et al. 2000). In effect, selling wine through wine tourism therefore allows the memories to be taken home in the bottle! (See Table 3.4.)

It is important to recognise that the recollection stage can last for many years. These experiences build up over time influencing where people go on holiday, how

TABLE 3.3 The five stages of the visitor experience

Stage	*Experience*
Decision making and anticipation	Decision to visit, planning, and thinking about the site visit
Travel to the site	Getting to the site
On-site behaviour	Behaviour on site or in the destination region
Return travel	Travel from the site
Recollection	Recall, reflection, and memory of site visit

TABLE 3.4 Stages of travel experience applied to wine tourism

Stage of travel experience	Wine experience and associated retail and promotional opportunities
Pre-visit (anticipation)	wine from destination/winery available through restaurant, retail outlet, or wine club previous experience at winery/wine region previous experience of other wineries promotional material and advertising for winery/wine region wine education websites stories in media (for example, television cooking and travel shows)
Travel to	wine en route (for example, at restaurant or on airline) airline promotional video/in-flight magazine article of destination that includes wine
Destination/on-site visit	winery experience (tasting, education/interpretation, service) setting, activities (for example, tours), food wine at hotel, restaurant, or café in region
Travel from	wine en route to home (for example, at restaurant or on airline)
Post-visit (reminiscence)	wine (from destination or winery) at home, restaurant, or wine club previous experience at winery/wine region previous experience of other wineries promotional material and advertising for winery/wine region photographs and souvenirs (including videos and books) wine purchased at cellar door mail order/newsletters/websites

Source: adapted from Mitchell et al. (2000).

they get there, where they stay, what they do, and whether they recommend it to other people. These various travel experiences, combined with the life stages of visitors (in terms of demographics and psychographics) means that we can talk of a family life cycle (Figure 3.3). For example, in Australia, leisure time varies by age and gender, with the most 'leisure-rich' age group (those aged 65 and over), having 60% more leisure time than the most 'leisure-poor' age group (35–44) (Lynch & Veal 1996). This is clearly related to work demands on overall available time, and time available for certain types of travel. Given the changing demographics of Australia's population, with people living longer and staying active and healthy, it is likely that the retired and semi-retired age group of those 65 years and older will become an increasingly important target market. Moreover, the fact that people are getting married later and having children later, or choosing not to have children at all, is also influencing tourism. Such decisions have substantial impacts on travel because of the amount of disposable income people have at various stages of their lives, with tourism and leisure being one of the major beneficiaries of increased disposable income.

Evidence from large-scale empirical studies supports many of the motivational factors identified above. For example, 'change of environment' is clearly a major factor in travel behaviour (Pearce 1987). In a major annual survey of Japanese

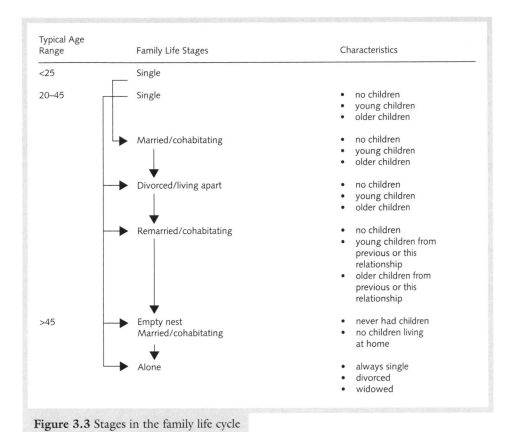

Typical Age Range	Family Life Stages	Characteristics
<25	Single	
20–45	Single	• no children • young children • older children
	Married/cohabiting	• no children • young children • older children
	Divorced/living apart	• no children • young children • older children
	Remarried/cohabitating	• no children • young children from previous or this relationship • older children from previous or this relationship
>45	Empty nest Married/cohabitating	• never had children • no children living at home
	Alone	• always single • divorced • widowed

Figure 3.3 Stages in the family life cycle

outbound travellers conducted by the Japan Travel Bureau Foundation in which people were asked about the purpose of overseas trips, most people (74.4%) replied that they intended to enjoy nature and scenery. The second most common response (55.3%) was to 'see famous historical sites and works of architecture', followed by a desire 'to taste food and try delicacies of the country' (50.5%). The other four major purposes of overseas trips were, in order, 'to enjoy shopping' (46.1%), 'to rest and relax' (39.0%), 'to visit art galleries and museums' (32.6%), and 'to experience a different culture' (32.4%) (Japan Travel Bureau 1991, p. 39).

From a tourism management and planning perspective it is important to recognise the extent to which different images, expectations and motivations lead to different types of tourism, travel patterns, destinations and use of tourism resources. For example, in examining wanderlust and sunlust travel, discussed above, it is apparent that one of the crucial differences between the two is the extent to which they are likely to generate international rather than domestic tourism. Clearly, this is a very important consideration for a national government or tourism agency which usually wishes to maximise the inflow of tourists while minimising the outflow of residents. According to Pearce (1987, p. 24), wanderlust tourism is more likely to be manifested in international travel than sunlust tourism, which in many cases can be realised in an individual's country. However, the extent to which this is true depends, among other factors, on the size and the geographical and cultural diversity of the country in question. Similarly, Plog (1974), in a study of the psychographic segmentation of tourists, suggested that tourists with different personalities seek different travel experiences, selecting particular forms of travel and types of destination. From a series of motivational studies, initially of flyers and non-flyers, Plog argued that travellers are distributed normally along a continuum from psychocentrism to allocentrism. At the one extreme are the 'psychocentrics', who tend to be anxious, self-inhibited, and non-adventurous, and who are concerned with the little problems in life. In contrast, the 'allocentrics' are self-confident, curious, adventurous and outgoing. According to Plog, travel is a way for these people to express their inquisitiveness and curiosity (Table 3.5). As previously noted (see page 70), according to Mason (2002), OE participants can be fitted within Plog's allocentric categorisation, with qualification. OE participants do travel great distances, but if their destination is Britain and they come from British stock, there will be cultural similarities, a virtually identical language, and a supportive community in terms of a good number of expatriates and the likelihood of friends and relatives. However, although the psychographic division of the travel market into wanderlust and sunlust tourism, or into allocentrics and psychocentrics, is a useful starting point from which to understand travel behaviour, it is clearly not specific enough to identify potential consumers and market segments for the tourism product. As Williams (1998, p. 10) noted:

> Plog's model has been widely criticised as over-simplifying a complex process by seeking an explanation based upon one element, and it lacks the dynamic qualities that are essential to explaining how some individuals can alter their behaviour patterns between different tourist trips.

The main application of psychographic studies has been as a complement to sociodemographic variables in market segmentation studies. Many tourist organisations conduct psychographic research as part of their market segmentation studies. However, some of the most detailed studies in Australia are undertaken by the Australian Tourist Commission (ATC) and the various state commissions, which

TABLE 3.5 Travel characteristics of psychocentrics and allocentrics

Psychocentrics	Allocentrics
Prefer mass-tourism destinations	Prefer non-tourist areas
Prefer commonplace activities at destinations	Enjoy sense of being an explorer of the destination area
Prefer sunlust destinations	Prefer novel destinations
Low-activity level	High-activity level
Prefer destinations they can drive to	Prefer flying to destinations
Prefer mass tourism accommodation, family-oriented restaurants and shops, and mass tourism attractions, such as theme parks	Small-scale accommodation, not necessarily modern or chain hotels (for example, boutique hotels, farm stays, bed and breakfast establishments), few mass tourism attractions
Prefer family and/or domestic atmosphere	Enjoy encounters with foreign cultures
Package tour travellers	Free independent travellers

Source: Plog, S.C. (1974) 'Why destination areas rise and fall in popularity', *The Cornell Hotel and Restaurant Administration Quarterly*, vol. 15, November, p. 15.

undertake ongoing market analysis to provide public sector agencies and the tourism industry with information to develop travel products and marketing programs, with a view to increasing the volume of holiday travel. For example, the following indicates the results of a segmentation exercise carried out by the ATC on the Japanese market (1993b).

To be considered potential medium-haul or long-haul travellers the Japanese respondents had to fulfil certain socioeconomic and demographic criteria (ATC 1993b):

- intending to travel on a holiday trip lasting two weeks or longer in the next three years;
- interested in visiting distant holiday destinations;
- willing to travel on a medium- to long-haul flight (six hours or more);
- willing to spend at least 100 000 yen per person on a holiday trip; and
- between 18 and 68 years of age and having a minimum household income of 6 000 000 yen.

The travel market was categorised according to: (i) the benefits sought by potential travellers (the essential motivations for taking a holiday); (ii) the experiences sought; and (iii) the type of traveller (the essential philosophy that each group had towards the planning and booking of a holiday trip). Five different categories of benefits were identified: Cultural Immersion (wanting a sense of purpose and accomplishment from the holiday), Family Resort (wanting a family holiday with all the comforts of home), Young Resort (encompassing sun, sand and an abundance of activity during the day and night), Upscale City (seeking upmarket experiences and lots of activities in an international city location), and Family Togetherness (seeking a good-value family holiday in comfortable surroundings).

Five different categories of experiences were also identified in relation to the emotional responses that can either attract or repel potential holiday travellers. Five different categories of travellers were identified in terms of their travel philosophy. The different categories were described as Independent (travellers who prefer to make their own travel arrangements and maintain flexibility in their travel plans), Package Lovers (who rely heavily on travel agents), Getaway (whose major travel motivation is to escape from the pressures of either home or work and who prefer preplanned travel such as a package holiday), Break-away (travellers with little tolerance for long-haul travel who leave arrangements up to the agent), and Late Bloomers (who rely extensively on their travel agents as they have little previous experience with overseas travel). Finally, the primary target groups were named to convey the essential nature of the market segment according to their desired benefits and experiences and their travel philosophy.

Such research has enormous implications for the tourism industry. Indeed, the above research was the foundation of the ATC's marketing and advertising strategies in Japan for much of the mid-1990s. An example of a domestic market segmentation exercise undertaken by the South Australian Tourism Commission (SATC) (2001a) is contained in Chapter 12 in the form of a study of wine tourism visitors to South Australia.

Different marketing strategies are then designed for each of these groups according to their travel requirements. Although the psychographic approach is useful in marketing, it also offers possibilities for further understanding the basic motivations for travel and for relating these to particular travel destinations, resort and hotel design, customer relations styles, and product development. In addition, psychographics can offer some insights into the development of particular destinations and the planning needs of those destinations.

THE INBOUND TOURIST MARKET

International tourist visitation to Australia has risen rapidly over the past thirty years. The number of overseas tourists coming into Australia is generally defined as the number of international visitors arriving for less than twelve months. Similarly, the number of Australian international tourists is generally measured by departures of Australian residents going abroad for less than twelve months (Bureau of Tourism Research 1993a). The major area of significant growth for short-term arrivals is in visitation from Japan and Asia (especially China, Hong Kong, Indonesia, Korea, Malaysia, Singapore, Taiwan, Thailand and, increasingly, South Asia) (Table 3.6). The primary reason for growth in these markets is the rapid economic growth of the Asia–Pacific region and a corresponding increase in personal disposable incomes, greater political freedom leading to a lessening of travel restrictions, improved transport links with Australia, and changes in social attitudes to travel as a result of the growth of consumerism in Asian societies (Hall 1994b; Hall & Page 1999). The 'traditional' markets of New Zealand, United Kingdom and Ireland, Europe, and the United States, although still significant, are declining in relative importance as Australia becomes more closely integrated with the economies of the Pacific Rim. For example, in 1990, Japan replaced New Zealand as Australia's major source of short-term arrivals. However, in 1999 New Zealand again became Australia's major source of short-term arrivals as the Japanese economy entered a period of recession.

Growth in outbound travel from tourism-generating regions also has a substantial impact on the total number of visitor nights spent by visitors from those regions in Australia. Table 3.7 illustrates the number of visitor nights for major markets. As expected, there is a significant relationship between the number of visitors and the total number of visitor nights. However, a factor which clearly influences the number of visitor nights is a change in the average length of stay which, in turn, is related to changes in the purpose of stay (Table 3.8).

A detailed geographical breakdown of international visitors to Australia by country of residence is provided in Tables 3.9 (Asia), 3.10 (Europe), and 3.11 (North America). Since the early 1990s the greatest increase in visitor numbers has been from Asian nations, especially the new industrial economies of Indonesia, Korea, Malaysia, Singapore, Taiwan, and Thailand (Table 3.9). However, although it is likely that Asia will be the source of approximately half of Australia's visitor arrivals by 2010, it should be noted that the financial crises in some Asian economies, which occurred in the latter half of 1997, substantially impacted some markets (Tourism Forecasting Council 1997c; Pacific Asia Tourism Association (PATA) 1998). For example, in late January 1998, the WTO revised its outbound figures for intraregional travel in the East Asia–Pacific (EAP) region from an estimated 8% growth for 1988 to a revised estimate of there being no growth. In terms of travel from EAP countries to outside the region, the change was from an original estimate of 6.3% growth to a fall of 2%. In addition, of great significance in terms of outbound tourism and

TABLE 3.6 International arrivals to Australia and forecasts by region 1980–2010 (000s)

Year	New Zealand	Japan	Other Asia	Europe	North America	Rest of world	Total	Change on previous year (%)
1980	307	49	–	244	–	–	905	–
1985	245	108	163	300	292	89	1143	–
1986	337	146	204	347	292	103	1429	25.0
1987	427	216	255	412	362	113	1785	24.9
1988	534	352	308	531	389	135	2249	26.0
1989	449	350	321	531	315	114	2080	–7.5
1990	418	480	348	549	304	116	2215	6.5
1991	481	529	389	531	325	116	2370	7.0
1992	448	630	506	577	312	131	2603	9.8
1993	499	671	704	637	332	154	2996	15.1
1994	480	721	927	721	344	169	3362	12.2
1995	538	783	1118	752	363	172	3726	10.8
1996	672	813	1311	799	378	192	4165	11.8
1997	686	814	1350	874	394	200	4318	3.7
1998	709	751	1081	951	446	229	4167	–3.5
1999	729	707	1211	1072	495	245	4460	7.0
2000	803	701	1351	1181	577	268	4882	9.5
2001	804	720	1520	1313	639	290	5288	8.3
2002	811	749	1723	1436	683	314	5715	8.1
2003	818	791	1963	1540	733	339	6184	8.2
2004	827	835	2214	1638	783	366	6663	7.7
2005	844	881	2493	1729	833	394	7174	7.7
2006	861	926	2798	1822	881	423	7711	7.5
2007	878	973	3132	1917	926	455	8280	7.4
2008	893	1020	3502	2014	972	488	8889	7.4
2009	907	1069	3912	2113	1015	524	9539	7.3
2010	918	1119	4365	2213	1055	562	10231	7.3

Numbers from 2001 onwards are forecasts

Source: Bureau of Tourism Research (1992a, 1992b); Tourism Forecasting Council (1997a); DISR (2000a).

TABLE 3.7 International visitor nights 1997–2010 (millions)

Year	North America	Europe	New Zealand	Japan	Other	Rest of Asia	Total world	Change on previous year (%)
1997	394.3	874.2	685.7	813.9	133.6	199.8	3101.5	–
1998	445.6	951.5	709.4	751.1	142.8	229.0	3229.4	4.2
1999	495.4	1072.3	728.8	707.5	162.6	244.8	3411.4	5.6
2000	577.1	1181.1	803.4	700.7	181.5	268.0	3711.8	8.8
2001	639.1	1313.3	804.4	720.3	204.2	290.3	3971.6	7.0
2002	682.5	1435.6	811.3	749.2	231.4	313.7	4223.7	6.3
2003	732.6	1540.3	818.0	790.6	263.7	339.5	4484.7	6.2
2004	783.2	1638.3	827.0	834.7	297.4	365.7	4746.3	5.8
2005	883.1	1728.6	844.0	881.1	334.9	393.8	5065.5	6.7
2006	880.9	1821.6	861.2	926.5	375.8	423.3	5289.3	4.4
2007	926.3	1917.0	877.7	972.8	420.7	454.5	5569.0	5.3
2008	972.0	2013.7	893.2	1020.4	470.7	488.0	5858.0	5.2
2009	1014.8	2112.7	906.6	1069.2	525.5	523.6	6152.4	5.0
2010	1054.7	2212.9	917.8	1119.2	586.4	561.6	6452.6	4.9

Numbers for 2000 onwards are forecasts

Source: Department of Industry, Science and Research (DISR), (2000) *Sport and tourism, strong outlooks for inbound tourism: 1999–2001*, Canberra. Reprinted with the permission of the Department of Industry Tourism and Resources.

TABLE 3.8 International visitor arrivals by purpose of visit 1991–2010 (000s)

Year	Business	Holiday	VFR	Other	Total	Change on previous year (%)
1991	260	1436	482	191	2370	–
1992	263	1623	500	218	2603	9.9
1993	309	1887	553	247	2996	15.1
1994	369	2094	655	244	3362	12.2
1995	436	2243	767	280	3726	10.8
1996	484	2503	852	326	4165	11.8
1997	528	2528	882	380	4318	3.7
1998	519	2265	857	527	4167	–3.5
1999	533	2581	848	497	4460	7.0
2000	593	2801	928	560	4882	9.5
2001	652	3032	988	615	5288	8.3
2002	712	3283	1049	671	5715	8.1
2003	775	3570	1110	728	6184	8.2
2004	840	3870	1172	781	6663	7.7
2005	909	4203	1231	831	7174	7.7
2006	983	4549	1296	883	7711	7.5
2007	1064	4915	1364	937	8280	7.4
2008	1155	5304	1437	993	8889	7.3
2009	1254	5717	1515	1053	9539	7.3
2010	1364	6153	1598	1116	10231	7.3
Average annual growth (%) 1999–2010						
	8.9	8.2	5.9	7.6	7.8	

Numbers from 2000 onwards are forecasts

Source: Department of Industry, Science and Research (DISR), (2000) *Industry science resources: Sport and tourism, strong outlooks for inbound tourism: 1999–2001*, Canberra. Reprinted with the permission of the Department of Industry Tourism and Resources.

TABLE 3.9 Asian visitor arrivals and forecasts 1985–2010 (000s)

Year	China	Hong Kong	Indonesia	South Korea	Malaysia	Singapore	Taiwan	Thailand	Rest of Asia	Total	Total growth (%)
1985	5	24	15	4	33	35	8	6	33	163	–
1986	6	34	18	5	39	45	12	8	38	204	24.7
1987	11	43	22	7	47	57	16	11	42	255	25.2
1988	18	49	30	9	52	64	19	16	51	308	20.6
1989	29	54	29	10	44	65	22	17	50	321	4.2
1990	24	55	34	14	47	76	25	20	54	348	8.5
1991	16	63	37	24	48	87	35	25	54	389	11.6
1992	19	75	46	34	60	117	64	34	59	506	30.3
1993	22	92	72	62	80	155	109	47	65	704	39.0
1994	30	110	106	111	95	188	143	67	79	927	31.7
1995	43	132	135	168	108	202	152	81	97	1118	20.6
1996	54	153	155	228	134	223	159	89	116	1311	17.3
1997	65.8	151.7	160.4	233.8	143.7	239.3	153.2	68.6	133.6	1350.1	3.0
1998	76.5	143.4	93.0	66.6	112.1	247.1	150.0	49.1	142.8	1080.6	–20
1999	92.6	139.6	91.1	108.6	139.8	267.0	147.5	61.9	162.6	1210.7	12
2000	123.9	150.0	95.2	163.0	150.0	273.1	141.1	73.4	181.5	1351.2	11.6
2001	163.1	160.8	101.5	186.8	171.4	299.2	150.3	82.9	204.2	1520.2	12.5
2002	216.6	174.9	111.9	222.4	198.2	310.9	160.6	95.7	231.4	1722.6	13.3
2003	282.1	186.4	128.7	263.6	228.3	327.5	171.2	111.5	263.7	1963	14
2004	357.3	200.1	143.7	303.1	256.2	346.7	180.2	129.2	297.4	2213.9	12.8
2005	444.6	212.3	158.2	352.8	283.2	367.9	190.1	149.4	334.9	2493.4	12.6
2006	540.3	225.1	173.7	407.8	312.8	390.7	199.4	172.2	375.8	2797.8	12.2
2007	651.6	238.0	190.4	468.3	345.4	412.7	208.5	196.4	420.7	3131.7	11.9
2008	781.1	251.0	208.4	535.2	381.3	434.6	217.4	222.5	470.4	3501.9	11.8
2009	930.2	264.0	227.8	608.8	420.7	457.2	226.1	251.2	525.5	3911.5	11.7
2010	1100.6	277.6	248.9	689.0	464.1	480.4	234.5	283.3	586.4	4364.8	11.6

Numbers from 2000 onwards are forecasts

Source: adapted from Tourism Forecasting Council (June 1997a), DISR (2000).

TABLE 3.10 European visitor arrivals and forecasts 1985–2010 (000s)

Year	France	Germany	Italy	Netherlands	Switzerland	UK (incl. Ireland)	Other Europe	Total	Total Growth (%)
1985	12	37	15	15	14	159	48	300	–
1986	14	42	17	16	17	183	58	347	15.6
1987	17	53	19	17	21	209	75	412	18.6
1988	21	66	25	22	26	273	97	531	28.9
1989	20	68	21	20	27	285	90	531	0.1
1990	23	78	24	21	30	288	90	549	3.3
1991	23	78	24	21	30	273	82	531	-3.2
1992	25	90	27	24	29	299	83	577	8.6
1993	31	106	32	28	31	321	89	637	10.3
1994	35	123	37	31	36	350	109	721	13.3
1995	35	124	37	35	35	365	121	752	4.3
1996	35	125	41	39	39	388	132	799	6.3
1997	40.0	128.9	45.8	42.1	38.6	410.6	142.9	848.9	6.2
1998	43.0	127.4	47.8	47.0	40.3	467.5	147.5	920.5	8.4
1999	49.1	144.5	51.4	52.3	45.1	528.4	161.0	1031.8	12.1
2000	56.8	152.5	60.7	59.7	49.8	560.3	194.8	1134.6	10
2001	67.5	170.9	68.8	65.7	57.2	611.7	216.6	1258.4	11
2002	77.9	189.4	78.0	72.9	63.4	654.7	236.7	1373	9.1
2003	87.0	201.7	86.3	78.8	68.7	697.0	254.0	1473.5	7.3
2004	95.2	211.1	93.0	83.0	73.3	741.9	270.2	1567.7	6.4
2005	102.5	216.9	99.1	85.9	77.4	786.7	285.1	1653.6	5.5
2006	110.1	223.0	105.5	88.7	82.0	832.6	300.4	1742.3	5.4
2007	118.3	228.8	112.3	91.7	86.8	879.3	316.1	1833.3	5.2
2008	127.0	234.3	119.4	94.6	91.8	926.9	332.1	1926.1	5.1
2009	136.3	239.7	126.8	97.5	96.8	975.4	348.4	2020.9	4.9
2010	146.1	244.6	134.6	100.4	102.0	1024.5	364.9	2117.1	4.8

Numbers from 2000 onwards are forecasts

Sources: adapted from Tourism Forecasting Council (1997a); DISR (2000).

TABLE 3.11 International visitor arrivals from North America and forecasts 1985–2010 (000s)

Year	Canada	United States	Total North America	Total growth
1985	41	197	237	–
1986	47	245	292	55
1987	53	309	362	30
1988	67	322	389	27
1989	54	261	315	–74
1990	54	251	304	–11
1991	53	272	325	21
1992	49	263	312	–13
1993	51	281	332	20
1994	54	290	344	12
1995	58	305	363	19
1996	61	317	378	15
1997	64.8	329.6	394.3	16.3
1998	71.7	373.9	445.6	51.3
1999	78.4	417.0	495.4	49.8
2000	89.0	488.1	577.1	81.7
2001	98.3	540.7	639.1	62
2002	110.1	572.5	682.5	43.4
2003	120.1	612.5	732.6	50.1
2004	127.7	655.5	783.2	50.6
2005	133.5	699.5	883.1	99.9
2006	139.3	741.6	880.9	–2.2
2007	145.2	781.1	926.3	45.4
2008	151.2	820.8	972.0	45.7
2009	157.3	857.5	1014.8	42.8
2010	163.5	891.2	1054.7	39.9

Numbers from 2000 onwards are forecasts

Sources: adapted from Tourism Forecasting Council (1997a); DISR (2000a).

the overall competitiveness of Australia as an international tourism destination, is the extent to which the devaluation of some Asian currencies will attract tourists, both in competition with Australia as a destination, and as an attraction to Australian outbound tourism.

One of the other major growth areas of visitation to Australia is from South Africa. Growth from this market has occurred because of a resumption of direct air links between the two countries, the breakdown of apartheid, and the rapidly growing South African population in Australia. However, the continued growth of short-term visitation from South Africa will probably depend on the political and economic stability of post-apartheid South Africa.

The International Visitor Survey (IVS) conducted by the Bureau of Tourism Research (BTR) is the primary mechanism by which specific socioeconomic and demographic information on international arrivals is gathered at government level in Australia. 'The IVS aims to provide a sound basis for market analysis by both government and industry bodies and to inform the Australian travel industry in general about the travel behaviour and attitudes of visitors to Australia' (BTR 1992c, p. 5). As part of the IVS, interviews are conducted with approximately 12 000 international visitors annually at Australia's major airports as they are departing the country. Data are collected on many aspects of international visitors' activities in Australia including such items as region of stay, accommodation, usage of transport, places visited, entertainment, enjoyment of stay, and expenditure patterns. The results of such research provides important information for marketing and planning.

OUTBOUND TOURISM

Although the focus of international tourism in Australia has been on inbound tourism, it has only been since 1987 that the number of short-term arrivals to Australia has outnumbered the short-term departures of Australian residents overseas. The number of Australians travelling overseas represents a significant flow of capital being lost overseas although, of course, substantial income is retained in Australia through the pre-purchase of travel through travel agents, travel on Australian international air carriers such as Qantas and Ansett, travel with Australian tour operators, and through the purchase of holiday items in Australia prior to departure. In 1995–96 it was estimated that an additional $4.6 billion was spent domestically by outbound tourists (for example, on travel agency services, travel to and from international airports, and international airfares paid to Australian carriers (ONT 1997h).

Table 3.12 shows the purpose of visit for Australians travelling overseas. Most significant in terms of Australian outbound travel behaviour is the increasing importance of business travel and visiting friends as travel motivations, although holidays are still clearly the primary reason for overseas travel. The main destinations for Australians are Asia (particularly Thailand and Bali), New Zealand, North America (especially the United States), the United Kingdom, and Europe (Table 3.13). The decline of Asian currencies relative to the Australian dollar has had a significant impact on travel patterns. For example, short-term resident departures for the nine months from January to September 1997 totalled 2.2 million, an increase of 7.9% compared with the same period in 1996. Departures in September 1997 numbered 304 200, up 8.1% on September 1996 (ONT 1997h). In addition to exchange rates, another key item in the determination of outbound travel flows is the perceived safety of destinations. Therefore, in recent years destinations such as Fiji have been dramatically affected by domestic political instability which has received a high profile in the Australian media. Similarly, travel to Indonesia by Australians has also been impacted because of terrorism, political instability, East Timor, and poor relations between Indonesia and Australia. However, although Bali (the main destination for Australians in Indonesia) is not promoted as being a part of Indonesia (Hall 2000d) the terrorist bombing of October 2002 will have a dramatic short-term impact on outbound travel.

DOMESTIC TOURISM

Although O'Clery (1990b, p. 30) described domestic tourism as 'the lifeblood of the Australian tourism industry', it is the poor cousin to the supposedly more glamorous world of inbound travel. Nevertheless it is the mainstay of the Australian tourism industry, accounting for approximately 70% of all tourist visitation in Australia, and

TABLE 3.12 Short-term resident departures by purpose of travel 1980–2010 (000s)

Year	Business	Holiday	VFR	Other[b]	Total
1980	161[a]	706	235	101	1204
1985	216[a]	891	288	116	1512
1990	367[a]	1194	439	175	2170
1991	348	1090	454	209	2099
1992	391	1144	491	250	2276
1993	426	1095	515	231	2267
1994	475	1105	561	213	2354
1995	540	1140	645	194	2519
1996	589	1263	684	196	2732
1997	637	1373	697	226	2933
1998	619	1494	753	294	3161
1999	667	1467	800	277	3210
2000	727	1541	848	304	3420
2001	775	1613	896	323	3607
2002	835	1672	945	338	3790
2003	888	1726	996	352	3961
2004	949	1777	1049	365	4141
2005	1007	1826	1106	377	4315
2006	1065	1871	1165	388	4489
2007	1127	1917	1226	399	4669
2008	1192	1964	1290	411	4856
2009	1260	2010	1357	423	5050
2010	1332	2057	1427	435	5251
Average annual growth (%) 1999–2010					
	6.5	3.1	5.4	4.2	4.6

[a] Includes business, convention, and accompanying business traveller

[b] Includes employment, education, other, and non-stated

Numbers from 2000 onwards are forecasts

Source: Australian Bureau of Statistics in BTR (1990c, 1991a, 1992a, 1993a); DISR (2000b).

much more in many areas, and it therefore provides a major stimulus for employment and regional development (Table 3.14). However, compared with inbound tourism, domestic tourism does not contribute as much per tourist to the national economy, and nor does it bring in foreign exchange to help offset Australia's balance of payments problems. Nevertheless, income derived from domestic tourism was valued at $41.9 billion in 1995/96 (ONT 1997h) and this is extremely important for many parts of regional Australia. Moreover, when domestic travel is undertaken instead of overseas travel, money is retained in the Australian economy that might have otherwise been lost. Such substitution of travel is quite possible in the holiday market, although less so in business and VFR travel. Critical factors for such switching between potential holiday destinations are cost (including exchange rate considerations), time available, and the nature of the holiday that is being sought.

Not surprisingly, domestic visitation levels are related to the overall population and size of each state. Thus Queensland, New South Wales, and Victoria clearly dominate the interstate market, thereby reinforcing the concentration of overseas visitors to Australia in those states (Tables 3.15 to 3.21). It should be noted that

TABLE 3.13 Short-term resident departures by main destination 1991–2010 (000s)

Year	New Zealand	US	UK	Indonesia	Hong Kong	Singapore	Thailand	Malaysia	Fiji	China
1991	318	309	221	175	130	100	72	71	90	15
1992	341	335	240	185	140	101	70	78	87	20
1993	347	300	241	199	132	98	72	84	78	27
1994	353	288	255	214	130	92	72	84	83	39
1995	371	314	265	222	157	95	75	89	75	53
1996	415	331	289	260	168	99	81	97	72	55
1997	407	352	322	311	156	105	89	98	76	72
1998	470	323	322	350	147	123	136	112	99	82
1999	489	347	313	281	136	141	137	120	115	91
2000	548	380	331	210	145	153	150	131	60	95
2001	591	395	341	230	154	166	164	133	62	110
2002	642	401	351	248	164	179	180	135	66	124
2003	667	417	358	269	170	187	196	139	69	133
2004	701	440	365	290	175	193	210	143	72	142
2005	725	460	370	311	178	199	221	148	75	153
2006	755	476	381	329	183	208	235	150	78	168
2007	789	489	392	349	189	216	249	153	81	185
2008	821	502	402	370	197	222	261	156	84	206
2009	851	514	410	393	206	227	273	161	87	226
2010	880	523	418	417	216	229	282	166	89	258
Average annual growth (%) 1999–2010	5.5	3.8	2.7	3.7	4.3	4.5	6.8	3.0	−2.3	9.9

Numbers from 2000 onwards are forecasts

Source: Department of Industry, Science and Research (DISR), (2000) *Industry science resources: Sport and tourism 2000, steady rise in outbound travel 1999–2010*, Canberra. www.sport-gov.au/forecasts/outbound/index (accessed May 2001) Reprinted with the permission of the Department of Industry Tourism and Resources.

TABLE 3.14 Domestic visitor nights by purpose of travel 1998–2010 (millions)

Year	Business	Holiday	VFR	Other	Total
1998	46.7	139.6	88.9	18.3	293.5
1999	44.2	143.9	86.8	19.2	294.2
2000	46.6	145.4	87.1	19.4	298.5
2001	48.5	146.2	87.6	19.3	301.7
2002	50.9	147.8	88.7	19.3	306.7
2003	53.0	149.8	90.1	19.4	312.3
2004	55.4	151.9	91.5	19.5	318.2
2005	57.8	155.2	93.1	19.6	325.7
2006	60.2	158.4	94.7	19.7	332.9
2007	62.6	161.4	96.2	19.8	340.0
2008	65.1	164.6	97.8	19.9	347.4
2009	67.8	167.8	99.3	20.0	354.9
2010	70.5	171.2	100.9	20.0	362.6

Average annual growth (%) 1999–2010

| | 4.3 | 1.6 | 1.4 | 0.4 | 1.9 |

Numbers from 2000 onwards are forecasts

Source: Department of Industry, Science and Research (DISR) *Industry science resources: Sport and tourism 2000: Positive long term outlook for domestic tourism: 1999–2010*, Canberra. Reprinted with the permission of the Department of Industry Tourism and Resources.

TABLE 3.15 Domestic visitor nights in Victoria by purpose of visit 1998–2010 (000s)

Year	Business	Holiday	VFR	Other	Total
1998	7668	26 977	18 999	2074	55 718
1999	6805	26 664	16 736	2335	52 540
2000	7420	27 937	17 695	2278	55 329
2001	7719	28 101	17 807	2269	55 896
2002	8094	28 402	18 033	2269	56 799
2003	8434	28 786	18 306	2278	57 804
2004	8819	29 182	18 587	2287	58 874
2005	9196	29 823	18 914	2300	60 233
2006	9570	30 430	19 236	2312	61 547
2007	9958	31 204	19 550	2323	62 856
2008	10 361	31 631	19 866	2333	64 192
2009	10 779	32 252	20 183	2343	65 558
2010	11 213	32 895	20 503	2353	66 965

Numbers from 2000 onwards are forecasts

Source: Department of Industry, Science and Research (DISR) *Industry science resources: Sport and tourism 2000: Positive long term outlook for domestic tourism: 1999–2010*, Canberra. Reprinted with the permission of the Department of Industry Tourism and Resources.

Victoria has been gradually increasing its share of the domestic market, in addition to increasing its share of overseas visitors.

Domestic tourism research provides socioeconomic information that is useful for regional and state tourism planning. For example, since the early 1980s there has been a gradual increase in the use of hotel and motel accommodation and staying with a friend or relative, at the expense of more 'traditional' accommodation such

TABLE 3.16 Domestic visitor nights in Queensland by purpose of visit 1998–2010 (000s)

Year	Business	Holiday	VFR	Other	Total
1998	10 576	35 236	20 119	3727	69 658
1999	11 250	40 333	20 401	6071	78 055
2000	11 217	39 357	20 081	5039	75 694
2001	11 669	39 589	20 208	5021	76 486
2002	12 237	40 013	20 465	5021	77 735
2003	12 751	40 554	20 774	5041	79 119
2004	13 332	41 111	21 093	5060	80 596
2005	13 902	42 014	21 465	5089	82 469
2006	14 468	42 869	21 829	5116	84 282
2007	15 055	43 706	22 186	5139	86 087
2008	15 664	44 561	22 545	5162	87 932
2009	16 296	45 437	22 905	5184	89 822
2010	16 952	46 343	23 268	5206	91 769

Numbers from 2000 onwards are forecasts

Source: Department of Industry, Science and Research (DISR) *Industry science resources: Sport and tourism 2000: Positive long term outlook for domestic tourism: 1999–2010*, Canberra. Reprinted with the permission of the Department of Industry Tourism and Resources.

TABLE 3.17 Domestic visitor nights in South Australia by purpose of visit 1998–2010 (000s)

Year	Business	Holiday	VFR	Other	Total
1998	3231	8859	6299	1843	20 232
1999	2643	8890	6182	1548	19 263
2000	3008	9244	6184	1758	20 194
2001	3129	9298	6223	1751	20 402
2002	3281	9398	6223	1751	20 733
2003	3419	9525	6398	1758	21 100
2004	3575	9656	6496	1765	21 492
2005	3728	9868	6610	1775	21 981
2006	3880	10 069	6723	1784	22 456
2007	4037	10 265	6833	1793	22 928
2008	4201	10 466	6943	1801	23 410
2009	4370	10 672	7054	1808	23 904
2010	4546	10 885	7166	1816	24 412

Numbers from 2000 onwards are forecasts

Source: Department of Industry, Science and Research (DISR) *Industry science resources: Sport and tourism 2000: Positive long term outlook for domestic tourism: 1999–2010*, Canberra. Reprinted with the permission of the Department of Industry Tourism and Resources.

as caravan parks. This trend might be due to changes in preferred travel style and decreased amounts of disposable income available for travel during periods of economic recession. Primary motivations for travel can also change over time. The reason for the rise and fall of pleasure/holiday travel is primarily related to the overall

TABLE 3.18 Domestic visitor nights in Western Australia by purpose of visit 1998–2010 (000s)

Year	Business	Holiday	VFR	Other	Total
1998	6800	12 863	6533	3574	29 770
1999	5342	14 644	7084	2135	29 205
2000	6214	14 326	6751	2971	30 263
2001	6465	14 410	6751	2971	30 263
2002	6779	14 565	6880	2960	30 629
2003	7064	14 761	6984	2972	31 782
2004	7386	14 964	7091	2983	32 425
2005	7702	15 293	7216	3000	33 211
2006	8016	15 604	7339	3016	33 975
2007	8341	15 909	7459	3030	34 739
2008	8678	16 220	7579	3044	35 521
2009	9028	16 539	7700	3057	36 324
2010	9392	16 869	7822	3069	37 152

Numbers for 2000 and onwards are forecasts

Source: Department of Industry, Science and Research (DISR) *Industry science resources: Sport and tourism 2000: Positive long term outlook for domestic tourism: 1999–2010*, Canberra. Reprinted with the permission of the Department of Industry Tourism and Resources.

TABLE 3.19 Domestic visitor nights in Tasmania by purpose of visit 1998–2010 (000s)

Year	Business	Holiday	VFR	Other	Total
1998	1198	4980	2656	343	9177
1999	1366	4554	2138	464	8522
2000	1319	4965	2373	416	9073
2001	1372	4995	2388	414	9169
2002	1439	5048	2418	414	9319
2003	1499	5116	2455	416	9486
2004	1568	5187	2492	418	9664
2005	1635	5301	2536	420	9891
2006	1701	5408	2579	422	10 111
2007	1770	5514	2621	424	10 330
2008	1842	5622	2664	426	10 554
2009	1916	5732	2706	428	10 783
2010	1993	5847	2749	430	11 019

Numbers from 2000 onwards are forecasts

Source: Department of Industry, Science and Research (DISR) *Industry science resources: Sport and tourism 2000: Positive long term outlook for domestic tourism: 1999–2010*, Canberra. Reprinted with the permission of the Department of Industry Tourism and Resources.

state of the economy and the exchange rate. Nevertheless, as noted above, domestic tourism remains extremely important for regional economies and employment, and will continue to provide the 'bread-and-butter' of the Australian tourism industry for a number of years to come.

TABLE 3.20 Domestic visitor nights in Northern Territory by purpose of visit 1998–2010 (000s)

Year	Business	Holiday	VFR	Other	Total
1998	2464	2467	1490	1262	7683
1999	1532	3172	909	817	6430
2000	2039	2937	1185	1081	7242
2001	2121	2954	1193	1077	7345
2002	2224	2986	1208	1077	7495
2003	2318	3026	1226	1081	7651
2004	2423	3068	1245	1085	7822
2005	2527	3135	1267	1092	8021
2006	2630	3199	1289	1097	8215
2007	2736	3261	1310	1103	8410
2008	2847	3325	1331	1107	8611
2009	2962	3391	1352	1112	8817
2010	3081	3458	1374	1117	9030

Numbers for 2000 onwards are forecasts

Source: Department of Industry, Science and Research (DISR) *Industry science resources: Sport and tourism 2000: Positive long term outlook for domestic tourism: 1999–2010*, Canberra. Reprinted with the permission of the Department of Industry Tourism and Resources.

TABLE 3.21 Domestic visitor nights in Australian Capital Territory by purpose of visit 1998–2010 (000s)

Year	Business	Holiday	VFR	Other	Total
1998	1003	1481	2395	374	5253
1999	1948	1593	2232	189	5962
2000	1528	1601	2292	294	5715
2001	1590	1610	2306	292	5799
2002	1667	1628	2336	292	5923
2003	1738	1650	2371	294	6052
2004	1817	1672	2407	295	6191
2005	1894	1709	2450	296	6350
2006	1972	1744	2491	298	6505
2007	2052	1778	2532	299	6661
2008	2135	1813	2573	301	6821
2009	2221	1848	2614	302	6985
2010	2310	1885	2656	303	7154

Numbers for 2000 and onwards are forecasts

Source: Department of Industry, Science and Research (DISR) *Industry science resources: Sport and tourism 2000: Positive long term outlook for domestic tourism: 1999–2010*, Canberra. Reprinted with the permission of the Department of Industry Tourism and Resources.

THE RELATIONSHIP BETWEEN THE MARKET, MOTIVATIONS, AND THE DEVELOPMENT OF A TOURIST DESTINATION

This chapter has provided an outline of the changing Australian tourism market in terms of inbound, outbound and domestic travel. Such information is critical for understanding the patterns and processes behind tourism development in Australia as the supply and demand of the tourist product are intimately related. Plog (1974) suggested that the market for a given destination evolves and that the destination appeals to different groups at different times. The destination is 'discovered' by 'allocentrics'. However, as it becomes more well known and develops, it attracts more visitors (for example, the 'mid-centrics'). The destination then loses its appeal to the 'allocentrics', who move on. Because the population is said to be normally distributed, this means than an area receives its largest number of visitors when it is attracting the 'mid-centrics'—at a stage when it is neither too exotic nor too familiar. But, from this point on, the implication is that the market will decline. As Plog concluded, 'Thus, we can visualize a destination moving across the spectrum, however gradually or slowly, but far too often inexorably toward the potential of its own demise' (1974, p. 16).

The above pattern of development can also be seen in the hypothetical model of the evolution of a tourist area discussed in Chapter 2. The critical consideration for a sustainable Australian tourism industry is therefore the question of how many tourists will be coming to Australia in the future and how many can Australia absorb?

Forecasting is an inexact science. The one certainty about the future is that it is uncertain. Nevertheless, a number of predictions have been made about the future growth of tourism in Australia, particularly with respect to inbound travel. The Liberal Party–National Party coalition's target at the 1993 federal election of 10 million visitors by 2000 was somewhat optimistic, but Commonwealth government agencies forecast 5–7 million international arrivals. In 1993 the BTR forecast 3.641 million visitors in 1996 and 5.151 million in 2001 (BTR 1993a). In contrast, the ATC (1993b) had a more optimistic range of short-term arrival targets of 4.308 million in 1996, 6.819 million in 2000, and 7.583 million in 2001. More recently, the Tourism Forecasting Council (TFC) predicted that Australia would have 6 million international visitor arrivals in 2000 and 8.8 million in 2005, with the major predicted growth areas for inbound travel into Australia being Asia and Japan (TFC 1997a, d). The actual number for 2000 was 4.882 million (see Table 3.8, page 88) with Australia receiving 4 816 600 international arrivals for the year to January 2002 (preliminary figures in DITR 2002c). However, recent economic events in South-East Asia and their repercussions in other economies have led to a substantial rethink regarding the potential growth of inbound tourism and the contribution of Asian markets (TFC 1997c; Thomas 1998). The more recent impacts of the events of 11 September 2001 have added to the uncertainty. The TFC long-range forecasts as at October 2001, are listed in Table 3.22.

There are inherent difficulties in predicting the future of tourism. Who, for example, could have predicted the 1989 air pilots' dispute months or even days before it happened? Similarly, the economic difficulties faced by many major markets in South-East Asia in late 1997 and early 1998 were not predicted by many tourism forecasters. The terrorist attacks in New York and Washington in September 2001

TABLE 3.22 Tourism Forecasting Council long-range forecasts (October 2001)

	2000	2010	Average annual growth 2000–10
International visitors			
From all markets	4.9 million	9.4 million	6.6%
From Japan and Asia	2.1 million	4.8 million	8.9%
From Europe	1.2 million	2.2 million	6.2%
From New Zealand	0.8 million	0.9 million	1.0%
From North America	0.6 million	0.9 million	4.4%
From rest of world	0.3 million	0.6 million	7.2%
Domestic visitors			
Visitor nights	293 million	339 million	1.4%

Source: Department of Industry, Tourism and Resources (DITR) (2002), Impact, February 2002, Canberra. Reprinted with the permission of the Department of Industry, Tourism and Resources.

were, of course, impossible to predict, as was the subsequent period of international concern over airline travel in the following months. The collapse of Ansett Australia was similarly unforseen. Nevertheless, forecasting is still an important exercise as it provides managers, policy-makers and planners with a basis on which to react to alternative development scenarios (Archer 1987; Calantone et al. 1987; Witt & Witt 1992; Faulkner 2001). However, alternative extreme scenarios may also need to be considered (Faulkner 1994), for example:
• What if the price of oil and aviation fuel doubles?
• What if there is a global financial crisis?
• What if domestic air services are again disrupted by a pilots' dispute?
• What if airline services are impacted by the collapse of another airline?
• What if the ozone layer precipitously disintegrates, resulting in severe constraints on outdoor activities?
• What if a major military conflict erupts in Asia or Europe?
• What if there is a widespread boycott of the major events?

TOURISM INSIGHT

WTO INTERNATIONAL TRAVEL ESTIMATES

According to the World Tourism Organization (WTO) international tourist arrivals totalled approximately 689 million in 2001, compared with 697 million in 2000 which was the year with the highest arrivals on record (possibly as a result of special millennium events). WTO has estimated that, from January to August 2001, arrivals worldwide grew by 3%—more than one point lower than the average annual gain of 4.3% in tourist arrivals over the past ten years. However, in the last four months of 2001 there was an estimated drop of 11% in arrivals worldwide and substantial decreases in every region: Africa (–3.5%); Americas (–24%); East Asia/Pacific (–10%); Europe (–6%); Middle East (–30%);

and South Asia (–24%). The only other year since 1980 that has shown negative growth in world tourism was 1982, when international arrivals declined by 0.4%. The Gulf War year of 1991 recorded a small increase of 1.2% in international arrivals.

According to the WTO (2002a), holidaymakers chose to travel by car or rail rather than by air. Consequently, tourists visited destinations that were closer to home rather than long-haul destinations, and they chose more familiar places that were perceived as being safer. In France, for example, passengers on domestic flights declined by 15% in November, while rail passenger numbers increased by 9% during that same period. These shifts in travel habits benefited rural tourism accommodation, ski resorts, camping grounds, and bed & breakfast establishments.

WTO's (2001) Tourism 2020 Vision has forecast that international arrivals are expected to reach more than 1.56 billion by 2020. Of these worldwide arrivals in 2020, 1.18 billion are expected to be intraregional travellers and 377 million are expected be long-haul travellers. The WTO has forecast that, by 2020, the top three receiving regions for international tourists will be Europe (717 million tourists), East Asia and the Pacific (397 million) and the Americas (282 million), followed by Africa, the Middle East, and South Asia (Table 3.23).

TABLE 3.23 WTO international tourist arrivals by region 1995–2020 (millions)

	Base year 1995	Forecast 2010	Forecast 2020	Average annual growth rate (%)1995–2020	Market share (%) 1995	Market share (%) 2020
Total	565.4	1006.4	1561.1	4.1	100	100
Africa	20.2	47.0	77.3	5.5	3.6	5.0
Americas	108.9	190.4	282.3	3.9	19.3	18.1
East Asia/Pacific	81.4	195.2	397.2	6.5	14.4	25.4
Europe	338.4	527.3	717.0	3.0	59.8	45.9
Middle East	12.4	35.9	68.5	7.1	2.2	4.4
South Asia	4.2	10.6	18.8	6.2	0.7	1.2
Intraregional[a]	464.1	790.9	1183.3	3.8	82.1	75.8
Long-haul[b]	101.3	215.5	377.9	5.4	17.9	24.2

Notes:

[a] Intraregional includes arrivals where country of origin is not specified

[b] Long-haul is defined as everything except intraregional travel

Source: World Tourism Organization (WTO) (2001), Tourism 2020 Vision, WTO, Madrid.

As noted above, the future of tourism is, by definition, uncertain. However, the policies, development practices, and management strategies put into place now must be able to respond adequately to the predicted changes in tourist visitation in Australia.

An understanding of the tourism market and tourism demand is important at three distinct levels. First, it provides an indication of why people travel, what they seek in the tourism experience, and how people in the tourism industry can best supply the required experience. Second, it demonstrates the importance of relating the motivation of the tourist (for example, the nature of demand) to changes in the travel market and, flowing on from that, the importance of changes in the nature of the destination as a supply component of the tourism market. Third, it can suggest ways in which tourist satisfaction can be maximised and how the economic, social and environmental returns of tourism can best be gained for the destination and the host community. Therefore, a crucial issue which needs to be addressed in the search for a sustainable tourism industry is whether we can plan for tourism demands and desired tourist experiences in a manner that improves rather than damages the destination—a question which will be examined in further depth in the remainder of this book.

SUGGESTIONS FOR FURTHER READING

The majority of general tourism textbooks discuss the nature of the tourism marketplace and tourist motivations. Students should also consult specific texts on tourism marketing. The best sources of information on inbound and domestic tourism in Australia are the reports produced annually by the BTR. Students should also examine the range of publications produced by the Australian Tourist Commission and the state and territory tourism commissions for further information on international and domestic market segmentation studies. For an excellent account of tourism forecasting in Australia, students should consult the proceedings of the 1993 Australian Tourism Research Workshop, and current forecasts can be seen in the various publications of the TFC and on the ONT website.

Data and forecasts on Australian inbound, outbound, and domestic tourism can be found at the following websites:
* Australian Tourist Commission:
  www.aussie.net.au

* Bureau of Tourism Research:
  www.btr.gov.au

* Department of Industry, Tourism and Resources:
  www.industry.gov.au/index.cfm

  (The DITR website includes links to TFC forecasts.)
Data and forecasts on international tourism can be found at:
* World Tourism Organisation:
  www.world-tourism.org

* World Travel and Tourism Council:
  www.wttc.org

  Tourism Insight on the web
  www.prenhall.com/hall_au
  has the following insights:

* University Student's Holiday Behaviour: A Case Study from New Zealand (Neil Carr).
* International and Domestic University Students and Tourism: The Case of the Australian Capital Territory, Australia (Brent Ritchie, University of Brighton, Brighton, England; Mark Priddle, University of Canberra, Australian Capital Territory, Australia)
* Australians going to New Zealand: the friendly border (Glen Croy. Department of Tourism, School of Business, University of Otago, Dunedin, New Zealand)
* Case Study—Australian Visitors to Dunedin, New Zealand (Kristy Rusher Department of Tourism, School of Business, University of Otago, Dunedin, New Zealand)

WHY DO WE TRAVEL? TOURIST MOTIVATIONS AND MARKETS

Key concepts

Key concepts discussed in this chapter were:
tourism market, market segmentation, geographic segmentation, demographic segmentation, socioeconomic segmentation, psychographic segmentation, segmentation by purpose of travel, motivations, sunlust, wanderlust, anomie, ego-enhancement, allocentrics, psychocentrics, forecasting.

Questions for review and discussion

1 Why do people travel?
2 With reference to the tourism insights on student travel, as well as general motivation theory, discuss why you travel.
3 How can tourism and hospitality managers best satisfy travellers' needs?
4 Why do people want to travel to Australia for a holiday? Relate your answer to the motivations of tourists.
5 How do exchange rates affect travel flows?
6 How important is VFR tourism?
7 Compare the actual number of visitor arrivals with the various forecasts made by the Tourism Forecast Council noted throughout this chapter. Explain the variance.
8 How significant is educationally motivated tourism?

IMAGING AND BRANDING THE DESTINATION

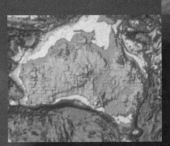

4

WRITTEN WITH GLEN CROY AND REID WALKER

New South Wales, Australia—sun-drenched beaches, rugged mountains, arid outback landscapes and lush forests. We offer a spectacular range of locations, plenty of sunshine and crews that equal the best of Hollywood but with costs up to 30% less than the USA. New South Wales has them all . . . moonscapes, cityscapes, country, urban, ocean, snow and rainforest—you can shoot period, western, science fiction and city thrillers . . . (New South Wales Film and Television Office 2002)

THE IMPORTANCE OF DESTINATION IMAGE

IMAGE is a very personal, subjective evaluation of a destination, and includes all aspects that make up an individual's knowledge of that place, whether they are true or not. This perception is based on information built on interactions with sources ranging from very informal contacts (such as friends and family) to direct promotional material (such as brochures).

Destination image is an evaluation based on perceptions. These perceptions are built up through general images associated with the destination, images specific to the destination, and person-specific travel attributes (Figure 4.1). What is included to build the perception and subsequent evaluation depends on what the perceiver chooses as evaluative attributes to reinforce this subjective process.

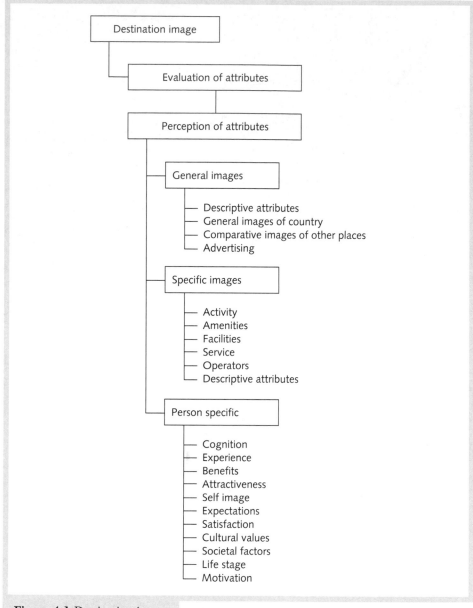

Figure 4.1 Destination image

Destination image is an integral component of the travel process and is the cornerstone of many attempts to market and promote tourism destinations. Destination image is important due to:
- its effects on prospective markets (Echtner & Ritchie 1993; Mackay & Fesenmaier 2000);
- its role in destination selection (Embacher & Buttle 1989; Teleisman-Kosuta 1989; Chon 1991; Hu & Ritchie 1993; Walmsley & Jenkins 1993; Alhemoud &

Armstrong 1996; Walmsley & Young 1998; Baloglu & McCleary 1999; Tapachai & Waryszak 2000);

- its role in creating expectations (Britton 1979b; Pearce 1982b; Mackay & Fesenmaier 1997; Coshall 2000); and
- its role in marketing strategy or market segmentation (Crompton 1979b; Calantone, di Benedetto et al. 1989; Reilly 1990; Chen & Hsu 2000; Mackay & Fesenmaier 2000; Sirgy & Chenting 2000; Baloglu & Mangaloglu 2001; Joppe et al. 2001).

Destination image is a principal component of the traveller's decision-making process, and consequently, is a prime component of destination marketing. Destination marketing is conducted to produce positive images of the destination for possible visitors. As recognised in Woodside and Sherrell's (1977) pioneering paper of a destination choice model, choice destinations eventuate from a set of destinations of which the traveller is aware ('aware set') (Figure 4.2). These destinations are further evaluated as unavailable, inept, inert, or evoked. There is also a set of destinations of which the traveller is unaware ('unaware set'). Woodside and Sherrell (1977, p.15) described the inept set as containing 'those brands a consumer has rejected from his purchase consideration'. The inert set contains brands that have no positive or negative evaluation, and the evoked set contains those from which a

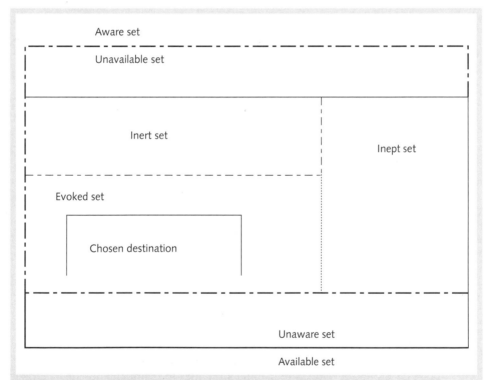

Figure 4.2 Travel destination sets in leisure behaviour
Source: Woodside, A.G. & Sherrell, D. (1977) 'Traveller evoked, inept, and inert sets of vacation destinations' *Journal of Travel Research*, vol.16, no. 1, pp. 14–18. Reprinted by permission of Sage Publications.

IMAGING AND BRANDING THE DESTINATION

purchase decision will be made—specifically a 'likelihood greater than zero of purchasing a brand or visiting a travel destination within some time period'.

Possible tourists base their decisions on a set of aware, available, and positively perceived destinations. As defined above, the awareness of a destination, or destination image, is the all-encompassing image which the possible traveller has of the destination. The availability of destinations is determined by fundamental decision factors, such as time available, money, distance (actual or perceived), family, attraction, and the like. A positive perception is determined by image evaluative components. Therefore, the evoked set is a small collection of destinations (Woodside & Sherrell 1977), among which destination image is the deciding factor. Of course, it is ideal for destination managers to have their destination in the evoked set. To do this, destination managers need to know where the destination is positioned (in terms of availability for the desired market segments), and what components of image produce a positive perception in these market segments. Consequently, because image produces the evaluative components and determines the destination choice, it is critically important that destination managers ensure that the image of their destination is within their control and managed accordingly. Destination management is more than marketing the destination. Destination image is the perceived 'sum' of the destination arising from the interface between the destination and existing, latent, and non-visitors (Figure 4.3). The management of the destination must promote the image in a strategic direction. Within this strategy, it is essential to identify the evaluative components of destination image, as held by the destination's ideal visitor groups, and to provide an image which satisfies the visitors' needs. Specifically, the image needs to create a positive evaluation and choice.

Figure 4.3 cannot be seen in isolation from the destination's business environment. There are many factors that influence and create destination image which are outside the direct control of the destination manager, particularly with respect to the images and information generated by the media. As noted, most of this is outside the control of destination managers, but strategies can be implemented to mitigate or reinforce the images portrayed in the media at national, regional, and local levels. The destination manager therefore has to know what message will create what image in the minds of possible visitors. It is therefore crucial that destination managers have an image management strategy.

IMAGE MANAGEMENT

Image management has been extensively developed at the product level within marketing. The images of corporate enterprises and, increasingly, the images of cities (see Chapter 13), have come under the spotlight in the last decade (Barich & Kotler 1991; Kotler et al. 1993; Hall & Hamon 1996; Marconi 1997). Cities, as destinations in competition with one another, have experienced increasing pressure (due to technological changes) to maintain their populations and vibrant corporate communities. They have since developed reimaging strategies to maintain and enhance their perception globally, and to develop the benefits gained from tourist visitation.

Like company image (Barich & Kotler 1991), destination image is made up of many components, with each playing a part in its creation and maintenance. Croy (2001) has undertaken research of destination image and the importance of these

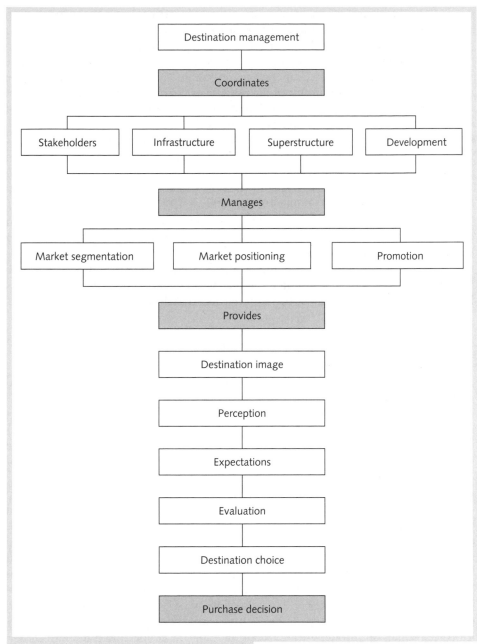

Figure 4.3 Destination image management

components in New Zealand. Rather than the segmented components of company image as identified in corporate studies, Croy (2001) identified evaluative components as defined by possible visitors. It was concluded that the identified evaluative components should be displayed within promotional materials, reinforcing the positive evaluative aspects of the destination. This aids in the movement of the destination from an inert, or inept, set into an evoked set—that is, the set of destinations from which a choice will be made (Woodside & Sherrell 1977).

However, care must be taken to ensure that the image displayed is realistic; otherwise it will detract from satisfaction (Croy 2001). It was also concluded that 'these considerations should become inherent in destination management, focusing future consideration on the maximising of the positive evaluative components, rather than just the image portrayed' (Croy 2001). In essence, Croy defined image management as being more than just the marketing of images.

Implicit within any consideration of destination image management is consideration of the source of image. The management of image includes much more than managing the information that a destination can officially and directly supply. The general media play a very large role in the creation and dissemination of destination image (Moutinho 1987; Butler 1990b; Altheide 1997; Fodness & Murray 1999), especially in the initial stages of destination image formation (Gartner 1993). In addition, destinations seek to develop and influence image through their branding and marketing campaigns. This chapter first discusses the role of the media in destination imaging and marketing, including the deliberate use of the media to attract visitors, before going on to examine the manner in which destination branding has been undertaken in Australia at the national and state level.

THE MEDIA

The study of the mass media as a depiction device of and in society has increased significantly in recent years, and this has given a new-found importance to mass popular representations of society, with a movement away from the previous focus on 'high' culture interpretations of the media (Wilson 1996). The media undoubtedly form a pervasive and invasive aspect of culture which has enormous influence on destination and place image, as well as on taste. For example, in the case of changing food fashions, the media have enormous influence. Increasingly, restaurants and chefs produce cooking and lifestyle books that also serve as a basis for radio and television programs which are simultaneously released as part of a total media package. In Australia television food programs such as 'Gondola on the Murray' not only showed the food but also introduced place elements (such as rural scenes) and images of the host meeting (and eating) with the producers of the foodstuffs which he used. Similarly, the chef Keith Floyd completed a whole series of cooking programs on world food cooked *in situ*, and Rick Stein has done similar work focused specifically on seafood (Randall 1999). The 'placefulness' of food (that is, the link between cuisine production and place) offers rich potential for tourism as an opportunity for place promotion through various media by explicitly connecting place with certain forms of production and consumption (Hall & Mitchell 1998). National and regional tourist organisations are often major sponsors and supporters of food programs (for example, in sponsoring Keith Floyd's travel to Australia), and advertising is also used (in the media or in supermarkets through food promotions) to connect travel to the place. The interrelationship between food and tourism is therefore intimately tied up with the production and consumption of images and the cultural meaning of place and space. Place connections and constructions are highlighted in much of the food media and are used to highlight the 'authenticity' of the food that is being presented and to develop images of the places in which the food is being cooked. Indeed, cooking shows which focus only on what the cook does in preparing the food, rather than associating the food with place, seem to be increasingly in the minority. As Randall (2000, p. 89) recognised, 'one common and significant feature of food texts is the limited amount of time actually devoted to the cookery/food elements'.

Research on the influence of cinematic representation of place is also growing in studies of the mass media (Aitken & Zonn 1994a) as well as in studies of tourism. The significance of such representations was noted by Aitken and Zonn (1994b, p. 5) who observed that:

> . . . the way spaces are used and places portrayed in film reflects prevailing cultural norms, ethical mores, societal structures, and ideologies. Concomitantly, the impact of a film on an audience can mould social, cultural, and environmental experiences.

The influence of feature films on tourism has been established, but only anecdotally (Riley & Van Doren 1992; Riley 1994; Tooke & Baker 1996; Riley, Baker & Van Doren 1998), and films have not gained the scrutiny within tourism that they have within the study of culture.

Film-induced tourism is a subset of media-related tourism, and 'involves visits to places celebrated for associations with books, authors, television programmes and films' (Busby & Klug 2001, p. 316). The British Tourism Authority described film-induced tourism as 'tourist visits to a destination or attraction as a result of the destination being featured on television, video or the cinema screen' (1999, p. 1). This approach was also supported by Evans (1997) who suggested that film-induced tourism involves tourists visiting locations or attractions that they have viewed on film, video, or television. The idea that film and television can influence a person to travel and can influence their destination perceptions is relatively new (Riley, et al. 1998). As the previous chapter indicated, a range of motivations can influence a person to travel, and what is viewed on the screen is one more motivational factor (Butler 1990b; Riley, Baker & Van Doran 1998). Motivations can be a need to escape, a quest for untainted environments, a desire for cultural and educational enhancement, or even a wish to undertake a pilgrimage (Riley & Van Doren 1992). However, given the growth of communications technology, the idea of film and television as motivating influences has become even more prominent as 'less importance is placed on reading as a form of getting information about places' (Butler 1990b, p. 51).

Film-induced tourism can take several forms, and many opportunities are available to a tourist who seeks a film experience. They range from a visit focused solely on a film location experience, to a package tour, to a visit to a particular film icon. Such film icons are not always visual objects. Icons include natural scenery, historical background, storylines and themes, actors, symbolic content, and human relationships (Riley et al. 1998). To be of note, such icons must represent something which distinguishes them from other productions. A range of iconic examples is presented in Table 4.1.

Films can be deliberately utilised to influence visitation, and the potential viewing audience is far greater than that of conventional advertising media. As Riley (1994, p. 454) has observed:

> In successful box-office films, the increased awareness of destinations can be substantial and the received value of increased tourism can also be substantial when compared to the budgets needed for advertising the same destinations.

IMAGING AND BRANDING THE DESTINATION

TABLE 4.1 Iconic representations featured in film

Film	Location	Iconic attraction
'Bridges of Madison County'	[1] Covered Bridges, Iowa, USA	love theme, romance
'Field of Dreams'	[2] Dyersville, Iowa, USA	love of baseball
'Close Encounters of the Third Kind'	[3] Devils Tower, Wyoming, USA	alien encounters
'Crocodile Dundee'	[4] Kakadu National Park, Australia	Australian bush culture, the 'ocker' and larrikinism
'Thelma and Louise'	[5] Arches National Park, Utah, USA	self-empowerment
'The River Wild'; 'A River Runs Through It'	[6] Montana, USA	wilderness and natural scenery

Notes:

[1] www.madisoncounty.com.

[2] www.fieldofdreamsmoviesite.com/distance.html

[3] www.newyoming.com/DevilsTower/

[4] www.ntholidays.com

[5] www.americansouthwest.net/utah/arches/national_park.html

[6] www.destinationnw.com/montana

Source: adapted rom Riley et al. (1998).

Films do not incorporate the 'hard sell' often associated with normal advertising. Rather, they raise awareness of a location and can allow for a more in-depth understanding of a place than is possible with other advertising (Riley 1994). Riley and Van Doren (1992) noted several ways in which film and television make for effective destination marketing:

• long periods of location exposure;
• involvement and identification with locations through the storyline—bringing personal meaning;
• enhanced location image through special effects, actor appeal, and perfect picture settings;
• reinforcement of locations through re-release in other media;
• contact with different market segments through the universal appeal of film;
• a non-sales environment; and
• easy access of the medium.

Film and television can also be used in the branding of a destination. Table 4.2 provides a number of examples of the branding of destinations in the United Kingdom through their association with productions. For example, the film 'Braveheart' sought to reinforce existing attractions celebrating William Wallace in Stirling, Scotland (although, ironically, most of the film was filmed in Ireland).

A significant part of the attraction of many of these destinations is that the films and television series are also connected with a series of books or other media. This occurred, for example, in the case of 'Heartbeat' and the release of accompanying CDs.

Few Australian films have reached an international audience to the extent that they have become part of branding strategies. Exceptions are 'Crocodile Dundee' which was utilised to help sell northern Australia (and the Northern Territory in particular) in the late 1980s (O'Regan 1988), and 'Babe', which was used in the promotion of the Southern Highlands of New South Wales in the late 1990s. More

TABLE 4.2 The branding of film locations in the United Kingdom

Location	Film or television series	Branding name
North Yorkshire	'All Creatures Great and Small'	Herriot Country [1]
Goathland	'Heartbeat'	Heartbeat Country [2]
Stirling	'Braveheart'	Braveheart Country [3]
Tyneside	'Tilly Trotter'	Catherine Cookson Country [4]
Cornwall	'Rebecca'	Daphne du Maurier Country [5]

Notes:

[1] www.yorkshire-explorer.co.uk

[2] www.touristnetuk.com/ne/nym/Heartbeat/index.htm

[3] www.stirling.co.uk

[4] www.uktouristinfo.net/counties/tyne/index.htm

[5] www.dumaurier.org/country.html

recently, New Zealand has sought to promote itself as 'Middle Earth' in the wake of the success of the 'Lord of the Rings' film trilogy, much of which was filmed in New Zealand.

The significance of the feature film industry is immense. To put this industry, and specific films, into perspective, the 'Star Wars' series had a combined box office taking of US$1.5 billion (*The Numbers* 2000), which is more than the annual budget of the United Nations. As is implied with such large box office takings, the viewing of feature films is growing as a leisure activity (Tooke & Baker 1996). Because of this, film and television can impact extensively on a location, not only during production, but also after the movie has screened (Tooke & Baker 1996; Riley, Baker & Van Doren 1998). Consequently, many film producers are now looking globally for unique picturesque locations as production sets. This trend is also driven by internationally competitive production costs (International Trade Association 2001). Thus, although Hollywood has long been identified as the world centre of the film industry, film locations have progressively been moving away from the United States and other traditional locations for some time. 'Runaway production', as this phenomenon is known, is costing the US economy billions of dollars in lost earnings annually (International Trade Administration 2001). The most common locations for runaway productions are in continental Europe, the United Kingdom, Canada and Australia. Several Australian states have taken initiatives to develop film and television production and to attract domestic and international productions. For example, to gain the

TABLE 4.3 Film and television shoots in NSW in February 2002

Television series	Production company
'Farscape'	Henson
'Grass Roots'	ABC and Eastway Communication
'Home and Away'	Channel 7
'All Saints'	Channel 7
'Always Greener'	Channel 7 and Red Heart
Feature films	*Production company*
'The Matrix' II & III	Silver Pictures

Source: derived from New South Wales Film and Television Office (2002).

economic and imaging benefits of production, New South Wales has established a Film and Television Office to assist in the development of the state's film and television industry. State and Commonwealth governments have provided a number of financial incentives to encourage production. Table 4.3 records the film and television productions under way in New South Wales in February 2002. The federal government provides a tax rebate for producers of foreign and larger budget films, and New South Wales provides a number of assistance programs including project development, production investment, a young filmmakers fund, and support for industry and audience development. These include:

- Film and TV Industry Attraction Fund—an incentive fund for 'footloose' productions that are interested in filming in New South Wales; the fund aims to increase NSW market share in film and television production;
- Regional Filming Fund—provides grants for filmmakers wishing to film for a week or more in regional New South Wales; and
- a payroll tax rebate at Fox Studios.

New Zealand has also sought to attract film production, as witnessed in the production of 'Lord of the Rings' for which the New Zealand government provided generous tax incentives (Campbell 2001b). In addition, the New Zealand government spent more than NZ$3 million in promoting the tourism and high-technology aspects of 'Lord of the Rings' after the first film in the trilogy was released late in 2001. Indeed, the responsible minister, Peter Hodgson, noted that the movie had the potential to rebrand the country: 'This [film] has come out of a country which a lot of viewers might associate with sheep' (Campbell 2001b, p. 24).

TOURISM INSIGHT

ATTRACTING FILM PRODUCTION TO NEW ZEALAND: THE ROLE OF LOCAL GOVERNMENT

Although New Zealand has not generally been identified as a film-production location, it is now being utilised more frequently. According to Woodward (2000), large productions have been located in New Zealand recently by Hollywood and 'Bollywood' interests. ('Bollywood'—a term coined from a combination of Bombay and Hollywood—is the centre of Indian film production, producing more than 800 films per annum for an estimated audience of 500 million). 'Vertical Limit' and 'Lord of the Rings' are the two most well-known American big budget films recently produced in New Zealand. 'The Piano', a critically acclaimed film by Australian-based Jane Campion, was also filmed in New Zealand. Previously, other smaller international productions, such as 'Willow', 'The Rescue', 'White Fang', and 'The Frighteners', were also filmed in New Zealand. There have also been a number of television movies (for example, 'The Lost World'), television series (for example, 'Xena: Warrior Princess' and 'Hercules'), and commercials filmed in New Zealand (Film New Zealand 2000).

The New Zealand Film Commission (2000) oversees the production of films in New Zealand by New Zealanders, and the local territorial authorities, regional tourism organisations, and local film offices are the primary facilitators for international production companies. These offices have been actively involved with the attraction of film producers to New Zealand. They have also initiated, as part of their duties under the Local Government Act, facilitation processes for film and television production.

RESEARCH
AIMS

Research was conducted by the present authors to elicit the objectives in the development of the film industry, and to assess the methods used to maximise the potential promotional and touristic benefits of the film industry. The management of image was also investigated.

METHOD

All of New Zealand's local government offices and regional tourism organisations (RTOs) were surveyed in early 2001. At this time, there was increasing local government involvement with film production due to the dramatic benefits associated with filming (Film New Zealand 2000; Queenstown-Lakes District Council 2000; Campbell 2001a). There was also significant publicity about the 'Lord of the Rings' trilogy, which was being filmed in New Zealand at the time (Campbell 2001a, 2001b), and about regional development policy (Ministry of Economic Development 2001). It was believed that these three events would facilitate the implementation of the survey instrument because the local government offices would have been actively considering, or at least have had some information regarding, the subjects covered in the survey.

Mail-out–mail-back surveys were distributed to all local government offices in New Zealand. Of the 96 offices surveyed, 52 returned surveys in a useable state, providing a valid response rate of 54%.

RESULTS AND DISCUSSION

Of the respondents, 79% had had their region used for film production in the past. However, only 45% of respondents stated that their economic development strategic plan included film production at any level. This lack of support or identification of the benefits of film for economic development could have been due to a perception that there was minimal direct economic contribution to be derived, keeping in mind that much of New Zealand film production is low key and low budget, and that there is a lack of research identifying actual impacts. The perceived benefits of film, as identified by its inclusion in strategic plans, are displayed in Table 4.4.

The low response for cultural development could have occurred because this is outside the roles of most respondents (who were primarily from economic development offices), but it is of concern that this aspect is being overlooked. The downplaying of image improvement is also of concern given that image is one of the keys to successful destination promotion. Again, this might have been understated due to the economic development perspective of respondents, rather than a lack of appreciation of possible postproduction effects.

IMAGING AND BRANDING THE DESTINATION

TABLE 4.4 Benefits of film in region

Benefit	%
Economic	89
Create employment	67
Increase visitor arrivals	67
Improve image	45
Cultural development	22

Note: totals more than 100% due to multiple responses

Comments made by some respondents from rural regions definitely reinforced the importance of image to tourism. One respondent stated that film was used to improve the profile of the region both nationally and internationally. This was further developed in a series of questions regarding film as a form of promotion of their area. Of the respondents, 5% believed that films produced in their area could not be used as promotion for their area. This was in contrast to the 71% who believed that it could be so used. The other 24% were uncertain of the ability of film to promote their area.

It was thought that fear of the potential for negative images to be displayed in films might prompt organisations to be selective in their encouragement of productions. Results showed that 49% of respondents were uncertain as to the role that their organisation could play in this selectivity (Table 4.5). This result was due, in part, to uncertainty regarding the role of the local offices in exercising this selectivity. Nonetheless, due consideration was given to the negative images, as indicated by such statements as: 'we would try to dissuade films of a derogatory nature that may project a poor image of the area'.

Respondents stating non-selectivity focused on the direct economic impact of film production, rather than on the postproduction effects on image or promotion. Respondents' understanding of the effects of negative image were also investigated, particularly as to whether organisations would accept films that portrayed regions in a negative way (Butler 1990b; Croy 2001).

Retention of the community's identity was also explored. This was then compared with the importance of contracts for end-credit acknowledgment for the region. As has been noted in the literature, this statement highlights organisations' realisation of the touristic potential of film. Cases exist of viewers watching a film's credits to ascertain the location of areas featured in a film (Riley & Van Doren 1992). A film's merit needs to be assessed in terms of its

TABLE 4.5 Film as promotion of destination image

Attribute of promotion	% No	Uncertain	Yes
Selective of genre filmed in region	25	49	26
Acceptance of film negatively portraying region	52	41	7
Important to retain identity	26	40	34
Importance of end-credit acknowledgment	8	12	80
Contract for end-credit acknowledgment	12	30	58

promotional value, as films can increase awareness in a positive manner and therefore move the destination into the evoked set of destination choices (Woodside & Sherrell 1977). This explains the subsequent increase in visitor numbers after locations have been used for film production.

The respondents were also asked to state the importance they placed on having an Internet site to provide film information on the area, either for tourists or film-production companies. Of the respondents, 69% indicated that this was either important or very important, replicating the high importance that film commissions place on Internet use as an information source for film production (Preston 2001). This emphasis on the Internet is demand-driven by film-production organisations as they seek the ideal location, and increasingly by audiences finding out more about the film. The result is an increasing rate of Internet usage and a trend towards e-commerce in general within the film industry (New South Wales Film and Tourism Office 1998). Only 8% of respondents stated that Internet sites were not important.

Respondents were then questioned on the importance of using films produced in the area in promotions to tourists. This question generated a high importance rating with 58% rating this as either important or very important. This again highlights the appreciation of film for attracting tourists and therefore the importance of image and image management. This result is also indicative of the importance of film and its stars as a promotion and image-enhancement tool, which 52% of respondents noted as important or very important. As Williamson (1991, in Riley 1994, p. 453) has stated 'no pocket brochure can match the wide screen miracle of Technicolor, Dolby, and high profile spokesmen'. Of interest was the large neutral response to this question. One third of respondents were neutral regarding the use of film or film stars in travel promotions.

Overall, having festivals and facilities to celebrate films was not considered to be of great importance to the respondents. Only 29% of respondents thought that the issue was either important or very important. This is an interesting result, especially in view of the media attention associated with film festivals in Australia, New Zealand, and around the world.

This study has shown that RTOs and local government have yet to fully appreciate the opportunities that are presented by film production as an economic development tool. More importantly, for rural areas, not only the direct effects of film production, but also the postproduction effects on image and film-induced tourism need to be understood and appreciated. Recognition of these opportunities must be developed within these organisations to maximise the economic development potential of film production.

BRANDING AUSTRALIA

Competition for the tourist dollar has intensified in recent years as destinations attempt to gain a share in the world's largest industry. This competition has led to many developments in tourism products, services and destinations, not least of which is

IMAGING AND BRANDING THE DESTINATION

the importance of differentiation. One method of differentiation available to destination marketers is to develop distinctive marketing and branding strategies. In marketing terms a brand represents a unique combination of product characteristics and functional and non-functional added values, which, taken together, have taken on a relevant meaning linked to that brand. According to Morgan and Pritchard (2002, p. 12):

> . . . brand advantage is secured through communication which highlights the specific benefits of a product, culminating in an overall impression of a superior brand. The image the product creates in the consumer's mind, how it is positioned, however, is of more importance to its ultimate success than its actual characteristics.

Ideally, brand marketers seek to occupy a market niche which is not occupied by any other brand so that their brand cannot be substituted by any other. However, in tourism terms this can be extremely difficult. For example, overseas destinations such as Bali, Fiji and Hawaii have tended to utilise very similar branding strategies in the Australian marketplace which focus on blue skies, sunny beaches, clear sea water, and palm trees, in a manner which makes each brand virtually indistinguishable from another. Despite the difficulties in differentiating similar products, destination marketers should be seeking to differentiate their destination product by stressing attributes which will match their market needs more closely than other brands and communicating such brand and product images in a manner which is consistent with the attributes of the target market.

The 'romance' of the Pacific Islands is reinforced by the use of images of palm trees and sandy beaches

It is increasingly being argued that consumer brand choice is a statement about lifestyle and consumers' emotional relationship with a destination (or other tourism product) as much as it is about image (Urdde 1999). Therefore, tourism marketers are increasingly focusing on product differentiation through brand loyalty and emotional appeal, rather than through discernible, tangible benefits (Westwood et al. 1999). However, as Morgan and Pritchard (2002, p. 12) observed, 'mere emotion is not enough, the key is to develop a strong brand which holds some unique associations for the consumer'. Nevertheless, in the longer term, to be successful, brands and associated images must also be founded on the realities of the destination product that the tourist actually consumes. Therefore, according to Morgan and Pritchard (2002), to create an emotional attachment with consumers a destination brand must:
• be credible;
• be deliverable;
• be differentiating;
• convey powerful ideas;
• enthuse trade partners; and
• resonate with the consumer.

Although this sounds good in theory it is extremely difficult to do in practice for two primary reasons. First, destinations are seeking to promote themselves in an extremely congested and competitive marketplace in which there is often a high degree of substitutability and also much copycat marketing, and in which campaigns, brands and images perceived as successful in one destination can be adopted by other destinations (Anholt 1998; Hall, D. 1999). Second, political pressures from different stakeholders within a destination might mean that some attributes of a destination are used or not used because stakeholders wish to have their own aspirations presented in a brand (and its associated campaign), rather than marketers selecting attributes most suited to the needs and aspirations of the target market (Morgan & Pritchard 1998; Buhalis 2000; Ritchie & Crouch 2000).

An additional issue which emerges from investigating the nature of destination branding is the difficulty that destinations can have in changing destination image while still remaining credible in the mind of the consumer. For example, Canada is often perceived as 'moose, mountains and mounties', Scotland as 'bagpipes, misty highland hills and tartan', New Zealand as 'Maori (often maidens in grass skirts and/or as warriors performing a haka), green hills and sheep', and the islands of the South Pacific in terms of 'sand, sea, palm trees and smiling tropical maidens in grass skirts'. Such images have been built up over time from a multitude of official and non-official sources, including the wider media. However, changing such images can be extremely difficult given the extent to which they are imbued in the consciousness of many consumers, and making too radical a change in image and branding might well mean that consumers will find such images unbelievable. For example, in the case of New Zealand, Maori do not wear grass skirts or perform haka in everyday contemporary life—although there are a lot of sheep! And what of Australia? Arguably, images of Australia are strongly influenced by perceptions of 'kangaroos, koalas, Aborigines (with images of boomerangs or corroborees), the outback, and the ocker'. Such images were reinforced by films such as 'Crocodile Dundee' and were utilised extensively by the Australian Tourist Commission in the 1980s when international tourism to Australia really took off (Spearitt 1990). Yet, the reality for Australia is that the vast majority of Australians live in cities, and Australia is one of the most urbanised countries in the world, with most recreational activity being urban based, including extensive visitation to museums and galleries. However, the Australian Tourist Commission (ATC) Brand Australia campaign launched in 2001 continued to utilise 'traditional' images. According to the ATC (2001a): 'The Brand Australia campaign positions Australia as a friendly, colourful and stylish destination and will be seen by 300 million people in 11 countries'. ATC research (2001a) showed:

> . . . that the free-spirited, Aussie personality is one of the most powerful assets we have . . . The design was developed after consumer testing identified the kangaroo as the country's most recognisable symbol, while the colour variations represent the diversity of the coastal and interior climates of Australia.

Table 4.6 identifies some of the branding campaigns and target markets for a number of the countries and regions in which Brand Australia was to be used.

Branding is only one promotion and marketing technique, but the successful utilisation of branding can have significant implications for the success of destinations in attracting their target markets. Key attributes commonly identified as determining the significance of branding as a marketing tool include: (i) brands that can identify the product; (ii) brands that can offer the consumer security; and (iii) brands that add value while also offering an indication of price, quality and psychological benefits (Randall 1997). Tourism Queensland (2001a) suggests that:

- branding is about developing a unique personality or 'feel' for each destination; that is, a unique selling point; and
- branding is about fine tuning a destination's marketing to meet the needs of a specific target market; but
- branding is *not* about trying to promote all of a destination's products in a single advertisement.

Although the first two statements are unquestioned, the application of the third is more problematic given the often political nature of the process by which product attributes are selected, with some attributes being included while others are left out, depending on the role of stakeholders in the process. Although multibranding has long been acknowledged as essential for tourism businesses (Delaney-Smith 1987), its application at both the destination and target audience level is often confused, particularly in a federal system such as Australia in which destination branding occurs at the national, state, and regional levels. For instance, Figure 4.4 presents examples of Australian and Queensland brands promoted to the New Zealand market in 2001.

Figure 4.4 A 'layer cake' of brands: the case of Queensland

TABLE 4.6 Some characteristics of the Brand Australia campaign

Region	Branding	Rationale	Target Markets
North America	'Australia—meet the locals'	'With research showing that Americans find the Aussie sense of humour and laid-back lifestyle highly appealing, the "meet the locals" campaign was developed using real Australian characters and promising adventure, escape and an off-the-beaten-track holiday'	'Older sophisticated travellers aged 45 plus, who seek discovery of other cultures with safety and comfort; and younger single adventure-seekers who are aged 25 to 49 and seek great stories to tell'
New Zealand	'And you thought you knew'	'The campaign for New Zealand features an array of exhilarating holiday images designed to broaden perceptions of Australia beyond the experiences Kiwis know so well'	'Experienced youthful travellers aged 25 to 44 are the primary target market because they have the money, the enquiring and adventurous spirit, and the potential to seek quality holiday experiences in different parts of Australia'
Europe	'Discover the other side of yourself'	'European travellers needed to be convinced that a holiday in Australia offers them freedom, escape and an enriching and unforgettable experience'	'Successful young independents aged 25 to 35, who are well-educated with a disposable income and sense of adventure'
Asia	'Australia—see you there'	'The visual message being delivered is that a holiday in Australia can be a life-changing experience of fun, and social and emotional freedom'	'25 to 34 years. They are well-educated professionals who are open to Western culture, and take a major long-haul holiday every one or two years. They frequently seek a prestigious destination that offers "bragging rights"'
Japan			'Female travellers aged between 20 and 34 with overseas travel experience, single or married, are the key target'

Source: adapted from Australian Tourist Commission (2001a).

IMAGING AND BRANDING THE DESTINATION

121

Differentiation and multibranding are considered to be essential, but the potential problems created by the application of these concepts are worth identifying. Differentiation, the ultimate goal of branding, is absent from the majority of Australian tourism organisation branding strategies, because the key attributes of the brands are often very similar. Although many of the brands include some form of identification, many fail to symbolise price, quality, or a summary of the destination offering. The branding strategies employed at national and state levels in the Australian tourism industry display many similarities in the slogans, icons, and themes as well as in the components of the strategy. Furthermore, from a demand perspective, the lack of differentiation and brand proliferation can create feelings of confusion in the international marketplace in particular. In addition, one cannot assume that all the brands used by Australian tourism organisations are individual brand entities because a number of levels of brand exist. For example, Randall (1997) suggests that brands can take the form of a product brand, a line brand, range brands, or umbrella brands, with these company, family, and source brands endorsing company, corporate, and banner brands.

One of the recent trends within branding strategies has been the introduction of loyalty programs, and many products are now involved with one or more such programs. Products that are involved include credit cards, airlines, petrol stations, rental car companies, supermarkets and accommodation providers. As yet, loyalty programs have remained at the product or service level in Australia. However, the application of such an approach at the destination level is currently limited. The ramifications of such a development are interesting. For example, the motivation for repeat travel to a destination (whether state, region or city) would be likely to increase, at least initially, if airpoints, free accommodation, trips, meals, or other incentives were offered.

For many years, the use of celebrity spokespeople making endorsements has been a popular method of promotion (Kotler, Haider & Rein 1997; Belch & Belch 1998). One of Australia's more famous celebrities, Elle Macpherson, was used in a successful Brand WA campaign in the UK. Whether or not Elle Macpherson's presence is a contributing factor in the success of the campaign is difficult to ascertain beyond doubt. However, 'in the 12 months to June 1999, 27.7% of all requests for information to the ATC hotline were for Western Australia, up from 11.6% in June 1998' (WATC 2001a, p. 40). Similarly, in the Australian Capital Territory, stars from the Canberra Cosmos and Matilda football (soccer) teams were used in the promotion of Olympic football games in Canberra, in order to attract youngsters from within and outside the region to the games (CTEC 2000).

Events have also taken a dominant position in the promotion of Australian states and their brands. Some states utilise events as urban regeneration and economic development tools, whereas others use events as a significant part of their tourism strategy, none more so than Western Australia, Victoria and New South Wales. For example, Western Australia, through its brand 'Best on Earth in Perth', and the events associated with it, has obtained millions of dollars worth of media exposure.

Another popular method for state and brand promotion is the use of publicity that is gained through media familiarisations. All of the states actively seek to attract media personnel to their regions—in some cases spending large portions of their promotions budgets. For example, Victoria was able to achieve nearly 900 media familiarisation visits in the 1999/2000 financial year (Tourism Victoria 2000) and

Western Australia managed \$3 million worth of exposure from 36 familiarisations (WATC 2001).

The Internet is also becoming an important component of brand and image promotion and reinforcement. In 1999 Australia ranked third behind Finland and the USA in terms of per capita use of the Internet (Department of Communications, Information Technology and the Arts (DOCITA) 1999). However, according to DOCITA, 'consumer use of Internet commerce is in its infancy' (1999, p. 5). In 1999 Australian consumers spent about \$100 million on the Internet, which represented less than 0.1 per cent of total retail sales (DOCITA 1999, p. 5). However, access and use of the Internet is not evenly distributed. For example, a greater proportion of residents in capital cities have Internet access (22%) than those living in other areas (14%). Higher-income groups, typically the primary target market for many destination campaigns, also have a higher rate of access to the Internet. Younger age groups also had the greatest proportion of Internet users—18–24 years old (62%), 25–39 years old (40%), 40–54 years old (29%), and 55 years and over (7%) (DOCITA 1999, p. 11). For tourism, the Internet is growing as an e-commerce purchasing tool, as well as a marketing tool. For example, Tourism New South Wales (TNSW) noted, with respect to its website <**www.visitnsw.com.au**>, that 'even light Internet users use it for general awareness of holiday types and destinations' (Tourism New South Wales 2000, p. 43). TNSW went on to observe: 'In June 2000, the site had received 50 681 visitors which was a 51% increase on the same period in 1999. The total number of visitors to the site in 1999/2000 was 440 554.' For TNSW (2000, p. 43), its website has become an essential component of its business, providing:

- a more consumer-oriented site, with friendlier, smarter navigation;
- a one-stop shop for travel products and destination information on all areas of New South Wales;
- a greater focus on regional New South Wales where each region and town is able to highlight its own unique identity using information in Visnet;
- a greater ability to support online advertising and sponsors;
- introduction of an online booking/enquiry form in which consumers can choose to have their enquiry handled by a supplier, a travel agent, or a visitor information centre;
- trial of an online call centre facility; and
- use of specially created maps, providing location snaps wherever appropriate.

TOURISM INSIGHT

THE INTERNET AND THE EUROPEAN TRAVEL MARKET

The Internet has become a major tool for planning and purchasing tourist travel. According to Hultkrantz (2002), 26% of adult Americans consult the Internet first when choosing or planning a vacation; 22% consult travel agents, 11% use guide books, and 10% consult newspapers and magazines first. In Europe, 6.4% of all trips abroad were initiated on the Internet in 1999. In 2000, 38% of the Europeans had used the Internet in the past three months to prepare holidays (Eurobarometer 2000). In addition, the 'book to look' quota seems to be rapidly increasing. For example, one of the main Swedish tour operators reported that direct sales over the Web had increased from 1% of all sales in Spring 2000 to 17% in Spring 2001. Skiing holidays, travel to specific events, and city breaks are all more likely to be booked online than offline by Europeans (Hultkrantz 2002).

Usage is expected to continue to grow rapidly as more consumers are connected, consumers become more experienced, the number of sites expands, and various early problems are overcome. The number of European households with Internet access increased by 55% in seven months from March to October 2000 (European Commission 2001a, 2001b). Four of every ten Europeans have online access, and two of every ten are connected at home (Eurobarometer 2000). In the three countries in which close to half of the population has home Internet access (Denmark, the Netherlands, and Sweden), 42–46% use the Internet for holiday planning, whereas, at the bottom end, in those countries in which only 6–10% have access at home (Greece, Portugal, and Spain), 25–30% of the population use the Internet for holiday planning. It seems that access to the Internet is no longer a major barrier, at least in European countries, to its use for holiday planning purposes (Hultkrantz 2002). Therefore, for the marketing of Australian product into the European market, the Internet has become a critical distribution channel and a vital component of tourism technology.

CHAPTER SUMMARY

Destination image is a very significant part of destination management and has been shown in the literature to be significant due to its effects on destination selection, purchase behaviour, and the appropriate marketing of a destination. One key group of components requiring more attention and research is the evaluative components of destination image that are critical in the process of destination choice and, consequently, in the purchase decision. Films, as producers of these images, have been identified as a tourist-inducing element that can turn places of little or no note into astounding tourist attractions. Although all films do not have such a significant effect, film, television, and the media in general clearly do affect the image of place. Destination managers should therefore implement an image-management strategic plan to help ensure the sustainable and successful development of the destination. However, as with many aspects of sustainable tourism, a long-term view is needed in the development of such a strategy because a successful desired brand (and its image positioning) can take many years to achieve.

For destination management, the image portrayed and perceived by potential visitors is very important, and it should therefore be given special attention in destination-management plans. The components of destination image, as displayed in the media, are critical for destination management and marketing. Within the image-management strategic plans, an accurate assessment must be undertaken of the evaluative components of the destination, especially the components which the ideal visitors use in making their evaluation. Mitigation or enhancement strategies should be developed within the strategy for use when opportunities or threats evolve. Such opportunities and threats can be produced by many events, including hallmark events, disasters, and terrorism.

There are also many areas requiring further research, including the relationships among destination management, economic development, media, and tourism. The study of film is relatively new in tourism research and studies have been completed on the anecdotal effects on image and film-induced tourism. Research is needed at the destination level to assess the evaluative components of image and to measure the effect that the media, and in particular films and television, have on image.

Branding is clearly a popular and often successful way to differentiate a destination. However, the relative success of branding in Australia in differentiating the states and regions requires more debate, because the branding strategies are often very similar. This brand proliferation can result in consumer confusion. The promotion techniques that are used in Australia are also very similar, although this is less of a problem because it is the message, rather than the delivery, which is of greatest concern. The development of loyalty programs by some states will no doubt be of great interest to academics and practitioners, and the use of the Internet, events, and media familiarisations will undoubtedly continue well into the future. In Australia, the national and state tourism agencies are significant broadcasters of destination images, and it is their role in tourism in Australia to which we will now turn.

SUGGESTIONS FOR FURTHER READING

For some excellent discussions of issues associated with destination imaging, branding, and advertising see Morgan and Pritchard (1998, 2000) and Morgan et al. (2002). A comparative discussion of the destination branding of Australia and Wales is to be found in Morgan and Pritchard (1999). Morse (2001) and Brown et al. (2002) comment on the use of the Olympics by the ATC as a means to promote tourism. The Western Australian brand campaign is discussed in Crockett and Wood (1999, 2002).

Some useful websites include:
• The 'Lord of the Rings' official web site:
>   **http://lordoftherings.net/index_flat.html**

• Tourism New Zealand:
>   **www.purenz.com**

• New South Wales Film and Television Office:
>   **www.ftosyd.nsw.gov.au**

• British Tourism Authority Movie Map:
>   **www.visitbritain.com/moviemap/index.htm**

• Australian Tourist Commission:
>   **www.aussie.net.au**

• On Tourism Insights on the web
>   **www.prenhall.com/hall_au**

see *The Effect of Film on Tourism: A Case of Making a Sea Change?* by Sue Beeton, and *Use and Trust of Tourism Information Sources Amongst University Students* by Neil Carr.

FOR DISCUSSION AND REVIEW

Key concepts

Key concepts considered in this chapter included:
image, media, evoked image, inept image, inert image, destination image management, branding, film, runaway production

Questions for review and discussion

1   Discuss the existing branding strategies for your region. Identify the strengths, weaknesses, opportunities, and threats.
2   Discuss a new branding strategy for your region. Consider the following:
>   (a) icons, slogans, message;
>   (b) target markets; and
>   (c) promotional techniques.
3   To what extent have the media influenced images of a destination? Refer to the role of film or that of television news coverage.
4   What are the major sources of information which you use to determine your travel?

GOVERNMENT AND TOURISM: THE NATIONAL LEVEL

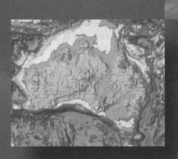

5

The answer [as to why governments should be involved with tourism] should not lie solely in economic reasons, for rarely in history has any society been a willing host to people from another culture or even another locality, yet in order to generate foreign exchange without having to exhaust assets which cannot be replaced, governments around the world are openly inviting tourists to visit their countries.

Every government must have a policy for tourism both at national and local level. To adopt a laissez-faire *philosophy and stand on the sidelines is to court confrontation between hosts and guests leading to poor attitudes, bad manners and an anti-tourism lobby. Only the most determined tourists will visit those places where they are overtly made to feel unwelcome and where they perceive difficulties with regard to their personal safety (Wanhill 1987, p. 54).*

Source: reprinted from Wanhill, S. (1987) 'UK—politics and tourism' *Tourism Management Journal*, vol. 8, no. 1, pp. 54–8, with permission from Elsevier Science.

TOURISM is now an important policy concern for most governments. There is an almost universal acceptance by governments around the world, regardless of ideology, that tourism is a 'good thing', with most tourism policies being designed to expand the tourist industry. Although tourism is often regarded as a private sector activity, Smith (1989b, pp. x–xi) has observed:

. . . government agencies at every level from the international down to small towns have adopted a progressively more active role in the use of tourism as a development tool . . . government agencies currently promote tourism as a panacea for underemployment in economically depressed areas.

Governments shape the economic climate for industry, help provide the infrastructure and educational requirements for tourism, establish the regulatory environment in which business operates, and take an active role in promotion and marketing. In addition, tourism suits the political needs of governments because they can give the appearance of producing results from policy initiatives in a short time. However, the tendency to privatise and commercialise functions that were once performed by governments has been almost universal in Western nations since the late 1970s and has affected the nature of many national governments' involvement in the tourism industry (Hall 1994a). According to Davis et al. (1993, p. 24), three principal reasons for this trend can be identified: 'governments are interested in reducing the dependency of public enterprises on public budgets, in reducing public debt by selling state assets, and in raising technical efficiencies by commercialisation'. Given the present debate surrounding the privatisation of government operations in Australia, such as airlines, the respective roles of the government and private sectors in the development of tourism is a timely topic for discussion.

Different levels of government tend to have different sets of objectives to achieve via tourism development (Airey 1983). As Williams and Shaw (1988c, p. 230) observed, 'The study of [tourism] policy formation is made more complex because the aims of the local state may diverge from those of the central state'. Nowhere is this more apparent than in a federal political system such as the Australian system, in which three main levels of government exist—national, state, and local.

Public policy is the focal point of government activity. Public policy-making, including tourism policy-making, is first and foremost a political activity. Public policy is influenced by the economic, social and cultural characteristics of society as well as by the formal structures of government and other features of the political system. Policy is therefore a consequence of the political environment, values and ideologies, the distribution of power, institutional frameworks, and the decision-making processes (Hogwood & Gunn 1984; Hall & Jenkins 1995; Hall et al. 1997b; Hall 2000a) (Figure 5.1).

Public policy 'is whatever governments choose to do or not to do' (Dye 1992, p. 2). This definition covers government action, inaction, decisions, and non-decisions, as it implies a deliberate choice between alternatives. For a policy to be regarded as public policy, at the very least it must have been processed, even if only authorised or ratified, by public agencies (Hall et al. 1997b). This is an important caveat because it means that the 'policy may not have been significantly developed within the frame-work of government' (Hogwood & Gunn 1984, p.23). Tourism public policy is therefore whatever governments choose to do or not to do with respect to tourism (Hall & Jenkins 1995). As a number of studies has indicated (Craik 1990, 1991a, 1991b; Jenkins 1997, 2001; Macbeth 1997; McKercher 1997), various groups perceive and influence public policies in significant and often markedly different ways. These include pressure groups (for example, tourism industry associations, conservation groups, and community groups), community leaders and significant individuals (for example, local government councillors), members of the bureaucracy (for example, employees within tourism commissions or regional development

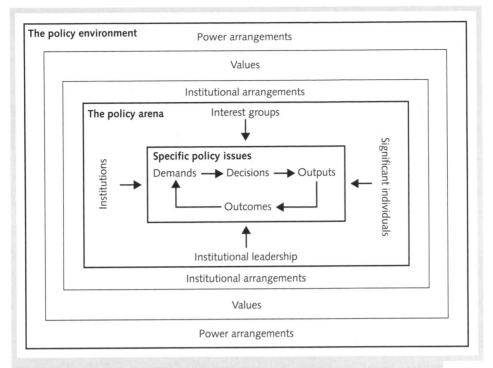

Figure 5.1 Elements in the tourism policy-making process
Source: Hall, C.M. (1994) *Tourism and Politics: Policy, Power and Place.* Copyright John Wiley & Sons Limited. Reproduced with permission.

agencies), and others (for example, academics and consultants). However, there is increasing scepticism and uneasiness about the effectiveness of government and the intended consequences and impacts of much government policy, including policy relating to tourism. For example, Richter observed that 'critics of current tourism policies are becoming aware and are more than a little cynical about the excesses and "mistakes" occasioned by national tourism development schemes' (1989, p. 21). In Australia at the beginning of a new century such an observation might hold true if there were open debate and discussion regarding tourism policies in the first place. However, with very few exceptions there is little questioning of the role that government authorities and corporations undertake with respect to tourism, and of their policies and their relationship with industry, except to the uncritical extent that what they do 'must be good for tourism'. Few ask questions as Jenkins (2001, p. 215) has done: 'Do the interests of these corporations reflect the interests of Australia? Do they act in the Australian public's interest?'

The present chapter examines the roles played by government in the development of tourism. Attention is focused on all three levels of government—Commonwealth, state, and local—and the various mechanisms that are used to influence the growth of tourism. A key issue from the perspective of promoting a sustainable approach to tourism in Australia is the issue of coordination. Therefore, the difficulties of achieving tourism coordination among the different levels of government within the Australian federal system is examined in detail. The chapter concludes with a discussion of some of the future directions that government might take if sustainable development of the Australian tourism industry is to be achieved.

THE ROLE OF GOVERNMENT

The International Union of Tourism Organizations (1974), in its discussion of the role of the state in tourism, identified five areas of public sector involvement in tourism: coordination, planning, legislation and regulation, entrepreneurship, and stimulation. To these, two other functions can be added—a social tourism role which, although not well developed in Australia, is very significant in European tourism; and a broader role of interest protection (Hall 1994a). The present section discusses these seven functions of government.

Coordination

Coordination is necessary both within and among the different levels of government in Australia if effective tourism strategies are to be developed and if duplication of resources among the various government tourism bodies and the private sector is to be avoided. According to the Australian Government Committee of Inquiry into Tourism (1987a), despite the existence of formal consultative mechanisms, coordination has not taken place to any significant degree in Australia and is regarded as one of the major shortcomings of tourism policy and administration. The need for coordination has become one of the great truisms of tourism policy and planning (Hall 1994a; Testoni 2001). For example, Lickorish et al. (1991, p. vi) argued that there is:

> . . . a serious weakness in the machinery of government dealing with tourism in its co-ordination, and co-operation with operators either state or privately owned. Government policies or lack of them suggest an obsolescence in public administration devoted to tourism . . . Political will is often lacking.

The nature of coordination and its application in the Australian scene is discussed in further detail below.

Planning

> [A] desire to plan exists in the tourism sector, but . . . few countries have been in a position to follow a policy of continuity regarding tourism development. Furthermore, the virtual absence of legislation seems to prejudice applying a directive plan (WTO 1980, p. 22, in D.G. Pearce 1992, p.13).

Planning for tourism occurs in a number of forms (development, infrastructure, promotion and marketing), involves various structures (different government organisations), and occurs on various levels (international, national, regional, local, and sectoral) (Hall 1994a, 2000a; Testoni 2001). In several nations, such as Israel, national tourism development plans have been drawn up in which government decides which sectors of the industry will be developed, the appropriate rate of growth, and the provision of capital required for expansion (Mill & Morrison 1985). As in most forms of economic planning, it is desirable to balance the development of supply (attractions, facilities and infrastructure) with the promotion of demand (the number of tourists). Government tourism planning therefore serves as an arbiter between competing interests. As Lickorish et al. argued '. . . without governments' involvement in tourism planning, development of the industry will lack cohesion, [and] direction, and short-term initiatives might well jeopardise longer-term potential' (1991, p.70). Nevertheless, although planning is recognised as an important element in tourism development, the conduct of a plan or strategy does not guarantee appropriate outcomes for stakeholders.

Because of the constitutional and political difficulties that it faces, the Commonwealth government has not taken an active role in direct national tourism planning in a statutory setting. Rather, it has focused on the development of a national tourism strategy in which the national government assumes more of a coordinating role (Department of Tourism (Cth) 1992; ONT 1997f, 1997g). However, planning initiatives have occurred at the state level where responsibilities for statutory planning are more clearly defined. Despite these difficulties, the Commonwealth has assumed a direct input into the tourism planning process at all levels of government through the Bureau of Tourism Research (BTR) and the Australian Tourist Commission (ATC) which provide tourism research and marketing and promotion services. The Commonwealth government has also been involved in direct granting schemes (Weigh 1988; Jenkins 1997).

Legislation and regulation

Government has a number of legislative and regulative powers which directly and indirectly impinge on the tourism industry. Commonwealth government involvement in this area ranges from policies on passports and visas to policies on industrial relations. At both the state and Commonwealth levels, general measures such as industry regulation, environmental protection, and taxation policy significantly influence the growth of tourism.

The level of government regulation of tourism is a major issue within the industry (Blunn 1988a, 1988b; Palmer 1989; ONT 1997f, 1997g). Undoubtedly, although the tourism industry recognises that government has a significant role to play, particularly when it comes to the provision of infrastructure, marketing, and research, the predominant argument is that the industry must be increasingly deregulated. The comments of Wright (1988, pp. 29, 33) are indicative of this approach:

> . . . regulation must exist but in a greatly reduced form and must be supportive rather than prohibitive . . . All unnecessary regulations must be removed to enable industry to operate successfully in the highly competitive world tourism arena.

Historically, the greatest advocate for a reduced level of government regulation of tourism has been the industry itself. For example, the Australian Tourism Industry Association (ATIA), in its *Tourism 2000 Strategy* document, demanded that governments reduce impediments to tourism development: 'The problem is that governments get in the way. They over-regulate industry. The industry requires them to get out of the way in the national interest—if not their own' (cited in Wright 1988, p. 31). However, although government faces demands from most of the tourism industry for deregulation, it simultaneously receives calls for increased regulation of tourism. The most prominent source of demands for tourism industry regulation is probably the environmental lobby (Bramwell & Lane 1993). In addition, it should be noted that tourism, like many other industries, seeks direct government assistance at times of crisis, such as in the period following the terrorist events of

GOVERNMENT AND TOURISM: THE NATIONAL LEVEL

11 September 2001 in the USA. For example, in an article headed, 'tourism represents one million votes', the Managing Director of the Australian Tourism Export Council argued: 'The industry is in serious need of support right now. A delay in the delivery of any rescue package until after the election does not meet the critical short-term needs of the industry'.

Because tourism is a predominantly private-sector industry, development decisions by enterprises must be geared to produce a profit. As McKercher (1993a, p. 10) has noted, there is:

> . . . [a] preference for investment in profit centres (such as swimming pools) rather than in cost centres (such as sewage systems) . . . Mitigation protection programmes will receive lower priorities, unless there is an opportunity for profit generation or a legislative imperative forcing such investment . . . [and therefore] . . . the very nature of the tourism industry makes voluntary compliance with environmental programmes virtually impossible.

This creates a regulatory vacuum in which government must operate to establish clear environmental guidelines. Although the relationship between tourism and the environment has the potential to be symbiotic (see Chapter 10), control of undesirable tourism activities becomes essential if certain aspects of the environment are to be protected from tourists and associated facilities. Environmental lobbyists, particularly in environmentally sensitive areas such as national parks or the coastal zone, often seek the extension of government regulation to ensure that tourism remains 'controlled' (Richins & Pearce 2000). The regulatory conflict is perhaps not so much over whether controls should be in place, but as to what the nature of the controls should be, with industry often seeking to place the locus of control on themselves (that is, a self-regulating framework), whereas environmentalists typically seek to have control placed with a government body, such as an environmental protection authority distinct from the tourism industry (Hall 1994a).

Government as entrepreneur

Government has long had an entrepreneurial function in tourism. Governments not only provide basic infrastructure such as roads and sewage, but also own and operate tourist ventures including hotels and travel companies. According to D.G. Pearce (1992, p. 11):

> . . . because of the scale of development and the element of the common good, provision of infrastructure is a widely accepted task of public authorities and one which can greatly facilitate tourist development and selectively direct it to particular areas.

Perhaps the most notable examples of Australian government entrepreneurship in the travel industry have been Qantas and Australian Airlines. Historically, Australian governments at all levels have had a long history of involvement in promoting tourism through bureaux, marketing ventures, and the lending of money to private industry for specific tourism-related developments. However, the role of government in tourism is increasingly being questioned from a public which is seeking smaller government. For example, the New South Wales government divested itself of direct responsibilities for such properties as Cave House at Jenolan Caves in the Blue Mountains, and the Commonwealth government has sold off Qantas.

The role of government as an entrepreneur in tourist development is closely related to the concept of the 'devalorisation of capital' (Damette 1980). This is the process by which the state subsidises part of the cost of production, for example by assisting in the provision of infrastructure or by investing in a tourism project for which private venture capital is otherwise unavailable. In this process, private costs are transformed into public or social costs. The provision of infrastructure, particularly transport networks, is regarded as crucial to the development of tourist destinations. There are numerous formal and informal means by which government at all levels can assist in minimising the costs of production for tourism developers. Indeed, the offer of government assistance for development is often used to encourage private investment in a particular region or tourist project—for example, through the provision of cheap land or government-backed low-interest loans.

Stimulation

According to Mill and Morrison (1985), governments can stimulate tourism in three ways. First, governments can assist through financial incentives such as low-interest loans or a depreciation allowance on tourist accommodation, although 'their introduction [has] often reflected both the scarcity of domestic investment funds and widespread ambition to undertake economic development programmes' (Bodlender & Davies 1985 in D.G. Pearce 1992, p.11). In Australia, the Commonwealth government has been criticised by sectors of the tourism industry for not providing the investment incentives available to tourism elsewhere in the Pacific Rim (MacDermott 1992). The second approach is to sponsor research for the general benefit of the tourism industry rather than for specific individual organisations and associations. Until recently there has been relatively little attention paid to tourism-specific research by either the Commonwealth or the states. However, at the Commonwealth level, the establishment of the BTR has gone some way towards redressing this situation. The third way is through marketing and promotion aimed at generating tourism demand in general (for example through national and state tourism organisations), or through investment promotion aimed at encouraging capital investment for specific tourism attractions and facilities. Tourism demand promotion has been the main area in which Australian governments have had a high profile in recent years, although there have been increasing demands from government for greater industry self-sufficiency in tourism marketing and promotion.

Tourism promotion

The Government has a legitimate and necessary role in the promotion of tourism. The tourist industry comprises many individual operators and small businesses who are not in a position to undertake the expensive destination marketing that is necessary in order for the consumer to be in a position to make an informed choice. It is therefore appropriate for Government to take a lead in such marketing (Queensland Tourist and Travel Corporation 1993, p. 3).

. . . marketing of inbound tourism in large measure has the market failure and public good characteristics that indicate private sector under-provision and justify public sector support via government funding of marketing activity (Access Economics 1997, p. 29).

One of the main activities of government is the promotion of tourism through tourism marketing campaigns (Ascher 1982). In Australia, government tourism marketing and promotion includes not only Commonwealth and state government agencies, but also regional and capital city tourist authorities. Tourist commissions and agencies have the task of identifying potential target markets, the best methods of attracting them, and (once they want to buy the tourist product), where to direct them.

Furthermore, as well as encouraging visits by foreign travellers, tourism promotion agencies attempt to retain as many domestic tourists as possible to ensure a minimum of 'leakage' from the national, state, or regional tourism system. In Australia this has been epitomised in the 'See Australia First' campaigns which have emphasised the natural heritage and attractions of Australia. An example was the $16 million national domestic tourism initiative launched in November 2000 under the banner 'See Australia' (Brown 2000).

Given the calls for smaller government in Western society in recent years, there have been increasing demands from government and from 'economic rationalists' for greater industry self-sufficiency in tourism marketing and promotion (Jeffries 1989). The political implications of such an approach for the tourism industry are substantial. As Hughes noted: 'The advocates of a free enterprise economy would look to consumer freedom of choice and not to governments to promote firms; the consumer ought to be sovereign in decisions relating to the allocation of the nation's resources' (1984, p. 14). Such an approach means that lobbyists in the tourism industry might be better off shifting their focus on the necessity of government intervention to issues of externalities, public goods, and merit, rather than concentrating on employment and the balance of payments (Hall 1994a). 'Such criteria for government intervention have a sounder economic base and are more consistent with a free-enterprise philosophy than employment and balance of payments effects' (Hughes 1984, p. 18). Nevertheless, as D.G. Pearce (1992, p. 8) has recognised:

> . . . general destination promotion tends to benefit all sectors of the tourist industry in the place concerned; it becomes a "public good" . . . The question of "freeloaders" thus arises, for they too will benefit along with those who may have contributed directly to the promotional campaign.

However, the 'freeloader' or 'freerider' problem can be regarded as rational business behaviour in the absence of some form of government intervention in tourism promotion. As Access Economics (1997, p. 29) has observed:

> There will be a strong incentive for individual producers of tourism/travel services to minimise their contribution to cooperative marketing, or even not to contribute at all, and other private sector producers have no power to coerce such producers and the beneficiaries of tourism activity anyway.

Given the supply-side fragmentation of tourism discussed in Chapter 1, and the substantial degree of market failure that exists with respect to generic destination promotion, government needs to determine the most appropriate form of government intervention. Access Economics (1997) reviewed a number of different forms of intervention including:
• forcing businesses to pay a funding levy;
• 'user pays' and cooperative funding systems;
• levies on foreign exchange earnings;
• making government funding conditional on industry funding;
• levies on tourism investment;
• funding from a passenger movement charge;
• a bed tax;
• funding from consolidated revenue; and
• funding from a goods and services tax (GST).

After examining these various potential forms of government intervention, Access Economics concluded that the most appropriate form of government intervention was the appropriation of funds from consolidated revenue through budgetary processes. Several reasons were put forward for this conclusion.

1 The inability to capture the benefits of generic marketing activity is severe in the light of the fragmented nature of the tourism industry.

2 Levies, user-pays charges and business tax arrangements, including bed taxes, will institutionalise the 'freerider' or 'freeloader' problem.

3 The benefits of successfully marketing Australia as a generic travel destination are dispersed across the Australian community.

One of the more unusual features of tourism promotion by government tourism organisations is that they have only limited control over the product they are marketing, with very few actually owning the goods, facilities and services that make up the tourism product (D.G. Pearce 1992). This lack of control is perhaps testimony to the power of the 'public good' argument used by industry to justify continued maintenance of government funding for destination promotion. However, it might also indicate the political power of the tourism lobby to influence government tourism policies (Craik 1990; Hall & Jenkins 1995; Jenkins 2001).

Social tourism

Social tourism can be defined as 'the relationships and phenomena in the field of tourism resulting from participation in travel by economically weak or otherwise disadvantaged elements of society' (Hunzinger, quoted in Murphy 1985, p. 23). Social tourism involves the extension of the benefits of holidays to economically marginal groups, such as the unemployed, single-parent families, pensioners, and the handicapped. The International Bureau of Social Tourism defines social tourism as meaning: 'the totality of relations and phenomena deriving from the participation in tourism of those social groups with modest incomes—participation which is made possible or facilitated by measures of a well defined social character' (Haulot 1981, p. 208). Australian agencies such as Anglican Homes, YMCA, and the Boy Scouts all offer forms of social tourism. European governments have had a long tradition of providing holidays for the disadvantaged (for example, through the Swiss Travel Saving Fund). However, Australian governments have had little involvement in the provision of social tourism opportunities, and this role has, instead, been undertaken by welfare agencies and trade unions.

According to Murphy (1985, p. 24):

> Social tourism has become a recognized component and legitimate objective for modern tourism. By extending the physical and psychological benefits of rest and travel to less fortunate people it can be looked upon as a form of preventative medicine.

The unfortunate apparent lack of support for social tourism in Australia probably stems from the myth that Australia is an egalitarian country with few people living in poverty, and the idea that such a support mechanism would constitute the strengthening of a 'welfare mentality'. However, as Haulot (1981, p. 212) has so admirably stated:

> Social tourism . . . finds justification in that its individual and collective objectives are consistent with the view that all measures taken by modern society should ensure more justice, more dignity and improved enjoyment of life for all citizens.

Indeed, in recent years, greater attention has begun to be paid to ethical and welfare issues in tourism development (Hall & Brown 1996), and these might begin to refocus attention on the issue of social accessibility to holiday opportunities.

Government as interest protector

The final role played by government in tourism is that of interest protector. Although not specific to tourism, such a role has major implications for the development of tourism policy (Jenkins 2001). The defence of local and minority interests has traditionally occupied much government activity, because government has a role in balancing various interests and values in order to meet national interests, rather than narrow sectional interests (including those of a specific industry such as tourism).

This, of course, does not ignore the fact that tourism interests are represented within the structure of government. As Davis et al. (1993, p. 26) has observed:

> Statutory authorities and a myriad of state agencies were established to protect sectional groups, to represent key interests in the policy process and to protect the social order via welfare provisions to many sections of business and society in general.

Nevertheless, tourism policy could potentially be subsumed beneath a broader range of government economic, social, welfare, and environmental policies. Ideally, policy decisions should reflect a desire to meet the interests of the relevant level of government (national, provincial/state, or local), rather than the sectionally defined interests of the tourism industry (Hall 1994a; Hall & Jenkins 1995).

THE ISSUE OF COORDINATION

To provide direction for tourism policy development and industry planning at the beginning of the new millennium, the then Minister for Industry, Science and Tourism, the Hon. John Moore MP, announced his intention to develop a National Tourism Plan (NTP). In view of the diversity of the tourism industry there was a need for a coordinated approach to its future development that took account of the interests of all relevant stakeholders. This required the involvement of all levels of government in close partnership with industry (ONT 1997f).

Because tourism is a manifold activity consisting of numerous units with divergent and often conflicting interests, the coordination of tourist activities devolves to the state, which is concerned with the optimum promotion and development of tourism in the national interest. This coordinating role is expanding as complex problems arise from the fast growth of tourism (International Union of Official Travel Organisations 1974, p. 68).

Of all the roles of government, probably the most important is that of coordination. The successful implementation of its various roles in tourism development is, to a large extent, dependent on such coordination. For example, Harris, Kerr, Forster and Company (1996, p. 65) argued in their report on Australia's tourism industry that tourism:

> . . . should be regarded as an industry requiring co-ordination, planning and research and a high level of co-operative action by State and Commonwealth Governments and private enterprise organizations directly engaged in the travel industry.

However, although considerable attention has been given to the importance of a coordinated government approach to tourism, many Australian commentators have failed to indicate exactly what is meant by the concept (Blunn 1988a, 1988b; Faulkner & Fagence 1988; Lamb 1988; Wright 1988; McKercher 1993a; Testoni 2001).

'Coordination' usually refers to the problem of relating units or decisions so that they fit in with one another, are not at cross-purposes, and operate in ways that are reasonably consistent and coherent' (Spann 1979, p. 411). Coordination occurs both horizontally and vertically within an administrative and policy system. In the Australian federal system coordination is made all the more complicated because of the plethora of tourism organisations at the national level (for example, the BTR, the Department of Industry, Tourism and Resources, the Tourism Forecasting Council, and the Australian Tourist Commission), the state level (with each state and territory having a separate tourism organisation), and the local level (with local governments often having tourism promotion and economic development bodies).

Two different types of coordination are covered under Spann's (1979) definition—administrative coordination and policy coordination. There is a need for *administrative* coordination if there is agreement on the aims and objectives of policies among the parties involved, but no agreement on the mechanism for coordination, or inconsistency in its implementation. There is a need for *policy* coordination if there is conflict over the essential objectives of the policy to be implemented. Undoubtedly the two types of coordination are sometimes hard to distinguish, because coordination nearly always means that one policy or decision becomes dominant over others.

Coordination is a political activity and can therefore be extremely difficult, especially if there is a large number of parties involved in the decision-making process, as in the case of the tourism industry. As Edgell observed (1990, p. 7), 'there is no other industry in the economy that is linked to so many diverse and different kinds of products and services as . . . the tourism industry'. However, it must be noted that the need for coordination becomes paramount only when it is not occurring. Most coordination occurs in a very loose fashion that does not require formal arrangement (Parker 1978). In addition, it is arguable that a situation of conflict can also be productive in the formulation of new ideas or strategies for dealing with problems. Furthermore, the need for coordination is issue-specific. Nevertheless, the continued calls for a coordinated strategy for tourism development indicate that there are problems in the Australian tourism industry that require both administrative and policy measures.

The demands for a coordinated strategy for tourism development in Australia arise from six, sometimes contradictory, sources.

1 The Australian federal system is inherently unstable and dynamic in certain policy areas, such as tourism, in which responsibility is not clearly defined under the Constitution.
2 Each level of government, including local, regional, and state authorities, has its own goals and objectives in the promotion of tourism development and in the marketing of the tourism product.
3 The tourism industry is extremely broad in composition. This means that the articulation of industry needs is fragmented by the different requirements of segments of the industry.
4 There are strong demands for deregulation from segments of the tourism industry, particularly because of compliance costs and a desire to speed up tourism development processes.
5 There are strong demands for increased regulation of the tourism industry because of its potential environmental and social impacts on host communities.

GOVERNMENT AND TOURISM: THE NATIONAL LEVEL

6 The rapid growth of the tourism industry in the 1980s has meant that substantial pressures have been felt in the provision of physical and social infrastructure within the industry.

Clearly government must have a major role in the coordination of tourism in Australia and, logically, the Commonwealth is the level of government which is most suited to fulfil such a role (Australian Government Committee of Inquiry into Tourism 1987a). As Helber argued, ultimately it is the responsibility of government to address the cumulative effects of tourism on the community: 'To accomplish this, governments . . . must lead the process of tourism development. They must be pro-active instead of reactive. To lead and facilitate tourism development, long range comprehensive and strategic planning is essential' (1988, p. 18). Nevertheless, if the Commonwealth is to take the lead in the coordination of tourism development, it is necessary to identify: (i) the present structure and responsibilities of government in Australia; (ii) the current involvement of all levels of government in tourism management, promotion and marketing; (iii) the relationships among the various levels of government; and (iv) the barriers to the fulfilment of a national tourism strategy. However, as the following discussion of the above issues demonstrates, such a task will not be easy.

THE STRUCTURE OF AUSTRALIAN GOVERNMENT

Tourism is not explicitly mentioned in the Australian Constitution. Therefore, the legal responsibility for tourism has developed under the division of powers for those areas which impinge on the tourism industry. For instance, powers over quarantine, aviation, customs and excise, corporations, and international trade come under the auspices of the Commonwealth. Section 51 of the Constitution details the areas in which the Commonwealth has the legal ability to act. All responsibilities not specified as belonging to the Commonwealth are under state control. Therefore the states have the greatest responsibility for domestic tourism. However, it should be noted that the lack of specific powers to deal with tourism under the Constitution has increased the potential for duplication of responsibilities and therefore the likelihood of disagreement between the states and the Commonwealth, and among the states themselves.

The responsibilities of government

Government faces the delicate task of choosing between alternative policy options. For government at all levels, tourism is but one of a number of alternative economic development opportunities. For instance, government might reject a tourism project on the basis that an alternative (non-tourism) use of land better suits the national, state, or local interest. The role of government is not to agree to tourism development because the tourist industry believes that it is serving the national interest. The role of government is to consider the rights of the community, its living environment, and its quality of life. Therefore, the ultimate responsibility of government is to the notion of a broad public interest rather than the narrow sectoral interests of the tourism industry (Jenkins 2001).

The division of responsibilities for tourism between the Commonwealth and state governments was established in the Statement of Government Objectives and Responsibilities in Tourism set out in the Tourist Minister's Council Agreement of 1976

(Australian Government Committee of Inquiry into Tourism 1987a). Under that agreement, the Commonwealth has prime responsibility for the international aspects of tourism and the formulation and implementation of policies which operate at a national level. The states and territories have responsibility for promotion and marketing of state attractions and for the development of tourist facilities through such measures as zoning and licensing. However, it must be stressed that many responsibilities are shared between the states and the Commonwealth, and although the respective governments have an official policy of maximising cooperation among the government sectors, this ideal situation is often not achieved in the real world of federal–state relations.

One of the difficulties in applying the Tourism Minister's Council Agreement to the contemporary situation is that the agreement ignored the substantial responsibilities of local government and private industry in tourism development. Furthermore, these responsibilities change according to developments in legal responsibility (as in the clarification of Commonwealth powers in relation to World Heritage Property), and according to changes in government policy (as in the divestment of domestic marketing and promotion responsibility by the ATC). Therefore, a more accurate estimation of the division of the primary responsibilities among the various levels of government and private industry is provided in Table 5.1.

Table 5.1 indicates that responsibilities for tourism are located throughout the three levels of government in Australia and private industry. Although the responsibilities are associated with the division of powers between the Commonwealth and the states under the Constitution, it should be noted that there are substantial areas of overlap between governments. The following pages examine the various responsibilities and structures of the different levels of government in Australia in the context of the problem of developing a coordinated approach towards tourism in Australia.

THE COMMONWEALTH GOVERNMENT

The Commonwealth has an overall role of facilitation and coordination in the Australian tourism industry. The Commonwealth is primarily concerned with the national and international dimensions of tourism. However, the Commonwealth's role varies according to the development of government policy and the redefinition of Commonwealth powers through changing interpretations of the Constitution. Nevertheless, the Commonwealth establishes the general framework within which tourism operates in Australia (Leiper 1980). As the Secretary of the Department of the Arts, Sport, the Environment, Tourism and Territories (DASETT—the forerunner to the present-day federal tourism department) reported (Blunn, 1988a, p. 45):

> Successive Commonwealth Governments have seen their most important activity in support of the tourism industry, or, indeed, any Australian industry, as providing a favourable economic climate best suited to the free operation in the market place.

The cornerstone of Commonwealth tourism policy for much of the 1990s was the national tourism strategy entitled *Tourism—Australia's Passport to Growth*, released by the federal government on 5 June 1992 (Department of Tourism (DOT) (Cwlth)

TABLE 5.1 Division of primary responsibilities for tourism in Australia

Responsibility	Commonwealth (DITR*)	Commonwealth (other departments**)	Commonwealth/ state	State	Local	Private sector
International Relations						
Tourism organisations	X					
International agreements	X	X				
Transport						
Air		X	X	X		X
Railways		X	X	X		
Sea		X	X	X		
Roads		X	X	X	X	
Coach		X		X		X
Visitor entry formalities						
Health regulations		X				
Visas, passports		X				
Customs and excise		X				
Quarantine		X				
Research and statistics						
Industry	X	X		X		X
Overseas visitors	X	X		X		X
Domestic travel	X	X		X	X	X
Regional	X	X		X	X	X
Planning						
Commonwealth land		X			X	X
States and territories		X		X	X	X
Development assistance						
Foreign investment	X	X		X	?	
Taxation concessions	X		X	X	X	
Overseas market	X			X		
Guarantees		X		X		
Loans		X		X	?	
Direct grants/subsidies	X	X		X	?	
Destination marketing						
Overseas	X		X	X		X
Domestic			X	X	X	X
Consumer affairs						
Trade practices		X	X	X		X
Travel agents regulation		X	X	X		X
Consumer protection				X		X
Workforce						
Employment		X	X	X		X
Training		X	X	X		X
Environment	X	X	X	X	X	?
Infrastructure	X	X	X	X	X	X
National standards		X	X			
National Parks		X	X	X		?
Regulatory services						
Building standards		X	X	X	X	X

* Including the BTR and the ATC
** Primarily the Department of Foreign Affairs and Trade

1992). According to the DOT (1993b, p. 1), the national strategy was specifically formulated to:

- provide a clear statement of the federal government's objectives for the future development of the tourism industry;
- provide a sound basis for the formulation of government tourism policy and industry planning during the 1990s; and
- enhance community awareness of the economic, environmental, and cultural significance of the tourism industry.

The national tourism strategy was based on four broad economic, environmental, social, and support goals, which were 'intended to guide the balanced and coordinated development of Australia's tourism industry' (DOT (Cwlth) 1993b, p. 11). However, the composition of policy goals, and their relative priority, vary in accordance with: (i) the changes in policy which occur through a government's lifespan; (ii) changes in government; and (iii) demands from industry, interest groups, and the electorate (Jenkins 2001). For example, the environmental goal is a relatively recent addition to the overall tourism objectives of government, and can be dated to the initial rise of conservation concerns in the late 1960s and early 1970s (Committee of Inquiry into the National Estate 1975) and international and national interest in concepts of sustainability during the 1980s (see Chapter 1). Similarly, the attention given to the social dimensions of tourism might change according to the political ideology of the party in government. Nevertheless, as DASETT (1988a, p. 2) reported:

> A balanced approach to the achievement of [tourism policy] goals is necessary. For example, it would be undesirable to concentrate on attaining high economic returns from industry growth at the expense of long-term environmental degradation of natural attractions. Similarly, a preoccupation with protecting the public interest may result in an over-regulated industry structure that stifles economic performance.

With the defeat of the federal Labor government in 1996, a reorientation of tourism policy took place in light of the policy objectives of the Liberal Party–National Party coalition. The most obvious of these was the abolition of the DOT and its replacement by the Office of National Tourism (ONT) as part of the Department of Industry, Science and Tourism (DIST). More recently, the ONT functions have been replaced by a sport and tourism division within the Department of Industry, Science and Resources (DISR), which later became the Tourism Division within the Department of Industry, Tourism and Resources following the 2001 federal election. Under the business plan of the sport and tourism division its mission was: 'To contribute to Australia's economic and social well-being through the development of sustainable, internationally competitive and innovative sport and recreation and tourism industries' (Sport and Tourism Division 2001). It is of interest, in light of the notion that government should also be acting in the public interest, that the division saw its clients and stakeholders as follows: 'Our primary clients are the Federal Government and our ministers. Our key stakeholders include other Commonwealth agencies; State, Territory and local governments; peak industry bodies; and industry leaders and businesses in our sectors' (Sport and Tourism Division 2001). No mention was made of the Australian public being a stakeholder.

When the Howard government took office in 1996 it also announced the development of a national tourism plan to replace the previous government's national

GOVERNMENT AND TOURISM: THE NATIONAL LEVEL

strategy. According to the ONT (1997f), in its discussion paper which was designed to incorporate industry involvement in the development of the plan:

> In general, the Commonwealth's involvement in industry development is usually justified where there is market failure (for example, inadequate investment in generic tourism promotion, limited or unreliable data on the tourism industry or inadequate conservation of the natural environment), or social or equity goals that the community wants pursued (for example, education, health, employment and safety issues). Government involvement in any area is carefully evaluated to ensure that the benefits of intervention outweigh the costs.

These changes were accompanied by substantial job losses in the Commonwealth tourism area, and by greater private-sector influence in determining the shape of government tourism policy—particularly by Tourism Council Australia (TCA, then the peak industry body) and the Tourism Task Force. However, given the substantial influence of industry in tourism policy determination in Australia (Jenkins 2001), changes in Commonwealth policy with respect to tourism tend to be incremental and marginal, with little questioning of the assumptions behind policy setting. For example, it is now almost taken for granted that the Commonwealth government substantially funds national tourism marketing campaigns, despite the fact that national government funding for commodity marketing campaigns has been substantially curtailed over the past twenty years. Why should tourism be different?

Just as policy changes are indicators of government priorities in tourism, alterations to the structure of the government bureaucracy also provide insights into such priorities. Tourism has generally been a low priority of government in Australia. Until the mid-1960s, when the ATC was established, tourism was a minor concern of the federal government. Since the early 1970s, and in particular since the expanded role of government during the Whitlam years, tourism has gradually increased its profile. Indeed, as discussed below, it is possible to detect the increasing commercial priorities of government tourism policies in the changing composition of the tourism bureaucracy.

The discharge of Commonwealth responsibilities

Virtually every country has a national body responsible for tourism. This can be a ministry, a constituted part of a government department, or an organisation with a separate legal status (for example a government corporation) (D.G. Pearce 1992, p. 7). According to Lickorish et al. (1991, p. 145), the role of a national tourist organisation usually includes the following functions:
• research;
• information and promotion within the country;
• oversight of standards of lodgings and restaurants;
• control of activities of private travel agencies;
• publicity overseas;
• technical and juridical problems;
• international relations;
• development of selected tourist areas; and
• overall tourism policy and promotion.

In Australia the functions of a national tourism organisation are undertaken by several separate government bodies. As of early 2002, the Commonwealth, through the responsible Minister, discharges its direct responsibilities for the tourism portfolio through four government organisations: the Tourism Division of the Department of Industry, Tourism and Resources (DITR), the Australian Tourist Commission (ATC), the Bureau of Tourism Research (BTR), and the Tourism Forecasting Council (TFC). Each of these bodies is responsible for a particular role. The BTR undertakes research and provides support for the forecasting role of the TFC, the ATC promotes and markets tourism internationally, and the DITR is responsible for broader coordination, regulation, and planning roles.

Tourism Division of the Department of Industry, Tourism and Resources

The position of tourism in the bureaucratic structure varies with the relative priorities of government. In 1974 tourism was part of the Department of Tourism and Recreation; in 1985 tourism was part of the Department of Sports, Recreation and Tourism; and in the late 1980s it was part of the 'super-department' of the Arts, Sport, the Environment, Tourism and Territories (DASETT). Although many people in the tourism industry would perhaps have preferred to see tourism associated with the industry and commerce portfolio, the relationship of tourism to areas such as the arts, sport and environment might have allowed the formulation of a broader approach to tourism development than might otherwise have been the case. In recognition of the significance of the tourism industry to the Australian economy and the impact of tourism on Australian society, the Commonwealth created a separate Department of Tourism (DOT) in December 1991. In March 1996, following the election of the Liberal Party–National Party coalition to government, the DOT was abolished and merged with Industry and Science, and an Office of National Tourism was created as part of the Industry, Science and Tourism portfolio. According to Jenkins (1997, p. 186): 'The Coalition government is committed to downsizing of the public sector, and history tells us that Coalition commitments to tourism departments, despite the growth of international and domestic tourism, have not been strong'. To an extent Jenkins was correct.

Under DIST, the objective of the tourism subprogram was to 'improve the international competitiveness of Australia's tourism industry by assisting in the development of an economically viable, environmentally sustainable and socially responsible tourism industry' (DIST 1997a, p. 43). DIST consisted of three functional branches which administered various components of the subprogram: Tourism Transport and Business Development; International Tourism and Industry Development; and Regional and Environmental Tourism. Tourism then came under the sport and tourism division of the Department of Industry, Science and Resources, and then under the tourism division within the Department of Industry, Tourism and Resources following the November 2001 election. Under the Liberal–National coalition government elected in 2001, the new Minister for Small Business and Tourism was the Hon. Joe Hockey with the Hon. Ian Macfarlane sitting in Cabinet for Industry, Tourism and Resources. In an interview with *Australian Leisure Management* (2002, p. 38) regarding his appointment, Mr Hockey discussed the rationale for uniting the tourism and small business portfolios:

> When he appointed me to this position, the Prime Minister told of the large number of small businesses involved in, or reliant on, the tourism industry in Australia, so it was a fairly natural fit for small business to come together with tourism. This elevated the tourism industry into a mainstream industry—an important step forward. It's also very

important for tourism to be part of the industry portfolio so that it can have access to mainstream industry initiatives . . . Tourism now stands alone as an industry and needs to be treated as a mainstream industry and not a weekend industry. It is a massive employer, it has a significant impact on the economy and, with my experience coming from Treasury, I intend to improve the recognition of the value of tourism.

Source: First published in 'Yes Minister: Tourism', *Australian Leisure Management*, no. 31, pp. 38–40.

However, similar arguments regarding the visibility of tourism had been part of the rationale for the Labor government of the early 1990s having tourism under a separate ministry.

The relative continuity in federal tourism policy is reinforced when one notes that the principal role of DOT was to advise the Minister responsible for Tourism and 'to develop and implement Government policies and programs that: encourage the tourism industry to take up opportunities for tourism development; and reduce constraints on, and impediments to, industry development' (DOT (Cwlth) 1993a, p. 3). Indeed, the general thrust of the Commonwealth role has been consistent since the inquiry into tourism in the mid-1980s. According to the Australian Government Committee of Inquiry into Tourism (1987a), there are three basic objectives to this tourism role. First, to encourage and improve the quality of a range of tourism opportunities suited to the needs of tourists in Australia. Second, to develop a viable and efficient tourism industry. Third, to achieve these objectives with due regard to the natural and social environments of Australia.

Following the federal election in March 1996 the federal Liberal–National coalition government announced its intention to develop a national tourism plan (NTP) to provide a policy framework for the development of Australia's tourism industry to 2005. As part of the NTP planning process the ONT commissioned a report by Jon Hutchison of the Sydney Convention and Visitors Bureau to provide for industry input in the development of the NTP (ONT 1997f, 1997g). The plan was intended to 'provide strategic direction for tourism policy development and industry planning into the new millennium. Its success depends on strong support from the industry, both in developing the Plan and in its implementation' (ONT 1998b).

The desire of new governments to be seen to be active in tourism matters was also reflected in the announcement, on 11 February 2002, by the Minister for Small Business and Tourism, of the federal government's intention to develop a 10-year Strategic Plan for Tourism (DITR 2002b):

The strategy will identify opportunities and obstacles to sustainable tourism growth and encourage the building of partnerships between the various sectors of the industry and governments. It is envisaged that the strategy will:
- establish clear tourism growth targets, which will be developed in consultation with the industry and other key stakeholders;
- identify and address regulatory and financial impediments to achieving growth rates;
- identify and address social, cultural and environmental issues which are critical to achieving sustainable growth;
- identify significant overlaps and synergies in organisational structures and activities and seek to harmonise these in order to reduce duplications and to leverage outcomes; and
- provide a timeframe and process for implementing the strategy.

A discussion paper was released in May 2002 with submissions addressing the discussion paper, and with other relevant issues to be then sought from interested parties (DITR2002b, 2002h). It was expected that a draft strategy, taking into consideration views expressed in consultations and submissions, would be released for public comment in the middle of the year. The final strategy was expected to be submitted for government consideration by the end of 2002.

The emphasis on industry input reflects the overall philosophy of the Liberal Party–National Party government, which has stressed stronger links with industry in its policy directives (Liberal Party–National Party 1996; DIST 1997b). Nevertheless, the focus of the Hutchison report (ONT 1997g) and the strength of ties with the tourism industry is a continuation of the directions which had increasingly been taken during the time of the DOT, such as the creation of the Tourism Forecasting Council (TFC).

The TFC was established in 1993 to improve information on which tourism policy, planning, and investment decisions are made. The TFC brings together a combination of tourism industry representatives, members of the construction and finance industries, and government representatives to develop a range of consensus forecasts on tourism activity (DIST 1997a). Areas in which the TFC have undertaken forecasting include international and domestic demand, the impact of the Olympics, and accommodation and infrastructure demand and supply. The creation of the TFC, particularly when an existing agency—the BTR—appeared to be mandated to undertake such work (see below), might seem strange to some readers. Its creation was a reflection of three things. First, the need for consensus in forecasting among agencies—the forecasts of the BTR were historically more conservative than the forecasts and/or targets of Tourism Council Australia and the Australian Tourist Commission. Second, a desire by government to give stronger representation to industry, and to Tourism Council Australia in particular, in forecasting and policy formulation in order to satisfy industry interest. Third, to provide an overall research role for government in areas not researched by private enterprise. According to DIST, in the absence of government funding, 'it is unlikely that adequate resources would be available to produce quality consensus forecasts of tourism activity, resulting in the inefficient allocation of investment funds in the tourism industry' (1997a, p. 47).

Australian Tourist Commission

Promotion is one of the key functions of government involvement in tourism. To this end, the Australian Tourist Commission (ATC) was established by an Act of Parliament in 1967 as a statutory authority of the Commonwealth. Section 15 of the *Australian Tourist Commission Act 1967* specified that the 'Commission is established for the purpose of the encouragement of visits to Australia from other countries; and of travel in Australia, including travel by people from other countries'. In 1987 the ATC was reconstituted under a new *Australian Tourist Commission Act*. Under the Act, the principal objectives of the Commission are (ATC 1993a, p. 10):
- to increase the number of visitors to Australia from overseas;
- to maximise the benefits to Australia from overseas visitors; and
- to ensure Australia is protected from adverse environmental and social impacts of international tourism.

The emphasis of the ATC is a reflection of 'the Government's view that at the national level tourism promotion should focus on selling Australia as a destination in its own right, with product specific marketing being the prime responsibility of the industry' (Blunn 1988a, p. 47). The ATC (2001) has identified five primary corporate objectives under its corporate plan for 2001/2–2005/6 related to fulfilling its statutory requirements. These are:

- to increase visitor arrivals into Australia from 4.9 million in 2000 to exceed the TFC forecast of 7.17 million in 2005;
- to increase market share in all countries where the ATC is actively marketing;
- to increase total visitor expenditure from $18 billion in 1999 to $31 billion in 2005;
- to seek vigorously to increase the geographical dispersal of overseas visitors (and indirectly sales of regional tourism product) to 35% of visitor nights spent outside the top 8 regions by 2005 and, in doing so, to work with relevant STOs and industry partners on the promotion of regional and remote Australia; and
- to promote the principles of ecologically sustainable development and to seek to raise awareness of the social and cultural impacts of international tourism in Australia.

The increase in funding for the ATC's activities, which occurred during the early years of the Hawke government, can be cited as one of the primary reasons for the rapid growth in overseas visitation to Australia. In particular, the ATC marketing campaigns featuring Paul Hogan were extremely successful in boosting inbound tourism from the North American market. The substantial increase in funding to the ATC in the early 1990s was also related to the contribution that the ATC's marketing made in influencing overseas consumer decisions to visit Australia (Crouch et al. 1992). However, the promotion of Australia overseas is not restricted to the Commonwealth, and many private companies, as well as all the states and territories, operate their own international marketing campaigns—often in cooperation with the ATC—to maintain or expand their market shares of overseas tourists.

In the domestic arena, the mid-1980s witnessed a National Tourism Campaign to encourage Australians to holiday within Australia and to increase community awareness of tourism as a significant contributor to the economy. The campaign, which also featured Paul Hogan in a series of television advertisements from 1984 to 1986, was a cooperative venture between the ATC and the state and territory tourism authorities from 1983–84 to 1986–87. Initially, the campaign focused on motivational material such as 'Australian Made Holidays' to promote domestic tourism. However, the 1986–87 campaign was directed at the travel industry with a special emphasis on the need for improved standards of service and training (ATC 1987).

Despite the positive benefits of the National Tourist Campaign in promoting domestic tourist activity, one of the main recommendations of the report of the Australian Government Committee of Inquiry into Tourism (1987a), otherwise known as the Kennedy Inquiry, was that the Commonwealth should restrict itself to international marketing, whereas the states and territories should be responsible for their own domestic marketing and promotional campaigns. Although the report's recommendations were implemented by the Commonwealth, the impact of the pilots' dispute on tourism meant that the federal government committed itself to a substantial domestic marketing and promotion campaign to be coordinated by the ATC, and therefore prolonged the commission's involvement in the domestic tourism industry. However, an improved relationship between the ATC and the various state tourism commissions in terms of cooperative overseas marketing through the 'Partnership Australia' program has meant that the focus of the ATC is now almost entirely on the international tourism arena.

Bureau of Tourism Research

> A longer term, strategic approach is essential if tourism is to achieve its potential as a focus for economic growth over the next decade. Such an approach requires a more effective integration of research with the decision making and planning processes undertaken by both the private sector and the government (BTR 1992c, p. 1).

The Bureau of Tourism Research (BTR) was established in late 1987, in accordance with the recommendations of the Australian Government Committee of Inquiry into Tourism (1987a), to provide government and the private sector with the statistical and analytical support necessary for effectively planned and balanced tourism development. The BTR was a response to the perceived need for a coordinated approach to tourism research and the desire to overcome gaps and deficiencies in the provision of data and, in particular, delays in providing statistical information on overseas visitor arrivals. Therefore, the establishment of the BTR was perhaps a somewhat belated recognition of the important role that research plays in the tourism development process (Hall 1988a).

The BTR is a non-statutory intergovernmental agency administered through the ONT. It reports directly to the Minister for Industry, Tourism and Resources and to the Tourism Ministers' Council (TMC) through the Australian Standing Committee on Tourism (ASCOT) on policy matters and the use of its core budget. The BTR is jointly funded by the Commonwealth and state and territory governments and also derives revenue from the sale of data and through its consultancy services.

> The BTR's mission is to provide independent, accurate, timely and strategically relevant statistics and analyses to the tourism industry, government and the community at large in order to enhance the contribution of tourism to the wellbeing of the Australian community (DOT (Cwlth) 1993a, p. 50).

The key tasks of the bureau include the administration and development of a national statistical database and forecasting facility; the production of regular statistical bulletins and specific reports; and the provision of statistical and research advice to government and industry. Core activities of the BTR include the conduct of the International Visitor Survey, the National Visitor Survey (replacing the former Domestic Tourism Monitor (DTM)), the Domestic Tourism Expenditure Survey, regional tourism studies, economic impact analysis, and tourism forecasting, including providing technical support to the TFC (DIST 1997a).

Indirect Commonwealth involvement in tourism

The Commonwealth is directly responsible for the international aspects of tourism development and the formulation and implementation of national policies. However, there is a large number of federal bodies which indirectly affect tourism growth. For instance, the Department of Immigration and Multicultural and Indigenous Affairs (DIMIA) is responsible for the issuing of visas and visa requirements for travellers to Australia. Slow visa issuing can act as a deterrent to travel. In addition, the DIMIA also facilitates entry to, and departure from, Australia through its administration of the entry and departure cards which forms the basis for much of the basic travel statistics to and from Australia. The Australian Bureau of Statistics also plays a major role in the collection of both national and international tourism statistics.

Other Commonwealth departments and agencies can also have an effect on tourism development. For example, the policies of Foreign Affairs and Trade, Transport and

Regional Development, Treasury, and Sports and the Arts, all help to determine the shape of the Australian tourism product, and export and promotional authorities such as Austrade also have a key role to play in encouraging inbound tourism. Clearly, the responsibility of each agency needs to be coordinated with others, and each agency must be kept informed of developments within the tourism industry to ensure that potential conflicts between the various segments of government are minimised and the benefits maximised.

Facilitation, regulation, and consultation

The level of tourist industry regulation and the provision of infrastructure are major issues for government. In Australia the Commonwealth government, no matter which party is in power, has emphasised a major commitment to reducing the level of government regulation of the tourist industry where appropriate, and to facilitating the ability of tourists to travel. Perhaps the most striking measure in this area has been the move by the Commonwealth to deregulate the domestic airline industry to encourage greater competition between airlines and, hence, it is hoped, the provision of better services for customers. In addition, the Commonwealth moved to manage the major airports on a more commercial basis through the establishment of the Federal Airports Corporation and, more recently, to sell and/or lease airports. However, the clearest indication to the tourism industry of an attempt by the Commonwealth to review the regulatory framework for tourism was the 1989 Industries Assistance Commission of Inquiry into Travel and Tourism, which examined the impediments to the competitiveness of the Australian travel and tourism sector.

Despite the attention that has been paid to the issue of deregulation, the significance of conservation issues in Australia has meant that demands for environmental protection might well encourage a countervailing trend for government regulation of the physical impacts of tourism. Such conflict should not be regarded as unusual. Conflict is an everyday occurrence in the policy-making process and reflects the difficulties that governments have in satisfying the demands of the many interest groups that are involved in the formulation of policy. Furthermore, the government's attempts to regulate and deregulate the tourism industry simultaneously demonstrate the problems in achieving a coordinated and sustainable approach to tourism development.

To help delineate a coordinated policy on tourism the Commonwealth has established a number of consultative forums. ONT provides the Secretariat for the TMC, the Australian Standing Committee on Tourism (ASCOT), and the TFC (see above).

The TMC, established in 1959, is comprised of the Australian (Commonwealth, state, and territory) and New Zealand ministers responsible for tourism. The Chairperson of the ATC and the Minister for Tourism of the Australian Territory of Norfolk Island have observer status. Annual meetings are held and the chair rotates on a calendar-year basis.

ASCOT consists of the representatives of the Commonwealth, state and territory tourism agencies, and provides a mechanism for coordinating government tourism activities and providing advice to the TMC. New Zealand participated for the first time as a member in September 1992. Established in 1976, ASCOT is responsible to the TMC. The main objective of ASCOT: 'is to improve cooperation and coordination in formulating and implementing government policies and activities that affect tourism and to provide advice and recommendations to the Tourism Ministers' Council' (DOT (Cwlth) 1993a, p. 18).

Tourism policy and international relations

By its increasingly international nature, tourism is inseparable from the field of international relations. Tourism is as much an aspect of foreign policy as it is a commercial activity, and global tourism now forms an important component of international relations (Edgell 1990; Mowlana & Smith 1990; Hall 1994a). As Edgell (1978, p. 171) noted: 'To admit foreign visitors and to facilitate their travel within a nation's borders is a political action. It is also an action which, to some extent, is bound to have an impact on domestic politics'.

Australia's international tourism policies have been developed to fulfil a variety of economic, diplomatic, and political goals including:
- increasing inbound tourism;
- attracting foreign exchange;
- improving Australia's balance of payments;
- improving the promotion and image of Australia overseas;
- attracting overseas investment;
- ensuring the safety and security of tourists as well as Australians generally;
- supporting Australia's sovereignty over the Australian Antarctic Territory;
- providing for regular consultations on tourism matters;
- ensuring Australia's biosecurity;
- enhancing mutual understanding and goodwill; and
- meeting Australia's national interests.

One of the most important aspects of Australia's international tourism policy is in the area of international trade issues and agreements. International tourism trade issues are usually dealt with on either a bilateral or multilateral basis, although unilateral action might be taken by governments when they feel that their interests are being impeded. Bilateral trade agreements relating to tourism are usually in the areas of transport (for example, air transport agreements), foreign investment, or overall trade relations. Multilateral negotiations are often conducted under the auspices of international organisations, such as the World Trade Organization(WTO) and the Asia–Pacific Economic Cooperation (APEC), which have recently begun to include trade in service industries (such as tourism) as key areas in which trade barriers need to be reduced. In addition, Australia's bilateral closer economic relationship (CER) with New Zealand has had a range of impacts on trans-Tasman trade, including trade in tourism-related goods and services (Commonwealth of Australia and Government of New Zealand 1991; Hall 1994b, 1997b).

Historically, Australian and New Zealand tourist organisations have lobbied their respective governments since 1990 to create a single-entry destination between the two countries (Coventry 1990). The ATC and the New Zealand Tourism Board (NZTB) have conducted joint research in Asia, Europe, and North America. However, there is considerable debate over whether the two destinations should be marketed jointly. Organisations such as Air New Zealand and the McDermott Miller Group (1991) have argued for the development of a 'Destination South-West Pacific' concept, including Australia and New Zealand, which would establish a regional tourism alliance in much the same way as 'Visit ASEAN Year' and the European Travel Commission. Although the development of joint marketing campaigns seems inevitable, particularly as the extension of CER virtually establishes a single domestic tourism market, the desire to maintain national identity will probably override regional promotion in the short term. Nevertheless, as Australia and New Zealand become further integrated economically (for example, discussion on a common Australian and New Zealand currency) and politically (for example, New Zealand is a member of the TMC and the ASCOT), the development of joint Australian and New Zealand product will become increasingly commonplace (Hall 1994b).

TOURISM INSIGHT

TOURISM POLICY IN WHOSE INTERESTS?

As Hall and Jenkins (1995) observed, one of the great problems in examining the role of interest groups in the tourism policy-making process is deciding on the appropriate relationship between an interest group and government. At what point does tourism industry membership of government advisory committees or of a national, regional, or local tourism agency represent a 'closing up' of the policy process to other interest groups, rather than an exercise in consultation, coordination, partnership, or collaboration? As Deutsch (1970, p. 56) recognised:

> . . . this co-operation between groups and bureaucrats can sometimes be a good thing. But it may sometimes be a very bad thing. These groups, used to each other's needs, may become increasingly preoccupied with each other, insensitive to the needs of outsiders, and impervious to new recruitment and to new ideas. Or the members of the various interest group elites may identify more and more with each other and less and less with the interests of the groups they represent.

The relationship between the tourism industry and government tourism agencies clearly raises questions about the extent to which established policy processes lead to outcomes that are in the 'public interest' and that contribute to sustainability rather than merely meeting narrow sectoral interests. Mucciaroni (1991, p. 474) noted that 'client politics is typical of policies with diffuse costs and concentrated benefits. An identifiable group benefits from a policy, but the costs are paid by everybody or at least a large part of society'. As Hall and Jenkins (1995) argued, tourism policy is one such area, particularly in terms of the costs of tourism promotion and marketing. However, the implications of this situation also affect the overall sustainability of tourism and of communities. The present focus by government tourism agencies on partnership and collaboration is laudable. But the linguistic niceties of partnership and collaboration need to be challenged by focusing on who is involved in tourism planning and policy processes and who is left out (Jenkins 2001). The policy arguments surrounding networks and collaboration need to be examined within broader ideas of 'governance' and an examination of the appropriate role of government and changing relationships and expectations between government and communities. Unless there are attempts to provide equity of access to all stakeholders. collaboration will be one more approach consigned to the lexicon of tourism planning clichés (Hall 1999).

According to the ONT (1997f) the tasks of the Commonwealth can be under-stood in the following terms:

Challenge: To provide for the coordinated and unified development of the tourism industry.

In view of the diversity of the tourism industry it is important to provide for its coordinated development. While each sector of the industry has its particular needs, each sector is interdependent and there are many synergies in the aspirations of different sectors.

What are the roles of representative bodies within the industry? Is there a need to rationalise the number of organisations? What are the leadership needs of the industry? Should the industry develop closer ties with more broadly based industry bodies?

Do the Tourism Ministers' Council and the Australian Standing Committee on Tourism provide for the effective coordination of Commonwealth and state/territory tourism policies?

At the international level, how might bilateral and multilateral tourism relations be enhanced to improve the prospects for the Australian tourism industry?

The Commonwealth government is the logical head of any coordinated structure for tourism in Australia. Although the Commonwealth has a substantial role to play in tourism development, particularly at the international level, the Commonwealth's ability to coordinate is restricted by its lack of legal standing in many areas and by opposition from industry, the states, and the territories, where there is a perception that the Commonwealth is infringing on their areas of responsibility or expertise. Furthermore, the Commonwealth's coordinating abilities are restricted by the very nature of tourism itself with its large range of interest groups and values intervening in the policy-making process. The Commonwealth is faced with a paradox in the field of regulation, with demands for increased industry deregulation on one side and calls for minimisation of the environmental impacts of tourism on the other.

Despite the difficulties that governments face in developing tourism policy, little debate has occurred as to what the actual role of government should be. Indeed, what passes as policy 'coordination' can sometimes be described as policy 'capture' (Hall 1999; Jenkins 2001). As noted above, coordination and policy development are inherently political. Tourism coordination might well mean improved relationships among government, organisations such as the ATC, the TFC, the DITR, and industry bodies, but it might also mean a lack of articulation of policy alternatives and a situation in which the interests of the public are equated with the interests of industry. As Jenkins (1997, p. 187) observed:

Debate and argument concerning the positioning of tourism in the machinery of government at the federal level is warranted. There is widespread acceptance in academic publications, industry and public sector documents concerning the need for a public sector national tourist organisation to coordinate tourism planning, development, marketing and promotion . . . However, such arguments might be challenged. The industry is becoming more and more vociferous in its demands for tourism assistance from the Commonwealth. Their claims have met with much support. Yet, when issues of taxation revenues (vis-à-vis bed taxes) to support government action in tourism have been raised, the tourism industry, particularly by way of peak industry organisations such as the Tourism Council Australia, have eschewed such policies. The industry is apathetic in moves to coordinate activities. Industry-led strategies are lacking. Yet, the industry, while quick to argue its size and contribution to the Australian economy, appears to accept that the solution to industry fragmentation in development, marketing and promotion lies in government intervention.

The achievement of a coordinated tourism strategy in a federal system such as Australia's will clearly be dependent on the degree of goodwill and the allocation of responsibilities among national, state, and local governments. Therefore, the next chapter turns to an examination of the state, territory, and local responsibilities for tourism, the trends in management and organisation, and the implications of those trends for the achievement of a coordinated and sustainable approach to tourism development.

SUGGESTIONS FOR FURTHER READING

Although government plays a major role in tourism development, the study of government and tourism has not received the treatment it deserves. However, several texts provide an overview of the role of government and semi-government tourist organisations in tourism policy-making and development; see Hall (1994a), Hall and Jenkins (1995), and Elliot (1997).

Although rather dated, King and Hyde (1989) contains several good case studies of state tourism commissions. More recent discussions of the Australian context can be seen in Hall, Jenkins and Kearsley (1997a) and in Jenkin's (2001) excellent study of the politics of tourism in New South Wales. The websites of the government departments and the various political parties should also be consulted.

Several critical studies of Australian government involvement in tourism are to be found in Faulkner and Fagence (1988), and Craik (1991a, 1991b), and Jenkins (1997, 2001) provide good accounts of some of the political elements of tourism policy formulation in Australia. Useful primary material on changing government tourism policies and the development of the national tourism strategy are to be found in the Senate Standing Committee on Environment, Recreation and the Arts (1992) and associated evidence. Carroll (1991) provides a brief overview of Commonwealth involvement in tourism from 1945 to 1990, and Leiper (1980) offers a valuable overview of government involvement in tourism in the 1970s. Readers wishing to be up to date with government involvement in the tourism industry should consult the annual reports of the government organisations referred to above, and should refer to the DITR and ATC websites. As of late 2002 the DITR (2002h) discussion paper on a ten year plan for tourism along with copies of submissions were still located on the DITR website.

INTERNET SITES

- the Australian Government homepage provides an entry point into many different dimensions of the Australian federal government:
  www.gov.info.au

- the Department of Industry, Tourism and Resources entry point provides access to the tourism-specific area of the Department at:
  www.industry.gov.au/index.cfm

- the corporate website entry point for the ATC is:
  www.atc.net.au

- the ATC's consumer homepage is at:
  www.aussie.net.au

- the BTR's site is located at:
  www.btr.gov.au

- the Governments of Australia entry point provides access to the various levels of Australian government at:
  www.gov.au

FOR DISCUSSION AND REVIEW

Key concepts

Key concepts considered in this chapter included:
coordination, planning, legislation, regulation, government entrepreneurship, stimulation, social tourism, division of powers, government policy, consultative forum, advisory body, inquiries.

Questions for review and discussion

1 What are the functions of public-sector involvement in tourism and to what extent do they occur in Australia?
2 Why is coordination such a necessary part of tourism planning and development?
3 What is the division of responsibilities for tourism among the private sector, the Commonwealth government, state government, and local government?
4 How is the marketing and planning of tourism affected by the structure of Australian government?

GOVERNMENT AND TOURISM: THE NATIONAL LEVEL

STATE, REGIONAL, AND LOCAL GOVERNMENT APPROACHES TO TOURISM

6

The Northern Territory Government does not see a significant role or need for the co-ordination of foreign tourist development between the States, including the Northern Territory, by the Commonwealth Government (Northern Territory Government submission in Senate Standing Committee on Environment, Recreation and the Arts 1992, p. 248).

In its role of developing a national tourism strategy the Commonwealth needs to promote a typical Australian holiday format which makes best use of available and distinctive assets (South Australian Government submission in Senate Standing Committee on Environment, Recreation and the Arts 1992, p. 249).

UNDER the Australian Constitution, the states have substantial responsibility for many aspects of tourism. The states and territories are primarily responsible for domestic tourism, including infrastructure and facility development, planning, and regulation. Nevertheless, as the Australian Government Committee of Inquiry into Tourism (1987a, p. 23) acknowledged, in reality: 'the State/Territory role is much broader, and in recent years there has been a blurring of responsibilities . . . particularly so in domestic and international tourism marketing'.

Many of the tourism development objectives of the states bear a great deal of similarity to the aims and objectives of the Commonwealth. The potential overlap of aims, objectives, and responsibilities among the various governments points to one of the great problems in achieving a coordinated approach towards tourism development in Australia—namely, agreement on the direction of tourism policy and how it should be implemented. The following pages outline some of the features of state and territory involvement in tourism development. Of particular significance are the different emphases given to regionalism and experiential tourism product in the various state and territory tourism marketing strategies. However, one of the features common to all states is the increasingly commercial orientation of government tourism bodies.

AUSTRALIAN CAPITAL TERRITORY

Canberra is a planned city, and a conscious creation of an emerging nation. It is still only partly developed and it is still maturing. By international standards it is still small . . . During the next decade, in the lead up to the centenary of Federation, the National Capital needs to reflect and symbolise the changing and maturing character of the nation as a whole (National Capital Planning Authority 1991, p. i).

Canberra is one of Australia's major urban tourist destinations. As the national capital, Canberra is rich in cultural and political attractions which, although not developed specifically for tourism, have served to encourage visitation such that tourism has come to represent a key element in the Australian Capital Territory's (ACT) economic base. In addition, Canberra serves as a gateway to the natural attractions of the ACT and of the surrounding hinterland within NSW, including the Snowy Mountains. Although many Australians do not think of Canberra as a major tourism destination, tourism is a major contributor to the ACT economy and a major employer (Australian Capital Territory Tourism Commission 1993; Chief Minister's Department 1993; Canberra Tourism & Events Corporation & Tourism Industry Council (CTEC & TIC) 2001). Tables 6.1 and 6.2 provide some visitor profiles for the ACT.

Despite the significance attached to tourism within the present ACT government's economic development strategies (CTEC & TIC 2001), substantial difficulties appear to have emerged in getting the 'right' promotional and development strategies in place, while also establishing a suitable administrative structure. The difficulties of achieving appropriate coordination in tourism administration and a pattern of tourism development which meets the diverse needs of various stakeholders within the tourism industry is, of course, not isolated to the ACT. However, the ACT government faces a peculiar set of circumstances in that it also has to overcome the various negative images of Canberra that have built up in Australia as being 'full of public servants and politicians, boring, [closed] on Sundays, hard to get around with too many roundabouts [and] cold' (Canberra Tourism Development Bureau 1989, p. 26). These images are a result of the frequent rounds of 'Canberra bashing' (Standing Committee on Tourism and ACT Promotion 1993). The ACT government also faces particular responsibilities in planning and managing the nation's capital, and all the associated issues of retaining and presenting national identity and heritage.

TABLE 6.1 International overnight visitors to the ACT, 1998-99

Country of origin	Number of visitors 1998(000s)	Number of visitors 1999 (000s)	% change
New Zealand	9.6	7.0	−28.9
United States	23.8	21.2	−11.2
Canada	7.7	7.0	−9.1
UK/Ireland	22.9	26.9	+17.5
Germany	12.2	10.4	−14.8
Other Europe	29.4	24.8	-15.6
Taiwan	38.5	24.4	−36.6
Japan	18.7	8.7	−53.5
Hong Kong	2.4	4.1	+70.8
Singapore	4.7	2.9	−38.3
Malaysia	1.1	2.4	+118
Indonesia	2.1	4.8	+128
Korea	2.5	5.4	+116
Thailand	4.0	5.0	+25.0
China	13.4	7.3	−45.5
Other Asia	6.6	4.7	−28.8
Other	8.0	13.5	+68.8
Total	207.7	180.7	−13.0

Source: Canberra Tourism and Events Corporation (2001) *ACT Tourism Masterplan 2001–2005.*

TABLE 6.2 International visitors (overnight and day trips) to the ACT, 1998

	Number of visitors	% of ACT market
Holiday	132 118	63
Visiting friends and relatives	27 599	13
Business	22 446	11
Convention and conference	5027	2
Employment	2217	1
Education	16 562	8
Other reasons	3906	2
Immigration	113	0
Total	210 510	100

Source: Canberra Tourism and Events Corporation (2001) *ACT Tourism Masterplan 2001–2005.*

Tourism development and administration in the ACT

In creating a framework in which tourism operates within the ACT, the Commission's policies partially mitigate against the future development of a successful tourist industry (National Capital Development Commission 1981, p. 121).

The first report to have paid attention to tourism in the ACT appears to have been that of the Senate Select Committee on the Development of Canberra in 1955, which concluded that every encouragement should be given to the development of Canberra as a tourist, cultural and educational centre, in keeping with its function as the nation's capital. The committee noted that, even though Canberra was a city of only 30 000 people, it was already attracting 250 000 visitors a year, and argued for the establishment of a number of national cultural institutions which would reinforce Canberra's identity in the minds of Australians.

Similar issues were raised in the inquiry into the Australian Capital Territory Tourist Industry conducted in 1961 by the Joint Committee on the Australian Capital Territory (JCACT). The committee highlighted many of the same concerns that surround the ACT tourism industry today—the adequacy of facilities for visitors; the adequacy of accommodation and transport links; the development and promotion of tourist attractions; and the integration of Canberra with the surrounding regions in terms of tourism promotion and marketing. The committee laid the foundation for the tourism agenda which still exists in the ACT to this day, and was particularly interested in the prospects for cultural tourism and the manner in which tourism could be linked to 'fostering interest in Canberra as the Commonwealth's seat of government and the National Capital, and acceptance of it as an important symbol of Australian ideals and achievements' (JCACT 1961, p. 6).

The members of the joint committee paid specific attention to the development of a national library, an art gallery, and a national museum, the last of which is still awaiting commencement of construction. In addition, the committee recommended that consideration be given to the establishment of a hall of Aboriginal culture, a hall of New Guinea and Territories culture, a hall of national history, a museum of folk and social history, and a national hall of photography, with the provision of indoor and open air theatres for drama, music, ballet, opera, and theatre also being required. The main thrust of the report concerned the manner in which tourism serves to reinforce national identity and national pride. As the committee noted (JCACT 1961, p. 9):

> The Committee considers that it is a legitimate function of the Federal Government to foster interest in Canberra as the seat of Government of the Commonwealth and as a symbol of Australian ideals and achievements. The capital of a nation, whether its greatest city or not, whether it has grown naturally or been brought into existence specifically to serve as the centre of administration, has been traditionally, and is to-day, a source of national pride and an inspiration for patriotic purpose. Athens, Ancient Rome and Jerusalem were such. London, Paris, Edinburgh and Washington are such today. In times when national cohesion is weak and patriotism a flickering flame, it is significant that there has often been no centre of political life or one which inspires no loyalty.

Given the almost full employment of the early 1960s it should not be surprising that the employment potential of tourism received little mention in the joint committee's deliberations. Tourism was seen as primarily serving an educative function that would broaden Australia's understanding of the creation of the national capital and encourage a more patriotic spirit. Cultural tourism was significant, but only in terms of the imaging of a nation and the presentation of national icons.

By 1972 the picture had changed considerably. In that year the JCACT (1972, p. 42) noted that there was still a need for the 'development of buildings and other works consistent with Canberra as the repository, and place for continuous and accessible display of matters on national importance such as art works, Australiana and the like'. However, it also noted (JCACT 1972, p. 42) that there was a need for 'co-ordination of effort of elements of the visitor industry to provide for effective development and attractive advertisement of Canberra to inform and interest Australians and other people'.

In April 1979 the Minister for the Capital Territory forwarded to the JCACT suggested terms of reference for an inquiry into tourism in the ACT. The committee had a wide brief for the inquiry with particular attention to be paid to the desirable role for tourism in the future development of the ACT. The primary focus of the report was on the potential economic and employment benefits of tourism and the use of tourism as a mechanism for regional economic development, although mention was made of the potential of tourism to serve educational functions and strengthen tourist consciousness of the national and cultural heritage (JCACT 1980, p. 20). The committee also concluded that the most effective way of promoting the ACT would be to establish an ACT Tourist Commission which (JCACT 1980, p.116):

> . . . would operate along the lines of the Australian Tourist Commission but would continue to have day-to-day involvement in the marketplace through the operation of information and service centres which would provide travel services to both tourists and local residents.

In addition to the report of the joint committee, the National Capital Development Commission (NCDC 1981, p. 85)—then the statutory authority responsible for the planning, development and construction of Canberra—also reported on tourism in the ACT: 'planning for tourism requires a comprehensive approach which takes into account the various aspects of tourism as they interact within, and form part of, the community'. The NCDC had no direct responsibility for the administration or promotion of tourism in the ACT. However, the commission did have a major involvement in tourism through its land use policies and its influence on the location and scale of attractions, facilities and infrastructure. Under the NCDC's Tourism Subject Plan 1978–88, tourism accommodations and attractions were concentrated in a series of zones: the city centre and the central area, town centres, northern approach zone (Barton and Federal Highways), southern approach zone (Jerrabomberra and Canberra Avenues), and other Canberra (primarily rural areas). As the committee noted (NCDC 1981, pp 90–1).

> As a result, the delineation of zones has precluded the development of a concentration of accommodation at a specific location. This may have created an effective barrier to the development of associated tourist facilities (e.g. entertainment) in conjunction with accommodation.

Indeed, the NCDC (1981, p. 103). went on to note that its policies in terms of memorials, national cultural and political sites, and other built attractions, 'necessitate a level of mobility by the tourist which is not necessarily required to the same extent in alternative tourist destinations'. The impacts of the NCDC policies on tourism development remains to the present day, and provide the physical framework within which tourism in the urban areas of the ACT have to operate.

The imperative for the development of a tourism development plan remained throughout the 1980s, particularly given the opportunities presented by the opening of the new Parliament House and the bicentennial celebrations of 1988, and concerns at the range of major problems which were perceived as besetting tourism in the ACT. According to the Joint Committee on the ACT (JCACT 1986, p. 6): 'complaints ranged from inadequate promotion, insufficient funding, unsatisfactory marketing, poor and uncoordinated collection of visitor statistics and inappropriate administrative arrangements'.

The provision of a development plan was a direct response to the fragmented nature of tourism planning under the NCDC and the need for improved policy and planning coordination. In addition, the joint committee recommended a further restructuring of tourism administration in the ACT. It recommended (1986, p. ix): 'that an ACT Development Board incorporating the Canberra Tourist Bureau and the Canberra Development Board be established to promote, develop and provide economic assistance to tourism and hospitality in the ACT'. The new tourism authority was regarded as being necessary 'to coordinate tourism and economic developments in an effective manner', with the new organisation also being required to 'focus on the development of local opportunities and industries rather than being primarily concerned with activities outside the Territorial border as is the case at present' (1986, p. 4).

In July 1988 the Canberra Development Board released its tourism strategy, which represented the first attempt to provide a comprehensive development plan for tourism in the ACT. The plan reflected the increasing desire of government to provide greater economic development for Canberra through tourism. The aim of the plan was 'to assist in promoting growth and diversification of the local economy by encouraging the private sector to develop tourism opportunities, while remaining sympathetic to the unique environment of Canberra and its character as the national capital' (Canberra Development Board 1988, p. 1). A more strategic approach to tourism planning and the provision of tourism product in the ACT was also apparent in the development of a tourism marketing strategy by the Canberra Tourism Development Bureau (1989). The strategy paid specific attention to matching the unique attractions of the Canberra region with relevant domestic and international market segments through product development, price considerations, distribution channels, and promotional activities, and served as a clear blueprint for tourism marketing in the territory. Of particular interest in the marketing strategy was the focus on a number of 'key result areas' (1989, p. 10) which were considered as being of crucial importance in the marketing of Canberra's tourism product. These included a campaign to improve the image of Canberra as a holiday and meetings destination ('Canberra—The Natural Capital'), a focus on special events and the conventions industry, pursuing a multicultural marketing strategy, target promotion of the short-break market from Sydney and Melbourne, and the targeting of the special-interest tourism market, particularly sports and cultural groups. To a great extent, the focus of the 1989–90 strategy still serves as the basis of ACT tourism marketing.

With the coming of self-government the ACT is still trying to find an appropriate formula for tourism planning and development. The need to be more cost-effective in promotion and marketing runs parallel to the desire of the ACT government to broaden the economic base of the territory and to create more employment opportunities. Given the chequered history of government and administrative debate over tourism in the ACT, it should therefore not be surprising that a further inquiry into tourism has been conducted by the Standing Committee on Tourism and ACT Promotion, a committee of the Legislative Assembly of the ACT (1993). Again, not surprisingly, given the outputs of the various other inquiries into tourism in the ACT over the past thirty years, the standing committee noted that there was 'a degree of uncertainty in sectors of the industry about its long and short term goals', although it did go on to observe that 'this may well reflect an industry involving a wide range of large and small enterprises as well as governmental institutions' (1993, p. 9). The

STATE, REGIONAL, AND LOCAL GOVERNMENT APPROACHES TO TOURISM

committee believed that it was imperative that the ACT Tourism Commission (ACTTC), 'in consultation with the tourism industry', develop 'an integrated tourism strategy for the ACT which incorporates regional factors and interdependence' (1993, p. 10). Nevertheless, significant problems emerged in such a strategy because, although national institutions are a significant tourist drawcard to the ACT, 'it is regrettable that a number of them do not appear to regard themselves as part of the tourism industry', and did not appropriately cater to the needs of visitors, particularly during the summer months (Standing Committee on Tourism and ACT Promotion 1993, p. 22).

The relationship between national institutions and the tourism industry lies at the heart of the difficulties of developing an integrated tourism strategy for the ACT. Undoubtedly Canberra is a cultural tourism destination *par excellence*, but the divides between public-sector and private-sector goals, and between national and ACT government objectives, are extremely hard to bridge, given long-standing organisational cultures that have only recently been made aware of their responsibilities to visitor needs.

Following self-government and the desire of the ACT government to broaden the economic and employment base of the ACT, tourism has become an important component of the regional development strategy. The establishment of the new Canberra Tourism and Events Corporation (CTEC) in July 1997, the development of a new comprehensive holiday package, and the construction of a new visitor centre (Canberra Tourism 1997), are all testament to the importance attached to tourism by the ACT government. The mission of CTEC is to 'maximise the social, cultural, economic and employment benefits of tourist visitation to the ACT commu-

Political tourist attraction. Parliament House, Canberra, is one of the most visited attractions in the ACT.

nity through the provision of quality tourism events, marketing and services' (CTEC 2000b, p. 7), with four goals being identified:

- to promote the ACT as a premier Australian tourism destination in partnership with the local tourism industry and the government;
- to manage Floriade and the Rally of Canberra;
- administer events funding programs;
- to promote the ecologically sustainable development of the local tourism and travel industry; and
- to provide tourism and travel information and booking services.

In addition, a new marketing strategy (CTEC 2000a) sought to highlight 'that priority should continue to be given to communications that seek to change the personality of Canberra from "cool, stuffy, reserved and closed" to more open, welcoming and approachable' (CTEC 2000a, p. 3). CTEC also sought to reposition Canberra 'to "our national capital" rather than "Canberra"' (2000a, p. 3). The marketing strategy also consciously sought to take advantage of the positive profile of the city gained during the hosting of soccer during the 2000 Olympics, as well as the sporting success of the ACT Brumbies in Super 12 rugby and the Canberra Raiders in rugby league.

Historically, tourism development in Canberra could, at best, be described as being in a partially confused state. This has primarily been a result of disagreements among different industry sectors over the direction of tourism in the ACT. However, it is also a reflection of deep-seated differences in perception over the role of the national institutions which make up such an important part of Canberra's tourism product, image, and identity in that there has existed a conflict in the eyes of some between the form and function of Canberra as a national capital and Canberra as a tourist destination.

In 2001 a new tourism master plan for the ACT was released as a joint initiative between government and industry (CTEC & TIC 2001) and it will be interesting to see whether the processes and frameworks established by this plan will assist Canberra in not only being perceived more positively but also in receiving recognition for its rich variety of tourist attractions.

NEW SOUTH WALES

> Our message will be that the Games might be over, but for Sydney and New South Wales things have only just begun. We'll repeat a few key messages to alleviate misconceptions that are barriers to travel, for example: Sydney is affordable; Sydney is accessible; Sydney is a new city, a fresh city, an Olympic city; Sydney and New South Wales in 2001 are at the heart of a new nation, a young and vibrant nation (Tourism New South Wales 2000, p. 27)

Since the early 1980s, substantial changes to the focus and structure of government tourism administration, marketing, and promotion in New South Wales have occurred. In 1982 the state government amalgamated the Department of Tourism and the Department of Sport and Recreation to form the Department of Leisure, Sport and Tourism to provide for 'more effective and efficient co-ordination and management' (Tourism Commission of NSW 1985, p. 1). The restructuring process was further enhanced by the establishment of the Tourism Commission of New South Wales in 1985 as a corporation under the New South Wales *Tourism Commission Act*

1984. The creation of a commission was due to a perception by government that 'the further development of the tourism industry . . . would be greatly facilitated by the establishment of a commercially oriented organisation solely responsible for the co-ordination of this important industry' (Tourism Commission of NSW 1985, p. 1). As Hollinshead (1990, p. 46) observed: 'the 1985/86 annual report of the New South Wales Tourism Commission is as much a manifesto of entrepreneurial interest as it is an exposition of legislative responsibility'. Under the commission's charter its purpose is: 'to achieve economic and social benefits for the people of New South Wales through the development of tourism', and its role is 'to promote travel to and within New South Wales and co-ordinate the development of ventures relating to tourism' (Tourism Commission of NSW 1988, p. 5). Tables 6.3 to 6.6 provide a profile of visitation to the state.

In the late 1980s and the 1990s the commission was further restructured to reflect the changing priorities of state government. The commission sought to (NSW Tourism Commission 1993, p. 4):

- establish a government framework in which private-sector tourism could develop to its full potential;
- establish cooperation among government and the relevant industry bodies;
- ensure that opportunities to develop or sustain tourism-related businesses were identified and communicated to key players;
- protect NSW's market share and increase visitor nights to and within NSW, including retailing of NSW tourism product;
- ensure effective management of human, financial, and technical resources within the organisation;
- fulfil the statutory requirements of operating as a government body.

TABLE 6.3 Origin of domestic overnight visitors and visitor nights in New South Wales, 1998–99

	Overnight Visitors (000s)				Visitor nights (000s)			
	1998	*1999*	*% change*	*1999 % total*	*1998*	*1999*	*% change*	*1999 % total*
Sydney	10 156	9856	−3.0	37	30 903	31 874	3.1	34
Regional New South Wales	9059	9113	0.6	34	29 485	29 035	−1.5	31
Melbourne	2448	2259	−7.7	9	10 400	9472	−8.9	10
Regional Victoria	876	728	−16.9	3	3763	3281	−12.8	3
Brisbane	1252	1227	−2.0	5	5073	5288	4.2	6
Regional Queensland	917	850	−7.3	3	5379	4571	−15.0	5
South Australia	497	503	1.2	2	2579	2933	13.7	3
Australian Capital Territory	1515	1539	1.6	6	4238	4153	−2.0	4
Rest of Australia	413	461	11.6	2	3042	3263	7.3	3
Total	27 132	26 536	−2.2	100	94 862	93 871	−1.0	100

Source: Bureau of Tourism Research (BTR), (2000) *Tourism trends in New South Wales: New South Wales state profile: year end December 1999,* Canberra, p. 4.

TABLE 6.4 Domestic overnight visitor activities in New South Wales, 1998–99

	Overnight visitors 1998 (%)	Overnight visitors 1999 (%)
Outdoor ecotourism	33	30
Go to the beach (include: swimming, surfing, diving)	24	22
Visit national parks, bushwalking, rainforest walks	13	11
Visit botanical or other public gardens	3	2
Active outdoor/sport	24	23
Go fishing	9	9
Play golf and other sports	10	8
Other outdoor activities	9	8
Arts/heritage	13	10
Attend theatre, concerts or other performing arts	3	2
Visit museums or art galleries	4	3
Attend festivals/fairs or cultural events	3	2
Visit historic/heritage buildings, sites, or monuments	5	4
Local attractions, tourist activities	9	7
Visit amusements/theme parks	2	2
Visit wildlife parks/zoos	2	2
Visit wineries	2	2
Social/other	74	77
Visit friends or relatives	44	39
Pubs, clubs, discos etc.	12	20
Go on a day trip to another place	6	6
Attend an organised sporting event	3	3
Total '000	27 132	26 536

Note: The percentage of visitors who participated in specific activities may sum to more than the percentage of visitors who participated in the broader activities categories as visitors may have participated in more than one activity. For example, in the outdoor ecotourism activity group, visitors may have visited the beach as well as national parks. As such they are counted against both these specific activities, but only once against the broader outdoor ecotourism activity.

Source: Bureau of Tourism Research (BTR), (2000) *Tourism trends in New South Wales: New South Wales state profile: year end December 1999,* Canberra, p. 11.

By the mid-1990s the tourism commission had been further corporatised and it changed its name to Tourism New South Wales (TNSW). According to the TNSW's corporate plan (1997a, p. 1) its mission was to:

Lead, organise and provide strategic direction to increase the efficiency and effectiveness of the tourism industry in New South Wales and market New South Wales as the destination of choice for Australian and international visitors; in order to generate economic, environmental, social and cultural benefits to the State.

Its strategic objectives (TNSW 1997a) were to:
• increase industry efficiency and effectiveness, yield and economic benefits to the state;
• increase benefits from travel by targeted markets to and within New South Wales;
• achieve and sustain demonstrated community and government support for the development of the tourism industry;
• optimise the tourism benefits to the state up to, during, and beyond 2000 as a result of the staging of the Olympics and Paralympics; and
• deliver quality service in all aspects of Tourism New South Wales' operations to internal and external stakeholders.

TABLE 6.5 International visitors' country of residence by state or territory visited, 1999

Country of residence	NSW (%)	Vic (%)	Qld (%)	SA (%)	WA (%)	Tas. (%)	NT (%)	ACT (%)	Total (%)*	Total (000s)
New Zealand	43	22	40	4	5	2	1	1	120	646
Japan	57	12	76	2	7	1	7	1	162	660
Hong Kong	62	18	39	5	8	1	3	3	138	128
Singapore	31	29	28	5	29	2	1	1	127	234
Malaysia	36	29	24	6	27	2	1	2	125	126
Indonesia	39	32	14	3	32	2	4	6	131	81
Taiwan	62	34	71	2	2	1	1	18	191	133
Thailand	61	31	17	6	15	2	2	9	144	54
Korea	84	15	49	4	3	1	1	5	163	100
China	82	42	37	3	6	1	**	8	179	87
Other Asia	54	28	34	3	11	1	3	5	138	98
United States	71	31	45	10	10	5	12	6	189	385
Canada	72	37	47	15	14	5	16	9	216	75
United Kingdom	65	31	47	14	23	3	16	5	203	505
Germany	69	38	52	22	20	5	38	7	252	139
Other Europe	69	36	48	17	19	3	24	6	223	385
Other countries	53	21	43	6	9	2	5	5	144	260
Total	**58**	**26**	**48**	**8**	**13**	**2**	**9**	**4**	**168**	**4097**

* This is the measure of the extent to which visitors visited more than one state or territory; for example 130 per cent means that, on average, visitors visited 1.3 states or territories in Australia

**Subject to sampling variability too high for practical purposes

Source: Bureau of Tourism Research (BTR), (2000) *Tourism trends in New South Wales: New South Wales state profile: year end December 1999,* Canberra, p. 18.

The vision of TNSW is 'to advance New South Wales as Australia's premier tourism destination' (TNSW 2001, p. 1)

As with similar tourism bodies in other states and territories, the goals of the TNSW reflect a desire to run the organisation on a commercial basis and have a facilitating role in tourism development, rather than one of direct investment, although the extent to which this assists rural regions tends to reflect broader government philosophies and priorities. For example, in the late 1990s with the election of the Carr Labor government, increased funding became available for regional marketing, especially to boost interstate and international visitation (TNSW 1997b).

One significant element of tourism development in NSW was the launching in 1990 of a Tourism Development Strategy developed by a joint industry and government task force (NSW Tourism Commission 1990). The strategy identified numerous opportunities and constraints and made 144 recommendations in the areas of environmental planning and development, government support, marketing, training, transport, and wages and employment. As at June 1993, 40% of the strategy's recommendations had been implemented with a commitment having been made to a further 45% (NSW Tourism Commission 1993, p. 19). More recently, Tourism NSW has developed a tourism master plan to provide strategic directions for the state tourism industry. To a great extent the plan continued from where the strategy had left off (TNSW 1996a). However, in the case of both the strategy and the master plan, one of the main difficulties in planning at the commission or ministerial level is their somewhat limited responsibilities for implementation, given that much of such power

TABLE 6.6 International visitors to New South Wales and Australia—country of residence by purpose of visit, 1999

Country of residence	Holiday NSW (%)	Holiday Aust. (%)	Visiting friends and relatives NSW (%)	Visiting friends and relatives Aust. (%)	Business NSW (%)	Business Aust. (%)	Other[a] NSW (%)	Other[a] Aust. (%)	Total NSW (000s)	Total Aust. (000s)
New Zealand	44	61	35	46	21	25	8	14	281	646
Japan	90	88	3	8	5	6	4	14	376	660
Hong Kong	52	66	25	42	14	16	14	16	78	128
Singapore	57	72	15	29	25	17	7	16	74	234
Malaysia	55	69	24	39	13	12	13	22	46	126
Indonesia	52	48	25	39	11	15	17	35	32	81
Taiwan	79	80	10	17	5	7	9	20	83	133
Thailand	61	62	22	31	7	16	16	27	33	54
Korea	63	64	16	21	10	15	16	24	83	100
China	35	42	18	24	32	37	18	27	71	87
Other Asia	38	49	32	41	16	19	18	34	53	98
United States	61	62	18	33	20	27	12	19	273	385
Canada	69	66	30	51	10	18	8	13	54	75
United Kingdom	70	74	35	60	8	10	8	13	327	505
Germany	75	81	18	29	7	12	14	12	96	139
Other Europe	73	71	21	38	10	14	14	19	265	385
Other countries	44	59	35	44	10	17	19	31	138	260
Total (%)	65	69	22	35	12	16	11	18	110[b]	138[b]
Total '000	1528	2875	520	1462	294	661	255	756	2363	4097

Notes:
[a] Other includes: in transit; employment; education; medical reasons; and other
[b] Percentages sum to more than 100 per cent because some visitors had more than one reason for visiting
Source: Bureau of Tourism Research (BTR), (2000) *Tourism trends in New South Wales: New South Wales state profile: year end December 1999*, Canberra, p. 23.

rests with other state government agencies, local government, and the private sector. More often than not this situation means that strategic planning documents, although serving useful political and directional goals for some stakeholders, have little direct influence on tourism planning and development as they tend to deal in generalities rather than specific physical planning decisions. However, their effect on policy decisions can be substantial. The master plan sought to achieve the following outcomes for tourism to New South Wales (TNSW 1997c):

• consistent industry profitability that delivered increased local investment and employment;
• tourism products and a marketing system that attracted high yield markets;
• effective management of mass tourism from Asia and other emerging markets;
• Sydney as a cultural capital of the Asia–Pacific region and one of the world's leading convention cities;
• protection and appreciation of the environment by the tourism industry;
• New South Wales strongly branded as the complete nature–culture holiday experience;
• wider dispersion of tourism benefits through key tourist areas;
• improved standard of service to ensure high levels of visitor satisfaction;

- improved efficiency in government spending for tourism; and
- a tourism industry highly valued by the community and government.

Undoubtedly, one of the most significant aspects of tourism in New South Wales has been the substantial reorientation of the Tourism Commission's marketing strategy. Under the Labor government which held office for most of the 1980s, the state's marketing strategy focused on the development of 'a comprehensive planning framework to co-ordinate the planning and development of tourism in . . . nominated priority areas' (Tourism Commission of NSW 1987a, p. vii; 1987b). In contrast, the approach under the Liberal Party–National Party coalition of the 1990s was marked by an increased emphasis on 'efficiency' and the redefinition of the role of regional tourism structures (Jenkins 1993). The approach of the government at the beginning of the twenty-first century lies somewhere in the middle although, undoubtedly, there is a far greater corporate emphasis than in the 1980s.

A strategy for the 1990s and beyond?

Tourism New South Wales operates in a competitive environment. We compete with other Australian and international destinations. We are energetic and focused in our marketing of New South Wales as we seek to increase the State's market share of the lucrative tourism industry. Our aim is to bring increased economic benefits to New South Wales through tourism (Tourism New South Wales 2001, p. 1).

In November 1992 the state government appointed the Office of Public Management (OPM) to review the NSW Tourism Commission with respect to its strategic priorities, objectives, current activities, resource utilisation, and the efficiency and effectiveness of its marketing functions. As a result of the OPM review, the commission established a new set of strategic priorities—(i) tourism planning and liaison; (ii) tourism marketing; and (iii) tourism information and sales—which led, together with 'the call for a commercial product and price-driven focus, and a philosophy of adding value to NSW holidays', to the commission becoming 'a more focussed marketing organisation' (NSW Tourism Commission 1993, p. 14).

As part of the new focus, the commission placed greater emphasis on cooperative marketing at both the domestic and international levels, including the 'Partnership Australia' scheme with the ATC to maximise advertising efforts in overseas markets (NSW Tourism Commission 1993; TNSW 1997b). Like all states and territories, New South Wales was adopting an increasingly aggressive stance in its marketing and advertising strategies. Increased funds were allocated to supporting or bidding for international events, with substantial funds also being allocated to promoting the benefits of tourism to the New South Wales people (TNSW 1997d), and Sydney was given a new branding image as 'the free-spirited harbourside city' as part of a Sydney Tourism Strategy launched in September 1997 (TNSW 1997e, p. 1). Although this was later to be subsumed under the marketing opportunities provided by the 2000 Summer Olympics. In mid-2001 New South Wales utilised a new brand—'feel free'. According to TNSW (2002), 'Feel free is brand New South Wales. Feel free embodies the State's values'. These values are presented as:
- diversity; lots of experiences and tourism product;
- freedom; to be yourself and to have your type of holiday; and
- liberation; welcoming, tolerant and non-judgemental people.

'Feel free' has evolved from New South Wales' past two branding campaigns—'Seven Wonders' and 'Experience it'. 'Feel free' is regarded as building on the accumulated effect of destination driven marketing in the 'Seven Wonders' campaign and experiential marketing in the 'Experience it' campaign. According to TNSW, 'Feel free':

- allows consumers to differentiate New South Wales from competitors;
- has the power to give meaning to 'affiliation'—you feel free in New South Wales because the people are welcoming and tolerant;
- has synergy with, and supports, brand Australia.

TNSW's approach is indicative of the trend away from a central tourism planning function for state government tourism agencies towards a marketing and promotional function. However, given the ongoing changes in tourism organisation, fundamental questions emerge with respect to New South Wales' ability, as with all states and territories, to balance the supply and demand sides of the tourism market system. As New South Wales enjoys a supposed Olympics and tourism-led economic recovery, important issues surrounding the supply of tourism product and infrastructure are likely to be ignored by the state government and left to market solutions.

NORTHERN TERRITORY—'YOU'LL NEVER NEVER KNOW IF YOU NEVER NEVER GO'

> There appears to have been a great deal of confusion over the years in terms of the correct positioning of our product in the market place. Market positioning should be based entirely on the strengths and assets of the Northern Territory and its Tourism Industry (Northern Territory Tourist Commission (NTTC) 1993a, p. 14).

The tourism industry is the Northern Territory's largest employer and second-largest revenue earner, after the mining industry. Tourism is estimated to account for 14.5% of all employment in the Northern Territory (directly and indirectly), compared with 10.0% for Australia overall. In 2000/01, tourism was estimated to have contributed $936 million directly to the Northern Territory economy. The total worth of the tourism industry (including indirect effects) was estimated at $1.842 billion for the year (NTTC 2002a). In 1999/2000, 65% of all visitors came to the Northern Territory for holiday or pleasure travel with 78 000 more international visitors coming to the territory for holiday or pleasure than in the previous year (NTTC 2000). In the same time period 'business visitors had the highest average daily expenditure ($144 per day), followed by holiday, pleasure visitors at $129 per day' (Territory Tourism 2000, p. 16). The 2000/01 financial year was even more successful with visitor numbers exceeding 1.5 million for the first time. Visitor numbers, nights, and expenditure increased upon the previous year's results by 10%, 12%, and 11%, respectively (NTTC 2001b). (Tables 6.7 to 6.10 provide a profile of visitors to the Territory.)

TABLE 6.7 Northern Territory total visitor numbers, nights, and expenditure 1998–2001

	1998/99	1999/2000	2000/01	% change
Visitor numbers	1 288 000	1 447 000	1 569 000	10
Visitor nights	6 461 000	7 292 000	8 174 000	12
Visitor expenditure ($m)	753.0	848.2	936.0	11

Source: Northern Territory Tourism Commission (NTTC), (2001) *Territory tourism selected statistics 2000–01*, p. 5.

TABLE 6.8 Northern Territory visitor numbers, nights, and expenditure by usual place of residence 2000–01

	Visitors	% change	Nights	% change	Expenditure ($M)	% change
Intra-territory	116 000	22	325 000	21	48.2	5
Interstate	473 000	–5	2 481 000	–10	373.4	–5
Domestic	553 000	0	2 806 000	–7	421.7	–4
International	484 000	1	1 703 000	1	330.8	20
Total CAS	**1 037 000**	**0**	**4 508 000**	**–4**	**752.5**	**5**

Note: The New Tax System was introduced on 1 July 2000. As expenditure is quoted in current prices, price movements related to the tax changes (GST introduced, bed tax abolished) have not been taken into account.
Source: Northern Territory Tourism Commission (NTTC), (2001) *Territory tourism selected statistics 2000–01*, p. 5.

TABLE 6.9 Northern Territory visitor numbers by usual place of residence 2000–01

	NT Visitors	NT % change	Top End	Katherine	Regions Tennant Creek	Centre
Intra-territory	**399 000**	**24**	**217 000**	**75 000**	**24 000**	**113 000**
NSW/ACT	217 000	19	93 000	46 000	29 000	93 000
Vic./Tas.	131 000	–12	77 000	26 000	18 000	60 000
Qld	102 000	11	59 000	29 000	18 000	25 000
SA	112 000	16	46 000	15 000	15 000	57 000
WA	71 000	4	47 000	11 000	5 000	21 000
Interstate	**633 000**	**8**	**323 000**	**128 000**	**81 000**	**255 000**
North America	71 000	–6	10 000	**	**	64 000
UK/Ireland/ Scandinavia	165 000	16	62 000	18 000	9 000	110 000
Other Asia	30 000	**	26 000	**	**	**
Other Europe	106 000	–12	30 000	15 000	8 000	76 000
Japan	54 000	4	4 000	**	**	50 000
New Zealand	21 000	**	9 000	**	**	11 000
Germany	53 000	–19	10 000	**	**	40 000
Other	37 000	13	15 000	**	**	19 000
International	**537 000**	**4**	**166 000**	**49 000**	**31 000**	**375 000**
Total	**1 569 000**	**10**	**706 000**	**253 000**	**141 000**	**743 000**

Notes:
(i) ** indicates that sample size are too small for estimation.
(ii) Care must be taken when interpreting data from individual countries or states as in some cases results are derived from small sample sizes.
(iii) As visitors may travel to more than one region during their Territory trip, regional visitation figures will not add to the Territory total.
Source: Northern Territory Tourism Commission (NTTC), (2001) *Territory tourism selected statistics 2000–01*, p. 8.

The importance of tourism for the Northern Territory economy has been consistent for most of the past fifteen years (NTTC 1993a, 1996a, 1997a, 1997b). As the Senate Standing Committee on Environment, Recreation and the Arts (1988, p. 25) reported following its inquiry into the potential of the Kakadu National Park region: 'because the Northern Territory has fewer strings to its economic bow than Australia as a whole, tourism is of more paramount importance to the Territory'.

TABLE 6.10 Northern Territory visitor expenditure by category 2000–01

Accommodation	23%
Aboriginal art	3%
Food, drink	22%
Pleasure shopping	10%
Other	10%
Tours	14%
Transport	19%

Source: Northern Territory Tourism Commission (NTTC), (2001) *Territory tourism selected statistics 2000–01*, p. 11.

The Northern Territory Tourist Commission (NTTC) was established by a 1979 Act of the Northern Territory Assembly and commenced operations on 1 January 1980. The NTTC replaced the Northern Territory Tourist Board which had commenced operations in 1962. The 1979 Act has been amended several times since. As a result of a 1992 review, the commission was restructured to provide greater emphasis on marketing the Northern Territory and acting as a facilitator for tourism development (NTTC 1993b). The charter of the NTTC 'is to market and influence the development of the Northern Territory as a competitive tourism destination for the continuing benefit of all Territorians' (NTTC 2002a).

The five-year corporate plan developed in 1993 was noteworthy for its explicit mention of environmental and social factors in the supply of tourism experiences and for the manner in which the plan incorporated stakeholders within the planning document. For example, the final two points under the heading 'Our vision and commitment to our customers' in the 1997–98 corporate plan stated (NTTC 1997b, p. 5):

- We will commit to planning processes that are responsible and undertake strategies that result in the sustainability of the Territory's tourism assets; and
- We will identify opportunities and encourage the involvement, where appropriate, of Aboriginal Territorians to share in the economic benefits from tourism.

In addition, to ascertain the efficiency of the NTTC, the commission has established a series of performance indicators which not only evaluate performance by increases in the three major benchmarks of the industry—visitor numbers, visitor nights, and visitor expenditure—but also on the ratio of visitor expenditure to the expenditure of the commission. This is expressed as both a return to the Northern Territory economy of income, compared with the commission's expenditure, and as a percentage ratio of the commission's expenditure to visitor expenditure. According to the commission (NTTC 1993b, p. 24): 'Our success will be in our ability to influence greater visitor numbers and therefore visitor expenditure, while controlling our own expenditure'. Although the performance indicators adopted by the NTTC were somewhat more sophisticated than some of the other states and territories, they still did not attempt to evaluate the net contribution of tourism to the Northern Territory. In one sense this was somewhat surprising, given that the mission statement did have a broader set of directions for tourism in the Northern Territory than elsewhere in Australia—the performance indicators should reflect the organisational mission. The influence of goals underlying the 1993 corporate plan has been substantial. The 2000/01 NTTC annual report stated that corporate and marketing focus was shaped by five issues considered critical to the future success of tourism in the Northern Territory. These issues and corresponding goals are outlined in Table 6.11.

TABLE 6.11 NTTC critical issues and goals

Critical issue	Goals
Market focus	Increase consumer demand to visit the NT. Maximise product accessibility to facilitate easy information gathering and purchase by consumers in all target markets.
Industry leadership	In partnership with industry develop quality Territory tourism product relevant to market demand. Effective communication with industry, the community, and government about the benefits of tourism to the Northern Territory.
Destination resource capability	Increase the number of options available for consumers to travel to the Northern Territory as a tourism destination. The development of infrastructure in key regions of the Northern Territory.
Territory discoveries	Through commercial arrangements, support and distribute a diverse and unique range of packaged NT tourism product consistent with the NTTC's marketing strategy.
Organisational capability	To ensure the NT Tourist Commission has the capacity to achieve its objectives.

Source: Northern Territory Tourism Commission (NTTC), (2001) *Annual report 2000–01*, Darwin, p. 4.

The main objective of the Northern Territory's market positioning strategies has been 'to portray the Northern Territory as a unique and distinctive destination aligned to individual market expectations' (NTTC 1993a, p. 14). The Territory was the first state or territory to agree to the joint international marketing strategy with the ATC called 'Partnership Australia' (NTTC 1993b). Therefore, in terms of concentrating on the unique tourist experiences which will differentiate the Northern Territory in the marketplace and give the Territory a competitive edge compared with other Australian destinations, the NTTC has concentrated on the provision of 'unique cultural experiences' (particularly Aboriginal-based tourism), nature-based tourism (including adventure and ecotourism), and maximising the 'reality of our year long summer in the Top End' (NTTC 1993a, p. 14). To this end a tourism development master plan was released by the Northern Territory in 1994, with a series of regional tourism plans also being developed which focused on regional identity in tourism terms, marketing, development strategy, and SWOT analyses (NTTC 1996b, 1996c, 1996d; 1997c). In 1997/98, the goals of the NTTC (1997b, p. 8) with respect to market positioning were:

- to promote the Northern Territory as Australia's premier nature-based holiday destination;
- to change consumer perceptions to see the Northern Territory as friendly, comfortable, exciting and accessible;
- to maximise the benefits and opportunities for the Territory's tourism industry from major sporting, cultural and special events; and
- to establish the Northern Territory as the home of the Australian spirit embodied in the character of the people, its cultural diversity, and its pioneering heritage.

More recently a 2000–2005 tourism master plan was developed by the Territory's Department of Industries and Business (DIB) in conjunction with the preparation of regional tourism development master plans for each of the four tourism regions—Top End, Katherine, Tennant Creek, and Central Australia. Major issues which were identified in the master plan included (NTTC 2001):

- promoting effective partnerships with Aboriginal land owners, the parks network and tourism industry, acting as a catalyst in which all stakeholders will derive economic and social benefits;
- negotiating increased capacity into Northern Territory's major airports;
- providing or negotiating year-round access to major tourism attractions territory-wide; and
- creating an environment in which a new wave of tourism infrastructure developments can be achieved.

However, responsibility for tourism infrastructure has since been returned to the NTTC from DIB following a public-sector restructuring after the election of the first Territory Labor government. Therefore: 'The Tourism Development Masterplan, which was prepared by DIB in 2000 to provide a framework for tourism infrastructure development, will be reviewed by the NTTC's Industry Development division to make sure it remains relevant' (NTTC 2002a).

One of the most important dimensions in the development of tourism in the Territory is the issue of accessibility to its main markets. As with several other destination areas located away from the major international gateways and domestic tourism-generating regions in Australia, the Northern Territory was severely impacted by the 1989 air pilots' dispute and the collapse of Ansett Australia. As the NTTC recognised, 'the three big obstacles to people holidaying in the Northern Territory, are accessibility, affordability and seasonality. The solutions to all these problems rest largely on a good relationship with the aviation industry' (1993b, p. 15). To overcome these obstacles the NTTC and the Northern Territory government developed a number of measures, which included the establishment of a Tourism Aviation Committee, to coordinate aviation matters, and developed several innovative tour packages, including budget holiday packages to the Top End and the Red Centre and a Darwin–Singapore package with Ansett Australia and Singapore Airlines. The latter was particularly noteworthy, as the package indicated the strong relationship between the Territory and Asian travel markets. According to the NTTC (1993b, p. 15):

> The package sold about 20 000 room nights. Research showed that 75% of people who took the package would not have gone overseas if we had not offered it, and 60% of them would not have come to the Territory.

The Northern Territory has achieved high visibility in Australian tourism in recent years with tourism icons such as Uluru and Kakadu featuring prominently in both domestic and international tourism marketing. The campaign featuring Daryl Somers promoting the territory as a fun, accessible and enjoyable place—'You'll never never know if you never never go'—doubled domestic interest in visitation (NTTC 1993b). Undoubtedly, the restructuring of the NTTC and the associated innovative marketing strategies which the commission adopted were aimed at ensuring that these targets were met. However, the next challenge which faces tourism in the Northern Territory is to ensure that the resource base on which the unique products of Territory tourism are based are developed in a sustainable manner.

QUEENSLAND

> Tourism creates jobs, wealth and tax revenue and offers Queensland the potential to be expanded and developed in a sustainable manner (Queensland Tourist and Travel Corporation (QTTC) 1993, p. 3).

Queensland is more dependent on tourism for employment and income generation than any other state. Tourism is Queensland's second-largest—and one of its fastest-growing —industries. Tourism employs almost 150 000 people—9% of all persons employed. One job is created in Queensland for every 167 domestic visitors or 65 international visitors. Tourism contributes $6.1 billion to the state's economy, representing 6.2% of gross state product (Tourism Queensland (TQ) 2001b). Queensland has been one of the most aggressive states in tourism development and marketing in recent years, and has overtaken New South Wales as the main holiday state destination for overseas visitors, a trend which is likely to continue given the development of further resorts in northern Queensland and the increasing number of direct international flights to the region. In addition, Queensland is also the major destination for interstate holiday travellers.

Queensland attracted more than 18.1 million overnight visitors in the year ended June 2000. Of these, 16.1 million were overnight domestic visitors and a further 2.0 million were from overseas. In addition, there were 30.9 million day trips taken in Queensland over the same period. Holiday and leisure travel was the main reason for visiting Queensland for 7.4 million (46.2%) of overnight domestic visitors and 1.4 million (72.8%) of Queensland's international visitors (TQ 2001b). Domestic tourism is therefore an important and longstanding component of the Queensland commercial accommodation market (QTTC 1997b). However, international visitors spend almost twice the amount of domestic visitors. (QTTC 1997c). 'Compared with the average Australian traveller, people who have visited Queensland on a holiday of 3 nights or more in the last 12 months are more likely to be Young Families (15%) and Older Households (14%)' (TQ 2000, p. 3) (Tables 6.12–6.17 provide a profile of visitors to the state). The three most significant visitor destinations in terms of numbers of visitor arrivals are the Gold Coast, Brisbane, and the Sunshine Coast, although the northern Queensland communities of Cairns and Townsville are also very important destinations. Holiday and leisure is the main reason for visitors going to Tropical North Queensland, the Gold Coast, the Sunshine Coast, and Brisbane, although Brisbane is more evenly distributed among holiday/leisure, visiting friends and relatives (VFR), and business (TQ 2001b).

The primary government tourism agency is Tourism Queensland (TQ), formerly the Queensland Tourist and Travel Corporation (QTTC), which operates as a statutory authority within the Queensland Department of Tourism, Racing and Fair Trading (TQ2001b). The QTTC was established in 1979 as a statutory authority through an Act of State Parliament. As in other states, the corporation developed from an existing government department of tourism, assuming the functions of the former Queensland Government Tourist Bureau and taking on additional responsibilities for tourism development and marketing. The purpose of the corporation, as detailed in the *Queensland Tourist and Travel Corporation Act 1979*, was to develop and market the tourism industry and to maximise its economic benefit to Queensland (QTTC 1988a). From the early 1990s on, the corporation's mission statement also noted that social and environmental benefits should be maximised, as well as

TABLE 6.12 Top six activities participated in by domestic visitors to Queensland

Activity	%
Visit friends & relatives	38
Eat out at restaurants	36
Going to the beach (incl. swimming, diving)	34
Go shopping	27
Walking around/sightseeing	24
Pubs/clubs/discos	20

Source: Tourism Queensland (2000) *Fact sheet—Queensland,* Brisbane, p. 2.

TABLE 6.13 Queensland visitor profile 1999

	Visitors (000s)	Visitor nights (000s)	Average length of stay (nights)
Total	16 362	78 083	4.8
Intrastate (Qld)	11 527	39 552	3.4
Total interstate	4 835	38 531	8.0
NSW	2961	18 273	6.2
Vic.	1176	12 435	10.6
Other interstate	698	7823	11.2

Source: Tourism Queensland (2000) *Fact sheet—Queensland,* Brisbane, p. 2.

TABLE 6.14 Top five international markets to Queensland 1999

Country of residence	Visitor arrivals	% of total international visitors	% growth (1999 on 1998)
Japan	499 158	25.6%	−3.8%
New Zealand	260 339	13.3%	3.4%
United Kingdom	237 882	12.2%	20.2%
USA	174 181	8.9%	16.3%
Taiwan	95 125	4.9%	−0.2%
Total international visitors	1 950 166	–	7.4%

Source: Tourism Queensland (2000) *Fact sheet—Queensland,* Brisbane, p. 4.

TABLE 6.15 Top six activities participated in by international visitors to Queensland

Activity	%
Go shopping (for pleasure)	86
Go to the beach	73
Visit national parks	58
Visit wildlife park/zoos	52
Visit botanical gardens or other public gardens	48
Go on guided tour/excursion	46

Note: Percentages add to more than 100 because respondents participated in more than one activity
Source: Tourism Queensland (2000) *Fact sheet—Queensland,* Brisbane, p. 4.

TABLE 6.16 International visitor numbers to Queensland by region of origin 1995–99

Origin	1995	1996	1997	1998	1999	Annual growth rate (%)
New Zealand	179 144	234 836	244 607	251 776	260 339	10
Japan	565 114	585 724	584 619	519 005	499 158	–3
Hong Kong	50 781	62 914	59 692	54 984	49 102	–1
Singapore	72 723	69 068	66 121	64 681	65 718	–3
Malaysia	25 821	32 987	33 749	20 553	29 868	4
Indonesia	24 981	29 784	29 407	9176	11 093	–18
Taiwan	103 926	98 588	95 710	95 296	95 125	–2
Thailand	16 523	14 991	15 470	7953	9439	–13
Korea	108 542	150 235	163 220	24 593	49 217	–18
China	n/a	22 558	24 420	26 269	31 839	12
Other Asia	26 610	13 420	26 165	29 368	32 952	5
USA	132 294	128 303	130 203	149 795	174 181	7
Canada	26 313	25 810	27 569	27 676	35 366	8
United Kingdom	131 561	150 444	172 528	197 912	237 882	16
Germany	70 069	64 038	72 173	70 603	72 517	1
Other Europe	127 231	142 459	154 087	162 082	185 032	10
Other countries	68 734	75 360	83 867	103 726	111 340	13
Total visitors	1 730 368	1 901 521	1 983 606	1 815 448	1 950 166	3

Note: In 1995 China was included in Other Asia

Source: Tourism Queensland (2000) *Fact sheet—Queensland*, Brisbane, p. 5.

TABLE 6.17 International visitor nights to Queensland by region of origin 1995–99

Origin	1995 (000s)	1996 (000s)	1997 (000s)	1998 (000s)	1999 (000s)	Annual average growth rate (%)
New Zealand	2777	3056	3343	3025	3576	7
Japan	2492	3208	3305	3193	2916	4
Hong Kong	509	507	445	497	392	–6
Singapore	443	491	428	576	555	6
Malaysia	270	208	230	248	252	–2
Indonesia	247	314	405	408	91	–22
Taiwan	447	516	640	646	852	17
Thailand	114	110	257	116	141	5
Korea	396	1105	1227	398	402	0
China	n/a	599	337	161	389	–13
Other Asia	269	154	506	503	1102	42
USA	1409	1306	1501	1554	2469	15
Canada	841	388	603	820	748	–3
United Kingdom	2932	3198	3040	3799	4593	12
Germany	984	866	1078	1063	962	–1
Other Europe	2667	2849	2642	3167	3771	9
Other Countries	1306	965	1089	1570	1718	7
Total nights (000s)	18 103	9 840	21 075	21 747	24 928	8

Note: In 1995 China was included in Other Asia

Source: Tourism Queensland (2000) *Fact sheet—Queensland*, Brisbane, p. 5.

the economic benefits (QTTC 1993). In October 1997 two new administrative structures—the Planning and Development Division and the Regional Planning Department—were established within the QTTC as a result of a merger with the Office of Tourism within the Department of Tourism, Small Business and Industry (1997a).

'TQ's primary role is to market and develop Queensland's tourism destinations and to maximise social, environmental and economic benefits to the state' (Tourism Queensland 2000, p. 1). Under its mission statement TQ 'is committed to enhancing the development and marketing of Queensland's tourism destinations in partnership with industry, government and the community' (Tourism Queensland 2000, p. ii). In 1997 the Queensland government developed a framework for the future of tourism in Queensland which aimed 'to create a commercially attractive operating element for the tourism industry' (QTTC 1997f, p. 3). The four strategic objectives of the framework were (QTTC 1997e, p. 5):

• to provide strong industry leadership coordination and management;
• to undertake targeted marketing to improve the yield and economic return from domestic and international visitor markets;
• to foster investment in infrastructure, services, and employment growth; and
• to seek environmental and social sustainability.

The commercial goals of the QTTC are evident in the importance attached to the self-generation of funds as a proportion of the total funding budget of the corporation. The major source of these funds has come from the selling of Queensland tourism product through Queensland Government Travel Centres and the Australian Travel and Leisure Automated Systems (ATLAS) although, since 1990, the corporation has also entered into cooperative marketing programs that have generated private-sector contributions (QTTC 1988b; 1993; 1997e; 1997f; 2000a; 2001b). In addition to its domestic activities, the QTTC also maintains a number of overseas offices, and Queensland has historically been the most aggressive of the Australian states in the overseas market. This is probably because of the parochial perception of Queensland as a state apart from the rest of Australia and, related to this, the strong development-oriented policies of the National Party governments from the 1950s to the 1980s (Fitzgerald 1984; Jones 1986). However, in recent years, the prospects for joint marketing and promotional campaigns with the Australian Tourist Commission have increased, particularly in light of the rising costs of overseas promotional activities.

Queensland was undoubtedly the focal point of much of Australia's tourism growth during the 1980s and early 1990s. This development arose for several reasons. First, the climate and physical environment of Queensland have proved to be attractive to domestic tourists from the southern states and overseas tourists in search of sun, sand, and surf. Second, the Great Barrier Reef has become a major international drawcard. Third, areas of northern Queensland—particularly Cairns and Townsville—have been extremely entrepreneurial in their tourism marketing and development, including, for example, the establishment of Cairns as an international airport. Fourth, and probably the overriding factor, Queensland governments—particularly the National Party governments of Joh Bjelke-Petersen—have played a major entrepreneurial role in tourist development through the provision of cheap land for developments, financial assistance, assistance with local government planning decisions, and the use of the QTTC as a major marketing arm for Queensland tourist developments.

State government involvement in tourism in Queensland has changed substantially since the days of Bjelke-Petersen, particularly with respect to the need to ensure that developments are environmentally responsible. However, aggressive marketing and promotion of Queensland has been an ongoing, although sometimes controversial, feature. An example was the high profile Queensland 'Yo! Way to Go' campaign, launched in November 1992, 'which established an innovative approach to advertising Queensland tourism' (QTTC 1993, p. 6). The 'Yo!' campaign, which featured a 'tits-and-bums' approach to promoting tourism in Queensland, was highly controversial because of its depiction of women, and it generated public opposition to such an extent that it was discontinued. Nevertheless, as the QTTC's chief executive officer's report stated (QTTC 1993, p. 12): 'The Yo! Way to Go! advertising campaign was certainly noticed, and was undoubtedly a factor in the record-setting sales performances'. In the second half of the 1990s, Queensland placed greater emphasis on regional destination product development and promotion. Although the overall Queensland brand and the positioning line 'Beautiful One Day, Perfect the Next' has been maintained, separate regional marketing strategies are being developed in conjunction with the various regional tourism associations. According to the QTTC (1997a, p. 14): 'Comprehensive market research identified five destinations which have generated a "critical mass" of consumer awareness and desirability, and where regional tourism industries are mature enough to service brand marketing strategies'. These were Tropical North Queensland, the Gold Coast, the Sunshine Coast, the Whitsundays and Brisbane.

Large-scale tourism development in Queensland is concentrated in four main regions: Northern Queensland (Cairns and Townsville), Brisbane, the Sunshine Coast, and the Gold Coast. Northern Queensland was severely affected by the 1989 air pilots' dispute in terms of the domestic market, with the overseas market only marginally affected, and was also affected by the collapse of Ansett Airlines in 2002. However, as noted above, the expansion of the Cairns and Townsville airports, particularly the former, has led to a substantial increase in international direct flights to the region. The Sunshine Coast probably benefited from the pilots' dispute in the short term and was able to develop its attractiveness as a short-stay destination for the Brisbane market and for interstate domestic travellers. However, the region is seeking to increase its level of international visitation by promoting itself as an alternative to the Gold Coast.

The Gold Coast has long been regarded, rightly or wrongly, as Australia's premier tourist destination. However, the Gold Coast perhaps epitomises Queensland's future development problem. The Gold Coast has tended to be attractive to the mass tourism market and, although mass tourism will undoubtedly be with us for a long time yet, there appears to an international trend away from large-scale developments towards smaller, less-contrived tourism destinations (see Chapter 12). The challenge for Queensland, as for the Gold Coast, is how to diversify the range of attractions available to the tourist while ensuring that development is more environmentally sound and community-based than it has been in the past.

SOUTH AUSTRALIA—'DISCOVER THE SECRETS OF SOUTH AUSTRALIA'

By building awareness of South Australia as a quality destination, able to provide an out-of-the-ordinary holiday in a safe, accessible environment, we will be able to achieve our target of $2 billion per annum injection into the South Australian economy through our tourism industry (Rann 1993, p. 5).

There is only one way that South Australians should view tourism—as a world of opportunity. Opportunity because this huge global industry is expected to double over the next ten years. As it does, South Australia must be there to stake its claim (South Australian Tourism Commission (SATC) 1996a, p. 5).

Tourism is as significant to the South Australian economy as the state's automotive or agricultural sectors in terms of jobs supported. In 1999 tourism generated $3.1 billion of expenditure and supported 36 000 full-time equivalent jobs (SATC 2001b, p. 14). During 2000 South Australia attracted more than 6.2 million travellers resulting in 26.3 million visitor nights. Of these nights just over five million were international visitors and just over 11 million were intrastate travellers (SATC 2001b). Table 6.18 provides a table of visitor origin.

A South Australian government tourism authority has existed in various forms since 1908 when a 'Tourist Bureau' was established to advertise the scenic attractions of the state. The initial function of the bureau was limited to the provision of an information service. Since that time, numerous administrative and entrepreneurial functions have been added, but it was not until 1979 that tourism responsibilities were amalgamated into a separate body. In 1987 a review was conducted of the Department of Tourism in conjunction with a major market research study of tourism in South Australia. As a result of the review, the marketing, planning, and development of the department were restructured without an increase in the total number of staff members employed. Of considerable significance was the changing of the name of the department to Tourism South Australia to reflect the new entrepreneurial character of the organisation and the change in marketing direction (Tourism South Australia 1988). In 1993 the structure of tourism in South Australia underwent further modification with the division of Tourism South Australia into two different organisations—the South Australian Tourism Commission (SATC), responsible for marketing and promotion; and the Office of Tourism Industry Development (OTID), which was responsible for all the functions carried out by the former Planning and Development Division of Tourism South Australia (OTID 1993). The OTID has since been abolished, with some of its activities being resumed by the SATC and the Minister for Regional Development, although a tourism policy and planning group still exists within the SATC. 'The group's vision is to ensure that South Australia is acknowledged as a global leader in achieving successful, responsible and sustainable tourism development' (SATC 2002b).

Planning functions have become increasingly important in South Australia in recent years. Strategic planning initiatives relating to research, education, investment,

TABLE 6.18 Summary of visitor origin to South Australia

	Visitors	Nights
International (1999–2000)	6%	21%
Interstate 12 mths ended March 2002	32%	34%
Intrastate 12 mths ended March 2002	62%	45%
Total	100%	100%

Source: South Australian Tourism Commission (SATC) (2002) *South Australian tourism indicators*, Adelaide, p. 1. **www.tourism.sa.gov.au**; pers.comm.

and the development of a South Australian tourism plan were given a high priority in the 1980s (South Australian Government 1988; Tourism South Australia 1990), with promotion and marketing being more significant in the 1990s (SATC 1996a, 1996b). However, perhaps the most significant development in the strategic planning area was the development of a series of state tourism plans (South Australian Tourism Development Board 1987a, 1987b; Tourism South Australia 1991; SATC 1996b) and regional tourism plans (Robe Tourism Working Party 1990; PPK Planning 1993a, 1993b).

The major objective of the South Australian Tourism Plan 1987–89 was to achieve sustainable growth in the economic value of tourism in South Australia. The overall aim of the plan was to ensure a coordinated approach by government and industry to the maximisation of the state's tourism potential (South Australian Tourism Development Board 1987a, 1987b). The emphasis on sustainability had grown further by the time of the development of the 1991–93 tourism plan, to the point where the state's tourism mission to the end of the century had been defined as being to 'achieve sustainable growth in the net value of tourism activity to South Australia' (Tourism South Australia 1991, p. 13). However, it is important to note that Tourism South Australia recognised that 'the mission of the Government and the tourism industry is essentially economic, but via the concept of qualitative growth it embraces social and environmental concerns' (1991, p. 13). Nevertheless, despite such a far-reaching approach to the overall integration of planning and marketing within the context of tourism development, this planning direction was not maintained in the restructuring of state government involvement in tourism in the mid-1990s, and the economic and political agenda of the Liberal government of that time. In contrast, the strategy for 1996–2001 aimed to (SATC 1996b, p. 10):

• establish a strong marketing position and a distinctive brand;
• strengthen South Australia's appeal as a holiday destination;
• make the tourism industry stronger (including regional tourism);
• ensure tourism is sustainable;
• identify initiatives that achieve simultaneous economic and community benefits; and
• forge partnerships between all relevant stakeholders.

By 2001 the mission for the SATC was to develop and promote 'the best that South Australia has to offer', with a vision that the 'SATC is an inspiring organisation, leading the way in the world's most dynamic industry' (SATC 2002a, 2002c). The SATC's (2002a, 2002c) goals were:

• increased numbers of visitors who stay longer and spend more;
• enhanced quality of visitor experiences offered while protecting South Australia's tourism assets;
• generation of more jobs throughout South Australia;
• greater community and industry prosperity and pride in South Australia; and
• a committed corporate team and a positive corporate culture.

Marketing focus

Under the *South Australian Tourism Commission Act 1993*, the commission is a statutory corporation established with the objectives of 'securing economic and social benefits for the people of South Australia through—(a) the promotion of South Australia as a tourist destination; and (b) the further development and improvement of the state's tourism industry'. According to the then South Australian Minister of Tourism, Mike Rann, the decision to replace Tourism South Australia with a tourism commission was 'more than cosmetic. The change to a more private sector styled statutory corporation, with a strong focus on tourism marketing, will have clear benefits for our tourism industry' (Rann 1993, p.1). The private-sector commercial orientation of the SATC is also seen in the Minister's comments regarding the commission's direction (Rann 1993, p. 1):

> The direction, administration and operation of the new Tourism Commission will be clearly and firmly in the hands of those with private sector expertise operating in partnership with the South Australian Government. This will provide the opportunity for a much greater sense of 'ownership' of the Commission's marketing and promotional direction by the tourism industry in our state, with all parties making a contribution and all being accountable. This partnership should promote greater shared commitment to tourism growth, rather than alibis and excuses or wasteful territorialism.

According to the SATC (1996a, p. 9), the key goal of the commission is 'to promote and expand South Australia's tourism industry for the benefit of residents and visitors'. To meet this goal the SATC developed several objectives (1996a, p. 9):
- to achieve a sustained increase in the number of visitors to South Australia and increases in length of stay and expenditure;
- to achieve a coordinated approach to the promotion of South Australia by public and private sector organisations;
- to support the development of appropriate new tourism product and infrastructure that positions South Australia as an appealing and different destination;
- to improve investor confidence in South Australia;
- to support the conservation and enhancement of the state's environmental and cultural heritage;
- to achieve a reputation for excellence and professionalism in serving visitors to South Australia through the commission's travel centres;
- to foster this reputation for excellence across the industry as a whole;
- to achieve an improved awareness of tourism and tourism related issues; and
- to achieve a better distribution of tourism business among the regions of South Australia.

The transfer of the planning and development functions to the Office of Tourism Industry Development and the restructuring of Tourism South Australia has also led to a redirecting of the budget with greater emphasis on marketing and promotion in the domestic and international markets, particularly with respect to special-interest travel markets such as cultural and ecotourism (Rann 1993) and wine tourism (SATC 2001a).

According to the *South Australian Tourism Plan for 1996–2001*, 'The priorities for South Australia are to create a distinct market position and brand, attract new investment and promote key destinations' (SATC 1996a, p. 13). To do this the SATC is seeking to overcome the two main disadvantages for South Australia as a tourist destination. 'It is not seen as a "tourist" place in the conventional sense and its image is intangible and hard to define' (SATC 1996a, p. 15). In response to this situation the SATC argues: 'The State must build on its strengths and turn its perceived weaknesses into strengths by clearly differentiating itself from other destinations in response to emerging market trends. It cannot hope to succeed by attempting to copy other States' (1996a, p. 15). To achieve this, the SATC is pursuing a positioning strategy of being 'surprisingly different' with a branding strategy that is based on the human 'senses', as expressed in the 1997–98 domestic marketing slogan 'Come to your senses, Come to South Australia'.

The tourism plan was being reviewed in 2001–02 for the period to 2006 (SATC 2001c, p. 1):

> The plan has been developed by the tourism industry and the State Government, as a guide for industry associations, government agencies and all other stakeholders [and] will outline a firm direction for the industry and help guide and develop sustainable tourism throughout South Australia. An inherent component of the new plan is to do things in an authentic 'South Australian' way.

According to the SATC (2001b, p. 2), the key objectives of the draft plan include:
- setting realistic goals;
- targeting productive segments;
- dispersing the benefits to regions;
- strengthening the industry;
- improving operator profitability;
- developing industry 'shock absorber' capacity to cope with unexpected challenges;
- improving tourism infrastructure;
- aligning government policies; and
- aligning and strengthening the industry marketing mix.

As a result of the review process a range of key themes emerged as being appropriate for development. These included (SATC 2001b, p. 1):
- lifestyle: wine, food, relaxation, and accessibility;
- drive market;
- mature-aged travellers;
- escapism;
- nature-based experiences: the Outback, Flinders Ranges, Coorong, and coastal (Eyre Peninsula, Kangaroo Island, Yorke Peninsula); and
- niche markets: Aboriginal, walking, wine tourism, cycling, birdwatching, and backpackers.

The SATC's planning and marketing strategy therefore continues the focus of the product strategy of Tourism South Australia. The strategy aimed to make South Australia a distinctive 'specialty' destination for 'discerning travellers to enjoy accessible and surprising nature, heritage, food, wine and festive experiences—with the emphasis on friendly, personalised hospitality, authenticity, quality and value for money' (Tourism South Australia 1989a, p. 9). Within this strategy (Tourism South Australia 1989a, p. 8) the priority target segment was described as travellers who:
- are discerning and confident;
- are experiential but fairly passive;
- have a preference for creature comforts;
- are food and wine oriented;
- have a strong sense of authenticity and heritage;
- are interested in ideas and creativity;
- are environmentally conscious; and
- have indulgent spending habits but are nevertheless practical.

The Tourism South Australia 1989 product-development strategy sought to place greater emphasis on increasing tourism value than on increasing tourism volume—

a key tenet of a sustainable approach to tourism development. However, given the changed emphasis of the SATC and the current directions for tourism, discussed above, it is likely that greater emphasis will be given to increasing tourist numbers in South Australia while the present tourism structure remains in place.

TASMANIA—'DISCOVER AUSTRALIA'S NATURAL STATE'

> Tourism has never been more important to the economic welfare of Tasmania and its people. It will become the foundation on which future generations of young people build their careers and prosperity. More than ever, we understand the scale of the challenge ahead of us, and the imperative to succeed. That is why Tourism Tasmania has been transformed into a commercially-focussed, service oriented organisation committed to delivering results. Tourism is the world's fastest growing industry, and Tasmania offers world class tourism product. But our industry is also one of the most competitive—nationally and globally. Increasing competition means Tasmania must be smarter, quicker, keener and more aggressive in Australian and international tourism marketplaces. Tourism Tasmania has been created to ensure we promote, market and sell tourism more effectively (Tourism Tasmania 1997a, p. 6).

Although Tasmania attracts only a small proportion of the nation's domestic and international tourist market, tourism is a significant part of the state economy and 'further expansion of the tourism industry' is seen by the state government 'as a means of creating more jobs' (Department of Tourism, Sport and Recreation 1992, p. 4). Total travel expenditure in Tasmania during 1998 amounted to $900 million. This generated employment for an estimated 18 300 people, 10.3% of total employment in the state (Tourism Tasmania (TT) 2002c). In 1996–97, visitors to Tasmania spent $595 million during their stay, with the tourism industry contributing $735 million to gross state product in 1995 (TT 1997a). Tourism Tasmania regards tourism as having the potential to be the state's top income earner and employer, and has established objectives such that, by 2007, tourism will provide more than $1 billion in visitor expenditure, 870 000 total visitors (620 000 domestic and 250 000 international) and 9600 new jobs (compared with 1995) (1997a). Tables 6.19 to 6.24 provide a profile of visitors to Tasmania.

Domestic travellers are the mainstay of the Tasmanian tourism industry, accounting for approximately 85% of all adult visitation. Victoria is the largest market, accounting for 46% of adult interstate visitors in 1996–97. However, because a large proportion of the Victorian visitors are on short-stay business travel, they account for only 35% of interstate visitor nights. Tasmania is visited by approximately 2% of international travellers to Australia. However, in state terms, their impact is significant, accounting for 15% of all visitation to Tasmania and spending an average of $96 per night and $1256 per trip, thereby contributing $86.9 million in income to the state economy. This compares with an average of $134 per night and $1223 per trip for domestic visitors who contribute $508.4 million in total (Tourism Tasmania 1997b).

Tasmania was the last Australian state or territory to create a separate tourism commission. Until early 1997, tourism was part of the Department of Tourism, Sport and Recreation. However, tourism had been given a corporate identity under the title of Tourism Tasmania, which focused on sales, marketing, and promotion. The objectives from the department's mission statement (1992, p. 8) relevant to tourism were:

TABLE 6.19 Visitors to Tasmania 1999/2000

	1999/2000	%
British Isles	24 300	4.6
North America	22 000	4.1
Continental Europe	17 700	3.3
New Zealand	10 400	1.9
Japan	3300	0.6
Other Asia	8200	1.5
Other overseas	3400	0.6
Total overseas	**89 300**	**16.8**
Victoria	197 300	37.1
New South Wales	117 800	22.2
Queensland	53 500	10.1
South Australia	29 300	5.5
Western Australia	27 000	5.1
ACT	14 200	2.7
Northern Territory	3200	0.6
Total Australia	**442 300**	**83.2**
Total visitors	**531 700**	**100.00**

Source: Tourism Tasmania (2000) *Tasmanian visitor survey 1999/2000*, Hobart, p. 10. **www.tourismtasmania.com.au**

TABLE 6.20 Visitors to Tasmania by purpose of visit 1999/2000

	1999/2000	%
Leisure/holiday	290 500	54.6
Visit friends/relatives	113 300	21.3
Business/employment	85 100	16.0
Conference, etc.	25 800	4.9
Other reason	16 900	3.2
Total visitors	**531 700**	**100.0**

Source: Tourism Tasmania (2000) *Tasmanian visitor survey 1999/2000*, Hobart, p. 10. **www.tourismtasmania.com.au**

- to promote sustainable growth in the tourism industry;
- to encourage the development of appropriate tourism infrastructure and activities; and
- to encourage an improvement in the quality of tourism services.

On 1 February 1997, Tourism Tasmania was established as a statutory authority under the *Tourism Tasmania Act 1996*. Under its 'Statement of Corporate Intent 1997–1999', Tourism Tasmania's mission was 'to promote Tasmania as a premier tourism destination through strategic marketing and sustainable development in partnership with industry, in order to maximise economic and social benefits for all Tasmanians' (TT 1997a, p. 41). The strategic directions for Tourism Tasmania were expressed in its core corporate objectives as follows (TT 1997a, p. 41):

TABLE 6.21 Tasmanian visitor nights 1999/2000

	1999/2000 nights	%	average stay (nights)
British Isles	298 700	6.1	12.3
Continental Europe	261 900	5.4	14.8
North America	193 500	4.0	8.8
New Zealand	118 800	2.4	11.5
Japan	25 600	0.5	7.7
Other Asia	77 600	1.6	9.5
Other overseas	49 200	1.0	14.5
Total overseas	**1 025 200**	**21.0**	**11.5**
Victoria	1 376 100	28.3	7.0
New South Wales	1 075 400	22.1	9.1
Queensland	602 800	12.4	11.3
South Australia	297 900	6.1	10.2
Western Australia	319 900	6.6	11.9
ACT	132 500	2.7	9.3
Northern Territory	41 300	0.8	12.9
Total Australia	**3 845 900**	**79.0**	**8.7**
Total nights	**4 871 100**	**100.0**	**9.2**

Source: Tourism Tasmania (2000) *Tasmanian visitor survey 1999/2000*, Hobart, p. 12. **www.tourismtasmania.com.au**

TABLE 6.22 Visitor expenditure in Tasmania 1999/2000

	1999/2000 $ million	%	$ per visitor	$ per night
British Isles	25.3	4.5	1040	85
North America	21.9	3.9	1000	113
Continental Europe	19.9	3.6	1130	76
New Zealand	12.0	2.1	1160	101
Japan	2.7	0.5	820	106
Other Asia	10.6	1.9	1290	136
Other overseas	3.6	0.6	1060	73
Total overseas	**96.1**	**17.2**	**1080**	**94**
Victoria	169.2	30.3	860	123
New South Wales	133.7	24.0	1130	124
Queensland	69.3	12.4	1300	115
South Australia	34.3	6.2	1170	115
Western Australia	37.9	6.8	1410	118
ACT	12.9	2.3	910	98
Northern Territory	4.6	0.8	1440	111
Total Australia	**461.8**	**82.8**	**1040**	**120**
Total expenditure	**557.9**	**100.0**	**1050**	**115**

Source: Tourism Tasmania (2000) *Tasmanian visitor survey 1999/2000*, Hobart, p. 13. **www.tourismtasmania.com.au**

TABLE 6.23 Length of stay of visitors in Tasmania 1999/2000

	Visitors	%
1 to 3 nights	127 000	23.9
4 to 7 nights	192 500	36.2
8 to 14 nights	149 100	28.0
15 to 30 nights	48 700	9.2
31 nights or more	14 300	2.7
Total	531 700	100.0

Source: Tourism Tasmania (2000) *Tasmanian visitor survey 1999/2000*, Hobart, p. 18. **www.tourismtasmania.com.au**

TABLE 6.24 Ten most popular activities undertaken by visitors to Tasmania in 1999/2000

Visiting national parks	54.7%
Browsing at markets	49.1%
Visiting historic houses	38.3%
Wildlife viewing	34.3%
Visiting antique shops	33.6%
Visiting gardens	29.7%
Bushwalking (under 2 hours)	28.4%
Visiting casinos	24.0%
Bushwalking (2 hours to full day)	18.3%
Visiting wineries	15.7%

Source: Tourism Tasmania (2000) *Tasmanian visitor survey 1999/2000*, Hobart, p. 20. **www.tourismtasmania.com.au**

• marketing—to influence target markets to travel to Tasmania;
• development—to facilitate development of export ready product and infrastructure to meet identified market opportunities;
• distribution—to ensure effective distribution of Tasmanian tourism products;
• coordination—to maximise existing and new partnerships with stakeholders to ensure Tasmania is marketed and developed as a premier visitor destination utilising the available resources to the maximum benefit;
• management—to ensure that Tourism Tasmania manages its business by balancing resources with priorities.

In September 1998, Tourism Tasmania was administratively incorporated into the Department of State Development. However it continued to operate under the *Tourism Tasmania Act 1996*, governed by a seven-member board appointed by the state government. 'Tourism Tasmania's brief is to promote Tasmania nationally and internationally as a world-class visitor destination, in the process providing jobs and revenue to the people and State of Tasmania' (TT 2002a). Under its 2001 corporate plan, the vision of Tourism Tasmania is: 'To ensure tourism achieves it full potential as a strategic growth industry and becomes a cornerstone of the Tasmanian economy generating income, employment and investment for the benefit of all Tasmanians' (TT 2002b).

As with other states, Tasmania has also been formally establishing a state brand. According to Tourism Tasmania (1997a, p. 24), 'Brand Tasmania':

. . . represents a combination of our accessible and diverse natural environment, together with our unique animals and plants, supported by authentic colonial history and quality, fresh foods and wine. It has been designed to complement the positioning of Australia by the Australian Tourist Commission.

The marketing and product development strategy for Tasmania is focused primarily on special-interest tourism opportunities such as nature-based and heritage tourism, special events, conferences, and conventions. The specialty travel dimensions of visitation to Tasmania are reflected in the most popular activities of travellers, which are visits to historic sites (54% of all visitors), visits to craft shops (50%), and browsing at markets (43%) (TT 1997b).

Tasmania's island status and geographical location in terms of domestic and overseas markets creates special marketing and promotion problems. As Mosley (1963, précis) reported:

> One of the most interesting features of the Tasmanian recreational scene since the middle of the last century has been a traffic of tourist visitors from the mainland. Increases in the number of arrivals over a period of a hundred years coincided generally with improvements in the communications between Tasmania and the mainland, and the main facet inhibiting present growth is seen to be limited capacity for the transport of visitor's cars.

Perhaps more than any other state or region, the success of tourism in Tasmania is dependent on the availability of secure transport networks. The future of tourism in Tasmania is therefore dictated in great part by transport capacity. Currently, fly–drive and ship–drive holiday packages are given high priority by Tourism Tasmania. However, as evidenced by the 1989 air pilots' dispute and the collapse of Ansett Australia in 2002, loss of transport connections have a far greater impact on Tasmania than other Australian destinations, and substantially affect consumers' perceptions of Tasmania as a reliable destination to visit. Therefore, to improve its domestic and overseas marketing, Tasmania has placed substantial emphasis on mainland-based travel centres and domestic advertising campaigns, and on joint overseas promotion with the Australian Tourist Commission and the Victorian Tourism Commission (Australia's Southern Tourism Promotion).

VICTORIA—'YOU'LL LOVE EVERY PIECE OF VICTORIA'

Victoria provides a good example of the changing nature of government's role in tourism development and marketing in Australia. Government involvement in tourism in Victoria has undergone considerable change in the past 25 years in terms of administrative structure, organisational goals and direction, and the relationship of government tourism structures to political ideology. For example, following the election of a Liberal Party–National Party coalition government in 1992, the Victorian Tourism Commission (VTC) was recreated as Tourism Victoria under the *Victorian Tourism Commission (Tourism Victoria) Act 1992*. The effects of the amendments to the original 1982 Act, which established the commission, were to change both its name and its board structure. In addition, a restructuring of state government administration resulted in Tourism Victoria being incorporated into a new Department of Arts, Sport and Tourism (Tourism Victoria 1993).

This section of the present book highlights the development of a coherent state tourism strategy in the 1980s under the Victorian Tourism Commission (VTC) and the repositioning of government involvement in the 1990s away from planning and development and towards marketing and promotion.

The Victorian Tourism Commission and the development of a state tourism strategy

The VTC in the 1980s offers a good example of the role of government authorities in the development of an integrated tourism strategy which combines marketing and planning goals. Established under the *Victorian Tourism Commission Act 1982*, the main function of the commission was the marketing of Victoria as a domestic and international holiday destination. The creation of the VTC was a reflection of a greater commercial orientation for government tourism agencies in the 1980s and the then new state Labor government's priorities in terms of employment generation and regional development. The commission saw its mission as providing strong leadership to the Victorian tourism industry and stimulating tourism development, with its major responsibility being the promotion of tourism for the long-term economic benefit of Victoria (Cathie 1984; VTC 1988). As part of the Labor government's development goals, the commission established Victour Properties Pty Ltd in 1983 as its entrepreneurial arm, with responsibilities for the development, management, and operation of several Victorian tourist facilities. Undoubtedly the company assisted in the development of tourist attractions and facilities at a time when private-sector involvement was harder to obtain in tourism projects than it is at present. However, because of the large amount of state debt at the end of the 1980s, the company was wound up.

Probably the most outstanding feature of the development of Victorian tourism in the 1980s was the development of a state tourism strategy which integrated marketing and planning objectives (Cathie 1984; Government of Victoria 1987). The main objectives of the tourism strategy were:
• to identify Victoria's competitive advantages in tourism journeys and destinations;
• to promote more intensive use of the state's tourist assets;
• to enhance the attractiveness of the state to Victorians, interstate visitors and overseas visitors;
• to improve the management and marketing of tourist attractions; and
• to identify opportunities for complementary tourism development.

What distinguished the Victorian approach from other state and regional strategies was the 'resort zone concept', with its emphasis on a 'cluster and connect approach' which sought to distinguish 'geographically concentrated tourism assets' (that is, tourist regions or zones) (Cathie 1984, p. 3; VTC 1984), and its relationship with other elements of the Victorian government's economic strategy for Victoria. The zonal concept involved the identification of areas in which the Victorian government encouraged tourism development and the tourism corridors which linked the various zones. In addition, the concept provided for the integration of the tourism hinterland with the focal point being provided by the attractions in the resort zones. Several criteria were adopted in the selection of resort zones (Cathie 1984, pp. 4–5):

Natural Resource Base—zones to incorporate areas with high potential for intensive recreation and, generally, natural resources offering potential for the development of year-round outdoor recreation (both active and passive) opportunities.

Attractions/Activities—zones to contain attractions or activities of such significance to enable them to draw upon the Victorian, interstate, and overseas markets. The zones to have the potential for 'Cluster' attractions, which can be promoted as a group to attract year-round visitation.

Image/Geographic Homogeneity—zones to have common features upon which to develop a regional identity (cultural, historical, etc.) which could be readily associated with the geographic area and not other areas.

Basic Infrastructure—zones generally to have available basic infrastructure facilities (for example, a variety of accommodation to facilitate tourism development).

Principal Service Centre—the zones to contain or be near service centres which are able to provide services to tourists and to developments within the zones.

Transportation—the zones must have good access from or along major transportation routes, particularly roads. The zones need to contain efficient internal transport networks, or the potential to develop such networks, providing access between attractions, facilities, and service centres.

Population—the zones to be relatively close to major markets, or to be accessible from these markets. This factor also includes access to labour sources to service tourist plant.

Under the strategy, seven regions were recognised as being suitable for development, management, and promotion as tourist zones with the support of the Victorian government (Cathie 1984, pp. 4, 20–7):

- Central Melbourne and selected day trip corridors;
- Goldfields (incorporating the central Victorian goldfield districts of Ballarat and Bendigo);
- Riverland (incorporating the area from Echuca to Mildura);
- North-East (incorporating the alpine areas, 'Kelly Country', and north-east wineries);
- Grampians;
- Gippsland Lakes; and
- Southern Ocean zones (incorporating the area from Port Campbell to Port Fairy).

In addition to identifying resort zones, the Victorian tourism strategy noted the importance of the 'tourism corridors' which link the various tourism centres. However, as the strategy reported: 'A tourism corridor is far more than just the road linking zones, although this is one of the major attributes. The road forms a nucleus from which tourists can move out to enjoy a continuous series of tourism experiences' (Cathie 1984, p. 5). Examples of tourism corridors included the Great Ocean Road, which links Melbourne with the Southern Ocean zone, and which offers many opportunities for coastal sightseeing, and the Hume Highway, which links Melbourne to the North-East zone, and which also has many attractions along the corridor including historic townships and vineyards.

The strategy clearly played a major role in identifying and promoting Victoria's tourist assets. In particular, the linkage of tourist attractions along defined routes allowed for the more efficient utilisation of information sources and also enhanced the trend towards the provision of quality, special-interest tourism experiences. Of course, the strategy also had a functional purpose, that of encouraging Victorian and interstate or overseas travellers to spend more money in Victoria. Undoubtedly, the Victorian tourism strategy provided a great boost to the state's tourism industry. The first stage of the strategy (1983–86) was characterised by its emphasis on product identification through regionalisation. The second stage (1987 onwards) provided for the redirection of the tourism strategy towards the marketing, promotion, facilitation and enhancement of the state's existing tourist assets, and the restructuring of the VTC and other state bodies such as the Alpine Resorts Commission, to achieve this goal. This second stage therefore served as a basis for the establishment of Tourism Victoria in 1992 and the reorientation of Victorian government involvement in tourism.

Tourism Victoria

> TOURISM VICTORIA is the vehicle by which the Victorian Government expresses its support for tourism, liaises with the tourism industry and through which a cohesive promotion of Victoria to domestic and international markets occurs (Tourism Victoria 1993, p. 6).

Upon election in 1992 the Liberal Party–National Party coalition government 'heralded an aggressive strategy to reposition tourism as one of the State's major growth industries' (TV 1993, p. 6), in order to generate employment, attract investment, reduce state debt, and increase market share. The economic emphasis of Tourism Victoria is reflected in its mission 'to maximise employment and the long-term economic benefits of tourism to Victoria by developing and marketing the state as a competitive tourist destination' (TV 1997a, p. 1; 2002b). To achieve its mission, Tourism Victoria (1997a, p. 1) set four broad goals:

- marketing goal—to increase visitor numbers, length of stay and visitor expenditure by positioning Victoria as a distinct and competitive tourist destination;
- leadership goal—to take a leadership role in the tourism industry, encourage professional standards and the development of cooperative arrangements which maximise industry effectiveness;
- infrastructure goal—to improve the tourism assets of Victoria by identifying infrastructure opportunities and facilitating development projects; and
- management goal—to encourage the effective use of resources by conducting the business of Tourism Victoria in accordance with professional commercial management principles.

The four organisational goals are notable for the extent to which they emphasised economic and commercial factors at the expense of broader social and environmental objectives. Unlike the Victorian tourism strategy of the 1980s, the set of corporate priorities listed above for Tourism Victoria were not integrated within a broader social justice strategy. Instead, the primary focus was on an increase of market share in terms of both intrastate and interstate domestic tourism and international visitation. Although Tourism Victoria shifted away from the planning emphasis of the 1980s, the tourist regions identified in the previous strategy did provide the geographical basis for the four major national marketing campaigns undertaken by Tourism Victoria in 1992–93: 'Ski Victoria', 'Summer in the Victorian High Country', 'the Goldfields Campaign', and 'Great Victorian Motoring Holidays'. Indeed, regional Victoria became even more important in terms of tourism promotion, and Tourism Victoria identified thirteen 'product regions' which served as the basis for regional and state marketing underneath the overall campaign of 'You'll love every piece of Victoria' (TV 1997b). Indeed, the regional focus was recognition that 'For Victoria to successfully promote itself as a holiday destination, based largely on the concept of touring, all elements of the tourism experience must be improved rather than relying on the motivational strength of marketing programs' (TV 2001).

For each region, consultants developed a series of regional tourism development plans. Each plan was funded by the state government and by the region. Each plan outlined a vision for the region, a relationship to the 1997–2001 strategic business plan (TV 1997b), the characteristics of the region, development issues, challenges, strategies, the visitor and target markets, and issues of access and transport, accommodation, product development, visitor information services, industry leadership, professionalism and standards. To support these regional initiatives Tourism Victoria also assisted in the development of partnerships with the newly restructured local government organisations to encourage tourism development in regional Victoria (TV 1995, 1997c; Country Victoria Tourism Council (CVTC) 1997).

> To facilitate an integrated planning approach to tourism, Tourism Victoria encourages local councils to develop a consistent approach to the way in which tourism is managed at a local level. The adoption of a consistent approach . . . will ensure a sound policy framework is achieved (CVTC 1997, p. 24).

The following elements were regarded as significant in preparing a tourism development plan by local government in Victoria (CVTC 1997, p. 24):
• incorporate tourism into the Land Use Strategy Plan:
— describe key existing features that support product strengths;
— discuss key planning issues relevant to tourism development;
— formulate goals, policies and actions to implement vision that complements the overall tourism plan.
• incorporate tourism into the Economic Development Strategy:
— assess the contribution of tourism to the local economy;
— integrate with other council strategies.
• identify tourism in Council Municipal Strategic Statement and Planning Scheme:
— include key tourism objectives and statements encouraging activities;
— promote maximum flexibility in planning schemes in the interpretation of ancillary uses of a tourism nature.

Tourism Victoria, in conjunction with the Victorian government, has therefore developed an aggressive strategy of regional product development, improved promotion and marketing, and a concentration on Victoria's major product strengths which Tourism Victoria (1997b, p. 78) has identified as:
• meetings, incentives, conventions and exhibitions;
• events;
• arts, theatre, and culture;
• food and wine;
• natural attractions;
• skiing; and
• shopping.

Undoubtedly Victoria's tourism strategy has had substantial success in contributing to employment growth and industry performance. For example in March 1997, employment in commercial tourist accommodation had risen by 3.6% over the previous twelve months, with Victoria accounting for 57% of the national increase in jobs in tourist accommodation (Tourism Victoria 1997a), and the total takings of Victoria's hotels and motels had increased from $420 million for the twelve months to September 1993 to $570 million for the twelve months to June 1996 (Tourism Victoria 1997b). Victoria also managed the impacts of the Asian financial crisis on tourism better than many other states attracting a record 1 034 000 overseas visitors (aged 15 years and older) during 1998, a 27% share of all international arrivals to Australia. There were 272 000 Asian arrivals to Victoria for the year ending December 1998, a decrease of 11% (compared with a national decrease of 21%). Visitor numbers to Victoria from Singapore and China increased (up 9% and 11% respectively) (Tourism Victoria 2001b) (see Table 6.25).

Between 2000 and 2002 the Tourism Strategic Plan for Victoria was again revised. Building on the framework established in previous plans, Tourism Victoria (2002a) described the plan in the following terms:

> . . . developed in consultation with business and industry representatives throughout the State, it is not simply a plan for Tourism Victoria, but one that aims to reflect the vision of the tourism industry. The Plan's time frame will stretch from 2002 to 2006 to ensure the strategic opportunities associated with the Commonwealth Games, to be held in Melbourne in 2006, are fully realised.

TABLE 6.25 Victoria's major international markets by ranking, 1999

Visitors		Visitor nights (000s)	
1 UK	155 192	1 UK	2600
2 New Zealand	140 925	2 New Zealand	1784
3 USA	118 647	3 USA	1659
4 Japan	77 923	4 Singapore	1329
5 Singapore	67 044	5 Japan	1265
6 Germany	52 516	6 China	1159
7 Taiwan	45 852	7 Malaysia	1153
8 China	36 727	8 Indonesia	1122
9 Malaysia	36 131	9 Germany	877
10 Canada	27 645	10 Taiwan	631
11 Indonesia	25 977	11 Canada	586
12 Hong Kong	23 498	12 Thailand	500
13 Thailand	16 794	13 Hong Kong	398
14 Korea	14 582	14 Korea	381

Source: Tourism Victoria (2000) Tourism Victoria Annual Report 1999–2000.

WESTERN AUSTRALIA

> The Tourism Commission has a role to ensure that tourism industry growth is accelerated. It achieves this by identifying potential new markets, marketing the State as an appealing tourist destination, removing impediments to the growth of the industry and actively encouraging infrastructure development (WATC 1991, p. 6).

> In general, Western Australians do not fully appreciate the benefits that a viable tourism industry brings to this state (WATC 1997a, p. 8).

Tourism is a significant component of the Western Australian economy. Tourism is worth more than $12 million a day to Western Australia and provides the state's economy with a significant export earner, worth more than $1 billion each year (WATC

TABLE 6.26 Origin of international visitors (15 yrs and over) and nights in Western Australia 1999/2000 (% change on 1998/99)

Country	Visitors	% change on 1998/99	Nights	% change on 1998/99
New Zealand	35 600	16.3	758 000	−8.3
Japan	52 900	13.8	919 000	−6.5
Hong Kong	10 100	−2.9	305 000	−38.0
Singapore	69 500	10.5	1 203 000	−24.1
Malaysia	40 300	43.4	528 000	−20.1
Indonesia	23 800	−15.9	970 000	30.9
Thailand	10 800	36.7	247 000	116.7
USA	34 700	−8.7	478 000	−38.0
Canada	12 800	14.4	348 000	52.0
United Kingdom	121 100	8.6	2 973 000	17.9
Germany	29 300	38.9	546 000	34.8
Other Countries	130 200	13.6	3 922 000	21.9
Total (excluding US Navy)	571 100	11.7	13 197 000	5.2
US Navy Personnel	18 900	−12.5	61 900	5.2
Total (including US Navy)	**590 000**	**10.8**	**13 258 000**	**5.0**

Visitor nights are from the *International Visitor Survey*, Bureau of Tourism Research. US Navy visitor nights are a WATC estimate based on US Navy information.

Base: International visitors are defined as overseas residents aged 15 years and over who spent at least one night in Western Australia. Also includes US Navy Personnel.

Note: Estimates may not add to total due to rounding.

Source: Western Australian Tourism Commission (WATC) (2001) *Research Brief on Tourism*, Perth. Courtesy of Western Australian Tourism Commission.

2000a). In 1999 between 72 000 and 78 000 Western Australians were employed in the state's tourism industry, accounting for approximately 8.5% of the workforce (WATC 2000a). This represents an increase of approximately 20 000 tourism-related jobs since 1996 (WATC 1997a, 1997b, 1997c). 'More than 3,500 tourism businesses currently operate in Western Australia of which 95% comprise small enterprises employing less than five persons and many are located in rural and remote locations' (WATC 2000, p. 3). In 1996, international visitor arrivals to the state exceeded 5 000 000 for the first time (WATC 1997b). By 2000 this figure had increased by almost 20%. However, domestic tourism is also extremely important (WATC 2001).

The state tourism organisation, the Western Australian Tourism Commission (WATC) was established as a statutory authority in January 1984. As with other state tourism bodies the WATC has seen considerable change in its mandate and organisation in recent years as the state has attempted to maximise the potential economic returns from tourism. For example, in 1992, the commission's mission was to 'facilitate and support the growth of the Western Australian tourism industry for the longer term economic and social benefit of the State', and in terms of promotion the objective of the WATC was to 'improve the viability of the tourism industry by generating greater tourism activity through supporting and co-ordinating the promotion of Western Australia as an attractive tourist and convention destination within Australia and overseas' (WATC 1992, p. 54). The corporate plan for 1997–2001 stated that the WATC had a vision to 'create an effective partnership between the private sector and government to make tourism a premier industry in Western Australia', with a mission to 'accelerate the sustainable growth of the tourism industry for the longer term social and economic benefit of the State' (1997c, p. 2; 2000a, p. 1).

The WATC corporate plan of the late 1990s detailed objectives in terms of two overall program initiatives—marketing the destination, and tourism industry development. The overall objective of the WATC in terms of tourism development was 'to promote, foster and facilitate investment in, and the development of, new tourist infrastructure; products and services and the improvement of existing tourist facilities and services in Western Australia' (WATC 1997c, p. 19), and the overall objective in terms of promoting the state was 'to promote Western Australia as an attractive tourist, event, and convention destination within Australia and overseas' (WATC 1997c, p. 10). Four subsidiary objectives were identified under this heading (WATC 1997c, pp. 16, 17, 18):

- national marketing—'in partnership with the industry promote Western Australia as a desirable holiday destination in the interstate and intrastate target market segments, and to undertake marketing strategies which will maximise the economic benefit to the state';
- international marketing—'in partnership with the industry and the Australian Tourist Commission, promote Western Australia as a desirable holiday destination in the identified core and future international markets to maximise the economic benefits generated from international tourism';
- events tourism—'to develop, attract, support and as appropriate, manage events which are capable of adding substance to Brand WA, generating substantial visitor expenditure and which can cost effectively market Western Australia nationally and internationally'; and
- convention and incentive travel—'to develop, attract and support conventions, conferences, meetings and incentive travel which is capable of generating visitor expenditure by increasing the number of delegate-nights to conventions, the amount of pre and post convention touring activities and the amount of delegate expenditure'.

TABLE 6.27 Purpose of visit of international visitors (15 yrs and over) and nights in Western Australia 1999/2000

Purpose	Visitors	% change on 1998/99	Nights	% change on 1998/99
Holiday	327 800	17.4	4 881 900	24.7
VFR	143 400	–0.6	3 107 000	–1.6
Total Leisure (inc US Navy)	471 200	11.3	7 988 900	12.9
Business	57 500	39.6	435 000	–21.9
Other	61 300	–9.9	4 835 000	–3.2
Total (including US Navy)	590 000	10.8	13 258 000	5.0

Base: International visitors are defined as overseas residents aged 15 years and over who spent at least one night in Western Australia. Also includes US Navy Personnel.

Note: Estimates may not add to total due to rounding.

Leisure visitors are those who come primarily for a holiday or to Visit Friends and Relatives (VFR), and includes US Navy.

Please Note: The 'other' category for purpose of visit mainly includes people visiting for education purposes, hence the significant number of nights they stay. It can also include those who visit mainly to attend a convention, conference, exhibition or a sporting event, as well as for any other reason that is not of a leisure or business nature.

Source: Western Australian Tourism Commission (WATC) (2001) *Research Brief on Tourism*, Perth. Courtesy of Western Australian Tourism Commission.

The mission and objectives of the WATC therefore demonstrated both continuity and change. Continuity was demonstrated in terms of the emphasis the commission attached to marketing and economic considerations and visitor growth, and the virtual absence of social and environmental considerations. Change was demonstrated in terms of (at least a partial) recognition of the significance of sustainability, even if this was recognised primarily in economic terms. An indication of the economic dimension of sustainability could be found in the performance indicators which the WATC used to evaluate the effectiveness of its tourism development strategy. The four indicators were:

• number of new products developed;
• number of new project sites progressed;
• number of new projects involved in which have come to fruition; and
• level of satisfaction with services provided (WATC 1997c, p. 19).

No measures of performance were provided in terms of environmental effects of tourism development or acceptance of such developments by the local community (see Chapters 9 and 10). The economic emphasis of the WATC is perhaps not surprising given that, according to the WATC (1991, p. 7), the commission:

> . . . was established to accelerate the development of the tourism industry and increase its economic impact on the State. The Commission measures its performance by assessing the growth of, and the flow-on benefits to the State derived from, the tourism industry.

As a result of the Western Australian government's commitment to tourism, several significant developments have occurred in recent years. One of the most notable developments was the development of 'Brand WA' to give the state a more 'meaningful identity' in the global tourism marketplace and to increase consumer awareness (WATC 1997c, p. 11). According to the WATC (1997c, p. 11) Brand WA reflects Western Australia's 'core personality—fresh, natural, free, spirited', and is intended to function as a core positioning statement which will be reflected in all WATC marketing strategies. It is also intended to be related to the ATC's development of 'Brand Australia' which emphasises 'Big Nature—Big City' (p. 12). Significantly, as a key aspect of its Brand WA strategy, the WATC 'created a marketing campaign designed to dispel the perception of Western Australia as a place that lacked exciting events' (WATC 2000b, p. 25), and launched the 'Best on Earth in Perth' events package. The WATC (2000b, p. 23) has estimated that the core events of the package—Telstra Rally Australia and the Hyundai Hopman Cup—'now deliver a combined economic impact to the State of $28 million each year. For example, Rally Australia has steadily increased its impact from $11 million in 1994 to $21.2 million in 1999'.

Under the Brand WA strategy, several target markets were identified. Within the important domestic market the primary market was 35–59-year-old singles and couples, the secondary market was young families travelling with one child under the age of 12, and the tertiary market was the 60 years and over market segment. In the international marketing arena the priority markets were identified as Singapore, Malaysia, Indonesia, the United Kingdom, Japan, and Europe (WATC 1996, 1997c).

Another significant development for tourism in Western Australia was the production of a nature-based tourism strategy (WATC 1997a). According to the WATC: 'The nature based tourism product of the State provides the basis for State and destinational differentiation. Many of these areas lend themselves to high value, low volume tourism. In addition there is a growing demand for nature based and

[A]boriginal cultural experiences' (1997c, p. 21). The strategy's vision was 'to ensure that Western Australia maintains its natural advantage and establishes itself as the leading nature based tourism destination in Australia' (WATC 1997a, p. 18), and was based upon five principles:

- conservation of the natural environment;
- involving and benefiting local communities;
- improving knowledge;
- providing quality products and services; and an
- efficient and effective industry.

The strategy and its vision illustrate the way in which the natural environment has become a commodity to be used in competition among the states and destinations for the tourism dollar. The strategy treated the environment as 'an integral part of "Brand" Western Australia' which will 'provide the State with an exceptional opportunity to capitalise on the growing worldwide demand for nature based tourism experiences' (WATC 1997a, p. 1). Undoubtedly tourism can make a contribution to conserving and maintaining ecological values (see Chapter 10). However, although the strategy noted the importance of sustainability, and stated that 'nature based tourism must be environmentally, culturally, socially and economically sustainable' (WATC 1997a, p.18), there was no identification in the strategy of the indicators which can be used to measure just how sustainable nature-based tourism really is.

The objectives and structure of the WATC have remained relatively constant since its formation. The most significant administrative restructuring occurred on 1 January 1991, when Eventscorp was transferred from the Western Australian Development Corporation to the WATC and the Perth Convention Bureau was absorbed by the commission as the Perth Convention Unit (WATC 1992). The Eventscorp Unit aimed to attract major sporting and cultural events to Western Australia, such as the Commonwealth Bank Rally of Australia, the Hopman Cup, the World Swimming Championships and the Whitbread Round-the-World Yacht Race. The Perth Convention Unit has since been renamed the Perth Convention and Incentive Unit and became responsible for attracting conventions and incentive travel to Western Australia.

The sheer size of Western Australia means that the WATC pays substantial attention to the intrastate tourism market. The market provides more than 80% of total visitor trips (WATC 1997d). In 1998-99 there were 10 390 000 intrastate visitor nights to Western Australia (WATC 2000b). By encouraging greater intrastate travel the commission can also help retain income within Western Australia rather than have it flow out on interstate and international holidays. The relative isolation of Western Australia in terms of the main domestic and international markets creates transport network problems similar to those of Tasmania. It has long been recognised that an increasingly price-conscious market means that discounted airfares and chartered flights play a major role in ensuring the attractiveness of Western Australia as a domestic travel destination (WATC 1992).

In both the domestic and international marketing arenas the WATC is developing cooperative marketing programs. In addition, the WATC has an extensive overseas marketing network. However, given increased cooperation between the ATC and the various state and territory tourism commissions for the promotion of Australia overseas as a tourism destination, it remains to be seen whether or not Western Australia will overcome its traditional parochialism and see itself as part of Australia or, like Queensland, remain a state apart in its marketing and development strategies.

COORDINATION AT THE STATE AND TERRITORY LEVEL

The difficulties of coordinating tourism at the state and territory level is a mirror image of the problems encountered at the Commonwealth level, except for one major difference—there is a total of eight state and territory governments. As the above account of state government involvement in tourism indicates, the trend towards the corporatisation of government tourism activities is replicated in the objectives and structures of each of the state and territory tourism authorities. The states and territories also encounter the conflicting forces which surround the regulation of the industry. However, from a national perspective the activities of the state and territory tourism authorities pose a coordination nightmare in the presentation of the Australian tourism product in the international marketplace. As the Australian Government Committee of Inquiry Into Tourism reported: '[I]n recent years there has been a blurring of responsibilities between the Federal and State/Territory Governments . . . and the States have increasingly become involved in aggressive international marketing of themselves' (1987a, p. 23).

Queensland has probably been the most aggressive state in the overseas marketing of its tourism product (King & Hyde 1989). For example, in the North American market the QTTC actively campaigned to capitalise on the interest generated in northern Australia by the 'Crocodile Dundee' movies. However, there is a danger that state tourism marketing overseas will confuse the marketplace, especially as knowledge about a country tends to diminish with increasing distance. The dangers of aggressive state promotion in the European market were expressed in submissions to the Australian Government Committee of Inquiry Into Tourism (1987a, p. 147):

> A regionalisation of Australian tourism is not appropriate . . . The efforts of individual Australian territories and federal states to represent themselves on the European (German) market can in the long term only harm Australian tourism . . . (Theodore Geus—Frankfurter Allgemeine Zeitung)

> The worst that could happen to Australia on the German market would be that the individual states of the fifth continent argue about the favours of the German holiday maker instead of canvassing jointly for a destination which Germans consider as a unity. The average German does not want to go to Queensland or Victoria, he wants to go to Australia . . . (Thomas Hopfgartern).

These issues regarding interstate competition and brand confusion exist to the present day (see Chapter 4). In addition to the damage that competition for the tourist dollar can do to the image of Australia in the mind of the overseas consumer, the duplication of effort in doing so can be regarded as a waste of scarce resources that could be better allocated elsewhere. However, the vagaries of the Australian states and territories are such that governments are intent on boosting the high profile of the tourism industry to their electors. In such a situation it is extremely unlikely that a high degree of coordination will ever be achieved among the states, as too many governments are afraid of missing out on a potential slice of the tourism pie. Indeed, programs such as Partnership Australia, which attempts to unite the ATC and the states and territories in joint promotional efforts, came into operation only because of the carrot dangled to the states and territories in the form of increased money for tourism promotion.

LOCAL GOVERNMENT AND TOURISM

> Due to the increasing recognition of tourism as a key industry sector, the role of local government is becoming more important in initiating, facilitating and supporting the development of tourism (CVTC 1997, p. 24).

Local government has a critical role to play in tourism development (Richins & Pearce 2000). Local authorities are at the forefront of tourism planning and development control and are the level of government closest to the demands of local residents. Local government has traditionally played an entrepreneurial role in attracting tourism through the establishment of tourist bureaux or the promotion of tourist attractions (Green, Tonge & Sceats 1980). As with other levels of government, local government increasingly perceives tourism as a mechanism for providing employment opportunities and local economic growth. In addition, tourism can help to provide services and facilities which would otherwise not be obtained. However, despite its significance, the role of local government in tourism has tended to be neglected by state and Commonwealth governments and, sometimes, by the tourism industry.

In terms of a direct involvement in tourism, local authorities usually act as the destination organisation for their own area, but often also act as providers of tourist attractions, facilities and services (Burkart & Medlik 1981; Local Government & Shires Association of New South Wales 1988; CVTC 1997). Within local authorities, tourism-related functions are usually undertaken by two separate departments— one concerned with leisure, recreation, parks, tourism, attractions, amenities, entertainment, and promotion, and the other involved with the physical planning process. Voluntary business and/or promotion associations might also receive funding from local government and might be closely involved in the development of local tourism planning strategies (Jenkins 1993).

In addition to its more traditional tourism role, local government can play a very significant coordinating role. As noted above, local government is the closest to the people, and is therefore best suited to coordinate tourism development at the local level. This point has been stressed by M. Reynolds (1988, p. 67) who reported: 'Local government and regional development organisations have the potential to integrate the sometimes disparate economic, social and environmental goals that sometimes exist in local communities in relation to tourism development'. However, although there are several barriers to the successful attainment of an integrated approach to tourism development, there are growing signs that such an approach is being accepted as necessary by some local government authorities (CVTC 1997).

The state government–local government relationship

Local government has a somewhat awkward position within the structure of Australian government. Local government derives none of its powers from the Australian Constitution. Despite attempts to have the role of local government enshrined in the Constitution, the difficulties of constitutional change and the politics that surround such change might well mean that the present position will last for many years to come. Local government derives its powers from state constitutions and Acts of parliaments. The powers and role of local government vary markedly from state to state in Australia, and despite the traditional perception of local government as the providers of rubbish disposal and road maintenance, it must be stressed that local government also has extremely significant welfare, community development, and environmental planning functions.

Local government is often seen as the hand-maiden of the states for two major reasons. First, their legal powers are derived from state legislation. Second, much of their funding is sourced from state grants. Local government derives a proportion of its funding from the collection of rates from properties within the authority boundary. Further funding can also be obtained in the form of direct Commonwealth grants for certain projects. However, the state governments serve as a primary source of funds for many local government authorities around Australia.

Each state government provides funds from its own resources for local government authorities. The money might be provided in the form of a direct grant because the local government authority is undertaking work at the request or requirement of the state government. Under this mechanism, '[l]ocal government has therefore become the medium for such services as roads, libraries, aged persons' homes, recreation, museums, tourism facilities and swimming pools' (Chapman & Wood 1984, p. 77). Unfortunately, the exact extent of tourism-related spending by local government authorities is extremely hard to determine because of both definitional problems and the lack of clear figures. Nevertheless, despite the difficulties in obtaining data on the financial role of local government in tourism development, it is possible to identify the planning function through the examination of tourism plans and development strategies. Coordination of local tourism development through the use of land-use plans and planning regulations to cover such items as permissible building height, or the construction of tourist developments in environmentally sensitive areas, is a key function of local government (Bates 1989; Stanton & Aislabie 1992a; Richins & Pearce 2000). However, as Jones (1977, p. 236) reported, '"co-ordination" is a widely used term in the management literature and is much more easily said than done. Local government could not attempt co-ordination by command because it does not have the powers'.

One of the great difficulties facing local authorities throughout Australia is the ability of developers to appeal against local government planning decisions through either the political or legal process at the state level. Such a technique has been applied in all of the Australian states and is often justified by declaring tourism projects to be in the state interest. Although this might indeed be the case, it still raises questions about the ability of local government to represent local interests which are the *raison d'être* of local authorities. Furthermore, such actions appear to be at odds with the development of a community planning approach to tourism which emphasises the primacy of the local community in the tourism development decision-making process (Murphy 1985) (see Chapter 11).

In addition to the planning coordination role of local government, local authorities also serve an important promotional function in tourism. Local authorities might promote tourism through the activities of a local tourism officer and a tourist bureau and/or support of a local tourism committee which often has substantial private-sector membership. Authorities often jointly promote an area through cooperative partnerships with surrounding authorities to promote a regional identity. For example, the Sunshine Coast derived its identity through the joint marketing approach of the local councils in the coastal strip between Brisbane and Fraser Island.

Cooperation among local authorities might considerably reduce promotion costs and should assist in retaining tourists within a region for a longer period of time (Goodall & Ashworth 1988). For example, the shires of northern New South Wales and south-east Queensland have cooperated in joint marketing campaigns. However,

STATE, REGIONAL, AND LOCAL GOVERNMENT APPROACHES TO TOURISM

despite the need for a positive approach to regional tourism development, local government boundaries are sometimes perceived as barriers which can establish an 'us-or-them' approach to tourism promotion. For example, the Joint Committee on the Australian Capital Territory (which focused on hospitality) emphasised the need for further cooperation among regional tourism authorities, and noted that the lack of such a relationship 'was an impediment to the successful promotional marketing of the ACT' (1986, p. 14)—a situation which began to be corrected only in the late 1990s. Indeed, there is a 'layer cake' of tourism strategies and plans, from the federal, to the state, to the local level in Australia. This provides a major challenge for effective coordination among the various levels of government.

Difficulties in coordination

> Co-ordination is not, of course, simply a matter of communicating information or setting up suitable administrative structures, but involves the exercise of power (Hogwood & Gunn 1984, pp. 205–6).

The ongoing development of state and regional tourism strategies by the New South Wales government and the Tourism Commission of New South Wales (1987a, 1987b) in the 1980s serve to illustrate the difficulties in coordination among the various levels of government (Senate Standing Committee on Environment, Recreation and the Arts 1992). The 1987 New South Wales Tourism Development Strategy and the more recent state tourism plan identified priority areas for tourism development (including the New South Wales north coast) and the need for a comprehensive planning framework to coordinate the planning and development of tourism. The framework operated at state, regional, local, and site levels. The state level emphasised the potential economic benefits of tourism and the objectives of the state strategy. However, the other three levels are also of major consequence for local government's role in tourism development. According to the Tourism Commission of NSW (1987a, unpaginated):

> *Regional Tourism Development [Strategies]:* . . . provide guidelines for coordinating public sector policy on tourism planning and development at a regional level; identify areas within a region suitable for tourism development; and suggest broad strategies to promote growth.
> *Local Tourism [Plans]:* . . . are prepared for areas of high tourism development potential. They address local planning issues such as statutory and development controls, the adequacy of existing infrastructure, the scope for future investment, perceived market trends, etc. These plans address supply-led potential, that is, the types of facilities and infrastructure that need to be provided to attract and service various market segments . . . responsibility for preparing Local Tourism Plans will generally rest with Local Councils with the Tourism Commission providing advice.
> *Site Management [Plans]:* . . . contain the most detailed information about site specific development sites. These Plans incorporate site specific recommendations including site appraisals and design and construction concepts and plans. Site Management Plans advance development concepts to the feasibility assessment stage. Responsibility for the preparation of these plans will generally rest with the landowner. Where necessary the Tourism Commission will provide advice and assistance.

The development framework described above is clearly related to the ability of local government to plan for local conditions and demands. However, it should be noted that the tourism planning framework advocated by the Tourism Commission of New South Wales (1987a, 1987b; Bates 1989) emphasised the economic aspects of tourism and the need to assist in its development. Although these are essential elements in any tourism strategy, little attention is given to the attitudes of local communities to tourism development. For example, the *North Coast Region Tourism Development Strategy* (Tourism Commission of NSW 1987a) did not specify the role of the community in developing regional strategies, although attention was given to the issue of environmental protection. More recently, other states and territories have attempted to develop regional tourism strategies which are designed to be integrated with state strategies, for example, the Northern Territory, Victoria and Western Australia (see above), and, of course, various national strategies and plans have also been developed (see Chapter 5).

Government and tourism: coordination and sustainable development

> While active governmental involvement in tourism development may serve to avoid or mitigate . . . potential problems, it may also serve to exacerbate them . . . [T]he crucial question is not whether government plays a role in tourism development, but what kind of role is played. It is therefore important to give serious consideration to the types of policy choices faced by planners, and to their potential consequences (Richter & Richter 1985, p. 203).

Local government clearly has a major role to play in the process of tourism development. The gradual adoption of a community basis for tourism planning by Australian local authorities heralds the possibility of the development of a uniquely Australian tourism product that has the support of local people and which is in sympathy with the local environment. However, local government will not achieve a prominent role in tourism until the Commonwealth and state governments allow local government to participate fully in the development of tourism policy (Senate Standing Committee on Environment, Recreation and the Arts 1992). As Chapman and Wood commented: 'The organisations for intergovernmental relations in Australia are relatively primitive and undeveloped. They do not account for the growth of government powers and the intermingling of the roles of each level of government' (1984, p. 168).

Local government, the level of government closest to many of the problems associated with tourism development and that which is most suited to a community planning approach, is excluded from nearly all of the ministerial councils and consultative committees. For efficient coordination of responsibilities and activities, the Australian federal system requires an intergovernmental structure which includes all levels of government. Indeed, Chapman and Wood argued that recreation and tourism were 'shared functions in which local authorities should enjoy a voice at the highest levels' (1984, p.168). Therefore, there is a need for a willingness to change the respective roles that the various levels of government play in the development of the Australian tourism product. According to George, 'The local government level is the most critical in terms of individual projects and achieving results' (1987, p. 91). The time has come for government (particularly state governments) and the tourism industry to allow local government to participate fully in tourism development and to ensure the coordination of tourism at all levels of government.

The domestic market is the great battlefield for the state tourism authorities' struggle for the tourism dollar. In the domestic marketplace each state is competing against others for the Australian traveller. Each state attempts to promote the attractions that it has to offer to its own residents, to the rest of Australia, and to overseas visitors. On this battlefield, some agreement exists between the states and the Commonwealth in as much as they are convinced that more Australians should travel within Australia. Undoubtedly, substantial economic benefits would result if Australians substituted domestic for overseas travel. However, questions can still be raised regarding duplication and wastage among the various state marketing campaigns.

THE GOVERNMENT RESPONSE

> There is an emerging trend among tourism agencies in Australia towards an increasing emphasis on advertising at the expense of research, strategic marketing and other activities which provide the ingredients of a more balanced and rational approach to the development of the tourism industry (H.W. Faulkner 1991, p .2).

> . . . in a federal system, which disperses power among different levels of government, some groups may have more influence if policy is made at the national level; other groups may benefit more if policy is made at the state or provincial level . . . In summary, institutional structures, arrangements, and procedures can have a significant impact on public policy and should not be ignored in policy analysis. Neither should analysis of them, without concern for the dynamic aspects of politics, be considered adequate (Anderson 1984, p. 18).

Government in Australia faces a conflict. On one side it has to meet the demands of concerned environmental and social groups regarding the negative impacts of tourism, while on the other it has to satisfy industry demands for deregulation of the tourism and travel industry and greater emphasis on marketing and promotion. Although concerns regarding the negative social and environmental aspects of tourism have been raised at the federal level, the prime responsibility for planning and development issues lies with the states. State government involvement in tourism is marked by increasing attention to the promotion and marketing of tourist product, and to the states as destinations, rather than the development implications of tourism for the wider benefits of society (Hall 1994b). The Victorian, New South Wales, and Queensland tourist commissions have all expanded their promotion campaigns and marketing divisions at the expense of planning and development functions. The focus of the states, as well as some sections of the federal government, often seems to be more directed to tourism numbers rather than the net benefits that tourism can bring to a destination.

Changes in the bureaucratic structures of tourism agencies can reflect substantial shifts in policy direction, and these can have substantial impact throughout the tourism industry and the wider community. The function of statutory authorities such as state and territory tourism commissions is substantially different from that of government departments. The fundamental difference is the direct influence of non-departmental people acting as commissioners, or, in effect, as directors. 'The implications of a Board of Directors linked to private industry within the confines of a QAGO (Quasi Autonomous Government Organisation) are that perhaps the balance of power swings to private developers' (Jenkins 1993, p. 284) who have a more commercial orientation towards tourism (Jenkins 2001).

The transfer of funds from policy, planning, and research areas to the promotional functions of state government agencies led the then Director of the BTR,

Dr Bill Faulkner, to comment publicly on the emergence of 'advertising fundamentalism', whereby research programs were being downgraded to spend more money on advertising. As Faulkner commented: 'It is unlikely that research into, for instance, the environmental and social impacts of tourism would be carried out under the market forces regime, even though problems in these areas could eventually render the tourism product of particular regions unsaleable' (1991, p. 2). That Dr Faulkner hit a raw nerve with his comments was indicated by the reply of the New South Wales Minister of Tourism, Mr Michael Yabsley, who stated: 'To accuse the commission of "advertising fundamentalism" merely highlights deficiencies in Mr Faulkner's own research into this subject' (Yabsley 1991). Over a decade later such a debate remains very relevant. The minister's comments reflect a deep division as to the role and character of government involvement in tourism in Australia and as to the future nature of tourism development. More often than not, success in tourism in Australia is measured in terms of numbers of visitors and their expenditure rather than the net benefits to be gained from tourist visitation and associated tourism development (Hall, Jenkins & Kearsley 1997a; Hall & Kearsley 2001).

Tourism policy is just one aspect of Commonwealth–state or state–state relationships. Coordination among the states suffers from the same tensions as any other aspect of the politics of Australian federalism. In the search for a coordinated tourism policy, state parochialism often overcomes the interests of the nation. Moreover, there is little agreement regarding the level at which final decisions on tourism development should lie. The additional issue of the extent to which state tourism and local authorities act in the industry interest rather than the public interest also remains an extremely significant, although underinvestigated, issue (Jenkins 2001). Perhaps most importantly, clarity and openness in the tourism policy and decision-making process would make a substantial contribution to the development of a sustainable Australian tourism product which the broader Australian community could support.

SUGGESTIONS FOR FURTHER READING

Several accounts of Commonwealth, state and local government involvement in tourism can be found in Elliot (1997) and Hall, Jenkins and Kearsley (1997a). The latter also includes a discussion of the New Zealand scene, as does D.G. Pearce (1992). However, studies of state and local government involvement in tourism in Australia are relatively few. State-oriented studies of tourism are to be found in Craik (1987, 1991), McMillen (1991a, 1991b), and West (1993), who focus on the Queensland situation. Knapman (1991) examines the Northern Territory from an economic perspective. In the local government area, reference should be made to the work of Bates (1989) and Stanton and Aislabie (1992a). Richins and Pearce (2000) provide a very good account on some of the pressures influencing tourism development at the local council level. Readers should therefore consult the annual reports of the various state and territory tourism commissions and local government authorities, and the various state and territory tourism websites.

- Australian Capital Territory:
      www.canberratourism.com.au

- New South Wales (holiday information and corporate connections):
      www.tourism.nsw.gov.au

- Northern Territory (corporate website):
      www.nttc.com.au

- Northern Territory (holiday information website):
      www.ntholidays.com.au

- Queensland (holiday information and corporate connections):
      www.qttc.com.au

- South Australia:
      www.tourism.sa.gov.au

- South Australia (holiday information website):
      www.southaustralia.com

- Tasmania (Tourism Tasmania corporate website):
      www.tourismtasmania.com.au

- Tasmania (holiday information website):
      www.discovertasmania.com.au

- Victoria (Tourism Victoria corporate website):
      www.tourismvictoria.com.au

- Victoria (holiday information website):
      www.visitvictoria.com.au

- Western Australia:
      www.wa.gov.au/gov/watc

- On Tourism Insights on the web,
      www.prenhall.com/hall_au

see *Towards Integrated Tourism Planning and Development: A Case Study of Australia's National Capital* by Brock Cambourne, and *Marketing Western Australia in a Competitive Minefield* by Ross Gregory and Jane Ali-Knight.

FOR DISCUSSION AND REVIEW

Key concepts

Key concepts considered in this chapter included:
regionalism, experiential tourism, stakeholders, strategic planning, special interest tourism, integrated tourism strategy, regional development strategy, commercially oriented tourism commissions, regional tourist associations, net contribution, marketing, promotion, planning and development functions, sustainable growth, coordinated approach.

Questions for review and discussion

1　How has the role of a state government in tourism changed?
2　What responsibilities do the states and territories have for domestic tourism?
3　What is a coordinated approach to tourism development at the state level?
4　Conduct a SWOT analysis of several states or regions. To what extent are there commonalities and differences among the areas you have studied?
5　What are some common goals of state tourism authorities?

STATE, REGIONAL, AND LOCAL GOVERNMENT APPROACHES TO TOURISM

INDUSTRY AND LABOUR

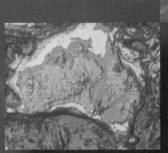

7

Conventional wisdom has it that a major benefit of tourism growth is its capacity to generate jobs. However, while tourism is a growing and major employer, there is evidence that many employment practices and processes associated with the Australian tourism boom may have long-term negative consequences for some workers and even for the industry itself (McMillen & Lafferty 1991, p. 82).

IT IS a widely held belief that service industries are one of the major potential growth areas of post-industrial societies (Bell 1974). A service industry is 'all those firms and employers whose major final output is some intangible or ephemeral commodity or, alternatively, that residual set of productive institutions whose final output is *not* a material good' (Gershuny & Miles 1983, p. 3). Until quite recently, it has been almost universally accepted that, as jobs were lost in manufacturing, mining, agriculture, forestry, and other industries through the adoption of new means of production, the expansion of service industries such as tourism would assist in the maintenance of employment levels.

The growth of service industries is closely related to changes in consumer demands which are, in turn, related to sociocultural and demographic changes in society. Several reasons can be given for changes in consumer demand, including greater affluence, increased leisure time, a high percentage of women participating in the workforce, greater life expectancy, changes in family structure, and the growing concern about the environment and the scarcity of resources.

The processes of globalisation, industrialisation, and urbanisation 'result in loss of self-sufficiency which entails a growing demand for services that individuals and families can no longer provide for themselves. Demand is also created for new types of services' (Gershuny & Rosengren 1973, in Cowell 1984, p. 13). However, the very fact that the tourism product is a composite of several services leads to substantial problems associated with product development and supply (Holloway & Plant 1988). In addition, the very nature of most tourism services also gives them some distinctive characteristics. Services are:

- intangible—they are experiences; although people can keep reminders of the experience such as souvenirs;
- inseparable—production and consumption of tourism services occur simultaneously;
- variable—because tourism is geared towards the selling of experiences they vary substantially from one service experience to another;
- perishable—the 'product' cannot usually be stored from one day to the next; if a room has not been sold tonight, the opportunity for that sale is lost forever; experiences can be stored only in people's heads!

This chapter discusses various aspects of the industrial dimensions of tourism in Australia. The first section examines the various sectors which make up the Australian tourism industry and highlights several of the main issues which currently face these sectors. The second section discusses labour issues in the tourism industry and notes some of the advances that have been made with training, industrial relations, and career pathing in recent years. The final section examines the difficulties inherent in achieving tourism industry coordination and raises the question of whether tourism is best seen as an industry at all, or whether it should be regarded as a collection of industries with common elements of service to visitors, but each with its own set of industrial objectives.

SECTORS OF THE AUSTRALIAN TOURISM INDUSTRY

The scope and rate of tourism growth is dependent on the development of the physical and social components of the tourism industry. Several sectors of the industry can be identified, including the transportation system, accommodation sector, travel services sector, the meetings industry, the food and beverage industry, and the retail industry. The following pages briefly discuss some of the key issues which arise in each sector.

The transportation system

As was illustrated in Chapter 2, a clear relationship exists between transport development and tourism growth. As was demonstrated by the air pilots' dispute in 1989 and the collapse of Ansett Australia in September 2001, few industries are as directly dependent on transport as tourism. In particular, these events highlighted the relationships among the various components of the tourist transport system: the airline system, bus transport, rail transport, and self-drive holidays. The viability of tourist destinations was shown to be related to the ability of the transport infrastructure to enable the tourist to get from A to B and back again. The pilots' dispute also indicated the manner in which consumers were prepared to switch from one form of transport to another because of cost and time factors (Faulkner & Poole 1989). According to the Australian Tourism Industry Association (ATIA), (1990a), an estimated 457 000 people cancelled their holiday plans altogether, and a further

556 000 had to change their holiday plans due to the dispute. One of the long-term effects of the pilots' dispute appears to have been that people discovered alternative tourist destinations, particularly for short-break and weekend getaways, which were previously either ignored or unknown. Over a decade later, with the collapse of Ansett Australia, some destinations that relied on air connections in the major tourism-generating regions and their transport gateways again feared loss of tourism (Tourism Industry Working Group 2001).

The transport sector has undergone massive deregulation, particularly in the airline system. The ending of the two-airline system, which had allowed Australian Airlines and Ansett to operate virtually unopposed on the major trunk routes, led to the launch of new airlines, such as Compass Airlines. However, although consumers initially benefited from such developments, the cost-cutting measures that occurred as a result of increased airline competition, have meant that several airlines have since disappeared from Australia's newly open skies. Compass Airlines and Kiwi Airlines went bankrupt and Eastwest Airlines was absorbed by its parent company, Ansett. The 1993 Annual Report of Ansett Transport Industries noted that 'Eastwest's former market niche as a dedicated leisure and discount operator has been eroded by deregulation' (1993, p. 7). The North American experience of airline deregulation indicates that the potential benefits to the consumer of increased competition operate only in the short term as airlines amalgamate in order to take advantage of economies of scale, and as they concentrate on the more profitable routes. In addition, airline deregulation, combined with the rapid growth of inbound tourism, places further stress on the ability of Australian airports, such as Kingsford-Smith (Sydney), to handle increased passenger flow. Indeed, Leiper (2002) in discussing the collapse of Ansett Australia has argued: 'While the management might have been deficient, a deeper issue is the primary cause of the failure. It is the policy of competitive markets imposed on Australia's airline industry by successive Federal Governments in the 1990s'.

The Australian aviation sector has been through a period of rapid change since the beginning of the 1990s. The Commonwealth government further amended its aviation policy to introduce multiple designation on international airline services, merged Australian Airlines into Qantas, injected $1.3 billion into the merged entity, sold 25% to British Airways, and later floated the remaining 75% when economic conditions improved (and, arguably, at a more profitable level by delaying the development of a common aviation market with New Zealand) (Hall & Kearsley 2001; Leiper 2002). Ansett Airlines had to respond to the new aviation environment (Ansett Transport Industries Limited 1993, p. 6):

> Our strategy during the year was to fly our fleet harder, filling the extra seats created by careful application of our yield management systems, and, at the same time, attack our costs. As a result we put 9% more seats into the market without adding extra aircraft, we increased passenger numbers by 8% and we cut costs per aircraft seat by 7%.

As noted in Chapter 5, changes to Commonwealth government aviation policy also allowed Ansett access to international air traffic with rights to fly to Malaysia, Indonesia, Hong Kong, Japan, Singapore, and South Korea. All of these markets will be lucrative to airlines in terms of holiday traffic growth to Australia over the next decade. In addition, Indonesia (especially Bali) and Malaysia are attractive in terms of outbound holiday travel in the longer term, as the effects of the financial crisis in South-East Asia continue to ease. Just as significantly, the deregulation of the aviation market created a situation attractive to Air New Zealand, which purchased an initial 50% of Ansett in 1997 to enhance its international access and to gain access to the lucrative Australian domestic market. However, as subsequent events proved, the deregulated airline market proved uneconomic to the Air New Zealand-owned Ansett, particularly when budget airline carriers such as Virgin Blue competed with the two major airlines (Leiper 2002).

The collapse of Ansett Australia has meant that, in the short term at least, Australia returned to a duopoly situation with two carriers, Qantas and Virgin Blue, although this situation is quite different from the heavily regulated aviation industry of the 1970s. As a result of the collapse of Ansett, Virgin Blue expected to expand its share of the domestic airline market from 14% to 25% in the 18 months from February 2002. According to Sir Richard Branson, owner of Virgin Blue: 'In time we want to be a true alternative to Qantas on as many domestic routes as possible. We could at some stage set up another airline with smaller planes to fill in the gaps' (Benns 2002).

The reasons for the Ansett collapse are complex. As noted above, Leiper (2002) highlighted the difficulties of two airlines operating in a deregulated market the size of Australia's. According to Hughes (2002) Ansett's 'death spiral' began in 1980 when transport magnate Sir Peter Abeles, 'inexperienced in the airline business but eager to make his mark', purchased Ansett with co-owner News Corporation in a hostile takeover bid. In the 1970s Ansett was Australia's largest and most modern airline. According to Bob Ansett (son of the founder Reg Ansett): 'I think both News Corporation and TNT [Abeles' company] went in for the wrong reasons. They saw Ansett as something of a cash cow to feed their other business activities'. By the mid-1980s Ansett had ceased to dominate the business travel market, and too many different types of aircraft were purchased, leading to a growth in costs. As News Corporation sought a buyer for its share during the 1990s, capital investment was kept to a minimum, staff loyalty waned, and industrial unrest grew. News Corporation eventually negotiated to sell to Singapore Airlines, but Air New Zealand exercised its right to purchase the stake instead. According to Bob Ansett, 'The airline was into one of those dives where it seemed it was incapable of pulling itself out' (Hughes 2002).

The demise of Ansett also severely damaged Air New Zealand which reported a loss of NZ$75.6 million excluding unusual items for the 2001/02 financial year, and a loss of NZ$300.9 million from post-tax unusual items from continuing operations (Asia Travel Tips 2002). The company was able to keep flying only as a result of the support of the New Zealand government. In the aftermath of the Ansett collapse and the events of 11 September, Air New Zealand has changed route capacity on a number of Asian and trans-Tasman routes, and has increased the frequency of Freedom Air (Air New Zealand's budget carrier) on both domestic and trans-Tasman routes.

In contrast to the Ansett and Air New Zealand situation, in February 2002 Qantas announced a profit after tax of $153.5 million for the half-year ended 31 December 2001, a result that was 41.6% lower than the previous corresponding period. The profit before tax was $231.3 million, down 44.5%. Qantas chairman Margaret Jackson said that the six months to 31 December 2001 had been the most tumultuous in the history of aviation, as a result of the terrorist attacks on 11 September and the collapse of Ansett: 'It is impossible to directly compare the performance of this six months to the prior period because of the external factors such as 9/11, Ansett and the Olympics'. Qantas chief executive officer Geoff Dixon said that conditions in the aviation industry had been difficult even before 11 September 2001 (Asia Travel Tips 2002a):

> At the beginning of the period, the Australian and international economies were slowing, the Australian dollar was weak and jet fuel prices were high. Added to this was the heavy discounting in the domestic market which saw two of the four domestic airlines collapse.

Dixon said that after 11 September the demand for international travel fell dramatically—up to 30% on some key routes. According to Dixon, Qantas had taken some major steps to provide a platform for a profitable future when stability was restored to the industry. These steps included (Asia Travel Tips 2002a):

- withdrawal from poorly performing international routes and reduced flying to other destinations;
- increase in capacity in the domestic and regional markets to establish a strong presence throughout Australia;
- seeking a wage pause from its employees and greater productivity in future negotiations;
- purchase and phased introduction of 15 New Generation single-class Boeing 737-800 aircraft for domestic routes (with options on another 60 aircraft);
- deferral of the purchase of three A330 aircraft and the redeployment of some international aircraft to permanent domestic flying;
- launch of Australian Airlines on Asian routes where Qantas cannot be competitive;
- significant product improvements, including a $50 million upgrade of Qantas Club lounges as well as new interiors (including in-seat videos in all classes) in the 747-400 fleet; and
- raising of $663 million in equity to provide stability to the balance sheet and ensure that gearing levels remain one of the lowest in the industry.

The collapse of the 66-year-old Ansett airline was undoubtedly bad news for the Victorian economy, because the airline had its headquarters in Victoria, employed most of its 2800 staff in that state, and sourced most of its external business supplies and services from Victorian companies. Peter Brain, a director of the Melbourne-based National Institute of Economic and Industry Research, was reported in *The Age* in February 2002 as saying that the Ansett collapse would cost Victoria around $900 million. He said that the loss of expenditure in airline travel and the flow-on effects to associated industries would strip 0.4% off state income. However, the Victorian Treasurer, John Brumby, believed that Ansett's demise 'would not necessarily affect the Victorian economy unduly' (Webb 2002). Brumby said that tourism in Victoria remained strong, and that he believed much of the recent increase in business for Qantas and Virgin was being driven by passenger growth out of Melbourne. 'The major challenge going forward is to ensure sound domestic linkages [in Victoria] for the Star Alliance passengers . . . This is because something like 50 per cent of all passengers through Tullamarine airport fly as part of the Star Alliance' (Webb 2002).

The Ansett collapse led many people in the tourism industry to look back at the 1989 air pilots' dispute, which had also focused a great deal of attention on the transport component of tourism. The strike-related disruption to domestic airline services between August and December 1989 led to a substantial shift in the travel behaviours of tourists. For example, the decline in air travel caused a corresponding increase in private vehicle trips (Bureau of Tourism Research (BTR) 1991b). Private vehicle use is by far the main mode of transport for domestic tourists. The proportion of tourists using vehicles falls as the destination becomes further away from the generating region and, not unexpectedly, the use of planes as the main mode of transport is much higher for interstate travel, as compared with intrastate travel. The travel patterns of domestic tourists have been strongly influenced by the effects of transport deregulation. For example, according to Chu Te (1993), as a consequence of airline deregulation:

- long-distance, interstate destinations have become more attractive to Australian travellers;
- to-destination movements tend to be by aircraft and private vehicles, whereas trains and buses primarily serve the within-destination market; and
- there is a shift to the use of planes among interstate holiday travellers.

After plane travel, the next most significant form of commercial transport used by tourists is coach and bus travel. There has been a major increase in the level of competition within the long-distance coach industry in Australia (Bureau of Transport Economics 1985; Federal Bureau of Transport Economics 1987). Inter-city bus services represent the cheapest form of transport in Australia and, as well as growth in inter-city services, there is also increased competition in the touring and tour charter area (King 1988). As in the aviation industry, long-distance bus services have been deregulated, which has led to low fares and fierce competition among bus companies, and among different modes of transport, although concerns have sometimes been expressed regarding the safety of bus services in a deregulated environment.

Transport safety issues are important in the overall perception of a tourist destination. Motor vehicle crashes are the leading cause of injury and death for international tourists, and 'less visible but equally important are the tourist injuries, property damage and other hidden costs' (Wilks et al. 1999, p. 653). As Wilks et al. (1999, p. 647) observed:

> Australia has some specific issues that should be brought to the attention of international drivers. Most important are driving on the left-hand side of the road; the legal requirements to wear a seat belt; a lower legal blood alcohol limit than in many countries overseas; an awareness of the size of Australia and the distances involved when planning each day of travel; unique animal hazards; and finally, unusual road and environmental conditions.

Train services for interstate tourism have experienced something of a revival in recent years. Services such as the Indian–Pacific (between Perth and Sydney), and the Ghan (between Adelaide and Alice Springs) are among the great train journeys in the world. Furthermore, the proposed completion of the train line between Alice Springs and Darwin is expected to have substantial benefits for tourism. In Europe, train travel is regarded as an environmentally friendly form of tourist travel. However, Australia does not have as extensive a network of rail links as Europe, and most train travel for tourists is between the capital cities of each state. In recent years, proposals for a high-speed train link between Melbourne, Canberra, and Sydney, and possibly on to Brisbane and Adelaide, has been given a high profile. Although such a link would dramatically cut the travel time between the urban centres of south-east Australia, its financial viability is greatly dependent on the costs of alternative travel modes (Hensher 1989). Given the deregulated aviation market and the resultant reduction in airfares on major air routes, the construction of a fast train link between Melbourne and Sydney would not appear to be likely in the near future, although improved train services are likely to become available on the main rail routes.

The accommodation sector

In response to the expanding tourist trade, the number, scale and type of establishments servicing the tourist industry has grown rapidly (Saville 1994). In particular, there has been a noticeable increase in the luxury and hotel resort sector of the market over the past decade which, in turn, has been accompanied by the establishment of more specialised businesses, such as health resorts and boutique hotels, which also cater for the upper end of the market (James 1988). Five-star or international standard accommodation in Australia accounts for only approximately 5% of total accommodation, although it does provide approximately 20% of all guest rooms and 40% of total takings (Barge 1988). The rapid growth of tourism in the 1980s was so substantial that, according to Barge (1988), the number of guest rooms available between 1983 and 1988 rose by 63%, and the number of establishments by 42%.

As of 1995, the stock of hotels, motels, and guesthouses consisted of close to 5000 establishments and 167 000 rooms. Although 4-star and 5-star properties made up only 9% of the establishments, they made up 49% of the employment and 54% of the room takings (Industries Commission 1995). According to the ATIA and ATC (1994) by far the greatest impact on employment and income came from the hotel/motel component of the accommodation sector, which accounted for just over 100 000 jobs. For the year to September 1994, hotels, motels, and guesthouses had takings of $2847 million from 34 million room nights sold at an average room rate of $83.80 (TFC). By the end of 1997 the room supply in hotels, motels, and guesthouses had grown to 180 000 rooms with the fastest growth occurring in Queensland, New South Wales, and Victoria.

Since the early 1980s Australia has experienced three major periods of accommodation building commencements. In the first period (1984–87), economic conditions were buoyant and overseas visitor arrivals, especially from Japan, were rising rapidly. In this period the value of accommodation building commencements was just over $700 million per annum (1994 dollars). In the second period (1987–90), the major factors which influenced investment were high rates of growth in inbound tourism, increasing occupancy and room rates, the ready availability of finance, and the expectation of substantial capital gains. In this period the value of accommodation building commencements was just over $1400 million per annum (1994 dollars). However, the transfer of funds to the property market following the stock market crash of October 1987, meant that many hotels were developed in the expectation of capital gains rather than on the basis of sustainable cash flows from the tourist trade. Consequently, many properties failed as asset prices fell and interest rates rose. The third period (1990 on), has been characterised by large losses as a consequence of over-supply, lower rates of growth in international arrivals, reduced levels of Japanese investment, and the sale of existing properties substantially below replacement value—including several high-profile resort properties on the Queensland coast—and often below that of the initial cost of construction. In the period from 1990 to 1995 the value of accommodation building commencements was approximately $400 million per annum (1994 dollars) (Industries Commission 1995). As McVey and King observed, 'As so often happens, rapid expansion in capacity is usually followed by a lacklustre performance in operation' (1989, p. 37). Although the conditions for accommodation investment appeared to be improving in 1996 and 1997, it was feared that the impact of the Asian financial crisis on inbound tourism might well mean a continuation of the trends of the early 1990s throughout the remainder of the decade. The overall rate of growth is determined by the state of the economy, investor confidence, and changes in inbound and domestic tourism. For example, Sydney's hosting of the 2000 Summer Olympics meant a substantial increase in the accommodation stock for the Sydney region as well as for some of the other major tourist centres around the country. Of the 131 tourist accommodation development projects (worth $2 million or more) under way during 1999, just over half of these were in New South Wales with Sydney accounting for more than one-fifth of the total rooms. Developments were mainly upper market, with more than 80% of the rooms being 4- or 5-star grade (DITR 2002e). The value of construction work in hotels and similar establishments for 1995/96 to 2000/01 is shown in Table 7.1, and the level of investment is illustrated in Table 7.2. In the September 2001 quarter, the value of work done was down 39.0% on the September 2000 quarter, to $104.7 million (DITR 2002d, p. 2).

Australian hotels tend to be more reliant on domestic travellers than their overseas counterparts (see Table 7.3 for a breakdown of the domestic accommodation market in hotels and motels). Business travellers have long been a major market segment in Australian hotels, but the rapid growth in inbound tourism in the late 1980s, associated in part with the Australian bicentennial, has meant that tour groups, particularly from Japan, Taiwan, and Korea, are rapidly growing in importance, particularly in tourist regions in Queensland and New South Wales. The room-occupancy rates for accommodation establishments vary considerably, depending on location, seasonality, and accessibility. In addition, the operating profits for hotels and motels vary according to the standard and mix of accommodation, the composition of expenses, and food and beverage sales. However, in both the 2–3-star and 4–5-star sectors, payroll and related expenses constitute the largest single item of expense.

TABLE 7.1 New investment in hotels and motels in Australia 1995–2001

Year	$million
1995/96	638
1996/97	1000
1997/98	1052
1998/99	1233
1999/2000	1213
2000/01	483

Note: includes developments valued at more than $2 million which were under construction, approved, or completed during the calendar year

Source: Department of Industry, Tourism and Resources (DITR) (2001) Tourism accommodation development survey, Canberra. Reprinted with the permission of the Department of Industry, Tourism and Resources.

TABLE 7.2 New investment in hotels, motels and guest houses in Australia by number of rooms 1999–2000

Year	1-star	2-star	3-star	4-star	5-star	Ungraded	Total
1999	0	254	1797	7610	3234	567	13 462
2000	0	151	1878	5492	2731	126	10 378

Note: includes developments valued at more than $2 million which were under construction, approved, or completed during the calendar year

Source: Department of Industry, Tourism and Resources (DITR) (2001) Tourism accommodation development survey, Canberra. Reprinted with the permission of the Department of Industry, Tourism and Resources.

TABLE 7.3 Domestic visitor nights in hotels, motels and guest houses 1998–2010 (millions)

Year	Business	Holiday	VFR	Other	Total
1998	23.3	38.5	7.0	2.4	71.2
1999	24.3	40.3	6.2	2.8	73.5
2000	25.6	40.3	6.1	2.8	74.9
2001	26.6	40.2	6.1	2.8	75.7
2002	27.9	40.3	6.1	2.8	77.2
2003	29.1	40.6	6.2	2.8	78.7
2004	30.4	41.0	6.3	2.8	80.5
2005	31.7	41.7	6.3	2.8	82.6
2006	33.0	42.4	6.4	2.8	84.7
2007	34.4	43.2	6.5	2.8	86.9
2008	35.8	43.9	6.6	2.8	89.1
2009	37.2	44.7	6.7	2.8	91.4
2010	38.7	45.5	6.8	2.8	93.8
Average annual growth (%)	4.3	1.1	0.9	0.1	2.2

Note: numbers from 2000 onwards are forecasts

Source: Department of Industry, Tourism and Resources (DITR) (2000) *Industry science resources: sport and tourism 2000. Positive long-term outlook for domestic tourism: 1999–2010*, Canberra. Reprinted with the permission of the Department of Industry, Tourism and Resources.

In 2000/01 the number of room nights occupied in hotels, motels, guest houses, and serviced apartments increased by 0.4% to 41.1 million, and takings per room night occupied were $120.00, up 13.7% on 1999/2000. The average room occupancy rate was 57.5% (59.0% in 1999/2000). In the September 2001 quarter, room nights occupied were up 1.6% on the September 2000 quarter. Average room occupancy rate increased from 58.4% to 58.7% (DITR 2002e, p. 2). Table 7.4 records the number of guest rooms and occupancy rates for 1999.

Several problems emerged from the rapid development of hotel and resorts in Australia in the 1980s and early 1990s. First, there have been staffing pressures,

TABLE 7.4 Number of guest rooms and occupancy rates for Australian states and territories, 1999

	Licensed	Motels/ guest houses	Serviced apartments	Total guest rooms	Market share %	Average annual occupancy %
New South Wales	21 753	33 639	5 929	61 321	32	58.4
Victoria	10 903	16 282	4 132	31 317	16	56.8
Queensland	20 682	18 573	12 640	51 895	27	58.1
South Australia	4 090	5 166	1 207	10 463	6	55.1
Western Australia	9 429	5 752	3 414	18 595	10	54.3
Tasmania	2 929	1 752	865	5 546	3	52.2
Northern Territory	1 949	3 124	1 153	6 226	3	58.9
Australian Capital Territory	1 681	1 731	1 304	4 716	2	60.8
Total	**73 416**	**86 019**	**30 644**	**190 079**	**100**	**57.2**

Note: includes establishments with 15 or more rooms or units

Source: Australian Bureau of Statistics, Survey of Tourist Accommodation, 1999, in Bureau of Tourism Research (2000), *Tourism Trends in New South Wales: New South Wales State Profile: Year End December 1999*, produced for Tourism New South Wales, TNSW, Sydney, p. 44.

particularly in the key skilled occupations such as chefs and front of house (Department of Employment, Education and Training 1988; KPMG Peat Marwick Management Consultants 1991). Second, there have been pressures on the environment through the establishment of resorts in new tourism destinations. Third, there has been a relative lack of development of hotel reservation systems and associated automated systems as compared with the aviation sector (McVey & King 1989). In addition, there has been a relative failure to take up modern technology in comparison with overseas counterparts. For example, there has been a relative lack of use of hotel reservation systems as part of a marketing database, and of the Internet as a reservation and marketing tool (Ng & Hall 1997).

There is also uncertainty about the classification of accommodation in Australia. This is of great practical importance for the tourism industry. Accommodation can be segmented into a range of types—downtown commercial and luxury hotels, resort hotels, budget hotels, motels, and caravans and camping. Classification systems (that is, star ratings) tend to vary from state to state. However, there is no standard ratings system for accommodation in Australia. This means that consumer expectancies, particularly those of overseas visitors, might not be met, and tourist dissatisfaction can result.

Finally, it should be noted that the accommodation sector is changing in response to consumer demands. 'There will be a greater range of accommodation available to the tourist, ranging from back-packer hostels through to 5-star resorts' (Saville 1994, p.30). New accommodation products are being developed to take advantage of the increasingly segmented travel and leisure market (see Chapter 12). Examples of new Australian lodging products include budget destination resorts, guest houses (including bed and breakfasts), backpacker lodges, farmstays, nature lodges and self-catering cabins and apartments (van der Lee 1990; Saville 1994). Backpacking, for example, has become an important sector of Australia's tourism industry with an average length of stay of almost three times that for all visitors. Because of their long period of stay, backpackers are also high-yield visitors, despite relatively low average daily expenditures. According to the BTR, backpackers' average expenditure was $3886 in 1995 (compared with $1936 per person for all visitors in 1995) (ONT 1997i). As a result of these social and economic changes, international-style 4-star and 5-star hotels and resorts will possibly decline in relative importance as the travelling population changes, and as consumers increasingly seek better value in the tourist product and more authentic unique travel experiences.

The travel services sector

The travel services sector covers a wide range of operations, the most common of which are travel agents, tourist bureaux, and travel information services. Travel agents have undergone a major shift in organisation in recent years. The use of computer technology and the increased complexity of the tourist industry has led to demands for qualified staff and training. However, the Australian travel services sector has often been relatively slow to adopt new technology. For example, in the late 1980s, only 28% of Australian travel agents were automated, compared with more than 80% in the United States (McVey & King 1989). The adoption of communications technology and its utilisation for marketing activities are vital for travel agency survival when tourists are increasingly booking travel, accommodation, and activities on the Internet (Oppermann 1999).

Travel agents are increasingly likely to be part of larger operations, rather than individual operations. The reason for this shift is the use of horizontal and vertical integration of operations to ensure greater market share and return on investment. Indeed, the processes which are operating in the travel agent sector are a reflection of the broader trends towards concentration of capital throughout the tourism industry.

Travel agencies act as brokers between tourist operations (such as airlines, cruise-lines, hotels and tour companies) and consumers. Travel agents are one of the main avenues by which tourist products are sold. Travel agents are thus intermediaries in the marketplace who, according to Murphy, 'must successfully match a tourist image and tourist product if the travel experience is to have any chance of success' (1985, p. 16). Travel agents therefore have a vital role in ensuring the success of destinations, at both a regional and an operational level.

Murphy (1985) identified four phases in the process of matching tourist image with tourist product by travel agents. The first is the development of a tourist product and the image of a destination by tour wholesalers. The second is the selling of destinations and product by travel agents and consultants who advise their clients on the choice of appropriate tour packages. The third is the arrangement of accommodation and supplementary services to meet the consumer's tastes and budget, and the fourth is the satisfaction of the consumer. This last point is most important as it enables the process to begin again through reinforcing the viability of the product and the accuracy of the tourist image. As Murphy (1985, p. 16) noted:

> The final objective is to have a satisfied customer, who is likely to make a return trip and act as a goodwill ambassador, for this is the most effective way of nurturing the industry and fulfilling the goals of tourism.

Tourist bureaux are another important intermediary between the tourist product and the consumer. Convention and visitors' bureaux are essentially private, non-profit, cooperative organisations whose purpose is to promote and market their cities and regions as a tourist destination or venue for conferences and conventions. The organisation of a convention and visitors' bureau represents a partnership among the tourist industry, the members of a bureau, and the various levels of government who have joined together to promote the tourist destination (Barnes 1988). One of the key responsibilities of a bureau is to sell the infrastructure and tourist attractions of a region or city as a single entity. Although almost all industry participants in a bureau possess their own marketing programs, bureaux offer the capacity for destinations to develop a particular image as a 'cohesive and complete community product' (Barnes 1988, p. 246) which helps differentiate the destination in a highly competitive tourism market.

The MICE industry: meetings, incentives, conference and exhibition tourism

Meetings, conferences, conventions and exhibitions are short-term events which are of great economic significance to tourism (Law 1987; Pearson & McKanna 1988; Hiller 1995; Wootton & Stevens 1995). The term 'meetings' covers all off-site gatherings (including conventions, congresses, conferences, seminars, workshops and symposiums) which bring people together for the purpose of sharing information. Major markets include the corporate and the association markets (Astroff & Abbey 1995). The term 'incentive travel' is a motivational tool used by companies to encourage employees to increase their performance by rewarding increased productivity or the attainment of corporate goals. Although Australia is a relatively small player in incentive travel in global terms, the market is growing. For example, the BTR estimated that, in 1995, 78 000 visitors to Australia arrived on a sales-incentive trip, nearly 40% more than in 1994 (ONT 1997b). The term 'exhibitions' (also described as 'expositions') is used to describe events which are designed to bring together suppliers of products, industrial equipment, and services in an environment where they can demonstrate and promote their products and services (Montgomery & Strick 1995). Several cities, such as Brisbane, Melbourne and Sydney, have government-funded purpose-built exhibition centres. The majority of exhibitions or trade shows held in Australia are held in Victoria, New South Wales and Queensland, with an estimated expenditure of $825 million, based on the assumptions that the 'average visitor spend' was $20 and the 'average exhibitor outlay' was $10 000 (ONT 1997b).

Meetings and conventions offer a great deal of stability to the tourism industry because they are an integral part of business practice (Barnes 1988). Furthermore, meetings and conventions are typically booked well in advance, and larger meetings and exhibitions often have a 5–10-year lead time for their development, planning, and marketing. Therefore, 'they are far less vulnerable to short-term economic changes and . . . provide a buffer against short-term violent cyclical swings in . . . travel business' (Barnes 1988, p. 248). The growing involvement of Australia with other Pacific Rim economies has seen the rapid development of trade conferences, business conventions and exhibition tourism as one of main tourism growth areas. According to the International Congress and Convention Association (ICCA), Australia hosted nearly 6% of the world's association meetings in 1995, with Europe hosting 54%, Asia 20%, North America 13%, South and Central America 7%, and Africa 3%. According to the ICCA in 1995 Melbourne was ranked nineteenth in a comparison of the number of MICE events on a city-by-city basis (with 23 events) and Sydney was ranked twenty-seventh (with 17 events) (ONT 1997b). Target markets of the Sydney Convention and Exhibition Centre at Darling Harbour include: (i) Australian national associations which regularly hold national events or which are bidding for international or regional events; (ii) organising bodies of one-off special events such as religious or trade union gatherings; and (iii) one-off sporting or entertainment events (Westcott 1988).

The meetings market is approximately 80% domestic and 20% international. BTR figures for 1994–95 indicated that the domestic conference and seminar market accounted for more than 3% of all domestic travel, worth an estimated $880 million in expenditure (ONT 1997b). According to the Australian Bureau of Statistics, in 1995 nearly 90 000 international visitors to Australia stated that their main purpose for visiting was attending an international convention or conference—representing an increase of 38% on the previous year's figures. By comparison, the BTR's International Visitors Survey (IVS) estimated that, irrespective of their stated reason for visiting Australia, 155 000 visitors (nearly 5% of all visitors during 1995) attended a convention or similar function while in Australia (ONT 1997b).

A joint report of the Association of Australian Convention Bureaux and the Commonwealth Department of Tourism has indicated that meetings and conventions are worth around $2 billion a year for Australia. The meetings industry accounts for 7% of total overseas and domestic visits and 15% of all hotel room nights. In 1993, more than 105 000 major meetings were held in Australia, involving 4 340 000

INDUSTRY AND LABOUR

delegates and more $540 million in hotel income. In that same year, Australia hosted 201 international conventions and 515 national conventions, attracting more than 80 000 overseas delegates (Lee 1994). Expenditure in Australia in 1995 by visitors who identified attending a conference or trade fair as the main reason for travel was approximately $103 million. The expenditure of all those who attended such an event—irrespective of their reason for visiting Australia—or who accompanied a person who did attend, was estimated at around $302 million (ONT 1997b).

Despite the longstanding worldwide acceptance of trade fairs and exhibitions as a means of doing business, Australia and New Zealand have generally lagged behind in using them as a marketing and promotion tool. As Tayt (1988) observed, to attend overseas trade shows has generally been regarded as indicative of high status within industry, whereas domestic exhibitions have been less well perceived. Nevertheless, the substantial income to be generated from business travel, and from the MICE sector in particular, has led to a substantial growth in national and local awareness of, and competition in, this high-value market in both Australia and New Zealand (Courtney 1995; Heeringa 1996; ONT 1997b). A report by the BTR (1998) concluded that the main hindrance to growth of the MICE sector is the lack of data and research to encourage informed decision-making, particularly for investment purposes, whereas locations without dedicated MICE facilities believe that business could be increased if larger or more suitable facilities were available. However, this last point is somewhat problematic, because it is debatable whether the revenue generated from the additional visitors to these locations would exceed the costs of building the additional capacity, or provide the region with a fair rate of return on its investment. Nevertheless, state governments remain enthusiastic about supporting conference and exhibition centres because of the overall economic impact of delegates on their states.

Casinos

The granting of casino licenses in Australia is a state government responsibility. Since the opening of the first legalised casino in Australia in 1973 in Hobart, casino development has traditionally been utilised by Australian state governments to increase tax revenue. Australian casinos pay 4–20% of their revenues to state governments, plus federal company tax, and, in some cases, community benefits levies and employees' licence fees (McHugh 1995). Casinos are essentially the creatures of recession, and increased fiscal demands on government have overcome moral objections to casinos from various sections of the community, particularly the churches (Walkley 1993; Hall & Hamon 1996). Undoubtedly, gambling is a major economic activity in Australia. In 1999-2000, total real gambling expenditure in Australia was $13.34 billion, with casino gambling accounting for 17.7% of gambling expenditure. Outside casinos, the most significant form of gambling in terms of expenditure was gaming machines, which accounted for 57.4% of gambling expenditure. Historically, gaming machines have been a significant part of the Gold Coast tourism product, although their relative importance has declined with the development of the Gold Coast and Brisbane casinos (Tasmanian Gaming Commission 2001).

Casino development in Australia has gone through three stages, each related to recessionary economic conditions (Chenoweth 1991; F. Smith 1993). The first wave of casinos, built in the early 1970s at the time of the oil crisis were small European-style casinos developed in the smaller cities of Hobart, Launceston, Darwin and Alice Springs. These casinos were regarded as 'one-off' developments to stimulate tourism.

The 1982 recession led to the second wave of casino development, with casino licences being granted in Townsville, the Gold Coast, Adelaide and Perth. The last three were American-style high-turnover casinos. The Townsville and Gold Coast casinos were developed in already established tourist destinations. The Perth and Adelaide casinos were the first large casinos in the world to be built in large population centres and aimed at the local market, with the tourist market being a secondary consideration (Chenoweth 1991). Perth's Burswood Casino was used to redevelop an old industrial waste dump, and the Adelaide Casino was located in an old railway station. Neither was used as a central component of a larger urban redevelopment or re-imaging strategy (see Chapter 12), although both the Western Australian and South Australian state governments used tourism as a justification for their development. As McMillan (in Chenoweth 1993, p. 16) observed in discussing Australian casino developments:

> They're quite obviously there for the locals, despite the rhetoric about doing it for the tourists. That notion of casinos being a honeypot and tourists flocking to them is a myth. All the specifications are for stable, local populations. Tourists are just the icing on the cake.

The third wave of casinos was a government response to the recession of the late 1980s and early 1990s. The latest round of casino developments in Brisbane, Canberra, Melbourne and Sydney means that every state capital has a casino. In addition to traditional licensing factors—such as governments increasing their tax revenues and casinos attracting tourists—casino development has more recently become an integral component of urban redevelopment and reimaging strategies. For example, the Canberra Casino, which opened in 1994, was specifically designed to help revitalise the main downtown area, and funds from the casino licence were earmarked for arts and cultural developments in the inner city area. The Brisbane Casino was used to provide a financial basis for the restoration of the former Treasury building in which the casino is located. The Brisbane Casino development was utilised by the Queensland state government as a component of waterfront redevelopment strategies which included the development of a major cultural, convention and leisure complex on the site of the 1988 Expo. The two largest developments of this third wave of casinos were located in Melbourne (Victoria) and Sydney (New South Wales). Because these cities are, by far, the two largest in Australia, their casino licences were the most keenly contested and contentious, with considerable community, legal, and political debate surrounding the bidding and the planning processes (Hall & Hamon 1996). However, in both cities, the two casinos have now become central components of tourism promotion and undoubtedly have had a major impact on the regional economies.

The food and beverage industry

Food and beverage is an integral part of the tourist experience. Tourism provides an enormous economic contribution to the food and beverage industry. The concentration of tourists at a particular destination directly affects the location of restaurants and subsequent investment in the area.

Apart from the economic considerations involved, one of the most pertinent issues in food and beverage is service. Tourism is a people-oriented industry. Nevertheless, one of the great problems in Australia is persuading employees to be service-oriented. As Frost observed, there is a 'delusion that Australian egalitarianism is incompatible with the provision of service . . . Service is not a matter of servility, neither is it necessarily dependant wholly on price, it is a combination of attitude, common sense and craft skill' (1988, p. 209).

The issue of service is related to the development of social infrastructure. It is not sufficient for the development of a tourism industry to deal in numbers of staff alone. The skill level of staff is also a critical factor and quality service can exist only if there is investment in training. Frost (1988) estimated that in the United States approximately 50% of the workforce had their first job experience in the catering industry, and predicted that this percentage will be passed in Australia. Therefore, in the long term, the development of the food and beverage sector of the tourism industry might well be dependent on skill and training levels, a point discussed further below.

The retail industry

Shopping is recognised as a major tourism activity, and tourism makes a substantial economic contribution to the retail industry (Bussey 1987; Gratton & Taylor 1987; Anderson & Littrell 1996; Kincade & Woodard 2001). Retail facilities are therefore a key component in attracting tourists to particular destinations. Nevertheless, Australia lacks an international image as a tourism shopping destination, and the significance of international tourism to retail industries is 'generally poorly understood by those industries and the community in general' (DASETT 1988b, p. 5). However, cities such as Melbourne and Sydney are increasingly focusing on shopping and entertainment as major drawcards in the domestic market and, increasingly, in the international market, particularly New Zealand. As Clement commented, the rapidity with which tourists spend money over a given span of time is important. 'It tends to reflect not only net income from tourism, but also the efficiency of the travel plant— that is, the success of a country in getting tourists to spend a fair amount of money in relation to their length of stay' (1967, p. 79).

For many people, shopping is a major form of leisure, if not the dominant form of leisure. Increasingly, the relationship between shopping and leisure has carried over into the tourism domain as more people travel and as per capita disposable income rises. The majority of surveys of tourist behaviour highlight the fact that tourists spend much time and money on shopping. For example, two studies by DASETT (1988b, 1990) reported that shopping accounts for approximately one-fifth of overseas visitor expenditure, with the Japanese and New Zealand markets having some of the highest rates of expenditure on shopping (Haigh 1994). It should also be noted that some destinations, such as Hong Kong and Singapore, deliberately position themselves for tourist shopping opportunities (Hall 1997b). However, recognition of the relationship between shopping and tourism is not new. It has long been noted that different types of shopping districts arise because of obvious differences in place utility, desirability of extensive selection, and symbolic value of goods offered (Stansfield & Rickert 1970). Stansfield and Rickert (1970, pp. 219, 220) described the concept of a functionally specialised recreational business district (RBD) and its implications for town and tourism planning:

> The inclination of shoppers to walk distances greater than a few hundred feet is significantly different in the RBD than in normal shopping centers . . . The RBD is a social phenomenon as well as an economic one. It provides a means of entertaining as a unit family members who may not otherwise participate jointly in various forms of amusement or shop with each other in an atmosphere of relaxation . . . The RBD even experiences a different daily rhythm of pedestrian traffic than do other districts, again, in keeping with its emphasis on leisure time shopping.

The Southbank development in Melbourne is the first stage of a comprehensive waterfront development program that will see much of Melbourne's former docklands turned into a mix of tourism–leisure–retail development.

More recently, Getz (1993a, 1993b) has described the concept of a tourism business district (TBD) to highlight 'the multiplicity of visitor-oriented urban functions that makes the term "recreational" less appropriate than "tourism" in this context' (1993b, p. 586). (See Chapter 13 for a further discussion of urban tourism.)

As in the food and beverage sector, the success of tourism development is dependent not only upon the provision of plant but also on the manner in which tourist facilities are operated. For example, the Committee of Inquiry into Tourism Shopping in Australia reported that five of every ten overseas visitors were dissatisfied with the times that Australian shops were open (DASETT 1988b, p. 19). Therefore, the issue of trading hours, which limits the efficient use of tourism plant, is central to investment strategies in the tourism industry. The following pages examine the broader issues of social infrastructure in greater detail and the concerns which surround industrial restructuring, penalty rates, training, and education.

THE TOURISM WORKFORCE

The development of a skilled workforce capable of sustaining high standards of service is critical to a labour-intensive industry such as tourism. Tourism is a 'people' industry and friendly, efficient service is a major ingredient in ensuring satisfied customers and continued growth. The challenge facing governments and the industry is to develop adequate education and training systems to meet the skill needs of the industry and to develop attractive career opportunities for existing and potential employees. Tourism's potential to generate employment accentuates the magnitude of this challenge. . . . The future development of the industry is dependent on drawing on the breadth of skills already in the labour market and developing the skills of potential employees. A commitment by governments, employers and unions to facilitate equal opportunities for people to train for industry positions and participate in the work of the industry on an equitable basis will optimise the economic and social benefits of tourism.

Source: Department of Tourism (Commonwealth) (DOT) (1992) *Tourism: Australia's passport to growth a national tourism strategy*, pp. 47–48. Reprinted with the permission of the Department of Industy, Tourism & Resources.

INDUSTRY AND LABOUR

Labour-related issues pose one of the major challenges to the continuing growth of the Australian tourism industry (KPMG Peat Marwick Management Consultants 1991; Industries Commission 1995; DITR 2002e). Service industries such as tourism 'require a sophisticated, well educated work force and a stable and attractive environment' (Blunn 1988b, p. 12). Fourteen years later, the DITR (2002e, p. 4) reported that:

> . . . the development of a skilled workforce capable of sustaining high levels of service is critical to a labour intensive sector such as tourism. Tourism is a people sector, and friendly, efficient, professional service is a major ingredient in ensuring satisfied customers and continued growth.

In 1997/98 there were an estimated 513 000 people in tourism-generated employment, or 6.0% of total employment in Australia, which equates to 389 000 full-time jobs. The largest number of persons in tourism-generated employment was in retail trade, accounting for 27% of total tourism-generated employment. In 1997/98, 37% of persons employed in tourism were part time, with a relatively even split between males and females (DITR 2002e, p. 2). Work undertaken for the Tourism Satellite Account and for the Australian Bureau of Statistics also revealed that (DITR 2002e, p. 2):

- 71.9% of travel agency and tour operator services' employees are female;
- 39.2% of employees in the accommodation industry work part time, with 58% of all employees being female; and
- 68.9% of employees in cafés and restaurants are part time, with 55.4% of all employees being female.

As at November 2000 (DITR 2002e, p. 2):

- there were 1.3 million people employed in retail trade, 478 000 in accommodation, cafés, and restaurants, and 426 000 in transport and storage;
- 52% of those employed in the retail trade sector were female, of which 60% worked part time;
- 54% of those employed in the accommodation, café, and restaurant sector were female, of whom 57% worked part time;
- 24% of those employed in the transport and storage sector were female, of whom 29% worked part time;
- over the three sectors, 39% of employees worked part time;
- 55% of employees in all three sectors were aged between 15 and 34 years; and
- 30% of employees in the accommodation, café, and restaurant sector were born outside Australia.

By contrast, as at November 2000 just over 26% of the total number of employees in Australia were part time, and almost 44% of employees were female.

The Industries Assistance Commission (IAC) (identified labour issues as one the key items discussed in the Inquiry into Travel and Tourism. Specifically, the commission examined skill shortages, education and training, penalty rates, labour disputes, and the potential for productivity gains through award restructuring. Unfortunately, the picture that the commission painted of tourism did not augur well for the industry (IAC 1989, p. 140):

> Industry statistics, submissions and discussions with participants paint the following picture of hospitality employment [in Australia]. It is relatively poorly paid, lowly unionised and highly mobile. Few staff have formal qualifications. Many work part time, many are young and a large proportion is female. There is significant casual employment. Participants

said career prospects are generally poor, industry awards are frequently breached, and cash payments to employees are prevalent. There are complaints of inflexible working arrangements. However, occupations that are in short supply, in particular skilled and executive chefs, were said to be highly paid.

Similarly, Boland (1988) argued that the development of trained personnel and proper remuneration for employees, together with a definite career structure, were critical to the future of the tourism industry in Australia. However, the overall picture had changed little by the mid-1990s when the Industries Commission (IC), followed on from the work of its predecessor, the IAC, and examined the issue of training in the Australian tourism industry. According to the IC (1995, p. 21), the characteristics of the tourism workforce were as follows:
- on average, young;
- characterised by female, part-time employment;
- more casual and part-time employees than other industries, but the majority of hours nevertheless worked by full-time employees;
- lowly unionised;
- relatively low-skilled work;
- unsociable hours of work;
- relatively low pay;
- mobile workforce with high turnover rates; and
- a workforce with low levels of formal educational qualifications.

The more recent DITR (2002e, p. 4) report on the tourism workforce paints a similar picture noting that state tourism agencies and education departments report that the tourism workforce:
- is on average a young workforce with relatively low levels of formal qualifications;
- is characterised by female, part-time, and casual employment;
- has a high proportion of low-skilled jobs;
- has a relatively high proportion of hours worked outside normal business hours;
- is mobile with high levels of staff turnover;
- employs many young people such as students; and
- is affected by structural and cyclical influences on employment and training demand.

Given the substantial growth of tourism in Australia, the industry is clearly faced with a difficult task in finding and providing the skilled labour to fill the diverse jobs which are now available. One way in which the shortage of labour has been met is by immigration and work permits. In the 1980s, net immigration contributed 30–40% of skilled chefs and cooks and 20–25% of catering managers in hotels and clubs (IAC 1989). Immigration and short-term visas remain important today. Difficulties in securing the services of teachers of tourism and hospitality has also led many Australian educational institutions to recruit staff from overseas (DSRT 1985), and relatively poor salary levels by international standards still pose a challenge in attracting and retaining qualified staff.

Key features of the tourism and hospitality labour market are its seasonality, high level of casual and part-time labour, high level of voluntary labour, high labour turnover, and segmentation (KPMG Peat Marwick Management Consultants 1991; Timo 1994; DITR 2002e; Hall & Page 2002a). For example, 'in the restaurant sector, the number of permanent employees resigning voluntarily between June 1989 and June 1990 represented 78% of permanent employment at June 1989, while in the accommodation sector the proportion resigning voluntarily was

46%' (KPMG Peat Marwick Management Consultants 1991, p. 5). Similarly, the Victorian Department of Labour (1986, in Timo 1994) noted that 57% of kitchen hands, 54% of waiting staff, 50% of chefs/cooks, 48% of bar staff, 30% of managers/supervisors, and 29% of housekeepers/room attendants had been employed in their current job for less than a year.

Different employment strategies are adopted by management, depending on the size of the establishment and demand factors. For example, small employers tend to utilise semi-skilled casual workers who can respond to seasonal variations in employment demand, whereas larger establishments have a 'small core of permanent workers and a large, semi-skilled workforce employed increasingly on a part-time or casual basis, including housekeeping, waiting and kitchen staff' (Timo 1994, p.33).

Demand for tourism and hospitality services structures the work conditions of employees. This demand is invariably irregular and unpredictable. The nature of tourism is that service is a component of the total product produced. Thus the technical and social aspects of production and consumption operate in tandem. The result is that the demand for hospitality services often results in employees being required to work long, unsocial hours in an environment that requires them to be physically productive and display a high standard of social skills. Split shifts are often required to cater for the twice daily demand for hospitality services (Timo 1994, pp. 32–3).

The tourism industry is certainly not as glamorous as its image suggests. As Timo (1994, p. 33) noted, with respect to hotels and larger establishments, the following demands frequently apply:
• a high proportion of staff working 38–45 hours per week;
• management and supervisory staff working more than 50 hours a week;
• nearly 80% of staff being required to work on Saturdays and 60% on Sundays; and
• split shifts being used as a common rostering practice.

The tourism industry should not be surprised at the present concerns over labour. As the DOT (Cwlth) (1975, p. 11) recognised in the mid-1970s: 'Determination of the industry's manpower requirements, and provision of education and training programs to produce executives and competent employees at all levels of operations, is a further area which requires early consideration'.

As noted in Chapter 3, tourism in Australia has experienced enormous growth in the past decade or so, and is an important industry in the restructuring of the economy. However, 'long-term success and growth of the industry is contingent upon the development of a skilled labour force (Dawkins 1988, p. 6). Despite variations in the estimation of the employment demands of the Australian tourism industry (ATIA 1988; Barge 1988), it is readily apparent that the rapid development of inbound tourism is placing a great strain on the availability of labour and on labour relations. As the Department of Employment, Education and Training (DEET 1988, p. i) noted: 'severe shortages currently exist in the highly skilled hospitality occupations of hotel/motel managers, executive and foreign cuisine chefs and skilled waiters . . . shortages also exist at the entry level and for the less skilled occupations'. DITR (2002e) quoted Tourism Training Australia's forecast in *Tourism Workforce 2020* that 'between 2000 and 2005, employment in designated tourism occupations will continue to grow at 3.1% per annum, whilst jobs in the overall economy will grow at 1.7% per year'.

In particular, the present rate of development of tourism in Australia will influence human resource requirements, not only through the sheer numbers of employees, but also in a qualitative sense in terms of skilled staff, leading to increasing demands for both training and retraining programs (Department of Sport, Recreation and Tourism (DSRT) 1985; Tourism Training Review Group 1986; KPMG Peat Marwick Management Consultants 1991; Tolhurst 1994). In addition, the profile of the tourism industry labour force does not match the policy demands of successive federal governments, and particularly those of the Labor governments of the early 1990s, which sought to develop a more highly skilled and highly productive labour force 'in which wages costs are not low in an absolute sense, but unit costs are low because of the higher productivity of better trained workers' (IC 1995, p. 23).

Several reasons can be suggested to explain the present staffing problems. The relative youth of the Australian tourism industry has meant that career paths have only recently begun to be clearly defined or developed (James 1988). Until the entry of the National Tourism Industry Training Committee (NTITC), the forerunner of Tourism Training Australia (TTA), industry had never successfully articulated its training needs to the government. The TTA is the government-recognised industry training advisory body operating within the national vocational education and training network, and is the main government provider of funds for tourism training at the institutional level. However, it is worthwhile to note that, according to Barge (1988, p. 13), in 1988 'only 10% of national organisations are supporting the NTITC and, in the main, the internationals do not participate at all'. Since that time, however, far more components of the industry have come to be involved, as TTA has moved to set national training and competency standards for a number of areas within tourism, such as tour guiding and hospitality. Poor attitudes to training have existed in the industry at large, with some sections of the industry paying only 'lipservice to training' (Barge 1988, p. 12; James 1988). Indeed, DEET (1988, p. 27) noted that 'much of the industry appears to regard expenditure on training as an operating cost to be minimised rather than an investment to be optimised'. This is perhaps a reflection of the large number of small businesses within the tourism industry which, by their nature, tend to place a low priority on staff development (DSRT 1985).

The poor profile of tourism on federal government policy agendas is another factor in the failure to address training issues in the industry. For many years tourism was simply not regarded as a 'serious' industry that required the development of substantive policy initiatives. Successive Commonwealth and state governments did not respond quickly enough to the growth of the industry (Tourism Training Review Group 1986; Barge 1988). Unfortunately, there has also been a failure of educational institutions to meet the needs of certain segments of the industry. The DSRT (1985, p. 25), reported that 'some training institutions have been developing and introducing courses in the absence of demand data, thereby running the risk of establishing courses not relevant to the needs of the industry in the immediate vicinity'. Barge (1988) argued that TAFE places high emphasis on cooking and food science, and little emphasis on marketing and people skills. Furthermore, historically, there has been a lack of communication among educational institutions regarding problems of accreditation (DSRT 1985; DEET 1988; James 1988), and these have only just begun to be overcome. More recently, concerns have been expressed that, although more graduates are being produced in travel and hospitality, other areas (such as inbound tourism, tour guiding, tourist attractions, meetings and tour wholesaling) are not receiving enough attention (Hall & Weiler 1989; KPMG Peat Marwick

Management Consultants 1991; Tolhurst 1994). According to the DITR (2002e, p. 5), areas identified as having potential labour shortages are:

- management and business skills for medium-sized to small-sized enterprises;
- cross-cultural and language skills;
- commercial cookery skills;
- marketing and product development skills;
- customer service skills for front-line staff;
- management and operational skills for meetings, conferences, exhibitions and events;
- operational skills for tour guides;
- general skills in the provision of gaming services;
- information technology skills;
- skills for managers and supervisors relating to the implementation of food standards and regulations;
- skills to formulate safety plans;
- operational skills for local and inbound tour operators;
- special interest tourism skills, such as ecotourism and adventure and recreational tourism;
- entrepreneurial and sales skills; and
- skills to train tourism operators.

In this respect, the comments of the IC (1995, p. 28) are salutary in regard to the nature of tourism training and education:

> In reflecting the wishes of industry, TTA has encouraged the development of very skill-specific training. There are two potential problems with this approach. First, training resources may not be put to best use if people undertake training courses that provide very industry-specific vocational skills and they subsequently leave the industry. This is a feature of this industry as demonstrated by the high rate of turnover.
>
> In this situation, the interests of society may be better served by training that includes general skills, because these skills will be applicable in a range of employment situations and industries. If narrowly focused firm-specific skills are to be provided, then industry itself should fund the provision of such training. It would be inappropriate for this very specific training to be provided at no cost to firms by publicly-funded institutions.
>
> A second problem is the diversity of the industry. This makes it difficult to develop a standardised training curriculum which is suitable for the full range of businesses. Small businesses particularly have been identified by inquiry participants (including TTA) as not having their training needs met satisfactorily under current training arrangements. A broader curriculum may help.

Many employers in the tourism industry do not demand that their staff have formal training. On-the-job training in tourism is still the norm and a relatively low number of managers have any formal training. According to the IC (1995, p. 30):

> . . . employers generally prefer experience to formal qualifications when employing new staff. Perhaps it is because managers tend to have limited formal training themselves and so prefer job applicants with relevant work experience (and by implication, on-the-job training), rather than formal qualifications.

For many students of tourism, such a situation is of great concern. Two possibilities present themselves. First, it is possible that tourism actually is an industry which has inherent low skill requirements. Therefore, further levels of formal training and education would represent inefficient government and industry expenditure. The second possibility was expressed in the following terms by the IC (1995, p. 31):

> . . . training now being provided does increase productivity but employers have not yet come to realise it. In this case real productivity benefits may be occurring. Waste and unmet expectations of employees will still result however, until employers can be persuaded of the benefits of training that is being provided.

The present author is persuaded by the second position. If businesses are to adapt and respond appropriately to the demands of the global tourism marketplace, a well-educated tourism workforce is essential. However, to achieve this, generational changes in attitudes to training and education are essential, and it is highly likely that readers of this book will have to be a part of such cultural shifts if such change is to occur.

TOURISM: THE PARTIALLY INDUSTRIALISED INDUSTRY?

The diverse nature of the tourism industry makes it essential that there is a high degree of communication and coordination among the various segments of the industry to ensure that the Australian tourist product is effectively managed, marketed and promoted. One of the great problems in coordinating and managing the tourism industry is the difficulty of deciding exactly what the tourism industry actually is. For example, the IAC in its review of the travel and tourism industry, noted that 'there is no standard definition of what constitutes travel and tourism' (1989, p. 27) (see Chapter 1). The concept of 'partial industrialisation' is one attempt to describe such difficulties and the consequent problems of coordination, management, and strategic development. According to Leiper (1989, p. 25), 'partial industrialisation' refers to a condition:

> . . . in which only certain organisations providing goods and services directly to tourists are in the tourism industry. The proportion of (a) goods and services stemming from that industry to (b) total goods and services used by tourists can be termed the index of industrialisation, theoretically ranging from 100% (wholly industrialised) to zero (tourists present and spending money, but no tourism industry).

Partial industrialisation of tourism is significant for tourism development, marketing, and coordination (Leiper 1995). Although many segments of the economy benefit from tourism, only those organisations which perceive a direct relationship to tourists and tourism producers become actively involved in fostering tourism development or in marketing. However, there are many other organisations such as food suppliers, petrol stations and retailers (sometimes described as 'allied industries'), which also benefit from tourists, but which are not readily identified as part of the tourism industry.

Australia therefore has great difficulty in finding a peak body to represent the interests of the tourism industry. For example, the Industries Assistance Commission of Inquiry into tourism received submissions from a wide number of peak bodies, each of which represented a component of the tourism industry. Industry associations play a major role in developing strategic goals for tourism development and in lobbying government in the interests of their members. They also assist in raising the profile of the industry in the broader community. Tourism-related industry associations and bodies exist at national, state, and local levels. However, substantial competition can occur among bodies representing tourism interests. For instance, TCA and the Tourism Task Force have, at times, been in conflict over the appropriate policy direction for tourism in Australia. In addition, small businesses in Australia have generally been reluctant to establish an effective lobbying group. Therefore, the difficulties of developing a coordinated approach to tourism in the government sphere is replicated in private industry. Coordination among the various elements of the tourism industry is also impeded by the onus on individual companies to make a profit and to fulfil their own company interests. Nevertheless, there are times when industry associations can have a major impact on tourism policy. Indeed, it can be argued that the industry did have a very strong influence on government policy for a long time. Indeed, the priorities submitted to the federal minister by ANTA in 1973 remain the core of industry policy objectives:

• acceleration of overseas visitor arrivals;
• generation of domestic tourism demand;
• creation of a favourable investment climate; and
• ensuring a flow of appropriate information to industry.

CHAPTER SUMMARY

The present chapter has provided an overview of some of the key industry and labour issues that currently face the Australian tourism industry. As in the previous chapter on the role of government, we have seen that the private sector also lacks a coordinated approach to development. The private sector has failed to designate a peak body to represent the needs of the industry to government and lacks intra-industry cooperation. The concept of 'partial-industrialisation' goes some way towards explaining the difficulty of developing coordinated responses within the private sector. However, competition induced by the profit motive of companies is also significant.

This chapter has also identified some of the labour and industry development issues that are crucial to the future of the tourism industry. In particular, issues of training and education must be resolved before tourism can enjoy long-term development. Undoubtedly the education and skill level of the tourism industry underlies the economic viability and competitiveness of Australian tourism in the international marketplace. In dealing adequately with the concerns raised by the economic restructuring process in Australia, it is essential that tourism employers adopt the principles of sustainable development, and treat their staff as a valuable human resource whose needs must be met if the demands of consumers are to be met.

SUGGESTIONS FOR FURTHER READING

McMillen & Lafferty (1991) provide a challenging account of the nature of the tourism workforce, and the report of the IC (1995) is also important reading. Prideaux (1993) provides an overview of the possible effects of new transport technologies on the transport sector of the tourism industry. The leading international text on the conference sector is Astroff and Abbey (1995). The development of the casino sector in Australia is examined in McMillen (1991b). Readers should examine BTR's annual report on *Tourism Trends in Australia* for further details on the growth and structure of the Australian tourism and hospitality industry.

INTERNET SITES

Good overviews of sectoral information are available at these websites:
- ONT:
    www.tourism.gov.au

- BTR:
    www.btr.gov.au

- Readers should consult the various industry associations and organisations (see Appendix A) which have developed websites or are in the process of doing so.

- On the Tourism Insight on the web
    www.prenhall.com/hall_au

    see: *The Meetings and Conventions Industry* by Jenny Nichol.

FOR DISCUSSION AND REVIEW

Key concepts

Key concepts discussed in this chapter were:
post-industrial society, service industry, demographic pattern, partial industrialisation, peak body, investment, privatisation, foreign investment, transport sector, accommodation (lodging) sector, travel services sector, meetings industry, food and beverage industry, retail industry, MICE, skill shortage, education and training, human resources, industrial relations.

Questions for review and discussion

1 What are the factors that have led to the growth in service industries such as tourism?

2 Why does the partial industrialisation of tourism affect coordination within the tourism industry?

3 How do the characteristics of tourism affect the nature of tourism employment?

4 Why has the issue of casino development become so sensitive in Australian tourism?

5 Describe how the issues of training, career structure, and remuneration affect tourism in Australia.

6 To what extent are various forms of tourism transport substitutable by other forms?

7 Discuss the changes that have occurred in the Australian aviation sector since 1990.

8 Outline the key features of the tourism and hospitality labour market.

9 How important is the MICE sector to tourism?

INTRODUCTION TO TOURISM

THE ECONOMIC DIMENSIONS AND IMPACTS OF TOURISM

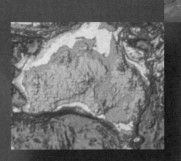

8

Tourism makes a major contribution to employment, can help develop the more isolated regional areas and it can improve Australia's balance of payments. Importantly, it can be counter-cyclical to our resource and agricultural export industries (WATC 1991, p. 6).

There is not a simple linear relationship between the growth of tourism and of the economic benefits for the whole community. In the initial stages tourism may create more jobs for locals while increased demand for food leads to intensification of agriculture. Later, with further development, negative consequences may become more apparent. These include overcommitment of resources to tourism diverting investment from other sectors, congestion, pollution, in-migration of labour, and conflicts with other land uses (Williams & Shaw 1988b, pp. 36–7).

Tourism has increasingly come to be seen by government and the private sector alike as a major source of economic and regional development. As Lord Parry observed, 'Tourism is no longer seen as incidental development but as a fundamental economic resource' (1988, p. 12). Nevertheless, despite the growing awareness of the economic significance of tourism in the Australian economy, students of tourism should not accept tourism's potential contribution to development without question. Indeed, it is through such questioning that we can come to a better understanding of the mechanisms by which tourism can contribute to the processes of sustainable economic development. 'The industry is shrouded in myths and stereotypes, and there is a need to critically examine recent trends in tourism, its economic organisation and its contribution to economic development' (Williams & Shaw 1988a, p. 1).

Much of the attention on the economic dimensions of tourism has concentrated on the contribution of tourism to the balance of payments and its potential to reduce levels of overseas debt (O'Clery 1990a; Rowe 1993). The balance of payments measure focuses on direct tourist expenditure. However, because of the broad nature of the tourism industry, some of the potential economic contributions of tourism to the national economy can be understated. To overcome this problem, Baretje (1982) recommended the use of a broader concept of 'tourism's external account' (Table 8.1). More recently the Industries Commission (1995), the World Travel and Tourism Council (WTTC) (1996) and Access Economics (1997) have recommended the adoption of a tourism satellite account (TSA) to measure the direct and indirect contributions of tourism to the economy more accurately.

The concept of a satellite account is a relatively new idea that originated in France as a way of addressing the problem of new and growing economic activities not recognised in the official measures of certain industries, such as tourism, energy, and information technology. Such an account is a model that is separate from, but linked to, the national accounts, and uses the same concepts and structure as the core accounts (DITR 2002g). The system of national accounts is a set of guidelines for organising information about an economy in a useful way. It provides concepts, definitions, classifications, accounting rules, accounts and tables to provide a comprehensive, integrated framework for production, consumption, capital investment, income, stocks, flows of financial and non-financial wealth, and related economic variables (Frechtling 1999, p. 164).

TSAs have been developed in a number of countries including Canada, New Zealand, Norway and, more recently, Australia (Smith & Wilton 1997). In Canada the TSA (DISR 2002d) showed that tourists represented:

TABLE 8.1 Tourism's external account

Expenditure	Receipts
Expenditure by tourists abroad	Expenditure 'at home' by foreign tourists
Transportation	Transportation
Investments (outward)	Investments (inward)
Dividends, interest, and profits paid out	Dividends, interest, and profits received
Commodity imports (tourism-induced)— capital and consumption goods	Commodity exports (tourism-induced)— capital and consumption goods
Salaries repatriated abroad	Salaries sent from abroad
Training	Training
Publicity and promotion	Publicity and promotion
Miscellaneous services	Miscellaneous services

Source: Baratje, R. (1982) 'Tourism's external account and the balance of payments' *Annals of Tourism Research*, vol. 9, no. 1, p. 62, with the permission of Elsevier Science.

- 93% of air passenger transport demand;
- 92% of short-term accommodation demand;
- 83% of vehicle rental demand;
- 22% of taxi demand; and
- 21% of food and beverage services demand.

The World Tourism Organization, the OECD and the WTTC (1997) encourage the development of an agreed international framework for TSAs to provide for better international comparisons. Although the accounts produced in international TSAs have not yet been standardised, they usually contain one or more of the following accounts (Frechtling 1999, p. 167):

- tourism consumption by commodity;
- tourism consumption impact on supply;
- production accounts of the tourism industry;
- tourism-related gross fixed capital formation;
- employment related to tourism;
- stocks and flows of fixed assets related to tourism;
- imports and exports of goods and services generated by tourism;
- tourism balance of payments; and
- tourism value added (contribution to GDP) by commodity and activity.

The Australian TSA was developed at a cost of almost a million dollars (DISR 2002d). The TSA identifies (DITR 2002i, p. 1):

> . . . industries which were closely related to tourism demand. It identified these industries as either "tourism characteristic industries", i.e. those industries where at least 25% of their output is consumed by visitors, or "tourism connected industries", i.e. those industries which produce a product which is consumed by visitors in volumes which are significant for the visitor and/or the producer.

Fortunately, much of the data required for the development of a TSA in Australia were already available in other forms. For example, on the demand side, the BTR's national visitor survey and international visitor survey provided almost all of the data needed on visitors' expenditure. On the supply side, the Australian Bureau of Statistics' (ABS) ongoing program of economic activity surveys and service industry surveys provided considerable data once their sample size had been increased and some additional items added. In addition, other ABS collections including the retail census, the public finance system, the balance of payments and other national accounts have been used (DITR 2002g).

The concept of gross value added (GVA) is vital for a comparison of tourism with other industries and sectors. According to the DITR (2002i, p. 1):

> Tourism GVA can be defined as the value of the output of goods/services which are consumed by visitors less the value of the inputs used in producing those goods/services. Tourism GVA therefore comprises part of the GVA of all those industries which produce goods/services which are consumed by visitors.

The composition of tourism GVA for 1997/98 is shown in Table 8.2.

In October 2001 the first Australian TSA was released for the financial year 1997/98 (DISR 2000d; DITR 2002g) (see Table 8.3). The response to the TSA results has been mixed, with some writers valuing the availability of an official measure of tourism's role in the Australian economy whereas others have been disappointed because 'results showed a lower economic contribution by tourism than had

THE ECONOMIC DIMENSIONS AND IMPACTS OF TOURISM

TABLE 8.2 Composition of tourism gross value added, 1997/98

Tourism characteristic and connected industries	Tourism gross value added ($m)	Compensation of employees (%)	Gross operating surplus (%)	Other net taxes on production (%)
Air and water transport	3 235	69	29	2
Manufacturing	2 572	50	47	3
Accommodation	2 388	82	15	3
Cafés, restaurants and take-aways	2 207	70	27	3
Retail trade	2 124	70	24	6
Clubs, pubs, taverns and bars	1 072	52	45	3
Motor vehicle hiring, taxis, and other road transport	1 024	51	42	7
Travel agency and tour operator services	835	81	13	6
Education	756	88	11	1
Other entertainment services	631	60	36	4
Rail transport	379	62	34	4
Libraries, museums and arts	366	52	46	2
Casinos and other gambling services	158	28	69	3
Ownership of dwellings	1 323	–	94	6
Total characteristic and connected industries	19 070	62	34	4
Tourism component of all other industries	3 318	54	42	4
Total	**22 389**	**60**	**36**	**4**

Note: 'Ownership of dwellings' is treated in the national accounts as an industry. In the tourism satellite account it relates to use of second homes for tourism purposes. Although it is not included in the analysis here, it is included in the table for completeness

Source: ABS Cat. No. 5249.0, Australian National Accounts: Tourism Satellite Account, 1997/98. Copyright Commonwealth of Australia. Reprinted with permission.

TABLE 8.3 Results of the Australian tourism satellite account 1997/98

Visitors consumed $58.2 billion worth of goods and services.

Of the total tourism consumption, 78% ($45.4 billion) was by domestic visitors whereas 22% ($12.8 billion) was by international visitors.

International visitors' consumption accounted for 11.2% of total exports.

Tourism GDP amounted to $25.2 billion (4.5% of total GDP).

Tourism's contribution to total gross value added (GVA) was 4.3%. This is was lower than 'Mining' (4.7%), but higher than 'Agriculture, forestry and fishing' (3.3%), 'Communication services' (3.2%) and 'Electricity, gas and water' (2.7%).

There were 513 000 persons directly employed in tourism-generated employment. This was 6% of total employment, showing that tourism is a relatively labour-intensive industry. Because many of the jobs were part time, this converts to an equivalent of 389 000 persons employed full time.

Tourism demand accounted for 97% of 'Travel agency and tour operator services' GVA, 89% of 'Accommodation' GVA, 64% of 'Air and water transport' GVA, 53% of 'Motor vehicle hiring' GVA, 38% of 'Taxi transport' GVA, and 30% of 'Cafes, restaurants and takeaway food outlets' GVA.

'Air and water transport' contributed 15% of total tourism GVA, 'Accommodation' contributed 11% of total tourism GVA, and 'Cafes, restaurants and takeaway food outlets' contributed 10% of total tourism GVA.

Source: Department of Industry, Tourism and Resources (DITR) (2002) *Research report no. 1: the Australian tourism satellite account*, Canberra, pp. 3–4. Reprinted with the permission of the Department of Industry, Tourism and Resources.

previously been estimated' (DITR 2002g, p. 4). For example, tourism labour productivity (Table 8.4) was relatively low compared with some industries (for example, 'manufacturing' or 'wholesale trade') although higher than others (for example, 'agriculture, forestry and fishing'). Tourism also had a 'significantly lower operating profit margin, 15.2%, than the average of all industries, 22.0%' (DITR 2002i). However, it should be noted that service industries overall tended to have a relatively low level of profitability. Despite these concerns about the figures, the results have been increasingly utilised in policy advocacy by industry and government and the next round of the Tourism Council of Australia (TCA) will see the development of a time series of data. These results will provide a more accurate assessment of the economic impacts of tourism at the national level than had previously been available.

In addition to the economic linkages provided by the external account and the TSA, calculations of the economic contribution of tourism to the national economy must also consider the role of domestic tourism and the emergence of demand for new types of goods and services from Australians travelling overseas or overseas visitors in Australia. However, although the contribution of tourism to the balance of payments is extremely significant, much attention is also paid to the potential employment benefits of tourism development.

TABLE 8.4 Labour productivity of the tourism sector by component industries, 1997/98

Tourism characteristic and connected industries	Gross value added ($m)	Tourism full-time equivalent employed persons ('000)	Labour productivity ($ per employee)
Air and water transport	3 235	27.6	117 200
Rail transport	379	3.8	99 700
Casinos and other gambling services	158	1.9	83 200
Manufacturing	2 572	35.7	72 000
Clubs, pubs, taverns and bars	1 072	15.4	69 600
Other entertainment services	631	10.3	61 300
Libraries, museums and arts	366	6.2	59 000
Education	756	14.5	52 100
Motor vehicle hiring, taxis and other road transport	1 024	19.9	51 500
Cafés and restaurants	929	22.9	40 600
Travel agency and tour operator services	835	22.4	37 300
Retail trade (incl. take-aways)	3 402	94.5	36 000
Accommodation	2 388	68.0	35 100
Total characteristic and connected industries	17 747	343.1	51 700
Tourism component of all other industries	3 318	45.4	73 100
Total	21 065	388.5	54 200

Notes:

(1) 'Ownership of dwellings', which has no employment, is not included in this table

(2) 'Take-aways' are included in 'Retail trade', rather than in 'Cafés and restaurants'

Source: ABS Cat. No. 5249.0 Australian National Accounts: Tourism Satellite Account, 1997/98 in Department of Industry, Tourism and Resources (DITR) (2002) Research Report Number 2: Tourism Productivity and Profitability, Canberra, pp. 3–4. Reprinted with the permission of the Department of Industry, Tourism and Resources.

TOURISM EMPLOYMENT

TOURISM DOLLARS = JOBS (1993 Queensland Tourism Week Slogan in QTTC 1993, p. 23)

One of the main justifications by government and industry for the development of tourism is the establishment of new jobs. As Roche (1992, p. 567) noted: 'probably the main political and social stimuli and motivations for developing a tourism industry at all derive from its assumed potential to generate *employment*'. This has been important throughout the industrial world, but perhaps more so in Australia, as the economy has been undergoing restructuring since the 1970s in the light of reduced protection for the manufacturing and rural sectors and reduced access to traditional markets (Hall et al. 1997). For example, a study of tourism development in the Illawara region in the late 1970s supported the use of tourism as a means of diversifying the base of the regional economy because the multiplier effect of tourism was found to be superior to that of existing industries (Ali, Blakey & Lewis 1979). A typical discussion of the employment benefits provided by tourism is provided by Brown (1985, p. 8) who claimed that:

> One of the most important characteristics of the [tourism] industry is its relative labour intensity in an age of great technological advancement and declining relative demand for labour. The industry and those industries closely aligned with it (which also tend to be labour intensive) provide many jobs both for the unskilled and highly skilled, and it has the potential to provide many further jobs, a large number of which can be introduced with minimum delay.

As a result of research conducted for the TSA it was estimated that in 1997/98 there were 513 000 people in tourism-generated employment (6.0% of total employment in Australia) which equated to 389 000 full-time jobs (DITR 2002e, p. 2). In 1995/96, the tourism industry was directly responsible for employment of around 694 000 persons (8.4% of the workforce) and indirectly for a further 334 000 persons. Taken together, direct and indirect employment thus totalled 1 028 000 persons (12.4% of all those employed) (BTR in ONT 1997h). This contrasted with the position at the end of 1989 when tourism accounted for approximately 442 000 jobs (5.8% of the workforce) (DASETT 1989b). It should be noted, however, that the 1997/98 figure cannot be compared with previous estimates as they used a different methodology and different data sets. Nevertheless, the significant potential of tourism for employment generation is often enthusiastically promoted by government. For example, the QTTC (1998a, p. 5) argued that 'every time the State's annual visitor population experiences a sustained increase of 300 international, 500 interstate, or 1500 Queensland holidaymakers, 10 new jobs are created'. In contrast, the BTR (1988) estimated that one job was created in the Australian economy for every 32 inbound tourists whereas, for domestic tourism, the ratio was one job for every 250 domestic tourists.

According to the BTR (1989a), during the peak season, 57% of total employment across all sectors of the hospitality sector of the tourism industry was female. Of all workers, 57% were part time or casual, and of these, 70% were female, whereas female workers occupied 40% of full-time positions. (See Chapter 7 for a further account of gender balance in the Australian tourism industry.) On the available figures, the tourism industry appears to show a substantial gender imbalance (IC 1995). According to McMillen and Lafferty (1991, p. 85):

The jobs done by women in tourism are characterised by lower pay, poorer conditions, less career mobility, limited access to training programmes and less effective trade union support than the traditionally male areas of employment. In tourism, the majority of women are concentrated in three broad categories, housekeeping, waiting and kitchen work. Within these categories, 75 per cent of all workers are women; only 36 per cent of managers and owners are women

Critical examinations of employment generation by tourism have been few and far between in Australia. Worland and Wilson (1988) reported that employment growth in the Victorian hospitality sector in the period 1979–1984 was almost entirely in the casual category. However, as Williams and Shaw (1988a, p. 5) emphasised, there is a need to:

> . . . avoid stereotypes and excessive abstraction. Consideration of the tourism-related demand for manufactured goods underlines this point, for the impact depends on where the goods are produced, whether it is by craftsmen or factory workers, on the alternative work opportunities available locally, and on the evaluation of these jobs by the individuals and by the community.

As the TSA has sought to do, attention needs to be given to the practical difficulties of identifying the flow-on effects of tourism in creating employment. For example, an employee at a restaurant in a tourism business district such as Sydney's Rocks area is dependent on a combination of business, local and tourist trade for his or her position. Furthermore, to analyse the quality of employment opportunities, there is a need to break down the employment generated by tourism into various categories of job types (that is, full time/part time, seasonal/year round, union/non-union, family-labour/wage-labour, manual/non-manual, skilled/unskilled). As the IC (1995, p. 21) observed:

> On the one hand, low skill, low pay casual jobs do not deliver high productivity and a consequent high standard of living. On the other hand, they do provide employment opportunities for people who are at high risk of unemployment. There is some evidence . . . that many of these tourism jobs do have a contribution to make to providing entry jobs to people who are currently unemployed or at risk of being unemployed.

One of the ironies of the perceived employment benefits of tourism is that areas that have tourism as a mainstay of the local economy tend to have high levels of unemployment (for example, the Gold Coast and the Sunshine Coast). According to Mullins (1990, p. 39), such a situation can be regarded as an 'imported problem', in that:

> . . . the Southern unemployed flock into these cities for the 'good life'. Yet data produced by the Commonwealth Department of Social Security on interstate transferees on unemployment benefits shows that the net number remaining in the Gold Coast and Sunshine Coast over any 12 month period barely makes 1 per cent of these cities unemployed.

Instead of 'dole-bludger' and 'surfer' migration, the explanation of unemployment situation rests in the nature of the two tourist regions. The economies of both areas are founded on two industries with considerable variation in demand—tourism, which is seasonal, and construction, which is cyclical. Therefore, 'high rates of unemployment seem inevitable' (Mullins 1990, p. 39), although as the economic base in such regions diversifies, unemployment levels should fall.

Another major consideration in the contribution of tourism to the national economy is the organisation of capital and, in particular, the penetration of foreign or international capital. The contribution of foreign capital to the Australian tourism industry has been very significant in recent years, with substantial investment coming from American, British, New Zealand, Japanese, and South-East Asian sources. Although such capital can play a significant part in the development of the tourist industry, it must be noted that, in the longer term, the leakage of income abroad through the payment of dividends, profits and royalties can have a substantial effect on the balance of payments.

The distribution and organisation of capital and tourists is spread unevenly between and within regions. As Peters (1969, p. 11) noted: 'tourism, by its nature, tends to distribute development away from the industrial centres towards those regions in a country which have not been developed'. Tourism can be highly polarised with concentrations along the coast in the more picturesque rural areas and in certain parts of major cities. Such concentrations of tourism can have significant flow-on effects to host communities through increased rents and house prices, localised inflationary effects, social and physical impacts, and potential alterations in the perceived quality of life.

There is a dearth of reliable estimates of the precise nature and strength of the elasticity of demand for tourism (Williams & Shaw 1988a). Nevertheless, tourism is generally characterised by a positive income elasticity of demand—in which demand rises proportionately higher than increases in the level of income. This is in part due to the perception of tourism as a luxury good. Indeed, tourism is also a significant component of the aspirations related to improvements in economic and social mobility (Waters 1967).

THE ECONOMIC IMPACT OF TOURISM: TOURISM MULTIPLIERS

By far the majority of tourism research has focused on the potential economic benefits that tourism can bring to a nation or a specific region. This situation should not be surprising, given the attention that is placed on tourism as a tool for regional development. To determine the specific impact of tourism, government and private industry frequently undertake economic impact studies which ascertain the effects of tourism development. As Frechtling (1987, p. 325) has observed:

> Economic impact studies are understood to include objective analyses of tourism activity's impact on resident wealth or income in a defined area. On the benefit side, this normally means the study provides estimates of travel and tourism spending on employment and income. On the cost side, this means estimating the costs, sometimes, non-monetary, to government and residents of travel activity in the area.

Many local and national economic impact studies focus on what is known as the 'multiplier effect'. This effect is concerned with 'the way in which expenditure on tourism filters throughout the economy, stimulating other sectors as it does so' (D.G. Pearce 1989, p. 205). Several different types of multiplier are in use, each with its own economic emphasis (Archer 1977; 1982). However, the multiplier can be regarded as 'a coefficient which expresses the amount of income generated in an area by an additional unit of tourist spending' (Archer 1982, p. 236). It is the ratio of direct and secondary changes to the direct initial change itself.

Economic impacts can be classified as being primary or secondary in nature (Archer 1982). Primary or direct impacts are a direct consequence of tourist spending, such as the purchase of food and beverages by a tourist in a hotel. Secondary impacts can be described as either indirect or induced. Indirect impacts are those arising from the re-spending of money in the form of local business transactions—for example, the new investment of hotel owners in equipment and supplies. Induced impacts are those arising from the additional income generated by further consumer spending—for example, the purchase of goods and services by hotel employees. However, it must be noted that for each round of spending per unit of initial tourist expenditure, leakage occurs from the regional economy until little or no further re-spending is possible. In sum, 'the tourism multiplier is a measure of the total effects (direct plus secondary) which result from the additional tourist expenditure' (Archer 1982, p. 237).

The size of the tourist multiplier varies from region to region and depends on the size of the area of analysis, the proportion of goods and services imported into the region for consumption by tourists, the rate of circulation, the nature of tourist spending, the availability of suitable local products and services, and the patterns of economic behaviour for tourist and local alike. As a measure of economic benefit from tourism, the multiplier technique has been increasingly subject to question, particularly as its use has often produced exaggerated results (Archer 1977, 1982; Cooper & Pigram 1980; Hughes 1982; Frechtling 1987; D.G. Pearce 1989; Bull 1994; Hall & Page 2002a, b). As Hughes (1982, p. 172) has argued in the case of Britain, other forms of economic activity can produce similar regional multipliers: 'They are not consistently superior and do not warrant the special status accorded them'. Nevertheless, despite doubts about the accuracy of the multiplier technique, substantial attention is still paid to the results of economic impact studies by government as a measure of the success of tourism development.

The size of the tourist multiplier is a significant measure of the economic benefit of tourism because it is a reflection of the circulation of the tourist dollar through an economic system. In general, the larger the size of the tourist multiplier, the greater the self-sufficiency of that economy in the provision of tourist facilities and services. Therefore, a tourist multiplier is larger at the national level than at a state level because, at a state level, leakage occurs in the form of taxes to the national government and in the importation of goods and services from other states. Similarly, at a regional and local level, multipliers reflect high importation into small communities and tax payments to state and national governments.

According to Murphy (1985, p. 95), 'for practical purposes it is crucial to appreciate that local multiplier studies are just case studies of local gains and no more'. Several questions remain unanswered about the real costs and benefits of tourism on local and regional development—such as the identification of the winners and losers in tourism development. As Coppock (1977, p. 1.1) argued in relation to the use of tourism as a tool for economic development:

> Not only is it inevitable that the residents of an area will gain unequally from tourism (if indeed they gain at all) and probable that the interests of some will actually be harmed, but it may well be that a substantial proportion does not wish to see any development of tourism.

TENDENCIES IN THE INTERNATIONAL ECONOMIC DEVELOPMENT OF TOURISM

Williams and Shaw (1988a, 1988c) have identified two major tendencies in the development of tourism—internationalisation (or economic globalisation) and concentration. These tendencies are related to the increased internationalisation of the tourism product, the economies of scale available to tourism companies, and the need for individual companies to reduce costs in a highly competitive international market. The internationalisation of tourism is reflected in the activities of the major airline carriers and international groups such as Avis car rental, Thomas Cook Travel, Thomson, and Tjaereborg. However, the most noticeable evidence of internationalisation is to be found in the ubiquitous multinational hotel chains such as ClubMed, Holiday Inn, Hyatt International, Inter-Continental, Sheraton Hotels, Travelodge, and Trusthouse Forte (United Nations Centre on Transnational Corporations 1982; Hall & Page 2002a).

Despite the undoubted internationalisation of tourism, significant barriers still remain in the international market. The delayed respectability of tourism as a 'genuine' industry is part of an overall lack of attention given to service industries in international trade agreements such as GATT for most of the postwar period. It has only been since the 1980s, particularly through the actions of the Organization for Economic Cooperation and Development (OECD), that tourism has reached the international agenda for trade liberalisation that had previously focused primarily on manufactured goods. The World Tourism Organization (WTO 1984) identified seven major barriers to international trade in tourism services:

- specific quantitative or qualitative restrictions on tourist entry;
- non-tariff import charges on international tourists;
- participation in trade by government administration, particularly through the use of subsidies to discourage overseas travel;
- administrative and customs procedures and specific administrative prices which, by their length, complexity and cost, discourage international tourism;
- concessionary transport costs for tourists;
- prevention of the establishment of foreign-owned tourism companies; and
- discriminatory practices against foreign airlines (for instance, by restricting access to certain tourism destinations and entry-points).

International tourism trade issues are dealt with unilaterally and multilaterally, although unilateral action is favoured by governments when they feel that their interests are being threatened. Many bilateral trade agreements relating to tourism are in the areas of transport (for example, air transport agreements) and investment (for example, protection for foreign investment under 'most-favoured-nation' status). Multilateral negotiations are often conducted under the auspices of international organisations. Three international trade organisations with an interest in tourism are the International Monetary Fund (IMF), the OECD, and the World Trade Organization. Organisations with a more specific interest in tourism activities include the World Tourism Organization (WTO), the International Civil Aviation Organization (ICAO), the International Maritime Organization (IMO), the Customs Cooperation Council (CCC) and regional bodies such as the Tourism Council of the South Pacific (TCSP) (Hall 1994b, 1997a). In examining obstacles to international travel and tourism, Ascher (1984, p. 3) identified a number of government-imposed restrictions which affect tourist trade:

- government attention to tourism is focused more on promotion of inbound tourist business rather than on a more general approach that deals with reduction or removal of restrictions to tourism on a worldwide basis;
- government has not fully assessed the 'tourism impact' of its laws and regulations;
- government policies concerning international relations—political, economic, monetary, financial—often conflict with, and override, tourism policy;
- for the most part, the international organisations that address problems of tourism deal with them mainly in a piecemeal fashion and not with tourism as an integral unit;
- although there is some coordination among international organisations on tourism matters, greater cooperation would improve their effectiveness; and
- there is a lack of internationally accepted rules and principles for dealing with new problems as they arise, and no mechanism for dispute settlement.

The Ad Hoc Working Party on Obstacles to International Tourism for the OECD's Committee on Tourism identified forty specific obstacles to international travel and tourism in five different areas (Table 8.5)—(i) those affecting individual travellers; (ii) those affecting companies providing services to facilitate travel (for example, travel agents); (iii) those affecting companies providing transportation (for example, airlines, coach operators); (iv) those affecting companies providing reception facilities (for example, hotels); and (v) other obstacles such as discriminatory regulations.

Obstacles to tourism can also be classified by whether they constitute tariff or non-tariff barriers. Non-tariff barriers include travel allowance restrictions, restrictions on credit card use, limitations on duty-free allowances, and advance import-deposit measures (for example, compulsory deposits prior to travel). Tariff barriers include import-duty measures, airport departure taxes, and airport taxes and subsidies (for example, a consumer-subsidy measure such as an official preferential exchange rate for foreign tourists, or price concessions). Although tourism tariff barriers can be lowered by specific tourism agreements, tariffs are usually dealt with under: (i) broader multilateral negotiations on tariff reductions for goods and services (for example, GATT, or negotiations within a specific trading bloc such as the European Community, the Association of South East Asian Nations (ASEAN) or the North American Free Trade Agreement (NAFTA)); or (ii) bilateral agreements (for example, the closer economic relationship agreement between Australia and New Zealand) (see Chapter 5) (Hall 1994b; Hall & Page 2000).

Further reduction of barriers to travel may lead to even greater levels between Australia and Thailand.

Unless multilateral organisations such as APEC act on problems such as global climate change many of the coral islands of the Pacific may disappear completely under water.

Although concentration of ownership and capital is a major trend in tourism, particularly at the top end of the tourism market, it must be recognised that the majority of tourism-related businesses are small. As Brown (1985, p. 8) noted:

> The industry is characterised by the significant role of small businesses in the provision of tourist accommodation. Over 80% of all tourist accommodation rooms are in establishments having less than 100 rooms, with most small hotels and motels being operated by their owners.

Nevertheless, there has been an international trend towards horizontal and vertical integration and expansion of tourism enterprises. In Australia and New Zealand, examples of the horizontal trend were the buy-out of shares in Ansett by Air New Zealand and the purchase of a major shareholding in Qantas by British Airways. An example of vertical integration was the ownership of Great Barrier Reef island holiday resorts by Australian airline companies. However, most public attention has been paid to vertical integration by Japanese or South-East Asian corporations (Higgins 1993).

One of the major international trends in the accommodation sector has been the increasing polarisation between the expansion of large hotels and hotel chains and the smaller, usually family-owned, hotels. In Australia, little research has been undertaken on the patterns of ownership in the hotel and accommodation sector. According to Williams and Shaw's (1988b, p. 28) analysis of western European tourism: 'Smaller hotels are finding it increasingly difficult to compete, especially if they lack facilities such as private bathrooms, bars and swimming pools which are becoming a part of standard expectations'. This observation appears to hold true in Australia. However, it must be recognised that many smaller businesses have been able to overcome the competition offered by large corporations by concentrating their attention on certain segments of the tourism market such as bed and breakfasts and special interest tourism.

THE NATIONAL SCENE

Tourism is one of Australia's largest economic activities. Under the tourism satellite account method adopted by the World Travel and Tourism Council, which

THE ECONOMIC DIMENSIONS AND IMPACTS OF TOURISM

TABLE 8.5 Types of obstacles to international tourism

I   Obstacles affecting the individual intending to travel

1   Imposed by the home country: (a) currency restrictions imposed upon residents; (b) conditions and procedures for issue of travel documents; (c) customs allowances for returning residents; (d) restrictions on overseas travel

2   Imposed by the host country: (a) currency restrictions imposed upon visitors; (b) entry visas, identity documents, limitations on duration of stay; (c) formalities concerning entry of motor vehicles, pleasure boats or other craft; (d) formalities concerning applicability of drivers' licences, car insurance, etc.; (e) restrictions on acquisition of property by non-nationals (for example, holiday flats); (f) taxes on foreign visitors

II   Obstacles affecting companies providing services to facilitate travel (travel agents, tour operators)

3   Limitations on foreign investment/equity participation

4   Restrictions on the establishment of foreign owned entities (branches and subsidiaries)

5   Requirements for qualifications for operating professionally that are either directly discriminatory or more difficult for non-nationals to acquire

6   Restrictions on non-national personnel and employment (for example, visas, work permits)

7   Difficulties in obtaining licences to operate

8   Relevant restrictions on transfer of funds in and out of the country (not covered under I above)

9   Restrictions upon the ability of non-established foreign companies to solicit for custom, advertise, or sell direct to clients without locally established intermediaries

10   Distinction in EEC countries between EEC and non-EEC nationals with regard to the above items

III Obstacles affecting companies providing transportation (for example, airline, railways, coach operators, cruise liners)

11–18 Categories as under II (3–10)

19   Restrictions on non-national airlines, coach operators, or cruise liners

20   Limitations on movements of passengers by foreign airlines or cruise ships

21   Discriminatory landing dues, taxes or port charges

22   Lack of reciprocal recognition of qualifications (for example, air crew, site guides, coach drivers)

23   Requirements for government employees to use national airlines/ferry services

24   Discriminatory access to special terms from state enterprises (for example, airlines, railways), including differential commissions

25   Limitations on access to reservation systems

IV	**Obstacles affecting companies providing reception facilities (for example, hotels, resorts, car hire firms)**
26–33	Categories as under II (3–10)
34	Restrictions on imports of essential goods
35	Requirements for placing of contracts (for example, for site development) with local enterprises
36	Discriminatory tax regimes for foreign entrants (including tax holidays not available to nationals)
37	Restrictions on ownership by non-nationals (for example, only leasing permitted) and problems related to security of tenure or repatriation of investments
38	Limitations on access to reservation systems
V	**Other obstacles**
39	Discriminatory regulations on health inspection/consumer protection, and so on
40	Compulsory use of centralised governmental/municipal organisations or middle men
41	Others

Source: OECD Committee on Tourism, AD HOC Working Party on Obstacles to International Tourism in Ascher. B., (1984) 'Obstacles to international travel and tourism', *Journal of Travel Research*, vol. 22, p. 14. Reprinted by permission of Sage Publications Inc.

The Asia–Pacific Economic Cooperation (APEC) organisation is a major force for free trade in the Pacific Rim and for creating improved relations among the major economic powers in the region. APEC has no charter that forces contractual obligations on its members. Rather it works by consensus (Hall & Samways 1997). APEC was established in 1989 to provide a forum for the management of the effects of the growing interdependence of the Pacific Rim countries and to help sustain economic growth. Originally established as an informal group of twelve Asia–Pacific economies, APEC has since grown with the admission of the People's Republic of China, Hong Kong, and Chinese Taipei (Taiwan) in 1991, Mexico and Papua New Guinea in 1993, and Chile in 1994. A permanent secretariat is based in Singapore, and the APEC chair and ministerial meetings are rotated annually among members. The first ministerial meeting was held in Canberra, Australia, in 1989. Since then, meetings have been held in Singapore, Seoul, Bangkok, Seattle, Jakarta, Osaka, Manila, Vancouver, Kuala Lumpur, and Auckland (Hall & Page 2000).

The declarations and recommendations of the annual ministerial conference carry significant political and diplomatic weight and provide a framework for meeting APEC's commitment to 'free and open trade and investment in the Asia–Pacific', with the aim of dismantling all barriers to trade and investment before 2010 by developed member nations and before 2020 by developing nation members (Bureau of East Asian and Pacific Affairs 1996). As part of the APEC framework, ten working groups have been established covering broad areas of economic, educational, and environmental cooperation, including tourism 'on the basis that the tourism industry is of growing importance in promoting economic growth and social development in the Asia–Pacific region' (APEC Tourism Working Group (ATWG) 1995). The ATWG was formed in 1991 in recognition of the tourism industry's growing importance in promoting economic growth and social development in the region. The ATWG brings together tourism administrators to share information, exchange views and develop areas of cooperation on trade and policies. Participation by the private sector has involved representative travel organisations such as the Pacific Asia Travel Association (PATA), the World Travel and Tourism Council (WTTC), and the World Tourism Organization (WTO). The ATWG plans to expand participation of the private sector by inviting more representatives to attend as observers to ATWG meetings (ATWG 2000). The vision statement of the ATWG (1999) states that it 'will foster economic development in the Asia–Pacific region through sustainable tourism growth that is consistent with the enhancement of the natural, social and cultural environment', recognising that:

- tourism is one of the region's fastest growing industries and is of significant importance to the economic development of the APEC economies;
- tourism is important in fostering regional understanding and cooperation;

- the tourism industry in member economies is at different levels of development; and
- member economies share the common goal of quality development and services.

Under its objectives, the ATWG (1995) will 'endeavour to achieve long-term environmental and social sustainability of the tourism industry by setting priority on the following:

a. removing barriers to tourism movements and investment and liberalizing trade in services and tourism;
b. developing and implementing the concepts of environmental and social sustainability in tourism development;
c. facilitating and promoting human resource development;
d. enlarging the role of the business/private sector;
e. developing cooperation and programs in the fields of information-based services related to trade and tourism; and
f. sharing information among APEC economies.'

During its two meetings held in 1999 (Manzanillo, Mexico and Lima, Peru), the ATWG's program included trade and investment liberalisation and facilitation, and economic and technical cooperation, including the development of an APEC Tourism Charter. A tourism task force, comprised of Brunei Darussalam, Korea, Mexico, New Zealand, and Singapore, with inputs from PATA and the WTTC, identified four main APEC Tourism Charter goals. These were (ATWG 2000):

- sustainable management of tourism impacts and outcomes—environmental, economic, social, and cultural;
- increased mobility of visitors and demand for tourism goods and services in the APEC region;
- removal of impediments to tourism business and investment; and
- enhanced recognition and understanding of tourism as a vehicle for social and economic development, harmonisation and sharing of tourism information, and expanding the knowledge base.

The APEC Tourism Charter, adopted by APEC Tourism Ministers in Seoul in 2000, included policy measures which aimed to (ATWG 2000):

- contribute to the minimisation of the regulatory impediments to tourism;
- promote environmentally and socially sustainable tourism;
- reduce congestion and improve passenger processing facilitation;
- identify emerging issues in tourism;
- improve the understanding of tourism; and
- enhance visitor services and tourism infrastructure.

The actions of the AWTG are not spectacular in terms of the amount of media coverage that they receive in Australia. However, they are extremely influential in terms of the direction of tourism development, and they serve to strengthen the horizontal and vertical integration of the tourism industry within the Asia–Pacific region. In seeking greater freedom of trade and investment in the Asia–Pacific region, APEC is one of a number of organisations which are seeking to develop new regimes of international tourism trade, with corresponding increased supranational economic integration (Hall 2000a).

attempts to present a more accurate picture of the direct and indirect contributions of tourism to the economy, in 1996 tourism accounted for (WTTC 1996 in Access Economics 1997, p. 22):

• about 12% of wages, salaries, and supplements in Australia—nearly $30 billion;
• nearly 9% of profits—more than $11 billion; and
• 10.1% of all taxes paid—nearly $14.75 billion.

The major economic contribution of tourism has been in the international sphere. In 1996/97, international tourism to Australia generated export earnings of $16.0 billion (up 6.0% on 1995/96). This accounted for 13.7% of Australia's total export earnings (13.8% in 1995/96) and 66.3% of services exports (65.8% in 1995/96) (ONT 1998). The greatest contributing factor to export earnings was in terms of travel credits which increased from $6.197 billion in 1991/92 to $11.926 billion in 1996/97. Table 8.6 details Australia's direct export earnings from tourism from 1997/98 to 1999/2000 and forecasts for 2000/01 to 2009/10 (DISR 2000a).

The contractionary economic policies of the Commonwealth government in the late 1980s and early 1990s, which were aimed at reducing the deficit in Australia's external account, contributed to the subdued pattern of domestic tourism demand. However, domestic tourism still accounts for almost three-quarters of all tourism in Australia. Expenditure derived from domestic tourism was $41.9 billion in 1995/96. An additional $4.6 billion was spent domestically by outbound tourists (for example, on travel agency services, travel to and from international airports, and international airfares paid to Australian carriers) (ONT 1998). The appreciation of the Australian dollar in relation to the currencies of key inbound markets such as Japan and South-East Asia might have dampened the growth of international visitor numbers and might have encouraged overseas travel by Australians, particularly as the Australian economy came out of the recession of the late 1980s (Crouch 1993; Carmody 1994). Nevertheless, the growth of international visitor numbers has drawn

TABLE 8.6 Direct tourism export earnings 1997–2010 in 1997/98 dollar terms

Year	Visitor arrivals (000s)	Export earnings (billion dollars)
1997/98	4220.0	12.79
1998/99	4288.0	*13.00
1999/2000	4651.8	*14.10
2000/01	5084.6	15.41
2001/02	5501.4	16.68
2002/03	5949.5	18.03
2003/04	6423.4	19.47
2004/05	6918.3	20.97
2005/06	7442.6	22.56
2006/07	7995.9	24.24
2007/08	8584.8	26.02
2008/09	9213.9	27.93
2009/10	9884.9	29.96

Notes:
(i) average forecast annual growth in export earnings 1999/2000 to 2009/10 was 7.8%
(ii) * estimates
(iii) numbers from 2000/01 onwards are forecasts
Source: Department of Industry, Science and Resources (DISR) (2000) *Industry science resources: sport and tourism, strong outlooks for inbound tourism: 1999–2001.* Reprinted with the permission of the Department of Industry, Tourism and Resources.

the attention of government to tourism as an economic tool for regional economic development and restructuring.

The 'tourism gap' is the difference between short-term arrivals of overseas visitors and departures of Australian residents. In 1987 foreign tourists exceeded departures of Australian residents for the first time since 1971. Although the numbers do not provide detail on the net contribution of tourism to the current account and the balance of payments, they do give some broad indication of tourism's balance of trade. The extent to which the tourism gap represents a leaking of funds overseas is quite controversial. At the end of the 1980s it was estimated that tourism's balance of trade was in deficit by almost three-quarters of a billion dollars (McKanna 1989). Indeed, it is possible that as the Australian economy improves relative to other destinations, the balance of trade might again worsen as Australians travel overseas instead of domestically (Carmody 1994). According to McKanna (1989, p. 2):

> The deficit in tourism's terms of trade suggests that it could be a mistake to concentrate on one sector of the market. The Federal Government's focus on encouraging international visitors to our shores has helped to narrow the tourism deficit. But in targeting overseas visitors, it has neglected Australia's major market—domestic tourists.

Despite the undoubted significance of international tourism to Australia's balance-of-payments, domestic tourism also represents a positive contribution to Australia's economy, particularly when it may be acting as a substitute for overseas travel. For instance, in 1990, the NSW Tourism Commission (1990, p. v) argued that 'domestic tourism will remain the driving force of the industry, supporting two of every three tourist-related jobs and dollars earned at the turn of the century'. As income increases, a greater amount of disposable income is spent on non-essential commodities and services such as recreation and tourism (ABS 1986a, 1986b). In monetary terms, total domestic travel expenditure on Australian produced goods and services rose from just over $12.7 billion in 1987/88 (NSW Tourism Commission 1990) to $41.9 billion in 1995/96 (ONT 1998). However, the long-term development of domestic tourism and its consequent economic impacts, will tend to reflect the overall state of the Australian economy and the ensuing consumer spending patterns.

State and regional economic development

> [There is] a growing involvement of local authorities in policies to sustain existing tourist developments and encourage new ones, although often the actual impacts of tourism on local employment and the economy are imperfectly understood. The direction of causality between growing employment and increasing policy involvement is often obscure and in any case variable (Hudson & Townsend 1992, p. 64).

Tourism has been recognised by all state and territory governments as making substantial contributions to economic development. For example, former Western Australian Premier Brian Burke echoed the sentiments of all states when he commented that: 'From the Government's viewpoint, the tourism industry is a vital industry in expanding Western Australia's economic base. It is, under the present economic environment, one of very few industry sectors experiencing growth' (Burke 1985, p. 20). At the state level the economic and employment impacts of tourism are considerable (see Chapter 6). However, the pattern of employment generation and economic impact is geographically uneven both between and within the states because of the location of major destinations and tourism flows.

Tourism is has long been cited as a mechanism to assist in the promotion of regional economic development in Australia, particularly in agricultural or industrial areas that are undergoing economic restructuring (Moffat, Tselpi & Mayo 1973; Guldberg & Prosser 1974; Byrne 1977; Planning Workshop 1977; Town Planning Department, City of Wollongong 1983; Centre for Regional Economic Analysis 1988; Shoalhaven City Council 1988; Jenkins 1993, 1997; Jenkins, Hall & Troughton 1998). Similarly, tourism is regarded as a mechanism by which the north of Australia might be opened up for economic development (Australian Labor Party 1979; Northern Australia Development Council 1980). However, despite the recent emphasis of the Commonwealth government on regional economic development, the actual success of tourism as a tool for regional development is problematic. For example, although there has been a general global growth in employment in service industries such as tourism, many of these positions are part time. In the case of Britain's hotel and catering sector, Robinson and Wallace (1984) noted that, although there had been extensive growth in part-time female employment, such workers were badly paid and earnt about 4% less than the average for part-time female workers in all industries (see also Chapter 7 on the nature of tourism employment). The seasonal nature of many tourist destinations can militate against some of the economic goals of regional tourist development strategies. Indeed, Urry observed that 'the more exclusively an area specialises in tourism the more depressed its general wage levels will be' (1987, p. 23)—an observation that has substantial implications for the use of tourism as a development mechanism.

The potential for tourism to contribute to regional development depends on a broad range of economic, social and political factors, including the degree of linkage among the various sectors within the regional economy, the pattern of visitor expenditure, and the extent of leakage from the regional economic system. If substantial imports of goods and services are necessary to maintain the tourism industry, the relative worth of the industry in that region is doubtful. The question of 'Who benefits?' should be fundamental to any assessment of development policies. In the case of many peripheral economic regions, primary control of the flow of tourists to the destination region might lie with companies based in the tourism-generating areas, with a consequent potential loss of control over the development process.

In economically peripheral areas the creation of some jobs through tourism is probably better than no jobs at all, but given the substantial amounts of money that governments place in regional development schemes, a closer examination of the redistributive effects of tourism development within a region is warranted. For example, although tourism is relatively labour-intensive compared with some other industries, that labour input is vulnerable to minimisation by tourism plant owners who wish to restrict costs, thereby creating a situation in which employment is often casual, part time, and underpaid—and lower paid jobs dominated by women and migrants.

If tourism is promoted as an alternative to other economic activities (such as marginal agricultural or forestry operations, or the mining industry), it is difficult for employees to transfer to the tourism industry without massive investment in retraining schemes and dramatic shifts in traditional gender roles. In many situations, tourism provides limited employment alternatives. Tourism might provide the same number of jobs (or even more) in a region, but employment patterns might dramatically shift by gender, with a potential for the development of social problems because of breakdowns in traditional roles (Hall 1994a). The potential contribution of tourism thus needs to be seen within the totality of development options, including alternative land uses which might have a greater beneficial impact on the region (Delforce et al. 1986; Butler et al. 1998; Page & Hall 2002).

Given the restructuring of the Australian agricultural economy, many rural regions 'naturally look to tourism as a means to boost their development and, where alternative employment opportunities are limited, tourism is vital to the economic survival of these areas' (V. Smith 1985, p. 13). However, although coastal resort development or rural-based tourism activities, such as farm tourism, might appear to offer significant potential for economic development, the infrastructure necessary for tourism activity might have to be imported from metropolitan areas, with little economic spin-off for the receiving area. Similarly, as noted above in the discussion of tourist multipliers, smaller and less economically developed regions, have a greater propensity to import goods and services for tourists. As Lundgren has argued in a discussion of tourism in Quebec, 'as the indigenous economic system for all intents and purposes is non-existent, these destinations can only function through importation into the region of various tourist services. This makes the destination completely dependent upon the tourist generating areas' (1982, p. 11).

Although tourism is an integral part of development strategies in many rural areas, the actual contribution of these activities to the regional economy can be quite restricted by a lack of regional interindustry linkages (Powell et al. 1987). A similar conclusion was also reached by Wales, who reported in a study of the Richmond–Tweed area of northern New South Wales that 'the regional economic impact of tourism has been confined to a small range of economic activities and a narrow spatial area generating little in the way of a propulsive effect upon the wider spectrum of total regional activity' (Wales 1976, p. 3). Therefore, if tourism is to be regarded as a major component of any regional development strategy, further consideration needs to be given by government to maximising the intraregional linkages among the various tourism-related industries.

One attempt to give effect to regional tourism development was the Tasmanian government's assistance scheme for tourism-related projects under the 3:1 Co-operative Marketing Grant Scheme and the Tasmania Winter Marketing Subsidy. The grant schemes were channelled through regional tourist associations which gave each region an opportunity to assess proposals in the light of local and regional needs and priorities. According to the Tasmanian Department of Tourism, the philosophy was 'to ensure that people with the knowledge of local needs, particularly based on feed-back from visitors, have input into the decision making process' (Dept. of Tourism (Tasmania) 1987, p. 21). Similarly, the federal government has also operated direct funding for regional tourism, although the value of the scheme along with the means by which funding is distributed has been well criticised by Jenkins (1997).

The employment opportunities generated by tourism development have thus aroused a great deal of controversy regarding their true value to the host community. There is little critical analysis of the quality of tourism-related employment in Australia. However, a study of high-level, highly specialised ski resorts in Alpine France, which might be broadly comparable to Australia's ski resorts, reported: 'the combination of corporate capital, distant investors and a state planning mechanism has limited the participation of the valley populations chiefly to un-skilled, seasonal occupations' (Barker 1982, p. 407). Furthermore, economic development at the regional level can be constrained by a political failure to develop appropriate marketing strategies or networks. Commenting on the preparation of a regional tourism marketing plan in north-eastern California during the early 1980s, Smith et al. (1986, p. 432) noted that 'provincialism and turfdom still hamper progress'.

One further aspect of regional economic development is related to the nature of the market which particular regions attract. Although much of the focus of government tourism policy is on the international holiday market, primarily because of the perceived contribution it can make to the balance of payments, the VFR and domestic tourism markets might have greater potential to contribute to regional development and economic redistribution (D.G. Pearce 1987, 1993). The international tourism 'boom' of the 1980s was concentrated on Queensland and New South Wales, a trend which was broadly continued during the 1990s. However, 'VFR tourism by its very nature will tend to be more evenly distributed around the country' and be less susceptible to fluctuations and downturns in the international holiday market (Jackson 1990, p. 17). For example, in 1989, when other forms of tourism declined in the post-Expo year, VFR tourism continued to grow, with states with the lowest relative proportion of VFR travellers experiencing the greatest overall downturns in visitor arrivals. Furthermore, 'VFR tourism, in contrast to that of holidaymakers and business visitors, requires less infrastructural investment and its net benefits to the domestic economy as a whole are more direct. Whist tourist hotel chains can be, and increasingly are, foreign owned, VFR accommodation cannot be so' (Jackson 1990, p. 17).

TOURISM INVESTMENT IN AUSTRALIA

> Foreign investment is directed toward the supply of tourism services—it does not of itself imply increased inbound or domestic tourism numbers . . . Foreign investment does not appear to be associated with changes in the nature and quality of services nor the effectiveness of their marketing . . . However, foreign investment will lead to an increase in tourism if it results in reduced prices paid by tourists (Forsyth & Dwyer 1993, p. 28).

The amount and form of tourism investment has emerged as one of the major policy concerns surrounding tourism in recent years. A substantial increase in levels of private investment has been one of the keys to the development of the Australian tourism industry, particularly in the provision of tourist facilities.

Tourism facilities such as hotels and resorts provide the focal point for much private investment in tourist development, although government is also a substantial investor in tourism through the provision of infrastructure in the form of roads, airports, sewage systems, distribution networks, and communication links. Nevertheless, no tourist investment will occur unless there is a demand or a perceived potential for demand for the facility. 'A facility serves no purpose unless it is associated with an appropriate resource and is provided for a definite market' (Lawson & Baud-Bovy 1977, p. 9).

Investment in tourism combines a number of factors, including the establishment of facilities, the provision of infrastructure, the development of the service and supply factors which are characteristic of tourism and, ideally, the protection of the environment.

> Direct tourism investment involves ownership of the physical property, either through the development of new facilities, or by acquiring existing stock. Indirect tourism investment

Plate 1 Blue Mountains. The scenic beauty of the Blue Mountains has attracted tourists since the middle of the nineteeth century.

Plate 2 National Gallery, Canberra. The Australian Capital Territory is extremely dependent on the tourist market that is generated by its national institutions.

Plate 3 Melbourne Casino. Melbourne Casino, the largest casino in the southern hemisphere, has had a substantial impact on the tourist and retail markets in Melbourne.

Plate 4 Off-road vehicles and tourists, Cooloola Beach, Great Sandy National Park, Queensland. Queensland's Great Sandy National Park attracts many off road vehicles and tourists. However, the sheer number of tourists it attracts may necessitate more restrictions in order to conserve the tourist resource.

Plate 5 Coastal protection, Noosa, Queensland. The rock wall at Noosa is designed to protect tourist developments which have been constructed on the former dune system. Such coastal protection mechanisms are often a response to inappropriately located tourist facilities.

Plate 6 Canal estate development, Noosa, Queensland. Canal estate development may have major impacts on estuarine systems.

Plate 7 Coastal erosion problems, northern New South Wales. Sand has been dumped onto a beach after a major storm in an attempt to protect the caravan park from further erosion.

Plate 8 Port Arthur, Tasmania. Built heritage, such as Port Arthur, can be a major tourist attraction, but it may require substantial engineering works to make it safe for people to access.

Plate 9 Boardwalk, Creepy Crawly Trail, Tasmania. This raised boardwalk which assists in removing some of the impacts of people on a fragile environment has been designed to fit into the existing environment and make the visitor experience more enjoyable.

Plate 10 Art and craft gallery in old apple storage shed, Tamar Valley, Tasmania. With rural downturns, former farm buildings may be reused by the tourism industry.

Plate 11 Vineyard development, Tamar Valley, Tasmania. Wine tourism is a growing market for the vineyards of the Tamar Valley, especially the fly/drive market from Victoria and New South Wales. Such visits may also assist in promoting wines and wineries, as customers can place their names on mailing lists and purchase the products when they return home.

Plate 12 Lake Saint-Clair, Tasmania. Lake Saint-Clair in Tasmania is a starting point for many domestic and overseas travellers who are seeking to experience some of Australia's most well-known wilderness areas.

Plate 13 Waterfront development, Hobart. Waterfront development has been important in Hobart where, apart from the development of a new waterfront hotel, the majority of the development has concentrated on renovating old buildings and giving them new uses.

Plate 14 Fremantle Markets, Fremantle, Western Australia. The Fremantle Markets are a good example of a project which contains both tourist and community-oriented shopping elements.

Plate 15 National Gallery of Victoria, Melbourne. Venues such as the National Gallery of Victoria in Melbourne are host to many cultural tourism events.

Plate 16 Quarantine Station, North Head, Sydney. To ensure that historic buildings are conserved there is a proposal to turn the site into a high quality accommodation and interpretive experience.

Plate 17 Tourism impacting on wildlife behaviour. Guided tourist group feeding a dingo on Fraser Island, Queensland.

Plate 18 Camel rides at Victoria Markets, Melbourne.

Plate 19 Fresh produce attracts locals and visitors to Victoria Markets, Melbourne.

occurs through investment in either listed and unlisted tourism vehicles or listed and unlisted property trusts with tourism assets in their portfolios (DITR 2002j, p. 1).

Investment can be allocated to both revenue-earning facilities and non-revenue-earning facilities. Non-revenue-earning facilities are typically developed by government, examples of which include the provision of infrastructure and municipal services such as parks and recreation reserves, car parks, tourist offices, and police stations. In addition, the provision of non-revenue-earning facilities essential to tourism development might also be strongly desired by the existing community. For example, recreational facilities can be attractive to both tourists and residents. Revenue-earning facilities are mainly developed by private investors seeking a return on their funds and growth of capital, although private industry might also assist in the development of non-revenue-earning facilities to establish sufficient infrastructure for the development of their projects. The main types of revenue-earning facilities are: accommodation and catering (hotels and restaurants); commerce, recreation, and sports (shops, cinemas, theatres, golf courses, stadiums); and real estate development. As with the development of non-revenue-earning facilities, many of the revenue-earning facilities that are specifically designed for the tourist market can also be utilised by the local community (Lawson & Baud-Bovy 1977; Senate Standing Committee on Environment, Recreation and the Arts 1992).

Historically, government has played a substantial role in the development of tourist regions, particularly in areas where little tourism infrastructure previously existed. Nevertheless, the growing worldwide trend towards smaller, more efficient government has meant that the government role in traditional forms of tourism investments (such as hotels and resorts) is diminishing. For example, pressure on the Commonwealth government encouraged the development of a policy for the privatisation of Qantas and Australian Airlines in the 1980s to provide them with an injection of capital and to increase their ability to compete in the marketplace. Investment in tourism developments such as hotels, motels, and resorts has traditionally been restricted by the distinctive characteristics of the tourist business, as noted by Lawson and Baud-Bovy (1977):

- a high proportion of the costs are fixed or semi-fixed whereas demand is often seasonal;
- the tourist product is perishable;
- there is little flexibility in supply;
- the tourist product has a fixed location and cannot follow the customer;
- the accommodation industry utilises a workforce which is often unused during the low season; and
- the tourist industry is sensitive to political crises or economic downturns in generating and receiving countries.

However, increasing professionalism within the industry, the development of greater management and marketing skills, and the continued growth of the tourism and travel sector have produced a greater propensity for financial institutions to invest in the tourism industry and a diminished role for family-owned businesses. The largest sources of domestic equity capital are insurance companies and superannuation funds. Nevertheless, less than 1% of their investment is in tourism. A Macquarie Bank report (1995, in DITR 2002j) put forward several reasons for this poor level of investment in tourism as compared with other industries and sectors, particularly the general property sector:

- the poor investment track record of the industry;
- a lack of awareness of the improvements in the sector and the potential for future income and capital growth;
- tourism being perceived as a high-risk venture with inadequate return; and
- tourism assets not being easily categorised as either a property or a business concern.

Investment in the Australian tourism industry has grown substantially since the early 1980s. Unfortunately, the exact pattern of investment is difficult to determine due to a lack of information about many tourism and hospitality operations, particularly in sectors other than accommodation, such as attractions, duty-free stores, restaurants, and transport. Furthermore, accurate figures on tourism investment are hard to ascertain because of difficulties in defining what operations should be classified as belonging to the 'tourism industry' (Dwyer, Findlay & Forsyth 1990; Senate Standing Committee on Environment, Recreation and the Arts 1992; DITR 2002j). As the DITR (2002j, p. 1) observed in its excellent report on tourism investment:

> Investment is a difficult term to define and to measure. Measuring the level of investment in the tourism sector is particularly difficult, since tourism is a demand side activity, not an industry as traditionally defined and identified in the Australian and New Zealand Standard Industrial Classification (ANZSIC). There is not yet an internationally agreed method of measuring tourism investment.

Nevertheless, the DITR (2002j, p. 1) went on to note that 'by examining the change over time of investment in tourism-related industries, an indication of the trends in tourism investment may be determined'.

The DITR identified two major sources of data on tourism investment—the ABS and the Foreign Investment Review Board (FIRB). Utilising the results of the TCA to identify those industries with a relatively high tourism component of their GVA (more than 10%), the DITR reported that the investment rate, defined in terms of capital expenditure as a percentage of industry value added, 'for "cultural and recreation services" was considerably higher than the whole-economy rate, perhaps due to substantial public funding. The rate for "transport and storage" was also somewhat higher than the whole-economy rate. However, the rates for "accommodation, cafés and restaurants" and particularly "retail trade" were lower' (2002j, p. 4) (Table 8.7).

Another de facto measurement of investment in tourism is in terms of new capital expenditure by private businesses. New capital expenditure refers to 'the acquisition of new tangible assets either on own account or under a finance lease and includes major improvements, alterations and additions' (DITR 2002j, p. 5). Table 8.8 shows the actual and expected private new capital expenditure by private businesses in selected industries from 1998/99 to 2001/02. In accordance with the TCA, the most relevant industrial classifications to tourism are 'retail trade' and 'transport and storage'. A third means of measuring investment is through assessment of gross fixed capital formation. Gross fixed capital formation is the value of acquisitions less disposals of new or existing fixed tangible or intangible assets. Table 8.9 shows the percentage change in gross fixed capital formation between 1986/87 and 1999/2000 by industry. Of those industries most relevant to tourism, 'cultural and recreational services' and 'retail trade' had the greatest increase in gross fixed capital formation between 1986/87 and 1999/2000. Significantly, 'accommodation, cafés and restaurants' and 'transport' had a relatively low increase in gross fixed capital formation compared with the economy-wide average (DITR 2002j).

TABLE 8.7 Industry investment rates (%), 1997/98 to 1999/2000

Industry	1997/98			1998/99			1999/2000		
	Cap. exp. ($b)	IVA ($b)	Invest. rate (%)	Cap. exp. ($b)	IVA ($b)	Invest. rate (%)	Cap. exp. ($b)	IVA ($b)	Invest. rate (%)
Agriculture, forestry & fishing	5.5	12.4	44.4	5.2	12.5	41.4	5.7	14.7	39.0
Mining	11.1	23.8	46.8	11.6	23.4	49.5	9.1	22.9	39.7
Manufacturing	13.0	67.7	19.2	12.4	68.7	18.1	12.1	71.5	16.9
Electricity, gas & water supply	5.0	14.1	35.0	5.1	14.1	36.4	6.1	14.5	41.9
Construction	2.6	19.2	13.6	2.2	20.6	10.7	2.6	24.0	10.9
Wholesale trade	2.8	26.2	10.7	4.0	29.9	13.4	4.0	31.7	12.5
Retail trade	3.4	31.4	10.7	3.3	31.1	10.7	3.6	29.6	12.3
Accommodation, cafés and restaurants	2.9	12.9	22.1	2.2	14.0	15.6	2.7	14.2	19.1
Transport & storage	5.2	21.5	24.3	5.8	22.3	26.2	5.4	23.9	22.6
Communication services	5.3	16.2	32.7	6.2	16.7	36.9	8.6	19.5	44.2
Finance & insurance	na	na	na	na	na	na	na	na	na
Property & business services	5.4	42.2	12.9	6.3	47.0	13.4	7.8	53.9	14.4
Private community services	2.6	20.8	12.5	2.8	19.8	14.2	3.1	21.71	14.3
Cultural & rec. services	3.1	8.9	35.4	3.3	9.7	33.6	3.9	10.2	38.3
Personal & other services	0.8	4.6	17.1	1.0	4.9	19.6	1.0	6.0	16.7
All industries	**73.7**	**326.7**	**22.5**	**74.8**	**340.5**	**22.0**	**84.7**	**365.9**	**23.2**

Notes:
(i) na = not available
(ii) Cap. exp.= capital expenditure—includes acquisitions of fixed tangible assets (such as plant and machinery) and intangible assets (such as patents and licences)
(iii) Invest. rate = investment rate—defined in terms of capital expenditure as a percentage of industry value added
(iv) IVA = industry value added

Source: ABS Cat. No. 8142.0, Business Operations and Industry Performance, 1999/2000 in Department of Industry, Tourism and Resources (DITR) (2002) *Research report no. 3: tourism investment*, p. 3. Reprinted with the permission of the Department of Industry, Tourism and Resources.

TABLE 8.8 Actual and expected new capital expenditure by private businesses in selected industries (current prices, $m), 1998/99 to 2001/02

Selected Industries *	1998/99 (actual)	1999/2000 (actual)	2000/01 (actual)	2001/02 (expected)
Mining	8 725	5 288	5 248	9 500
Manufacturing	9 435	9 685	8 397	8 224
Construction	1 733	1 435	1 268	752
Wholesale trade	2 700	2 599	2 071	1 793
Retail trade	3 070	3 093	2 771	3 034
Transport and storage	3 891	3 659	3 040	3 811
Finance and insurance	2 599	2 925	3 187	2 708
Property and business services	5 974	6 163	5 848	4 375
Other services **	6 554	7 601	7 527	6 814
Total (selected industries)	**44 682**	**42 447**	**39 357**	**41 011**

Notes:

* these data exclude agriculture, forestry and fishing, government administration and defence, education, and health and community services

** includes electricity and gas, communications, accommodation, cafés and restaurants, cultural and recreational services, and personal services

Source: ABS Cat. No. 5625.0, Private New Capital Expenditure and Expected Expenditure to June 2002 in Department of Industry, Tourism and Resources (DITR) (2002) *Research report no. 3: tourism investment*, p. 4. Reprinted with the permission of the Department of Industry, Tourism and Resources.

Tourism and foreign investment

Foreign investment has been one of the most significant investment issues in the Australian tourism industry since the early 1980s. The 1980s witnessed a dramatic increase in the amount of foreign investment in tourism. For example, during the 1980s, the annual growth rates of direct foreign investment in Australia were 30% from the USA and Europe, 65% from Japan, and 110% from South-East Asian countries (Bull 1990). 'The aggregate level of new tourism investment projects approved over the period 1985–86 to 1990–91 was $14.833 billion' (Forsyth & Dwyer 1993, p.27). New South Wales and Queensland were the main destinations for foreign investment in the tourism industry (Senate Standing Committee on Environment, Recreation and the Arts 1992; Department of the Treasury 1993), although the extent of foreign ownership differs from state to state and from sector to sector. For example, in 1991 foreigners owned only 15.5% of all Australia's hotel and motel rooms of 3-star rating and above, but they owned almost half—49.5%—of all 5-star establishments. In Western Australia, 32.1% of accommodation rooms were foreign-owned, and in Queensland 25.9% were foreign-owned. However, the other states and territories were substantially lower. In NSW the figure was 14.4%, in the ACT it was 14.2%, in the Northern Territory 12.9%. Tasmania was 7.8%, Victoria was 2.4% and South Australia was 1.8% (F. Cameron 1991).

International direct tourism investment has developed for several reasons (Holloway 1985). First, host governments wish to encourage foreign investors to develop tourist infrastructure where locals do not possess the necessary expertise or finance. Second, multinational or transnational tourism corporations, especially tour operators or carriers, might invest in destinations to ensure the quality and supply of their product. Third, international investors not primarily engaged in tourism

TABLE 8.9 Gross fixed capital formation, by industry, 1986/87 to 1999/2000

Industry	1986/87 ($m)	1990/91 ($m)	1994/95 ($m)	1998/99 ($m)	1999/2000 ($m)	% change 1986/87 to 1999/2000
Communication services	2 378	3 392	5 036	7 621	9 728	309.1
Cultural & rec. services	904	1 163	1 925	3111	3 405	276.7
Ownership of dwellings	12 026	18 845	26 803	32 037	38 091	216.7
Health and community services	1 707	2 467	3 188	4 154	4 554	166.8
Personal and other services	591	1 048	904	1 263	1 557	163.5
Retail trade	2 399	2 986	4 546	5 672	5 989	149.6
Mining	4 797	7 022	9 122	14 911	11 075	130.9
Property and business services	5 379	7 564	6 149	9 642	10 583	96.7
Education	1 761	2 211	2915	3 213	3 457	96.3
Manufacturing	6 877	7 819	10 701	12 340	13 442	95.5
Agriculture, forestry & fishing	2 880	2 567	4 415	5 679	5 460	89.6
Finance & insurance	3 447	4 502	3 493	5 339	6 396	85.6
Wholesale trade	1 989	2 827	2 442	3 283	3 387	70.3
Accom., cafés & restaurants	1 810	2 693	2 437	3 281	2 872	58.7
Government admin. & defence	2 603	2 869	3 418	3 256	3 996	53.5
Construction	2 064	2 164	2 781	3 160	2 723	31.9
Electricity, gas & water supply	4 292	4348	5 319	7 316	5 590	30.2
Transport & storage	8 017	7 963	9 492	9 440	9 842	22.8
Total	65 921	84 450	105 086	134 718	142 147	115.6

Source: ABS Catalogue No. 5204.0, Australian System of National Accounts, 1999/2000 in Department of Industry, Tourism and Resources (DITR) (2002) *Research report no. 3: tourism investment*, p. 5. Reprinted with the permission of the Department of Industry, Tourism and Resources.

might extend into the tourism industry to expand their investment portfolio and maximise yields. Fourth, favourable exchange rates, tax variations, or interest rate differences might make tourism attractive for an international investor. According to Bull (1988, 1990), the second and third reasons are highly significant in understanding the pattern of foreign investment in Australia, particularly given the relatively high yields over the long-term available in the Australian tourism industry and its rapid rate of growth. Nevertheless, the first and fourth reasons might also be of some significance given the various government and private initiatives that are presently being offered in Australia to attract further foreign investment in tourism. Indeed, the tourism industry has often failed to attract domestic investors because of the relatively low rate of immediate return that the tourism industry offers. As Forsyth and Dwyer (1993, p. 29) observed:

> Given the shortages in Australia of long term equity for tourism investment, coupled with forecasts for continuing global and Asia Pacific tourism growth, it is not surprising that foreign investors have been prepared to supply it. While some of the foreign investment has 'crowded out' domestic investment, total investment in the industry has increased due to foreign involvement. The extra supply of tourism services, particularly accommodation, results in more competition for the tourist expenditure and thus lower prices.

To encourage tourism development, the Australian state and federal governments have provided a number of incentives to domestic and foreign investors in tourism. For example, buildings used to provide short-term traveller accommodation, if construction commenced after 26 February 1992, could be amortised at 4% per annum, whereas the capital cost of income-producing structural improvements, such as car parks, roads and covered walkways, was deductible over forty years at the rate of 2.5% per annum (ONT 1997a). In addition, the federal government simplified the approval processes for foreign investment (ONT 1997a):

- foreign investments of $5 million to $50 million in tourism proposals required notification only;
- proposals for acquisitions of more than $50 million were examined under national interest considerations within a commercially sensitive time frame;
- properties within a designated integrated tourism resort could be on-sold without individual transaction approval (normally, any residential real estate purchase by a person not ordinarily resident in Australia required approval to proceed);
- 50% of residential units in a project could be sold off-the-plan to foreign investors; this included the acquisition of units from extensively refurbished buildings, provided that the cost of the overall refurbishment of the building exceeded 50% of the acquisition cost of the building; and
- proposals by foreign interests to acquire developed non-residential commercial real estate were no longer required to have 50% Australian equity participation or to demonstrate that the equity was not available.

However, the level of foreign investment, particularly Japanese and Asian investment, has become a major political issue in recent years (Dwyer, Findlay & Forsyth 1990; Senate Standing Committee on Environment, Recreation and the Arts 1992; Stanton & Aislabie 1992b), especially since the late 1990s with the rise of the One Nation political party. Several reasons can be postulated for the Japanese showing such interest in the Australian tourism market, including a favourable exchange rate, a desire to export capital from Japan; Australia's relatively stable economic and political environment; a recognition of strong tourism interest by Japanese travellers in

Australia; Japanese investors seeking to integrate a product for sale to Japanese tourists; a desire to have a balanced international trade; and recognition of the mutual benefits of such investment (T. Smith 1988; Bull 1990; Hall 2001d). According to the Japanese Ministry of Finance, Japanese investors invested $2.3 billion in Australia in the period April to September 1989, much of it in real estate and tourism development (*The Australian*, 14 December 1989, p. 1). Japanese foreign investment in the tourism industry in the late 1980s was around nine times as great as the next highest country, with more than 90% of Japanese investment being concentrated in two states, Queensland (69%) and New South Wales (23%) (Dwyer, Forsyth & Findlay 1990). 'Portfolio and induced investment are generally seen as beneficial, and therefore less controversial, to a host economy. The benefits of "integrative" investment undertaken by enterprises from tourist generating economies in destinations may be less' (Bull 1990, p. 331). Nevertheless, it must be emphasised that the Japanese are not the only foreign investors in the Australian tourism industry, as substantial property portfolios are also held by American, British, Hong Kong, New Zealand, and Malaysian companies (Dwyer, Forsyth & Findlay 1990). The industry perspective of foreign investment has long held that:

> . . . we utilize every opportunity in encouraging further investment. We must act quickly to overturn negative public opinion such as recent publicity given to a reported groundswell against Japanese investment in Australia which has been interpreted by the Japanese in a much wider sense. They believe that because we do not want them investing in our country that we do not want them visiting here either. (Sargeant 1988, p. 53)

Japanese investment is generally regarded by the tourism industry as being essential to the long-term development of the Australian tourism product (Department of the Treasury 1993). As T. Smith (1988, p. 183) observed: 'Investment by Japanese corporations is usually, by nature and intent, long-term. The operating cash flow short fall invariably experienced in the early years of a typical new hotel's life is not a major deterrent as it is with Australian developers'. Substantial opposition towards Japanese investment in Australia exists because of a perception among some communities that the Japanese are taking over the economy, although it must also be recognised that opposition to Japanese investment also retains distinctly racist overtones that, if they persist, could cause great harm to the inbound tourism industry. The basic facts of Japanese investment are, as the Queensland Treasurer Keith De Lacy observed, 'overlaid by a range of perceptions and issues—emotions ranging from a genuine desire by Australians to control their own land . . . to rather ugly attitudes based on racism, war experiences and general xenophobia' (*The Australian*, 3 July 1990, p. 2). However, the reaction of many Australians to Japanese investment in the tourism industry might well change, given the substantial reduction in Japanese investment in the early 1990s following the collapse of share and property values in Japan and again at the end of the 1990s following the Asian financial crisis (Hall & Page 2000). Indeed, the tourism industry might suffer in terms of the development of infrastructure, facilities, and services as the Japanese and South-East Asian funds dry up (Higgins 1993; Hall 2001d). Nevertheless, although foreign investment is acknowledged by government as being important to the development of the tourism industry, 'it is important to ensure that the identity of the Australian tourism product is not unduly compromised to the extent that the industry is largely dependent on foreign capital' (DASETT 1988a, p. 48).

Given the debate that has often surrounded the extent of foreign investment in the Australian tourism industry it is surprising that little solid information on such investment is available. However, the excellent research of the DITR has shed new light on some of the patterns of such investment. Table 8.10 illustrates the flows and stocks of direct foreign investment in Australia by industry. A negative flow indicates that sales of investments were greater than purchases. It is of interest that 'accommodation, cafés and restaurants' experienced only moderate levels of foreign investment through most of the 1990s with a dramatic withdrawal of investment occurring in 1999/2000—probably in response to the after-effects of the Asian financial crisis and Japan's poor economic performance. However, as DITR (2002j, p. 6) noted: 'interpretation of the data is difficult as changes in values of flows and stocks are a combination of changes in volume, local valuation and exchange rates'.

The final illustration of the extent of foreign investment in tourism in Australia comes from the FIRB. Although the FIRB collects data on foreign investment proposals under the 'tourism' heading 'there is no strict definition of what is included in this category, it mainly comprises investments in accommodation facilities, with most of the rest relating to investment in tourist attractions and entertainment' (DITR 2002j, p. 7) (Table 8.11). However, caution needs to be exercised in evaluating these figures because: (i) they relate to proposals which might not go ahead or might be delayed in their implementation; (ii) they tend to reflect large investments (many smaller investments, and those that fall outside of the ambit of the Act are excluded).

Foreign investment and the balance of payments

Direct foreign investment in the tourism industry can have substantial impacts on the balance of payments. Table 8.12 demonstrates the implications of tourism investment on the inflow and outflow of payments. Ideally, the difference between Inflow (I) and Outflow (O) should remain positive to justify the continued maintenance of foreign investment. Tourism is a major contributor to Australia's balance of payments and current account. Nevertheless, tourism has been criticised by some as being a dangerous strategy for economic development because of its dependency on external (foreign) sources of growth. Although this criticism has usually been levelled within the context of less-developed countries (de Kadt 1979), considerable concern has also been expressed in Australia over the degree of foreign ownership of tourism resources and the longer-term implications that this might have for the balance of payments as profits are repatriated (David & Wheelwright 1989; Daly & Stimson 1993). For example, according to Daly and Stimson (1993, p. 24):

> The very high levels of Japanese participation in Cairns' tourist industry produced vocal reactions in the early 1990s. As the issues were debated the level of Cairns' dependency became more apparent. Its success as a tourist destination had come not only because of its attractions but significantly because it was tied into the international system that controls tourist flows: the international travel agents, tour operators, international hotel chains, and international airlines. Without tourism the Cairns economy would die, and without the international connections tourism within Cairns would fade. Thus the 'miracle' region within Australia's 'miracle' industry of the 1990s was left as a dependent outlier of the world's fastest growing but most competitive industry.

Although some control has been lost overseas by virtue of Australians selling equity, it should be noted that the Australian government still has a substantial degree

TABLE 8.10 Flows and stocks of foreign direct investment in Australia, 1991/92 to 1999/2000 (in $m)

Industry	1991/92	1992/93	1993/94	1994/95	1995/96	1996/97	1997/98	1998/99	1999/2000
Flows									
Agric., forestry & fish.	−511	20	−69	88	−10	−39	21	77	151
Mining	721	−169	456	1 396	586	883	3 232	1 104	2 839
Manufacturing	4 532	5 162	2 310	1 485	1 975	143	1 404	2 962	2 337
Electricity, gas & water	n.p.	n.p.	n.p.	n.p.	3 391	1 922	1 217	2 088	1 525
Construction	82	72	−181	201	−98	519	−193	252	942
Wholesale trade	−20	454	347	852	1 457	822	2 319	509	3 666
Retail trade	396	254	109	−879	−16	114	327	185	−150
Accomm., cafés & rests	155	−49	60	81	158	55	272	134	−649
Transport & storage	92	849	158	251	213	2 769	540	−214	805
Communication services	n.p.	156	63	n.p.	n.p.	24	−101	n.p.	43
Finance & insurance	1 317	2 092	1 049	2 088	3 111	2 093	414	1 016	−438
Property & bus. services	460	263	533	−73	731	284	−293	−362	767
Other industries	16	−86	n.p.	n.p.	n.p.	−368	−50	n.p.	−26
Unallocated	−69	138	175	1 350	484	2 110	1 186	1 496	650
Total	**7 602**	**9 157**	**5 722**	**6 888**	**12 490**	**11 332**	**10 296**	**11 412**	**12 464**
Stocks ($ millions)									
Agric., forestry & fish.	736	759	793	746	619	603	627	1 063	1 535
Mining	17 641	18 715	19 673	20 425	19 849	20 724	22 171	25 095	28 914
Manufacturing	34 638	43 923	44 355	45 551	46 820	46 490	52 410	56 656	64 873
Electricity, gas & water	n.p.	n.p.	n.p.	n.p.	4 055	6 937	8 405	10 337	11 213
Construction	1 069	1 256	1 096	1 285	1 945	3 072	2 493	2 423	3 004
Wholesale trade	12 910	13 157	14 190	16 178	17 521	17 389	19 217	18 574	22 523
Retail trade	3 809	3 930	3 442	2 804	2 765	2 886	3 027	3 380	2 367
Accomm., cafés & rests	2 153	2 391	2 951	3 050	3 185	2 921	3 373	2 958	2 135
Transport & storage	1 002	1 831	1 834	1 914	2 433	4 814	5 329	5 797	6 748
Communication services	n.p.	n.p.	n.p.	n.p.	n.p.	n.p.	n.p.	n.p.	n.p.
Finance & insurance	13 030	14 328	15 443	16 830	19 500	24 640	25 121	24 823	26 250
Property & bus. services	16 543	15 081	15 605	17 870	19 075	18 295	17 840	17 957	19 551
Other industries	251	n.p.	374	553	n.p.	n.p.	n.p.	n.p.	n.p.
Unallocated	368	33	10	8	56	102	−22	131	1
Total	**104 634**	**116 560**	**121 305**	**128 695**	**140 001**	**150 827**	**162 046**	**177 328**	**200 511**

Note: n.p. = not published
Source: Department of Industry, Tourism and Resources (DITR) (2002) *Research report no. 3: tourism investment*, pp. 6–7. Reprinted with the permission of the Department of Industry, Tourism and Resources.

TABLE 8.11 FIRB approvals of tourism investments, 1995/1996 to 1999/2000

	1995/96	1996/97	1997/98	1998/99	1999/2000
Number of investments					
Less than $50 million	18	44	69	52	n/a
Greater than $50 million	11	16	19	7	n/a
Total	**29**	**60**	**88**	**59**	**56**
Total investment value ($billion)					
Less than $50 million	0.2	0.5	0.8	0.4	n/a
More than $50 million	1.3	1.8	2.8	0.7	n/a
Total	**1.4**	**2.3**	**3.6**	**1.1**	**2.4**

Source: FIRB, various annual reports in Department of Industry, Tourism and Resources (DITR) (2002) *Research report no. 3: tourism investment*, p. 8. Reprinted with permission of the Department of Industry, Tourism and Resources.

TABLE 8.12 Tourism investment and the balance of payments

Stage	Inflow to balance of payments	Outflow from balance of payments
Investment	Capital inflow (capital account)	Dividends, interest and profits (current account)
Construction	–	Design and consultancy fees; import cost of materials
Operation	Receipts from foreign tourists; souvenir sales; taxes on foreign operators; wages received from foreign operators; saving from supplying domestic tourism product (import substitution)	Royalties and technical aid; imported materials and spares; imported consumer goods, particularly food and drink; remittance of wages by expatriate workers; extra expenditures on imports by nationals resulting from earnings from the demonstration effect of tourism
Marketing	–	Overseas promotion costs; overseas-based personnel costs
	Total inflow (I)	Total outflow (O)

of control over the development process should it wish to use its considerable legal powers. However, as Leiper (2002) observed with respect to the collapse of Ansett Australia:

> A complicating factor in the Ansett case was that the Australian Government had allowed Ansett to be sold off to a foreign company, Air NZ. This meant that detailed information about trends in Ansett's business performance was not being kept in Australia, but in New Zealand where Australian observers could not be closely aware of what was happening with Ansett in the short term. It also meant that decisions about Ansett by top managers and company directors were being made in New Zealand by persons whose first duty was to the parent company Air NZ. When the going got tough for both airlines in the middle of 2001, the directors apparently looked after the parent company's interests to the disadvantage of the subsidiary company in Australia.

The loss of equity to overseas investors helps share losses as well as potential profits, and can improve the prospects of visitation from certain tourist-generating regions. Furthermore, according to Forsyth and Dwyer (1993, p. 31):

To the extent that both domestic and foreign investors are making wise investments with their debt and equity, there is nothing particularly desirable or undesirable about increases in the current account deficit, or decreases in foreign debt, that might come about as a result of tourism or foreign investment in it.

As Australia has already witnessed, overseas visitation and domestic tourism activity is affected by a range of factors including safety (terrorist activity, airline safety, tourist safety), political instability in competing destinations, industrial disputes, the generally positive image of Australia, the relatively low value of the Australian dollar, and the hosting of a number of international events which has served to heighten overseas awareness of Australia as a tourist destination. Nevertheless, probably the most critical factor in the viability of tourism development, and hence investment, is the relative value of the tourism product. Because mass tourism destinations offering sea, sun, and sand show little differentiation in the marketplace, considerable fluctuations in demand can result even from relatively small price changes, including those resulting from exchange rate fluctuations. Given the distance of Australia from the source countries of many of its inbound tourists, the relative value of tourism product and the potential yield might therefore play a major part in the viability of tourism investments in Australia.

BROADENING THE ECONOMIC BASE: AMENITIES AND CLUSTERS

Although many regions and settlements are desperately trying to encourage greater rates of tourist visitation to broaden the host community's economic base, many established destinations are trying to attract other forms of economic activity to ensure that the local economy is not totally dependent on tourism. Scenic or amenity-rich tourist areas seek to attract light manufacturing, educational and research industries. However, many tourist destinations are too isolated or lack the appropriate infrastructure for economic development not associated with leisure, and face the prospect of failure in the new enterprise. An area which has used tourism as a lever to further economic development is far north Queensland. According to the Queensland Department of Local Government and Planning (QDLGP 1997) the region's economic development to date has occurred in three waves:
- initial growth of core tourism businesses (for example, tourist accommodation, tours, and attractions);
- growth of industries supplying goods and services to tourism-focused enterprises (for example, food production, taxi services, and vessel construction); and
- development of industries able to capitalise on the facilities and infrastructure created by tourism, including the transport infrastructure and marketing channels it has developed (for example, the diverse range of industries from agribusiness to high value-added services such as education, health, and tropical science).

According to QDLGP (1997), future priority development opportunities include:
- tradable services including education, environment, health, mining, and the arts;
- tourism, including business and cultural tourism;
- agribusiness—value-added exports;
- forestry; and
- marine-based industries.

These will initially be dependent on the business and transport networks made possible by tourism development—for example, airports, seaport infrastructure, and road routes. Over time the importance of tourism as the core user of such services can diminish as other industries are able to take advantage of international, domestic, and intra-state business opportunities. However, to become established they need to leverage off tourism.

The north Queensland experience has focused on the use of clusters as a mechanism for economic development. Clustering is a form of network structure particularly suited to building on the innovative and marketing capabilities of individual firms, particularly small and medium enterprises (Hall et al. 1998). Firms that are too small by themselves to sustain a significant research and development effort or to market internationally or interstate can, through network strategies such as clustering, gain the synergies of collaboration. They can achieve these outcomes without loss of the dynamics of competition, and this offers outcomes that are superior to those that would be attained by markets alone (Enright & Roberts 2001).

A cluster in a geographic region is defined as a concentration of companies and industries that are interconnected by the markets they serve and the products they produce, as well as by the suppliers, trade associations, and educational institutions with which they interact (Porter 1990). Such chains of firms are the primary 'drivers' of a region's economy, on whose success other businesses, such as construction firms, for example, depend for their own financial viability. An industry cluster includes companies that sell inside as well as outside the region, and also supports firms that supply raw materials, components, and business services to them. These clusters form 'value chains' that are the fundamental units of competition in the modern, globalised world economy. Clusters in a region form over time and stem from the region's economic foundations, its existing companies, and local demand for products and services (Waits 2000). In a number of regions where strong interconnections exist tourism acts as a good example of a cluster.

Regional cluster strategies are now evident in South Australia, north Queensland and the Hunter (Blandy 2000; Enright & Roberts 2001). The Australian wine industry is one of the few sectors to have adopted this approach (Blandy 2000; Enright & Roberts 2001), with considerable relationships to wine tourism as a constituent of the wine cluster (Hall et al, 1998; Hall, Johnson & Mitchell 2000). Enright and Roberts (2001) have noted that, despite considerable rhetoric, the actual incidence of clustering is limited in Australia. However, they argued that the existence of industry associations provides a ready base for governments to adopt an enabling or facilitating approach, using industry associations as intermediaries, in arrangements that are based on performance commitments (see also Marsh & Shaw 2000, pp. 57–64).

TOURISM INSIGHT

WINE CLUSTERS AND TOURISM

Wine has been recognised as an industry in which clustering is a significant competitive factor. Porter (1990) used the Californian wine industry as an example of successful cluster development. Similarly, Blandy (2000, p. 21) cited the example of the South Australian wine industry as 'the classic example of a successful industry cluster in South Australia . . . a group of competing, complementary and interdependent firms that have given strong economic drive to the State through the cluster's success in exporting its products and know how nationally and internationally'.

Cluster formation is regarded as a significant component in the formation of positive external economies for firms, including those of the wine industry, with tourism being recognised as a significant component (Porter 1990), and Telfer (2000, 2001) has argued that cluster development has been a significant component of wine and food tourism network development in the Niagara region of Canada.

Although one of the lessons of cluster development programs around the world 'is that there is no precise, "right" (one size fits all) formula for developing industry clusters' (Blandy 2000, p. 80), a number of factors has been recognised as significant in the development of clusters and the associated external economy which serves to reinforce the clustering process. These include:

- the life cycle stage of innovative clusters; for example, Audretsch and Feldman (1997) have argued that the generation of new economic knowledge tends to result in a greater propensity for innovative activity to cluster during the early stages of the industry life cycle, and to be more highly dispersed during the mature and declining stages of the life cycle;
- government financing and policies;
- the skills of the region's human resources;
- the technological capabilities of the region's research and development activities;
- the quality of the region's physical, transport, information, and communication infrastructure;
- the availability and expertise of capital financing in the region;
- the cost and quality of the region's tax and regulatory environment; and
- the appeal of the region's lifestyle to people that can provide world-class resources and processes.

However, several other factors can be noted as important in terms of cluster success in wine tourism (Hall 2001e, 2001f), and these can be readily applicable to other tourism regions:

- spatial proximity—the extent of substantial spatial separation of enterprises within a region due to physical factors can reduce interaction among enterprises;
- administrative proximity—the existence of multiple public administrative agencies and units within a region can disperse clustering and networking efforts;
- the existence of a 'champion' to promote the development of a network is regarded as important to encourage cooperation; ideally, this person should be from the private sector; and
- ensuring that informal and formal meetings are held between stakeholders to develop relationships.

It is of interest that one of the factors in influencing the development of wine and food tourism clusters are the region's amenity values. Such values can encourage lifestyle migration, thus importing people, entrepreneurial skills, and capital to a region. Therefore, cluster formation can be influenced as much by the social and physical geography as it is by economic geography.

Another promising means of broadening the economic base of destinations has been the rapidly growing retirement market (Karn 1977). The presence of retirees in communities can be useful in reducing the impacts of the seasonality of tourist visitation, and the influx of pension monies and investment for retirement housing can provide a major influx of capital funds. The Gold Coast represents the best Australian example of the phenomenon of the search for the sun by retirement settlers. However, the Sunshine Coast in south-east Queensland, and the central (Gosford, Woy Woy) and northern (Ballina–Byron Bay, Coffs Harbour, Tweed Heads) coasts of New South Wales are also major retirement areas (P.A. Murphy 1981).

The establishment of holiday homes has also developed as a means of broadening the economic base of rural townships. Significant economic benefits can be gained by the presence of second homes in a community, principally in the form of the payment of rates to local government and in payment to local services for management and maintenance of properties. Furthermore, some benefits can accrue to local businesses during the construction phase. However, considerable physical impacts can result from the construction of accommodation that is unsympathetic with the local landscape, and the cyclical nature of visitation to second homes by owners can lead to conflict between residents and visitors (Beattie 1987). Indeed, from a social planning perspective, second homes can have substantial impacts, as noted by Mills (1983, p. 45):

> The fact that such accommodation is sometimes left unoccupied for considerable periods has led to justifiable concern, and in some cases obvious hostility. It can clearly become a source of friction where local inhabitants seeking accommodation find themselves in competition with outsiders who may have greater financial resources, and thus cause a local housing shortage and a rapid escalation in property values to the disadvantage of the native population.

An alternative to second home development has been the establishment of time-sharing resorts. The idea first developed in France and the United States in the late 1960s and early 1970s and has since become an internationally accepted component of the tourism and leisure market. Multi-ownership, otherwise known as time-sharing, has recently become a significant factor in tourism development in certain parts of Australia (Hopper 1984). Time-sharing is offered worldwide as an economically and socially viable alternative to normal full-time ownership because it enables people to reduce maintenance costs, rating charges, and even the vandalism that is sometimes associated with unoccupied dwellings. However, significant problems can loom for the consumer in the management of such resorts.

The drawbacks of tourist development

If there are definite limits to tourism as the basis of local economic development strategies, it is difficult to avoid the question of whether, realistically, there is an alternative. The answer to this question will be place- and time-specific but, undoubtedly, there are local authorities and communities which, as of now, can see little alternative to a heavy, if not sole, reliance on tourism for work and incomes. What does the future hold for them? (Hudson & Townsend 1992, p. 66).

Tourism undoubtedly has the potential to contribute a great deal to economic development at the national, state, and regional levels. However, complete economic dependence on the tourism dollar is not an appropriate development strategy. As Mullins commented with respect to the Gold Coast and the Sunshine Coast, 'behind this carnival mask that is tourism urbanisation, there is a tragic face; high unemployment and low household income suggest rates of poverty and near poverty which are greater than in most other major Australian cities' (1990, p. 41). Although tourist growth has proven to be resilient over the past two decades, events can occur which lead to a levelling out in tourism growth or even a decline at particular locations. Such events can be beyond human control, as in the case of natural disasters such as floods, cyclones, or earthquakes, or they can be created by people, in the form of industrial disputes, overzealous pricing, or acts of war.

The vulnerability of the international tourist industry is most obvious at times of economic or political uncertainty, either in generating or receiving countries. The vulnerability of a destination to a changed pattern of tourist behaviour is increased when the tourist clientele comes mainly from one generating country or region.

One of the most significant drawbacks to tourism development is the seasonal nature of tourism which can lead to underemployment or unemployment at certain times of the year, as noted by the WTO (1984, p. 43):

> The most specialised destinations (some beach, mountain, hunting or fishing destinations at certain times of the year, etc.) are usually the most seasonal because of the seasonal factor associated with tourist utilization of their basic resources. Tourist destinations supported by large urban centres, while having high points of activity, have more continuous operation throughout the year because they depend upon a more diversified demand.

In addition to its often seasonal nature, tourism can also place inflationary pressures on local or regional economies. The inflationary impact is due mainly to three factors. First, the increased demand for land on which to build tourist facilities can place pressure on the availability of building sites and housing stock, leading to an increase in land values. Second, the rapid rate of creating tourist facilities can cause an increase in building costs. Third, the seasonal influx of a relatively higher spending population can cause a corresponding increase in food and beverage consumption. The inflationary impact depends on the relative size of the local market, compared with the tourist demand, and the economic structure of the region.

Tourism development also leads to a number of unquantifiable impacts which can be extremely significant for how tourism is viewed by the wider community. Indeed, Baud-Bovy and Lawson argued that 'the intangible effects of developing tourism may be very significant and even of over-riding importance' (1977, p. 22) and went on to cite the Economic Commission for Europe (1976) which, in a study of tourism development in Europe, argued that traditional investment analysis is inadequate in assessing the external effects associated with tourism and recreation. Similarly, in the Australian context, the North Coast Environment Council (1987, p. 2) noted that: 'The simplistic valuation of areas of natural environment only in gross dollar terms is inappropriate, since this is a narrow assessment of environments capable of satisfying a range of social values'. Nevertheless, efforts to establish the value of development proposals can be useful in determining aspects of intergenerational equity which are a component of ideas of sustainability (see Chapter 1) (Hundloe 1990).

In terms of establishing a sustainable economic development strategy, it is to be hoped that Australia does not reflect Heeley's (1981, p. 75) outline of the British experience of using tourism as a development tool:

> The Government's present objectives in tourism amount to little more than a statement of good faith in the balance of payments and regional economic development contributions of tourism and in the desirability of spreading tourist flows in time and space. They do not provide a basis on which to implant a national perspective on the strategies for tourism which are emerging at a regional and local level.

Successful sustainable economic tourism development 'must generate a minimum of additional costs to the community at large and provide widespread economic benefit while maintaining the range of values of the local resource' (North Coast Environment Council 1987, p. 4). Therefore, as the following chapters demonstrate, it is essential that the social and environmental consequences of tourism development are taken account of in the development process.

CHAPTER SUMMARY

This chapter has provided an overview of the broad economic framework within which tourism operates in Australia. The use of tourism as a mechanism for economic development, particularly in areas undergoing economic restructuring and in peripheral regions, requires a more critical examination of the worth of tourism than has been the case. The concepts of tourism's external account and the tourism multiplier were examined to illustrate their utility as conceptual tools in the analysis of tourism's economic impacts at various levels and tourism's contribution to the national economy.

The economic impacts of tourism were analysed at international, national, state, and regional levels. At all levels, tourism was illustrated to have substantial economic and employment benefits. However, it was noted that such benefits are not evenly distributed in time or space. It was therefore argued that host communities need to ensure that they are not solely dependent on tourism as a means of economic and regional development if they are to minimise the potential impacts of downturns in the tourist market. The chapter concluded with a discussion of the drawbacks of tourism development and the difficulty in quantifying many of the social and environmental impacts of tourism, which is critical to a sustainable tourism development strategy.

SUGGESTIONS FOR FURTHER READING

Few areas of tourism have been covered in more depth than its economic impacts. Most general texts have a chapter or two on the subject. Bull (1994) *The Economics of Travel and Tourism*, is a good standard text on the subject.

Cooper and Pigram (1984) provide a good overview of the role that tourism played within the Australian economy in the mid-1980s, and some of the implications of deregulation are outlined in the IAC (1989) and the Senate Standing Committee on Environment, Recreation and the Arts (1992). Readers seeking current information on economic aspects of tourism should consult the publications of the ABS, DITR, BTR, and the respective state tourism commissions.

Readers wishing to conduct further reading on problems with the use of multipliers and other measures of economic activity at a variety of levels should consult Archer (1977, 1982), Baretje (1982), Frechtling (1987), Bull (1991, 1994), and West (1993). An excellent account of the role of tourism as an agent for economic development within the European context is Williams and Shaw (1988a) 'Tourism and development: introduction', in *Tourism and Economic Development: Western European Experiences*. More detailed studies of the economic impacts of tourism in Australia are Haigh and Rieder (1989), Arnold et al. (1989), Senate Standing Committee on Environment, Recreation and the Arts (1992), West (1993), Skene (1996), WTTC (1996), and Access Economics (1997). Extremely useful discussions of the TSA are to be found in Smith and Wilton (1997), WTTC (1997), Frechtling (1999), Leiper (1999), and the DITR (2002g).

INTERNET SITES

Also see the following websites:
- Australian Bureau of Statistics:
  www.abs.gov.au

- Bureau of Transport and Regional Economics:
  www.dotars.gov.au/btre/research.htm

- Also refer to government websites as noted in Chapters 5 and 6.

THE ECONOMIC DIMENSIONS AND IMPACTS OF TOURISM

Key concepts

Key concepts covered in this chapter included:
balance of payments, external account, tourism satellite account, employment benefits, flow-on effects, organisation of capital, penetration of capital, leakage, elasticity of demand, regional development, multiplier effect, primary impact, secondary impact, induced impact, indirect impact, internationalisation, concentration, trade barriers, the tourism gap, economic base, holiday homes, second homes, retirement market, time-share resorts, seasonality, localised inflation, unquantifiable impacts, social values.

Questions for review and discussion

1 What is the multiplier effect and why is it important in the analysis of the economic impacts of tourism?

2 What are the major trends in the international economic development of tourism?

3 How can tourism contribute to regional economic development in Australia?

4 Describe how tourist destinations can broaden their economic base.

5 How do the characteristics of tourism affect investment in tourism developments such as hotels, motels, and resorts?

6 Why has the issue of foreign investment in tourism become such an emotive point in recent years?

THE SOCIAL AND CULTURAL DIMENSIONS OF TOURISM

9

Economic benefits cannot be ignored, least of all by people living in areas that have become reliant on the industry. But the strength of community feeling against fast tourism expansion does not appear to have been alleviated by the promise of economic riches (Tolhurst 1990, p. 10).

ALTHOUGH the social dimensions of tourism in destination areas have been major themes in international tourism research, particularly in less-developed countries, such issues did not begin to receive significant attention in Australia until the mid-1980s. It is of interest that this was a time when international tourists and hallmark events started to become more visible in Australia. However, the emergence of xenophobic reactions to international visitors and the development of negative reactions to tourism development in some destinations have meant that government and private industry are increasingly paying attention to public attitudes to tourism. For example, the New South Wales Tourism Commission *Tourism Development Strategy* (1990, p. 31) stressed the economic significance of the social impacts of tourism, noting that it is 'important to state that if residents believe that they are experiencing negative social impacts, then this belief, rather than any objective reality, will be the basis for their hostility to tourism and may act as an impediment to the growth of the industry'. Similarly, Craik (1988a, p. 26) argued that despite difficulties in quantifying the social impacts of tourism, 'in the same way as . . . bed requirements and even environmental impacts . . . it is perhaps the most important aspect of tourism development'. Therefore, an examination of the social impacts of

269

tourism is essential not only from a community planning perspective, but also from the perspective of tourism growth and development. Without such an examination, tourism planning becomes increasingly difficult (Hall 1988a). As G. Ross (1991b, p. 157) observed:

> If pleasant and satisfying experiences involving local residents are important in the destination images of tourists and in their decision-making processes, then a consideration of the well-being of local residents in the context of tourist development would seem critical. Should residents of tourist communities come to believe that continual tourist development is destroying their physical and social environment and that tourists are the symbols of this process, then a degree of unpleasantness may eventually characterize many resident-visitor interactions, which would ultimately damage the image of friendliness in the locals so prized by overseas tourists at present.

THE SOCIAL IMPACTS OF TOURISM

The social impact of tourism refers to the manner in which tourism and travel effects changes in collective and individual value systems, behaviour patterns, community structures, lifestyle, and the quality of life. The variables that contribute to resident perceptions of tourism can be categorised as extrinsic or intrinsic (Faulkner & Tideswell 1996). Extrinsic variables refer to factors which affect a community at a macro level—for example, the stage of tourism development, the ratio between tourists and residents, cultural differences between tourists and residents, and seasonality. Intrinsic variables are those factors which vary according to the characteristics of individuals in a given population—for example, demographic characteristics, involvement in tourism, and proximity to tourist activity.

The potential impacts of tourism on host communities have been recognised for many years and have been the focus of much work on tourism in less-developed countries (Farrell 1977; de Kadt 1979). However, tourism is also increasingly recognised as having the potential to induce dramatic social changes in industrialised countries such as Australia. The social impacts of tourism have historically been cast in a negative light. As Martyn (1970, p. 45) has noted, tourists 'appear to the local residents to pre-empt the best of everything—hotel rooms, food and rare wines, luxury products of all kinds, even the best looking girls'. Nevertheless, although a negative image of the tourist is often portrayed in popular culture, tourism has also been promoted as a force for better international understanding and a mechanism for providing employment and social services to local communities (NSW Tourism Commission 1989b).

Some of the basic principles of the social dimensions of tourism in destinations have been recognised for a number of years. According to Matthews (1978), the scale of social impact is determined by the numbers of tourists in relation to the host population and by the economic level of the host community as compared with that of the tourists. However, to this should also be added another factor—the cultural differences between host and guest. As Lundgren (1972 in D.G. Pearce 1989, p. 217) observed: 'the force of tourist-generated local impact seems to increase with distance from the generating country'. An additional critical factor, particularly in Australia, is the visibility of the tourists and the tourism industry. 'No one will dispute the ability of tourists, as a species, to irritate their hosts through sheer arrogant display of wealth and/or brazen disregard of their hosts' sensitivities and values' (Gray 1974, p. 386). The poorer the host community and the greater the degree of economic reliance of the hosts on the export of tourism services, the greater the irritants are likely to be. Nevertheless, one of the problems in accurately assessing the social impacts of tourism has been a lack of 'consistent method and standardised instrumentation' in measuring resident perceptions (Lankford & Howard 1994, p. 123).

One of the most significant social dimensions of tourism development is the extent to which non-local investment can reduce local control over tourist resources. As Krippendorf (1987, p. 55) has questioned: 'Why has the loss of local autonomy—certainly the most negative long-term effect of tourism—been practically ignored? Why does the local population tolerate it?' Indeed, this question has become even more pertinent as economic globalisation has become more accelerated, with the 'internationalisation of national economic spaces through growing penetration (inward flows) and extraversion (outward flows)' (Jessop 1999, p. 23) being one of the key characteristics of globalisation and, correspondingly, of international tourism. Jessop's observation regarding the effect on national economic space could equally well be directed at the effect on local areas. Clearly, community reaction to issues of globalisation are aimed at more than just tourism. Consider, for example, the rise of the One Nation political party in the late 1990s and some of the debates regarding refugees and migration during the 2001 federal election. International tourism and tourists become ready targets for dissatisfaction because of their visibility. Table 9.1 presents a hypothetical example of mass tourist destination development from such a perspective.

It must be emphasised that Table 9.1 is only a hypothetical model. It does not necessarily hold that the model will apply in all situations. Nevertheless, substantial evidence suggests that if planning controls are not in place or if little community consultation occurs, tourism development can overrun a destination community, particularly in less-developed nations (Mathieson & Wall 1982; D.G. Pearce 1989; Mowforth & Munt 1998). However, the potential loss of local autonomy is only one aspect of the social dimensions of tourism within destinations. The following pages examine a range of social issues associated with tourism.

Tourism and place

Substantial support exists for the hypothesis that if tourism activity is concentrated for an extended period of time in an area, the attitudes of permanent residents to tourism and tourists become negative (Pizam 1978; King et al. 1993). Tourism can produce resentment of the apparent wealth of visitors. A longer-term effect can be a breakdown or loss of an individual's sense of place as his or her surroundings are transformed to accommodate the requirements of tourism (Dovey 1989). A 'sense of place' arises where people feel a particular attachment or personal relationship to an area in which local knowledge and human contacts are meaningfully maintained. 'People demonstrate their sense of place when they apply their moral or aesthetic discernment to sites and locations' (Tuan 1974, p. 235). However, people might consciously notice the unique qualities of their place only when they are away from it, when it is being rapidly altered, or when it is being represented or marketed in a way they do not relate to.

The concept of sense of place is of significance to tourism development for a number of reasons. The creation of tourism precincts in inner-city areas can force

TABLE 9.1 Hypothetical stages in the development of a mass tourist destination

Stage	Community effects and response
Stage 1 Developers buy cheap land	Little attention is paid to the potential negative impacts on the community. Development is justified to locals in terms of employment and potential income for the local community. Some locals, usually propertied, gain monetary rewards through land speculation.
Stage 2 Site development commences	Little consideration is given to environmental and social concerns in the development process. Local authorities are persuaded to provide infrastructure such as roads, sewage, and water supply on the basis of the potential income to be injected into the local community by the tourist development. The architecture of the project is often in an 'international' style rather than reflecting the character of the local area.
Stage 3 Site development under way	Developers employ architects, building contractors, and furniture suppliers from outside the local community on the basis that the amount of local expertise is insufficient to meet the demands of the project. Some local community members are employed for temporary on-site labouring and sub-contracting.
Stage 4 Marketing of development project in main tourism-generating regions	Tourists arrive from outside the local community. Relatively little money trickles into the community from tourists because the majority of their spending is prepaid or is retained within the tourist development.
Stage 5 Fully established development	Local community members are employed in housekeeping and more menial positions. Food and drink is imported into the area to meet the demands of international clientele.
Stage 6 Fully established development	As employment and income benefits fail to materialise, local community resistance to the project increases with substantial anger directed towards tourists and development employees ('outsiders') living within the community. Substantial reassessment of the tourism development occurs.

Source: adapted from Lundberg (1972); Doxey (1975); Krippendorf (1987).

long-term residents to leave and can change the character of the community, as well as changing the physical make-up of the community. In Australia this certainly applies to a number of inner-city areas that have been associated with tourism development. In these instances, the identification of long-term residents with the physical and social structure of the neighbourhood can be deeply disturbed, leading to a condition of 'placelessness' (Relph 1976).

According to Relph (1976, p. 141): 'There are at least two experienced geographies; there is a geography of places, characterised by variety and meaning, and there is a placelessness geography, a labyrinth of endless similarities'. This observation predates more recent observations regarding the 'Disneyfication' or 'McDonaldisation' of places by which the landscape becomes placeless because cities are so similar with global brands and architecture overwhelming the integrity of the regional and local aesthetic (Mullins 1994; Meethan 1996, 2001). The standardisation of production and consumption in many aspects of Western urban life has been discussed by Ritzer (1996) in terms of the 'McDonaldisation' of production and consumption, with the 'golden arches' of McDonald's acting as a metaphor for the way in which globalisation affects society and the urban environment. According to Relph (1976, p. 141), cultures can continue 'the inevitable spread of placelessness', or transcend 'placelessness through the formulation and application of an approach for the design of a lived-world of significant places'. Relph (1976, p. 147) might well have been correct when he argued: 'A deep human need exists for associations with significant places. If we choose to ignore that need, and allow the forces of placelessness to continue unchallenged, then the future can only hold an environment in which places simply do not matter'. Nevertheless, more than 25 years since these words were written, it is likely that few people now live in a city, town, or suburb which does not have a McDonalds, a KFC, a Pizza Hut, Starbucks, Body Shop, or Gap.

Destinations faced with rapid tourism development might attempt to preserve components of the townscape, including buildings and parks. The conservation of heritage is often a reaction to the rate of physical and social change within a community. Generally, when people feel they are in control of their own destinies they have little call for nostalgia. The strength of heritage conservation organisations in many areas of Australia is perhaps a reflection of a desire to retain a sense of continuity with the past during a time of rapid change. In addition, the protection of historic buildings and the establishment of heritage precincts can also produce a significant economic return to destinations because of the desire of many visitors to experience authentic forms of tourism.

Australian Aboriginal people also have a strong sense of place. Traditional Aboriginal groups have an intense attachment to their estate lands (Strehlow 1947; Stanner 1965). As Tuan (1976, p. 32) observed: 'It is the home of ancestors, the dreaming place in which every incident in legend and myth is firmly fixed in some unchanging aspect of nature—rocks, hills, mountains, even trees, for trees can outlive many human generations'. For these reasons, conflict has occurred between the tourism industry—which wants to develop a landscape and presentation of people and place for its own needs—and Aboriginal groups in places such as Uluru, Kakadu, Katherine Gorge, and Cape York. As H. Ross (1991, p. 177) noted:

'Tourist' is a depersonalising classification referring to people in a temporary status. Aboriginal people like to 'place' non-Aboriginal visitors to their country in their own categories of social meaning, through a process of personalisation and incorporation. Those with whom they become intensely involved are allocated a place in the local kinship system, and expected to learn and observe kinship norms governing interaction with other people (close friendships, tutorships, and avoidance relationships) and correct behaviour towards the environment.

The tourism industry is 'now both the consumer and producer of cultural diversity' (Finlayson & Madden 1994). Therefore, it is of great significance that the NSW

Rainforest Sanctuary, South Bank, Brisbane. The redevelopment of the South Bank of Brisbane for the 1988 Expo had substantial social impacts on a small segment of the community. However, these impacts now seem to have been forgotten given the popularity of the leisure landscape it provides.

Tourism Commission (1990, p. vii) stated that 'Aborigines' traditional concepts of relationships, privacy, space, sacred sites and rites and the land all point away from a major participation in the tourist industry'.

Individual buildings, townscapes, and landscape,s help define the cultural char-acteristics of a region and help determine the attractiveness of a destination in the tourism marketplace. Buildings and landscapes also serve a significant function in the formation of identity, and perform an important role in the historic memory of a community (Haraven & Langenbach 1981). Such social features should not be lost on the Australian tourism industry. Nevertheless, it should also be recognised that change is also normal part of the life of a community.

Change is also a crucial element of tourism. The creation of a tourist precinct or the location of event facilities can rejuvenate an urban area through the construc-tion of new infrastructure. Traditionally this has been used to revitalise inner-city locations or areas that are regarded as requiring renewal. In Australia this approach has been utilised in Fremantle for the 1987 America's Cup defence, in Brisbane for the 1988 Expo (Kingston 1987), in Sydney for the 1988 Darling Harbour Bicen-tenary project (Thorne & Munro-Clark 1989; Hall 1998b) and the 2000 Olympic Games (Hall & Hodges 1996; Murphy & Watson 1997), and in Melbourne with the dockland redevelopment project of the late 1990s. In New Zealand such mech-anisms have been associated with the redevelopment of the Auckland waterfront (for the 2000 America's Cup) and the Wellington waterfront (Page 1996; Hall & Kearsley 2001). Indeed, so common is this strategy, that it is almost taken for granted that the benefits of such developments are universally accepted. Nevertheless, it is worth-while to examine critically some of the impacts of tourism development in Australia.

A useful example is the development of the South Bank area in Brisbane, now one of the key urban tourism areas of Brisbane. Visitors to the area are impressed by the availability of green space within the city, the beach area, the attractions, and the activities that are available. However, the justification for the development of the area from light industrial waterfront use to leisure and entertainment was the hosting of the 1988 Brisbane Expo (Park & Feros 1985). Indeed, according to the general manager of the Brisbane Expo, Neil Minnikin (1987, p. 3): 'The South

Brisbane site won approval because of its central position, its suitability for an event such as World Expo 88 and its potential for development from a run-down area to one of the most valuable, attractive precincts in Brisbane'. Nevertheless, Expo 88 had significant on-site impacts in the displacement of small businesses through land resumption and payment of compensation. The Brisbane City Town Clerk, E.K. Campbell (30 July 1987, in Olds 1988, p. 53), noted that 111 small businesses had been displaced, that 73 properties (130 claims—72 owners, 58 tenants) had been resumed. In addition, the long term redevelopment of the Expo site had substantial impacts on the surrounding communities (1987, p. 6). As Craik (1988b, p. 5) observed: 'It seems clear that whatever the shape of the re-development, it will favour large scale development of tourist and commercial activities geared towards those who can afford it'. Looking at the Brisbane River foreshore today and the South Bank area, it is clearly apparent that this has happened. However, given the time that has elapsed since the controversies surrounding the redevelopment, do people still care or are they happy with the changes that have taken place? Or have they just forgotten?

The creation of a post-industrial urban environment can therefore have a major impact on the people who traditionally occupy areas designated as suitable for renewal or rejuvenation because they are run down and have low real estate values. Usually these occupants are the poorer people in society. Although it might be argued that 'for many residents the growth of a tourist core to their city adds excitement, leisure opportunities and a sense of civic pride' (Australian Tourism Industry Association (ATIA) 1990, p. 17), the issue of which residents benefit and which lose out is seldom raised. Unfortunately, the creation of a 'desirable' middle-class environment can lead to increased rates and rents, accompanied by a corresponding breakdown in community structure, including ethnicity, as families and individuals are forced to relocate (Cowie 1985; Shaw 1985, 1986; D. Graham, 1988; Reynolds 1988; Page 1995; Olds 1998). Furthermore, as the Darling Harbour project and the associated monorail development have demonstrated, the creation of urban leisure precincts can be undertaken with little formal public participation in the decision-making process and in the consideration of the wider costs and benefits of undertaking such a project (Thorne & Munro-Clark 1989). In the case of the Darling Harbour redevelopment, the requirements of the project meant that participatory procedures and environmental safeguards were set aside (Hall 1998b). It has been noted that this involved 'the disabling of public discussion by the deliberate withholding of information', and a 'clear contempt shown specifically for concerns that relate to the urban environment as distinct from purely economic or technical reasons' (Thorne, Munro-Clark & Boers 1987, p. 20). However, more than a decade later, do people care? Have relationships in the community and surroundings really been substantially negatively affected in the long term, or have new sets of social and community relationships been developed?

Tourism-related social change in communities has become even more important as Australia has embraced economic globalisation and has become involved in greater competition for capital and visitors, often involving state and city competition. For example, the longstanding competition between Sydney and Melbourne has been described by Murphy and Watson (1997, p. 1) in these terms: 'One way Sydney is constructed is in relation to Melbourne, its denigrated other' . . . Melbourne is dull, Melbourne is serious, Melbourne is full of wowsers, in Melbourne it rains all the time. The two construct each other'. However, the competition between Melbourne and Sydney can also have social consequences.

The hosting of the 2000 Olympic Games in Sydney and Melbourne's successful bid to host the 2006 Commonwealth Games are both associated with the redevelopment and reimaging of the two cities to attract capital and investment. However, the reimaging of Sydney and Melbourne is not just a matter of selling bricks and mortar, or even attractive urban views, it is now also a matter of selling lifestyles. Both Melbourne and Sydney, particularly the former, promote access to a 'café culture' through wine and food opportunities, restaurants, and colourful markets full of local and foreign produce. All of these can now be accessed through guided tours, and lessons in how to cook the meat, fruit, and vegetables bought on the tour. Certain areas with a concentration of restaurants reflecting the local migrant populations are now marketed as 'authentic ethnic foods'. Inner-city suburbs, such as Fitzroy in Melbourne and Paddington and Balmain in Sydney, have been transformed from working-class neighbourhoods into gentrified middle-class suburbs representing an 'authentic' city lifestyle that is promoted in lifestyle magazines and television shows— thus influencing the aspirations of contemporary homemaking. Even some suburbs that have retained their ethnic mix are now drawn into the range of authentic 'colourful' tourist opportunities that have been 'commodified' for visitors from overseas, from interstate, or from the other side of town (Hage 1997).

Although it seems that everything has been turned into a saleable commodity available for consumption, this is not the case. A commodity has to be of a certain type, with a given symbolic value that reinforces preferred lifestyles. Furthermore, these commodities are not evenly distributed in urban space. They are disproportionately located in downtown and inner-city areas, with many of the outer suburbs forgotten by those who seek to 'sell the city', even though the outer suburbs are where the majority of residents live. Nevertheless, these commodities still 'seduce' (Hall 2002b). They are produced and/or packaged to seduce the visitor, to attract international capital (albeit for increasingly short periods of time), and to seduce the locals. Why has this occurred? It has occurred because, when globalisation, economic restructuring, and change seem to be the norm, and when employment is increasingly casualised and insecure, political élites need to be seen to be doing something. New brands, new developments, the hosting of events, and the creation of new leisure and retail spaces are all signs that something is being done. However, those who visit Melbourne and Sydney frequently note that the cities look the same, although they are trying to reimage themselves as places that are different. Melbourne's Southbank is to Sydney's Darling Harbour as the new Olympic Homebush stadium in Sydney is to Colonial Stadium and the sports centre in Melbourne. Both cities now also have large legal casinos with virtual monopolies on certain types of gambling entertainment. As Zukin (1991, p. 221) observed, the city is a site of spectacle, a 'dreamscape of visual consumption'. It is therefore not surprising that, at a time when little competitive edge can be found for either city in terms of the reconstruction of their physical space, emphasis is then placed on the lifestyle opportunities they offer to those who are able to afford them. Indeed, in some urban areas, the outcome has been described as 'the city as theme park' in which the architecture of the inner city utilises historic facades 'from a spuriously appropriated past' to generate consumption within an atmosphere of nostalgia and display. 'The result is that the preservation of the physical remnants of the historical city has superseded attention to the human ecologies that produced and inhabit them' (Sorkin 1992, p. xiv).

The creation and representation of place is a social process. By its very nature tourism is explicitly related to notions of place through tourism promotion and development. However, in both the developed world and less-developed countries, tourism development has been dominated by sectional interests and by an institutional ideology that represents tourism as a 'good' form of economic development. Such a process is inherently political (Hall & Jenkins 1995). As Harvey (1993, p. 8) noted: 'The question immediately arises as to why people accede to the construction of their places by such a process'. In many cases they do not, and communities sometimes resist the change inherent in tourism development. As Kelly and McConville (1991, p. 91) noted, 'political battles between residents and specially created redevelopment authorities have punctuated the urban renewal of Australian waterfronts'. However, although short-term opposition has saved the physical fabric of many Australian inner-city communities, it is worthwhile noting that the social fabric has been changed through gentrification and touristification of many areas leaving only heritage facades. Surely a community is more than a collection of buildings and local culture more than just a commodity? As Hewison observed: 'the time has come to argue that commerce is *not* culture, whether we define culture as the pursuit of music, literature or the fine arts, or whether we adopt Raymond Williams's definition of culture as "a whole way of life". You cannot get a whole way of life into a . . . shopping bag' (1991, p. 175).

Destination regions

In areas in which tourism has 'taken off' in Australia, there is often a seemingly contradictory attitude to the industry. For example, in the early 1980s Cairns was a 'laid-back' north Queensland town known for its marlin fishing and sugar industry, with few buildings more than four storeys high. Today, eight-storey and taller hotels stretch along the city's foreshore, and resorts and marinas, many of them sited on previously public land, run north along the coast to Port Douglas and Cooktown. As Tolhurst (1990, p. 10) observed:

> Locals have better job opportunities . . . Yet antitourism sentiment runs high. Cairns folk, as they have demonstrated at the ballot box, no longer talk about the wonders of tourism. Instead, they will complain about such projects as Tekin Australia's Hinchinbrook Harbour resort (in which the developer levelled 40 ha of melaleuca stands and mangroves).

The social impacts of tourism are thus not isolated to capital cities. Indeed, there is evidence to suggest that isolated rural communities are even more at risk from the potential negative effects of tourism, or at least have a more negative reaction to foreign tourists (J.A. Pearce 1980). Cairns City and the adjoining Mulgrave Shire in northern Queensland have been the focus of substantial tourism development since the mid-1970s. However, with the opening of the Cairns international airport in 1984, the rate of visitation increased markedly. The growth in tourism certainly generated substantial economic inputs into the local economy, with tourism accounting for 75% of the formerly sugar-dependent region's economic activity in the late 1980s and early 1990s (Office of Local Government 1987; Clark 1998; Tolhurst 1990; Queensland Department of Local Government and Planning (QDLGP) 1997). However, the potential economic benefits that tourism presents to the region have not been gained without perceived costs. For example, in the late 1980s Cameron McNamara (Office of Local Government 1987) and Clark (1988) both paid attention to the issues of the perceived costs and benefits of tourism in the Cairns/Mulgrave region. Clark (1988, p. 79), a Mulgrave Shire councillor, stated that, although:

. . . economic benefits are very real, opposition to tourism in the Cairns region has been focused on the negative environmental and social effects that have become evident. Thus, increasing crime rate and cost of living, lack of affordable housing, traffic congestion, proliferation of high rise buildings in Cairns City, destruction of rainforest and wetland habitats and noise pollution, have all been identified as concerns by the local community, both in the press and to me personally by ratepayer and resident organisations.

Although Clark (1988) conveyed a broad impression of the perceived impacts of tourism on the region, it does not give us any indication of the relative importance of such issues in the mind of the community. Unfortunately, many of the raw facts and figures which might give a closer approximation of 'reality' are not collected or, if they are, can be quite unreliable. For example, although there was a substantial increase in the growth of crime over the period from 1976 to 1987 (Clark 1988), and although this trend continued in the early 1990s (Kelly 1993), it is extremely difficult to attribute this directly to tourism development. Nevertheless, research by G. Ross (1991a, 1992a) suggested that perceptions by Cairns' residents that levels of crime had increased were well-founded, although he did note that a perception of increasing crime rates was stronger in short-term residents, possibly because they were less 'aware of the presence of crime in their community before the advent of a major tourism industry' (G. Ross 1992a, p. 22). Similarly, although there was a strong concern in the Cairns community that tourism development led to social displacement through rent increases and the loss of low-cost accommodation (Office of Local Government 1987), it is extremely difficult to gain any hard evidence of such displacement.

Despite difficulties in obtaining empirical evidence of negative impacts, resident perceptions that tourism is causing overcrowding, lack of privacy, and inflation all lead to adverse reactions to tourism development. Furthermore, in certain locations where the original community is 'swamped' by large-scale tourism development in a relatively short time—such as Broome in Western Australia and Port Douglas in Queensland—disruption to the community values of the local inhabitants undoubtedly occurs (Hudson

TABLE 9.2 Costs and benefits of tourism development in Broome, WA

Costs	Benefits
Marginalisation of Aboriginal and coloured people	Expansion of new services, and businesses
Too much power in vested interests	More infrastructure and community facilities
Destruction of multicultural flavour of the town and the original form of Shinju Matsuri	More sealed roads and kerbing and guttering
Increased racism	Increased variety of restaurants/ entertainment
High accommodation costs and shortages	Restoration of Broome architecture
High local prices	Better health system
Less friendly/more local conflicts	Tidier town
Loss of historical character of town and imposition of artificially created atmosphere	
Environmental impacts (for example, dune destruction)	
More crime and domestic violence	

Source: Hudson, P. (1990) 'Structural changes in three small north western Australian communities: the relationship between development and quality of life'. Paper presented at annual conference of regional science association, p. 10.

1990a, 1990b). Table 9.2 details the costs and benefits of tourism development in Broome. However, it must be emphasised that individual attitudes to tourism development are influenced by a person's position in the existing social and economic order, personal gains from the development process, and individual response to the changing environment (Hudson 1990b). In addition, it should be noted that individuals can perceive negative tourism impacts, and yet be favourably disposed to tourism's overall benefits to the community. In their study of the Gold Coast region, Faulkner and Tideswell (1996) referred to this phenomenon as the 'altruistic surplus', and suggested that this could be the result of the mature stage of tourism development in the region, whereby residents have adapted to tourism through experience and migration.

Both positive and negative attitudes to tourism have also been revealed in various studies of resident attitudes to tourism in northern New South Wales dating back to the late 1970s (Hall 1990; Brown & Giles 1994; Dutton et al. 1994). According to Pigram's (1987, p. 67) survey on tourism in Coffs Harbour, 'the overwhelming majority felt that the economic and otherwise benefits of tourism outweighed the disadvantages'. Nevertheless, despite the overall favourable or apathetic response of residents, several negative reactions to tourism did emerge from the study. According to Pigram (1987), the greatest impact of tourism on the local community was the perceived increase in the cost of goods and services because of the presence of tourists. The respondents also indicated that they believed that petty crime was worse during the tourist season, an observation supported by studies of crime at three north coast tourist resorts during the late 1970s (Walmsley et al. 1981, 1983). The natural environment of the Coffs Harbour area was perceived to be slightly worse as a result of tourism, with the greatest impact being on the beaches. However, in terms of attributes perceived as being improved by tourism, opportunities for public recreation registered highest (Pigram 1987, p. 63).

Grimwood's (1982) study of the social impacts of a proposed resort development at Yamba revealed a greater ambivalence of residents to tourism development than that noted in the work of Pigram (1987). Residents reacted negatively to the environmental impacts of proposed tourism development in their area, and more than 50% disagreed with the notion that the project would enhance community life (Grimwood 1982). In addition, 'although the majority of households agreed that the development would create employment within the region and economically benefit the existing region, a majority also disagreed with the notion that the development was necessary for economic growth' (Grimwood 1982, p. 52).

Reynolds' (1989) examination of community attitudes to tourism on the far north coast of Queensland generally reflected the findings of the previous work of Pigram (1987) in Coffs Harbour. According to Reynolds (1989), the positive impacts of tourism on the region as perceived by its residents were shopping opportunities, the quality of police and fire protection, job opportunities, an increase in resident income (and consequent rise in the standard of living), and an increase in the number of available recreation facilities. Conversely the negative impacts were perceived to be prostitution, vandalism, alcoholism, unemployment (and consequently the number of welfare recipients), increased cost of rental accommodation and land, more litter, and increases in traffic (compounding the poor condition of the roads).

Similar combinations of positive and negative perceptions of tourism and tourism-related development were also noted in the wider study of development in the northern rivers region of New South Wales by Dutton et al. (1994).

Despite the mixed responses, the results of the studies outlined above indicate that the implications of the social impacts of tourism for residents, the tourist industry, and the tourists do require greater attention than has been the case. Furthermore, they highlight the continued significance of anti-social behaviour patterns such as vandalism (or the 'hoon effect') for perceptions of tourism in host communities (Sandy 1983). However, tourism can also have a substantial impact on the development of more serious social problems, such as crime and prostitution.

Crime and prostitution

The relationship of tourism to crime and prostitution is a relatively overlooked, but nevertheless important, avenue of tourism research (Pizam & Mansfield 1996). Tourism centres and tourist events create a range of negative externalities (such as crime) that need to be considered within the tourism planning process. The response to actual or potential increases in rates of crime and prostitution can lead to government and private organisational adjustments in law enforcement practices, possibly resulting in increased expenditure on crime prevention (Rothman et al. 1979). Crime and prostitution are commonly regarded as detrimental to the character and public image of a neighbourhood or a tourist resort, and fear of criminal activity can be a major deterrent to tourists (Nichols 1976; P.L. Pearce 1988; Ryan 1991; Kelly 1993; Prideaux 1996; Pizam & Mansfield 1996). Conversely, the less salubrious attractions of the 'seedy side' of town have, since the earliest days of tourism, drawn visitors to them (Ryan & Kinder 1996).

A positive relationship between tourism and crime has been found in several overseas studies (Rothman 1978; Fujii & Mak 1980; Chesny-Lind & Lind 1986). In Australia, the research of Walmsley, Boskovic, and Pigram (1981, 1983), Kelly (1993), and Prideaux (1996) has tended to support overseas findings. In their study of criminal behaviour in tourist and non-tourist centres in northern New South Wales, Walmsley, Boskovic, and Pigram demonstrated that 'in coastal resorts, the peaks and troughs in the occurrence of crime coincided with highs and lows in tourist activity' (1983, p. 154). Nevertheless, they were not able to demonstrate conclusively that a causal relationship between tourism and criminal behaviour existed.

In a study of the development of the Gold Coast, Jones (1986) characterised the resort as '*A Sunny Place For Shady People*'. The high rates of crime in the region—described as 'the State's rape capital' (Kyburz in Jones 1986, p. 110)—were regarded by Jones as being closely related to the inherent nature of the local tourism industry. Furthermore, Jones (1986, p. 111) has maintained that the higher crime rates in the region are at such a level as to demand that: 'The Coast will simply have to put more resources into crime control and public safety, or face the possibility of being known as the regional crime capital of Australia'. Similarly, Cameron McNamara noted that tourism growth in the Cairns region had attracted a large population of temporary residents associated with problems of crime, vagrancy, and social stress. 'In general, tourism growth *per se* has not caused these problems. But such growth, in the absence of counter social policies, assists in sustaining some of these problems' (Office of Local Government 1987, p. 7.6); a conclusion which has found support in the more recent research of Ross (G., 1992a, 1992b), Kelly (1993), and Prideaux (1996).

A rise in crime and larrikinism was also associated with the hosting of the 1986–87 America's Cup defence in Perth (Hall, Selwood & McKewon 1995). According to the West Australian Police Department's America's Cup Division (1987, p. 5):

During the period October 7, 1985 to February 16, 1986, prior to the America's Cup series, the Fremantle Police preferred a total of 5,502 charges. During the corresponding period while the America's Cup Defence Series was being conducted a total of 7,483 charges were preferred by the America's Cup Division and Fremantle Police. This reflects a growth in the number of charges of 1,981 or 36%.

Over the same period, the number of arrests in Fremantle increased by 62.19%. The number of charges processed by the courts also increased: the Fremantle Traffic Court by 110.7%, the Fremantle Petty Sessions by 23.5% and the Children's Court by 44.7%. It is of interest that the 'overwhelming majority' of charges were preferred against permanent residents of the Fremantle area (America's Cup Division 1987, pp. 5–6; Appendices 'c' and 'd'). Police officers were instructed to avoid 'heavy-handed and insensitive' action against visitors, and this might have influenced the statistics (West Australian Police Department 1986, p. 19). It should be noted that the precise reason for these increases remains unclear, however the evidence does suggest that there was a strong relationship between the hosting of the event and an increase in petty crime (Selwood & Hall 1988; Hall 1989d; Hall et al. 1995).

Prostitution is a 'somewhat neglected topic' within the study of tourism (Graburn 1983, p. 437; Ryan & Hall 2001). Despite claims by Mathieson and Wall (1982, p. 149) that there is little evidence to confirm or deny a positive link between prostitution and tourism, there has been a long history of this relationship (Turner & Ash 1975). In contemporary accounts of tourism and prostitution, attention has tended to focus on the growth of prostitution in less-developed countries and, in particular, in tourist destinations in South-East Asia (Cohen 1982; Graburn 1983; Bishop & Robinson 1998; Hall & Ryan 2001). Indeed, considerable attention has now been given in Australia to the need to stop child prostitution in South-East Asia, especially given the potential roles of Australian nationals (Hall 1998c). However, a similar relationship exists in Western tourist destinations.

Just as Miami has become synonymous with vice, the combination of sun, sea, sand, and sex has become associated with tourism resorts in general. Tourist promotion can play on the more licentious characteristics of tourists and highlight the unseemly characteristics of tourist destinations (Desmond 1999). As Bailie (1980, pp. 19–20) commented:

> Tourism promotion in magazines and newspapers promises would-be vacationers more than sun, sea, and sand; they are also offered the fourth 's'—sex. Resorts are advertised under the labels of 'hedonism', 'ecstacism', and 'edenism' . . . One of the most successful advertising campaigns actually failed to mention the location of the resort: the selling of the holiday experience itself and not the destination was the important factor (1980, pp. 19–20).

The 'red light' districts of many cities, such as Sydney's Kings Cross, are often seen as tourist attractions which attract sensation-seeking tourists as participants or observers. When conditions become too threatening or dangerous visitors can be driven off, but if a degree of control over illegal activities is maintained, certain classes of tourists can be attracted. With few exceptions, there is an apparent 'blind spot' or reticence among academics to acknowledge the relationship between tourism and sex in Western society (Selwood & Hall 1988; Crick 1989; Ryan & Hall 2001). Nevertheless, if an effective analysis of the proposition that 'tourism is prostitution' reveals the proposition to be as true of metropolitan tourist resorts of the first world as it is of the third world (Graburn 1983, p. 441), such studies are necessary.

Most observers who have examined the motivations of tourists have overlooked the very explicit messages purveyed in tourist advertisements (Oppermann et al. 1998). For example, V.L. Smith (1979), although identifying the importance of socially sanctioned resorts in determining the choice of destination, failed to recognise the hedonistic nature of the tourist experience as being a motivational factor. Similarly, Crompton (1979), although perceiving that pleasure vacations provided an opportunity for tourists to do things that were inconceivable within the context of their usual lifestyles, failed to identify the sexual experience as being part of this phenomenon. Despite the self-confessed selling of hedonism by the tourist industry (Bailie 1980; Oppermann et al. 1998), it is interesting to note that several studies of tourist brochures and images have failed to identify the pervasive use of erotic and sensual images in promoting travel destinations (Buck 1977; Dilley 1986).

Although Sydney's Kings Cross is arguably the pace-setter of Australian pornography and prostitution, other communities also cater to hedonistic tastes. For example, the Hay Street brothels are a major feature of tourist visits to Kalgoorlie and provide an example of a 'gendered space' whereby prostitutes are forced into a certain area of the city into which tourists and clients can look, and sometimes enter. Similarly, illegal gambling and prostitution in the West End of Brisbane and the Gold Coast achieved national prominence with the revelations of the Fitzgerald Inquiry into official corruption in Queensland. As Jones (1986, p. 111) contended:

> Prostitution is widespread on the Coast, especially in the tourist zone around Surfers Paradise and call girls occupy many high-rise apartments in central Surfers. Many escorts and massage parlours advertise in the *Gold Coast Bulletin* . . . Modern tourism requires a well-regulated supply of women and the pragmatic Queensland industry knows that these services must be provided, especially if the Coast is to compete with Asia where sex has become the main objective of many package tours (1986, p. 111).

From the author's own travels to Queensland in 2000 and 2001, Jones' observation of prostitution on the Gold Coast still rings true. Jones' (1986) discussion of tourism on the Gold Coast highlighted the strength of the relationship between mass tourism and the sex industry. No matter how exploitative or morally unsavoury it might be to some elements of society, the strength of the relationship is such that it cannot be legislated away (Ryan & Hall 2001). Indeed, the Gold Coast Chamber of Commerce has proposed that prostitution be legalised at the Coast so that it can be controlled and criminal elements deterred from participating in prostitution.

Changes in legal structures are just one example of the effects that tourism can have on community attitudes. The next sections examine the broader impacts of tourism on sociocultural values.

THE SOCIAL DIMENSIONS OF EVENT TOURISM

A number of social benefits and costs was identified in a study of the Adelaide Grand Prix (Burns, Hatch & Mules 1986). Short-term social costs included the traffic congestion caused by the use of city roads for the race track, time lost as a result of traffic detours, property damage incurred by residents, increased thefts of vehicles and vehicle contents, noise, and accidents. Short-term social benefits were described as 'psychic income'. This category included the general excitement created by the event, good self-opinions, extra access to shopping, the opportunity to have guests, home hosting opportunities, and the pleasure of experiencing the event (Burns & Mules 1986, pp. 24–30).

Unlike most research on event tourism, the Adelaide Grand Prix study also paid explicit attention to long-term costs and benefits of hosting the event. Bentick (1986) indicated that the Grand Prix had the potential to attract the interest of entrepreneurs in South Australia, affect the attitude and confidence of local business people, workers and residents (an improved self-image), promote investment, and demonstrate the ability of the state to manage similar large-scale events. Longer-term benefits and costs of hosting the event were identified as being a potential loss of amenity, and an increase in crime, vandalism, hooliganism, and accidents.

Of particular interest in the context of long-term social effects of the Grand Prix is the so-called 'hoon effect' (Stuart Innes, *The Advertiser*, 10/1/86, in Fischer, Hatch & Paix 1986, p. 152)—a 'hoon' being 'a reckless, irresponsible driver . . . which may or may not have been encouraged by the staging of the Grand Prix' (Fischer, Hatch & Paix 1986, p. 152). For the five-week Grand Prix period in 1985, road casualties in South Australia were 5% higher than the previous year. Only a small fraction of this increase could be explained by reference to weather conditions, overall trends, or traffic volume. The Adelaide study inferred from this 'that the particular nature of the Grand Prix, its emphasis on speed and aggressive driving, contributed substantially to these accidents' (Fischer, Hatch & Paix 1986, p. 160). Furthermore, long-term behaviour modification might also result from the major sponsor's product (Foster's beer) and the excitement and general well-being generated by the event (Arnold, Fischer, Hatch & Paix 1989). Nevertheless, despite the undoubted significance of the 'hoon effect' as a social consequence of hosting a tourist event, study of the event was generally favourable to the social effects of the Adelaide Grand Prix.

A more recent study of the perceptions of a motor racing event is Fredline's (1996) study of resident perceptions of the Gold Coast Indy car race. Residents perceived a range of both negative and positive impacts of the event (Table 9.3). The most important benefits were perceived to be tourism promotion, greater social opportunities, improved community self-esteem, and increased employment and business benefits. Negative effects included noise levels, traffic congestion, overcrowding, and lifestyle disruption (Fredline & Faulkner 1998, 2000). According to Fredline (1996, p. 79):

> The fact that residents perceived these costs, yet still favoured the continuation of the Indy in future years, would appear to indicate that they consider the benefits of the event to outweigh the costs. It may also indicate the operation of an altruistic surplus effect . . . Residents may be prepared to accept these negative impacts because they perceive that the event benefits the community at large.

THE CULTURAL IMPACTS OF TOURISM

As an overarching term, 'culture' refers to the general symbol system of society. However, 'culture' contains several related elements, all of which can contribute to the touristic attractiveness of a destination. Figure 9.1 illustrates the three major components of culture that are 'commodified' into tourism product—(i) 'high culture' (for example, the performing arts and heritage attractions such as museums and art

TABLE 9.3 Statements regarding the Gold Coast Indy with which a majority of residents agreed

Negative statements

The Indy greatly inconveniences local residents through traffic congestion.

The Indy creates noise levels which annoy residents.

During the Indy it is difficult to find a parking space.

The Indy disrupts the lives of local residents.

The Indy causes overcrowding and make it difficult to use local facilities.

Positive statements

The Indy promotes the Gold Coast as a tourist attraction.

Showing the Indy around the world gives the Gold Coast an international identity.

Holding the Indy on the Gold Coast gives local residents an opportunity to attend an international event.

The Indy gives the Gold Coast an opportunity to show the world what we can do.

The Indy increases trade for local businesses.

The Indy increases employment opportunities on the Gold Coast.

There are increased business opportunities because of the Indy.

The Indy gives residents the opportunity to meet new people.

The Indy promotes Australian motor sport and gives young drivers more opportunities.

Source: Fredline, E. 'Resident perceptions of the Gold Coast Indy: an exploratory study'. Unpublished Honors Thesis, Griffith University, p. 81.

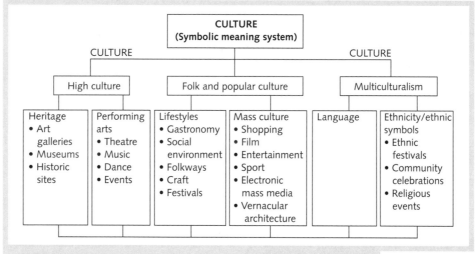

Figure 9.1 The three components of culture *Source:* Hall (1997c)

galleries); (ii) 'folk and popular culture' (for example, gastronomy, crafts, sport, and architecture; and (iii) 'multiculturalism' (which refers to cultural and racial diversity and language). Although all three dimensions of culture can be packaged as tourism products, the touristic element is greatest in high culture, which can be located in specific sites and attractions, as opposed to the more diffuse nature of folk and popular culture and multiculturalism. The ease with which various aspects of culture can be packaged for tourist consumption is significant. Because of ease of packaging, the 'culture' in 'cultural tourism' is often associated with easily commodified aspects

INTRODUCTION TO TOURISM

284

of high culture, such as museums and art galleries (V. Smith 1989; Hall & Zeppel 1990; Harron & Weiler 1992; Zeppel & Hall 1992; ONT 1997c, 1997d). Ritchie and Zins (1978, p. 257) identified twelve aspects of local culture that can determine the attractiveness of destinations to tourists:

- handicrafts;
- language;
- traditions, such as festivals or rituals;
- gastronomy;
- art and music, including concerts, paintings, and sculpture;
- history of a region, including visual reminders of the past;
- patterns and methods of work activity and the technology that is used;
- architecture, which can be distinctive of a region;
- religion, including its visible manifestations;
- educational systems;
- costume and dress; and
- leisure activities.

Despite the undoubted significance of cultural artefacts, behaviour, social relations and traditions for the attraction of tourists, the possibility exists that tourism will destroy the cultural resource on which it is based. When two cultures come into contact for a period of time an exchange of ideas occurs. This process is known as 'acculturation' (Nuñez 1989). However, the exchange process might not be equal as one culture can dominate another by virtue of the type of contact, the socioeconomic characteristics of the members of a culture, and the size of the population.

The process of acculturation is often associated with tourism in less-developed nations, although the cultural impacts of tourist development on Western destinations is increasingly being recognised. In Australia, considerable attention is being paid to the impacts of tourism on Aboriginal populations, particularly in the more remote, economically marginal regions, such as the Kimberley and much of the Northern Territory, where tourism is seen as a potential source of economic development (Palmer 1985; Altman 1987, 1988, 1989, 1991; Dillon 1987; Kesteven 1987; Gillespie 1988; Finlayson 1991; Parsons 1991; Ross, H. 1991; Altman & Finlayson 1993; Altman, Ginn & Smith 1993; QDLGP 1997; ATSIC and the ONT 1997; Hall 2000e; Simmons 2000). Despite concerns over undesirable social impacts, Australian governments have long held out hope that tourism might be a mechanism for the economic development of Aboriginal communities, particularly with respect to reducing Aboriginal unemployment. Aboriginal culture has also been perceived as a means of attracting tourists. For example, in the mid-1970s, the Commonwealth Department of Tourism and Recreation (1975, p. 7) argued:

> The development of tourism can provide an opportunity for many Aboriginal Australians to engage in worthwhile economic activities and increase their self-reliance. There are many areas in the States and the Northern Territory where Aboriginal participation would, in fact, enhance the appeal of a particular tourist attraction. The Department . . . would seek to encourage appropriate training programs and employment opportunities so that Aborigines could gain maximum benefits from participation in tourism projects.

Twenty-two years later the ONT (1997d) stated that the:

> . . . international tourism market's increasing sophistication, with more visitors now seeking experiences which match their own particular interests in preference to 'mass tourism'

experiences, involves visitors who tend to spend more than tourists on packaged tours, making them important contributors to Australia's export earnings.

For these reasons, there is a need to extend international interest in Australia beyond the traditional attractions of sun, surf, and wide open spaces. Potential visitors must be made aware that Australia is also a culturally distinctive and fascinating destination with a rich indigenous cultural heritage.

> . . . For many Aboriginal and Torres Strait Islander communities, tourism has the potential to provide a means to economic independence and a stimulus to preserving and reinvigorating their cultures.

The Royal Commission into Aboriginal Deaths in Custody (Commonwealth of Australia 1991) identified five principal areas in which Aboriginal people could participate in the tourism industry—employment, investment, the arts and crafts industry, cultural tourism, and joint ventures. However, as Altman and Finlayson (1993, p. 39) rightly observed, 'none of the five areas . . . [is] unproblematic for Aboriginal participants. Employment in tourism-related industries requires a high level of literacy and communication skills and the adoption of cultural styles which are foreign and daunting'.

Case studies of Aboriginal involvement in tourism developments do not provide universal support for the notion that tourism provides direct economic benefit to Aboriginal peoples either through employment or through increased income. Studies in the Northern Territory and north-west Australia by Altman (1987, 1988, 1989) and Dillon (1987), and in Victoria by Finlayson (1991) and Finlayson and Madden (1994), indicate that, as Altman and Finlayson (1993, p. 41) observed:

> . . . commercial opportunities are likely to be limited by a cultural priority for social outcomes that may be incompatible with commercial development . . . Even with a number of structural advantages, economic benefits may not accrue to Aboriginal interests, and if they do, they may be offset by related social and cultural costs.

For example, there is a fear among many Aboriginal groups that contact with tourists might devalue Aboriginal culture and lead to further social breakdown in some communities. S. Brennan (in Senate Standing Committee on Environment, Recreation and the Arts 1988, pp. 28–9) from the Bureau of the Northern Land Council commented that the Gagudju people in the Kakadu region:

> . . . do not like the idea of being a bit like a zoo, feeling that they are on display for tourists to come and see what an Aboriginal person looks like in his environment, to see whether he still walks around with a spear. They certainly do not like that concept of tourism.

One dimension of Aboriginal culture that has been a prominent component of Australian tourism for a number of years is the selling of Aboriginal art and artefacts. Boomerangs, motifs on clothing, bark paintings, and hunting weapons are all part of the souvenir package available to the tourist. The impact that the demand for such goods has had on Aboriginal groups is quite substantial, although debate continues as to whether souvenir production debases or revitalises Aboriginal culture. Nevertheless, it is apparent that culture is not static and will change and develop over time. As de Kadt (1979, pp. 14–15) observed:

> Even though curio production, 'airport art', and performances of fake folklore are of course stimulated by tourist demand . . . frequently arts, crafts, and local culture have been

revitalized as a direct result of tourism. A transformation of traditional forms often accompanies this development but does not necessarily lead to degeneration. To be authentic, arts and crafts must be rooted both in historical tradition and in present-day life; true authenticity cannot be achieved by conservation alone, since that leads to stultification.

The issues of cultural production, ownership and authenticity have also been noted by the ONT (1997d) which rightly observes: 'Stereotyped depictions of dot paintings, corroborees and didgeridoos, for example, may not be appropriate for particular communities. In all cases, individual communities need to be consulted about the use of indigenous cultural images'. As Simmons (2000, p. 428) commented, 'Commercial exploitation of Aboriginal art and cultural heritage continues despite protective legislation and the success of recent case law'. The key to acceptance of cultural forms that have been prepared for tourists probably lies in the degree of authenticity which both the host and the guest attaches to artefacts and performances. The next section examines the nature of authenticity and its significance for contemporary tourism.

Authenticity

> . . . tourists are seeking authentic cultural products. They do not want to find that the boomerang they bought in Sydney or Perth was made in Asia. Indigenous arts and crafts sold to tourists need to be genuine and must provide a fair return and due acknowledgment to those who created them . . . Aboriginal and Torres Strait Islander communities are the custodians of their culture. The use of their culture for tourism purposes needs to take place only with the agreement of those communities, and on the terms established by those communities to ensure respect for their culture and sites of cultural significance (ONT 1997d).

Authenticity is one of the key motivational forces for those travellers with an interest in foreign cultures and destinations, yet considerable confusion can arise over the perceived authenticity of particular tourist attractions. Commentators, such as Boorstin (1973, p. 103), have argued that the rise of modern tourism has led to the trivialisation of culture and the creation of superficial and contrived tourist experiences which he described as 'pseudo-events':

> In order to satisfy the exaggerated expectations of tour agents and tourists, people everywhere obligingly became dishonest mimics of themselves. To provide a full schedule of events at the best seasons and at convenient hours, they travesty their solemn rituals, holidays, and folk celebrations—all for the benefit of tourists.

Similarly, MacCannell (1973, 1976) has argued that the modern tourist is often caught in an all-embracing 'tourist space', constructed by the tourism industry in which authenticity is staged. Cohen (1979) identified a dual interpretation of 'authenticity' which distinguished between the perceptions of the tourist and the nature of the scene as provided by the hosts. As Cohen (1979) noted, 'staged authenticity' does not have to be an inevitable consequence of tourism development, and distinguished between four types of touristic situations in which authenticity can be perceived (Table 9.4):

- if both the hosts and the tourist accept that a situation is authentic (the ideal situation);
- if events and attractions are created or staged for tourists by the tourist industry but the tourist accepts the contrived scene as real (MacCannell 1973);

THE SOCIAL AND CULTURAL DIMENSIONS OF TOURISM

TABLE 9.4 Types of touristic situations

Nature of scene	Tourist's impression of scene as real	Tourist's impression of scene as staged
Real	(1) authentic	(3) denial of authenticity (staging suspicion)
Staged	(2) staged authenticity (covert tourist space)	(4) contrived (overt tourist space)

Source: Cohen, B. (1979) 'Rethinking the sociology of tourism', *Annals of Tourism Research*, vol. 6, (Jan–March), no. 1, p. 26. Reprinted with permission from Elsevier Science.

- if the reverse of the above occurs—that is, although the event is real for the host, the visitor might suspect that the scene is unauthentic and that the tourist is being manipulated; as Cohen (1979, p. 27) has suggested: 'the situation of "denial of authenticity" is of particular theoretical interest, since it represents the feedback effects of previous touristic learning on the tourist's approach to new situations'; and
- if an 'overt tourism space' exists, in which the scene is admittedly contrived by the tourist industry and is seen as such by the tourist.

Cohen's typology provides a useful conceptual device for analysing the nature of the tourist experience at particular attractions, and the level of satisfaction with the tourist experience. Research at Australian historic theme parks has suggested that authenticity, especially in terms of historical accuracy, is perceived by domestic travellers as an important motive for travelling to such parks (Pearce & Moscardo 1985; Moscardo & Pearce 1986). Nevertheless, the actual authenticity of such parks may be open to question as it is clear that they are staged events, regardless of the belief by tourists that they are gaining an 'authentic' experience. Similarly, considerable debate has been generated by the methodological problems in applying the concept of authenticity (Turner & Manning 1988; Selwyn 1994). However, it is to be hoped that more research will be conducted in this area, particularly as it relates to the historical interpretation of cultural heritage sites such as Aboriginal sites, national parks, and early European settlements.

The issue of authenticity also raises important questions about the psychological impact on the individual of overt tourism spaces. For example, a Sydney playwright (Sewell 1987, in Craik 1988a, p. 18), after staying at a Great Barrier Reef island, described the experience as: '. . . the existentialist's nightmare: a place stripped of all meaning and significance, where the human spirit has finally been overcome by its own fantastic imagination . . . [the] problem of life has, here, been resolved by removing all reference to it'.

Although the example provided by Craik might be an extreme instance of architectural alienation, it illustrates how a site, event, or landscape can have a significant meaning for an individual. As Huie (1988, in Craik 1988a, p. 25) commented: 'if we lose our identity, if we stop building things that are Australian, that have an Australian style, that are authentic, that are real in our community, we won't have a tourist industry to sell at all'.

LOCALLY APPROPRIATE TOURISM DEVELOPMENT

Tourism should not be manufactured for an external market. It should start with what's legitimate—or right—for its own people. If it does this, the destination will be distinctive (Tourism South Australia 1992).

The preceding sections have highlighted the broad range of effects that modern tourism can have on host populations. It is virtually impossible to shut out the tourism industry entirely from current and potential destinations. Therefore, the task that faces tourism planners and the tourist industry is to design tourism development that is acceptable to the host community and appropriate to its social, economic, and physical setting.

Considerable attention has been given to the development of socially acceptable guidelines for tourism expansion in Canada (Cooke 1982; D'Amore 1983; Murphy 1985). Cooke's (1982) study of social sensitivity to tourism in British Columbia provided some important insights into how the social impacts of tourism on a community can be ameliorated through appropriate planning. Cooke (1982, p. 26) identified several conditions that are appropriate and inappropriate to local tourism development. Conditions associated with locally appropriate tourism development included:

- tourists respecting local or ethnic traditions and values;
- opportunities for extensive local involvement in the tourism industry existing at three levels: (i) through decisions made by local government; (ii) through community-wide support for volunteer support programs for tourism; and (iii) through active participation in the direction of tourist development;
- tourism being an economic mainstay or viewed as a desirable alternative to other industries; and
- themes and events that attract tourists being supported and developed by the local community.

Conditions associated with locally inappropriate tourism development included:

- tourists not respecting local or ethnic traditions and values;
- uncertainties about the future direction of tourism development with local people feeling that they have little control;
- residents feeling that visitors are catered for ahead of locals, and that infrastructure and facilities have been designed for the benefit of tourists rather than the local community;
- growth in the host community proceeding faster than the residents feel is appropriate; and
- perceived conflicts over natural resource use.

Cooke's (1982) study of tourism development in British Columbia recommended that all tourism planning be based on the goals and priorities of residents. Indeed, she even went further and recommended that local attractions be promoted only when endorsed by residents. Such an approach would have a substantial impact on tourism development. For instance, opposition has often emerged to the development of casinos because of their perceived impact on host communities, particularly in relation to increased crime and prostitution, and the effectiveness of state governments in regulating casino gambling (Leiper 1990a). As Lynch and Veal (1998, p. 194) commented:

> The economic impact of a casino may be relatively easy to conceptualise and research, and assessment of certain social impacts—such as noise, congestion, crime levels and the incidence of problem gambling—can be equally straightforward, but taking account of the effects on society's moral sensibilities and concerns about global and local trends in the economy and labour market adds considerable complexity to the task of social impact assessment.

If opposition to the perceived social impacts of tourism developments exists, how should government react to such community perceptions?

If it is acknowledged that residents have a right to decide the type of tourism development that is appropriate to their locality, it is apparent that local government must have a major role in the development process. However, in Australia the importance of social impact assessment on the evaluation of tourism development is only gradually being recognised (Gorman 1988), and local planning processes that incorporate social concerns are presently restricted to a small number of municipalities.

The development of a 'residents first–tourists first' approach under an integrated, community-based planning system appears to be a step in the right direction. As Clark has argued in the case of the Cairns/Mulgrave region, in developing a sustainable industry 'the role of local government becomes clear; it must . . . put in place planning controls for the benefit of both the tourist industry and the local residents. Ideally these controls would be supported by the State Governments' (1988, p. 81). However, such support is not always forthcoming.

State government legislation throughout Australia makes it possible to overturn planning decisions made at the local government level. State governments can also enact legislation to bypass the role of local government in the tourism planning process, as in the use of the Integrated Resort Development Act by Queensland governments throughout the 1980s.

Concern over social impacts comes a poor second to the attention that is paid to the perceived economic benefits of tourism. Nevertheless, local government and residents of a destination do have policy and planning options available to them. 'One of the most important factors in a balanced development is the principle of local sovereignty in matters concerning the use of land. Local authorities must retain a firm grip on this their most effective instrument of control' (Krippendorf 1987, p. 119).

Five guidelines for socially sensitive tourism evolved from Cooke's study of community tourism development in British Columbia. Some people regard such guidelines as being restrictions on tourism development. Nevertheless, the guidelines were designed to assist in promoting appropriate sustainable tourism development within the overall context of community development and, as such, are especially relevant to Australia. As Cooke (1982, p. 26) argued:

> . . . the recommendations represent a constructive approach to the issue of tourism, by attempting to mitigate perceived problems associated with the industry and to maximise benefits. Therefore each guide is a method of maintaining or increasing the limits of local tolerance to tourist activities and of avoiding the pitfalls resulting from exceeding carrying capacity.

The following guidelines for socially sensitive tourism development have been adapted from Cooke (1982, pp 26–7) for the Australian situation.

1 At the local level, tourism planning should be based on overall development goals and priorities identified by residents.
2 The promotion of local attractions should be subject to resident endorsement.
3 The involvement of Aboriginal people in the Australian tourism industry should proceed only if the Aboriginal community involved considers that the integrity of its traditions and lifestyle will be respected.
4 Opportunities should be provided to obtain wide-scale community participation in tourist activities and events.

5   Attempts to mitigate the perceived negative consequences of tourism growth should precede the introduction of tourism or any increase in tourism activity.

The proposed set of guidelines illustrate the need for government and industry to be aware that the tourism experience is the result of a symbiotic relationship among the tourists, industry, and the host community. Tourism development and marketing strategies can succeed only if residents are supportive of the tourist industry and if they believe that benefits are accruing to the host community. Therefore, government and the tourism industry must recognise that successful tourist development has a local social framework which must be catered to before the needs of the tourist.

CHAPTER SUMMARY

The social impacts of tourism and the relationship between visitor and host are among the most important, yet under-researched, aspects of tourism in Australia. As a tourist destination develops, the host community can resent the presence of tourist 'outsiders'. This chapter illustrates that a variety of tourism-related social impacts, including the controversial issues of crime and prostitution, have been recorded in Australia. In particular, attention is focused on the effects of tourism within certain tourism settings and the broader cultural impacts of tourism.

Culture is shown to be a major determinant in the attractiveness of a destination for tourists and can provide an opportunity for marginal communities, such as many Aboriginal groups, to develop a strong economic base. However, undesirable social and cultural changes can result from the commodification of cultural artefacts, identity, and performances—including the perceived authenticity of the tourist experience and the role that tourism plays in altering senses of place. Nevertheless, consideration of socially acceptable guidelines for tourism through locally appropriate development practices could see the growth of tourist destinations and facilities that are attractive to host and guest alike.

SUGGESTIONS FOR FURTHER READING

Until relatively recently, detailed studies of the social impacts of tourism have generally been restricted to developing or economically marginal regions. However, far more attention is now being paid to this crucial aspect of tourism development, although Australian government and industry still pay little more than 'lip-service' to social impact research. Most introductory texts have a general chapter on social impacts.

More detailed discussion of the social and cultural effects of tourism and the relationship between 'host' and 'guest' is to be found in the influential writings of Crick (1989), P. Pearce (1988), and V.L. Smith (1989a). Excellent recent examinations of the social dimensions of tourism are also to be found in Mowforth and Munt (1998) and Meehan (2001).

THE SOCIAL AND CULTURAL DIMENSIONS OF TOURISM

The following websites are recommended:
- Aboriginal Tourism Australia (ATA):
  www.ataust.org.au

- Aboriginal and Torres Strait Islander Commission (ATSIC):
  www.atsic.gov.au

- Tourism Concern:
  www.gn.apc.org

- ECPAT-Childwise—Ending Child Prostitution, Pornography & Trafficking:
  www.ecpat.org

- ECPAT International:
  www.ecpat.net/eng/index.asp

- WTO Task Force to Protect Children from Sexual Exploitation in Tourism:
  www.world-tourism.org/protect_children/index.htm

On the Tourism insight website
  www.prenhall.com/hall_au

see:
- *A Decade of Action Against Child Sex Tourism: An ECPAT Perspective*, by Bernadette McMenamin;

- *Child Sex Tourism: Old Problems—New Solutions*, by Christine Beddoe, ECPAT (End Child Prostitution, Pornography and Trafficking) Australia/Childwise, South Melbourne, Victoria, Australia;

- *Indigenous Ecotourism in Australia*, by Heather Zeppel.

FOR DISCUSSION AND REVIEW

Key concepts

Key concepts discussed in this chapter included:
xenophobia, local autonomy, urban renewal, redevelopment, community structure, ethnicity, overcrowding, privacy, 'psychic income', self-image, 'hoon-effect', crime, prostitution, culture, acculturation, art, artefacts, authenticity, sense of place, locally appropriate tourism development

Questions for review and discussion

1 Why are the social impacts of tourism an important consideration in tourism development?
2 Are rural communities likely to experience more negative effects of tourism than urban locations?
3 Are crime and prostitution unavoidable by-products of mass tourism?
4 How can locally appropriate tourism development meet the needs of the tourist?

THE ENVIRONMENTAL DIMENSIONS AND IMPACTS OF TOURISM

10

From an ecological perspective, sustainable tourism means conserving the productive basis of the physical environment by preserving the integrity of the biota and ecological processes and producing tourism commodities without degrading other values. Having no form of tourism ... may well be the most advisable management strategy in terms of ... ecological integrity ... However, it is also unrealistic. In order to ensure that wilderness areas are preserved we must, somewhat paradoxically, allow people to visit these wild places so that policy makers can be persuaded to maintain their reserve status ... Vicarious appreciation through books and documentaries is important, but it is not sufficient to create a groundswell of public opinion for preservation ... (Hall & Wouters 1994, p. 369).

TOURISM is an environmentally dependent industry. Facilities and infrastructure are not sufficient in themselves to attract tourists. The natural and cultural environments of host regions provide major drawcards for tourism. As Mathieson and Wall commented (1982, p. 97):

> In the absence of an attractive environment, there would be little tourism. Ranging from the basic attractions of sun, sea and sand to the undoubted appeal of historic sites and structures, the environment is the foundation of the tourist industry

However, although the environment is one of the major drawcards for tourists, an increase in the number of visitors brought by tourism can impact on the integrity and quality of the environment. As Berry, writing about the Avon Valley near Perth, Western Australia, noted, 'the scenic landscape and its close proximity to Perth make it a major tourist destination. While this is welcomed by the merchants of York, it inevitably means added pressures on their landscape' (1986, p. 21).

There has been substantial growth in public attention to the environment in recent years. The preservation of historic buildings and townscapes and the perceived need to establish wilderness and national park areas are testimony to the development of a conservation ethic in Australian society. Heritage sites, and cultural and natural landscapes are significant components of the tourism resources of a region (Upper Yarra Valley and Dandenong Ranges Authority 1988; Kearsley et al. 1997). Indeed, they are often the major attractions for visitors. However, it has long been recognised that tourism resources can be damaged if there are too many tourists impacting on a region or site, or if there are inappropriate forms of tourist development. 'Those who handle tourism must be adequately educated to recognize the dangers and, equally, conservationists throughout the world should be made to understand that tourism, rather than being stopped, must be better planned and controlled' (Budowski 1976, p. 28). Similarly, one of the first books on tourism planning, by Baud-Bovy and Lawson (1977, p. 183) noted that:

> . . . tourism degrades irreversibly the very attractions which justified and attracted it, eroding natural resources, breaking up the unity and scale of traditional landscapes and their characteristic buildings, polluting beaches, damaging forests and rendering banal under the inundation of alien facilities of often mediocre uniform design a formerly unique country.

The rise of the environmental movement is one of the major changes in Australian society to have directly impacted on the tourism industry. Conservation groups such as the Australian Conservation Foundation and the Wilderness Society not only have led to improvements in conservation practices but also have encouraged public interest in Australia's natural areas (Nature Conservation Council of NSW 1988; Wilderness Society 1988; Hall 1992a; Mercer 2000). As was noted in Chapter 1 of the present book, conservation is an essential element of any sustainable tourism development strategy. 'Conservation can be defined as the management of the environment to achieve the greatest sustainable benefit to present generations while maintaining its potential to meet the needs and aspirations of future generations' (Tourism South Australia 1989b, p. 2).

A number of definitions of 'environment' can be found in Australian law. The benchmark Commonwealth *Environment Protection (Impact of Proposals) Act 1974* stated that the environment 'includes all aspects of the surroundings of man, whether affecting him as an individual or in his social groupings'. This broad definition is similar in intent to many of the legal definitions of environment in Australia which highlight the built, cultural, natural, and social components of the external surrounds of people (Fisher 1980; Fowler 1984; Mercer 2000). For example, Tourism South Australia (1989b, p. 2) in its *Environmental Code of Practice* defined the environment 'as the sum total of resources available to human beings, consisting of the physical environment of earth, water and air, the natural environment of landscapes, plants, animals and ecosystems, and the social environments of mankind—past and present'.

'Environmentalism' and 'environmentalist' are commonly used terms that are also frustratingly vague. According to O'Riordan and Turner (1983, p. 1):

> Although environmentalists are not the only people who object to much of what they interpret as modern-day values, aspirations and ways of life, it is probably fair to say that one of the two things which unite their disparate perceptions is a wish to alter many of the unjust and foolhardy features they associate with modern capitalism of both a state and private variety. The other common interest is a commitment to cut waste and reduce profligacy by consuming resources more frugally. Environmentalists do not agree, however, about how the transition should be achieved.

Despite confusion about what is meant by an environmentally 'responsible' approach to tourism development, it is becoming apparent that protection of the natural and cultural resources upon which tourism is based is essential for the long-term sustainable development of a location (WTO & United Nations Environment Program 1982; Hall & Lew 1998). As the next section discusses, tourism need not be damaging to the social and physical environment. Nevertheless, a 'thorough assessment of the land's condition, the local area, the proposals' ability to achieve long-term sustainable development, and the significance of the environmental impact is needed for rational land-use planning' (North Coast Environment Council 1987, p. 2).

THE RELATIONSHIP BETWEEN TOURISM AND THE ENVIRONMENT

> Conservationists and some resource managers now claim that the tourism industry runs the risk of spoiling its main attraction—the natural environment. It is also acknowledged that there will, increasingly, need to be some trade-offs between tourism and the environment. However, it becomes difficult to limit visitors once a location has gained a reputation as an attractive destination (Davis & Weiler 1992, p. 313).

The dependence of tourism on conservation 'is clear and well-known: without conservation there would be nothing for the tourist to see. But its contribution to conservation is perhaps less-considered' (Boyer 1984, p. 134). One of the most influential perspectives on the relationship between tourism and the environment is that of Budowski (1976), who suggested that three basic relationships can occur—conflict, coexistence, or symbiosis (Table 10.1).

Tourism and environmental protection have a long association. The first national parks in Australia, Canada, New Zealand, and the United States were created as much for the promotion of economic development through tourism as they were for the protection of landscape (Hall 1988b, 1992a, 1998, 2000b). Initially, tourism was perceived as being beneficial for the development of an appreciation of the environment and was strongly promoted as a justification for the creation of national parks. However, the flow of visitors to national parks and other non-urban areas at that time was minuscule compared with the growth in domestic tourism visitor numbers that occurred with the advent of the motor car. With the development of mass tourism the natural environment has been placed under enormous pressure, and there has been a transition, in many instances, from a state of coexistence to that of conflict (Hall & McArthur 1993, 1996, 1998; McKercher 1993c).

TABLE 10.1	The relationship of tourism to the environment
Conflict	Tourism and the environment are in conflict when tourism has a detrimental impact on the environment.
Coexistence	Tourism and environmental conservation can exist in a situation in which the two have relatively little contact, because (i) the two sets of supporters remain in isolation from one another, or (ii) there is a lack of development, or (iii) there are administrative barriers. However, this situation 'rarely remains static, particularly as an increase of tourism is apt to induce substantial changes' (Budowski 1976, p. 27).
Symbiosis	Tourism and environmental conservation can be mutually supportive and beneficial if they are organised to ensure that tourists benefit and the environment experiences improvements in management practices. This relationship can have economic advantages and contribute to the quality of life in host communities.

Source: adapted from Budowski (1976).

In contemporary Australia it might be said that expressions of all three relationships exist simultaneously. Tourism is still used as a justification for the establishment of national parks or for the retention of natural areas in a relatively undisturbed state (Fennell 1999; Weaver 2001), whereas, in other areas in which natural values are extremely high, tourism is often seen as a threat to ecological or aesthetic integrity (McKercher 1997). In Victoria's Alpine National Park, the number of licences granted to tourism operators increased more than fourfold between 1992 and 1997 to more than 110. According to Lindberg and McKercher (1997, p. 73):

> This level of growth, and the perception that parks policy now favors tourism interests over other users, has resulted in antipathy toward tourism emerging in stakeholders who feel disaffected by tourism's expansion . . . This may lead to ecotourism becoming the next target of the park movement.

Nevertheless, the relationship between tourism and the environment involves more than just national parks or high-value natural areas, and should encompass all aspects of the notion of 'environment'. The relationship between tourism and the environment is site dependent and is likely to change according to broader economic, environmental, and social concerns. What is regarded as an acceptable 'balance' between tourism and the environment at one time will be different at another. For example, until the Second World War it was generally acceptable to construct accommodation and other visitor infrastructure inside national parks. Now, environmental conservation arguments suggest that such infrastructure should be located outside parks if possible.

TOURISM AND THE NATURAL ENVIRONMENT

Tourism has the ability to encourage hundreds of thousands of people to take a more caring approach to the natural environment. It also has the ability, like any industry, to simply see wilderness as a resource to be appropriated for corporate profit irrespective of environmental impacts (*Wilderness News* 1988, p. 12).

Research on the effects of tourism on the natural environment is similar to research on the environmental impacts of recreation. The majority of the research has been undertaken on the effects of tourism and recreation on wildlife and the trampling of vegetation, with relatively little attention having been given to impacts on soils and air and water quality (Wall & Wright 1977; Mathieson & Wall 1982; Edington & Edington 1986; Parliamentary Commissioner for the Environment 1997).

The majority of studies have examined the impacts of tourism and recreation on a particular environment or component of the environment rather than a range of environments. According to Mathieson and Wall (1982, p. 94), there has been 'little attempt to present an integrated approach to the assessment of the impacts of tourism'. However, there is clearly a need to detect the effects of tourism on all aspects of an ecosystem. For example, the ecology of an area might be dramatically changed by the removal of a key species in the food chain, or by the introduction of new species such as trout in Tasmania (which were introduced for the benefit of recreational fishermen). In addition, it is important to distinguish between perceptions and the actual impacts of tourism. For example, many visitors believe an environment is healthy as long as it looks 'clean and green'. The ecological reality might be vastly different. An environment can be full of invasive introduced species such as pine trees which, although contributing to a positive aesthetic perception, can have extremely negative ecological implications.

Because research on impacts has focused on particular regions or environments, the ability to generalise the findings from one area to another has been limited. In Australia much of the research has concentrated on the coastal zone or on locations such as the Great Barrier Reef, the wet tropics of northern Queensland, Uluru, and Kakadu, for which Commonwealth funds are available for research, partly as a result of their World Heritage status. Yet, in a review of the environmental monitoring of tourism developments in Australia, Warnken and Buckley (2000, p. 459) noted that:

> Relatively few Australian developments (7.5%) were subject to formal environmental monitoring. Monitoring programs are more frequent for recent projects that required approvals from the Great Barrier Reef Marine Park Authority (GRBMPA) and these programs are also of significantly higher scientific quality than the others.

When monitoring did occur there was a higher incidence of BACIP designs (Before, After, Control, Impact, Paired Sampling). However, Warnken and Buckley observed that there was often a lack of control sites, and the implementation of monitoring programs was often subject to constraints in time and finance (2000, pp. 459–60):

> One common deficiency is the absence or inadequacy of predevelopment baseline monitoring; the before, after (BA) comparison in the BACIP design. Some human disturbances are unforeseen, and monitoring can take place only after the event. More commonly, however, entrepreneurs are simply reluctant to invest in monitoring until development approvals have been granted, and then want to commence construction immediately after having received approval, without time for predevelopment baseline monitoring.

Research in Australia is comparatively recent, and is generally of a reactive nature to site-specific problems such as the impacts of visitors on the Great Barrier Reef. In addition, few longitudinal studies exist to assess the long-term impacts of visitation. Only in such truly national parks as Kakadu, Uluru, and the Great Barrier Reef have any accurate assessments of long-term damage been performed. However, it is difficult to generalise conclusions from these environments to the more temperate landscapes of south-western and eastern Australia. In addition, several significant methodological problems have been identified by Mathieson and Wall (1982, p. 94) as requiring urgent attention:

- the difficulty of distinguishing between changes induced by tourism and those induced by other activities;
- the lack of information concerning conditions prior to the advent of tourism and, hence, the lack of a baseline against which change can be measured;
- the paucity of information on the numbers, types, and tolerance levels of different species of flora and fauna; and
- the concentration of researchers upon particular primary resources, such as beaches and mountains, which are ecologically sensitive.

Nevertheless, despite the difficulties that have emerged in studying the relationship between tourism and the natural environment, it is apparent that 'a proper understanding of biological, or more specifically, ecological factors can significantly reduce the scale of environmental damage associated with recreational and tourist development' (Edington & Edington 1986, p. 2).

The physical impacts of tourism

Tourism has a wide range of impacts on the physical environment (Cohen 1978; Valentine 1984; Pearce 1985; Romeril 1989; Buckley & Pannell 1990; Inskeep 1991; Minerbi 1992; Hunter & Green 1995; Mieczkowski 1995; Hall 1996b; Parliamentary Commissioner for the Environment 1997). The more obvious include the development of tourist resorts in the arid inland (Yulara resort at Uluru), the coastal zone (the Gold Coast), and mountainous areas (the Blue Mountains). However, other significant impacts include damage to vegetation in national parks and forest areas, problems in sewage disposal, and the removal of vegetation from sand dunes.

Tourism, vegetation, and wildlife

Vegetation and wildlife are key attractions in many Australian destination areas. The kangaroo and koala have been as significant to the development of tourism in Australia

Uluru, Northern Territory.

as the elephant and herds of wildebeest and zebra have been to the countries of eastern and southern Africa (Durst & Ingram 1988). In particular, the koala has been a major drawcard for Japanese tourists, and has allowed the redevelopment of tourist attractions such as the Lone Pine Sanctuary near Brisbane which has established colonies of the increasingly endangered animal. Similarly, vegetation has also become a drawcard in recent years for both inbound and domestic tourists. The rainforests of Queensland, New South Wales, and Tasmania are now an integral part of those states' marketing strategies, and the long-term development of tourism in those areas might well depend on the conservation of resources for both direct tourist experiences and as a setting for other activities, such as white-water rafting.

A variety of tourist-related activities impact on vegetation (Mathieson & Wall 1982; Edington & Edington 1986; Newsone et al. 2001). Plant collection is one of the more obvious forms of visitor damage to natural areas. Plants might be collected for replanting in 'visitors' homes, or flowers might be cut for decorative purposes. In Australia damage to native species has caused most Australian states to pass laws prohibiting the removal of wildflowers. However, problems exist in policing such laws and substantial damage can occur along roadsides.

In certain areas near camping grounds and along walking trails, vegetation is often deliberately chopped for shelter and firewood. This has necessitated the provision of firewood in many national parks and reserves to prevent damage to the surrounding trees, and many national parks now prohibit the lighting of open fires for cooking. These measures also serve to control the careless use of fire. Although much of Australia's vegetation is fire-adapted, wildfires caused by campfires getting out of control can cause severe damage to vegetation and wildlife, as well as endangering people and property. In addition, many people dislike the aesthetic damage caused by fires. Nevertheless, the appearance and long-term ecological well-being of many areas in Australia depend on fire being allowed to occur at certain times of the year.

One of the major problems along many tourist routes and walking tracks is the dumping of rubbish from vehicles or by recreationists. Apart from being unsightly, dumping can alter soil composition and introduce exotic species into plant communities. Apple and pear trees that have grown from fruit thrown from cars can be found along many Australian country roadsides. Similarly, tourist vehicles can introduce weeds into natural areas, as has happened in Kakadu National Park (Lonsdale & Lane 1994).

Camping and pedestrian or vehicular traffic have substantial impacts in a wide range of natural environments. 'Trampling damage is frequently unwelcome in scenic areas because it destroys attractive plant communities and creates eroded, unsightly soil surfaces' (Edington & Edington 1986, p. 78). Trampling damage caused by recreationists depends on the susceptibility of different plant communities and the amount of traffic at a particular site. For any trail or campsite there is a level of visitor use beyond which normal soil and vegetation cover can no longer be maintained. This level is known as the natural 'carrying capacity' of that trail. Evidence from North America suggests that, for a given intensity of use, damage to trails is greater in forests than on grasslands (Cole 1978; Weaver & Dale 1978). However, results from North American studies cannot be automatically transferred to Australian settings, because trampling effects differ among ecosystems (Edwards 1977; Keane, Wild & Rogers 1979; Gibson 1984; Calais & Kirkpatrick 1986).

The ability of a site to withstand trampling depends on the resiliency of the species and the frequency and pattern of trampling activity. The most fragile species can disappear with site or trail use, leaving more resilient species behind. Resiliency can be measured not only in terms of the ability of plants to withstand physical damage and the effects of soil compaction on nutrient and water uptake, but also by the success of plants in reproducing in a disturbed environment. With continued use of a site or trail the diversity of species can be reduced, and only the most resilient species will remain. However, some species are able to take advantage of the changed physical conditions and can colonise the impacted site or the edge of a trail. Similarly, streams and rivers are able to carry only a limited amount of boating traffic before damage occurs. For example, the banks of the Gordon River in Tasmania's south-west wilderness have become eroded because of the speed of tourist boats plying the river, and the frequency of trips made by these boats (Cook 1985).

The carrying capacity of trails and specific areas can be increased by the diversion of visitors onto other trails and site hardening through the use of wooden walkways or bituminised or gravel walking paths (Gale & Jacobs 1987; Hall & McArthur 1993, 1996; Newsome et al. 2001). Nevertheless, depending on the expectations of recreationists, any change in the perceived 'natural' appearance of a site can lead to a drop in visitor satisfaction levels. Trails also create other problems in natural area management as they provide an avenue for the introduction of weeds and exotic species, particularly in national parks. Although humans can introduce exotic species into natural areas by dumping rubbish or by carrying seeds in their clothing, one of the major sources of weed dispersal is by animals. In particular, the riding of horses by tourists in national parks can be a major source of introduced species on certain trails and at camping sites, and is perceived by some conservation groups as being potentially more damaging than foot-based travellers in national parks (Cubit 1990; Beeton 1997).

As noted above, wildlife is an essential part of the Australian tourism image. National parks such as Kosciuszko and safari parks such as the Dubbo Zoo are major tourist attractions in rural areas. Zoological and botanic gardens and aquariums are important urban tourist attractions which also serve an important conservation function, and certain exhibitions can be major tourist events (Mason 2000).

Hunting and photography are two of the most obvious tourist-related wildlife activities. Hunting is not a major tourist activity in Australia as there are few trophy animals to be had, except for wild water buffalo in the Northern Territory. Fishing is an important tourist activity, being one of the most popular recreational or sporting activities in Australia. Game fishing has a high tourist profile off the north-west coast of Western Australia and northern Queensland, particularly in the Cairns region. However, big-game fishing perhaps contributes more to the image of a region than to the direct attraction of visitation.

Bird-watching, scuba-diving, wildlife photography, and safari-type tours are some of the major tourist uses of wildlife, and are major growth areas in the field of special interest tourism (Durst & Ingram 1988; Hall 1989b; Weiler & Hall 1992; Davis 1993; Shackley 1996; Reynolds & Braithwaite 2001) (see Chapter 12). Despite their non-consumptive nature (Duffus & Dearden 1990), these activities can still impact on certain species by distorting behaviour through artificial feeding and habitat disturbance, or by disruption of breeding and feeding patterns. For example, to minimise disturbance, access by tourists to the seabird nesting islands of Michaelmas Cay (offshore from Cairns in northern Queensland) has to be managed carefully during peak nesting periods when more than 30 000 birds are on the site (Muir & Chester 1993). The ability of wildlife to withstand the impacts of tourists vary from species to species and from region to region, according to the intensity and type of development, species resilience, and the ability of wildlife to adapt to the tourist presence (Mathieson & Wall 1982; Hill & Rosier 1989; Newsome et al. 2001; Wilson & Tisdell 2001).

Whale-watching is an expanding segment of the tourist industry that relies upon the presence and activities of wildlife. The annual whale migration along the east coast of Australia has led to whale-watching being an important tourist activity off Fraser and Stradbrooke Islands and in certain areas off the Great Barrier Reef. Similarly, whale-watching is recognised as a potential attraction in the Shark Bay region of Western Australia, together with its well-established dolphin and dugong population (Dowling 1997). Kaikora in the South Island of New Zealand has also developed an international reputation as a whale-watching and marine life centre. However, international experience with whale-watching indicates that controls need to be put in place to ensure that animals are not hit by ships and boats (Kaza 1982). Furthermore, boats can separate mothers from calves, and can disturb the behaviour of pods (Edington & Edington 1986). Therefore, the federal government has enacted regulations to minimise the disturbance of whales by tourism operators. As Puddicombe (1986, p. 258) noted:

> Properly managed, whale watching could continue to contribute significantly to tourism and the economies of towns such as Warrnambool and Byron Bay and afford the opportunity to promote public awareness and understanding of cetacean conservation issues. Improperly managed, the industry could threaten the continued existence of Australia's great whales.

TOURISM INSIGHT

WHALE-WATCHING

Since the growth of the international environmental conservation movement in the 1960s and the 'save the whale' movements of the early 1970s, whales have been regarded as representatives of a country's overall marine conservation policy. Whales have become an international conservation icon species often referred to as charismatic fauna. These are generally 'cute furry animals, with big eyes' which possess emotive potential (see Cooper 1993), and include such animals as elephants, pandas, and harp seal pups (Freeman 1997). The public appeal of whales, particularly in the Western world, has been sustained through a proliferation of books, magazines, films (for example, 'Free Willy'), television shows, music, and works of art (Barstow 1986).

In addition to the media interest in whales, there has been a growing fascination with observing whales and dolphins in their natural environment (Barstow 1986). With the worldwide ban on commercial whaling there has been a shift from a consumptive use of whales to a non-consumptive utilisation. This has resulted in financially viable businesses based on taking tourists to watch whales in the open sea and a rapid worldwide growth in marine mammal-based tourism. Whale-watching has become an important economic, educational, and recreational activity. Organised whale-watching appears to have begun in the United States in the 1950s on small, isolated scales in Hawaii and California (Tilt 1985). It grew slowly at first, and the concept did not reach Europe, Australia, and New Zealand until the mid-1980s (David et al. 1997; Orams 1997; Muloin 1998; Hall & Kearsley 2001). During the late 1980s and early 1990s the whale-watching industry grew substantially. In 1995 around 5.4 million people a year participated in whale-watching trips in 65 countries and overseas territories, generating revenues in excess of US$500 million (Hoyt 1995). Duffus and Dearden (1993), in discussing the management of killer-whale-watching tourism and its benefits and costs, noted that the benefits of wildlife use involved both economic and non-economic values, including education and conservation values—which they defined as changing environmental attitudes.

Nevertheless, the overwhelming growth in the whale-watching industry has stirred some serious concerns over planning and management. Whale-watching can provide both benefits and costs to the whales and to humans. Much work is needed to develop techniques to quantify the biological risks and to define the ethical values of whale-watching (Franklin 1995; Hall & Brown 1996; Hughes 2001). Management must confront the human demands and the impact they have on the animals. Indeed, management officials often find it difficult to come up with ways to ensure tourist satisfaction and the continued success of marine mammal programs (Duffus 1996; Orams 1996, 1997). In relation to whales and dolphins, management concerns range from maintenance of the whale's habitat, harassment of the whales and dolphins by commercial and private vessels, and defining and enforcing the policies that affect tourists and whales (Blane & Jackson 1994; Davis et al. 1997; Constantine 1999).

One of the objectives of ecotourism is to change the behaviour and lifestyle of tourists such that their actions become more environmentally responsible during the tourism experience, and in the longer term (Fennell 1999; Weaver 2001). Opportunities to view whales therefore provide an important platform for public education regarding the natural environment (Orams 1996). It has even been argued that any negative impacts on populations of marine mammals that are constantly pressured by tourist boats and viewers might be counterbalanced by the education and awareness that whale-watchers receive (Decker & Goff 1987). This education can increase overall environmental awareness, and benefit all cetacean species. However, if inadequate education is provided, and the operator is simply exploiting a natural resource, such operations need to be extensively reviewed.

Tourism can have a number of direct and indirect impacts on wildlife (Shackley 1996). The most significant impact is removal or disturbance of habitat. For example, tourism developments in some coastal and estuarine areas, particularly the removal or reclamation of mangroves, can disturb the breeding and feeding grounds of birds (Williams & Smith 1986). Damage to feeding grounds can result in increased competition for food within an animal population or can force migration to alternative environments. Traditional feeding patterns of some species can also be altered by the presence of litter and garbage from tourist operations. However, it should be stressed that the impacts of tourism on wildlife have not been adequately researched in Australia, and that the effects of tourism on wildlife ecology generally remains under-researched.

The three-way relationship among tourism, wildlife, and local residents is critical in Africa, South America, and South-East Asia where the economic return from the establishment of national parks is critical to local development strategies (Barnes 1996; Shackley 1995, 1996; Sindiga 1996, 2000; Roe et al. 1997). However, with the possible exception of some of the national parks and reserves of northern Australia, where Aboriginal people have a major interest in management, wildlife has not been an important factor in tourism development. Nevertheless, the significance of wildlife to local tourism destinations whose attractiveness is based upon access to fauna and flora—such as the Shark Bay region of Western Australia and Kakadu National Park— means that such tourism resources must be protected. Furthermore, as noted above, wildlife and vegetation is an integral component of the Australian image, and is a tourist product that is rapidly growing in importance (D. Hall 1984).

Tourism and pollution

Pollution has emerged as a major issue for tourism in Australia. Although not sourced from tourism developments, the broader problems of sewage disposal in Sydney in the early 1990s, particularly along some of the beaches that had to be closed on certain days because of the amount of sewage in the water, damaged the 'clean, golden sands' image of the city. The issue of sewage disposal from coastal resorts poses a major problem for many Australian tourist destinations. The ocean discharge of primary or secondary (treated) sewage is not only aesthetically unsightly, but can also lower water quality, endangering personal health.

Localised water pollution problems can also exist in boating areas, such as marinas, harbours and waterways, where oil or wastes are discharged from boats. Water pollution is a particular problem in sheltered waterways that are not adequately flushed by tidal or wave action. In such areas the water can be covered in unsightly oil or garbage, and can also be dangerous for swimming.

Generally, little information is available on the effects of tourism on air quality. It is possible that motor car exhausts have a detrimental effect on the environment in some areas. However, in Australia, these effects have generally been too small to be noted at tourist destinations. Aviation pollution might also have some impact on the atmosphere, and possibly on the ozone layer. However, as with car fumes, such issues have not warranted attention.

Tourism can also affect the geology of an area. Apart from the erosive effects of walking on certain soil types, the major tourist activities that affect the geology of an area are climbing and fossicking. Although only a small number of people participate in climbing as a tourism activity, they can nevertheless impact on certain routes on cliff faces and mountains. Furthermore, in reaching certain sites, climbers can cause some damage to the surrounding areas. The growing use of climbing aids has meant that many climbs are marked by the trails of previous climbers, which can not only damage the rockface but also alter the nature of the climbing experience.

Fossicking, the searching for artefacts and natural deposits such as gemstones and minerals, is an important tourist activity in several Australian rural areas, particularly the New England region of New South Wales and the Kalgoorlie district in Western Australia (Jenkins 1988). Although some fossickers can cause localised damage to some sites by chipping at rocks or digging for samples, the most significant impact of fossickers is in their search for sites. Jenkins' (1988) study of fossickers in New England indicated that, although fossickers had a high degree of environmental awareness, many sites were poorly managed by local government, and some damage was also created by fossickers searching for gems on private land.

Fossicking and climbing are examples of two tourist-related activities which can affect environmental quality at certain locations. However, rather than focusing on activities it might well be more profitable to investigate the possibility that certain types of environment are more vulnerable to the impacts of tourism than others.

Tourism in arid Australia

Many overseas visitors to Australia have had a perception that Australia is a desert. In many ways this is true, because nearly three-quarters of continental Australia is arid land (Yencken 1985). For many people, the arid and semi-arid lands of Australia are empty and contain little of value apart from minerals and pastoral properties. However, since the early 1970s there has been a rapidly growing awareness that the arid interior also constitutes a significant tourism resource. Indeed, the opportunity to experience the 'outback' has become a key feature of Australian tourism marketing (Poole 1983; Wright & King 1983). Nevertheless, the fragile nature of arid lands makes them particularly sensitive to tourism development and poses major management problems.

The highly specialised and adaptive biological resources of the arid zone make them extremely susceptible to erosion and degradation (Messer & Mosley 1983; Woods 1983). As Sprigg (1974, pp. 56–7) commented in the landmark Report of the Committee of Inquiry into the National Estate:

> Vegetation in arid terrain tends to be sparse, dwarfed, often ephemeral and most delicately balanced ecologically. These areas require special care, protection and management, since they represent to modern man the 'last great land frontier' . . . Exploration, mining, petroleum production and tourism represent the greatest potential danger to these sensitive environments and require new understanding, conservation and care.

The effects of tourism on arid environments is typically concentrated at specific points (destinations and attractions) and along corridors (roads and tracks). One of the most noticeable impacts of tourists is the activities of off-road recreationists. Roads and tracks can create a substantial aesthetic disturbance in arid wilderness areas (Lesslie & Taylor 1983). For instance, Alexander (1981) reported that four-wheel drive tracks in central Australia often take many years to revegetate because of low rainfall. Nevertheless, for many visitors, off-road vehicles provide the only means of access to natural attractions which they would not otherwise be able to see.

Tourists are often perceived as being in conflict with the pastoral industry. For instance, Delforce, Sinden, and Young (1986), in a study of pastoralism and tourism in the Flinders Ranges of South Australia, reported that pastoralists frequently cited littering and gates being left open as significant management problems. However, only 9% of pastoralists could definitely attribute any losses of production directly to the actions of tourists. The study concluded that, 'for most pastoralists, although tourists cause many different problems, most of the problems are probably not very serious from a regional viewpoint' (Delforce et al. 1986, p. iii).

Substantial problems also exist for the development of tourism facilities in arid environments. The most significant factor for many developments is the high cost of construction and maintenance of facilities. Water supply is clearly a major problem in such a dry climate, and the distance from metropolitan regions entails costs in travel and supply. The aesthetic and environmental difficulties encountered in the siting of tourist plant mean that few facilities are developed to attract mass tourists. Yulara resort at Uluru (Ayers Rock) will remain the exception rather than the rule in arid zone tourism. Nevertheless, small-scale tourism, based on adventure and on nature-oriented tours run by professional operators, will undoubtedly remain a growth area in the Australian tourism industry (see Chapter 12).

Coastal tourism

Beaches, and for that matter, the entire Australian coastline, constitute an important economic resource which should be utilised in a manner that maximises commercial tourism potential without promoting indiscriminate or environmentally insensitive development (Burrell 1986, p. 375).

'Sun, sea, surf and sand' are essential elements of the Australian lifestyle (Dutton 1985) and are prominent components of the image that is sold as a part of the Australian tourism product. The Victorian government has recognised the coast as the state's 'most important tourist and recreation resource' (1988, p. 25). Furthermore, with three-quarters of the Australian population living within 40 kilometres of the coast, and more than a quarter within three kilometres, intensive recreational activity is focused on the beaches (Yapp 1986; Bird 1988). Therefore, it should not be surprising that recreation and tourism have had a major impact on the Australian coastal environment, particularly in such areas as northern Queensland, the Gold Coast, and northern New South Wales, where tourism development has been concentrated. However, the coast is a sensitive bio-physical and ecological system which needs to be carefully managed to ensure that its value as a tourism resource is maintained (Chape & Chalmers 1984; Agardy 1993).

The concept of coastal tourism embraces the full range of tourism, leisure, and recreationally oriented activities that take place in the coastal zone and the offshore coastal waters. These include coastal tourism development (accommodation, restaurants, food industry, and second homes), and the infrastructure supporting coastal development (retail businesses, marinas, and activity suppliers). Also included are tourism activities such as recreational boating, coast-based and marine-based ecotourism, cruises, swimming, recreational fishing, snorkelling, and diving (Miller & Auyong 1991; Miller 1993). Marine tourism is closely related to coastal tourism, but also includes ocean-based tourism such as deep-sea fishing and yacht cruising. Oram (1999, p. 9) defined marine tourism as including 'those recreational activities that involve travel away from one's place of residence and which have as their host or focus the marine environment (where the marine environment is defined as those waters which are saline and tide-affected)'. Such a definition is significant because, as well as having a biological and recreational basis, it also emphasises that consideration of the elements of marine and coastal tourism must also consider shore-based activities, such as land-based whale-watching, reef-walking, cruise ship supply, and yachting events, within the overall ambit of marine tourism.

Ocean and coastal tourism is widely regarded as one of the fastest-growing areas of contemporary tourism (Orams 1999). Although tourism development has been spatially focused on the beach for much of the past fifty years (as reflected in the slogan of the four tourism 'Ss' of sun, sand, surf, and sex), the ocean and the marine environment as a whole has become one of the new frontiers and fastest-growing areas of the world's tourism industry (Miller & Auyong 1991). The exact number of marine tourists remains unknown. Nevertheless, the selling of 'sun, sand and surf experiences', the development of beach resorts, and the increasing popularity of marine tourism (fishing, scuba diving, windsurfing, and yachting) have placed increased pressure on the coast—an area already used extensively for agriculture, human settlements, fishing, and industry (Hall & Page 2002). However, because of the highly dynamic nature of the coastal environment any development that interferes with the natural coastal system can have severe consequences for the long-term stability of the environment (Cicin-Sain & Knecht 1998). Indeed, the United States National Oceanic and Atmospheric Administration (NOAA) (1997) recognised:

> Of all the activities that take place in coastal zones and the near-shore coastal ocean, none is increasing in both volume and diversity more than coastal tourism and recreation. Both the dynamic nature of this sector and its magnitude demand that it be actively taken into account in government plans, policies, and programs related to the coasts and ocean. Indeed, virtually all coastal and ocean issue areas affect coastal tourism and recreation either directly or indirectly. Clean water, healthy coastal habitats, and a safe, secure, and enjoyable environment are clearly fundamental to successful coastal tourism. Similarly, bountiful living marine resources (fish, shellfish, wetlands, coral reefs, etc.) are of critical importance to most recreational experiences. Security from risks associated with natural coastal hazards such as storms, hurricanes, tsunamis, and the like is a requisite for coastal tourism to be sustainable over the long term.

As with many other aspects of tourism, concerns over the impacts of tourism on the physical environment, and related dimensions of sustainable development, have become substantial interests and have influenced research on ocean and marine tourism (Orams 1999). Improvements in technology, including transport (for example, tourist submarines) and recreational technology (for example, scuba diving), have also made the oceans more accessible to tourists than ever before. For example, marine parks, coral reefs, and areas which are in relatively easy reach of scuba divers have come to be widely regarded by governments and the private sector as significant natural resources that can be developed through tourism. Tourism development can have both positive and negative effects on the coastal and marine environment. Demands for water-borne recreation have resulted in substantial modifications to the coastline in the form of piers, sea walls, breakwaters, groynes, marinas, and facilities for beach users. The drainage of coastal areas and the creation of public picnic grounds are regarded by many as being an aesthetic improvement of the coastal environment. However, Australians are increasingly realising the ecological significance of the destruction of wetlands and the subsequent loss of species that has occurred in the name of shoreline 'improvement' policies (Senate Standing Committee on Environment, Recreation and the Arts 1992; Newsome et al. 2001).

Many of the effects of coastal development have occurred because of inadequate planning or simple ignorance of the dynamic nature of the shoreline. Development activities can result in the elimination of some plant and animal habitats, the destruction of geological features, water pollution, and damage to the aesthetic qualities of the coast. Human intervention in the coastal system has resulted in a dramatic increase in the initiation or acceleration of beach erosion. For example, the interception of northward drifting sand by breakwaters at Tweed Heads in northern New South Wales resulted in beach erosion on the Gold Coast because of a reduced sand supply (McGinnity & Jackson 1986). Similarly, on Phillip Island, Victoria, the stabilisation of sand dunes that had been moving along the Woolami Isthmus and nourishing the beach in Cleeland Bight was followed by erosion of these beaches (Bird 1988).

Coastal development has also altered the character of the coastline at Noosa Heads on Queensland's Sunshine Coast. One of the original reasons for the development of Noosa Heads as a beach resort was the fact that the Noosa Headland protects the beach area from the prevailing south-easterly wind and the cold southerlies. Ironically, the construction of the rock wall at Noosa in 1968–69, to prevent erosion of the valuable ocean frontage, has altered the capacity of the beach to regenerate because the steep-angled boulder wall has altered the natural slope and curve of the bay.

At several Australian tourist destinations, most notably the Gold Coast and Surfers Paradise, the absence of buffer zones between developments and the ocean has created substantial coastal management problems. Much of the development on the Gold Coast has occurred during periods of extremely mild weather (Jones 1986). However, the construction of buildings on former dune systems has left structures highly susceptible to beach fluctuation, especially the erosion which occurs during cyclones. As a result, certain areas (such as Palm Beach, which was developed in the 1920s), have had to be protected by heavy boulder walls because the frontal dune system to the seaward side of properties has been eroded during adverse weather conditions (McGinnity & Jackson 1986).

The protective capacity of sand dunes depends on the stabilising and binding properties of dune vegetation and the amount of human impact. Dune systems are extremely fragile and are particularly sensitive to the impacts of offroad recreational vehicles (ORVs). As Edington and Edington (1986, p. 31) reported: 'Of all the kinds of habitat damage caused by recreational vehicles, that sustained by certain types of coastal sand dunes must qualify as having the most direct implications for human welfare'. Many state governments have instituted a number of mechanisms to curb the effects of ORVs, including the provision of off-road vehicle parks, policing of environmentally sensitive areas, and fencing. However, the most effective management strategy is the development of an effective publicity and promotion campaign highlighting the responsibility of ORV recreationists to prevent environmental damage (Tucker, Green & Lewis 1986).

Much of the damage to the coastal environment has occurred because the land was not useful for agricultural or other purposes, and was therefore accorded a low value. For instance, the construction of the Noosa Island canal estate was enthusiastically received by the Noosa Shire Council in 1972. According to Shire Chairman Ian Macdonald (in Cato 1982, p. 104): 'The canal estate offers, at no cost to the ratepayer, additional waterfront land of high value, which yields substantial amounts of rates and generally assists the economy of the area'. Similarly, the managing director of Cambridge Credit, the initial developers of the estate, announced in his opening speech (in Cato 1982, p. 107): 'My company believes in conservation . . . we don't apologize for taking this land away from the mosquitos and the sandflies. We have turned an ecological desert into a fine estate'. However, it now appears that the estate has caused damage to the fauna and flora of Noosa Sound, reduced the quality of fishing, and lowered the environmental amenity of the area, as well as causing it to be endangered by periodic floods and cyclones.

Coastal areas are also susceptible to pollution. Excessive algal growths in inland waters enriched by sewage effluents have a variety of consequences, including 'water bloom' (Brook 1957), skin rashes, and gastrointestinal upsets. Furthermore, algae can be washed up on shore where they start to decay, smell, and provide a breeding ground for flies. For example, the Peel-Harvey estuarine system, a major tourist and daytripping region south of Perth in Western Australia, has experienced a number of severe summer algal blooms because of the large amounts of nutrients washed into the inlets from inland farming areas (Waterways Commission 1982). Sewage discharge can damage coral reefs as algal growth can overgrow sections of the reef, depriving reef species of food supply and shutting off light. Similarly, soil erosion caused by construction activity can also be damaging to coral reefs, because the increased water turbidity can reduce light penetration (Odum 1976), an issue that was a major concern in the construction of the Cape Tribulation Road in northern Queensland (Douglas Shire's Wilderness Action Group 1984; House of Representatives Standing Committee on Environment and Conservation 1984; Hall 1992a).

The above examples of the impact of coastal development illustrate the point that 'coastlines are key areas where planning measures and land-use controls must be implemented if that environment is to make a lasting contribution to the tourist industry' (Mathieson & Wall 1982, p. 114). All Australian states are taking steps to improve coastal management practices, and the activities of the Resource Assessment Commission in the early 1990s also raised awareness of coastal management issues. For example, the Victorian government has recognised that: 'Large-scale tourist development on the coast can . . . have substantial environmental and visual impacts. It is essential to protect the coastline from haphazard development, which can in fact destroy the features that make the coast attractive to visitors' (Victoria 1988, p. 25). Similarly, in 1989, the New South Wales government re-established the advisory Coastal Council and released a set of Guidelines for Coastal Development (Standing Committee on State Development 1989; New South Wales Government 1990).

Although many of the environmental impacts of tourism and associated coastal development can be mitigated through technical management (that is, improved sewage treatment) or restricted access (that is, visitor management programs), the social and political context within which coastal development occurs is extremely complex. For example, the NSW Standing Committee on State Development (1989) identified two state government organisations with a large role, and twenty-six organisations with a substantial interest in coastal management. In addition, there are numerous advisory committees, regional committees, and local government authorities that are also involved in coastal zone management. Therefore, the problem that faces the state and Commonwealth governments is the creation of measures that set out the coordination, responsibilities, and management priorities for the various institutions involved in coastal zone management, and the establishment of guidelines by which coastal development proposals can be evaluated (Resource Assessment Commission 1992a, 1992b, 1992c). In addition, as in all matters of environmental management in Australia, greater attention needs to be paid to the differing policies

THE ENVIRONMENTAL DIMENSIONS AND IMPACTS OF TOURISM

of local government authorities on tourism development. Sustainable development of coastal tourism is therefore recognised as being dependent on (NOAA 1997):

- good coastal management practices (particularly regarding proper siting of tourism infrastructure and the provision of public access);
- clean water and air, and healthy coastal ecosystems;
- maintaining a safe and secure recreational environment though the management of coastal hazards (such as erosion, storms, floods), and the provision of adequate levels of safety for boaters, swimmers, and other water users;
- beach restoration efforts that maintain the recreational and amenity values of beaches; and
- sound policies for wildlife and habitat protection.

However, such a statement, although laudable, fails to reflect the complexities and difficulties of the management and regulation of tourism with respect to the physical environment.

Unfortunately, there is usually little or no coordination among programs that promote and market tourism and those that aim to manage coastal and marine areas. Environmental and planning agencies often fail to understand tourism, and tourism promotion authorities tend not to be involved with evaluations of the effects of tourism, or with its planning and management. Implementation strategies often fail to recognise the interconnections that exist among agencies in trying to manage environmental issues, particularly when, as in the case of the relationship between tourism and the environment, responsibilities can cut across traditional lines of authority. Therefore, one of the greatest challenges facing coastal managers is how to integrate tourism development within the ambit of coastal management, and thus increase the likelihood of long-term sustainability of the coast as a whole (White et al. 1997; Cicin-Sain & Knecht 1998).

THE BUILT ENVIRONMENT

As with the natural environment, tourism has had mixed impacts on the built environment. Historic buildings are extremely important to the tourism industry. Australia does not possess historic churches, cathedrals, castles, or palaces of the type that attract visitors to Europe. Nevertheless, over the past two decades, and particularly as a result of the enthusiasm for Australia's past generated by the 1988 bicentennial and the centenary of federation in 2001, both Australian and overseas visitors have taken a greater interest in the built history of Australia. For example, Port Arthur in Tasmania, the West End of Fremantle in Western Australia, the convict settlement on Norfolk Island, and the Rocks area of Sydney are some of Australia's premier tourist attractions.

The potential contribution of tourism to heritage preservation through education and direct financial support is substantial. Although ethical considerations of heritage preservation are laudable, the costs of such preservation have to be met. Therefore, as Piesse (1970, p. 177) recognised more than 30 years ago, 'organised, cultural tourism would seem to provide for Australia the only economic justification and thus viable means to achieve greatly increased government interest and investment in the protection and preservation of historic sites and monuments, including Aboriginal relics'. Tourism has meant that many buildings have been restored and

TOURISM INSIGHT

CRUISE TOURISM

Cruise tourism has become significant for a number of ports because cruise tourists are higher-yield tourists who spend, on average, much larger amounts of money per day than other categories of international tourists (Dwyer & Forsyth 1996, 1998; Ritter & Schafer 1999). In a study of cruise tourism in Australia, Dwyer and Forsyth (1996) reported that home-porting cruise ships in Australia, with a marketing emphasis on fly–cruise packages for inbound tourists, had the greatest potential for generating large expenditure inflows to Australia. In addition, they reported that because of leakages due to foreign ownership and foreign sourcing of inputs, the average expenditure per passenger per cruise injected into the Australian economy is twice as great for a coastal cruise as opposed to an international cruise. Nevertheless, there is significant debate over the impacts of cruise ships. Ritter and Schafer (1998), for example, argued that the ecological impact of cruises is low; that spending by individual tourists is high, and that accultural processes are minimal, and they claimed that, although the number of jobs directly created as a result of cruises is low, it compares very favourably with most other forms of travel as a sustainable development option. In contrast, Marsh and Staple (1995), in a study of cruise tourism in the Canadian Arctic, concluded that given the environmental fragility of much of the region and the vulnerability of small, remote, largely aboriginal communities, great care should be exercised in using the area for cruise tourism. Similarly, in examining some of the cultural dimensions of the cruise ship experience, Wood (2000) argued that the global nature of the cruise market has meant that cruise ships have become examples of 'globalisation at sea' with corresponding deterritorialisation, cultural theming, and simulation. In addition, concern over the environmental impacts of cruise ships led the United States Environmental Protection Agency (EPA) to host a series of meetings in 2000 to solicit input from the public, the cruise ship industry, and other stakeholders on the issue of discharges from cruise ships. These meetings were part of an information-gathering effort on the part of the agency to prepare an in-depth assessment of environmental impacts, and existing and potential measures to abate impacts from these discharges. Cruise discharges are currently regulated through a combination of domestic and international pollution-prevention laws, and the EPA was assessing whether these laws adequately protect the environment and whether there are gaps in these laws which might pose a risk to the environment (Rethinking Tourism Project 2000).

has ensured that Australia's architectural heritage has been preserved not as a 'museum' but as something that is alive and pertinent to modern society. The Department of Tourism and Recreation (1975, p. 7) recognised that 'planned and balanced tourism development in association with interpretative programs can . . . provide the means of educating man to appreciate Australia's unique characteristics'. However, although tourism has stimulated the rehabilitation of existing historic sites and buildings, and has transformed old buildings and historic precincts into new tourist facilities, many examples of Australia's heritage have been lost. For example: 'Few people realise that a historically significant convict built slipway was filled to provide parking space for the commercial/recreational wharf at Port Arthur' (Egloff 1982, p. 3).

The siting of tourist facilities was, for many years, often unsympathetic to the needs and demands of both the human setting and the natural setting, and led to the introduction of administrative and planning controls to maintain environmental amenity. Many coastal and rural municipalities have imposed height restrictions on tourist developments to maintain aesthetic qualities. There is 'no logic in transferring the high-rise solution to a rural or remote location . . . most architecturally and environmentally successful examples of modern hotel design are related to the site on which they are built and the environment of which they are now part' (Mills 1983, p. 65). Nevertheless, although regulations might be in place, their enforcement does not always follow should a developer be able to persuade local and state governments of the virtue of their tourism development. For example, the development of the Sheraton Noosa went ahead despite the height of the building exceeding the then guidelines for height restrictions.

Different market niches require different accommodation developments. For example, special interest markets such as adventure and ecotourism often require facilities and services in relatively remote areas. Solutions have to be found for the associated problems of access, provision of power, and waste disposal. As the general community comes to expect that developments, particularly in environmentally sensitive areas, have little or no impact on the natural environment, solutions to these problems become increasingly important in the overall development of these projects. (Saville 1994, p. 30).

THE NEED FOR ENVIRONMENTAL PLANNING

Over the past two decades there has been an increased recognition that tourism, 'if it is to be successful and sustained, actually requires the protection of the scenic and historical heritage of destination areas' (Mathieson & Wall 1982, p. 97). Indeed, the Department of Tourism and Recreation (Cwlth) argued in the mid-1970s that although protection of the environment should be an essential prerequisite of any tourist development, 'carefully planned tourism activity can be fully consistent with the needs of the environment' (1975, p. 7).

However, the 1990s witnessed the emergence of a new set of environmental concerns. Increased public awareness of conservation and quality of life issues such as wilderness preservation, water quality, and coastal development have set the parameters within which tourism development will occur. For example, the ATIA reported that 'The tourism industry must be seen to be developing a practical response to public concern about the environment and actions already in hand must be publicised' (1990b, p. 8). Murphy (1985, p. 41) foreshadowed the current debate over tourism development in Australia:

> The biggest concern for destination communities should be conservation of their natural resources, for this is their *raison d'être*. Successful tourism development leads to increased numbers and the possibility of visitor-induced stress on a community's physical environment. The problem is most acute in those areas with outstanding scenic beauty or

recreation opportunities possessing good access to tourist generating regions. They are becoming overwhelmed with tourists and need to conserve their attractions by controlling growth.

Heritage tourism, with adequate interpretation and information, is a rapidly growing area of Australian tourism, and an essential element of the tourism strategies of many regions, such as South Australia (Tourism South Australia 1989a, 1991) and the Northern Territory (Davis & Weiler 1992). In the case of the Wet Tropics World Heritage Area, for example, attracting tourists was seen by 55% of respondents in a study of perceptions of World Heritage listing to be the greatest benefit of listing (Wet Tropics Management Authority 1994). If heritage is to be preserved, improved environmental planning measures will be required at all levels of government, and, from the private sector, heritage preservation 'certainly needs the profit generated from a sound commercial approach, marketing, market research and new product development' (Davies 1987, p. 104). In terms of management practices, Budowski (1976, p. 28) argued that 'some areas must remain completely protected and become "strict reserves"'. Some areas are so sensitive to human impact that no access should be allowed to them. Indeed, many national parks and reserves are zoned or managed so as to restrict or prohibit access to areas of scientific significance such as endangered fauna and flora (Dowling 1997). However, government cannot manage the tourism resource by itself. Therefore, mechanisms need to be found if the tourism industry is to invest successfully in conservation. Budowski (1976) has identified six such mechanisms.

1 The tourism industry should invest financial support in conservation organisations.
2 A national system of national parks, reserves, and other protected areas should be established to meet the needs of the tourist industry.
3 Greater cooperation should be established between tourist authorities and national park and conservation authorities.
4 The tourism industry should assist in the establishment of national park and natural area interpretation centres.
5 The tourism industry should educate consumers about appropriate behaviour in parks and reserves and the role and nature of environmental conservation.
6 The tourism industry should develop a code of ethics for tourism and the environment.

All of the above are occurring in Australia to varying degrees at national, state, and regional levels. However, there is, as yet, no coordinated response from the tourist industry that covers all of the above points. The former Australian Tourism Industry Association (ATIA) put considerable effort into the production of a self-regulatory code of practice to which members should adhere (ATIA 1989a, 1989b, 1990). See Table 10.2. According to ATIA (1990d), the code 'marks the beginning

TABLE 10.2 ATIA/TCA's code of environmental practice

Philosophy

To recognise both development and conservation as important and valuable expressions of human utilisation of the environment.

To recognise tourism as legitimate and valuable resource utilisation.

(continues)

THE ENVIRONMENTAL DIMENSIONS AND IMPACTS OF TOURISM

To work towards an improved understanding of the allocation process of land and other resources and establish uniform environmental policy guidelines for the tourism industry. To support local, regional and national planning concepts and participate in the associated processes.
To work towards the highest level of professionalism in the industry.

Assessment
To develop an appreciation of the land and an understanding of its capabilities to support alternative uses in order to establish a basis for environmentally sustainable activities.
To ensure assessment processes recognise individual and cumulative implications of each activity.
To establish and apply methods to enhance beneficial and minimise adverse effects on the environment.
To assess actual and potential effects on the environment from individual tourist developments and uses which may positively or negatively affect aspects of the environment.

Protection
In co-operation with relevant agencies help:
To review private sector tourism infrastructure environmental management and modify such management where necessary.
To contribute towards protection and management of those irreplaceable segments of the natural and created environment on which the industry relies and to review and modify protection management activities where necessary.
To protect and preserve existing habitat flora and fauna and natural and cultural areas of local, national or international significance directly related to and involved with tourism development and use.

Responsibility
To accept responsibility for the enterprise related environmental impacts of tourism development, operation and use and to undertake responsible corrective and remedial action where necessary.
To ensure that natural ecosystems are not used beyond their sustainable capability by the activities of the tourism industry.
To take account, where appropriate, of environmental policies and codes of environmental practice in developing tourism proposals, including the incorporation of such policies and codes in contract documents.
To co-operate with relevant authorities and communities, in order to integrate environmental requirements into tourism management and land use processes.

Information
To incorporate environmental policies and codes of environmental practice within tourism training programs.
To ensure all involved in tourism, both directly and indirectly, have the opportunity to develop a sound knowledge of the natural resources and environmental principles associated with a sustainable tourism industry.
To support the inclusion of conservation principles in education, training and planning for tourism.
To enhance visitors' appreciation and understanding of their surroundings within the conservation objectives for the area.

Public Interest
To consider the value of other legitimate developments and utilisations and respect those values in making decisions for tourism development and utilisation.
To participate in and facilitate positive discussions on tourism related land utilisation issues.

Source: ATIA (1990d).

of an education process to demonstrate to the industry that good environmental management equals good management, and is necessary for the long term viability of the Australian tourism industry'. Nevertheless, considerable doubts have been expressed regarding the efficacy of a self-regulatory code without accompanying consideration of the strategic planning and policy implications of tourism development (Craik 1991a, 1991b; Hall 1992c, 1993b; Senate Standing Committee on Environment, Recreation and the Arts 1992; Hall & McArthur 1998; Malloy & Fennell 1998). Similarly, the Western Australian government developed a set of guidelines for sustainable tourist development (Research and Planning Division WATC 1986; O'Brien & Associates 1988) and Tourism South Australia developed an environmental code of practice (1989b) and a planning handbook (1990). Nevertheless, self-regulation will probably be successful only to the extent that it relies on consistent and comprehensive legislation and regulations (Senate Standing Committee on Environment, Recreation and the Arts 1992; Malloy & Fennell 1998). In Australia this is not yet the case.

The planning dimensions of environmentally responsible tourism are increasingly clear. 'It is the responsibility of governments and in the best self-interest of developers to make certain that environmentally appropriate tourism planning and development are accomplished' (Inskeep 1987, p. 132). Community consultation is also being incorporated into the shaping of environment–tourism planning, although the implementation of such an approach in the planning process is still somewhat problematic (Dowling 1993a; Hall & McArthur 1996, 1998) (see Chapter 11). To develop a long-term approach to industry growth, tourist destinations must appreciate the fragility of certain resources and protect their resource base. However, to do so, both government and industry must be willing to cooperate, and transform the current relationship between tourism and the environment from that of either conflict or coexistence, to a relationship of symbiosis. Both parties must recognise that a symbiotic relationship docs not just mean agreement between government and the tourism industry, but means the incorporation of the perspectives of all interested and affected parties in the tourism development process.

TOURISM INSIGHT

WORLD HERITAGE

World Heritage properties are areas or sites of outstanding universal value recognised under the Convention for the Protection of the World's Cultural and Natural Heritage (the World Heritage Convention (WHC)), adopted by a United Nations Educational, Scientific, and Cultural Organization (UNESCO) conference on 16 November 1972. The convention is one of the pinnacles of world conservation. 'The philosophy behind the convention is straightforward: there are some parts of the world's natural and cultural heritage which are . . . unique and [so] scientifically important to the world as a whole that their conservation and protection for present and future generations is not only a matter of concern for individual nations but [also a matter of concern] for the international community as a whole' (Slatyer 1983, p. 138). The aim of the WHC is to provide an administrative, financial, and legal framework for the protection of areas or sites of outstanding universal value on which World Heritage status is bestowed, which must meet certain cultural and/or natural criteria, and which pass tests of integrity and authenticity. Cultural centres such as Venice, Rome, Kyoto, and Quebec City have received World Heritage status along with natural areas such as the Great Barrier Reef, Victoria Falls, the Galapagos Islands, and the Grand Canyon. As of the end of 2001 there were 721 properties inscribed on the World Heritage List consisting of 554 cultural (places of historical significance, monuments, groups of buildings or sites), 144 natural (natural features, geological and physiographical features, and natural sites) and 23 mixed properties in 124 different countries which are party to the convention. According to Environment Australia (2001):

> Inscription of a property on the World Heritage List can produce many benefits for Australia, and in particular, for local communities. Australia's World Heritage properties are a clearly identifiable part of our heritage. In the case of properties such as the Tasmanian Wilderness, Kakadu and Uluru-Kata Tjuta National Parks and the Great Barrier Reef, World Heritage listing has featured in promotions which have resulted in greatly increased tourist visitation from overseas and within Australia. In addition to possible increases in employment opportunities and income, local communities could also expect benefits from improved planning and management of the region. A major focus for Commonwealth Government assistance for World Heritage properties has been the provision of resources for strengthening management and improving interpretation and visitor facilities. World Heritage listing also cultivates local and national pride in the property and develops feelings of national responsibility to protect the area.

Under the terms of the WHC (UNESCO 1999, Sec. 24), each cultural property nominated should:

(i) represent a masterpiece of human creative genius; or

(ii) exhibit an important interchange of human values, over a span of time or within a cultural area of the world, on developments in architecture or technology, monumental arts, town-planning or landscape design; or

(iii) bear a unique or at least exceptional testimony to a cultural tradition or to a civilisation which is living or which has disappeared; or

(iv) be an outstanding example of a type of building or architectural or technological ensemble or landscape which illustrates (a) significant stage(s) in human history; or

(v) be an outstanding example of a traditional human settlement or land-use which is representative of a culture (or cultures), especially when it has become vulnerable under the impact of irreversible change; or

(vi) be directly or tangibly associated with events or living traditions, with ideas, or with beliefs, with artistic and literary works of outstanding universal significance (the committee considers that this criterion should justify inclusion in the list only in exceptional circumstances and in conjunction with other criteria cultural or natural).

In addition cultural properties have to meet the test of authenticity in design, material, workmanship, or setting and, in the case of cultural landscapes, their distinctive character and components. They must have adequate legal and/or contractual and/or traditional protection and management mechanisms to ensure the conservation of the nominated cultural properties or cultural landscapes. Natural properties must (UNESCO 1999, Sec. 44):

(i) be outstanding examples representing major stages of Earth's history, including the record of life, significant on-going geological processes in the development of land forms, or significant geomorphic or physiographic features; or

(ii) be outstanding examples representing significant on-going ecological and biological processes in the evolution and development of terrestrial, fresh water, coastal and marine ecosystems and communities of plants and animals; or

(iii) contain superlative natural phenomena or areas of exceptional natural beauty and aesthetic importance; or

(iv) contain the most important and significant natural habitats for in-situ conservation of biological diversity, including those containing threatened species of outstanding universal value from the point of view of science or conservation.

Such is the significance of World Heritage status that World Heritage sites have been described as 'magnets for visitors', and World Heritage designation 'virtually a guarantee[s] that visitor numbers will increase' (Shackley 1998, preface). Several authors have agreed that World Heritage status increases the popularity of a destination with visitors (Ashworth & Tunbridge 1990; Hall 1992; Drost Hall & McArthur 1998; Shackley 1998; Carter et al. 2001; Thorsell & Sigaty 2001). For example, in a survey of 118 natural World Heritage sites, Thorsell and Sigaty (2001) reported a total annual visitation of nearly 63 million people. Fifteen of the sites surveyed recorded more than one million visitors a year with the Great Smoky Mountains in the United States having the highest number (9 265 667). However, of the sites surveyed, the 32 sites in the USA, Canada, Australia, and New Zealand received more than 84% of all visitors. The average visitation for the 30 sites in Africa was 22 705 per year compared with 2.6 million visitors per year in the 16 sites in the USA and Canada. However, as Hall and Piggin (2001) indicated in a recent survey of tourism of World Heritage sites in OECD countries, a causal link between World Heritage listing and increased visitation over and above existing tourism trends is somewhat tenuous. Whatever the potential to attract tourists, World Heritage listing is clearly a significant factor for tourism management on the basis of the inherent qualities of the property (Hall, 1992; Shackley, 1998).

THE ENVIRONMENTAL DIMENSIONS AND IMPACTS OF TOURISM

Tourism is an environmentally dependent industry with environment and heritage providing the physical basis and being the drawcard on which the tourism industry and tourist experience is built. The relationship of tourism and the environment was examined with reference to Budowski (1976), who suggested that the relationship can be expressed as being in conflict, coexistence, or symbiosis. In Australia it can be argued that all three relationships exist simultaneously, depending on location and issue. However, such is the importance of the environment for Australian tourism, particularly in terms of Australia's attractiveness as an inbound destination, that a greater understanding of tourism's effect on the environment must be established.

A range of environmental impacts from touristic activity was discussed, although it was noted that research on the subject is incomplete and that substantial gaps remain in our knowledge base. Research has been focused on particular regions or environments, but there is a limited ability to generalise findings from one area to another. However, tourism was demonstrated to have substantial impacts on vegetation and wildlife and to be related to a general lowering of environmental quality in certain situations, although it was also recognised that tourism can assist in protecting certain sites through the creation of national parks and reserves. Similarly, tourism was also regarded as being a mixed blessing for the built environment, with loss of heritage on one hand, and financial incentives and regulatory controls on the other.

The chapter concluded with a discussion of the need for environmental planning for tourism and noted that if tourism is to be successful and sustained, the natural and built environments of destinations must be conserved. Incentives for conservation come from the profit motive and the potential for industry codes of ethics to restrict undesirable behaviour. Indeed, it was argued that a variety of mechanisms exist for the tourism industry to invest in conservation. However, government at all levels still has a major role to play, given that conflict or an uncomfortable coexistence still surrounds much tourism development in Australia.

SUGGESTIONS FOR FURTHER READING

For general introductions to environmental aspects of tourism see Inskeep (1991), Gunn (1994), Hunter and Green (1995), Mieczkowski (1995), and Weaver (2001). Shackley (1996) provides a very useful introduction to issues surrounding wildlife tourism. The best introduction to tourism in natural areas is Newsome et al. (2001).

The IAC (1989) *Travel and Tourism* report provides a good overview of most of the concerns surrounding the impact of tourism on the environment, particularly the respective roles of government and the private sector within an Australian framework (pp. 163–83). More detailed discussions of the environmental impacts of tourism and possible management mechanisms can be found in Wall and Wright (1977), Edington and Edington (1986), Williams (1987), Shackley (1996), and Newsome et al. (2001). Within Australia, increased attention is being given to the implications of the relationship between environmental conservation and the tourism industry. For example, the Senate Standing Committee on Environment, Recreation and the Arts (1992) produced a report on tourism and the environment. Several studies of the perceived environmental impacts of tourism are now available; see Cato (1989), Buckley & Pannell (1990), and Dowling (1993a, 1993b). The annual Australian tourism and hospitality research conference also usually has a substantial number of papers on issues relating to environmental aspects of tourism and sustainability. Several Australian and New Zealand case studies of the environmental impacts of tourism and their management can be found in Hall et al. (1997a), and several case studies are also available in Harris and Leiper (1995). An excellent overview of problems associated with coastal zone management can be found in the Resource Assessment Commission (1992a, 1992b, 1992c) coastal zone inquiry. An extremely useful report by the New Zealand Parliamentary Commissioner for the Environment (1997) on the management of the environmental impacts of tourism also contains valuable comparative material for Australian students.

INTERNET SITES

The following websites are recommended:
- Environment Australia:
    www.erin.gov.au

- United Nations Environmental Programme:
    www.unep.org

- World Conservation Union:
    www.iucn.org

- On the Tourism insights on the web
    www.prenhall.com/hall_au

see:
Marine Tourism, by Michael Lüeck;
Tourism in Antarctica (photoessay), by Thomas G. Bauer; and
Indigenous Ecotourism in Australia by Heather Zeppel.

FOR DISCUSSION AND REVIEW

Key concepts

Key concepts discussed in this chapter included:
heritage sites, cultural landscape, natural landscape, environmental movement, environment, conflict, coexistence, symbiosis, trampling, visitor impacts, wildlife attractions, carrying capacity, pollution, off-road recreation, buffer zones, built environment, environmental planning, environmentally responsible tourism.

THE ENVIRONMENTAL DIMENSIONS AND IMPACTS OF TOURISM

Questions for review and discussion

1 What are the three basic relationships that can exist between tourism and the environment?

2 How can changes in the environment caused by tourism be distinguished from the effects of other activities?

3 Describe some of the ways in which off-road vehicles can harm the environment.

4 How can tourism contribute to conservation of the built environment?

5 How can the tourism industry best invest in conservation?

6 How 'green' should tourism be in terms of planting species around tourism developments and landscaping?

TOURISM PLANNING AND DESTINATION DEVELOPMENT

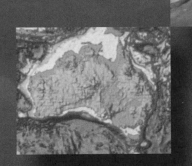

11

The advent of tourism, either at the community or national level, occurs almost invariably during periods of rapid change or precipitates local change. Elements within national governments may make policy commitments to the promotion and development of tourism as a quick expedient to shore up a quaking economy, and a local community may be 'discovered' overnight as one of the 'last' unspoiled tourist meccas (Nuñez 1989, p. 268).

It is no longer good enough to allow uncontrolled development . . . Regrettably much of the coast of New South Wales and Queensland suffers from continuous, boring urban development which offers the tourist little in the way of an alternative life style. The suburbia of the cities has been transplanted to natural beauty spots resulting in unidentifiable images, undistinguished environments and lack of amenity with consequent loss of tourist potential. Climate and natural scenic attractions are the major reason why the present resorts survive (Cox 1985, p. 46).

PLANNING for tourism occurs in a number of forms (development, infrastructure, promotion, and marketing); structures (different government and non-government organisations); scales (international, national, regional, local, and sectoral) and times (different time scales for development, implementation, and evaluation). However, planning is rarely exclusively devoted to tourism *per se*. Rather, planning for tourism tends to be 'an amalgam of economic, social and environmental considerations' which reflect the diversity of the factors which influence tourism development (Heeley 1981, p. 61). Nevertheless, the emergence of public concern over externalities has led to demands for improved planning for tourism in the belief that this will help ameliorate the negative impacts of tourism development. As Burkart and Medlik (1981, p. 235) commented:

> All tourism activity is increasingly regulated in the interests of the consumer; physical planning and development are increasingly regulated in the interests of the tourist as well as the resident. The need for physical planning has come to be widely recognized, if not always readily accepted.

As a general field of research, tourism planning has mirrored broader trends within the urban and regional planning traditions (Getz 1986, 1987; Inskeep 1991; Hall 2000a), primarily because it has been focused on destination planning rather than on individual tourism business planning. Moreover, planning for tourism tends to reflect the economic, environmental, and social goals of government and, increasingly, those of industry, at whichever level the planning process is being carried out. Therefore, planning can in many ways be regarded as going hand-in-hand with tourism policy.

Planning for tourism has traditionally been associated with land-use zoning or development planning at the local government level. Concerns have typically been focused on site development, accommodation and building regulations, the density of tourist development, the presentation of cultural, historical, and natural tourist features, and the provision of infrastructure, including roads and sewerage. However, in recent years, tourism planning at all levels of government has had to adapt its tourism planning program to include environmental considerations and concerns over the social impacts of tourism. And all of this planning activity is in potential conflict with modern demands for 'smaller government'.

To increase the financial contribution of tourism to government income, government is often entrepreneurial in its involvement with tourism. Government is increasingly involved in the promotion and marketing of destinations, and in the joint development of tourist attractions or facilities with the private sector. However, such activities are often carried on outside the statutory powers of government (Senate Standing Committee on Environment, Recreation and the Arts 1992). For example, although the state and territory tourism commissions are usually charged with development and marketing, they have no statutory authority to intervene in the planning process. Rather, this is the responsibility of the various state and territory planning departments.

The lack of a single authority responsible for tourism development at the state level has meant that local authorities and private industry have often been confused by the tourism development and planning process. Furthermore, the diverse structure of the industry has meant that coordination of the various elements of the planning process has been extremely difficult. As has long been recognised, the very nature of the industry makes planning important. As Gunn (1977, p. 85) observed, because of the fragmented growth of the tourism industry 'the overall planning of the total tourism system is long overdue . . . there is no overall policy, philosophy or coordinating force that brings the many pieces of tourism into harmony and assures their continued harmonious function'.

Tourism planning does not refer only to tourism development and promotion, although these are certainly important. Tourism must be integrated within the wider planning processes to promote economic, social, and environmental goals through appropriate tourism development (Testoni 2001). Therefore, tourism planning must be 'a process, based on research and evaluation, which seeks to optimize the potential contribution of tourism to human welfare and environmental quality' (Getz 1987, p. 3).

THE CHANGING ROLE OF GOVERNMENT IN TOURISM PLANNING

Demands for tourism planning are a response to the effects of unplanned tourism development. The rapid pace of tourism growth and development has often meant that responses to the impacts of tourism on destinations have been *ad hoc*, rather than predetermined strategies oriented towards development objectives. Such an *ad hoc* approach is the antithesis of planning. According to Murphy (1985, p. 156): 'Planning is concerned with anticipating and regulating change in a system, to promote orderly development so as to increase the social, economic, and environmental benefits of the development process'. Therefore, planning is a crucial element in ensuring the long-term development of tourist destinations. However, as the following pages illustrate, the focus and methods of tourism planning have not remained constant and have evolved to meet the new demands that have been placed on the tourism industry.

International tourism policies in developed nations can be divided into five distinct phases (Table 11.1). Of particular importance has been the increased direct

TABLE 11.1 International tourism policies 1945–present

Phase	Characteristics
1945–55	Dismantling and streamlining of the police, customs, currency, and health regulations that had been put into place following the Second World War
1955–70	Greater government involvement in tourism marketing to increase tourism earning potential
1970–85	Government involvement in the supply of tourism infrastructure and in the use of tourism as a tool of regional development
1985–late 1990s	Continued use of tourism as a tool for regional development, increased focus on environmental issues, reduced direct government involvement in the supply of tourism infrastructure, greater emphasis on the development of public–private partnerships and industry self-regulation
Late 1990s–present	International tourism policy marked by international regulation and agreement with respect to matters such as the environment, trade in goods and services, investment, and movement of people

Source: adapted from OECD (1974); Hall (1994a, 2000a); Hall and Jenkins (1995).

involvement of government in regional development, environmental regulation, and the marketing of tourism, although more recently there has been reduced direct government involvement in the supply of tourism infrastructure and greater emphasis on the development of public–private partnerships and industry self-regulation (Airey 1983; Hall 1994a, 2000a). The attention of government on the potential benefits of economic and regional development has provided the main driving force for tourism planning, 'but the result has been top-down planning and promotion that leaves destination communities with little input or control over their own destinies' (Murphy 1985, p. 153). As the following pages indicate, economic motivations have been foremost in tourism planning. However, attention is gradually becoming focused on the social and environmental aspects of tourism development.

Nevertheless, as Gunn (1979, p. 1) observed 'on the surface, the planning of tourism is a contradiction . . . tourism implies non-directed, voluntary and personal goal-oriented travel, and its corollary of free-enterprise development'. However, completely unregulated or unplanned tourism development would almost certainly lead to the degradation of the physical and social resource base upon which tourism depends. Therefore, what must be planned is not the travel experience itself but the opportunity to achieve that experience within an appropriate economic, environmental, and social setting for the hosts.

Although the desirability for tourism planning is generally accepted, the form and method of the most effective method of planning remains a contested concept. One of the seminal works on tourism planning by Clare Gunn (1988) identified a number of foundation points for the development of an overall approach to tourism planning.

1 Only planning can avert negative impacts, although for planning to be effective, all 'actors' must be involved—not just professional planners.
2 Tourism is symbiotic with conservation and recreation, not a conflicting use with irreconcilably incompatible objectives or effects.
3 Planning today should be pluralistic, involving social, economic, and physical dimensions.
4 Planning is political, and as such there is a vital need to take into account societal objectives and to balance these with other (often conflicting) aspirations.
5 Tourism planning must be strategic and integrative.
6 Tourism planning must have a regional planning perspective—because many problems arise at the interface with smaller areas, a broader planning horizon is essential.

The foundations identified by Gunn (1988) provide a useful basis for realising the benefits of tourism, although they do not provide the only means of minimising the costs of tourism. The consequences of tourism development are wide-ranging and often unpredictable. As a result, planning can often only articulate concerns or uncertainties; society must guide planners in assessing their acceptability. Furthermore, as the discussion below illustrates, planning occurs at different levels and within a number of planning traditions.

Planning at different levels

Tourism planning occurs at local, regional, and national levels within government and organisational structures, with a fourth dimension, that of tourism organisation planning, usually categorised under business planning (Hall 2000a). Although the national/regional/local breakdown might be suitable for planning within the

Australian government framework, there have recently been moves to undertake planning based on physical or ecological boundaries, or at a destination level, which might cross government boundaries. However, defining what actually constitutes a 'destination' is extremely difficult (Davidson & Maitland 1997) with the term often being equated with a 'resort' (Vukonic 1997) and also being applied at a number of levels. Smith (1995) provides a number of ways in which regionalisation can be identified in tourism research—through such measures as cartographic regionalisation, perceptual regionalisation, cognitive mapping, functional regionalisation, and destination zone identification. Drawing on the work of Gunn (1979), Smith (1995) identified a number of criteria that might be applied in the identification of destination zones.

1 The region should have a set of cultural, physical, and social characteristics that create a sense of regional identity.
2 The region should contain an adequate tourism infrastructure to support tourism development; infrastructure includes utilities, roads, business services, and other social services necessary to support tourism businesses and to cater to tourists' needs.
3 The region should be larger than just one community or one attraction.
4 The region should contain existing attractions or have the potential to support the development of sufficient attractions to draw tourists.
5 The region should be capable of supporting a tourism planning agency and marketing initiatives to guide and encourage future development.
6 The region should be accessible to a large population base; accessibility can be by road, air, or cruise ships.

Nevertheless, despite the value of such an approach, precise boundaries are still difficult to identify (Smith 1995). Moreover, from a public planning perspective it should also be noted that perceptual regions or destination zones can run over different government boundaries, making land use planning and even tourism promotion extremely difficult as it raises the potential for conflicts between different government jurisdictions. In attempting to overcome such difficulties, Davidson and Maitland (1997, p. 4) defined destinations in terms of 'a single district, town or city, or a clearly defined and contained rural, coastal or mountain area' which share a number of characteristics:

• a complex and multidimensional tourism product based on a variety of resources, products, services, and forms of ownership;
• other economic and social activities, which might be complementary to, or in conflict with, various aspects of tourism;
• a host community;
• public authorities and/or an elected council with responsibility for planning and management; and
• an active private sector.

As Hall (2000a) suggested, Davidson and Maitland's approach to tourism destinations is useful as it highlights the complexity of destinations and, therefore, the corresponding difficulties in planning. If planners are serious about making places sustainable, they need to treat them as the complex set of relationships and networks that they are. At a project-based level, planning is also regarded as essential for tourist development. The Shankland Cox partnership, a British based planning consultancy, has identified four basic studies that are regarded as essential in the preparation of a comprehensive plan for any tourism development (Mills 1983, p. 132):

- the tourist market: its origin, form, needs, rate of growth, and competition for it;
- the physical capacity of the area: its ability to absorb the requirements of tourism in terms of its natural attractions, infrastructure, and economic resources;
- the socioeconomic impact on local communities' migration and housing, and social infrastructure for the support population; and
- the environmental capacity of the area: the limits imposed upon tourist development to protect the quality of the area in terms of landscape, townscape, tranquillity, and culture.

Project-based planning represents the immediate face of tourism planning for most members of the general public. However, the efficiency and effectiveness of project planning depends on the emphasis given to its various elements by developers and the receptiveness of planning authorities to its usefulness as a planning tool. As the next section demonstrates, tourism planning occurs in a variety of forms, each of which emphasises different elements of project planning.

APPROACHES TO TOURISM PLANNING

Getz (1987) identified four broad traditions of tourism planning: (i) 'boosterism'; (ii) an economic, industry-oriented approach; (iii) a physical/spatial approach; and (iv) a community-oriented approach (which emphasises the role that the host plays in the tourism experience). As Getz (1987, p. 5) noted:

> . . . the four traditions are not mutually exclusive, nor are they necessarily sequential. Nevertheless, this categorisation is a convenient way to examine the different and sometimes overlapping ways in which tourism is planned, and the research and planning methods, problems and models associated with each.

The following sections review each of these traditions, and the chapter concludes with a discussion of the development of a sustainable model of tourism planning. The various approaches to tourism planning are outlined in Table 11.2.

Boosterism

Boosterism has been the dominant tradition in tourism development and planning in Australia since the early 1960s. Boosterism is a simplistic attitude that tourism development is inherently good and of automatic benefit to the hosts. Under this approach little consideration is given to the potential negative economic, social, and environmental impacts of tourism. Cultural and natural resources are regarded as objects to be exploited for the sake of tourism development. Therefore, in many ways, boosterism can be more aptly described as a form of non-planning.

Residents of tourist destinations are not involved in the decision-making and planning processes surrounding tourism development, and those who oppose such development can be regarded as unpatriotic or excessively negative. Research in this tradition focuses on the forecasting of tourism demand solely for promotion and development rather than for ensuring that levels of demand are appropriate to the resources and social carrying-capacity of a region. According to Getz (1987, p. 10):

Boosterism is still practised, and always will be, by two groups of people: politicians who philosophically or pragmatically believe that economic growth is always to be promoted and by others who will gain financially by tourism. They will go on promoting it until the evidence mounts that they have run out of resources to exploit, that the real or opportunity costs are too high, or that political opposition to growth can no longer be countered. By then the real damage has usually been done.

The economic tradition: tourism as an industry

In the economic tradition, tourism is seen as an industry that can be used as a tool by governments to achieve certain goals of economic growth and restructuring, employment generation, and regional development through the provision of financial incentives, research, marketing, and promotional assistance. Although the economic model does not claim tourism to be the panacea for all economic ills, the approach does emphasise the potential value of tourism as an export industry, sometimes nebulously defined, that can positively contribute to national and regional imbalances.

Within the economic tradition, government utilises tourism as a means to promote growth and development in specific areas. Therefore, the planning emphasis is on the economic impacts of tourism and the most efficient use of tourism to create income and employment benefits for regions or communities. Attention is given to the means by which tourism can be defined as an industry so that its economic contribution and production can be measured, and so that the role of government regulation and support can be adequately appraised. In Australia, the economic tradition was very much in evidence in the review of travel and tourism conducted by the Industries Assistance Commission (IAC) (1989) which examined the impediments to the development of the Australian tourism industry. Although noting the need for tourism to be seen within the context of overall national goals of social and economic development, the IAC emphasised the need for deregulation and improved marketing as being the keys to tourism development, and the relationship between tourism and the environment was approached from an economic (rather than an ecological) perspective (Burns 1989). This tradition has been maintained in more recent government reviews of tourism such as that undertaken by the Industries Commission (1995). It is worthwhile noting that, although other factors (such as

Casino development is often regarded as having the potential to cause significant social dislocation through increased crime, prostitution and problem gambling.

TABLE 11.2 Tourism planning approaches: assumptions, problem definition, methods, models, and literature

Planning tradition	Underlying assumptions and related attitudes	Definition of the tourism planning problem	Some examples of related methods	Some examples of related models	Some examples of related literature
Boosterism	tourism is inherently good; tourism should be developed; cultural and natural resources should be exploited; industry as expert; development defined in business/corporate terms	How many tourists can be attracted and accommodated?; How can obstacles be overcome?; convincing hosts to be good to tourists	promotion; public relations; advertising; growth targets	demand forecasting models	Australian Tourism Industry Association (1989a), (1989b), (1990b), (1990c)
Economic	tourism equal to other industries; use tourism to create employment, earn foreign revenue, improve terms of trade, encourage regional development, and overcome regional economic disparities; planner as expert; development defined in economic terms	Can tourism be used as a growth pole?; maximisation of income and employment multipliers; influencing consumer choice; providing economic values for externalities; providing economic values for conservation purposes	supply–demand analysis; benefit–cost analysis; product–market matching; development incentives; market segmentation	management processes; tourism master plans; motivation; economic impact; economic multipliers; hedonistic pricing	Industries Assistance Commission (1989); Burns (1989); Dept of Tourism (1995a); Dwyer et al. (1997)
Physical/Spatial	tourism as a resource user; ecological basis to development; tourism as a spatial and regional phenomenon; environmental conservation; development defined in environmental terms; preservation of genetic diversity	physical carrying capacity; manipulating travel patterns and visitor flows; visitor management; concentration or dispersal of visitors; perceptions of the natural environment; wilderness and national park management; designation of environmentally sensitive areas	ecological studies; environmental impact assessment; regional planning; perceptual studies	spatial patterns and processes; physical impacts; resort morphology; limits of acceptable change (LAC); recreational opportunity spectrum (ROS); tourism opportunity spectrum (TOS); destination life cycles	Gunn (1994); Inskeep (1991); Beaumont (1997); Dowling (1997)

Community	need for local control; search for balanced development; search for alternatives to mass tourism development; planner as facilitator rather than expert; development defined in sociocultural terms	How to foster community control?; understanding community attitudes to tourism; understanding the effects of tourism on a community; social impact	community development; awareness and education; attitudinal surveys; social impact assessment	ecological view of community; social/perceptual carrying capacity; attitudinal change; social multiplier	Murphy (1985); Blank (1989); Macbeth (1997)
Sustainable	integration of economic, environmental, and sociocultural, values; tourism planning integrated with planning processes; holistic planning; preservation of essential ecological processes; protection of human heritage and biodiversity; inter- and intra-generational equity; achievement of a better balance of fairness and opportunity among nations; planning as process; planning and implementation as two sides of the same coin; recognition of the political dimension of tourism	understanding the tourism system; setting goals, objectives, and priorities; achieving policy and administrative coordination between public and private sectors; cooperative and integrated control systems; understanding the political dimensions of tourism; planning for tourism that meets local needs and trades successfully in a competitive marketplace	strategic planning to supersede conventional approaches; raising producer awareness; raising consumer awareness; raising community awareness; stakeholder input; policy analysis; evaluative research; political economy; aspirations analysis; stakeholder audit; environmental analysis and audit; interpretation	systems models; integrated models focused on places and links among places; resources as culturally constituted; environmental perception; business ecology; learning organisations	Krippendorf (1987); Hall and McArthur (1996), (1998); Mathieson & Wall (1982); McKercher (1997); Lindberg and McKercher (1997)

Source: adapted from Getz (1987); Hall et al. (1997); Hall (2000a).

TOURISM PLANNING AND DESTINATION DEVELOPMENT

environmental, cultural, and social concerns) are usually mentioned in state and Commonwealth tourism strategies, the emphasis of government policy at both levels still remains on economic criteria such as growth, employment, and increasing visitor numbers (see Chapters 5 and 6).

One of the main characteristics of the economic approach is the use of marketing to attract the type of visitor who will provide the greatest economic benefit to the destination, given the destination's specific tourist resources. Both government and industry emphasise market segmentation studies, and the matching of product and markets. Economic goals are given priority over social and ecological questions. However, issues of opportunity costs, the assessment of visitor satisfaction, and the economic necessity of generating a positive attitude to tourists in host communities do mean that limited attention is paid to the negative impacts of tourism. For example, as noted in Chapter 6, South Australia has shifted from an approach that emphasised net value to one that focuses on increasing visitor numbers. Nevertheless, under the economic approach, the issue of who benefits and who loses from tourism development does not usually arise.

The physical/spatial approach

The physical/spatial approach has its origins in the work of geographers, land-use planners, and conservationists who advocate a rational approach to the planning of natural resources. Tourism is regarded as having an ecological base, with a need for development to be based upon certain spatial patterns that minimise the negative impacts of tourism on the physical environment.

This approach focuses on the related issues of physical and social carrying capacity (Stankey 1982; Beaumont 1997; Newsome et al. 2001), environmental thresholds (Hill, Koslowski & Rosier 1985; Koslowski, Rosier & Hill 1988; Hill & Rosier 1989) and acceptable or desirable rates of change (Prosser 1986; Wight 1998). To minimise the impact of tourists on the physical environment, managers seek to manipulate travel patterns by concentrating or dispersing tourists in sensitive areas. For example, many national parks and marine parks such as the Great Barrier Reef Marine Park have management plans that zone sections of the park in relation to certain levels of visitation. The ATC (1994) *Natural Holiday Guide* stated (in Lindberg & McKercher 1997, p. 72):

> . . . fortunately most of Australia's World Heritage sites are big enough to support a large number of tourists. As soon as an area starts to show signs of damage through overuse, the walking paths, roads, boating and other activities can be shifted to a different location.

However, Lindberg and McKercher (1997, p. 72) noted that 'the common strategy of dispersion may be misguided . . . From the perspective of minimizing overall environmental change due to ecotourism, shifting locations may be the wrong strategy, because the new location may be damaged before the old location recovers'.

Within the spatial tradition, geographers have emphasised: (i) the tendency for destinations to evolve and decline in relation to the market (an economic approach); and (ii) the resources of a region (the physical approach) (Butler 1980; Pearce 1987, 1989). It is therefore not surprising that the spatial tradition emphasises the production of tourism development plans that are based on the natural resources of a region and on the capacity or limitations of sites to withstand tourism infrastructure (Hill & Rosier 1989). However, although such plans provide valuable insights into the natural resources and travel patterns that occur within a region, they often fail to give attention to the social and cultural attributes of a destination.

Community-oriented tourism planning

In the late 1970s and throughout the 1980s, increasing attention was given to the negative environmental and social impacts of tourism. Although the negative effects of tourism were initially associated with less-developed nations (de Kadt 1979; Smith, V. 1989a; Harrison 1992; Mowforth & Munt 1998), it was gradually recognised that undesirable impacts were also occurring in more-developed nations, such as Australia. In response to the perceived negative effects of tourism development, alternative strategies of tourism development were espoused which highlighted the social and physical context within which tourism occurred. For example, although Gunn (1979) emphasised a *laissez-faire* perspective in the first two of his three goals of tourism planning (satisfactions to users and rewards to owners), the third goal (protected utilisation of environmental resources) did signify a new appreciation of the renewable nature of tourism resources. Similarly, McIntosh and Goeldner (1986, pp. 308, 310) highlighted the need for community control in their five goals of tourism development, in which they argued that tourism development should aim to:

- provide a framework for raising the living standard of local people through the economic benefits of tourism;
- develop an infrastructure and provide recreation facilities for both residents and visitors;
- ensure that the types of development within visitor centres and resorts are appropriate to the purposes of these areas;
- establish a development program that is consistent with the cultural, social, and economic philosophy of the government and the people of the host area; and
- optimise visitor satisfaction.

One of the clearest statements of the community approach to tourism development is to be found in Murphy's (1985) book *Tourism: A Community Approach*. Murphy advocated the use of an ecological approach to tourism planning that emphasised the need for local control over the development process. One of the key components of the approach is the notion that in satisfying local needs it is possible to satisfy the needs of tourists (Haywood 1988; Murphy 1988)—a 'win–win' philosophy that has long been advocated in Australia in the case of the Cairns–Mulgrave region (Cameron McNamara 1986; Clark 1988), South Australia (Tourism South Australia 1990, 1991; PPK Planning 1993a, 1993b), north-western Australia (Dowling 1993a, 1993b, 1997), and on the north coast of New South Wales (Dutton et al. 1994). Nevertheless, despite the undoubted attraction of the concept to many destinations, the operation and implementation of such a process present many problems.

Community tourism planning was a response to the need to develop more socially acceptable guidelines for tourism expansion (Cooke 1982; D'Amore 1983). Until the growth of public concern in Australia for environmental and social justice issues in the late 1970s and 1980s, many planning exercises took the form of placation after policy or development decisions had already been made. However, with the growth of more sophisticated community interest groups, the planning process in Australia has started to adapt itself to public concerns in a wide range of development issues, including tourism.

A community approach to tourism planning is a 'bottom–up' form of planning, which emphasises development in the community rather than development of the community. Under this approach, residents, rather than tourists, are regarded as the focal point of the tourism planning exercise. The community, rather then being treated as part of local government, is regarded as the basic planning unit. Nevertheless, substantial difficulties arise in attempting to implement the concept of community planning in tourist destinations. As Dowling (1993a, p. 53) noted, 'research into community attitudes to tourism is reasonably well developed, although incorporation of such views into the planning process is far less common'.

One of the major difficulties in implementing a community approach to tourism planning is the political nature of the planning process. Community planning implies a high degree of public participation in the planning process (Haywood 1988). As Arnstein (1969) argued, public participation implies that the local community has a degree of control over the planning and decision-making process. Therefore, a community approach to tourism planning implies that there is a need for partnership in, or community control of, the tourism development process. However, such a community approach has generally not been adopted by Australian government authorities. Instead the level of public involvement in tourism planning can be more accurately described as a form of tokenism in which decisions, or the direction of decisions, have already been prescribed by government. Communities rarely have the opportunity to say no.

A further problem in utilising a community approach to tourism planning in Australia is the structure of government in Australia. The nature of the Australian federal system leads to difficulties in ensuring that tourism policies at different levels of government are adequately coordinated (see Chapters 5 and 6). For example, a community decision not to allow tourism development at a particular site might well be at odds with a regional or state tourism plan drawn up by a state government. Alternatively, a local government decision to proceed with a tourism-related development might be opposed by the Commonwealth if it impinges on significant National Estate or World Heritage conservation values (Hall 1992a; Dowling 1993a, 1993b). Nevertheless, despite the difficulties in implementing a community approach to tourism development, it is becoming apparent that tourism in Australia requires a more detailed and integrated planning direction than it has had in the past. 'If tourism is to become the successful and self-perpetuating industry many have advocated, it needs to be planned and managed as a renewable resource industry, based on local capacities and community decision making' (Murphy 1985, p. 153), with an increased emphasis being given to the interrelated and evolutionary nature of tourist development.

TOURISM INSIGHT

COMMUNITIES, CONFLICT, AND COOPERATION

The concept of community has been significant in tourism, and tourism planning in particular, for more than twenty years. Indeed, the central role of the 'community' in tourism planning has come to be recognised as one of the tenets of sustainable and socially responsible tourism. However, although community-based planning is an important driver in academic and bureaucratic approaches to tourism development, this does not necessarily lead to either sustainable tourism development or even a reduction in the amount of conflict surrounding tourism development. Instead, a local focus allows for the dynamics of the planning process to be altered as stakeholders face their interdependencies at a place-specific level. A key point is that the 'local' should not be romanticised, as so often seems to be the case in discussions of tourism planning. As Millar and Aiken (1995, p. 629) observed:

> Communities are not the embodiment of innocence; on the contrary, they are complex and self-serving entities, as much driven by grievances, prejudices, inequalities, and struggles for power as they are united by kinship, reciprocity, and interdependence. Decision-making at the local level can be extraordinarily vicious, personal, and not always bound by legal constraints.

Nevertheless, a community-based approach provides the possibility that the necessity to consult over the use of shared resources and the needs of neighbours opens the way for resolution of conflicts regarding tourism. Perhaps more significantly, this can occur with a reduction in the extent of formal government procedures as part of a push towards 'smaller government' and 'public–private partnership' in much of the Western world. A community-based process of management and conflict resolution can provide for greater informality in personal relationships among stakeholders in which trust is able to develop (Hall 2000a). In examining the role of the community in tourism, it is impossible to separate the social, economic, and political processes which operate in a community from the conflict that occurs among stakeholders. Conflict and disagreement among members of a community over the outputs and outcomes of tourism are, in fact, the norm. As Millar and Aiken (1995, p. 620) commented:

> Conflict is a normal consequence of human interaction in periods of change, the product of a situation where the gain or a new use by one party is felt to involve a sacrifice or changes by others. It can be an opportunity for creative problem solving, but if it is not managed properly conflict can divide a community and throw it into turmoil.

Conflict resolution is a process of value change which attempts to manage disputes through negotiation, argument, and persuasion. In this process, conflict is eliminated, or at least minimised to the extent that a satisfactory degree of progress is made by the interested stakeholders. Substantial attention has been given to issues of conflict resolution in the field of resource and environmental management. However, relatively little attention to such issues has been forthcoming in tourism, a somewhat surprising situation given the extent to which research on tourism destination development and the social impacts of tourism have highlighted the dissatisfaction with tourism often felt by residents.

Conflict resolution can take a number of forms, ranging from information exchange, to mediation involving a neutral third-party, through to binding arbitration in which decision making is collectively handed over to a third party

TOURISM PLANNING AND DESTINATION DEVELOPMENT

by the affected stakeholders. In all such situations two primary objectives are sought. First, an agreed definition of resource use is sought. Second, the creation of a working relationship among the affected parties is desired—a relationship that will provide for effective implementation of the resource use agreement and ongoing monitoring, evaluation, and procedural mechanisms for dealing with new problems that might emerge.

Tourism planners therefore typically have to find accommodation among various stakeholders and interests in an attempt to arrive at outcomes that are acceptable to stakeholders within the wider community (Hall 2000a). Indeed, much of the recent burst of activity in the tourism literature regarding co-operation and collaboration in tourism destinations is a direct response to the need to find mechanisms to accommodate the various interests that exist in tourism development (Selin 1993, 1998; Selin & Chamez 1995; Jamal & Getz 1995; Selin & Myers 1998). However, although public participation is seen as a standard tourism planning mechanism to deal with controversial issues, it should be noted that the simple hosting of a public meeting—a common consultation strategy—will not, by itself, resolve conflicts. Indeed, such a meeting might well lead to even greater conflict among parties, and might serve to reinforce rather than change positions, thus decreasing the chances of agreement. As Millar and Aiken (1995, p. 627) observed:

> Public meetings may help to identify conflicts, but they cannot resolve or manage them. While it is true they allow everyone to have his or her say, the root causes . . . are often neglected. In the end, the government is often left with the task of sorting out what it considers to be the relevant facts.

The problem has often been a focus on the technique (for example, a public meeting), rather than on the process and the desired outcome. Too often, processes have been interest-based rather than values-based. If long-term agreement and common ground among stakeholders is desired, attention must be given to the values which are involved in the conflict. Public meetings and other forms of public participation might help to identify conflicts and opinions, but they do not necessarily manage or resolve them (Hall & McArthur 1998). Smith (1992), for example, recommended that decision-making processes be structured around four principles:

- real and regular consultation that seeks to be inclusive of all stakeholders and that begins early in any decision-making process;
- development of a common information base;
- action plans involving multiple stakeholders; although more costly in terms of time (and often money), savings can be gained in the longer term as parties to any agreement reduce the cost of regulation; action plans should also encourage ongoing dialogue and cooperation, and should anticipate difficulties in implementation and possible future potential conflict; and
- the use of a variety of effective mechanisms including mediation and zoning.

Substantial problems also exist in implementing public participation programs at the community level. Jenkins (1993) identified seven impediments to public participation in tourism planning:

- the public generally has difficulty in comprehending complex and technical planning issues;
- the public is not always aware of, or does not understand, the decision-making process;
- there can be difficulty in attaining and maintaining representativeness in the decision-making process;
- there can be apathy of citizens;
- the process involves increased costs in terms of staff and money;
- the approach prolongs the decision-making process; and
- there are adverse effects on the efficiency of decision making.

As noted above, tourism planning is not static. Planning approaches need to evolve to meet the demands that are placed upon them by the public. A community approach to planning provides a basis for the formulation of tourism policies that assist both residents and visitors. However, a community approach is only a starting point. In the new millennium, tourism planning must be able to accommodate the impacts of tourism on the social and physical environment to ensure the long-term viability of the tourism industry. In particular, tourism development has been the subject of much controversy in recent years especially on the coasts of Queensland and northern New South Wales (Mullins 1984, 1990; Jones 1986; Craik 1987, 1991a, 1991b), where it has had a dramatic effect on urbanisation. The next section examines some of the problems of achieving a sustainable approach to tourism planning.

A sustainable approach to tourism planning: Towards integrated tourism planning and development?

The primary objective of sustainable development is the provision of lasting and secure livelihoods that minimise resource depletion, environmental degradation, cultural disruption, and social instability (Chapter 1). The report of the World Commission of Environment and Development (WCED) (Bruntland Commission) (1987) extended this basic objective to include concerns of equity; the needs of economically marginal populations; and the idea of technological and social limitations on the ability of the environment to meet present and future needs.

Although tourism ostensibly seeks to meet the primary objective of sustainable development (that is, not to 'foul its own nest' and, in so doing, to continue over time to return benefits to society), there are many contradictions within the concepts of sustainable development and tourism which mean that complete satisfaction is extremely difficult (Bramwell & Lane 1993; Hall & Butler 1995; Hall & Lew 1998; Testoni 2001). For example, Pearce, Barbier, and Markandya (1986) noted that sustainability implies an infinite time horizon, whereas practical decision making requires the adoption of finite horizons. Although these factors complicate the attainment of sustainable development planning objectives, they are not 'hard barriers'. Rather, they serve to emphasise the preconditions for tourism to become sustainable. Paramount among these is an effective coordination and control mechanism—a system that is able to give practical and ongoing effect to the policy intent of sustainable development.

The complex nature of the tourism industry, and the often poorly defined linkages among its components, are major barriers to the integrative strategic planning that is a prerequisite for sustainable development. Tourism development is often fragmented and poorly coordinated—ideal preconditions for what Odum (1982) identified as the 'tyranny of the small decision'. The net effect of such small decisions is contrary to the objectives of sustainable development and yet is occurring within a policy context in which sustainable development objectives are being formalised. The poor record of synchronisation of policy and practice is one of the major impediments to attainment of sustainable development objectives (Hall 2000a). The existence of tourist infrastructure and 'ready-made' attractions are not sufficient in themselves to ensure the long-term future of Australia as a tourist destination.

An imbalance between the supply and demand of tourism, together with inadequate attention to factors determining economic, social, and environmental sustainability, have the potential to lead to undesirable and unforeseen consequences. The IAC Inquiry (1989) indicated that substantial problems of 'balance' exist in the Australian tourism industry. However, although the inquiry dealt with economic and, to a lesser extent, environmental problems, fundamental questions concerning social impacts were largely overlooked—again reiterating the difficulty of balancing the many objectives of sustainable development in an industry as complex as tourism (Craik 1990). Similarly, although the Commonwealth government's National Tourism Strategy (DOT 1992; 1993b) gave much emphasis to principles of ecologically sustainable development, the social basis of sustainable tourism development was not examined in any detail.

As Australian tourism developed in the immediate postwar era, there was little evidence to suggest that the nature and scale of tourism activities was not sustainable. For example, Claringbold, Deakin, and Foster (1984) observed that the range of artificial attractions and uses of the Great Barrier Reef from 1946 to 1980 were minimal by today's standards. It is only since the rapid growth of inbound tourism began in the early 1980s that questions about factors affecting sustainability, such as environmental and social constraints to development, have become prominent. Therefore, it is not surprising that the need for incorporation of sustainable development principles into tourism development emerged as one of the key management issues in Australian tourism only in the late 1980s (O'Brien & Associates 1988; ATIA 1989a, 1989b, 1990b). However, although the intention of such guidelines is commendable, their implementation is heavily dependent upon voluntary acceptance. The fragmented nature of tourism management in Australia emphasises the gap between policy and implementation. Few of the present guidelines seek to address this weakness. For example, the vertically integrated planning model of the NSW Tourism Commission (Chapter 6) failed to recognise that implementation of the planning framework lay not with the Commission but with a variety of other state and local government authorities.

The key to the resolution of such problems lies in making the tourism industry aware of the importance of incorporating sustainable development principles into planning and operations. Community planning provides a firm basis for a long-term approach to tourism development, but the tenets of community-based planning need to be extended to incorporate the coordination of the educational, integrative, and strategic aspects of tourism before a sustainable approach can be realised. Dutton and Hall (1989) identified five mechanisms by which this goal can be achieved: (i) cooperative and integrated control systems; (ii) development of industry coordination mechanisms; (iii) raising consumer awareness; (iv) raising producer awareness; and (v) strategic planning to supersede conventional approaches. These approaches are still relevant today.

Cooperative and integrated control systems

In a typical planning process, stakeholders are consulted minimally, near the end of the process, and often via formal public meetings. 'The plan that results under these conditions tends to be a prescriptive statement by the professionals rather than an agreement among the various parties'; in contrast, an interactive style 'assumes that better decisions result from open, participative processes' (Lang 1988 in Wight 1998). An integrative planning approach to tourism planning and management at all levels (from the regional plan to individual resort projects) assists in the distribution of the benefits and costs of tourism development more equitably, and a focus on improved relationships and understanding among stakeholders assists in agreement on planning directions and goals (Testoni 2001). However, cooperation alone will not foster commitment to sustainable development without the incentive of increased mutual benefits.

Tourism South Australia developed the most integrated planning model by a government authority for tourism in Australia. Tourism South Australia (1991, p. 28) noted that traditional approaches to tourism planning, as outlined above, 'are limited because they ignore research and evaluation of tourism demand (market needs and expectations) and tourism supply (resource utilisation consistent with demand preferences and environmental sustainability)' (also refer to the tourism market system outlined in Chapter 1). Therefore, to provide a unique, satisfying tourism experience which differentiates products and destinations in the marketplace, creates long-term appeal, and sustains the resource base on which tourism products and destinations are based, tourism planning must integrate market and resource-driven processes. According to Tourism South Australia (1991), such an approach provides for a 'synergistic' tourism planning process which is goal-oriented, integrative, market driven, resource driven, consultative, and systematic (Table 11.3).

A planning process for regional tourism that utilises a synergistic and integrated approach to tourism planning is illustrated in Figure 11.1. Such a process might not be applicable in all situations; rather, the succession of stages indicates 'the investigative logic that is required for proper tourism planning' (Tourism South Australia 1990, p. 28). The key elements identified in Table 11.4 are utilised in such

TABLE 11.3 Elements of a synergistic tourism planning approach

Goal-oriented	clear recognition of tourism's role in achieving broad community goals
Integrative	including tourism planning issues in the mainstream of planning for the economy, conservation, parks, heritage, land use and infrastructure
Market-driven	planning for development that meets the needs of people and will thus trade successfully in a competitive marketplace
Resource-driven	developing assets that build on the destination's inherent strengths while protecting and enhancing the attributes and experiences of tourism sites
Consultative	with meaningful community input to determine what is acceptable to the local population
Systematic	drawing on, or undertaking research to provide conceptual or predictive support for planners; in particular, drawing on the experience of other tourism destinations

Source: Tourism South Australia (1992) *Making South Australia Special*, Tourism South Australia, Adelaide, p. 28.

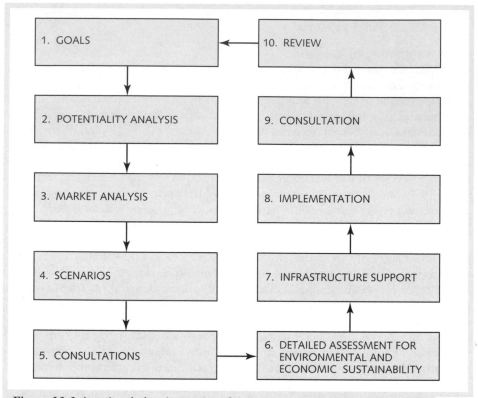

Figure 11.1 A regional planning process for tourism
Source: Tourism South Australia (1992) *Making South Australia Special*, Tourism South Australia, Adelaide, p. 29.

TABLE 11.4 Steps and outcomes in a regional planning process for tourism

Step	Outcomes
1. Goals	
Within the tourism and conservation philosophies of the state, establish what is to be achieved by the process	Clear statement of purpose
2. Potentiality analysis	
Examine broad market trends; Analyse area's tourism assets, strengths and weaknesses; Undertake competitor analysis; Determine community goals; Determine the existing and potential role of tourism in the area's economy	Statement of tourism's potential and priority in community development
3. Market analysis	
Analyse the tourism market—trends, market segments, characteristics and needs, growth potential; Identify fit between market forces and the area's assets and resources;	Target margets identified; statement of market positioning; major product gaps identified

(continues)

TABLE 11.4 *(continued)*

Step	Outcomes
Determine market position; identify major product gaps	
4. Scenarios	
Identify preliminary 'primary values';	Draft statement of desired future role
Identify alternative future tourism scenarios; examine implications of growth;	and character of tourism; statement of objectives and strategies
Select preferred scenario; identify constraints to achieving preferred scenario; establish tourism objectives and strategies	
5. Consultations	
Consult with key organisations and the community through interviews and workshops as appropriate;	Vision or statement of an agreed 'Desired Future Character'
Present results of investigations and proposals; identify community's primary values, key issues and problems	
6. Detailed assessment for economic and environmental sustainability	
Identify and evaluate natural and built tourism resources; specify potential development opportunities consistent with positioning;	Revise objectives and strategies; Tourism character areas identified specifying appropriate types and scales of development; development
Analyse environmental and landscape values; identify conflicts and constraints to tourism development	principles and planning specifications for character units; Major development opportunities and performance criteria specified
7. Infrastructure support	
Identify and detail infrastructure required to support investment and provide for visitor needs;	Prioritised program of infrastructure works
Identify and detail infrastructure required to manage visitors' impacts; identify and describe opportunities for the interpretation of features of visitor interest	
8. Implementation	
Devise implementation mechanism—program of work, organisational responsibilities and timelines; identify changes to existing legislation	Implementation strategy
9. Consultation	
Consult with key organisations and the community	Concise document outlining stages 1 to 8; draft supplementary development plan as required; amendment to tourism plan as appropriate
10. Review	
Monitor and review implementation procedures	Periodic reports on implementation and recommendations for plan amendments

Source: Tourism South Australia (1992) *Making South Australia Special*, Tourism South Australia, Adelaide, p. 29.

TOURISM PLANNING AND DESTINATION DEVELOPMENT

a manner as to ensure that the planning process is systematic, identifies the needs of the various stakeholders in the tourism planning and development process, and incorporates an understanding of the market and the tourism resource base. This planning process has been utilised in the preparation of regional tourism plans for Kangaroo Island (Tourism South Australia 1991; see also Hall & McArthur 1998), the Clare-Burra region (PPK Planning 1993b) and Victor Harbour (PPK Planning 1993a) in South Australia.

At a local level, elements of the strategic planning process can be employed to achieve a manageable, timely, and cost-efficient plan. Open community workshops and consultative processes can be especially useful to identify a range of issues which arise in tourism development (Tourism South Australia 1991, p. 31), including:

- *primary values*—What is it that residents and visitors value about the area?
- *aspirations*—What role do residents wish tourism to play in the economic and social development of the community?
- *fears*—What concerns do residents have about the impact of tourism on the community?
- *possibilities*—What are the special characteristics of the area that locals wish to share with visitors?
- *warts*—What are the things that detract from the area being a pleasant place to visit?

By going through a local tourism planning process (Figure 11.2) and determining responses to some of the issues raised above, destinations, townships, and local councils can be in a far better position to determine their positioning in the tourism

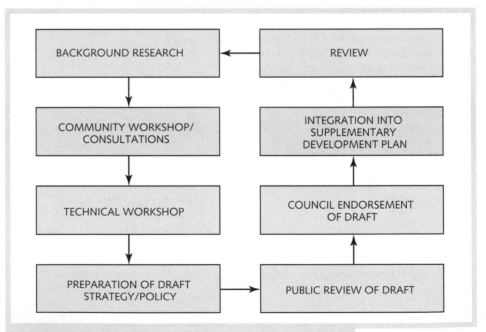

Figure 11.2 Local planning process for tourism
Source: Tourism South Australia (1992) *Making South Australia Special,* Tourism South Australia, Adelaide, p. 31.

market, product development, infrastructure development, development constraints, preferred futures, local needs, and the indicators by which success will be measured.

The role of an indicator is to make complex systems understandable. An effective indicator or set of indicators helps a destination, community, or organisation determine where it is, where it is going, and how far it is from chosen goals (Moldan & Bilharz 1997; Miller 2001). Sustainability indicators provide a measure of the long-term viability of a destination or community based on the degree to which its economic, environmental, and social systems are efficient and integrated (Gill & Williams 1994; Moldan & Bilharz 1997; Hall 2000a). Indicators are useful only in the context of appropriately framed questions (Hall & McArthur 1998). In choosing indicators, a clear understanding of management goals is essential. A typology of indicators might include:

- economic, environmental, and social indicators (measuring changes in the state of the economy, environment, and society);
- sustainability indicators (measuring distance between the current state and a sustainable state of the environment); and
- sustainable development indicators (measuring progress to the broader goal of sustainable development in a national context).

There has been a tendency to pick indicators that are easiest to measure and that reflect most visible change. Thus, important issues such as the social and cultural impacts of tourism might be dropped. In addition, appropriate indicators might not be selected because organisations might not want to be held accountable for the results of evaluations (Hall & McArthur 1998). According to Wight (1998), indicators to reflect desired conditions and use should ideally:

- be directly observable;
- be relatively easy to measure;
- reflect understanding that some change is normal, particularly in ecological systems, and be sensitive to changing use conditions;
- reflect appropriate scales (spatial and temporal);
- have ecological, not just institutional or administrative boundaries;
- encompass relevant structural, functional, and compositional attributes of the ecosystem;
- include social, cultural, economic, and ecological components;
- reflect understanding of indicator function/type (for example, baseline/reference, stress, impact, management, system diagnostic);
- relate to the vision, goals, and objectives for the destination region; and
- be amenable to management.

Development of industry coordination mechanisms

Although a range of formal and informal industry bodies exist, few of these bodies address complex issues such as sustainable development. The support by industry groups (for example, Ecotourism Association of Australia 1993) of environmental codes is indicative of possible directions if common needs can be agreed upon. However, for such guidelines to be effective, they must not constitute a 'lowest common denominator' approach to development and implementation. Government at all levels must use its influence to encourage greater industry coordination on planning issues by creating structures and processes that enable stakeholders to talk to each other and create effective relationships and partnerships.

TOURISM PLANNING AND DESTINATION DEVELOPMENT

THE TOURISM OPTIMISATION MANAGEMENT MODEL (TOMM)

The tourism optimisation management model (TOMM) is a recent and relatively untried model to monitor and manage visitors (McArthur 1996; 2000b; Hall & McArthur 1998). The conceptual emphasis of the TOMM is on achieving optimum performance rather than limiting activity. The TOMM positions a range of influences in the destination–visitor relationship to focus on the sustainability of the destination, the viability of the tourism industry, and empowerment of stakeholders. Besides environmental and experiential elements, the TOMM addresses the characteristics of the tourist market, the economic conditions of the tourism industry, and the sociocultural conditions of the local community. The model recognises the complex relationships among destination management and planning, the tourism industry, and supporting local populations. In this respect the TOMM is more politically sensitive than previous models to the forces that shape visitation and subsequent impacts (McArthur 2000a, 2000b).

The first TOMM was produced in late 1996 and implemented during 1997 (Hall & McArthur 1998; McArthur 2000a). It spanned public and private land in South Australia's Kangaroo Island, and was co-funded by the federal and South Australian Tourism Departments, and the South Australian Department of Environment and Natural Resources. The TOMM has attracted support not only from its three public sector funders, but also from local government, the local tourism association, the tourism industry, conservation groups, and members of the local community (Hall & McArthur 1998; McArthur 2000a). This has been achieved because of several key characteristics, including:

• the TOMM covers a range of dimensions of the destination–visitor relationship;
• a wide range of stakeholders collect data and therefore 'own' part of the intellectual property;
• the results of the monitoring are produced in easy-to-follow formats so that any untrained eye can pass over them and broadly deduce the health of the destination–visitor relationship; and
• management strategies can be jointly determined through shared understandings of the current situation and emerging trends.

The TOMM contains three main components—context analysis, a monitoring program, and a management response system (Manidis Roberts Consultants 1996; McArthur 2000b). The *context analysis* identifies the current nature of community values, tourism product, tourism growth, market trends and opportunities, positioning, and branding. This information is collected through literature reviews, face-to-face interviews with persons possessing relevant expertise, and a community workshop. The context analysis also identifies alternative scenarios for the future of tourism, used later to test the validity of the model.

The second stage of the development of a TOMM is the development of a *monitoring program*. The basis for a monitoring program is a set of optimal conditions which tourism and visitor activity should create (rather than impacts they should avoid). In this way the model avoids setting limits, maximum levels, or carrying capacities, and can offer the tourism industry opportunities to develop optimal sustainable performance. The monitoring program is essentially designed to measure how close the current situation is to the optimal conditions. The measurement yardstick is a set of indicators (one for each optimal condition). Table 11.5 provides a list of assessment criteria for selecting the most appropriate indicators for a TOMM. Each indicator has a benchmark and an acceptable range within which it is expected to operate. Table 11.6 provides an example of desired outcomes and their supporting indicators and acceptable ranges; in this instance they are environmentally orientated. The data generated from the monitoring program are then plotted to determine whether the status is within the acceptable range. Annual performance is presented via report charts already displaying benchmarks, and a relatively simple table that is principally designed to reflect whether each indicator is within its acceptable range or not. The presentation of data is therefore designed to provide a 'quick and dirty look' that all stakeholders can utilise (Hall & McArthur 1998).

TABLE 11.5   Assessment criteria for selecting indicators for Tourism Optimisation Management Model on Kangaroo Island

Criteria	Explanation	Example
Degree of relationship with actual tourism activity	The indicator needs to have a clear relationship with tourism activity to be relevant to the model	The number of fur seals at Seal Bay is more relevant than the number of possums at Stokes Bay
Accuracy	The indicator needs to represent the desired condition accurately	The number of traffic accidents is more accurate than the perception of parking difficulties
Utility	The indicator is more worthwhile if it generates additional insights	Visitation (number of visitors) has greater utility than perception of crowding
Availability of data	The indicator is more worthwhile if data already exists and is accessible, rather than needing to be collected from scratch	Data on the level of expenditure is more available than operator profit
Cost to collect and analyse	The indicator is more worthwhile if it requires minimal additional human resources to collect and analyse	The level of direct tourism employment is cheaper to monitor than the number of tourism products developed by local suppliers in response to tourist demand

Source: McArthur, S. (2000a) *Visitor management in action: an analysis of the development and implementation of visitor management models at Jenolan Caves and Kangaroo Island.* Unpublished PhD Thesis, University of Canberra.

TOURISM PLANNING AND DESTINATION DEVELOPMENT

TABLE 11.6 Management objectives and potential indicators for assessing the quality of the environment at Kangaroo Island

Optimal conditions	Indicators	Acceptable range
The majority of the number of visits to the island's natural areas occurs in visitor service zones	• The proportion of KI visitors to the island's natural areas who visit areas zoned specially for managing visitors	65 to 100% of visitors
Ecological processes are maintained or enhanced in areas where tourism activity occurs	• Net overall cover of native vegetation at specific sites	0 to 5% increase in native vegetation from base case
Major wildlife populations attracting visitors are maintained and/or enhanced in areas where tourism activity occurs	• Number of seals at designated tourist site • Number of Hooded Plover at designated tourist site • Number of Osprey at designated tourist site	0 to 5% annual increase in number sighted
The majority of tourism accommodation operations have implemented some form of energy and water conservation practice	• Energy consumption/ visitor night/visitor • Water consumption/ visitor night/visitor	3 to 7 kilowatts 20 to 40 litres of water

Source: McArthur, S. (2000a) *Visitor management in action: an analysis of the development and implementation of visitor management models at Jenolan Caves and Kangaroo Island.* Unpublished PhD Thesis, University of Canberra.

The third stage of development is a *management response* system. This system involves the identification of poor performing indicators, the exploration of cause-and-effect relationships, the identification of results requiring a response, and the development of management response options. The first part of the response system is to identify annually which indicators are not performing within their acceptable ranges. This involves reviewing the report charts to identify and list each indicator whose annual performance data are outside the acceptable range. It also involves identifying the degree of the discrepancy and whether the discrepancy is part of a longer-term trend. The trend is determined by reviewing previous annual data that have been entered onto the report charts. A qualitative statement is then entered under the degree of discrepancy. The second part of the response mechanism is to explore cause-and-effect relationships. The essential question relating to cause and effect is whether the discrepancy was principally induced by tourism activity or by other effects (such as the actions of local residents, initiatives by other industries, and regional, national, or even global influences). The third part in the system simply involves nominating whether a response is required. Specific alternatives for the response include a tourism-oriented response, a response from another sector, or identification that the situation is beyond anyone's control.

The fourth and final part involves developing response options, dependent upon whether they:

- require a response from a non-tourism sector (this involves identifying the appropriate body responsible, providing it with the results, and suggesting a response on the matter;
- were out of anyone's control (in this instance no response is required); or
- require a response from the tourism sector (involving the generation of a series of management options for consideration, such as additional research to understand the issue, modification to existing practices, site-based development, marketing, and lobbying).

After the tourism-related options have been developed, the preferred option is tested by brainstorming how the option might influence the various indicators. This requires the reuse of the predicted performance and management response sections of the model. Once several years of data have been collected, the model can be transferred to a simple computer program to streamline the reporting, predicting, and testing of options.

The final application of the model is to test potential options or management responses to a range of alternative scenarios. The first form of testing for application is the performance of a sample of individual indicators. The second form of testing the model's performance is against several potential future scenarios that have already been developed and presented in the contextual analysis. The testing helps ensure that the model has some degree of predictive capability.

Raising consumer awareness

In many cases the difference between a sustainable and non-sustainable tourism operation can be difficult for consumers to detect, particularly in the short term. Even in the long term various market segments react differently to different levels of impact. For example, some users of national parks continue to use areas even when they become crowded, whereas others divert to other areas. Nevertheless, if consumers are to enjoy the benefits of better quality experiences, while minimising the costs of that experience to their own or external communities, they are more likely to make informed judgments about the types of tourism products and services (Hall 1989b; Botterill 1991; Wood & House 1991; Elkington & Hailes 1992; Hall & McArthur 1998). For example, the shift in adventure travellers from consumptive to experiential services (from hunting to wildlife photography) is illustrative of the capacity of markets to readjust and make value judgments compatible with the values inherent in the philosophy of sustainable development (Barbier 1987).

On the demand side, tourist codes of behaviour have been developed to minimise the negative impacts of tourists on the social and physical environment (Dowling 1991; Ecotourism Association of Australia 1993; Mason & Mowforth 1996). For example, the Audubon Society, one of the largest conservation groups in the United States, has developed the Audubon Travel Ethic which draws attention to the appropriate behaviours and ethics to which individuals travelling with the Society should subscribe (cited in Valentine 1992, p. 122):

- the biota shall not be disturbed;
- Audubon tours to natural areas will be sustainable;
- the sensibilities of other cultures will be respected;
- waste disposal shall have neither environmental nor aesthetic impacts;
- the experience a tourist gains in travelling with Audubon shall enrich his or her appreciation of nature, conservation, and the environment;
- the effect of an Audubon tour shall be to strengthen the conservation effort and enhance the natural integrity of places visited; and
- traffic in products that threaten wildlife and plant populations shall not occur.

However, although alterations to the demand side of the tourism equation might be possible through modification of tourist behaviour by developing codes of behaviour, it can be argued that the tourists who read and take note of such material are those who represent the least worry in terms of negative impacts on the physical and social environment (Hall 1992c; Mason & Mowforth 1996). Therefore, if sustainable forms of tourism are to be developed, it clearly becomes essential to develop more sustainable forms of tourist product that are supplied to the consumer.

Raising producer awareness

Greater attention has been given to meeting the demands of different consumer segments than to the needs of the supplier of the tourist product. Such an approach is extremely short-sighted because there is clearly a need to balance the supply and demand of the tourist experience. For example, in the late 1980s and early 1990s, the New South Wales 'larger than life' marketing campaign promoted rural tourism, despite evidence that small operator-based farm tourism is poorly coordinated and can provide little, if any, financial benefits to operators of economically marginal farms (Hall 1989b). In addition, tourism operators need to pay more attention to welfare concerns (Hall & Brown 1996) and the needs of groups such as the aged and disabled (Murray & Sproats 1990). As Mills (1983, p. 81) reported:

> Provision for the disabled in any type of holiday situation can no longer be regarded as an optional extra. Any building which has been conscientiously designed for disabled users will in fact be more convenient and attractive for able-bodied users and will make the holiday break for those travelling with disabled holidaymakers more restful and beneficial.

In the environmental sphere, producer awareness can be raised through the production of environmental codes of conduct or practice (for example, O'Brien & Associates 1988; ATIA 1989a, 1989b; Tourism South Australia 1989b; Dowling 1991; UNEP 1995; Mason & Mowforth 1996; Hall & MacArthur 1998). However, such documents, although influencing the perceptions of some tourism developers, need to be reinforced by government regulation and environmental planning legislation if they are to have any overall effect on development practices (Malloy & Fennell 1998). Indeed, a cynical commentator might note that such developments have occurred only to reduce the likelihood of greater government intervention in the environmental dimensions of the tourism industry.

Strategic planning to supersede conventional approaches

Strategic planning is facilitated by greater involvement of host communities in the decision-making process (Gunn 1988; Dowling 1993a, 1993b). Such an approach

Part of the strategy of sustainable tourism is the development and use of codes of conduct to encourage appropriate behaviour towards host communities and the environment by various sections of the tourism industry, the tourist, and the public sector. Many are based on codes developed by global organisations, such as the United Nations Environment Programme (UNEP), the International Chamber of Commerce, and the World Travel and Tourism Council. For example, a resolution on a 'Tourism Bill of Rights and Tourist Code' was accepted at the Sixth General Assembly of the World Tourism Organisation (WTO) at Sophia in 1985 (WTO 2001a). The right of the tourist is an integral part of the philosophy of this very extensive document. This philosophy was developed to ensure that travel is available to all people, and that, through travel; understanding, education, conservation, and ultimately, peace, can be achieved. The American Society of Travel Agents (in UNEP 1995) supports this philosophy in its 'code of conduct' in which it states that: 'Travel is a natural right of all people and is a crucial ingredient of world peace and understanding— with that right comes responsibilities'.

As noted in the declaration, although travel is now deemed as a right of all people, with that right come social and environmental responsibilities. In 1985 the WTO approved a 'Global Code of Ethics for Tourism' which addresses the rights and obligations of stakeholders in the tourism industry. It attempts to present a balanced perspective that focuses on the need to minimise negative impacts of tourism on both the natural environment and the cultural aspects of host countries, yet also maximise the benefits to residents and the private sector created by tourism (World Tourism Organization 2001a).

Many other organisations and businesses have adopted codes of conduct and have used them to promote responsible tourism practices among the industry, as well as having used them as an educational tool for visitors. The use of codes of conduct by many tourism organisations highlights the industry's acknowledgment of the necessity to ensure sustainable development of the tourism industry and the resources on which it relies.

Codes of conduct have been developed not only for global use but also for specific purposes and specific places. The actions that have been advocated are therefore many and varied. They address issues of the natural environment, cultural sensitivities, and low-impact behaviours (UNEP 1995). However, the range and variety of codes of conduct can create confusion among travellers as to the correct behaviour to adopt while travelling. This is particularly true if certain behaviour is appropriate in one place but inappropriate in another. To add to this confusion, some codes of conduct, although designed to promote responsible travel behaviour, might not consider cultural and site-specific require-ments. Indeed, in some cases they can even be in conflict with each other.

The codes of conduct aimed at tourists tend to adopt an ethical approach, stating such things as 'Respect the frailty of the earth. Realize that unless all are willing to help in its preservation, unique and beautiful destinations may not be here for future generations to enjoy' (American Society of Travel Agents [ASTA] Ten Commandments on Eco-Tourism (1989) in UNEP 1995), or as in the Ecumenical Coalition on Third World Tourist's Code of Ethics for Tourists (1998): 'Instead of the Western practice of "knowing all the answers", cultivate the habit of asking questions' (in UNEP 1995). However, these are very broad statements that do not deal with individual sites. They address a more global approach to attitudes but do not address site-specific behaviour.

There needs to be a more ground-level approach to codes of conduct that outlines what tourists actually must do to ensure that they are being responsible at a particular site. However, because each site might have specific guidelines on appropriate behaviour, a global approach is difficult to adopt. To complicate matters, the task of communicating local environmental codes of conduct is difficult because a destination needs to consider the visitors' motivations for visiting the destination, as well as their time, entertainment, and involvement constraints. Visitors might not spend the time, money, or energy to find out what is appropriate behaviour, thereby relying on their own set of environmental values that have been developed through upbringing, education, or their own governmental regulations. But visitors' own environmental values might be in conflict with those of the destination. This can lead to visitors' believing that they are acting in an environmentally friendly way when, in reality, they are damaging the environment or having a major impact on the local community and environment. This raises many questions and not all can be answered simply. It is therefore important to look at the tourists' own environmental values, what they do at home on a day-by-day basis, and whether they continue these behaviours while travelling. These factors, along with an understanding of what motivates a person to visit a destination, and the constraints they experience in a tourism context, need to be considered when developing codes of conduct.

To date, it appears that codes of conduct can be divided into three main groups:
• cultural impacts;
• social impacts; and
• environmental impacts

Each of these groups has educational and ethical elements promoting minimal impacts. Most of them start with a directive to 'travel with an open mind', setting the scene to ensure that the traveller educates himself or herself about the host community and environment as the essential step in ensuring that minimal impact occurs.

Cultural elements
• tourists educating themselves about the host community, its history, and its culture (such as belief systems, local language, how to be a good guest); and
• respecting the host community's culture by asking permission to take photos of people and places of cultural significance, and by adjusting to the hosts' way of life (rather than tourists' expecting to live to their own mores while visiting).

Social elements
- purchasing behaviour that supports the local community by buying locally made goods, utilising locally owned and operated tourism operators, staying in accommodation places, patronising local hospitality and tourism companies, and buying products made only of renewable resources; and
- sensitivity to economic differences between the tourists and the host community by not displaying wealth, not promising things such as education, and not bartering.

Environmental elements
- tourists learning the geography of the area;
- learning about the environmental issues of the area;
- staying on trails;
- travelling in low-impact groups;
- adopting a pack-in–pack-out philosophy;
- not buying goods made from endangered species; and
- contributing to projects that benefit local environments and communities.

Sue Russell

is not presently widespread in Australia, and the achievement of genuine public involvement in planning will require a willingness on the part of decision-making agencies to solicit and take account of host community attitudes. Strategic planning needs to be proactive and responsive to community needs, and must perceive planning and implementation as part of an ongoing single process (Lang 1986). Dredge and Moore highlighted the need to integrate tourism in to town planning and emphasised that strategic plans need 'to be backed up by statements of implementation that guide the pattern of tourism development' (1992, p.15). More recently, the development of strategic planning mechanisms has been acknowledged as essential to the immediate management of the natural and human-made disasters that impact on tourism (Faulkner 2001), and to the management of longer-term recovery (Faulkner & Vikulov 2001).

Strategy is a means of achieving a desired end—such as the objectives identified for the management of tourism resources (Chaffee 1985). In the case of sustainable tourism planning and development, a strategy involves the use of appropriate visitor management, marketing, management, and planning practices to achieve three basic objectives: (i) ensuring the conservation of tourism resource values; (ii) enhancing the experiences of the visitors who interact with tourism resources; and (iii) maximising the economic, social, and environmental returns to stakeholders in the host community (McArthur & Hall 1993; Hall & McArthur 1998). As noted in the above discussion of regional tourism planning in South Australia, strategic analysis combines three different types of analysis:
- *environmental analysis:* which assists planners and managers to anticipate short-term and long-term changes in the operational environment;
- *resource analysis:* which helps the heritage managers to understand the significance of a site's physical and human resources in successful ongoing environmental adaptation;

TOURISM PLANNING AND DESTINATION DEVELOPMENT

- *aspirations analysis:* which identifies the aspirations and interests of the major stake-holders in the heritage site and assists management to formulate its own strategic objectives in light of the desires and interests of others.

As Richardson and Richardson observed: 'If performed effectively, strategic analysis can generate tremendous insight (particularly for first time users) into the factors which underpin present success/failure levels and into the organisational changes which make greatest sense in the context of the anticipated future' (1989, p. 58). Indeed, strategic analysis is part of the process by which tourism agencies and oper-ators can be turned into 'learning organisations' that can constantly adapt to the demands of their stakeholders (Garratt 1987; Tweed & Hall 1991). Measures which private and public sector tourism organisations can take to evaluate the strategic basis for tourism planning and development include:

- an aspirations analysis to determine who the important stakeholders are/will be and to ascertain their power positions, aspirations, and propensities for or against alternative potential developments;
- an environmental analysis of the insight this might stimulate on questions of organisational restructuring as well as potential product/market competitive developments;
- pertinent market segmentation exercises;
- analysis of the present and potential competitive market structure and identifica-tion of the inherent attractiveness of the markets, and the openings which might exist for managers to exploit; and
- analysis of the wider and more futuristic environment to anticipate futures which the organisation might seek to exploit, change or avoid as necessary (Hall & McArthur 1998; Hall 2000a).

Some recent and comprehensive examples of a strategic approach to tourism and visitor management in Australia are the Wet Tropics of Queensland (Chester & Roberts 1992; Wet Tropics Management Authority 1992, 1994, 1995), the Australian Alps (Australian Capital Territory, New South Wales, and Victoria) (Mackay & Virtanen 1992) and Kangaroo Island in South Australia (Manidis Roberts Consul-tants 1996). For example, after taking into account information gained from a commu-nity consultation process in the case of the development of a Wet Tropics World Heritage area management plan, the Wet Tropics Management Authority (WTMA) developed a draft vision statement which provided the initial basis for the organisa-tion's operations and for its stakeholders understanding of the agency's task:

> The management of the Wet Tropics of Queensland World Heritage Area will be an example and inspiration to Australians and other nations. Maintaining and restoring the World Heritage values of the Area will be paramount. The management will reflect a sense of community ownership and serve a function in, and contribute to, the community. People will be encouraged to use and enjoy the Area and appreciate its World Heritage values, but in ways that do not jeopardise those values. The values will be presented in ways that help develop better appreciation, understanding and community support for ongoing protection of the Area's unique qualities. The Authority will seek to establish harmonious relations with land holders and management agencies within, and neighbours adjacent to, the World Heritage Area, to ensure management will protect World Heritage values. The impact of essential infrastructure and facilities will be minimised. The Authority will undertake to increase appreciation, awareness and understanding of the Area's cultural values and will encourage participation by the community, in particular Aboriginal people, in the management of the Area. Degraded areas will be rehabilitated and threatening influences

such as pollutants, weeds, feral animals and diseases will be controlled. Scientific research will be encouraged to increase the knowledge and understanding of the World Heritage Area and facilitate better management. The values of the Area must be preserved for future generations to treasure and enjoy (Wet Tropics Management Authority 1992, p. 7).

Source: Wet Tropics Management Authority (1992) *Wet tropics plan: strategic directions*, Cairns.

By 1997 the vision was 'The Wet Tropics Area enjoyed, protected and treasured now and forever' (WTMA 1997).

The increasing recognition by government and industry of the nexus between successful development and sustainable development augurs well for a more socially responsive and environmentally sensitive Australian tourism industry. Following the rapid growth of the 1980s and 1990s, the design, planning, and management of tourism environment requires more than the simplistic adoption of codes and guidelines. A sustainable tourism industry requires a commitment by all parties involved in the planning process to sustainable development principles. Only through such widespread commitment can the long-term integration of social, environmental, and economic objectives be attained.

PLANNING FOR THE QUALITY TOURIST EXPERIENCE

Without planned developments which really capture the essence of our country and landscape, Australian tourism will not attain its potential (Cox 1985, p. 50).

For many years the comment has been widely made that an international hotel in one country is usually indistinguishable from one in another country (Saville 1994, p. 30).

Tourist facilities must be well planned, environmentally sensitive and help establish the overall attractiveness of a destination in order to survive in the tourism marketplace (Cox 1985, p. 50).

Israel (1985, p. 62) argued that Australian tourism and resort development should establish 'an architecture of pleasure' which would emphasise the distinctive character of tourism in Australia. Fortunately, some measures are being taken in hotel and resort developments that do stress the uniqueness of the destination. For example, Saville (1994, p. 30) noted that there is:

. . . an increased importance being given to a sense of regionalism in the design of hotels . . . More recent developments have often reflected an acknowledgement of the building styles and materials traditionally used in the region. This is then followed through to the interiors with the use of locally sourced finishes and furniture.

The quality of the tourism experience is clearly a critical element in the attractiveness of a tourist destination. The challenge for industry is how to ensure that quality is maintained or improved through the sustainable development of the elements which make an area attractive—from the physical through to the social. Therefore, planning and development must become process-based to meet the long-term demands of the market and the most appropriate use of tourist and resort facilities. According to Gunn (1979, p. 190), regional strategic planning is needed to provide the impetus and catalyst for integrated tourism development and a framework for specific feasibility and development at a site level. Planning should be a positive process in which the local people become involved (Dowling 1993a). As Dasmann et al. (1973, p. 115) argued: 'The more local people benefit from tourism the more they will benefit from a commitment to preserve the environmental features which attract tourism'. Tourism developers and operators have a crucial role to play. Visitors have only limited influence. The tourism developer, in conjunction with government and the destination community, has the opportunity and the responsibility to enhance the special qualities of the place upon which business depends.

CHAPTER SUMMARY

This chapter has examined the crucial role of planning in tourism development. Planning for tourism occurs in a variety of forms and structures and on a variety of scales, and is rarely devoted solely to tourism. Rather, desirable planning includes other economic, social, and environmental considerations.

Five different forms of tourism planning were identified: (i) boosterism; (ii) an economic, industry-oriented approach; (iii) a physical/spatial approach; (iv) a community-oriented approach; and (v) a sustainable approach. The last approach combines elements of physical/spatial and community planning in a manner that aims to ensure that development is equitable, that it minimises resource depletion and environmental degradation, and that it minimises the negative social effects of tourism. Sustainable development planning for tourism also aims to ensure a quality experience for the visitor in accordance with local needs. Through such an approach it is hoped that both the host community and the tourist can benefit from tourism development.

SUGGESTIONS FOR FURTHER READING

Several excellent accounts of the scope of tourism planning have been written. In particular, the pioneering work of Lawson and Baud-Bovy (1977) contains numerous practical examples of the way in which tourism infrastructure and facility planning can benefit host and guest alike. See also Pearce (1989), Inskeep (1991), and Gunn (1994). Gunn is the standard text on more traditional physical-/spatial-oriented tourism planning measures at the regional, destination, and site levels, and has been updated to include a discussion of the application of the principles of sustainable development to tourism. Refer also to Hall (2000a) which integrates destination and organisational approaches to tourism planning within a comprehensive planning framework. Those wishing to investigate further the difficulties and potential of community planning should see Haywood (1988), Murphy (1988), and Hall & McArthur (1998). Issues surrounding sustainable tourism planning are also well-covered in Hall and Lew (1998) and in Testoni (2001).

Dredge and Moore (1992) provide an extremely valuable account of the integration of tourism in town planning with specific reference to a number of Queensland examples. Dowling (1993a, 1993b) examines resident-visitor attitudes with respect to tourism development in the context of regional tourism planning for the Gascoyne region of Western Australia. This approach is complemented by the more traditional land use planning approach of Priskin (2001). Hall et al. (1997) provide a variety of planning case studies in Australia and New Zealand and it is instructional to compare the planning assumptions and methodologies outlines in different studies, particularly those of Macbeth (1997) and Dwyer et al. (1997).

INTERNET SITES

Refer to the individual state and territory government websites noted in Chapter 6 for details of state planning organisations.

On the Tourism insights on the web
www.prenhall.com/hall_au

see *Towards Integrated Tourism Planning and Development: A Case Study of Australia's National Capital* by Brock Cambourne, and *Indigenous Ecotourism in Australia* by Heather Zeppel.

FOR DISCUSSION AND REVIEW

Key concepts

Key concepts discussed in this chapter include:
tourism planning, form, structure, scale, externalities, physical/ecological boundaries, boosterism, economic approach, physical/spatial approach, community-oriented planning, socially acceptable tourism, environmental issues, social justice, sustainable development, control systems, coordination mechanisms, consumer awareness, producer awareness, strategic planning, quality tourist experience.

Questions for review and discussion

1 What is tourism planning?
2 Why is tourism planning desirable?
3 What are the major approaches to tourism planning?
4 Why is a community approach to planning difficult to implement?
5 What are the mechanisms by which a sustainable approach to tourism planning can be achieved?
6 Why have many resorts not provided the opportunities for escape from the urban environment?

TOURISM PLANNING AND DESTINATION DEVELOPMENT

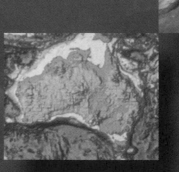
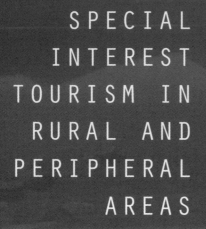

SPECIAL INTEREST TOURISM IN RURAL AND PERIPHERAL AREAS

FARM, FOOD, WINE, ADVENTURE, AND NATURE-BASED TOURISM

12

A S TOURISM has developed in the Western world, the travel market has become increasingly segmented and specialised, with the development of new styles of leisure and tourism (World Tourism Organisation (WTO) 1986). Faulkner and Walmsley (1998, p. 101) argued that:

> the increased diversity of highly specialised products designed to satisfy the needs of niche markets can be construed as a response to increased segmentation . . . Similarly, the emergence of 'events' as a significant element of contemporary tourism is a further manifestation of the increasing relevance of the differentiation of the market into specific interest groups.

Since the early 1970s, for example, there has been a marked shift towards active holidays. Holloway (1985, p. 39) noted that: 'Changing social patterns have given rise to new patterns in holiday-taking; special interest holidays to cater for the expanding range of interests of a leisure society, e.g. activity holidays for those whose sedentary occupations encourage more energetic forms of travel'. Similarly, Helber (1988, p. 21) reported a trend towards 'experience oriented' holidays with an emphasis on action, adventure, fantasy, nostalgia, and exotic experiences.

The development of new forms of tourism is of great significance to the tourism industry. If destinations are to achieve sustainable tourism growth and development, the industry must supply appropriate product to meet tourist demands. However, it is also important that 'new' forms of tourism are critically evaluated in terms of both demand and supply. As part of such an evaluation, several commentators are now starting to question whether the notions behind sustainable tourism and ecotourism are new labels for old concepts (Wall 1994; Butler 1998; Hall 1998a).

The present chapter and Chapter 13 examine some of the new directions or types of tourism that have emerged as significant to tourism development in Australia and New Zealand in recent years. This chapter examines tourism in rural and peripheral areas, including farm and wine tourism as examples of more specialised forms of rural tourism, as well as considering adventure tourism and ecotourism. The following chapter discusses more urban-based forms of tourism such as cultural and heritage tourism and event tourism.

Of particular importance in examining the development of more 'specialised' forms of tourism activity is an analysis of the way in which the term is used and the size of the activity that is being described. This is especially significant when trying to evaluate the business opportunities that are presented by such developments, and the extent to which such forms of tourism impact on destinations and communities. The next section examines the nature of specialist forms of tourism and, in particular, seeks to distinguish between specialty tourism and special interest tourism.

SPECIALTY TOURISM AND SPECIAL INTEREST TOURISM

Special interest tourism (SIT) has been defined by Read (1980, p. 195) as:

> . . . travel for people who are going somewhere because they have a particular interest that can be pursued in a particular region or at a particular destination. It is the hub around which the total travel experience is planned and developed.

SIT can therefore be said to occur when the traveller's motivation and decision making is primarily determined by a particular special interest (Hall & Weiler 1992). Similarly, Derrett (2001, p. 3) defines SIT as 'the provision of customised leisure and recreational experiences driven by the specific expressed interests of individuals and groups'. However, she also related it to the development of 'new tourism', defined by Poon (1997, p. 47) as the 'phenomenon of large scale packaging of non-standardised leisure services at competitive prices to suit demands of tourists as well as the economic and socioenvironmental needs of destinations'.

Although only a limited psychographic profile exists of special interest tourists, it would appear that they broadly correspond to the allocentric category of Plog's (1974) psychographic continuum (see Chapter 3). Allocentrics focus on life's varied activities and prefer unfamiliar, novel trips. Cultural and historical travel motivations appear significant (Hall & Zeppel 1990; Tourism South Australia 1992; Zeppel & Hall 1992; Huie 1993), and Snepenger (1987) indicated that the characteristics of the novelty seeking or 'explorer' tourist segment had substantial implications for tourism marketing and management.

The limited studies of novelty and speciality within the tourism market reflect the difficulties in classifying travellers. As Mathieson and Wall argued: 'Categories based on single travel motivations do little more than indicate very general tendencies in the choice of travel destinations. They do not explain the nature of tourist phenomena nor their manifestations' (1982, p. 19). For example, V. Smith's (1989b) typology of tourists classifies special interest travellers as: 'explorer', 'elite', 'off-beat', or 'unusual'. Despite difficulties in neatly categorising special interest travellers, special interest tourism can be characterised, at least in part, by the tourists' search for novel, authentic, and quality tourist experiences (Hall 1989b; Derrett 2001). Indeed, with much marketing zeal, Read (1980, p. 202) suggested that the 'obscure' term of special interest travel be discarded and replaced by the notion of REAL travel: 'Travel with only four additives. That travel would be REWARDING; it would be ENRICHING; it would be ADVENTURESOME; and it would be a LEARNING experience'. However, of even greater importance is the need to recognise that special interest tourism relates to the primary motivations of the tourist to participate in a trip or activity rather than just the provision of activities which meet such motivations. Special interest tourism therefore refers to cases in which the traveller's motivation and decision making are primarily determined by a particular special interest (the demand characteristics). Specialty tourism refers to the supply characteristics of providing more specialised tourism experiences within the context of the setting (for example, rural tourism) and/or the activities (for example adventure tourism). Although there is an overlap between the two concepts, it is important to distinguish between the two because the size of the market that could be described under the rubric of special interest tourism is substantially smaller than that which participates in specialty tourism activities (Figure 12.1). For example, during the course of a trip a tourist could participate in a number of specialty tourism activities with none of them constituting either the primary or even a secondary motivation to undertake the trip or choose a particular destination.

Special interest tourism has been a significant target market of governments and companies in Australia and New Zealand since the early 1980s. For example, the Australian Tourism Industry Association (ATIA) (1982, p. 33) identified 'functional interest destinations and resorts related to health, fitness, fossicking, gliding, sports, boating, canoeing, riding, safaris, etc.' as one of the more significant development opportunities in the boosting of tourism growth. The National Tourism Committee also placed considerable emphasis on the special interest market as 'a growth area of travel with potential for much further development' (1988, p. 27), and noted 'a world-wide trend towards "travel with a purpose"—this means what it says, travelling with a goal to work to, dates to use as a starting point, a motivation' (1988, p. 25). At a state level, all of the various tourism agencies have targeted the special interest sector. For example, the Tourism Commission of NSW (1987b, 1990) produced a marketing strategy that stressed the experiential base of tourism and emphasised the designing of specifically targeted holiday packages and products, particularly in rural areas.

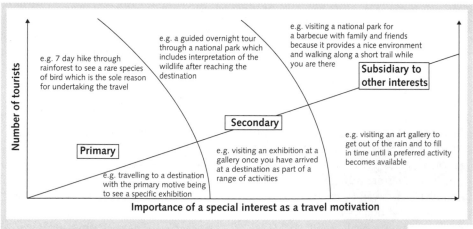

Figure 12.1 Relative importance of special interest as a travel motivation

According to the commission (1987b), the 'new enthusiasts' and the 'anti-tourists' market segments, represented a combined total of 34% of the domestic tourism market and offered major potential growth areas for special interest tourism.

The majority of recreation and tourism studies on specialty tourism have been directly linked to a wider concern with the need to cater for expanding demand. The analytical focus has tended to be on the consumption of tourism rather than on its production and supply. In the Australian context this approach is seen in the marketing campaigns of the various state tourism commissions. In particular, the New South Wales 'larger than life' campaign focused on the rural tourism product with apparently little consideration as to whether the product was in place. Although tourism is market-driven, equal consideration needs to be given to ensuring that a viable product exists. The development of a sustainable approach to tourism development includes attention to both the consumer and the producer of the tourism product. As Bouquet and Winter (1987, p. 7) noted, the 'way in which host populations receive, promote, resist or incorporate various forms of tourism surely deserves much more considered appraisal'. Nevertheless, specialty tourism is often considered to be more beneficial to host communities than is mass tourism (Weiler & Hall 1992; Lindberg & McKercher 1997; Hall & Lew 1998; Derrett 2001). Figure 12.2 contrasts some of the perceived characterisations of specialty tourism and mass tourism, although it must be noted that the empirical evidence for regarding specialty tourism as being more sustainable is increasingly debatable (Butler 1998) given that it depends significantly on the indicators that are used and the unit of analysis.

The following section analyses some of the major growth areas of specialty tourism in Australia and elsewhere, including farm tourism, wine tourism, adventure travel, and ecotourism. These activities occur primarily in rural areas (including the urban fringe) and peripheral areas. Therefore the reasons for the development of rural tourism are outlined to provide an appropriate context to the growth of these new areas of tourism development in Australia.

Perceived Attributes of 'Mass Tourism'					
High numbers of tourists	High levels of dependency on external financing and investment	Price	Spatial concentration of tourism infrastructure	High level of pressure on the social and physical environment	Inauthentic or staged tourist experiences
TOURIST NUMBERS	LEVEL OF DEPENDENCY	PRICE/QUALITY TRADE OFFS	SPATIAL DISTRIBUTION	ENVIRONMENTAL PRESSURES	LEVEL OF AUTHENTICITY
Low numbers of tourists	Low levels of dependency on external financing and investment	Quality	Spatial dispersion of tourism infrastructure	Low level of pressure on the social and physical environment	Highly authentic tourist experiences
Perceived Attributes of Speciality Tourism					

Figure 12.2 Perceived attributes of speciality and mass tourism

RURAL TOURISM

Many rural areas in Western countries are markedly different from what they were only a generation ago. During the past twenty years in particular, rural areas have experienced numerous far-reaching, economic, social, political, and institutional changes that have had profound effects on the ways in which people in rural areas live and govern themselves (Marsden et al. 1993). Rural economies are much more open to global forces, they are more economically, culturally, and environmentally diverse, and their populations are becoming more concentrated in larger centres (Sorensen & Epps 1993). Rural areas are continuing to evolve under the pressures of globalisation and economic restructuring. Little wonder, then, that although 'rurality varies as a concept from region to region and through time' (Lane 1994, p. 18), it remains an important focus for government policy (Getz & Page 1997; Hall & Jenkins 1998).

Changes to rural areas have been inextricably linked to developments in global and local economies, and tourism has emerged as one of the central means by which rural areas can adjust themselves economically, socially, and politically to the new global environment. The regional restructuring associated with globalisation has usually involved attempts by regions to widen their economic base to include tourism as part of a 'natural' progression towards a tertiary economy, as employment in traditional Western agriculture declines and farm sizes diminish. (Hudson & Townsend 1992, p. 64).

Australia and New Zealand, which traditionally have had a strong reliance on the rural economy, have not been immune to the changes in the global economy. Indeed, there is a growing recognition in both countries of the importance of rural tourism as an element of the wider tourism experience, and through it, its contribution to rural economies Department of Tourism (DOT) (Cth) 1993c.

As has been noted throughout this book, tourism is increasingly being used as a tool for regional development in terms of economic growth and employment generation. This implies the selective expansion of tourist flows with a view to achieving one or more of the following goals (Hall & Jenkins 1998):

- to sustain and create local incomes, employment, and growth;
- to contribute to the costs of providing economic and social infrastructure (for example, roads, water, sewage, and communication);
- to encourage the development of other industrial sectors (for example, through local purchasing links);
- to contribute to local resident amenities (for example, sports and recreation facilities, outdoor recreation opportunities, and arts and culture) and services (for example, shops, post offices, schools, and public transport); and
- to contribute to the conservation of environmental and cultural resources, especially because scenic (aesthetic) urban and rural surroundings are primary tourist attractions.

Government has a variety of policy instruments to try to achieve these goals. Policy instruments are government actions which influence the behaviour of economic agents by providing incentives, usually financial, for appropriate behaviour and activities, and disincentives for inappropriate behaviour and activities. Examples of policy instruments for rural tourism development are illustrated in Table 12.1. Five different categories of policy instruments are identified, although several instruments could fall into more than one category:

- regulatory instruments—regulations, permits, and licences that have a legal basis and that require monitoring and enforcement;
- voluntary instruments—actions or mechanisms that do not require expenditure;
- expenditure—direct government expenditure to achieve policy outcomes;
- financial incentives—including taxes, subsidies, grants, and loans, which are incentives to undertake certain activities or behaviours and which tend to require minimal enforcement; and
- non-intervention—government deliberately avoids intervention to achieve its policy objectives.

Government at all levels therefore has a substantial number of instruments available to achieve desired policy outcomes. However, although the goals of rural tourism development are fairly clear at the regional level, little research has been conducted on the most appropriate policy mix to achieve such objectives, and there is often minimal monitoring and evaluation of policy measures (Hall & Jenkins 1995, 1998; Hall et al. 1997a). More often than not, promotion of rural tourism development has been seen in isolation from economic development activities in other sectors of the regional economy. As a component of regional planning, rural tourism should therefore seek to:

- stimulate local business;
- create employment opportunities;
- be a recognised and understood factor in regional social and economic development;
- be clearly positioned in terms of its contribution to the various components of regional development; and
- be identified as a means of developing regional infrastructure, facilities, and services, including recreational facilities that can be used by rural residents and tourists.

Given the problems of unemployment, underemployment, population loss, and low rates of economic growth in many rural regions, it is not surprising that tourism has been given substantial emphasis in rural Australia because of its development potential. As the DOT (Cth) (1993c, p. 24) noted:

> Diversification of traditional rural enterprises into tourism would provide considerable benefits to local rural economies including:
> - wider employment opportunities;
> - diversifying the income base of farmers and rural towns;
> - additional justification for the development of infrastructure;
> - a broader base for the establishment, maintenance and/or expansion of local services;
> - scope for the integration of regional development strategies; and
> - an enhanced quality of life through extended leisure and cultural opportunities.

The DOT (Cth) released a discussion paper (1993c) and a national strategy (1994b) which outlined elements and strategies of rural tourism product development and planning. The department defined rural tourism as 'a multi-faceted activity that takes place in an environment outside an urban area and represents to the traveller the essence of country life' (DOT 1993c, p. 2). In this approach, the setting is important rather than the activities *per se*. The following activities and experiences were identified by the department as constituting rural tourism: agricultural/country life, nature-based, Aboriginal, cultural, sports/adventure, beaches/lakes/rivers, and relaxation. Nevertheless, despite the enthusiasm of government departments, there is a longstanding, widespread, erroneous perception that tourism offers salvation

TABLE 12.1 Rural tourism development policy instruments

Categories	Instruments	Examples
Regulatory instruments	1. Laws	Planning laws give considerable power to government to encourage particular types of rural tourism development (for example, land use zoning)
	2. Licences, permits, and standards	Regulatory instruments for variety of purposes especially at local government level (for example, setting materials standards for tourism developments, or setting architectural standards for heritage streetscapes)
	3. Tradable permits	Often used in the USA to limit resource use or pollution; requires effective monitoring for this instrument to work
	4. Quid pro quo	Government requires businesses to do something in exchange for certain rights (for example, land given to a developer below market rates if the development is of a particular type or design)
Voluntary	1. Information	Expenditure on educating the local public, businesses, or tourists to achieve specific goals (for example, appropriate recreational behaviour)
	2. Volunteer associations and non-governmental organisations	Government support of community tourism organisations by direct grants or by provision of office facilities; very common in tourism; (for example, local or regional tourist organisations, heritage conservation groups, mainstreet groups, tour guide programs, local farmstay or homestay associations)
	3. Technical assistance	Government provides technical assistance and information to businesses regarding planning and development requirements
Expenditure	1. Expenditure and contracting	Government spends money directly on specific activities (for example, infrastructure, such as roads, mainstreet beautification programs); contracting used as a means of supporting existing local businesses or encouraging new ones
	2. Investment or procurement	Investment directed into specific businesses or projects; procurement to provide businesses with secure customers for their products
	3. Public enterprise	Governments create their own businesses (for example, rural or regional development corporations or enterprise boards); successful businesses can be sold to private sector

	4. Public–private partnerships	Government in partnership with private sector to develop certain products or regions; perhaps a corporation with specific mandate to attract business to a certain area
	5. Monitoring and evaluation	Government monitors rural economic, environmental, and socioeconomic indicators; useful for government assessment of rural tourism development objectives; also valuable source of information to private sector
	6. Promotion	Government promotes a region to visitors with or without private financial input; allows individual businesses to reallocate their own budgets by reducing promotion.
Financial	1. Pricing	Pricing measures used to encourage appropriate behaviour or to stimulate demand (for example, use of particular walking trails, lower camping or permit costs)
	2. Taxes and charges	Used to encourage appropriate individual and corporate behaviour (for example, pollution charges); taxes and charges used to help fund infrastructure development (for example, regional airports)
	3. Grants and loans	Seeding money provided to businesses to encourage product development or retention of heritage and landscape features
	4. Subsidies and tax incentives	Although often regarded as inefficient, subsidies encourage certain types of social and environmental behaviour not covered by market economics (for example, heritage and landscape conservation)
	5. Rebates, rewards, and surety bonds	Financial incentives to encourage individuals and businesses to act in certain ways; surety bonds ensure that businesses act in agreed ways (if not the bond money is spent by government for the desired purpose)
	6. Vouchers	Affect consumer behaviour by providing a discount on a specific product or activity (for example, to shop in a rural centre)
Non-intervention	Non-intervention (deliberate)	Government decides that policy objectives are being met; government resources then better spent elsewhere

Source: Hall, C. M. and Jenkins, J.M. 'Rural tourism and recreation policy dimensions' in *Tourism and Recreation in Rural areas*, 1998. Copyright John Wiley and Sons Limited. Reproduced with permission.

from local economic crises (Clout 1972). Indeed, optimism over the potential employment and economic benefits of tourism 'owes much to a policy climate that has been uncritical over a range of issues' (Hudson & Townsend 1992, p. 50).

Cautionary comments regarding tourism development in rural areas have existed for almost as long as government has promoted rural tourism development. For example, as Baum and Moore (1966, p. 5) observed in the United States in the 1960s:

> . . . there are and there will be increasing opportunities for recreation [and tourism] development, but this industry should not be considered to be a panacea for the longstanding problems of substantial and persistent unemployment and underemployment besetting low-income rural areas . . . The successful development of a particular recreational [and tourism] enterprise or complex of enterprises requires the same economic considerations as the planning and development of economic activities in other sectors.

Similarly, the Canadian Council on Rural Development (1975, p. 5) reported:

> Tourism and recreation demands for rural resources can provide income and employment opportunities for rural people and therefore assist in a 'stay' option for those who prefer rural living. The supply and demand relationship however remains a controlling factor underlining that tourism and recreation are not a panacea to the economic problems of depressed areas but that they can be an important supplement to existing economic activities . . . benefits are likely to accrue only to those with the necessary imagination, managerial skills and financial capability. Other factors identified which determine the degree to which rural communities can be expected to benefit from tourism and recreation are: the diversity of recreational facilities available; accessibility to markets; and the retainment locally of tourist expenditures.

The formulation and implementation of rural tourism and recreation policies presents several conundrums to government. Unrealistic expectations of tourism's potential are unfortunately combined with ignorance or wilful neglect by decision makers of the potentially adverse economic, environmental, and social consequences of tourist development that threaten to curtail its benefits (Hall & Jenkins 1998; Jenkins et al. 1998). Yet, as Duffield and Long (1981, p. 409) observed: 'Ironically, the very consequences of lack of development, the unspoilt character of the landscape and distinctive local cultures, become positive resources as far as tourism is concerned'.

There is considerable evidence that more people in Western industrialised nations are visiting and appreciating rural areas (DOT (Cwlth) 1993c, 1994b; Butler et al. 1998), and that many more people are ready to use rural areas for recreation if they are accessible. However, as many people utilise rural areas for recreational activities, competition among resource users and economic, physical, and social impacts on the rural environment are inevitable. Nevertheless, as Hudson and Townsend (1992, pp. 52–3) observed:

> Non-tourist activities that are incompatible with one type of tourism may be perfectly compatible with another. Thus, the broader question of the relations between tourism and other economic activities could be related to segmentation of the tourist market and to policy choices to develop one sort of tourism rather than another. Exploring possible combinations of activities, relative to the specific attributes of particular places, could identify windows of opportunity to which local authority policies might respond in formulating an overall programme for local economic development and employment.

It should also be noted that substantial competition among activities occurs on the urban fringe. According to Weaver and Lawton (2001) the three major forms or tourism established in peripheral urban regions include theme parks, 'boutique strips', and natural areas for touring, walking, and outdoor recreational activities. To these can be added events, market garden visits, garden tours, heritage tours, and, in many areas of Australia, wine tourism. The following sections examine a number of different forms of specialty tourism that occur in rural and peripheral areas. Among the key planning and policy issues to emerge in these discussions are the linkages among different sectors and the difficulties that relationship-building poses for economic development.

Farm tourism

Farm tourism refers to active working farms that supplement their primary agricultural function with some form of tourism business (Pizam & Pokela 1980; Murphy 1985). 'While farm tourism can be termed as "off-farm" production, as it does not relate [to] the actual animal/crop production on the property, nevertheless, *spatially* it is not "off" the farm at all' (Stehlik & Jennings 1999, pp. 8-9). The development of vacation farms in Australia began during the 1970s. Lowe (in Younger 1988), the founder of Border Promotions (an Australian farmhost and farm holiday booking agency), stated that in 1973 he first had a group of American tourists stay on his farm. In 1978 Australia was estimated to have 300 host farms. Ten years later R. Smith (1989, p. 1) reported that the size of the Australian farm tourism industry was 1500 establishments with an estimated income of $50 million. The current number of establishments is extremely hard to estimate as many farm stays are not part of any formal tourism marketing network, and are not formally registered as a farm accommodation business with local authorities. Many are available only on a casual or seasonal basis.

In 1995, Australian Farm & Country Tourism (AFACT), which was established in 1987 as the national industry association to represent farm and country tourism across Australia, had a registered membership of just over 350 operators ranging from farm stays and station stays to country retreats, cabins, and cottages (Greene 1995). The vision and mission statement of AFACT is detailed in Table 12.2. It is of interest that the vision explicitly recognises the role of tourism in preserving rural communities and the role of tourism in promoting rural produce.

Broadly three types of farm tourism experiences can be recognised (Stehlik & Jennings 1999; Hall & Kearsley 2002):

• farm stays—accommodation in a farm setting;
• farm attractions—including demonstration of farming attractions such as shearing; and
• experiential farm stays—including accommodation and involvement in farm activities.

The main attractions of farm tourism for the consumer appear to lie in the nostalgia for the perceived simplicities and characteristics of the agrarian life, the educational experience that farms can present to urban children, and the perception that it is an inexpensive form of holiday (ATIA 1990c; DOT (Cwlth) 1993c). The location and production of farm tourism appears to be related to three factors:

• the marginality of agricultural activity;
• the presence of tourism and recreational resources near the farm; and
• accessibility to major tourist-generating regions.

TABLE 12.2 Australian Farm & Country Tourism Inc.: Vision, Mission and Objectives

Mission statement

To promote the growth, profitability and professionalism of the farm and country tourism industry through representation and servicing of the interests of members.

Vision

Develop a professional reputation as the regional representative body of a unique industry. AFACT registered membership to number 2000 by the year 2003.

AFACT growth to continue in the light of growth of inbound tourism, and a growing domestic farm and country holiday domestic market.

AFACT to work to ensure a quality, Australian experience to both the domestic market and international traveller.

AFACT to encourage new opportunities and marketing avenues for members.

AFACT to maintain a good working relationship with all levels of government to develop tourism in rural Australia, playing a part in preserving the rural communities from the economic and social decline caused by agricultural rationalisation.

AFACT to foster the image of this ecologically friendly industry as a sustainable export earner by governments and the community, earning valuable foreign exchange.

The education experience to be enhanced by rural, eco and cultural exchange.

AFACT to progressively develop a national office, a sophisticated, user friendly reservation system, with an executive director for policy making, lobbying and marketing, a secretarial staff, and state field officers for member liaison, property inspection and product development.

AFACT to market our individual and unique holiday concept positioning our product up with the most sought after holiday destinations.

Farm and country tourism to increase the exposure of value added industries, eg: wool, wood and food products to international and Australian tourists.

Farm and country tourism to progress to being a vibrant efficient industry earning millions in foreign exchange and enhancing goodwill for Australia.

Objectives

Promote the growth of the rural tourism industry in Australia.

Progressively increase the annual number of bed nights in farm and country operator's establishments.

Achieve internationally recognised status for Australian Farm and Country Tourism membership.

Achieve national and international industry recognition for the objectives and needs of the Australian rural tourism industry.

Attain industry and government recognition and support for AFACT as the peak representative body for Australian farm and country tourism.

Have 70% industry participants as full fee paying members of AFACT by the year 2003.

Source: Australian Farm & Country Tourism Inc. **www.farmwide.com.au/nff/afact/AFACTJUN.pub**

The growth of farm tourism was originally most evident in marginal agricultural regions. However, more recently, farm stays and rural home stays have also been developed on the urban fringe on small holdings within easy reach of cities. Examples of these areas include the Yarra Valley in Victoria and the Barossa Valley in South Australia. The conventional wisdom is that farm tourism has potential for growth because of the increased demand for simple, inexpensive vacations by tourists and the need for income supplementation for farmers in a time of agricultural restructuring when the small scale of many of these operations results in very low entry and exit barriers (Geale 1985; Carlin 1987; Embacher 1994; Butler et al. 1998; Hogh 2001). As Mills (1983, p. 120) commented: 'the principal possibilities are the adaptation of redundant farm buildings for holiday purposes and the development of leisure and holiday centres based on working farms or similar enterprises'. Nevertheless, as Jenkins (1993, p. 282) noted in the case of rural New South Wales, there is:

> . . . a widespread, if erroneous, perception that tourism offers salvation from local economic crises. Given the recent downturns in rural economies in NSW, it is perhaps understandable that much attention has been given to the economic benefits of tourism, particularly in those rural areas struggling to keep pace with and adapt to dynamic domestic and world economies. Unfortunately, however, the environmental and social impacts of tourism are frequently ignored, neglected or strategically omitted from the decision-making process.

Similarly, a cautious perspective has been adopted by Lawrence (1987, p. 48):

> . . . while there remains some scope for an expansion of tourism-related activities and for value-added activities on some farms (for example, packaging and selling tropical fruits to road travellers), the average beef-sheep-wheat farmer has limited interest in, and opportunity for, such activities. Pluriactivity may become an important option for the 60,000 or so non-commercial farming units. It is likely to be of little help to Australia's commercial farmers—the very ones suffering the present crisis.

Lawrence's arguments are supported by R. Smith (1989), who observed that, whereas rural theme parks and tourist resorts appeared to be attracting large numbers of people, the farm holiday sector was not showing the same growth and development as the farm tourist resorts or day destinations—as a direct result of a lack of market development of farm holidays as a product. In the case of farm resorts, R. Smith (1989, p. 2) noted that: 'the development of a market niche obviously requires an enormous amount of effort, expense and expertise to achieve a high level of occupancy'. Similarly, farm proprietors in Western Australia 'found advertising to be expensive and not very effective' (Fry 1984, p. 55).

A more recent perspective on the development of rural tourism relates its growth to aspects of lifestyle migration by which people seek to locate in areas in which their perceived quality of life will be greater. However, they still require amenity values

For many children living in urban areas farm tourism provides one of the few opportunities to learn where produce comes from.

including education, health care, communication, and transport. Therefore, they often locate on the urban fringe to have both an enhanced environment and urban access. For these people lifestyle blocks and rural tourism therefore offers the possibility of being able to have an income from serving daytrippers and short-break visitors from the urban areas (Page & Hall 2002).

Farm stay visits tend to be short (one or two nights, often for weekend getaways), and the visitors tend to be of higher socioeconomic status. Earlier studies noted that vacation farms are often seen as budget holidays (Fry 1984). However, increasingly, more boutique-style farm stay accommodation has been developed. Slightly different results were identified in a July 1985 market survey of the potential of the farm tourism market in Sydney, Melbourne, and Brisbane (Geale 1985). The results of the survey of 900 persons led to the identification of five market segments in terms of their attitudes and perceptions of farm holidays: family-oriented, nature lovers, excitement and adventure seekers, outdoor enthusiasts, and acquisitors of farm life. In terms of farm preference, all segments listed 'mixed' farms as their first choice with 6–10 nights as the preferred length of stay, and a maximum price tolerance of $40–50 per night. Private cars were the preferred mode of transport and the market was strongly oriented towards family groups, except for the 'nature lovers' of whom 71% stated that their expected holiday group would be friends (P. Graham 1988).

In New Zealand 3% of international visitors experienced at least one night on a farm or homestay in the year 1995/96, and this accommodation type accounted for 7% of all nights spent in New Zealand. Oppermann (1998) reported that guests remain very briefly at each farmstay, with respondents to his survey indicating that the average length of stay was 1.5 nights. Most guest groups consisted of a couple (80%). About 10% were single travellers and 10% were couples with children. As Opperman (1998) noted, a large share of the total international visitor nights, especially in homestays, bed and breakfasts, and rental houses, can be attributed to a very small number of people. Nonetheless, as Oppermann (1998) observed, farmstays do play a role in accommodation provision for international visitors in New Zealand, with more than 300 farmstays being available. However, little information is available on the extent to which farmstays cater to the New Zealand domestic market.

The social aspects of farm tourism have been identified as a significant motivational factor in studies of farm tourism in Australia and New Zealand (Fry 1984; Younger 1988; P.L. Pearce 1990; Oppermann 1998; Hall & Kearsley 2001; Hogh 2001). 'But for the farmer's wife's interest and determination, few tourism enterprises would exist. To some women, the "social" benefits of meeting a variety of people outweighed the "economic" benefits' (Frater 1983, p. 168). Indeed, Stehlik and Jennings (1999, p. 9) in a study of the gendered nature of farm tourism in Australia noted that farm tourism remains:

> . . . based on the domestic and non-valued work role of women. Although in this role the women are definitely value adding. However, the money goes back into the farm (in some cases this appears to be the underlying reason why the farm survives), rather than establishing a separate income for women.

Oppermann (1998) reported that 41% of the respondents in his survey rated social contacts ahead of economic gain as their main reason for venturing into farm tourism. Nevertheless, despite the social and economic appeal of farm tourism, farmers frequently underestimate the costs of commencing a farm tourism operation. With respect to vacation farm facilities in Bellengen Shire in New South Wales, 'all prospective operators view a vacation farm as being a viable proposition, even though 50 per cent of them had insufficient funds at present to commit to such a venture' (Younger 1988, p. 63). As Younger argued: 'Most new vacation farm operators enter the industry expecting the proposal to make substantial returns. However, many find the proposal is not as profitable as anticipated' (1988, p. 65), an observation supported by Oppermann's (1998) research, which also reported that farmstays experienced substantial problems of seasonality in visitor demand. Indeed, he argued that 100 nights is a crucial barrier below which farmstay operations are considered unprofitable. However, profitability might well depend on the extent to which labour costs by the hosts are realistically calculated into the equation. If little or no capital investment is required—for example, in cases in which rooms formerly occupied by children are used—the profitability threshold is lower than cases in which such investment is required. Similarly, when the labour time cannot be used for other income purposes—for example, because there is no other part-time work or work at home available—time investments in farm tourism yield an income which would not otherwise be available (Oppermann 1998). For many farm tourism operator, additional income—which allows them to maintain a desired rural lifestyle—and the social opportunities that hosting guests offers, are the critical factors in continuing businesses which would otherwise be regarded as extremely marginal operations.

Wine tourism

Wine tourism can be defined as visitation to vineyards, wineries, wine festivals, and wine shows for which grape wine tasting and/or experiencing the attributes of a grape wine region are the prime motivating factors for visitors (Hall 1996a; Macionis 1996, 1997; Hall & Macionis 1998; Foo 1999; Hall et al. 2000). Cambourne et al. (2000) extended the definition of wine tourism beyond the location of vineyards and wineries, to encompass tourism activity influenced by and occurring within the regional territory. That is, wine tourism becomes *tourism activity influenced by the physical, social, and cultural dimensions of the winescape and its components.* According to Cambourne et al. (2000), conceptualising wine tourism in a non-wine specific context not only creates awareness of the potential expansion of economic linkages, but also recognises the importance of social and environmental linkages which encourage stakeholders to identify their roles, responsibilities, and opportunities for further development.

Wine tourism operates on different scales and at various levels. Jack Rasterhoff, Chief Executive of the Victorian Wineries Tourism Council drew attention to this when he stated (in Fuller 1997, p. 35):

> There are a number of perspectives to wine tourism. For the small wineries it provides cash flow and assists them in achieving a better sales mix at a higher price or yield. It also enables them to successfully brand their product and winery. For larger wineries the effect is different. While wine tourism is an economic necessity for small wineries, large wineries often support cellar door activities as a publicity or public relations commitment. There are also big benefits for the State as a whole, in terms of regional employment and providing a diversity of tourism products to a region.

The Winemakers' Federation of Australia Strategy 2025 states that: 'For many small wineries, especially those with a strong lifestyle business motivation, wine tourism [cellar door visitation] can be the core business function' (Australian Wine Foundation 1996, p. 7). For small wineries, particularly in emerging or non-traditional wine-producing regions, wine tourism is often an economic necessity which provides cash flow, assists them to achieve a better sales mix at a higher yield, and provides opportunities to brand their products and wineries successfully. Wine tourism can thus offer many benefits to an individual winery. For example, Dodd (1995) argued that wine tourism can:

- provide an opportunity for customers to try new products at little or no cost;
- build brand loyalty;
- increase margins;
- provide an alternative distribution outlet (particularly significant for small wineries);
- provide a source of marketing intelligence for wineries;
- provide an educational opportunity in a non-threatening environment to develop wine appreciation; and
- create awareness and improve knowledge of wines and the wine industry.

Welcoming visitors into a boutique winery is an important way of introducing wines to the public and is the only way for a winery to become known if production is small and if the product is underrepresented on retail shelves (Aplin 1999). Indeed, the most profitable way to sell wine is through a tasting room (Kendziorek 1994). Aplin (1999, p. 32) noted that 'cellar-door sales for smaller wineries make up a significant part of a winery's income, and just as importantly, it is income that the winery can pocket in full; there is no one in the middle taking their cut'. Due to increased selling and distribution costs, and greater competition in the wider market, there is a clear reduction in average revenue as the wine is sold further from the winery (Bigsby et al. 1998). For example, in their study on the economic impacts of the Marlborough wine industry, Bigsby et al. (1998) found that cellar door sales generate the highest revenue per litre in comparison to other market outlets.

However, wine tourism needs to be seen as part of the overall development of a wine business rather than as an end in itself. For some small wineries, offering cellar-door sales takes time away from other business activities, particularly during harvest, and the small-scale production of many boutique wineries means that they might have to close the cellar door to visitors for some periods of the year if they run out of stock, thereby potentially leading to visitor dissatisfaction. Developing a tasting room can require a substantial initial investment as well as ongoing operational expenses in the salaries of staff.

Although tourism is important for many wineries in terms of the ability to sell wine either directly to visitors or to place such customers on a direct mail order list, tourism is often seen in very disparaging terms, with the implication being that those who are seriously interested in wine are not tourists (Bradley 1982; Hall & Johnson 1997). For example, in their survey of the attitude of New Zealand wineries to tourism, Hall and Johnson (1997) quoted a Canterbury winery's attitude which was not atypical: 'I don't really support tourism—most countries I have travelled to which are heavily tourist orientated were ruined countries'. However, not all attitudes to tourism are so negative. In her standard work on wine, Robinson (1994, p. 980) records that:

> Wine-related tourism has become increasingly important. For many centuries not even wine merchants traveled, but today many members of the general public deliberately make

forays to explore a wine region or regions. This is partly a reflection of the increased interest in both wine and foreign travel generally, but also because most wine regions and many producers' premises are attractive places. Vineyards tend to be aesthetically pleasing in any case, and the sort of climate in which wine is generally produced is agreeable during most of the year. Getting to grips with this specialist form of agriculture combines urban dwellers' need to commune with nature with acquiring privileged, and generally admired, specialist knowledge. And then there is the possibility of tasting, and buying wines direct from the source, which may involve keen prices and/or acquiring rarities.

Wine-related tourism is now being explicitly recognised as an important component of the Australian tourism product. The Bureau of Tourism Research (BTR) (1996) estimated that 282 400 visitors, or almost one in every eleven international visitors, visited a winery during their stay in Australia, representing a 20% increase on a previous 1993 survey. At a state level, estimates of the size of the wine tourism

TOURISM INSIGHT

THE SOUTH AUSTRALIAN WINE TOURISM MARKET

In June 2000, the South Australian Tourism Commission (SATC) commissioned a substantial research project designed to investigate the wine tourism market in South Australia. The methodology for the research involved industry consultation, the conduct of focus groups in Adelaide, Melbourne, and Sydney, and more than 600 interviews conducted at cellar doors in the five main wine regions of South Australia: the Barossa Valley, Clare Valley, Fleurieu Peninsula, Limestone Coast, and Adelaide Hills. The research results indicated that 887 000 people visited one or more winery cellar doors annually in the five regions. Of these visits 78% were day trips (includes interstate and overseas visitors staying elsewhere, for example, in Adelaide) whereas 22% stayed overnight in the regions surveyed (SATC 2001a). Other results of the survey included:

- of the daytrip visitors, 19% were travelling with a tour group in a bus or minibus;
- of the overnight visitors 42% were staying in a hotel/motel, 30% stayed in a bed and breakfast (compared with 8% for all domestic visitors in South Australia), 12% stayed in a caravan park, and 15% stayed in some other form of accommodation;
- total cellar door attendances were around 4.0 million over the 5 regions and involved 422 000 visitor nights.

Compared with the overall visitor population in South Australia, wine tourists were younger (55% were aged between 25 and 44 years compared with 38% for all domestic overnight visitors), more likely to be employed in professional or white-collar jobs (72%), and were more likely to be resident interstate or overseas. Excluding South Australian day-trip visitors, 73% of the cellar door sample were resident interstate or overseas compared with 36% of all overnight visitors.

Apart from the opportunity to taste wine at cellar doors (90%), and to purchase wine (80%), the main factors influencing the decision to visit a wine region were 'to spend quality time with partner' (68%), 'nature and natural attractions' (49%), followed by 'local produce' (48%). Aspects of the cellar door experience associated with lower levels of satisfaction included: availability of food at cellar doors (40% satisfied), facilities for children (41% satisfied, where applicable), and quality of food at cellar door (46% satisfied, where applicable) (SATC 2001a).

When compared on the basis of origin market 'to entertain visitors' was a more important reason for South Australian daytrip visitors (45%) as was purchasing wine at the cellar door (85%). For South Australians staying overnight in the region the opportunity to spend quality time with their partners was an important factor (78%), and for interstate visitors the opportunity to spend quality time with partner (74%) and history and heritage (54%) were important. Compared with the total sample, international visitors were more interested in nature and natural attractions (61%), history and heritage (55%), and meeting local winemakers (48%) (SATC 2001a).

The SATC (2001a) study identified three major market segments:

Wine-focused

Members of this segment were primarily focused on tasting wine at cellar doors and purchasing wine at cellar door outlets. They were somewhat more interested in meeting local wine makers. They displayed a low level of interest in activities such as leisure shopping, history and heritage, and nature and natural attractions. Members of this group were more likely to be male, aged 25 to 34 years, and employed in a professional occupation. A higher proportion were also South Australian residents undertaking a day trip.

Browsers

Members of this group indicated a wide range of interests including, history and heritage, local produce, quality restaurants, nature and natural attractions, art galleries, antique shops, and leisure shopping. Entertaining visitors was also a moderately important activity for this group. Wine tasting and purchasing were important, but no more so than for members of the other segments. They were likely to be attracted to markets, fairs, and events in a region. Members of this group were slightly more likely to be female. Other characteristics were generally consistent with the overall sample.

Time out

Although interested in tasting and purchasing wine at winery cellar doors, this group was distinguished by an interest in spending quality time with their partners. They were less likely to be entertaining visitors or to be interested in meeting local winemakers. They were more likely to stay overnight in the region, and were slightly older. They were more likely to be young couples, or families with children. When compared with the total sample, a higher proportion of this group was resident interstate.

Source: South Australian Tourism Commission **www.southoz.com**

market have also been substantial. Tourism New South Wales (TNSW) estimated that approximately 1.5 million domestic and international tourists will visit a winery in New South Wales every year, and the Victorian Wine Tourism Council reported almost two million visits to Victorian wineries in 1994–95, generating almost $120 million for regional Victoria (Macionis 1996). The BTR indicated that 45% of all international visitors to South Australia in 1995 visited the state's wineries (Ruberto 1996).

Although relatively little systematic research is available, the regional impact of wine tourism is likely to be substantial. For example, in South Australia, the McLaren Vale Winemakers have estimated that the annual value of the region's wine tourism industry to be in excess of $50 million, of which $8.7 million was attributable to wine sales alone. In New South Wales, the Hunter Valley Vineyards Association estimated annual visitation to the region's vineyards to be more than 500 000 visitors. Based on an average expenditure of $246 per visitor, the total tourist expenditure generated by the wine industry was estimated at $123 million per annum, with additional indirect expenditure of approximately $158 million per annum (Winegrape and Wine Industry in Australia 1995 in Macionis 1996).

Wine regions can overlap with tourism-destination regions in both a spatial and a perceptual sense. Merret and Whitwell (1994, p. 174) remarked that wine is 'one of those rare commodities which is branded on the basis of its geographical origin', a situation which clearly overlaps with regional destination promotion. In Australia the economic potential of wine tourism has been recognised at state government level not only in terms of explicit promotion of wine tourism packages by state tourism commissions, especially New South Wales, South Australia, and Victoria, but also through the establishment of wine tourism organisations in South Australia and Victoria to provide better coordination between the wine and tourism industries. In the case of Victoria, the establishment of the Victorian Wine Tourism Council (VWTC) has led to an aggressive promotional campaign for wine tourism, and has provided a basis for surveys of tourism activities and visitors (Golledge & Maddern 1994; Maddern & Golledge 1996).

Several reasons for visiting wineries have been recognised (Macionis & Cambourne 1994; Maddern & Golledge 1996; SATC 1996b):
- sampling and purchasing;
- festivals and events;
- socialising with family and friends;
- country setting/vineyard destination;
- other attractions and activities;
- learning about wine and winemaking;
- eating at winery (restaurant, café, or picnic);
- tour of a winery;
- meeting the winemaker; and
- entertainment.

Maddern and Golledge (1996) also noted that 72% of winery visitors incorporated food-related activities as part of their trips to the region. This motivation and focus was also recognised in the South Australian Tourism Plan 1996–2001 (SATC 1996b), which aimed to position South Australia as the Australian state for 'gourmet living' by encouraging working links among the tourism, wine, and food industries. According to the plan, 'If we can change the way in which the wine and tourism industries currently operate in relative isolation of one another and forge a stronger working partnership there will be simultaneous benefits to both industries' (SATC 1996b, p. 21).

Despite the potential links between the wine and tourism sectors, linkages can be extremely hard to forge. For example, the Victorian Parliament Economic Budget Review Committee (1985, p. 186) inquiry into the wine industry noted that 'many small and intermediate wineries had not realised the potential of winery based tourist facilities' and that:

> . . . if wineries are to attract visitors, one way is to increase the range of facilities available—both sales facilities and special features. This would encourage not only increased private and family patronage, but also coach tours to those wineries with suitable facilities. Such developments would benefit the winery directly, and contribute to the growth of tourist related services in the region itself.

International research has suggested that many wineries which recognise the potential synergies of wine and tourism have benefited through additional on-site wine and related merchandise sales. Formal and informal agreements among wineries, tour operators and the food and hospitality industry highlight the significance of horizontal and vertical linkages for increasing business and regional income (Hall et al. 1998; Hall, Johnson & Mitchell 2000; Telfer 2000, 2001). Indeed, the significance of such cooperative arrangements is now beginning to be recognised for the Australian wine industry overall (Marsh & Shaw 2000) (see Chapter 8).

The economic potential of wine tourism has been recognised by several state governments, not only through the promotion of wine and wineries as a tourism product but also through the establishment of wine tourism organisations to provide better coordination between the wine and tourism sectors. In 1993 the Victorian State government formed the Victorian Wine Tourism Council (VWTC), with terms of reference to develop strategies to promote the wineries of Victoria as important state tourism assets and productions in their own right (Golledge & Maddern 1994; Maddern & Golledge 1996). South Australia followed in 1996, with the formation of the South Australian Wine Tourism Council, a joint wine and tourism body based on the VWTC model, given the task of 'championing' wine tourism in South Australia. Although New South Wales has yet to institute a specific wine tourism body, it has constituted a Culinary Tourism Advisory Committee, which released a food and wine tourism development strategy in November 1996 (TNSW 1996b; Macionis 1997; Hall & Macionis 1998). The functions, aims, and activities of these organisations are detailed in Table 12.3. However, despite such formal relationships between wine and tourism—and to a lesser extent food—many wineries do not perceive themselves as being in the business of tourism. For example, Macionis (1997), in a study of wine tourism in the Canberra wine district, noted that a number of wineries overtly resisted cooperating with other wineries and with the regional tourism organisations in promoting wine tourism because they did not see the visitors to their winery as tourists. Similarly, Hall and Johnson (1997) reported in a national survey of wineries in New Zealand that linkages were poorly established between the wine and tourism industries at the national level, although there were improved linkages at the local level in terms of placing information about wineries in visitor information centres. Indeed, they noted that wineries appeared to take the attitude that wineries contributed more to tourism than tourism to wineries.

TABLE 12.3 Functions, aims and activities of state wine tourism bodies in Australia

	Victorian Wine Tourism Council	South Australian Wine Tourism Council	New South Wales 'Food and WWE Tourism' Plan
Year formed	1993	1996	1996
Mission	To increase the economic contribution to Victoria by increasing the number of visitors to Victoria's wineries and wine regions.	Raising the profile and championing wine tourism in South Australia.	To weave food and wine into every part of the tourist experience and its promotion.
Priority aims and issues	1. *Product development and regional tourism promotion through:* (i) the production of promotional material such as Great Victorian Winery Tours Booklet; (ii) the development and marketing of a comprehensive calendar of events; (iii) the development of a conventions and events marketing strategy; (iv) supporting the development of regional festivals.	1. *Product development and infrastructure:* (i) ensure provision of appropriate development in wine regions, such as specialised accommodation and convention facilities; (ii) provide wine tourism education forums; (iii) develop tourism infrastructure and interpretive material in wine regions.	1. *To package and market food as an integral part of the tourism experience:* (i) feature the food and wine experience as a major component in packaging and promotional activities; (ii) promote industry and community awareness of culinary tourism; expand and enhance food and wine tourism experiences; explore food and wine visitation, promotions, and trade shows.
	2. *Promotion of Victorian wines:* (i) encourage participation and promotion of the wineries category of the Victorian Tourism Awards; (ii) promote and support wine shows and festivals.	2. *Promotional activities:* (i) production of motivational brochures; (ii) extend visiting journalists' program; (iii) maximise the benefits of ATC's theme year of 'Good Living' (1997); (iv) develop wine region positioning and branding activities, such as SATC logo.	2. *Encourage the delivery of food and wine experiences:* (i) develop wine-growing regions as centres for quality food and wine; (ii) develop achievement awards which recognise the development of quality food and wine tourism packages.
	3. *Industry communication:* (i) develop a database of key wine and tourism bodies; (ii) develop and cultivate relationships with key industry publications and editors; (iii) support journalist familiarisation programs.	3. *Research:* (i) identify wine tourism motivations and experience gaps; (ii) undertake competitive analysis.	3. *Foster greater coordination and cooperation between the food, wine, agricultural, and tourism industries:* (i) access appropriate sectoral experience; (ii) encourage cooperative marketing and wine tourism packages.
	4. *Identify impediments to and opportunities for Victorian wine tourism:* undertake research on tourism numbers.	4. *Develop attractions within wine regions:* (i) further develop wine-based festivals; (ii) develop facilities including restaurants, guided tours, food and wine trails; (iii) establish a national wine centre.	

Source: adapted from Macionis (1996, 1997); Hall and Macionis (1998).

The creation of linkages between the wine and tourism sectors, as with tourism and other components of the agricultural economy such as food production (Telfer & Wall 1996), are good examples of Leiper's (1990a, 1990b) description of tourism as being partially industrialised (discussed in Chapter 7). Although many organisations that are explicitly part of the tourism industry (such as regional tourism organisations) can recognise the role of rural businesses (such as wineries, fruit stalls, and farms) as visitor attractions, the rural businesses themselves might not. Only a small proportion of their visitors are from overseas, with the majority often being daytrippers or visitors on short breaks. Tourism is seen as something else—typically, it's regarded as what people do overseas, not here! However, if tourism's contribution to rural economies is to be maximised, it is essential that linkages and relationships be developed. Such relationships not only have substantial short-term benefits for businesses—for example, many small wineries rely on cellar-door sales for much of their income—but can also lead to longer-term customer relationships with their product (Mitchell et al. 2000; Mitchell & Hall 2001).

Adventure travel

'Adventure tourism is symbolic of holidays with a difference. A sense of pioneering and physical effort is required to experience new environments through the challenge of activities like mountaineering, trekking, canoeing or rafting' (Tallantire 1993, p. 279). Adventure tours are a rapidly growing segment of the Australian tourism industry which have no doubt been spurred on by the success of the 'Crocodile Dundee' movies and the development of a positive appreciation of the Australian environment. Australian adventure, wilderness, or 'outback' tourism is a relatively new form of commercial travel that has become available only since the mid-1960s, but which has recently achieved considerable prominence in the tourism marketplace (Centre for Studies in Travel and Tourism 1988; Fishman 1989; Hall 1989b; Hall 1992d).

Marsh argued that adventure travel in wilderness areas 'is important because of the satisfaction it provides . . . the economic benefits and employment it affords and because it serves to justify nature preservation' (1986, p. 47). Adventure travel can provide a very satisfying experience for participants. Nevertheless, it is apparent that, as in the case of farm tourism, attention has generally been focused on the consumer rather than the producer of the tourism experience.

Kayaking has become an important adventure travel activity.

National parks and reserves, wilderness areas and scenic rivers provide the setting for many adventure and wilderness tourism operations (Da Costa 1988; Hall 1992a). The Australian Council of Nature Conservation Ministers (CONCOM) has argued that: 'Wilderness areas are established to provide opportunities for the visitor to enjoy solitude, inspiration and empathy with his or her natural surroundings' (1986, p. 4). The values associated with outdoor recreation highlight the importance of the 'wilderness experience' as a motivating factor in adventure tourism. Several themes emerge in an examination of the wilderness experience including the aesthetic, the spiritual, and the escapist (see Table 12.4). However, given its essentially personal nature, the wilderness experience is extremely difficult to define. Nevertheless, the values accorded to wilderness recreation listed in Table 12.4 do point to the various motivating factors associated with the wilderness travel.

Associated with the values of the wilderness experience is the idea that wilderness can provide mental and moral restoration for the individual in the face of modern civilisation (Boyden & Harris 1978; Hall 1992a). The encounter with wilderness is regarded as forcing the individual to rise to the physical challenge of wilderness with corresponding improvements in feelings of self-reliance and self-worth. 'In the extreme, wilderness generates a feeling of absolute aloneness, a feeling of sole dependence on one's own capacities as new sights, smells and tastes are encountered' (Ovington & Fox 1980, p. 3). In addition to recreation values, a range of scientific, ecological, and educational values can also be associated with wilderness (Table 12.5).

Although the values of wilderness are well recognised, for management and legislative purposes such values need to be identified formally, and areas that have high wilderness values need to be legislated as wilderness under law (as in New South Wales) or managed as wilderness in park and reserve management plans (as in Western Australia). Wilderness has to be appropriately defined and inventoried through a formal assessment process. Australia has been at the forefront of such efforts since the late 1970s through governments and researchers providing detailed resource information to assist in the debates regarding use of natural resources (Lesslie et al. 1988; Hall & Page 2002). These contributions include a federal government funded

TABLE 12.4 Components of the wilderness experience

Component	Nature of experience
Aesthetic/perception	Appreciation of wild nature and scenery
Religious/spiritual	The experience of God or self in the wilderness
Escapist	Finding freedom away from the constraints of urban living and alienation
Challenge	The satisfaction that occurs in overcoming dangerous situations
Historic/romantic	The opportunity to re-live or imagine the experiences of pioneers or the 'frontier' that helped form national culture and society
Solitude	The awe of being alone in a vast and indifferent setting
Companionship	The desire to share the setting with companions and reinforce social bonds and ties
Discovery/learning	Discovering or learning about nature in a natural setting
Vicarious appreciation	The pleasure of knowing that wilderness exists without actually ever having seen it

TABLE 12.5 The scientific values of wilderness

Value	Description
Genetic resources/biodiversity	Sources of potentially useful genetic materials; as more of the world's natural ecosystems are removed or simplified the remaining natural areas assume even greater importance as storehouses of genetic material.
Ecological research and biological monitoring	Protection for large natural ecosystems in which research can occur, including ecosystem dynamics, comparative ecology, ethology, surveys of fauna and flora, and the relationship of base ecological data to environmental change.
Environmental baselines	Reference areas in the monitoring of environmental change both within the biome and globally.
The evolutionary continuum	The evolutionary continuum of adaptation, extinction, and speciation can occur without the direct interference of humans.
Long term	Flora and fauna conservation, particularly those which require large territories.

Sources: Smith (1977); Frankel (1978); Hendee et al. (1978); Hall (1992).

national wilderness inventory conducted in the 1980s and early 1990s (Lesslie 1991; Hall 1992a; Hall & Page 2002a).

Definition is the major problem in the inventory of wilderness. The definition, and its accompanying criteria, provide the source from which all else flows. Two different conceptions of wilderness are generally recognised—one anthropocentric, the other biocentric. From the anthropocentric view, human needs are considered to be paramount. Adherents of this approach tend to ascribe a recreational role to wilderness. In contrast, the biocentric (or ecocentric) approach defines wilderness 'in ecological terms and [equates] wilderness quality with a relative lack of human disturbance' (Lesslie & Taylor 1983, p. 10).

Kirkpatrick's (1980) study of south-west Tasmania identified wilderness as a recreational resource, 'as land remote from access by mechanised vehicles, and from within which there is little or no consciousness of the environmental disturbance of western man' (Kirkpatrick & Haney 1980, p. 331). Kirkpatrick assigned absolute wilderness quality scores based on the more readily quantifiable characteristics of wilderness: remoteness and primitiveness. These characteristics are the two essential attributes of wilderness which fulfil biocentric and, potentially, anthropocentric perspectives on wilderness. The attributes of remoteness and primitiveness can be expressed as part of a continuum which indicates the relative wilderness quality of a region (Helburn 1977; Hall 1992a) (Figure 12.3). Remoteness is measured 'as the walking time from the nearest access point for mechanised vehicles', whereas primitiveness, which 'has visual, aural and mental components', is 'determined from measures of the arc of visibility of any disturbance . . . and the distance to the nearest disturbance' (Kirkpatrick & Haney 1980, p. 331). The identification of remoteness and primitiveness as the essential attributes of a wilderness area helped create the methodological basis for the initial wilderness inventory of South Australia by Lesslie and Taylor (1983) and provided the basis for the national survey of wilderness (Lesslie & Taylor 1985; Lesslie 1991).

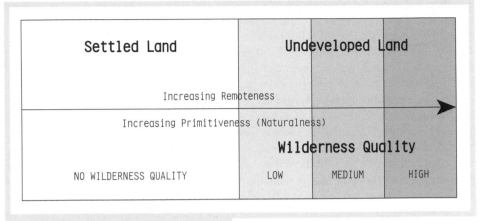

Figure 12.3 The wilderness continuum

One of the basic observations underlying the national wilderness inventory was that 'areas which satisfy biocentric considerations need not be consistent with areas which satisfy anthropocentric considerations' (Lesslie & Taylor 1983, p. 11). Because of the social nature of a wilderness experience, the area required to satisfy recreational criteria for wilderness can be much smaller than the area required for maintaining the ecological balance of a region. Therefore, the experiential criterion for wilderness is substantially different from the ecological criterion, and the concept of a 'wilderness experience' must be separated from that of 'wilderness area' for inventory purposes. As Lesslie and Taylor (1983, p. 14) observed, there has been an 'almost universal tendency to confuse the *benefits derived from wilderness* with the *nature of wilderness itself*'—a point of crucial importance in the delineation, inventory, and management of wilderness. Hence, the two attributes which are definitive of wilderness, *remoteness* (distance from the presence and influences of settled people) and *primitiveness* (the absence of environmental disturbance by settled people) need to be based at the high-quality end of the wilderness continuum to accommodate the anthropocentric and biocentric dimensions of wilderness (Taylor 1990; Lesslie 1991).

The evaluation of wilderness in the Australian National Wilderness Inventory was 'based upon the notion of wilderness quality as a continuum of remote and natural conditions from pristine to urban' (Lesslie et al. 1991, p. 6). Lesslie and Taylor (1983) identified four indicators of wilderness quality—remoteness from settlement, remoteness from access, aesthetic primitiveness (or naturalness) and biophysical primitiveness (or naturalness)—which could be mapped on the basis of existing data and which served as the basis on which the national inventory was developed. A spatial framework utilising the techniques of geographic information systems (GIS) was used to sample variation in values of the four wilderness quality indicators. There are two major advantages in using a GIS to formulate wilderness evaluation databases. First, the approach is open-ended: new data can be added and current data modified. Indeed, in Australia, 'information about access and land use is often poorly recorded and lacking in currency. Even the most recently available information may be inaccurate and out of date. This makes the compilation of a reliable database difficult, particularly because of the necessary dependence on published sources for much of the required information' (Lesslie et al. 1991, p. 13). Second, the process is spatially flexible, enabling scale to be matched to purpose. Furthermore, maps showing the distribution of wilderness identified in the inventory can be generated rapidly and efficiently to assist decision making. However, the development of such techniques does not necessarily mean that decision making occurs without controversy. Indeed, in Australia controversy has been the norm with respect to the impact of developments on wilderness and areas with high natural values.

McKenry (1977) provided an analysis of the degree to which the values of wilderness are disrupted by activities such as forestry, mining, grazing, and road construction, which still holds to the present day. Table 12.6, based on McKenry's research, records the level of compatibility between wilderness values and common disruptive activities. The significant factor which emerges from Table 12.6 is that, because of the intrinsic characteristics of wilderness as primitive and remote land, the range of uses that can occur within wilderness areas without diminishing the values of wilderness is extremely limited and requires careful management. Tourism is possibly a better use of land than other forms of development in terms of impact on wilderness values, but even this is debatable. To what extent can tourism be allowed to grow in wilderness areas before damage occurs to the environment and to the nature of the wilderness experience itself? Wilderness and natural area images are key components of national and state tourism advertising campaigns, but how will growth in nature-based adventure and ecotourism affect the resources on which they are based? (Mercer 2000)

The size of the adventure travel market in Australia is difficult to ascertain. Hall (1989b) and McKercher and Davidson (1995) have noted that the sector has a poor understanding of its customers and their motivations. In addition, the market is characterised by a large proportion of people who undertake adventure travel activities outside formal tours conducted by commercial operators. The formal adventure travel industry is marked by a high turnover of operators and is extremely interconnected, with much contracting of adventure travel services between operators.

TABLE 12.6 Interactions between values associated with wilderness and common disruptive activities

Common disruptive activities	Water resources	Traditional Aboriginal habitat	Wildlife resources and habitat	Plant resources and habitat	Research and education	Wilderness recreation resources	Vicarious appreciation of wilderness	Reserve resource pool
Hydro	1–2	5	3–4	3–4	4–5	4–5	4–5	4–5
Forestry	3–4	5	3–4	3–4	3–4	4–5	4–5	2–3
Mining	3–4	5	3–4	3–4	3–4	4–5	5	4–5
Agriculture	3–4	5	3–4	4–5	3–4	5	5	4–5
Grazing	3–4	4–5	2–3	3–4	2–3	3–4	3–4	2–3
Road	2–3	4–5	2–3	2–3	2–3	4–5	4–5	2–3
Tourism	3–4	5	3–4	2–3	2–3	4–5	4–5	2–3
Off-road	2–3	4–5	2–3	2–3	2–3	4–5	2–3	1–2

Scale of Disruption to Wilderness Values: 1 No incompatible interaction (mutually compatible); 2 Slightly incompatible; 3 Substantial incompatibility; 4 Slight compatibility only; 5 Totally incompatible (mutually exclusive)

Source: adapted from McKenry (1977, p. 209).

Rockclimbing has become a significant adventure travel activity, however, it has come under recent criticism for some of the environmental impacts arising from the use of climbing technology.

Adventure travel has achieved significant economic importance in some areas of Australia. The tourism marketing strategies of Tasmania and the Northern Territory are heavily oriented towards promoting wilderness and national parks areas as adventure travel destinations, and the highland areas of Victoria and New South Wales are also major destinations. The attractiveness of an area for a special interest tourism activity, particularly adventure travel, depends to a great extent on the physical attributes of the region (Hall & McArthur 1991b). In Australia, these regions are often regarded as economically marginal with little alternative economic activity apart from primary industries, such as mining or forestry. Therefore, as economic restructuring occurs, some areas can end up replacing economic dependence on one resource with dependence upon tourist resources (Hall 1992d).

Despite the undoubted interest of consumers in adventure travel, the formal adventure travel industry in Australia appears to be confronting significant problems in marketing its activities to the consumer. Many businesses have a short lifespan. Lack of capital and business experience have posed problems for many operators. Many smaller adventure businesses are run on a part-time basis by interested individuals who have relatively little business or adventuring experience, and consequently often face substantial financial difficulties (Frew 1989; McArthur 1989; Hall & McArthur 1991a; Gardner & McArthur 1994). Further research needs to be undertaken on the economic importance of adventure travel for the areas in which it occurs. Nevertheless, the expenditure of adventure tourists can be substantial. Blamey (1995) reported that scuba divers and snorkellers spent 42% more on average than inbound visitors as a whole, and horse riders and outback safari tourists spent more than twice that of all inbound tourists on average. Rock climbers spent 75% more on average than inbound visitors as a whole. One of the justifications for the creation of national parks and reserves has often been the contribution that tourism can make to regional development (Healy 1994; Driml & Common 1995). However, it is possible that if operators and their provisions come from outside the local area, relatively little direct economic benefit is gained for the tourist-receiving region.

Ecotourism

> Is ecotourism a contradiction in terms? How can places of great natural beauty, or wildlife, be preserved once tourists start visiting in their thousands, bringing with them the need for services and development? Is it possible to have a guilt-free holiday? Can you visit a place without damaging it in some way? . . . It's difficult, but with careful planning and research and a responsible attitude, you can holiday all round the world while ensuring that your conscience remains clear (*Guardian* 2002).

Ecotourism is a fast-growing sector of the tourism industry. It offers excellent potential to generate foreign exchange earnings, private sector investment, employment, and other economic and social benefits, particularly in rural areas. Ecotourism provides an incentive for the conservation and sustainable management of public and private lands.

> Ecotourism involves learning about and appreciating nature in a non-damaging way. It is also about the development of an internationally competitive tourism industry, firmly based on responsible management practices. Ecotourism is both an important niche market and a catalyst for the wider tourism industry to develop on an ecologically sustainable basis. The principles of ecotourism can help Australia to develop a long-term sustainable tourism industry generating jobs and wealth while at the same time protecting the country's natural assets—its unspoilt natural environments (ONT 1997e).

> Ecotourism is fast becoming the modern marketing manager's source of inspiration for the new sale. It's got a lot going for it: it gives great pictures; it offers pretty much what people want when they wish to escape from pressured polluted urban living, and it offers a sort of moral expiation of guilt for our contribution to the degradation of our own planet (Helu-Thaman 1992, p. 26).

Although interest in the natural environment has always been a component of modern tourism and led, for example, to the creation of national parks in the nineteenth century (Runte 1987; Hall 1992a) (see Chapter 11), the sheer scale of current interest in the environment as the *raison d'être* of travel is a more recent phenomenon. Active tourist participation, interest, and concern for the environment is generally described as 'ecotourism'.

In few regions around the world has interest in ecotourism been as pronounced as it has been in Australia and New Zealand (Hall 1993b; Waever 2001). 'Ecotourism' has become one of the 'buzzwords' of the tourism industry to the point where its definition has become a matter of some confusion and debate and where it has, arguably, become a cliché (Hay 1992; Weiler 1992; DOT (Cwlth) 1994a). Nevertheless, although there remains debate over exactly what they are, ecotourism and nature-based tourism remain important and influential concepts (Ross & Wall 1999; Fennell 1999, 2000). The discovery of 'the environment' by tourism marketers is no accident. Tourism is subject to broader shifts in societal values and the emergence of a conservation ethic in Western society has been commodified for the needs of the tourist industry. Conservation and the development of 'environmentally friendly'

Are family camps in the bush a form of ecotourism?

product has now become a major selling point of tourism destinations and specific tourist packages (Huie 1993). As Ryan et al. (1999, p. 148) noted: 'Originally, ecotourism was proposed as a means to deal with negative environmental affects of mass tourism by encouraging to small groups to act in environmentally friendly ways'.

One area in which there has been an explosion in tourism numbers is in visits to the world's polar regions. More than 10 000 tourists visit the Antarctic each year, mainly by ship, although only a relatively small proportion of these visit the Australian Antarctic Territory. A significant proportion of those taking cruises to the Antarctic or Arctic regard the trip as a 'once in a life time event' largely because of the high cost. They are determined, however, to make the most from the trip and generally report very high levels of satisfaction (Mason & Legg, 1999). In addition, Qantas operates overflights of Antarctica each summer.

The ONT (1997e) estimated that there were 600 ecotourism operators in Australia in early 1997, with the sector (like the adventure operations) being characterised by small businesses, of which approximately 85% employed fewer than twenty staff. Indeed, Cotterill (1996) reported that the majority of ecotourism businesses had four or fewer staff, although he also reported that the average life of enterprises is ten years, which is substantially longer than those identified in the adventure sector (Hall 1989b). In 1997 ecotourism businesses in Australia were estimated to have an annual turnover of approximately $250 million and to employ a total staff of approximately 6500, the equivalent of 4500 full-time staff (ONT 1997e). However, growth in the sector has been slow, and the industry is yet to mature to a level of stability. The reasons for this slow 'coming of age' are many and complex, but perhaps the key reason is a lack of marketing capital and strategic business skills to compete on world markets. As Bingham (1994, pp. 35, 36) reported with respect to ecotourism in Tasmania:

> Already there is evidence that ecotourism, far from being a boom segment in the state's tourism industry, is struggling with little or no growth and a high failure rate amongst the small operators in the field . . . Estimates show that only 20 per cent of operators have any real stability, while many just survive from season to season.

Awareness of the relationship between tourism and the environment occurs in both the demand and supply components of the tourist product. Therefore, the term 'ecotourism', as it is commonly used in Australia, refers to two different dimensions of tourism which, although interrelated, pose distinct management, policy, planning and development problems (Hall 1992c):

- ecotourism as 'green' or 'nature-based' tourism which is essentially a form of special interest tourism and refers to a specific market segment and the products generated for that segment; and
- ecotourism as any form of tourism development which is regarded as environmentally friendly.

In both of its common usages, ecotourism is regarded as a positive dimension of tourism. Who can argue with the concept of a form of economic development or income generator which helps preserve the environment? The concept of ecotourism has become propagandised and has become 'good' or 'desirable' (Hall 1992c; 1993b). Nevertheless, some words of caution have been heard. As Berle (1990, p. 6) commented:

> Ecotourism is big business. It can provide foreign exchange and economic reward for the preservation of natural systems and wildlife. But ecotourism also threatens to destroy the resources on which it depends. Tour boats dump garbage in the waters off Antarctica, shutterbugs harass wildlife in National Parks, hordes of us trample fragile areas. This frenzied activity threatens the viability of natural systems. At times we seem to be loving nature to death.

Concern over the impacts of inappropriate forms of ecotourism have concentrated on the effects of ecotourists on the physical environment (Wall 1997). After all, the impact of the footprint of an ecotourist is the same as that of a 'mass' tourist! (Hall 1992c). Therefore, organisations such as the Ecotourism Association of Australia (EAA) (1993), the ecotourism sector's peak representative body with about 500 members Australia-wide (ONT 1997e), have developed codes of conduct (to reduce negative impacts) (Table 12.7) and accreditation standards (to improve product quality) (Lindberg & McKercher 1997). Valentine (1992) has argued that it is essential that conservation is put back into our understanding of ecotourism, particularly as ecotourism represents the potentially symbiotic relationship between tourism and environmental conservation suggested by Budowski (1976) (see Chapter 10). More often than not, ecotourism has come to be regarded as tourist visitation to national parks and reserves (Eagles 1999). However, such a notion of ecotourism not only provides an extremely limited approach to ideas of environment, ecology, the maintenance of bio-diversity, and sustainability but also, as indicated in the Australian national tourism strategy (DOT (Cwlth) 1992) and ecotourism strategy (DOT (Cwlth) 1994a), leaves the social and community dimension out of the sustainable tourism development equation (Cater 1993; Hall 1993b; Wight 1993, 1998).

Since the early 1990s both the ATC and the various state tourism commissions have embraced ecotourism and nature-based tourism as a promotional mechanism for the development of new tourist product. For example, the Victorian Department of Conservation and the Environment (1992a) produced an ecotourism brochure which listed thirty-eight different products available in the state, ranging from visits to national parks to trips to the zoo. In addition, the department has produced a detailed strategic policy and marketing document on the value of the ecotourism market to Victoria (Department of Conservation and the Environment 1992b). However, as in the case of the Commonwealth government's search for ecological

TABLE 12.7 Ecotourism Association of Australia's guidelines for ecotourists

Before you go . . .
Ensure that you prepare well for the trip by reading about the places you are about to visit. Choose your ecotours after asking the following questions:
- Does the ecotourism operator comply with the Ecotourism Association Code of Practice for Ecotourism Operators?
- Is a percentage of the economic benefit going back to or staying in the local community/environment?
- Does the tour operator have local guides and use local services and supplies when needed?

While you are away . . .
Minimise the negative impacts of your visit by:

Social impacts
- being culturally sensitive and respecting local customs;
- remembering that you are a guest;
- trying to allow enough time in each place.

Environmental impacts
- leaving an area cleaner than when you found it;
- being efficient with natural resources;
- travelling by your own muscle power wherever possible;
- staying on the trail;
- taking only pictures to remember the places visited;
- being careful not to introduce exotic plants and animals;
- not exploiting an area when food gathering;
- respecting animal escape distances;
- familiarising yourself with local regulations;
- not using soaps or detergents in natural water bodies;
- considering the implications of buying plant or animal products; asking if they are rare or endangered species, or taken from the wild.

Economic impacts
- spending money on local enterprises;
- not encouraging illegal trade by buying products made from endangered species.

When you return . . .
Foster and generate a natural and cultural understanding of places you have visited. Consider the environmental and cultural effects of your visit. Provide feedback to tour operators, your travel agent and government agencies (who manage the areas visited).

Source: Ecotourism Association of Australia membership brochure. Reproduced with permission of the Ecotourism Association of Australia.

sustainability, although employment, benefits to nature conservation, and positive economic returns are highlighted, the broader social dimensions of ecotourism are ignored (Hall 1993b). Furthermore, ecotourism is often perceived as an activity that occurs within national parks and World Heritage areas rather than on other public lands or even on private property. The majority of nature-based tourism experiences in Tasmania are based around World Heritage Area national parks. Yet by their nature these areas can go only so far in providing further growth for the industry, particularly when much of it is fragile alpine country. Although Tasmania's state forests do not offer the same marketing advantages as World Heritage Areas, they do have a

ASSESSING RESOURCE SUITABILITY FOR NATURE-BASED TOURISM

Priskin (2001), in a study of natural resources for nature-based tourism in the central coast region of Western Australia, identified a number of categories in which the assessment of an area's capacity for nature-based tourism could be undertaken. Four categories were identified: attractions, accessibility, supporting infrastructure, and level of environmental degradation. Each category was comprised of a set of indicators relevant to the category being assessed in a matrix form. The common assessment frameworks could then be applied to different sites which were then given a weighted score to illustrate the importance of the indicators. The method bears similarity to the approach developed for the national wilderness inventory in Australia (Lesslie 1991) (see above) in that the scores could be entered into a GIS database with the results available as a set of maps. However, this was not undertaken in the Priskin study although the potential was recognised.

Attractions

Ten indicators were selected to assess the attractiveness of a site to nature-based tourists:
• species diversity of flora;
• scenic diversity;
• recreation opportunity;
• adventure opportunity;
• bay or inland water body;
• rocky coastline;
• sandy beach;
• vistas;
• scientific interest; and
• geological features (for example, caves).

Accessibility

Accessibility was assessed using the indicators of 'road type' and 'vehicle class' (4-wheel drive or 2-wheel drive). The greater the access the higher the score.

Supporting infrastructure

Seven indicators were used to inventory visitor infrastructure:
• toilet facilities (including showers);
• picnic tables;
• seats;
• barbecue facilities;
• availability of rubbish bins/disposal;
• disabled access; and
• availability of shade and shelter.

Level of environmental degradation

Ten indicators were used to evaluate the level of environmental degradation:
- litter;
- weeds;
- disease in the environment;
- impact of fire from non-natural events;
- visitor caused erosion;
- vegetation trampling;
- dune destruction and erosion caused by tourists;
- landform erosion;
- non-purpose built tracks caused by off-road vehicles; and
- squatter shacks.

Such research can be extremely valuable for recognising the potential of an area for the development of nature-based tourism. As Priskin (2001, p. 645) recognised: 'By knowing the condition and amount of a resource base, decision-makers are better placed in making decisions about resource capability, land use compatibility and impacts'. However, as she went on to acknowledge: 'While neither the method nor the results of this research solved difficulties inherent in the area, the study provided a considerable amount of information in a readily usable form for the planning and management process and this was particularly useful to Local Government Authorities' (2001, pp. 645–6).

number of attributes which allow tourism operators to provide experiences not possible in other tenures, particularly greater resilience to impact, greater access, and freedom of activity (Gardner & McArthur 1994). Therefore, the Tasmanian Forestry Commission has been particularly active in working towards the further development of nature-based tourism (including ecotourism) in state forests.

Ecotourism has become a major thrust of the Commonwealth government's tourism strategies (DOT (Cwlth) 1992, 1994a; ONT 1997e). Under the ecotourism strategy, ecotourism was defined as 'nature-based tourism that involves education and interpretation of the natural environment and is managed to be ecologically sustainable' (1994, p. 3). More recently, the ONT (1997e) defined ecotourism as 'nature-based tourism that involves interpretation of the natural and cultural environment and ecologically sustainable management of natural areas'.

Ecotourism is seen as ecologically and socially responsible, and as fostering environmental appreciation and awareness. It is based on the enjoyment of nature with minimal environmental impact. The educational element of ecotourism, which enhances understanding of natural environments and ecological processes, distinguishes it from adventure travel and sightseeing (ONT 1997e).

Between 1993/84 and 1996/97, approximately $10 million was targeted by the Commonwealth government at nature-based tourism activities with programs to be implemented in industry accreditation, market profiles and research, energy and waste minimisation practices, infrastructure projects, ecotourism education, baseline studies and monitoring, integrated regional planning, business development, conferences,

SPECIAL INTEREST TOURISM IN RURAL AND PERIPHERAL AREAS

385

and workshops. Some of the research and consultancies undertaken as part of the national ecotourism strategy has been relevant to areas other than ecotourism; after all, all tourism is environmentally dependent (see Chapter 10). However, ecotourism as such is probably best appreciated as a relatively small market niche within the wider spectrum of nature-based tourism—most people who are described as ecotourists want only a brief sample or a 'look in' at the environment, rather than a seven-day walk slogging through the wilderness. As Ryan et al. (1999, p. 158) astutely observed: 'The experience of ecotourism lies in the intensity of interaction with the site'.

Commentators such as Priskin (2001, p. 639) have noted that 'nature-based tourists cannot be classified into a single group because their activities and hence profiles may overlap with other forms of tourism'. Nevertheless, information is available on nature-based activities and attractions including national park visitation. According to Blamey (1995), Japanese and other Asian tourists are the most common inbound visitors to national parks (21% and 19% respectively of all such visitors), although they have the lowest propensities to do so on a per visit basis. Visitors from Switzerland have the highest propensity to visit natural areas (74%) followed by Germany, Canada, Scandinavia, and other European countries (all above 65%). The economic expenditure of nature-based tourists can be substantial. Blamey (1995) reported that the average expenditure per trip for international visitors undertaking bushwalks during their stay was $2824 in 1993, or 58% above the average expenditure of all inbound visitors ($1788).

Given the high turnover of small businesses which comprise the ecotourism suppliers, and the emphasis on selling the Australian environment, and particularly its national parks and reserves, it will be interesting to see over the next few years whether it will be a case of 'loving the environment to death' or a dissatisfied market which has failed to have the experiences they were seeking. The question is whether nature-based tourism in Australia can become a sustainable tourism sector.

Will contact with native wildlife encourage the development of positive attitudes towards the environment?

CHAPTER SUMMARY

This chapter has provided an overview of several growth areas in rural-oriented special interest and specialty tourism. A common theme which emerged throughout the chapter was the use of tourism as a mechanism for economic restructuring in rural areas and as a tool for economic development. However, despite the optimism with which national, state, and local government embrace rural tourism, several obstacles remain. A number of issues need to be addressed in rural tourism community planning, including:

- seasonality in visitation rates, visitor expenditures, employment, and incomes;
- development of infrastructure and tourist-related services;
- the recreational needs of the local residents;
- positive and negative economic, physical, and social impacts on host communities;
- conservation of natural and cultural heritage; and, ultimately
- the development of a sustainable tourist industry.

Rural tourism development, marketing, and planning needs to be integrated with wider concerns (economic growth and development, social change, public policy developments) in the pursuit of some future goals with respect to the physical construction of the countryside and the achievement of defined national, regional, and local social and economic objectives (Groome 1993; Butler et al. 1998)—an issue addressed in the next chapter.

SUGGESTIONS FOR FURTHER READING

The most detailed accounts of special interest tourism to-date are contained in Hall (1989b), Weiler and Hall (1992), and Douglas et al. (2001). However, the seminal work by Read (1980) should also be consulted.

For an excellent global account of issues associated with rural restructuring see Marsden, et al. (1993). For a discussion of rural restructuring in Australia see Lawrence (1987) and Sorensen and Epps (1993), and for the New Zealand situation, which provides an interesting comparison with Australia, see Pawson and Le Heron (1995) and Pawson and Scott (1992). Critical discussions of rural tourism and recreation issues are to be found in Lane (1984), Butler et al. (1998), and Hall and Page (2002). A wealth of good case study material on rural tourism is available in Page and Getz (1997), Hall et al. (1997), and Butler et al. (1998). Wine tourism is given a comprehensive overview in Hall et al. (2000).

The growth of ecotourism and its relationship to more educational and adventure motivations is examined in Hall (1984), Heywood (1990), Boo (1990), and Weaver (2001). Readers wanting a broad overview of the nature-based tourism area should see Lindberg and McKercher (1997), Fennell (1999, 2000), Ross and Wall (1999), Weaver (2001), and Newsome et al. (2001). Useful overviews of ecotourism in Australia are to be found in the various conference proceedings of the Ecotourism Association of Australia, and good case studies include Ryan et al. (1999) and several case studies in Hall et al. (1997). More critical assessments of ecotourism are to be found in Cater (1993), Wight (1993), Hall (1993b), Wheeler (1994), Wall (1997), and Hall and Lew (1998).

INTERNET SITES

Useful websites include:
- Australian Farm & Country Tourism Inc.:
  www.farmwide.com.au/nff/afact/afact.htm

- Farm and Country Tourism Victoria Incorporated (FACTV):
  www.factv.com

- Victorian Wine Tourism Council (VWTC):
  www.visitvictoria.com/wineries

- Ecotourism Association of Australia:
  www.ecotourism.org.au

- International Ecotourism Society:
  www.ecotourism.org

- In Balance Magazine:
  www.inbalancemagazine.co.uk

- Environmental Transport Association:
  www.eta.co.uk

- Green Guides:
  www.greenguideonline.com

- Green Choices:
  www.greenchoices.org

- Tourism Concern:
  www.gn.apc.org

- On the Tourism insights on the web
  www.prenhall.com/hall_au

see: *Marine Tourism* by Michael Lüeck, *Tourism in Antarctica* (photoessay) by Thomas G. Bauer, and *Indigenous Ecotourism in Australia* by Heather Zeppel.

Key concepts

Key concepts discussed in this chapter included:
experiential travel, special interest tourism, active holidays, novelty, authenticity, nostalgia, rural tourism, rural restructuring, globalisation, farm tourism, wine tourism, economic marginality, adventure travel, wilderness experience

Questions for review and discussion

1 How can special interest tourism be distinguished from other forms of travel?
2 What is farm tourism and can it ensure the survival of the family farm in Australia?
3 What are the major motivations for cultural and heritage tourism?
4 What is ecotourism?
5 Is it possible to 'love nature to death'?
6 How can you use tourism to support preservation activities without endangering the attraction?

SPECIAL INTEREST TOURISM IN RURAL AND PERIPHERAL AREAS

URBAN TOURISM DEVELOPMENT

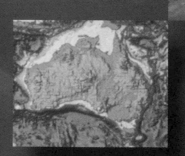

13

RETAILING, CULTURE, HERITAGE, EVENTS, AND THE CITY AS PRODUCT

As a major, yet typically unappreciated and unacknowledged, avenue of accumulation in the late twentieth century, tourism is one of the most important elements in the shaping of popular consciousness of places and in determining the creation of social images of those places (Britton 1991, p. 475).

ALTHOUGH urban centres have long attracted tourists, it is only in recent years that cities have consciously sought to develop, image, and promote themselves to increase the influx of tourists (Law 1993; Page 1995; Murphy 1997). Following the de-industrialisation of many industrial and waterfront areas in the 1970s and 1980s, tourism has been perceived as a mechanism to regenerate urban areas through the creation of urban leisure and tourism space. This process appears almost universal in the industrialised nations (Law 1985; Bramham et al. 1989a; Cameron 1989; Watson 1991; Hall 1992b; Roche 1992; Richards 1996a; Page & Hall 2003). Table 13.1 provides a number of Australian and New Zealand examples of urban imaging strategies. Such a situation led Harvey to ask: 'How many museums, cultural centres, convention and exhibition halls, hotels, marinas, shopping malls, waterfront developments can we stand?' (1988, cited in Urry 1990, p. 128). Events and inner city renewal projects to attract tourists and new investment have been used to revitalise the South Bank by the City of Brisbane and the Queensland state government, and Sydney utilised the 2000 Olympic Games to the same effect. Urry (1990, p. 119) observed that 'in recent years almost every town and city in Britain has been producing mixed development waterfront schemes in which tourist appeal is one element'. However, according to Mommaas and van der Poel (1989, p. 263), the development of a more economically oriented city development policy style, aimed at the revitalisation of the city, has led to 'projects, developed in public–private partnerships, [that] are meant not for the integration of disadvantaged groups within society, but for servicing the pleasures of the well-to-do'.

The primary justification for the redevelopment of inner city areas for tourism is the perceived economic benefits of tourism. The nature of the urban core is changing. Although the commercial function of central business districts is still important, leisure and tourist functions are increasingly significant. According to Jansen-Verbeke (1989, p. 233): 'The entire urban core is presently looked upon as a recreational environment and as a tourism resource'. The ramifications of such an approach are far-reaching, particularly the way in which cities are now perceived as products to be sold. As Bramham et al. (1989b, p. 9) observed: 'it is no longer unusual to see the city as a tourist product, although on the level of local policy this may still be more an expression of certain political ideas than a coherent policy with practical consequences'.

Urban imaging processes are clearly significant for tourism planning and development. Contemporary urban imaging strategies are important elements in policy responses to the social and economic problems associated with de-industrialisation and associated economic restructuring, urban renewal, multiculturalism, and social integration and control (Roche 1992) in the same way that rural tourism has developed in response to the need to encourage regional development. Indeed, according to Mommaas and van der Poel (1989, p. 264) the imaging of the city to attract the middle class employment market, and the associated focus on the economic benefits of tourism has 'reinforced the idea of the city as a kind of commodity to be marketed'.

TABLE 13.1 Examples of urban imaging strategies in Australia and New Zealand

City	Components of urban imaging strategies
Adelaide	Adelaide Grand Prix; cultural tourism; bid for 1996 Commonwealth Games
Brisbane	1982 Commonwealth Games; 1988 Expo; South Bank Development; bid for 1992 Olympic Games
Canberra	Kingston Foreshore development; event strategy; cultural tourism
Hobart	Waterfront redevelopment; cultural tourism
Melbourne	Bid for 1996 Olympic Games and 2006 Commonwealth Games; dockland redevelopment including new stadium; development of the South Bank cultural precinct; hosting of Australian Grand Prix; Melbourne casino; event strategy
Perth	America's Cup 1986/87; cultural tourism; special events
Sydney	Darling Harbour redevelopment; cultural tourism; special events; winning bid for 2000 Olympic Games; Sydney casino
Auckland	Sky Tower (Auckland casino); America's Cup 2000; waterfront redevelopment
Christchurch	Casino development; event strategy
Dunedin	'It's All Right Here' and Spirit of Dunedin campaign
Wellington	'Absolutely Positively' campaign; waterfront redevelopment including Te Papa (Museum of New Zealand); event and cultural tourism strategy; including bid for 2006 Commonwealth Games

URBAN TOURISM·DEVELOPMENT

According to Hall (1992b), the principal aims of urban imaging strategies are to:
- attract tourism expenditure;
- generate employment in the tourist industry;
- foster positive images for potential investors in the region, often by 'reimaging' previous negative perceptions; and
- provide an urban environment which will attract and retain the interest of professionals and white-collar workers, particularly in 'clean' service industries such as tourism and communications.

Urban imaging processes are characterised by some or all of the following:
- the development of a critical mass of visitor attractions and facilities, including new buildings/prestige centres (for example, Darling Harbour in Sydney, Southbank in Melbourne, casino development);
- hallmark events (for example, Sydney 2000 Olympic Games, 1988 Brisbane Expo, Commonwealth Games, America's Cup, hosting of the Grand Prix);
- development of urban tourism strategies and policies often associated with new or renewed organisation and development of city marketing (for example, 'Canberra— A Hard Act to Follow'); and
- development of leisure and cultural services and projects to support the marketing and tourism effort (for example, the creation and renewal of museums and art galleries and the hosting of art festivals, often as part of a comprehensive cultural tourism strategy for a region or city such as Melbourne, or new museum development on the Acton Peninsula in Canberra).

Of considerable significance to urban tourism and reimaging strategies is the rivalry between the New South Wales and Victorian state governments for investment and, hence, the generation of economic growth and employment. This rivalry is typically concentrated on attracting investment to the two state capitals of Sydney and Melbourne, and is illustrated by the aggressive competition that exists for the hosting of events, and the urban redevelopment and reimaging programs that have been established for both cities. For example, Melbourne's unsuccessful bid for the 1996 Olympic Games was followed by Sydney's successful bid for the 2000 Olympics. In the case of Melbourne, the bid was tied to the redevelopment of the Docklands area, and the key feature of the Sydney bid was the redevelopment of the former industrial site and waste dump at Homebush Bay on Sydney Harbour as the main stadium complex of the Games. In both cities the bidding for events by state governments has been integrated into the development of new cultural policies that focus on attracting visitors to the city, and into broader urban redevelopment programs that seek to develop cultural, housing, leisure, and entertainment complexes in waterfront areas (Hall & Hamon 1996).

Elements of these imaging strategies are discussed in greater detail below with reference to cultural and heritage tourism and event tourism. It should be noted that although these activities are not exclusively urban, they are more often located in urban rather than rural environments.

Tourism and urban retail districts

Retail districts have always been places of special significance in the urban setting. Unlike individual residences, which separate people and provide space for privacy and reflection, retail places serve as centers of public show and interaction. More than any other part of a city, they display the life and vitality of a community (Lew 1989, p. 15).

The decline of the social and economic significance of traditional retail centres began with the rise of the automobile in the 1950s and the dominance of the suburban shopping centres and malls in the 1960s. Since that time urban and regional planners and mainstreet retailers have been grappling with the problem of revitalising the downtown areas. In the 1960s and early 1970s one solution was the wholesale destruction of areas of the inner-city in the name of urban renewal and the replacement of these areas by (often award-winning) concrete boxes which were economic and social disasters. However, the problems of the mainstreet and the downtown districts did not fade away.

From the 1970s processes of gentrification have led to a revival in the fortunes of many inner city retail areas, with many small developers taking advantage of low property values to renovate old buildings. The establishment of new businesses has had substantial implications for the revival of traditional retail districts (Jansen-Verbeke 1986). As Lew (1989, p. 15) noted, in relation to the American experience:

> The gentrification process brought new ideas and energy to older retail areas at a time when the American public began to experience a nostalgia for what was perceived as the simpler values and lifestyles of a rapidly disappearing past . . . Considerable time, effort and money have brought some remarkable changes to many inner city landscapes, and the resulting impact in any one city is a mixture of pre-existing design elements and the ideas and innovative concepts superimposed by the new gentry.

The American experience in inner-city development has been repeated throughout the Western world. For example, in Australia, areas such as Carlton and Fitzroy (Melbourne), Paddington (Sydney), Northbridge (Perth) and Fremantle have all experienced revivals thanks to the inner-city migration of the middle classes. The redevelopment of areas of the inner city to create areas of high heritage value has been paralleled by the regeneration of retail areas in smaller towns and cities.

One of the main driving forces in the regeneration of older retail districts is tourism. Potential tourist visitation can serve as a justification for the redevelopment of a downtown area, or it can be a consequence of the establishment of a more attractive area which encourages increased leisure shopping by people outside the immediate community (Kent et al. 1983). For example, pedestrianisation of streets in retail areas is often a response to competition from suburban shopping centres through the creation of shopping areas that provide leisured space and encourage social interaction (Roberts 1987). As a result, 'the growth of tourism as a form of economic development is having a major impact on the urban landscape of some cities and reflects a changing attitude toward inner cities as well as a need to diversify repressed economies' (Lew 1989, p. 15).

Tourism is increasingly creating a specialised and distinct form of retail district. This distinct tourism-oriented retail district is marked by a change in function and form of main street retailing with the introduction of leisure shopping, specialty retailing (for example, cafés, non-essential shops, art galleries, specialty stores, and antique shops), and pedestrian areas. Such retail districts are often marked by their small-scale, distinct ambience, which is, in turn, related to heritage features. Such leisure or tourism shopping areas (TSAs), also referred to as tourist shopping villages, are part of the broader phenomenon of leisure shopping and have substantial implications for heritage conservation, tourist promotion, and small-town development planning (Getz 1993a). However, the number of visitor-oriented functions can make

The Darling Harbour complex is a major leisure space which has redeveloped a former dock area. According to Harvey (1988), imaging a city through the organisation of spectacular urban space is a mechanism for attracting capital and people (of the 'right' sort) in a period of intense inter-urban competition and urban entrepreneurialism.

it difficult for a discrete, all-encompassing, tourism district to be easily located. Burtenshaw et al. (1991) identified a number of overlapping functional areas in a tourist city:
- 'the historic city' (historic monuments, museums, art galleries, theatres, concert halls);
- 'the culture city' (museums, art galleries, theatres, concert halls);
- 'the night life city' (theatres, concert halls, nightclubs, entertainment, red light districts, cafés, restaurants); and
- 'the shopping city' (cafés, restaurants, shops, offices).

To these can be added a 'business city' which also has links with tourism because of the demands of business travellers and conference and exhibition delegates and a 'sports city' whereby sports facilities (such as stadia) and events are also related to local tourism infrastructure (Page & Hall 2003). Thus, multifunctional urban areas can be easily identified. For example, Parnell in Auckland and Oxford Street in Sydney are examples of visitor-oriented shopping precincts and focal points for night life (Hall et al. 1997). Waterfront areas, such as those of Hobart, Wellington, Melbourne, Sydney, and Brisbane also serve to concentrate cultural activities such as museums, art galleries, and concert halls, and provide shopping opportunities. The significance of night-life districts such as Kings Cross in Sydney was recognised by Ashworth and Tunbridge (1990, p. 65):

> Restaurants and establishments combining food and drink with other entertainments, whether night-clubs, discos, casinos and the like, have two important locational characteristics that render them useful in this context: they have a distinct tendency to cluster together into particular streets or districts . . . and they tend to be associated spatially with other tourism elements including hotels, which probably themselves offer public restaurant facilities.

Shopping and urban tourism

Law (1985, 1993) noted that the typical components of urban tourism are conferences and exhibitions, heritage, waterfronts, museums and art galleries, shopping, eating and drinking, entertainment, theatres and concert halls, sports facilities, vantage points (such as lookouts in buildings), and connections (pedestrian and transit systems). Similarly, Jansen-Verbeke (1986) has argued that the inner-city environment provides a leisure function for a wide range of visitors and the local community. In her model of the inner-city tourism system, she noted the main components as 'activity places' and 'leisure settings', with secondary elements of 'hospitality and shopping services' and conditional elements of accessibility and the provision of tourism infrastructure, such as the provision of visitor information services and guides.

More recently, Jansen-Verbeke (1990, 1991) reported in her study of leisure shopping in the Netherlands that those shoppers with a leisure motive tend to stay longer in a shopping area and take part in more activities, such as eating and drinking. Although not categorically proving the relationship between visitor attitudes and activities relative to the attractiveness of the shopping area, she has noted (Jansen-Verbeke 1991) a number of specific criteria which might assist in the planning and design of shopping areas which attract leisure-oriented visitors and locals alike:

• clustering of a wide variety of shops, catering, leisure and other activities and attractions;
• good accessibility and parking;
• pedestrian priority over vehicles;
• a positive image;
• attractive design (aesthetics);
• availability during leisure time (for example, Sundays);
• hospitableness (visitor orientation, adequate information, symbolism, identification);
• social affective value; and
• liveliness or animation, with surprises.

It is readily apparent that many of the retail area and leisure space characteristics sought by tourists are the same as those desired by local people seeking to enhance their physical and social environment. However, tourist shopping and the leisure space preferences of tourists are extremely important because tourist expenditure represents a source of funding and a justification for both the private and public sector to revitalise retail areas, townscapes, and streetscapes (Table 13.2) (also see

TABLE 13.2 Authenticity and place issues in tourism-oriented retail areas

Authentic ←			→ *Inauthentic*
Spontaneous retail mainstreet districts, developed unselfconsciously over a period of time	renovation program, usually as part of an historic preservation effort; an attempt to preserve the past in an authentic manner.	facades placed over existing store fronts, often integrated with re-creation of heritage values, heritage preservation efforts and new retail developments	re-created or downtown 'Disneyfacation'
Oxford Street, Paddington, NSW	Salamanca Place, Hobart, Tasmania	Parnell, Auckland; The Rocks, Sydney; Arrowtown, NZ; Fremantle, WA	Cockington Green; Australian Heritage Village, ACT

Source: After Lew, A. A. (1989) 'Authenticity and sense of place in tourism-oriented retail areas' *Journal of Travel Research*, vol. 27, no. 4, pp. 15–22.

Chapter 7). Nevertheless, there is a number of planning issues which need to be addressed in turning streets into tourism venues. Table 13.3 outlines issues and impacts identified in retail area redevelopment.

Retail area evolution

As noted above, leisure and tourism shopping influence what types of shopping areas exist in a community and how they evolve. Attention needs to be given to the most appropriate mix of resident- and visitor-oriented retailing businesses. Development of visitor-oriented services (for example, specialty gift shops) can displace resident-oriented business or can lead to the expansion of shopping and service opportunities (Getz 1993a). Clearly, the latter is preferable, particularly given community concerns and a desire for creating economic spin-offs into the surrounding community. Nevertheless, as Getz (1993a, p. 23) observed:

> It is . . . difficult for a planning agency to control the process, as normal commercial land use designations do not differentiate between resident and tourist-oriented services. Possibly zoning laws [and business opening hours] can be used to discriminate on the basis of scale or type of development.

Furthermore, it is important that development controls through local governance and local entrepreneurship be encouraged wherever possible to maintain community support for development initiatives and investment.

Authenticity, heritage and place

Local-oriented and derived images—the opposite of mass images—express the uniqueness of community and place. The reuse of historic buildings and streetscapes has enabled many communities to retain elements of their heritage. However, the

TABLE 13.3 Potential positive and negative impacts in retail area redevelopment associated with tourism

Potential positive impacts	Potential negative impacts
increased tourist visitation	inadequate parking
increased local use	building disrepair
civic pride	vacancies
improved image	future agenda
economic and employment flow-on effects	street disrepair
heritage conservation	building design
site for festivals and events	sewage system
improved streetscape	second-storey vacancies
provision of pedestrian comfort zones	loss of local community access and control
increased financial return to local government	economic dependence on tourism
	crime
	inadequate shop space
	inauthentic development
	loss of heritage
	increase in rates for business
	relocation or closure of traditional retailers
	localised inflation

Sources: Jansen-Verbeke (1986, 1990, 1991); Law (1985, 1993); Lew (1989); Hall and Zeppel (1990); Getz (1993a, 1993b).

deliberate theming of architecture and heritage in tourist shopping and street developments runs the risk of being perceived as unauthentic or inappropriate by host and guest alike (Lew 1985, 1989; Zeppel & Hall 1992; Getz 1993a; Page & Hall 2003) (see Table 13.2). Nevertheless, as Lew (1989, p. 21) observed:

> For smaller towns, a well implemented theme provides a symbolic identity to which residents can feel a sense of attachment, whether or not the symbol is authentic. Time covers the scars of creation and eventually all but the most contrived designs are realized to be true and authentic creations of people working together.

The task of tourism development in the urban setting, therefore, is to provide the proper arrangements of the built environment to match the images and concerns of the tourists and local community.

Marketing

For many retail areas it is vital that they be marketed to host and guest alike to ensure that they are meeting their clients' needs. In the case of tourist marketing, it is important that retail areas be marketed in conjunction with other local attractions, particularly those that are thematically related to the retail area (for example, heritage) and accommodation. For smaller rural towns the integration of mainstreet with other elements of the tourism sector assists in prolonging visitor stay, and hence increasing expenditure, further encouraging community support for the provision of new and existing core leisure spaces. In addition, festivals and events can be used to generate ambience and animation in leisure spaces to encourage tourist and local visitation and use (see the section on event tourism below).

Amenity and social planning

Problems with congestion and traffic flow have long been recognised as a potential problem in the establishment of tourist-oriented retail areas (see Chapter 9). Therefore, assessment of the physical carrying capacity of a tourist streetscape is essential in meeting community concerns over impacts on shopping and traffic flows. Furthermore, 'key issues are likely to be residents' fear of the loss of traditional shopping and its replacement by tourist-oriented services, higher costs in stores and general disruption' (Getz 1993a, p. 24). A longer-term issue, particularly for smaller communities, is the development of over-dependence on the tourist dollar for income and employment.

Planning strategies

Tourism-related development is often highly emotive in nature because of the perception of an 'us and them' situation by which locals perceive that the visitors receive the benefits of retail area and mainstreet redevelopment. However, it is often the case that locals and visitors are seeking similar benefits in the design and availability of attractive leisure spaces with a strong leisure shopping function. Therefore, it is possible to create win–win situations for host and guest alike. Nevertheless, evidence suggests that it is essential to gain full community support (local businesses as well as the local citizenry) to undertake successful redevelopment. In the case of tourist shopping villages, Getz (1993a, p. 25) has argued that, given the principles of community-based planning (see Chapter 11), a preferred approach is to:

URBAN TOURISM DEVELOPMENT

- offer the community advice on preparing a tourism strategy;
- implement an adaptable planning and control process that fosters community-based planning;
- undertake a cost–benefit assessment, using long-term sustainability, rather than immediate profit, as the key criterion for measuring net benefits;
- gradually assist local investment and development efforts;
- balance the needs of residents and visitors, based on research into attitudes and behaviour;
- avoid large-scale and sudden changes;
- avoid unalterable changes;
- plan the service sector developments to respect the scale, nature, and character of the place; and
- anticipate and address traffic congestion and other negative impacts before they occur.

A community approach is essential for the successful development of leisure spaces. The development options and strength of convictions held by different constituencies, interest groups, and significant individuals must be assessed. As Lew observed (1989, p. 20): 'Pending development is frequently characterized by a conflict between community concerns to maintain the local uniqueness of a natural or cultural resource and business concerns to incorporate mass images into the development for promotional purposes'.

Heritage, image, and economic development concerns are the three main issues that colour the relationship between tourism and the development of streets and spaces. If there is exceptionally strong attachment to place and heritage resources, conservation development in relation to tourism must be clearly articulated to local citizens and interest groups. Although the development phase tends to be 'guided' by local concerns, it should be noted that the current growth in cultural and heritage tourism can best be met by the development of authentic, community-based tourism products, which portray the uniqueness of a place to outsiders. Indeed, it is the emphasis on uniqueness that will give many communities their competitive advantage in the tourist marketplace.

The development of leisured space provides the basis for the reimaging of communities to outsiders to attract both tourists and new investment. It can also help to boost civic pride and raise community self-confidence. Image development is primarily a concern of the business and local government sector, with little involvement of the local citizenry. According to Lew (1989), theme adoption and compliance should be promoted by private business organisations. Therefore, it is essential that strong business associations and support are created and appropriately marketed if the reimaging process is to be successful as part of the goals of streetscape redevelopment.

Finally, it is apparent that the economic objectives of redevelopment must have the support of local citizens. In many cases the local community, as consumers, is far more important than tourist visitation although, of course, the income and employment generated by tourists provides the justification for retail area redevelopment and provides the critical marginal income that allows the private sector to invest in new plant and infrastructure. If a community has only a mild interest in tourism or is even anti-tourist, a tourist-related redevelopment will usually not work. Furthermore, not all retail areas and communities can successfully attract tourists in sufficient numbers to make redevelopment financially viable. Because of a lack of accessibility or a lack of unique or notable human or natural tourism, resources in some areas do not attract tourists. Therefore, successful tourism-related leisure spaces are marked by appropriate imaging, conservation of heritage, and the retention of those elements of the streetscape to which communities have the greatest attachment. This involves an emphasis on uniqueness, and most fundamentally (and perhaps paradoxically to some), putting the locals first.

CULTURAL AND HERITAGE TOURISM

Cultural tourism is sustainable tourism. It is successful in the long term because it recognises and builds on what is important about a place or culture. It works with the community to identify the special character of the destination—its special character, its sense of place and sense of continuity. Cultural tourism ensures that new developments are so consistent with the character of the place that they become part of it (Tourism South Australia 1992).

Cultural tourism encourages us to showcase those qualities and experiences that make us distinctly Australian and to demonstrate to the world our excellence in internationally recognised art forms. The cultural and tourism industries and the wider Australian economy can benefit through the development and pursuit of the dual themes of cultural identity and excellence (Office of National Tourism (ONT) 1997c).

The diversity of cultural attractions and their popular appeal have made cultural and heritage tourism a major area of growth in the special interest tourism market. The present section examines this culturally based travel trend by providing an overview of the general characteristics of cultural tourists, the strategies adopted in marketing cultural tourism, and the management difficulties that can arise in the development of cultural and heritage tourism.

Defining culture and heritage

Culture is a key element in international relations. Australia's image as a modern, multicultural, dynamic society can be shaped by cultural promotion, cultural exchange and by the export of cultural goods and services. Increasingly, Governments are recognising that Australian culture has potentially, a world market.

Australian culture and cultural activity is of vital interest to the key growth and export earning industry of inbound tourism (Statistics Working Group of the Cultural Ministers Council 1996).

'Culture', perhaps even more than 'tourism', is an extremely difficult term to define. The term is used in two general ways (Tomlinson 1991; Richards 1996b; Meethan 2001). First, culture as a process, which refers to 'the social field of meaning production' (Clarke 1990, p. 28). Culture in this sense refers to the manner in which people make sense of themselves and their identity in social groupings such as nation, ethnicity, and community. Second, culture can be seen as a commercial 'product' that is consumed. Although there is substantial overlap between the two concepts, much of what is regarded as 'cultural tourism' is aligned more closely to the latter meaning.

The notion of culture as a commodity or product has become especially strong in recent years in Australia, particularly in the policy settings of the federal Liberal-National government. For example, the Statistics Working Group of the Cultural Ministers Council (1996) wrote of 'Australia's Balance of Trade in Culture' and concluded:

URBAN TOURISM DEVELOPMENT

. . . in 1994–95 Australia earned $902 million in foreign exchange from culture, of which $750 million was due to exports of goods. By comparison, imports of cultural goods in 1994–95 totalled $3,364 million an increase of 12.0% over the previous year. This represents a trade deficit of $2,614 million, and exports did not exceed imports in any of the cultural goods categories examined.

According to the Statistics Working Group (1996) 'the Statistical Advisory Group to the Cultural Ministers Council identified those activities which it considered were predominantly cultural in nature'. Their statistical framework defined culture as including:
- heritage;
- museums;
- zoological and botanical gardens;
- literature;
- libraries and archives;
- music;
- performing arts;
- visual arts;
- film and video;
- radio; and
- television.

Heritage does not refer only to old buildings. At its most basic, heritage represents the things we want to keep. Heritage is the things of value that are inherited. If the value is personal, we speak of family or personal heritage; if the value is communal or national we speak of 'our' heritage. For example, the World Heritage Convention, which has had an enormous influence on the conservation of cultural and natural areas of international significance in Australia aims to conserve places that have universal values for the whole of humankind (Hall 1992a). More often than not, heritage is thought of in terms of acknowledged cultural values. For instance, a residence is not usually deemed as heritage unless it can be seen as part of the symbolic property of the wider culture or community—as an element of the identity of that culture or community. The linkage between heritage and identity is crucial to understanding not only the significance of heritage as something to be valued, but also the difficulties managers face in identifying and conserving heritage (Hall & McArthur 1996, 1998). However, questions of identity, meaning, and values indicate the likelihood of there being conflicting notions of ownership attached to heritage, and therefore conflicting sets of values and interests with which the manager has to contend (Beeton 1997; McKercher 1997). Indeed, the emergence of multiple perspectives on heritage has led to an expanded meaning of heritage beyond simply the things we want to keep (Hall & McArthur 1998).

Tunbridge and Ashworth (1996) identified five different aspects of the expanded meaning of heritage:
- a synonym for any relict physical survival of the past;
- the idea of individual and collective memories in terms of non-physical aspects of the past when viewed from the present;
- all accumulated cultural and artistic productivity;
- the natural environment; and
- a major commercial activity (for example, the 'heritage industry').

There is significant overlap among these various conceptions of heritage. However, according to Tunbridge and Ashworth (1996, p. 3):

> . . . there are intrinsic dangers in the rapidly extending uses of the word and in the resulting stretching of the concept to cover so much. Inevitably precision is lost, but more important is that this, in turn, conceals issues and magnifies problems intrinsic to the creation and management of heritage.

Ironically, the uncertainty about what constitutes heritage is occurring at a time when heritage has assumed greater importance *because* of its relationship to identity in a constantly changing world. As Glasson et al. (1995, pp. 12–13) recognised: 'One reason why the heritage city is proving such a visitor attraction is that, in easily consumable form, it establishes assurance in a world which is changing rapidly'.

The formulation of what constitutes heritage is intimately related to wider political, social, economic, and technological changes which appear to reflect 'postmodern' concerns over the end of certainty and the convergence between cultural forms which were once seen as separate aspects of everyday life—for example, between education and tourism or, more relevant to heritage, between marketing and conservation. Much discussion in heritage studies has focused on the recognition of multiple meanings of heritage, particularly with respect to the recognition of other voices in heritage, such as those of indigenous peoples. Although the cultural construction and complexity of heritage is now readily acknowledged (Hudson 1987; Corner & Harvey 1991; Hooper-Greenhill 1992; Tunbridge & Ashworth 1996), what has not been readily forthcoming is the translation of this understanding into practical approaches for heritage managers who are faced with the day-to-day reality of multiple demands on heritage and the quality of the heritage product (Hall & McArthur 1998).

Cultural tourism

The ONT (1997c) defined 'cultural tourism' as 'tourism that focuses on the culture of a destination—the lifestyle, heritage, arts, industries and leisure pursuits of the local population'. The term 'cultural tourism' 'encompasses historical sites, arts and craft fairs and festivals, museums of all kinds, the performing arts and the visual arts' and other heritage sites which tourists visit in pursuit of cultural experiences (Tighe 1986, p. 2). Visiting Aboriginal art sites, experiencing special events such as ethnic festivals, and enjoying the re-enactment of historically significant moments are also part of cultural and heritage tourism. Cultural tourism was defined by the World Tourism Organization as including 'movements of persons for essentially cultural motivations such as study tours, performing arts and other cultural tours, travel to festivals and other cultural events, visits to sites and monuments, travel to study nature, folklore or art or pilgrimages' (Secretary General, World Tourism Organisation (WTO) 1985). Cultural tourism is experiential tourism, based on being involved in, and stimulated by, the performing arts, visual arts, and festivals. Heritage tourism, whether in the form of visiting preferred landscapes, historic sites, buildings, or monuments, is also experiential tourism in the sense of seeking an encounter with nature or feeling part of the history of a place (Hall & Zeppel 1990). Cultural tourism has been a significant element in several state tourism strategies since the early 1990s, most notably that of South Australia and, more recently, Victoria.

Built on the profile of long-standing cultural initiatives such as the Festival of the Arts, the South Australian cultural tourism strategy promoted the cultural assets of

URBAN TOURISM DEVELOPMENT

As well as being an architectual icon in its own right, the Sydney Opera House is also a focal point to arts-oriented tourists.

the state to the local market, as well as to interstate and international travellers (Tourism South Australia 1992). In the late 1980s South Australia established a 'speciality position' in the tourism marketplace by promoting the 'complementary imagery of festivals, events, lifestyle, hospitality, graciousness, charm, heritage, culture and friendly character' (South Australian Tourism Development Board 1987a, p. 13) which it has sought to maintain to the present-day. Significantly, the tourism development principles adopted in South Australia include enhancing the cultural, built, and natural heritage; ensuring authenticity and integrity in the tourism experience, and providing opportunities for memorable experiences with emphasis on involvement and learning (Tourism South Australia 1992). According to Tourism South Australia (1992), the following working principles need to be adopted in cultural tourism:

- emphasise quality before quantity;
- ensure value for money;
- ensure authenticity and integrity;
- respect, preserve and, where appropriate, enhance the state's natural and built heritage;
- provide memorable experiences with the emphasis on involvement and learning; and
- ensure development is in keeping with local character.

The 'bottom–up' approach taken in actively promoting cultural and heritage tourism in South Australia ensures that the local community benefits by being involved in art, heritage, and culture, along with the interstate and overseas visitors who come to experience the 'Festival State'.

There are a number of aesthetic, intellectual, emotional, and psychological factors motivating tourists to seek out and enjoy cultural experiences (Figure 13.1). Four broad categories of heritage tourism can be identified (Table 13.4). Visitors to art galleries are seeking to encounter beauty, authenticity, uniqueness, and exclusiveness. The individual visitor becomes involved in the often solemn contemplation of art works and the encounter creates a very personal aesthetic experience. In contrast, visitors to museums are seeking discovery, novelty, diversity, and knowledge. Museums are information centres that primarily offer a learning experience, often with interactive

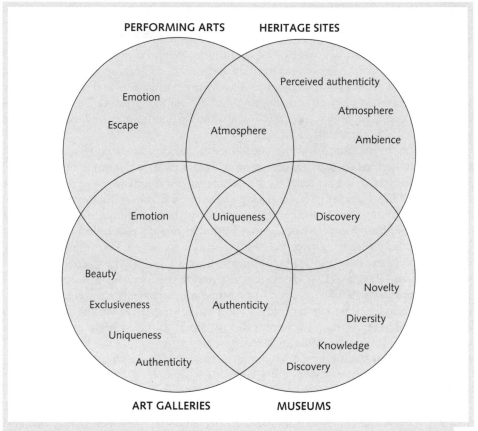

Figure 13.1 Motivating factors in cultural and heritage tourism
Source: Hall, C.M. & Zeppel, H. 'Cultural and heritage tourism: the new grand tour?' (1990)
Historic Environment, vol. 7, no. 3–4, pp. 86–98. Published by Australia ICOMOS.

TABLE 13.4 Categories of heritage tourism

Category	Example
Museums and art galleries	Open air museums, special exhibitions, regional museums, sculpture gardens
Arts festivals	Adelaide Festival, theatre, dance, opera, and music festivals
Heritage Sites	
(a) Natural	Scenic landscapes, botanic gardens, national parks and reserves, designated outdoor recreation areas, historic gardens
(b) Cultural	Historic buildings, sites and monuments, heritage theme parks, architecture, archaeological sites, cultural landscapes
Folklore	Ethnic and indigenous cultural traditions, handicrafts, cultural centres, dance performances and ceremonies, folk festivals and other community celebrations

displays (such as the Powerhouse Museum in Sydney). Visitors to historic houses, Aboriginal art sites, and other heritage sites are seeking to experience authenticity (or what is perceived as authenticity), atmosphere, and ambience. Heritage sites can also convey a sense of place and bring to visitors an awareness of the historical context of an area. However, visitors to performing arts events are seeking a more emotional experience and an escape from the everyday world. 'Audiences seek to satisfy many needs in part at least through consumption of these cultural products', special cultural and artistic experiences 'are sources of arousal to compensate for the deficiencies of ordinary life' (Hughes 1987, pp. 209, 212).

The growth in cultural and heritage tourism can be attributed to an increasing awareness of heritage, greater affluence, more leisure time, greater mobility, increased access to the arts, and a reaction to the demands of modern society (Brokensha & Guldberg 1992). For example, it has long been noted that in rediscovering heritage, people are looking back with a certain nostalgia to the way things used to be. 'This increased emphasis on retrospection, whether due to a psychological need for continuity, the desire to transcend contemporary experience, or the urge to know one's roots, characteristically leads to some form of appreciation and concern for the past' (Konrad 1982, p. 412). Heritage sites provide the focus for this psychological motive in travelling. This exploration of culture and heritage is a travel activity now open to all classes of people to enjoy. 'The past belongs to everyone: the need to return home, to recall the view, to refresh a memory, to trace a heritage, is universal and essential' (Lowenthal 1981, p. 236).

The Australian bicentennial celebrations in 1988 and the celebrations of the centenary of Australian federation in 2001 have also encouraged a greater awareness of Aboriginal and European heritage. People within Australia are now, more than ever, seeking to identify with the varied aspects of Australian culture and heritage (DASETT 1988a). The growth in Aboriginal arts, in particular, reflects the emergence and assertion of Aboriginal culture, heritage, and identity in contemporary Australian society, and the desire by both Australian and overseas visitors to experience indigenous Australian culture (Ryan & Huyton 2000).

Overseas visitors who come to 'experience' Australia are increasingly seeking to enjoy not only the scenery but also the arts and culture as well. A survey of cultural tourism activities of international tourists to Australia in 1995 noted that museums and art galleries, national parks, historic sites or homes, and cinemas were all high-ranking entertainment venues for international tourists (Department of Communication and the Arts 1996). For example, 31% of United States visitors went to a museum or art gallery. Such tourists have a desire to be involved in cultural experiences to learn and to be enriched by heritage encounters on their travels. In keeping with this trend, Australia's cultural and heritage assets are increasingly being recognised and promoted as enriching and educational tourism experiences.

Who are the cultural tourists?

In Australia, the need for research on cultural tourism has been recognised only since the late 1980s (Australia Council 1989a; Brokensha & Guldberg 1992; Hall & McArthur 1993; Department of Communication and the Arts 1996). The lack of local market research was such that by the late 1980s 'no comprehensive data' had 'been collected on domestic tourist attendance at arts events and facilities, nor information on their interests, motivation or other characteristics' (Spring 1988, p. 350).

To correct this situation the statistical advisory group of the Cultural Minister's Council recommended that the Australian Bureau of Statistics have a separate industry category for the collection of statistics on the products and services provided by the culture–leisure industry (*Images* 1988), and the Australia Council also produced research on cultural tourism (1990b, 1990c, 1991, 1992). This research has been reinforced by the activities of the Department of Communications and the Arts (1996) and the Statistics Working Group of the Cultural Ministers Council (1996). The results of such research are significant. For example, in the twelve months ending March 1995, 3.9 million Australians visited museums while 3.1 million visited art galleries. One-quarter of all international visitors during 1995 (aged 15 years and over) visited museums or art galleries, while 32% of international visitors during 1995 (aged 15 years and over) visited historical/heritage buildings, sites, monuments, and towns (ONT 1997c). The results of the international visitors' survey have also identified the propensity of various international tourist groups to visit cultural and heritage attractions in Australia (Bureau of Tourism Research (BTR) 1996; Department of Communication and the Arts 1996). The Australia Council (for the Arts) has also undertaken a study in conjunction with Saatchi and Saatchi Australia to identify the value that Australians place on the arts. This study identified five main arts market segments in contemporary Australia (Australia Council 2000a):

- arts lovers (17%)—who were very positive about the arts and were in favour of change;
- satisfied (21%)—who were generally quite positive about the arts and who did not see particular reasons for the arts to change;
- interested (25%)—who were open to a positive experience of the arts but could see ways in which the arts could change to improve their attitudes towards them;
- disinclined (25%)—who were not particularly interested in the arts at the time, but could see changes that would make them feel more positive about the arts; and
- disengaged (11%)—who had little or no interest in the arts, gave them a low value, and were not interested in seeing them change in the future.

The large number of Australians with generally positive attitudes towards the arts is obviously of significance for cultural tourism because of the extent to which arts activities—such as events, galleries, museums, and arts and crafts—are important domestic tourism activities. According to the Australia Council (2000b):

> In one year in Australia there are 12 million attendances at public art galleries, 6.7 million admissions to live theatre, 5 million admissions to musical theatre (including opera), 3.4 million attendances at dance performances, 4 million attendances at classical music concerts, and 19.5 million attendances at popular music concerts.

Table 13.5 outlines the attendance at museums, galleries, live theatre, and musical performances by international visitors to Australia. The table indicates the substantial proportion of international visitors who attend cultural activities in Australia and highlights the degree of repeat visitation to such events (also see Australia Council 1991, 1992). According to the Australia Council (2000b), 28% of international visitors go to art galleries or museums and 18% attend a performing arts event. 'In 1996, they purchased $67 million worth of Indigenous art or souvenirs (a doubling over a five-year period), comprising 26 000 Indigenous paintings, 51 000 carvings and sculptures, 29 000 craft items, 12 000 books on Indigenous art, and 15 000 recordings of Indigenous music'. However, relatively little information is available

TABLE 13.5 International visitor attendance at entertainment venues, by country or region of origin, 1995 (%)

Venue	New Zealand	Japan	Hong Kong	Singapore	Malaysia	Indonesia
Nightclubs, discos or karaoke	8	5	4	7	3	4
Museums or art galleries	14	9	16	18	15	11
National parks	18	20	29	29	27	23
Historic sites or houses	7	13	7	12	21	4
Cinemas or movie theatres	12	3	13	14	23	18
Theatre, opera or ballet	14	2	3	1	11	4
Classical music	1	0	0	0	2	2
Contemporary music	0	1	1	2	3	0
Sporting venues	9	4	2	1	1	5
Adventure activities	4	10	6	5	1	1
Theme or amusement parks	12	20	18	24	20	20
Animal parks, zoos or aquariums	20	35	18	31	28	37
Adult entertainment	5	0	2	0	1	8
Other entertainment	10	21	4	6	17	11
None	36	17	26	23	24	20

Venue	Taiwan	Thailand	Korea	Other Asia	United States	Canada
Nightclubs, discos or karaoke	2	12	9	11	15	7
Museums or art galleries	23	24	13	25	31	22
National parks	33	18	40	20	31	54
Historic sites or houses	9	12	15	15	17	25
Cinemas or movie theatres	15	15	7	7	17	8
Theatre, opera or ballet	8	13	6	3	9	4
Classical music	0	0	0	0	2	0
Contemporary music	1	3	2	2	2	6
Sporting venues	2	4	3	3	5	0
Adventure activities	2	3	10	1	15	14
Theme or amusement parks	37	17	28	9	4	6
Animal parks, zoos or aquariums	47	35	45	33	36	35

Adult entertainment	2	6	1	4	0	24
Other entertainment	11	6	12	7	15	14
None	16	28	9	36	22	22

Venue	UK	Germany	Scandinavia	Other Europe	Other Countries
Nightclubs, discos or karaoke	26	14	35	15	10
Museums or art galleries	24	36	31	33	10
National parks	39	54	30	38	17
Historic sites or houses	17	28	22	27	7
Cinemas or movie theatres	26	20	29	21	16
Theatre, opera or ballet	8	6	15	12	7
Classical music	0	3	0	4	2
Contemporary music	5	5	10	4	2
Sporting venues	13	6	14	3	5
Adventure activities	12	13	23	16	5
Theme or amusement parks	12	6	3	8	6
Animal parks, zoos or aquariums	30	47	38	44	13
Adult entertainment	2	1	9	3	0
Other entertainment	14	7	10	12	2
None	18	16	9	11	46

Source: Department of Communication and the Arts (1996) *Cultural Tourism in Australia*, Canberra.

about cultural participation by domestic tourists in Australia (Brokensha & Guldberg 1992; Hall & McArthur 1993).

In South Australia, economic studies have been conducted on the impact of the Adelaide Festival of Arts (Brokensha & Tonks 1985; McDonald 1988; SATC 1997). At the festival, 29% of the box office takings came from non-Adelaide residents and 60% of the interstate visitors came from Victoria (Lloyd 1989). Adelaide festival visitors spent more and stayed longer than other tourists in the city. They spent 86% more on their stay than all other visitors. Interstate festival visitors alone spent 17.5% more than typical interstate visitors each day and also stayed for longer (more than 11 nights on average). The 1988 impact study demonstrated that South Australia received an estimated economic benefit of nearly $3 million as a result of staging the Adelaide festival. Total attendances for the 1996 festival were estimated at 705 000 with more than 1000 country visitors and 7600 interstate or overseas visitors attending ticketed events (SATC 1997). In 2000, total attendances were estimated at more than 860 000, including attendances at free events, and total attendances for the 1998 Adelaide Fringe Festival were estimated at 857 000, with 230 000 paid attendances. (SATC 2000). Museum visitation in Australia is also a major leisure time activity. As Holding (1989, p. 7) observed:

> Recent statistics . . . suggest that a visit to a cultural institution is as popular to the average Australian as attending a football game. It is estimated that museums alone have attracted some twelve million visits annually. Major museums reach up to thirty-two percent of the domestic population annually and up to fifty percent of the population over five years.

The popularity of visiting art galleries and museums in Australia seems to indicate a newfound awareness and public interest in cultural matters which has major implications for the pattern of domestic and international visitation and for the manner in which the Australian tourist product is marketed (Bennett & Frow 1991; Brokensha & Guldberg 1992; SATC 2000).

Heritage management

The development of cultural and heritage tourism should ideally proceed within a heritage management framework that gives priority to the conservation and preservation of unique heritage resources. The growing popularity of cultural tourism and the expanding heritage industry emphasise the necessity for effective tourism management to protect heritage sites and provide visitor services (Hall & McArthur 1993, 1996). In the private sector, the heritage industry includes the rapidly growing number of tours provided for visitors to experience the natural, cultural, and built environments of an area. This industry requires reliable information and guidelines on the promotion and presentation of heritage tours and heritage sites. The operation of historical theme parks by private enterprise should also be reviewed in terms of the authenticity and integrity of the historical tourism experience being offered to visitors. For example, Sovereign Hill at Ballarat is an historically accurate recreation of an 1850s gold mining town. The buildings, shops, domestic animals, and role-playing characters in historical costumes recreate the working life and atmosphere of a gold rush town in the period 1851 to 1861. In developing Sovereign Hill, all historical details of the township, gold rush life, and costumes were researched for historical accuracy by relevant committees of the Ballarat Historical Park Association (Loh 1989).

In the public sector, the management of heritage resources by government agencies has to balance the often conflicting needs of conservation and tourism. The issues involved in public heritage management include matters of funding, staffing, public access, visitor facilities, heritage presentation and interpretation, and the ongoing maintenance of heritage sites. Because heritage resources are irreplaceable, the most critical issue in heritage management is that of conservation. Governments, as the main controllers of heritage resources, need a heritage conservation policy to guide and control tourism development (Hall & McArthur 1993). 'Long term planning for heritage tourism with an integral, continuing conservation policy is essential in ensuring a quality experience for the visitor at each heritage site' (Millar 1989, p. 13).

The increasing popularity of cultural and heritage tourism will create yet more heritage management problems which need to be resolved. The pressures of mass tourism can cause structural damage at heritage sites and can lead to visual pollution in the form of traffic, parking areas, signs, and crowds, with a consequent decrease in visitor satisfaction. Conservation of atmosphere or ambience at heritage sites should also be considered in heritage management. This is important if visitors are to experience the spiritual, spatial, and aesthetic qualities of historic buildings, landscapes, and other heritage sites. To fund the proper management of heritage sites many government agencies are implementing a user-pays policy, whereby visitors are paying for access to national parks, museums, and special exhibitions at art galleries. Municipal authorities can also levy accommodation taxes with a designated portion of the revenues set aside for the arts (Backas 1983). In South Australia, a cultural sponsorship organisation known as Foundation South Australia is funded through a levy on tobacco licensing fees (Department for the Arts 1989).

Heritage management refers to the conscious process by which decisions concerning heritage policy and practice are made, and how heritage resources are developed. The field of heritage management therefore encompasses analysis, management, and development (Hall & McArthur 1998). As Middleton (1994, p. 3) recognised:

> Like it or not, around the world in the 1990s heritage and management are inevitably and inextricably linked. For many it is a very uneasy marriage of interests. Few people involved with heritage resources consider themselves part of an *industry* in which the management practices developed in business and commerce can be readily applied.

The realisation that heritage managers need to adopt appropriate approaches from the business world is leading to a transformation in heritage management strategies. Middleton (1994, p. 5) has identified three aspects of a management strategy for heritage resources:
• managing the heritage resource;
• managing access; and
• managing organisations.

Managing heritage resources, be they collections, historic houses, national parks or traditional festivals is the primary duty of management of heritage bodies (Middleton 1994). However, as Middleton emphasised, there is clearly a need to expand the notion of what heritage management is about if managers are to respond to the changing environment in which they are operating. Middleton and other authors (Hooper-Greenhill 1992; Hall & McArthur 1993, 1996; Harrison 1994) have emphasised the need for managers to consider issues of access, quality, visitor demands, marketing, and organisation, as well as traditional resource conservation. Indeed, Hall and McArthur (1998) argued that management needs to consider the primacy of stakeholders in heritage, given that the heritage manager is engaged in managing not so much a resource *per se* but the multiple attitudes, values, perceptions, interests, and wants of stakeholders with respect to heritage. This represents a fundamental shift in much heritage management thinking. It does not deny the importance of physical conservation and restoration of heritage. Rather, it argues that such activities need to be seen in the context of the (at times conflicting) demands of various stakeholders who determine that something *is* heritage and that it therefore requires the development of appropriate management strategies and practice.

Heritage as a tourism commodity?

> There is a growing demand throughout the world for tourism experiences that involve interaction with indigenous people and exposure to indigenous cultures. As home to one of the world's oldest living cultures, Australia is well placed to open the window of opportunity presented by this rising interest (ONT 1997d).
>
> For whatever meanings of Aboriginality are current in any domain they are always constructed in opposition to meanings of white society. Aborigines are what whites are not. Sometimes this difference is seen as a threat, but sometimes, as in tourism, it can be seen as a compensation, as a means of liberating whites from the limitations of the society they have built and of offering them alternative ways of thinking (Fiske et al. 1987, p. 129).

In a desire to cut government spending, many traditionally 'public' assets—such as national parks, historical monuments and sites, museums, art galleries, and zoos—are having to adopt a more commercial orientation, if not outright corporatisation or privatisation. The attraction of the tourist dollar becomes a new management goal. But the tourist dollar does not come without a cost. Historic townships, national parks, rock art, and archaeological sites often show the unwanted effects of visitation in the form of physical damage, overcrowding, and insensitivity to the local community. For example, problems of visitation identified by the English Tourism Board and the Department of Employment (1991) included increased risk of fire, pilferage, graffiti, accident risks for cars, atmospheric pollution, impaired ambience, destruction of architectural and archaeological integrity, traffic congestion and parking problems (both private cars and coach tours), and crowding. Indeed, many concerns have been expressed not only about the quality of the visitor experience but also about the quality of heritage itself (Tabata et al. 1992; Boniface 1995; Hall & McArthur 1998).

The cultural and heritage resources of any country should not be seen as existing solely to serve the needs of the tourism industry (Cossons 1989; Hall & Zeppel 1989). Heritage and the performing and visual arts have come to be regarded as an industry. As Hewison (1988, p. 240) observed:

> We already have a changed language in which we talk about the arts. We no longer discuss them as expressions of imagination or creativity, we talk about 'product'; we are no longer moved by the experiences the arts have to offer, we 'consume' them. Culture has become a commodity.

For example, the current popularity of Aboriginal art has created a large market for traditional and contemporary Aboriginal art forms to meet the demand for tourist souvenirs, art galleries, and private collectors (Simmons 2000).

The size of the market interested in indigenous culture is substantial—380 000 international visitors (11% of the total) visited indigenous sites and attractions in 1995. This represents an increase of more than 50% from 1994. According to the ONT (1997d), the greatest demand for Aboriginal tourism product came from United Kingdom, European, and North American visitors, with growing interest from the Asian market. The economic returns are substantial—sales of Aboriginal arts and souvenirs to international visitors are estimated to be worth at least $100 million each year (ONT 1997d). According to the Department of Communication and the Arts (1997), 20% of international visitors in 1995 had an interest in Aboriginal art and craft, although European visitors were more than twice as likely to take an interest in Aboriginal items as Asian visitors. As an example of this, 53% of German visitors had an interest in Aboriginal items, compared with 13% of Japanese. Visitor interest in Aboriginal art also varied depending on places visited. For example, over 50% of travellers who visited the Northern Territory had an interest in Aboriginal art and craft compared with 9% of visitors to Tasmania. Interest in these items was also higher in the younger age groups. More than 20% of visitors aged between 15 and 34 years had an interest in Aboriginal art and craft, including 30% of those aged 20 to 24 years.

In becoming a marketable commodity, Aboriginal art can become removed from its traditional social and cultural context (Simmons 2000). Art forms such as the Papunya Tula paintings of Central Australia are now being produced in large quantities to meet tourist demand. This has led to reduced quality, sameness, and the potential denigration of meaning in the artwork through the commercialisation and trivialisation of important events from the Aboriginal creation period or 'Dreamtime' (Hollinshead 1988). As Altman and Finlayson (1993, p. 48) observed: 'It is imperative that any government initiatives for Aboriginal participation [in the tourism industry] recognise the fragility of the Aboriginal cultural product so that undue pressure is not placed on Aboriginal suppliers of cultural tourism to meet the needs of the tourism market'. Culture and heritage, as expressed through the arts, can be both stimulated and degraded by the impact of tourism (Hughes 1987, 1989). With the advent of mass tourism and its attendant market impact, the materials, form, and content of much Aboriginal art have been adapted to meet external tourist demands. However, the demands of the tourism industry are such that a universal return to traditional Aboriginal art and cultural forms is almost impossible and, perhaps from an economic perspective, undesirable.

The role of the corporate sector in promoting and developing cultural tourism in Australia also needs to be considered. The Adelaide Festival of Arts and the Festival of Perth, for example, both rely heavily on private business sponsorship to bring their programs of cultural events to the public. Special exhibitions at art galleries are also often sponsored by businesses (Roux 1987). Businesses regard arts and heritage sponsorship as a supplementary marketing tool to reach a target audience, with the public relations aspect creating an up-market corporate image. However, in seeking corporate funding for heritage projects, measures need to be taken to ensure that heritage attractions do not become solely the vehicles for corporate advertising, rather than being the authentic and meaningful experiences they were meant to provide for visitors and communities alike.

URBAN TOURISM DEVELOPMENT

EVENT TOURISM

Short-term staged attractions or hallmark events have been major components of the growth of tourism in Australia in the past decade or so. Hallmark tourist events, otherwise referred to as 'mega' (Ritchie & Yangzhou 1987) or special events (Burns et al. 1986) are major fairs, festivals, expositions, cultural, and sporting events held on a regular or one-off basis. Hallmark events have assumed a key role in international, national, and regional tourism marketing strategies in Australia, providing host communities with opportunities to secure prominence in the tourism marketplace for short, well-defined, periods of time (Ritchie 1984; Hall & Selwood 1987; Hall 1989e, 1992b; National Centre for Studies in Travel and Tourism 1989; Getz 1997; Goldblatt 1997; McDonnell et al. 1999; Gessel 2000; Frost 2001).

Hallmark events are different in their appeal from the attractions normally promoted by the tourist industry, because they are not continuous or seasonal phenomena. Indeed, in many cases, hallmark events are strategic responses to the problems that seasonal variations in demand pose for the tourist industry (Ritchie & Beliveau 1974). However, the ability of an event 'to achieve this objective depends on the uniqueness of the event, the status of the event and the extent to which it is successfully marketed within tourism generating regions' (Ritchie 1984, p. 2).

Events can help construct a positive image and help build commercial and public awareness of a destination through the media coverage which they generate (Department of Sport, Recreation and Tourism 1986; Van Der Lee & Williams 1986; Tourism Victoria 1997a, 1997b; Gessel 2000). For example, South Australia has for many years been known as the 'Festival State' to many Australians because of the success of the bi-annual Adelaide Festival of Arts and associated activities (SATC 2000). More recently, Victoria has been aggressively promoting itself as the event state, with Tourism Victoria (1997b) reporting that its research indicates that Melbourne is now recognised as the Australian city which hosts major international sporting and cultural events, ahead of Sydney, Adelaide, Brisbane, and Perth.

The positive image which events are able to portray to the public, and the media exposure they offer, explain the lengths to which governments and politicians go to host major national and international events (Hall 1989f). Examples can be seen in the bidding process by which Australian cities and state governments competed for the right to host the 1996 and 2000 Olympic Games, the competition between Victoria and New South Wales to host the Australian Motorcycling Grand Prix, and the conflict between Victoria and South Australia over the hosting of the Australian Formula One Grand Prix.

Many state governments have now established specific event units to assist in the bidding for major sporting and cultural events (Tourism Victoria 1997a, 1997b). For example, in 1992, Eventscorp, the events unit of the West Australian Tourism Commisssion (WATC), was involved in the staging of events which injected an estimated $18 million into the state economy and raised more than $5 million from the private sector as sponsorships, spectator revenue, and other event income. Criteria used by Eventscorp in assessing the viability of events included (WATC 1992, p. 23):

- a targeted return of $7 economic impact generated by the event to each $1 of Eventscorp funding;
- a dollar-for-dollar private sector financial support to complement government funding;

- significant identifiable national and international media exposure; and
- the utilisation of existing infrastructure, tourism, and sporting facilities, and the development of additional facilities when appropriate.

Table 13.6 records examples of various hallmark tourist events in Australia and New Zealand. Although several of the events are not specifically designed for the purpose of attracting tourists, such as perhaps the Sydney Gay and Lesbian Mardi Gras (Seebohm 1990), they nevertheless make important contributions to the tourism industry of the host community. For example, the month-long Mardi Gras celebration provides one of the biggest economic boosts by any festival, sporting event, or special event to any local economy in Australia (Marsh & Greenfield 1993; Ryan & Hall 2001).

Hallmark events are not restricted to major large-scale events. Short-term staged events such as carnivals, festivals, and fêtes in small towns can also be described as hallmark events and can be of significant economic importance to the local community through attracting visitors and retaining local expenditure. Such events not only serve to attract tourists but also assist in the development or maintenance of community or regional identity. Therefore, community festivals and local celebrations can be described as hallmark events in relation to their local and regional significance. Such an observation notes the importance of the economic, marketing, social, and geographical *context* within which hallmark events take place (Hall 1989c). Investment decisions regarding sporting and recreational events should not always be made on economic grounds alone, as it is 'impracticable to place a value on the enhanced well-being of the populace' (Patterson & Hagan 1988, p. 13).

The amount of local involvement and the actions of government in the planning of events appear to be crucial in deriving maximum benefit for the host community.

TABLE 13.6 Examples of hallmark tourist events in Australia and New Zealand

Classification	Examples and locations
Carnivals and festivals	Todd River Regatta (Alice Springs); Beer Can Regatta (Darwin); Gay and Lesbian Mardi Gras (Sydney); Moomba Carnival (Melbourne); Floriade (Canberra); Melbourne Food Festival
Major commercial and agricultural events	Royal Agricultural Show (Sydney); National Agricultural Fair (Orange); Taste Australia (Adelaide, Melbourne)
Major political events	CHOGM (2002); Australian Labor Party national conventions; visits by monarchy; APEC meeting (Auckland 1999)
Major sporting events	Olympic Games (Melbourne 1956, Sydney 2000); rugby World Cup (2003); AFL Grand Final (Melbourne); rugby league Grand Final (Sydney); America's Cup (Fremantle 1986/87; Auckland 1999/2000, 2002/03); Grand Prix racing (Melbourne); Spring Racing Carnival and Melbourne Cup (Melbourne); Bathurst 1000 (Bathurst, NSW)
Cultural and religious events	Festival of Sydney; Festival of Adelaide; Festival of Perth; Spoletto Festival (Melbourne); International Comedy Festival (Melbourne); Blessing of the Fleet (Fremantle)
Historical milestones	Australian bicentenary (1988); centenary of Australian Federation (2001)
World fairs, expositions, and conferences	International Expo (Brisbane 1988); International Lions Convention (Brisbane 1990)

URBAN TOURISM DEVELOPMENT

The more an event is seen by the impacted public as emerging from the local community, rather than being imposed on them, the greater is that community's acceptance of the event. However, the international dimension of many events often means that national and regional governments assume responsibility for the event's planning. Indeed, because of the interests that impact upon upper levels of government, local concerns can be lost in the search for the national or regional good, with special legislation often being enacted to minimise disturbance to the hosting of an event (Hall 1989f, 1989g). The short timeframe in which governments and industry have to react to the hosting of events can lead to 'fast track planning' in which proposals are pushed through the planning process without the normal economic, social, and environmental assessment procedures being applied.

A classic example of the failure of governments to give adequate attention to the broad impacts of hallmark events was the hosting of the 2000 Olympics by Sydney. The bid for the Games had more to do with Sydney and New South Wales politics than a rational assessment of the economic and tourism benefits of hosting the Games. Waitt (1999, p. 1057) commented:

> As a political device, the bid was employed to imbue social consensus in an era distinguished by a sense of alienation, anomie and increasing social inequalities within cities by income, ethnic identity and life opportunities. During the 1990s, Sydney was not exempt from these problematic features of city living.

As research on large-scale events such as the Olympics or World Fairs has indicated, the net costs of the event often far outweigh any net benefits, except in terms of potential political and economic benefits for urban élites (Hall 1992b, 1996c). The Sydney Games were therefore designed to assist with urban redevelopment and imaging more than with concern over the spread of social, economic, and environmental impacts (Hall & Hodges 1996; Waitt 1999). Indeed, before the Games it was even argued that they would create a great deal of turbulence in the marketplace with the Games actually serving to repel rather than attract some tourists (Leiper & Hall 1993). Tony Thirlwell (1997, p. 5), chief executive officer of Tourism New South Wales (TNSW), confirmed that there was a need for some 'reality checks' to be brought home to New South Wales in the light of the Atlanta Olympics experience:

Olympic related construction, Sydney

The simple fact that people travel to Olympic Games for sports events cannot be over-stated . . . Zoo Atlanta, Six Flags Over Georgia and other attractions . . . suffered adversely because of the Olympic Games. Revenue losses were caused by Olympic distortion of attractions' usual visitation patterns and by costs of their attempts to leverage off the Olympics.

Nevertheless, the expectations for the long-term effects of hosting the Olympics were high. According to TNSW (1997, p. 1): 'an extra 2.1 million overseas tourists are expected between 1994 and 2004—a $4 billion tourism boost' (1997f, p. 1). In addition, TNSW reported the results of a survey which showed that outside Sydney '39% of respondents said they would definitely or probably travel to Sydney for the event', with the survey also finding 'that 73% of Sydneysiders were interested in attending Games events' (1997g, p. 9). Yet clearly, these numbers were not neces-sarily translated into action. Table 13.7 portrays the facts and figures surrounding the Games as reported by the Australian Tourist Commission (ATC) (2001c).

The Games were also regarded as important in increasing the exposure of Sydney in the international media and contributing to the ability of the Sydney Conven-tion and Visitors Bureau to win major international conferences. For example, the ATC (2001c) described the Olympics as having:

> been . . . a huge success for the Australian tourism industry. Travel agents and industry partners have reported a surge in enquiries about Australia from potential travellers. Visitors to the ATC's Web site australia.com increased 700 per cent during the Games compared to average September 1999 figures. Australia is definitely 'the' place that's being talked about around the world.

Of course, talking about a place needs to be converted into action. Therefore, the ATC invested substantial amounts of money on promotion and marketing. The four key elements of the ATC strategy included:
- the launch of more than 90 joint tactical advertising campaigns, worth more than $45 million and involving more than 200 industry partners, promoting holiday deals to Australia;
- an aggressive $6 million direct marketing campaign including the redevelopment of the ATC's website, <**australia.com**>;
- undertaking research on how the Olympic exposure has shifted Australia's image internationally; and
- continuing to build the lucrative meetings, incentive, convention, and exhibition (MICE) sector (ATC 2001c).

Australian studies of hallmark events, as with tourism studies in general, have tended to focus on the forecast of visitor numbers and the economic impacts of events. However, research in this area has generally been of poor quality and 'much of what has been done has been rather misleading' (Burns & Mules 1986, p. 8) with often excessive estimates of the benefits of hosting of events (Hall 1989e). As Patterson and Hagan (1988, p. 27) noted, there is a 'necessity to treat claims made by organ-isers, or others close to the event, with a modicum of caution'. Overstated large benefit/cost ratios have emerged for several reasons. First, there has been a failure to account for the economic impact that would have occurred anyway but has switched from one industry to another. Second, there has been the 'unfortunately common mistake' of attributing all the benefits received from the event to government expen-diture, instead of establishing the marginal impact of that contribution' (Burns &

Mules 1986, pp. 8, 10). Third, counting of taxation benefits of expenditure generation as 'additional to the multiplier "flow-ons" has taken place when they have already been included'. Fourth, 'output' rather than 'value-added' multipliers have been uncritically employed, which can result in major overestimates of the economic impact of events (Burns & Mules 1986, pp. 8–9). Fifth, there has been a general failure to delimit the size of the regional economy that is to be studied—the smaller the area to be analysed, the greater will be the number of 'visitors' and hence the greater is the estimate of economic impact.

Several studies have been conducted of the economic impacts of Australian hallmark events (Lynch & Jensen 1984; Burns & Mules 1986; Centre for Applied Business and Research 1987; Minnikin 1987; Patterson & Hagan 1988; Hagan & Patterson 1991; McCann & Thompson 1992). However, opportunity costs, leakage from the state or region due to foreign and interstate investment and administrative and social costs have generally not been taken into consideration. In addition, the costs of policing events can be quite substantial. For example, the Fourth World Cup in Athletics staged in Canberra in October 1985 necessitated the devotion of 12 565 police labour hours (Australian Federal Police 1986, p. 25). Similarly, no consideration was given to the considerable costs which were associated with the 250-member police task force established for the duration of the 1986–87 America's Cup Defence in Western Australia (Hall 1989d; Hall & Selwood 1989), and the Sydney Olympics obviously entailed substantial security operations.

Debate has also been substantial over the economic benefits of the Formula One Grand Prix held in Melbourne. According to Tourism Victoria (1997a, p. 24), the 1997 Grand Prix:

> . . . was watched by an estimated overseas audience of more than 300 million people . . . total attendance at the race was 289,000 over the four days . . . An independent assessment of the 1996 . . . Grand Prix indicated that it provided a gross economic benefit to the Victorian economy of $95.6 million and created 2,270 full year equivalent jobs.

In contrast, a thorough evaluation of the 1996 Grand Prix by Economists at Large and Associates (1997, p. 8) for the Save Albert Park Group concluded the following about the claim of $95.6 million of extra expenditure:

- it was a misrepresentation of the size of the economic benefit;
- the claimed gross benefits are overstated or non-existent; and
- ironically, compared with what might have been achieved, Victorians were poorer when they could have been wealthier if the government had chosen a more 'boring' investment than the Grand Prix.

Debate over the impact of the event still continued in 2002. According to the Grand Prix organisers 127 000 people attended the 2002 Australian Grand Prix in Melbourne with the four-day Formula One event achieving a record-breaking 371 800 people, which was 2300 more than the 2001 crowd. However, the Save Albert Park group again questioned the veracity of the Grand Prix Corporation's claims regarding crowd numbers. According to group spokesman Ross Ulman (in Dubecki 2002): 'The Grand Prix Corporation is not telling the people of Victoria where their numbers are coming from'. Members of Save Albert Park each year manually counted the number of spectators at every entrance to the track circuit over the four days. They found their numbers were consistently 100 000 fewer over the four days than the official figures (Dubecki 2002).

Nevertheless, despite both the overt and 'hidden' costs of hosting events, substantial gains can be made through event tourism if strategies are carefully considered, if appropriate strategies are developed, and if there is meaningful consultation with affected stakeholders.

CHAPTER SUMMARY

This chapter has provided an overview of several growth areas in urban tourism development. Like the issues noted in the previous chapter with respect to rural areas, tourism is recognised as a major mechanism that can be used to respond to problems of economic restructuring in urban areas. However, substantial concerns are now being raised regarding the implications of place promotion and the way in which tourism-related development, including the hosting of mega events, can affect urban communities.

On the demand side, the profile of the consumer in the range of activities discussed in this chapter tends to support Pearce's assertion that the 'future trends for tourism seem to suggest that travellers will be especially concerned not with just being "there", but with participating, learning and experiencing the "there" they visit' (1988, p. 219). The analysis and development of the special interest product has tended to focus on the consumer, not the producer or how to get the product to the market. Such an approach might have dire consequences for the long-term development of special interest travel and for Australian tourism in general. Government and industry need to be aware that the tourism experience is the result of a symbiotic relationship between producer, consumer, and the host community. As Read (1980, p. 1999) observed:

> The local people must be involved—be a part of the tourism experience—and recognize that the 'special interest' tour group is not merely a group of people coming to gawk at zoo-like culture. Our experience has shown that the kind of traveller who is attracted by a 'special interest' is indeed looking for [a] rewarding, enriching, adventuresome, learning experience.

Tourism development cannot be sustained if the product that attracts consumers is not fully in place. Special interest tourism will be a prime force in the expansion and diversification of tourism. The ATC and the various state and territory tourism commissions have embarked on campaigns to encourage international tourists to experience aspects of Australian culture. However, the development of cultural and event tourism has often occurred without due consideration of the effects of tourism on local communities. If Australia is to take advantage of the growth in specialty travel, it must be realised that long-term tourism development is the result of the symbiotic relationship between consumers and producers, rather than the marketing-led approach that is generally advocated by government and industry alike.

URBAN TOURISM DEVELOPMENT

Useful general discussions of urban tourism on an international scale can be found in Page (1995), Murphy (1997), and Page and Hall (2003). Australian and New Zealand case studies of tourism in urban areas can be found in Hall, Jenkins, and Kearsley (1997a). Chapters discussing various dimensions of planning for urban tourism in particular places can be found as follows: Auckland (Page & Lawton 1997), Western Sydney (Dwyer et al. 1997), and Dunedin (Kearsley 1997b).

Overviews of the event tourism literature are contained in Getz (1991a, 1991b, 1997), Hall (1992b), Goldblatt (1997), and McDonnell, Allen, and O'Toole (1999). Although somewhat dated, an excellent case study of a sporting event is Burns, Hatch, and Mules (1986). Marsh and Greenfield (1993) produced an excellent report on the impact of the Sydney Gay and Lesbian Mardi Gras. The report by Economists at Large and Associates (1997) on the 1996 Australian Grand Prix also serves as an excellent example of how the economic evaluation of events should be conducted. Frost (2001) provides a useful account of some of the issues associated with the hosting of commemorative events.

Overviews of the cultural and heritage tourism literature are available in Harron and Weiler (1992), Zeppel and Hall (1992), Richards (1996a), and Boyd and Timothy (2002). Critical international perspectives of the heritage field and its relationship to tourism are to be found in Hewison (1987, 1988), H.L. Hughes (1989, 1997), Bianchini and Parkinson (1993), Norkunas (1993), and Hall (1997a). A variety of case studies of heritage management in Australia and New Zealand are to be found in Hall and McArthur (1993, 1996), including a study of Aboriginal tourism (Wells 1996).

INTERNET SITES

The following websites are recommended:
- Australian Museums and Galleries on line, which contains a national directory, a museum search service and a resource page with useful international links is located at
    www.amol.org.au

- Australia Council for the Arts:
    www.ozco.gov.au/index.htm

- Australian federal government culture and recreation portal:
    www.acn.net.au

- Australian National Maritime Museum:
    www.anmm.gov.au

- National Aboriginal Cultural Institute:
    www.tandanya.on.net

- Save Albert Park (also contains an excellent economic critique of the Grand Prix):
    www.save-albert-park.org.au/sap.html

FOR DISCUSSION AND REVIEW

Key concepts

Key concepts discussed in this chapter included:
urban tourism, economic restructuring, retail shopping districts, cultural tourism, heritage tourism, cultural identity, heritage management, interpretation, conservation, commercialisation, commoditisation, corporate funding, hallmark events, fast-track planning, supply of tourism product.

Questions for review and discussion

1   What is urban reimaging?
2   What is the relationship between urban tourism and economic restructuring?
3   How is culture commodified?
4   What problems does the hosting of hallmark events present for tourism planners?
5   How can you use tourism to support preservation activities without endangering the attraction?

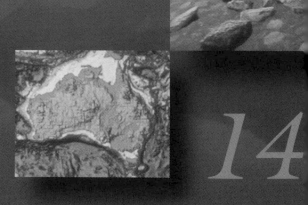

THE FUTURE DIRECTION OF TOURISM

14

When the tourist movement is viewed internationally one cannot but feel that the danger exists that undue stress may be laid on immediate and transient benefits to the detriment of the future and more permanent interests. To the extent that this is being done the future is being sacrificed to the present; the danger of this is the more imminent, the more governments fail to recognize their responsibility in the development of their tourist industry, which then becomes an issue for private and local initiative. A wise tourist policy requires that a balance be struck between the present and the future in the first instance, and between the tourist industry and the exploitation of other industries in the second instance. A country which tends to concentrate unduly on its tourist industry in preference to other branches of economic activity is exposing itself to a great danger. The tourist industry is still to a very great extent a luxury industry and as such extremely susceptible to variations in economic activity. Therefore, the larger the proportion of the population engaged in activities connected with the tourist industry, the greater the danger that with a decline in international prosperity a relatively large proportion of the population will be thrown out of employment (Norval 1936, p. 147).

Is sustainable development possible within a capitalist economic system? (Professor Jost Krippendorf in Januarius 1993, p. 30).

TOURISM lies at the crossroads. Never before has tourism been of such importance to the economy. However, with newfound recognition has come a range of pressures on government and industry to ensure that tourism does not adversely affect the physical and social environment. Therefore, this book has argued that tourism must be developed on a sustainable basis which provides for the protection of the resource base and the appropriate long-term growth of the tourism industry.

This final chapter examines a variety of issues which must be addressed if government and industry are to determine in what direction tourism will head over the next decade. In particular, it analyses some of the broader societal concerns that provide the framework within which tourism operates. The most fundamental question that must be addressed is that of the sustainability of tourism development. To avoid the dangers of boom-and-bust style development, the tourism industry needs to be encouraged to grow in such a manner that the tourist product retains its uniqueness and vitality if it is to continue to attract overseas visitors and to retain and encourage domestic tourism.

WHAT KIND OF TOURISM?

> Most ideological debate about tourism starts from the premise that the basic cluster of activities which we call tourism is likely to continue in the foreseeable future. The debate is not so much concerned with tourism versus no tourism as it is with what kind of tourism (Matthews 1978, p. 74).

Tourism should be available to all. It can be a great liberating force that enables individuals to see beyond their own personal worlds, and to appreciate the beliefs, ideas, and perceptions of other people. Tourism has even come to be regarded as a force for peace (Commission of the European Communities 1982). However, as with all forms of development, tourism has its negative aspects. According to Craik (1991b, p. 8):

> . . . governments are embracing tourism as the industry of the future and hoping that the benefits will outweigh the costs. The reality is that, as tourism becomes part of more local, regional and national economic strategies, the range and degree of impacts is increasing . . . Inevitably, changes attributable to—or coinciding with—tourist development are becoming more intense and increasing in scope. Over time, this phenomenon transforms the amenity, culture and lifestyle of destinations.

Negative impacts should not be brushed aside by government and industry, nor be managed by codes of ethics and responsibility which give lip service to community-oriented strategic planning and environmental and social concerns and, in the end, do nothing. We live in an imperfect world, yet that is not a reason to fail to establish a tourism industry that attempts to meet the economic, social, and environmental demands that are placed upon it. As Lew and Hall (1998, p. 203) commented: 'The goal of sustainable tourism development is there, just beyond our reach—and it's continuing inaccessibility provides a world of opportunity for stimulating research, discussion and action'.

This book has put forward the case for the establishment of a tourism industry that has a long-term perspective of development and that tries to ensure its future by not damaging the resources on which it is based. This has been argued because of the necessity to develop a tourism product that will be uniquely Australian, that will enhance both society and the environment, that will maximise employment, and that will lead to a higher quality of life for both host and guest. To ensure that the tourism industry not only survives but also grows, far more strategic planning and coordination is needed within the industry than ever before. Most of all, tourism must be responsive to the needs of destination communities as well as the desires of the tourist.

Crucial to the development of Australian tourism is a realisation that tourism, like any other product, is subject to a life cycle and to economic, social, political, and technological change. As Chapter 2 illustrated, tourism changes in response to broader shifts in society and to changes in technology, particularly in transport and communications. The success of inbound tourism throughout much of the 1980s and 1990s is no guarantee that tourism will continue to grow in the future, as witnessed by the effects of the 1990s Asian financial crisis on visitor numbers from Korea, Indonesia, and Malaysia to Australia, as well as the impact of the terrorist attacks of 11 September 2001. As a former New South Wales Minister for Tourism stated: 'The industry has been through a fantastic growth pattern but it is going to take a lot of work to keep those numbers rising. Those who expect tourism to keep growing naturally are in for a rude shock' (West 1989, p. 1). There is a need for increased sophistication in market segmentation research and target marketing to compete on the world market, as seen in the example of appropriate development of the special interest travel segments identified in Chapters 12 and 13. Moreover new competitors continue to emerge to seek to attract tourists in both the domestic and international markets.

The Australian tourism industry must be educated regarding the benefits of independent research on a broad-range of tourism-related issues. As Jafari (1998, p. 273) noted: 'One cannot help but wonder when tourism research will graduate from the bounds of economics and marketing to amplify the subject in its fullest dimensions'. Unfortunately, the necessary relationships and understandings between the academic community and the private sector are only partially developed. However, awareness of the need for improved education and training in the workforce, as discussed in Chapter 7, will, it is hoped, assist in forging new relationships among the various segments of the tourism industry.

Greater attention paid to the potential of research to contribute to tourism development would assist in identifying future labour force and training requirements. In 1975 the Department of Tourism and Recreation (Cwlth) argued that the 'determination of the industry's manpower requirements and provision of education and training programs to produce executives and competent employees at all levels of operations, is a further area which requires early consideration' (1975, p. 11).

SPACE TOURISM: ANOTHER NEW TOURISM?

In April 2001, millionaire businessman Dennis Tito become the first private citizen to pay for the privilege of travelling in space. Tito's trip to the International Space Station on a Russian Soyuz TM-32 space vehicle was, for years, only hypothetical. Although the USA has certainly put private citizens into space on previous occasions through its space shuttle program, none was required to pay for the opportunity. As such, the Russians not only put the first individual in space in April 1961, but also sent up the first tourist almost forty years later to the day. Supporters of space tourism (for example, <**www.space future.com**>) are now, more than ever, convinced that space tourism could soon become a reality. In fact, the concept of space tourism is not recent. The idea of hotels in space appeared in the late 1960s, and at that time Pan Am began taking registrations of interest from individuals interested in travelling in space. More recently, Virgin Atlantic has registered the name 'Virgin Galactic Airways' with the intention of providing space travel within the next decade.

Although supporters of the development of space tourism products point to substantial rates of visitation to tourist attractions offering space or astronomical educational themes, this cannot be used to forecast demand for space tourism products. Demand for a product is linked with price. More extensive market research is clearly needed, as Crouch (2001) has pointed out, to determine what amount potential tourists would be willing to spend on a trip in space. As many market researchers are quick to point out, interest does not necessarily translate into purchase. At present, it is not clear whether space tourism will benefit from the economies of scale that have come to characterise the mass tourism product on Earth. The enormous cost of propelling a vehicle into space is likely to translate into substantial prices for tourists, and potentially less demand. Investment in space tourism could consequently be adversely affected.

The impacts of space tourism need to be considered, both on Earth and in space. Should space tourism ultimately become commercially successful, what needs to be considered is the cumulative impact of the launch of numerous space vehicles, which will be heavier, require more fuel, and thus emit substantially more emissions at higher altitudes where the atmosphere is much more fragile. Similarly, although much attention has been given to the environmentally destructive behaviour of many types of 'alternative' and 'mass' tourists on Earth, the degree and type of impact in space is, at this point, speculation. However, those responsible for the development of space tourism have an opportunity to learn from mistakes made on Earth with respect to the potentially destructive nature of tourism.

Websites of interest:

Boeing Space Systems: **www.boeing.com/bdsg/space.html**

International Society to Preserve the Beauty of Space: **http://beautyof space.org**

David Timothy Duval

Unfortunately, government and industry did not adequately respond to such an observation until the late 1980s with consequent substantial shortfalls in trained staff (Chapter 7). In addition, numerous tertiary tourism courses were established in the late 1980s and early 1990s without an adequate assessment of industry needs and the employment destinations of graduates (Hall & Weiler 1989).

The lack of industry support for the development of a substantial tourism research base is also a reflection of the uncoordinated nature of tourism in Australia and the difficulty in developing effective national and regional planning strategies. The importance of tourism is rarely perceived and, when it is recognised, the response is often fragmented and parochial (Pigram 1986). Furthermore, government and industry preoccupations with the potential economic benefits of tourism have meant that longer-term structural implications, environmental concerns, and social and cultural questions associated with tourism are frequently not addressed (Hall 1988a, 1993a; Craik 1990, 1991a, 1991b). Although the Commonwealth government (in the national tourism strategy (Department of Tourism 1992)) and various state and territory commissions have noted the importance of sustainability, they have tended to do so in environmental, economic, and business terms, rather than in terms of the social dimensions of tourism. As noted in Chapter 1, and as stressed throughout this book, sustainable tourism development requires the integration of economic, social, and environmental considerations (Figure 14.1). By taking just one of these elements out of the sustainable equation, the prospects for sustainable tourism will be diminished.

Community-based planning and the adoption of principles of sustainable development at all levels of government and the private sector are regarded as key mechanisms for achieving a coordinated approach to tourism development. Appropriate tourism development which seeks to maximise benefits and minimise costs in both the short term and long term requires the involvement of all parties in the development process. However, Australia has been slow to adjust its planning mechanisms to incorporate principles of sustainability and community involvement. Attention has been given to economic and, increasingly, environmental concerns, but little attention has been given to the social dimensions of sustainability. As Heenan (1978, p. 32) argued:

> In their quest for viability and legitimacy, enlightened investors and community leaders must balance local and outside needs and interests . . . if the constructive impact of tourism is to be realized, collaborative approaches between diverse stakeholder groups will be needed. To survive and prosper in the decades ahead, tourism must develop some multiple constituencies.

Furthermore, under a sustainable approach to tourism planning, industry and government must recognise that not all communities will want tourism development, nor does tourism automatically benefit every member of a destination community. A 'boosterism' approach to tourism planning and development (Chapter 11) is totally inappropriate to the demands that will be placed on tourism destinations in the next century. As Coppock (1977, p. 1.1) observed:

> Good for whom? . . . Not only is it inevitable that the residents of an area will gain unequally from tourism (if indeed they gain at all) and probable that the interests of some will actually be harmed, but it may well be that a substantial proportion does not wish to see any development of tourism.

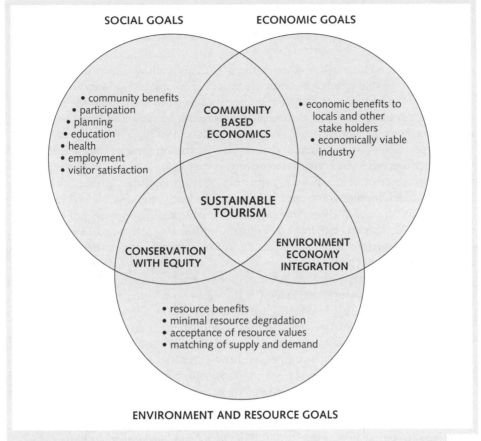

Figure 14.1 Sustainable tourism values and principles model
Source: After Sadler (1990) and Wight (1993)

The new colonial plantation economy?

Tourism by its very nature becomes focused on particular nodes: tourists generally visit one or a few countries on a trip and focus on a small number of locations within those countries. Investment patterns necessarily reflect this.

The nature of the tourist–finance nexus leads to high levels of dependency between source and destination areas. This current form of dependency creates difficulties every bit as tenacious as the commodity–manufacturing links of the early postwar period. Further, the manifestations are quite specific in space, and communities thrive or fail according to the stage and nature of this dependency relationship (Daly & Stimson 1993).

The promotion of tourism should not be regarded as an end in itself or a panacea to the economic ills of an area; rather, there is a need to establish a diversified economic structure which is not solely dependent upon tourism. The demand for tourist facilities can be highly elastic, even capricious, and there are many opportunities for destination substitution. As Lengyel (1975, p. 753) commented:

The travel component in the total cost of a holiday is . . . an important consideration which, like a number of other factors such as economic conditions in the countries where tourists come from and political conditions in the countries which are to receive them, are quite beyond those who cater for visitors.

Similarly, many locations need to realise that they are either unsuitable for tourism development or that greater benefits could accrue to the community from alternative forms of development. 'Most communities . . . can only hope for small-scale economic advantages and in such areas tourism can be no more that one element in a wider development strategy' (Williams & Shaw 1988c, p. 239).

A future challenge for decision makers will be the renewal of tourist resorts and facilities that have been constructed over the past two decades. As the Australian tourism product cycle reaches maturity and facilities age, they present potentially enormous redevelopment problems. If Australian industry does not reinvest in tourism, how will the built and physical environment be maintained and what will the impact on local labour markets be? Indeed, Williams and Shaw (1988a, p. 239) argued, in future 'some tourist resorts will replace steel or textile communities as the major concern of regional economic policies'.

Another major area of concern is the degree to which tourism in Australia becomes controlled by overseas interests, at least at the more profitable top end of the market. Matthews (1978, p. 79) described tourism as potentially a new colonial plantation economy in which 'Metropolitan capitalistic countries try to dominate the foreign tourism market, especially in those areas where their own citizens travel most frequently'. Air services, bus companies, hotels, resort developments, recreational facilities such as golf courses and food and beverage, are all potential markets related directly to tourism which might become owned by foreign interests. According to Best (1968), the elements of a plantation tourism economy are that:
• tourism is structurally a part of an overseas economy;
• it is held together by law and order directed by the local élites; and
• there is little or no way to calculate the flow of values.

Although Matthews' thesis was developed in relation to the influence of American and multinational corporations on Caribbean tourism development, Australia should attempt to learn from the overseas experience of tourism development. The first and last points (above) are already of concern to many Australians, although the Tourism Satellite Account (TSA) is now shedding new light on the economic contribution of tourism. Elements of the second point can be seen in the modifications to local laws when large-scale tourist events (such as the America's Cup, the Commonwealth Games, the Olympic Games, and Expo 88) are held. It can be argued that to describe tourism as a 'plantation economy' is an extreme perspective on foreign investment and ownership. Nevertheless, widespread public concerns over local control of resources and a critical examination of the benefits of tourism development do at least caution us not to accept blindly that all tourism is good for us. As Matthews (1978, p. 80) observed:

> Tourism may add to the numbers of jobs available and it may increase the trappings of modernity with modern buildings and new services, but if it does not contribute to the development of local resources, then it differs little from the traditional agricultural plantation.

Environmental concerns

Much of the criticism of the tourism industry in recent years has been over the potential damage that tourism can bring to the physical environment. However, as

Chapter 12 argued, tourism can also be of great benefit to the environment and assist in the establishment of national parks, the preservation of significant heritage sites, and the enactment of legislation that helps to conserve scarce cultural and natural resources. Nevertheless, the Australian tourism industry must develop more sophisticated design and planning mechanisms that will encourage a symbiotic relationship with the environment. In addition, the tourism industry should be concerned about the potential effects of global environmental issues such as the ozone layer and climatic change on tourism in Australia. Climatic change, for example, might impact on such tourist attractions as the coastline through a predicted rise in sea-levels, and might also severely affect the Australian ski fields.

The establishment of environmental codes of ethics and development guidelines is a valuable first step in the development of a sustainable tourism industry. However, codes and guidelines do not have the same authority as legislation in restricting incompatible tourist activities. Australia has long suffered from a utilitarian attitude to the environment which has meant that an Australian conservation ethic has been extremely slow in developing (Lines 1991; Hall 1992a). It is therefore imperative that government takes the lead in ensuring that tourist development and activities are compatible with existing land uses and do not harm environmentally sensitive areas. Indeed, to ensure the long-term viability of tourism resources in destination regions, it is likely that in some areas tourist activities will be severely curtailed or even prohibited.

The potential damage that uncontrolled tourism development can do to the environment has been recognised since the early 1970s. For example, the Commonwealth Department of Tourism and Recreation (1975, p. 35) reported that 'Australia has, potentially, some of the world's great attractions but we are either not developing them or are developing them inadequately. In some cases ill directed development is slowly destroying them'. The Australian tourism industry must learn from past experience of the dangers of unfettered development, particularly along the much sought-after coastal strip. One of the great attractions of holidaymaking in Australia is the opportunity to vacation in a place where the trees are still standing. It is the responsibility of the tourism industry, among others, to ensure that this remains the case.

The industrialisation of leisure and tourism: image over substance?

> The timber industry processes timber. The metal industry processes metal. The tourist industry processes tourists (Krippendorf 1987, p. 19).

The growth of tourism in the postwar period illustrates the comprehensive reach of industrialisation to encompass leisure activities as well as work. Tourism is marketed today in response to assumptions of what the people of an industrial society want. These assumptions are generally based on people wanting material and service products and the status that society attaches to them. However, as discussed in Chapters 11 and 12, the tourism market is becoming increasingly segmented in a manner that reflects concerns of consumers with the quality of life and the quality of the tourist experience. As Hiller (1975 in Matthews 1978, p. 78) asked: 'the question becomes, is there some way that through the travel experience we might be able to satisfy our non-product oriented needs?'

In contemporary postmodern society the commercialisation of leisure has meant that tourism is often treated purely as a commodity to be sold through the established rules of marketing. 'Postmodernism . . . signals nothing more than a logical extension of the power of the market over the whole range of cultural production' (Harvey 1989, p. 62). Krippendorf (1987, p. 20) has admirably illustrated the issue:

> The techniques are the same as in selling cars, vacuum cleaners, detergent or other consumer goods. But because they deal in desires and dreams, landscapes, people and cultures, travel sellers, one would presume, carry a much greater responsibility. However, they don't seem to be aware of it—or else they simply do not want to realize it. The 'producers' of the item called travel are not charitable institutions but commercial undertakings, a fact that they admit quite openly. Why a journey is undertaken is of no consequence to them—what matters is that it is undertaken. Their primary interest is the short-term growth of their own business and not the long-term development of a well-balanced tourist trade. It would be naive to censure them for it, because they act in accordance with established principles of the free-market economy. But today we must try to see where the limits of this freedom lie.

Image is a crucial part of the tourism industry. Indeed, a good case can be put forward that tourism is the image industry, positioning and fashioning destinations and products to be consumed by the much-needed tourists with their contribution being not just to tourism businesses but also to servicing the national debt. Indeed, maintaining a positive image seems to be the *raison d'être* for many government tourist organisations who are now primarily promotional bodies. As Waitt (1999, p. 1073) noted: 'From a political perspective, the value of hosting the Olympics rests not with the residue of stadia, but with its symbolic qualities of informing the rest of the world of Australia's achievements and progress'. For instance, the Office of National Tourism (ONT) (1997d) stated that 'the lead up to the Sydney 2000 Olympics and the Centenary of Federation in 2001 presents exciting opportunities to promote an image of contemporary Australia as a vibrant, sophisticated, friendly, culturally rich and diverse nation'. Yes, they do, but to what extent does the image match the reality of modern Australian life? And, more particularly, if one was to oppose this image and the holy grail of the Olympics, for example, how would industry react? To return to Waitt (1999, p. 1073), 'this formula of social control, attributed to the Romans, argues that by providing the disadvantaged a taste of bread and a day of entertainment, they will forget their troubles and believe in the authority's benefit . . . "Share the Spirit"'. More often than not the desire to project a positive image, albeit perhaps a well-meaning desire, overwhelms the capacity for informed debate on tourism and its positive and negative dimensions and the possibilities of choosing alternative development strategies.

When people undertake a holiday what are they really trying to achieve? Are they attempting to improve their quality of life, or are they merely following marketing dictates about what they should be doing and where they should be going? Krippendorf (1982, 1986b, 1987) has emphasised that tourism must be about enriching lives and experiences. Tourism should be seen as a meaningful part of a whole lifestyle and not as a separate component: 'to find or regain a state of moderation and human measure, a harmonized, cooperative world, in which each part is a centre, living at the expense of nobody else, in partnership with nature and in solidarity with future generations' (Krippendorf 1987, p. 11).

As part of a change in tourism fashion, consumers and suppliers are becoming increasingly critical of the tourist product. For example, Hewison observed that the postmodernist stage of heritage tourism creates 'a shallow screen that intervenes

TOURISM INSIGHT

TRAVELS IN HYPERREALITY?

In a postmodern society dominated by the mass media and increasingly complex communication technologies, it is becoming more difficult to remove oneself from the unreal, the constructed, and the 'hyperreal'. As virtual reality and computer-generated graphics begin to enter mass communications such as major motion pictures, what is around the corner for the 'hyperreal' experience remains to be seen. One thing is clear; 'hyperreality' and 'hyperreal' tourism are unquestionably the new 'fields of dreams' for tourism. 'Hyperreality' is where the real becomes intertwined with the simulated or unreal, creating a new set of experiences. Schofield (1997, p. 334) described 'hyperreality' as the 'third order of simulacra' which 'represents the stage where simulation models actually constitute the world and the distinction between real and unreal is imperceptible or invalid'. Simulacra are 'representations or copies of objects or events', the 'first order' of which are the 'counterfeit of the original' and the second are the mass reproduction of 'industrial simulacra' which appeared during the Industrial Revolution (Schofield 1996, p. 334, after Baudrillard 1983). In a 'hyperreal' society, advertising and the electronic mass media dominate, pleasure is derived from highly stimulating experiences and consumption is of images or signs and not products. Schofield (1997, p. 332) also suggests that 'the contemporary tourist experience is inseparable from this'.

'Hyperreality' has given rise to the notion of the 'post-tourist' (or 'post mass tourist'), whose experience is through Urry's (1990) 'framed images'—for example, the tour brochure, camera or video lens, car or bus window, television or silver screen (Schofield 1997, p. 334). The 'post-tourist', then, might gain a 'hyperrealistic' experience both through the electronic media (the television or big screen for example) and at the destination—the boundary between the context and '(un)reality' of one overlapping with the other—as in the case of a theme park or Disneyland or even heritage tourist attractions where history is re-enacted for the visitor. However, travelling in hyperreality raises numerous issues about the nature of the tourism experience.

If visitors expect 'hyperreality' (with involvement or triggered imagination) and, instead, experience 'reality' which might be different but not necessarily better or worse, will they be dissatisfied as Harrison (1997) suggests?

Will their images of the destination and experience be more positive or negative if they are not satisfied?

Is the expected experience 'staged authenticity', or is it 'authentic', or is there a need for a further category of 'hyperauthenticity'?

What effect do major motion pictures with negative or antisocial images of a destination (for example, 'Train Spotting') have on 'hyperreality' and expectations? Do negative images lead to a 'hyperreal' experience or do we exclude them from our images? Do we expect to have a negative 'hyperreal' or real experience?

Richard Mitchell

THE FUTURE DIRECTION OF TOURISM

between our present lives, our history. We have no understanding of history in depth, but instead are offered a contemporary creation, more costume drama and re-enactment than critical discourse' (1987, p. 135). Similarly, although the institutionalised commercialisation of spectacles such as Darling Harbour in Sydney, the Sydney Olympics or the Australian Grand Prix are often regarded as a success because they create a positive and high-quality image of place, little consideration is given of the effects of such urban renewal schemes on urban poverty and homelessness, community breakdown, and social dislocation (Hall 1989f, 1989g, 1993a; Harvey 1989; Hall & Hodges 1996).

Krippendorf argued that there is a need for a more critical socially and environmentally responsible approach to tourism marketing: 'Clichés is what people want and clichés they will get. Travel destinations are changeable at will. They can be leafed through just as one leafs through the pages of travel catalogues' (1987, p. 22). Therefore, the process of self-actualisation through discovery, education, enhanced social relationships, and relaxation that travel and holidaymaking can provide might depend less on what happens in the holidays than it does on everyday life. To overcome the depreciation of tourist experiences that commercialisation can bring will require not just a critique of the tourism industry but also an awareness of the overall effect of commodification and urban entrepreneurialism on people's lives. 'People who cannot find self-actualisation at home, won't find it on holiday either. The four or so weeks just won't do the magic trick of producing emancipation. Things that do not work in everyday life cannot suddenly find function on holiday' (Krippendorf 1987, p. 66).

Although the marks of symbolic and economic capital and rampant commercialism are to be found throughout Australian tourism, pockets of resistance have emerged to the internationalisation of the Australian tourism product. In the search for a more authentic tourism experience, segments of the industry and consumers have assisted in the development of new products, such as those discussed in Chapters 12 and 13—products that are small-scale and appropriate to community, producer, and tourist needs. A lowest common denominator approach to the selling of tourism can satisfy much of the market. But surface image and spectacles will not provide a long-term basis for industry development. Eventually, people find the reality behind the image. Tourism South Australia (1991) in determining their tourism plan for early 1990s recognised that the concepts of sustainable growth and net value were fundamental to their mission. For Tourism South Australia, sustainability referred to the present and long-term needs of people and therefore necessitated the incorporation of principles of long-term trading and quality of life in tourism planning and development (see Table 14.1). Unlike many other Australian tourism organisations, both public and private, Tourism South Australia (1991, p. 13) recognised that:

> Tourism activity—like any activity—has benefits and costs. Both long term trading and quality of life benefits will be achieved by observing the additional principle that: major new initiatives demonstrate a net value to the State or region (net value is achieved where economic, environmental and social benefits exceed economic, environmental and social costs.

Unfortunately, such an enlightened attitude is the exception rather than the rule in Australian tourism. Indeed, the changes to the nature of government involvement in tourism in South Australia meant that the state began to follow the 'numbers

TABLE 14.1 Principles of long-term trading and quality of life in tourism development

Long-term trading principles

Integrating tourism strategy with a nation's or region's overall economic strategy

Maintaining a distinctiveness from other destination choices and between regions

Recognising a region's cultural, historical, environmental, and lifestyle attributes

Encouraging development that complements these attributes

Developing specialty products and experiences

Placing an emphasis on encouraging increased visitor expenditure, length of stay, and repeat visitation (providing variety and value for money)

Responding to the market (within the above context meeting the needs of visitors in those market segments targeted as offering the best overall benefits)

Basing product development on the needs of the local travel market (the fact that the locals underpin the relevance and viability of the product means that it will be more appealing to interregional, interstate, and international visitors seeking change and difference)

Quality-of-life principles

Integrating tourism strategy with conservation strategies (recognising the interdependence of tourism development and conservation)

Expressing clearly stated visions for areas and developments and ensuring that they are consistent with the broad vision of the region's tourism industry

Being environmentally responsible

Being socially and culturally responsible

Involving the community in planning and development for tourism (tourism can be successful only to the extent that locals are willing to host visitors—these hosts must be consulted if new development is to achieve a sense of belonging

Source: Tourism South Australia (1992) *Making South Australia Special*, Tourism South Australia, Adelaide, p. 13.

game' of other state and national tourism organisations, and aimed to achieve increases in visitor arrivals, expenditures, and bed nights without due consideration of the net benefit of such growth. Indeed, one of the lessons of the South Australian experience, and possibly of many other states and destinations as well, is that sustainability is all well and good while the numbers of visitors are rising but many politicians and industry and public sector leaders can often find it very difficult to argue that smaller numbers are better, even though the net yield per tourist might actually have substantially increased.

Much of the desire for environmentally and socially responsible tourism will no doubt become highly commercialised. However, the search for alternative forms of tourism by consumers who are disenchanted with the present objectification of the tourist might provide a framework for the development of an Australian style of tourism which incorporates local values and wider economic, social, and environmental concerns. Indeed, the SWOT analysis of Australian tourism that was developed as part of the industry discussion paper for the national tourism plan (ONT 1997f) (see Table 14.2) highlights many of the points raised in this book and in its earlier editions (1991, 1994, and 1998), and highlights many of the issues that need to be addressed.

At least, in part, visitors are likely to increasingly accept the importance of 'responsible tourism' in which the individual is aware of, and tries to minimise, the potentially negative aspects of tourist activities. As part of this process tourists will

Strengths

Unique natural heritage

Climatic advantages

Comparatively safe, friendly and clean environment

Relative proximity to, and within a similar time zone of, emerging Asian markets

Some tourism icons with a worldwide reputation (for example, Opera House, Great Barrier Reef, Uluru National Park)

Strong international marketing program

Growing international interest in Australia's indigenous culture

Good infrastructure base for emerging sectors (for example, conventions, sporting events)

Good transport links to major markets

Multicultural nature of Australia's society

Few barriers to entry for prospective tourism operators

Well-trained staff

Weaknesses

Distance from European and American source markets

Still primarily perceived as a 'mono-product' image (sun, surf, koalas, kangaroos, Great Barrier Reef, Uluru)

Perception of a lack of cultural attractions

Poor image as a shopping destination

Low level of yield in some industry sectors

Low recognition of the economic significance of tourism in government, the industry and community generally

Distance between domestic destinations

Inconsistent service and product quality

Inadequate information base

Seasonality of some source markets and of some domestic destinations

Limited 'tie-in' potential with other destinations (except New Zealand)

Complex and often slow planning approval processes

Different regulations at three levels of government adding to business costs

Limited access to and use of vocational and management training in smaller establishments

Opportunities

Located on rim of fast-growing Asia–Pacific region

Growing awareness of, and interest in, Australia as a tourist destination

2000 Olympics and Centenary of Federation

Opportunity to increase world share of high yield segments (for example, conventions)

Scope for greater diversification of product base (for example, cruise shipping, rural tourism, educational tourism, indigenous tourism)

Greater use of technological innovation

Increased involvement of indigenous people in tourism

Many world-class natural heritage sites still 'undiscovered'

Conversion of outbound travel to domestic travel

Spread the benefits of tourism to regional Australia

Development of health and fitness-related tourism

Development of Australia as a gateway for Antarctic tourism

Threats

Emergence of competing destinations in the Asia–Pacific region

Diminished perception of Australia as a safe and friendly destination

(continues)

TABLE 14.2 *(continued)*

Environmental degradation in areas subject to high utilisation

Poor investor perception of tourism industry

Time lag between demand changes and industry/investor response

Potential deficiencies in transport infrastructure (for example, slow development of Sydney's second airport)

Possible image fragmentation overseas due to competing State campaigns

Negative community attitudes to tourism in some areas

Increasing cost structures

Source: Office of National Tourism (ONT) (1997) *Towards a national tourism plan: a discussion paper.* Reprinted with the permission of the Department of Industry, Tourism and Resources.

need to accept that there will be a set of responsibilities to which they should try to adhere. Jeffreys (1987, p. 10) identified a number of such responsibilities:

- learning about the places they are visiting, the values of those places and how they can protect them;
- respecting the cultural and social values and privacy of residents in the places they are touring;
- abiding by laws, regulations, and guidelines designed to protect the environment;
- leaving places in the same or better environmental condition;
- choosing activities, tour operators, and tourist attractions which are caring of the environment; and
- contributing, financially or otherwise to the ongoing efforts to protect and maintain the environment.

Perhaps considered by some to be naïve or overly optimistic, such a set of responsibilities should not be seen as irrelevant to the marketplace. Consumers are increasingly concerned about the environmental and social justice implications of their purchases, including many of the high-yielding tourists whom Australia would like to attract. For example, the Tourism Industry Association of New Zealand (TIA) reported in March 2002 that research in Britain confirmed that consumers are increasingly looking to support those companies and destinations that focus on improving and maintaining their environmental and social sustainability, with 85% of people feeling tourism should not damage the environment and 64% being willing to pay $30–$75 more to ensure standards were met. This reinforced the results of a similar survey by Tourism Concern which found that respondents were willing to pay 5–10% on top of all holiday costs if this provided benefits to local communities and/or helped resolve environmental issues (TIA 2002). As Chapter 12 discussed, one of the fastest-growing tourism markets is the area of nature-based or ecotourism in which tourists travel in small groups and minimise their impacts on the environment. In this period of widespread environmental and social concern, ecotourism has the potential to be in the vanguard of wider changes in the way that the relationship between tourism and the environment is viewed. However, it must be remembered that tourism is still about having fun.

Table 14.3 presents another set of possible futures for international tourism to the year 2020. Conducted in the form of a PEST analysis (see Figure 2.2) the table highlights a number of potential outcomes and events that relate to tourism. They are educated guesses. However, it needs to be realised that we make the future; it is not preordained. Therefore, in conclusion we turn to how that future will be made.

TABLE 14.3 A PEST analysis of possible future trends in global tourism

Trends	short-term to 2005	mid-term 2006–10	longer-term 2011–20
Political	ongoing emphasis on public–private partnerships in tourism; tourism continues to be given high political prominence because of its perceived economic and employment value; ongoing emphasis on free trade; continued financial support for tourism promotion; normalisation of relations between Cuba and the USA leads to dramatic tourism increase in Cuba	tourists increasingly subject to attack in some developing countries; increased resistance to free trade agreements as government subsidies are withdrawn, especially in Europe as assistance for rural tourism activities is reduced; European Union continues to grow to include Eastern European nations	increased conflict between developing and developed countries over global economic strategies as it becomes apparent to large numbers of the population in developing countries that they will never be able to have Western lifestyles due to population/resource constraints; Israel and Palestine undertake joint tourism promotion funded by the USA and the EU
Economic	continued trade wars among Europe, Japan, and the United States; continued growth of user-pays philosophy in visitor management; continued development of alliances among tourism, leisure, entertainment, sport, and communication corporations	Asian economic growth returns to early 1990 figures mainly due to the growth of the Chinese economy; formal horizontal and vertical integration among tourism, leisure, entertainment, sport, and communication corporations; network strategies continue to be utilised by smaller secondary tourism businesses	substantial free trade in APEC area; Japan replaced as major tourism-generating market in Asia by China and India; economic growth targets come under increased pressure because of natural resource constraints; reduced economic growth and higher fuel costs lead to substantial reductions in the rate of world tourism growth
Social	continued growth in proportion of population over 55 in developed nations; continued growth of consumerism in Asian countries; fast food sector and restaurant sector continues to grow as fewer people prepare their	ageing populations in developed countries increasingly have to rely on own funds rather than state pensions for their retirement; cruising continues to grow as a travel market as population ages; despite ongoing improvements in communications technology, business and conference travel	development of mass 'health tourism' in the developed world as medical technology continues to lengthen lifespan of some; increasing focus on domestic and short-haul travel as cost of long-haul travel dramatically increases due to fuel costs; religious and spiritual-related travel

	own meals at home; increasing recognition by the tourism industry of the needs of single-parent families; education standards continue to increase in the tourism industry	continue to grow because of the desire for personal contact; skills and reskilling required in the workplace	increasingly important due to uncertainty and rapid change
Technology	continued growth of Internet; reorientation of travel agencies as information brokers as increasing numbers of tourists book their own travel	widespread introduction of new generation double-decker jumbo jets further reinforcing development of 'hub and spoke' transport patterns; dramatic growth in train travel in conjunction with air travel as high-speed train systems continue to be integrated with aviation hubs; virtual tourism used to sell visits to destinations	increased cost of aviation fuel as world oil supplies come under increasing pressure leading to dramatic impacts on visitor arrivals; public transport given renewed emphasis as price of fuel increases; air balloons increasingly used for commercial flights; space tourism commercially available; virtual tourism attraction in its own right
Environmental	national parks and reserves continue to be established to promote tourism	water shortages start to curtail some resort developments in the south-west USA; biological diversity continues to diminish; increasing restrictions placed on access to national parks due to impacts of large numbers of visitors (pricing used as a major tool); ongoing loss of biodiversity, rainforest areas particularly hard hit; damage to ozone layer leads to health warnings to international travellers to Australia, New Zealand and southern South America because of the increased danger of skin cancer	several island destinations in the Caribbean, the Indian Ocean, and the Pacific are evacuated due to rising sea-levels; freshwater shortages severely affect tourism development in many parts of the world; ski tourism in traditional alpine resorts in Europe, North America, and Australasia becomes increasingly expensive due to unpredictable snow cover; several significant species such as tigers, rhinoceros, elephants, pandas, chimpanzees, and gorillas all but extinct save for their presence in privately run tourism sanctuaries

Source: adapted from Hall (2000c).

THE FUTURE DIRECTION OF TOURISM

THE POLITICS OF TOURISM

We do not need any more theory, but practical politics. We have a long way to go but we now have easily enough knowledge to put the policies into action. For some years the recommendations, resolutions, propositions and lists of demands from institutions and individuals for a new political orientation have been fundamentally the same. It is just that politics itself will not go along with this. If we really want to change something we will not get anywhere with anaemic theories and recommendations. Scientists are political lightweights. Politicians only adopt the demands of scientists when they correspond to their own plans; if they don't, the demands are quickly described as 'pure theory'. It would be better if we devoted all our energies to education and tried, with all available resources and in all possible ways, to reach those who in the end have political power—the people themselves—firstly those in tourist areas, but also the urban population. It is a question of exposing all our insights, of simplifying them and making them comprehensible. We must encourage action, sometimes even opposition and disobedience, and courage itself. A change of attitude among politicians will only take place under pressure from the public, the electorate (Krippendorf 1982, pp. 146–7).

Source: Krippendorf, J. (1982) 'Towards new tourism policies: the importance of environmental and sociological factors' *Tourism Management* (journal) vol. 3, no. 3, pp. 135–148 with permission of Elsevier Science.

Tourism is inherently political in nature (Hall 1994a, 2000a). 'The struggle for economic rewards continues to dominate the politics of tourism, and politics continues to be an exercise in who gets what' (Matthews 1978, p. 95). Unfortunately, little has been written on the politics of tourism in Australia (Jenkins 2001 being a notable exception). This is perhaps surprising given the significance of tourism to the Australian economy. However, it is probably an indication of the general standing that tourism has within both the academic and the wider community, plus the possibility that many researchers do not want to bite the hands that feed by critically examining tourism policy and the assumptions which underlie them, nor by critically examining the closed set of relationships between industry and government that creates them (Jenkins 2001). Nevertheless, the crucial issues of coordination, strategic planning, adapting to restructuring, globalisation, the creation of social capital, social, economic, and environmental responsibility and sustainability should mean that the politics of tourism can no longer be ignored.

The substantial problems that Australian tourism faces are a reflection of the political nature of the industry. The Australian tourist industry illustrates and magnifies two fundamental difficulties in the structure of tourism. First, there is fragmentation of organisations that participate in the formulation of public policy, leading to a proliferation of goals and control mechanisms that operate at different spatial scales and/or in different sectors of the industry. Second, there is uncertainty over the balance between the roles of the public and private sectors in supplying and regulating different aspects of the tourist product (Ashworth & Bergsma 1987; Hall & Jenkins 1995; Jenkins 2001). However, although structural problems in the Australian tourism industry are significant, more fundamental political issues need to be addressed if sustainable tourism development is to be achieved.

Politics is about control. At the local, regional, and national levels, various interests attempt to affect the determination of policy, policy outcomes, and the position of tourism in the political agenda. With few exceptions, the tourism agenda has been controlled by industry with a small number of corporate bodies and significant individuals having an undue influence over tourism development in this country (Jenkins 2001). However, the domination of one sectoral interest over other interests and community concerns is antithetical to the goal of sustainable development. Sustainability and long-term development require not only an environmentally responsible industry but also the incorporation of broader community and social concerns in the development of tourist opportunities. Sustainability implies greater equity both in input into the decision-making process and in tourism policy outcomes than has been the case. Therefore, the concluding and most important concern for the achievement of a sustainable Australian tourism industry is that of who gets what, where, and how? There can be no more important question.

CHAPTER SUMMARY

This chapter has discussed some of the key issues for the future direction of Australian tourism. Most critical of all issues is the question of what kind of tourism Australia wishes to have. Following on from this it is apparent that the economic, social, and environmental aspects of tourism need more attention than has been the case in Australia. Furthermore, it can be argued that the long-term effects of the commercialisation and industrialisation of tourism and leisure require considerable analysis to improve the quality of the tourist experience for host and guest. The chapter concluded by observing that tourism is inherently political in nature and that tourism has, and will continue to be, an exercise in who gets what. Therefore, if sustainable development is to be a goal of government and the tourist industry, community and social concerns will need to be incorporated into the decision-making process of tourism opportunities.

SUGGESTIONS FOR FURTHER READING

The majority of introductory textbooks on tourism, leisure, and recreation contain a section on the future. Specific recent articles on the future of tourism include Walton et al. (2000) and Hall (2000c). Potential future trends in Australian tourism are presented by the Bureau of Tourism Research and the Tourism Forecasting Council. However, from a broader social perspective it is worth reading Krippendorf (1982, 1986b, 1987) to judge the prospects for a more environmentally and socially oriented form of tourism. Also consult the Commonwealth Government's plans and strategies for tourism so as to examine the future directions which are being mapped out (e.g. DITR 2002h).

THE FUTURE DIRECTION OF TOURISM

Websites worth visiting are:
- Virtual Reality Tours Australia:
  www.vrtours.com.au

- Travel Western Australia:
  www.westaustralia.net

- The city of Leeds in England in virtual reality:
  www.vrleeds.co.uk/the-pages/main-info.html

- Space tourism initiative:
  www.gwu.edu?~spctour

- Armchair travel for virtual travel:
  www.armchair-travel.com

FOR DISCUSSION AND REVIEW

Key concepts

Key concepts discussed in this chapter included:
sustainability, ideology, life cycle, appropriate development, colonial plantation economy, destination substitution, environmental concerns, industrialisation of leisure and tourism, postmodern society, socially and environmentally responsible tourism marketing, responsibilities of the tourist, ecotourism, politics of tourism.

Questions for review and discussion

1 Should tourism in Australia be regarded as the new colonial plantation economy?

2 How can greater environmental and social responsibility be incorporated in tourism marketing?

3 How accurate is the Office of National Tourism's (Table 14.2) SWOT analysis of Australian tourism?

4 How can sustainable and long-term development be achieved within the Australian tourism industry?

5 The last question in the Discussion Paper for the 10 year tourism plan for Australia stated: 'What consultative mechanisms are needed to enable governments to receive ongoing advice, representative of all tourism sectors, on tourism issues?' (DITR 2002h), p. 89). Given that the community is such an important part of sustainable tourism development why aren't they consulted?

REFERENCES

Abel, L. 1994, 'Holidays and health in nineteenth and early twentieth century South Australia', *Journal of the Historical Society of South Australia*, no. 22, pp. 82–97.

Access Economics 1997, *The Economic Significance of Travel & Tourism & Is There a Case for Government Funding for Generic Tourism Marketing*, Tourism Council Australia, Property Council of Australia and Tourism Task Force, Canberra.

The Adelaide Observer, 5 January 1856.

Agardy, M.T. 1993, 'Accommodating ecotourism in multiple-use planning of coastal and marine protected areas', *Ocean and Coastal Management*, vol. 20, no. 3, pp. 219–38.

The Age, 21 December 1861.

— 15 January 1958.

Aiken S.R. 1994, *Imperial Belvederes: The Hill Stations of Malaya*, Oxford University Press, Singapore.

Airey, D. 1983, 'European government approaches to tourism', *Tourism Management*, vol. 4, pp. 234–44.

Aitken, S. & Zonn, L. (eds) 1994a, *Place, Power Situation and Spectacle: A Geography of Film*, Rowman and Littlefield, Baltimore.

— 1994b, 'Re-presenting the place pastiche', pp. 3–25 in *Place, Power Situation and Spectacle: A Geography of Film*, eds S. Aitken & L. Zonn, Rowman and Littlefield, Baltimore.

Alexander, L. 1981, Conservation and exploration: A case study of the Simpson Desert Conservation Park, unpublished Master of Environmental Studies thesis, Centre for Environmental Studies, University of Adelaide, Adelaide.

Alhemoud, A. & Armstrong, E. 1996, 'Image of tourism attractions in Kuwait', *Journal of Travel Research*, vol. 34, no. 4, pp. 76–80.

Ali, S., Blakey, K.A. & Lewis, D.E. 1979, *Development of Tourism in the Illawarra: Economic Effects and Prospects, An independent study undertaken for and supported by the Department of Tourism, New South Wales*, Economic Research Bulletin 11, Department of Economics, University of Wollongong, Wollongong.

Altheide, D.L. 1997, 'Media participation in everyday life', *Leisure Sciences*, vol. 19, pp. 17–29.

Altman, J.C. 1987, *The Economic Impact of Tourism on the Warmun (Turkey Creek) Community*, East Kimberley Working Paper No. 19, Centre for Resource and Environmental Studies, Australian National University, Canberra.

— 1988, *Aborigines, Tourism and Development: The Northern Territory Experience*, North Australia Research Unit, Darwin.

— 1989, 'Tourism dilemmas for Aboriginal Australians', *Annals of Tourism Research*, vol. 16, pp. 456–76.

— 1991, 'Reply to Parsons', *Annals of Tourism Research*, vol. 18, pp. 317–18.

Altman, J. & Finlayson, J. 1993, 'Aborigines, tourism and sustainable development', *Journal of Tourism Studies*, vol. 4, no. 1, pp. 38–50.

Altman, J.C., Ginn, A. & Smith, D.E. 1993, *Existing and Potential Mechanisms for Indigenous Involvement in Coastal Zone Resource Management*, Consultancy report to Coastal Zone Inquiry, Resources Assessment Commission, Resources Assessment Commission, Canberra.

Anderson, J.E. 1984, *Public Policy Making*, 3rd edn, CBS College Publishing, New York.

Anderson, K. & Gale, F. (eds) 1992, *Inventing Places: Studies in Cultural Geography*, Longman Cheshire, South Melbourne.

Anderson, L.F. & Littrell, M.S. 1996, 'Group profiles of women as tourists and purchasers of souvenirs', *Family and Consumer Sciences Research Journal*, vol. 25, no. 1, pp. 28–56.

Andrews, E. 1993, '25 April 1916: first Anzac Day in Australia and Britain', *Journal of the Australian War Memorial*, vol. 23, p. 13.

Andrews, G. 1983, 'Australia's inshore passenger services', *Heritage Australia*, vol. 2, no. 2, pp. 40–3.

Anholt, S. 1998, 'Nation-brands of the twenty-first century', *Journal of Brand Management*, vol. 5, no. 6, pp. 395–404.

Ansett Transport Industries Limited 1993, *56th Annual Report*, Ansett Transport Industries Limited, Melbourne.

Anzachouse 2001, **http://www.anzachouse.com/14DayItinAD.shtml**

Aplin, J. 1999, 'Winery tourism', *WineNZ*, February/March, p. 32.

Archer, B.H. 1977, *Tourism Multipliers: The State of the Art*, Bangor Occasional Papers in Economics No. 11, University of Wales Press, Bangor.

— 1982, 'The value of multipliers and their policy implications', *Tourism Management*, vol. 3, pp. 236–41.

— 1987, 'Demand forecasting and estimation', pp. 77–85 in *Travel, Tourism and Hospitality Research: A Handbook for Managers and Researchers*, eds J.R.B. Ritchie and C.R. Goeldner, John Wiley and Sons, New York.

The Argus, 25 June 1857.

Arnold, A., Fischer, A., Hatch, J. & Paix, B. 1989, 'The Grand Prix—road accidents and the philosophy of hallmark events', pp. 186–94 in *The Planning and Evaluation of Hallmark Events*, eds G.J. Syme, B.J. Shaw, D.M. Fenton & W.S. Mueller, Avebury, Aldershot.

Arnold, R., Davies, S. & Pearce, D. 1989, *Some Economic Implications of Tourism Expansion*, Inquiry into Travel and Tourism, Discussion Paper No. 2, Australian Government Publishing Service, Canberra.

Arnstein, S. 1969, 'A ladder of citizen participation', *Journal of American Institute of Planners*, vol. 35, pp. 216–24.

Ascher, B. 1982, 'Obstacles to international travel and tourism', *Journal of Travel Research*, vol. 22, pp. 2–16.

Ashworth, G.J. 1992, 'Planning for sustainable tourism: a review article', *Town and Planning Review*, vol. 63, no. 3, pp. 325–29.

Ashworth, G.J. & Bergsma, J.R. 1987, 'New policies for tourism: Opportunities or problems?', *Tijdschrift voor Economische en Sociale Geografie*, vol. 78, no. 2, pp. 151–5.

Ashworth, G.J. & Tunbridge, J. 1990, *The Tourist–Historic City*, Belhaven, London.

Asia–Pacific Economic Cooperation (APEC) 2000, *Seoul Declaration on an APEC Tourism Charter: A Ministerial Statement of Purposes and Intent, July 7, 2000*, APEC Secretariat, Singapore.

APEC Tourism Working Group 1995, *Asia–Pacific Economic Cooperation (APEC) Tourism Working Group*, APEC Secretariat/Singapore Trade Development Board, Singapore.

— 1999, *Terms of Reference (Updated 3 December 1999)*, APEC Secretariat/Singapore Trade Development Board, Singapore **http://apec-tourism.org/terms-of-reference/**

— 2000, *Activities by Groups: Tourism (Updated 9 February 2000)*, APEC Secretariat/ Singapore Trade Development Board, Singapore **http://www.apecsec.org.sg/workgroup/tourism_upd.html**

Asia Travel Tips 2002a, 'Qantas reports half-year profit of $153.5 million', *Asia Travel Tips*, 25 February.

— 2002b, *Air New Zealand Interim Report Financial Year 2002*, **http://www.asiatraveltips.com/7March2002AirNewZealand.htm**

Astroff, M.T. & Abbey, J.R. 1995, *Convention Sales and Services*, 4th edn, Waterbury Press, Cranbury.

ATSIC and the ONT 1997, *National Aboriginal and Torres Strait Islander Tourism Industry Strategy*, ATSIC and the ONT, Canberra.

Audretsch, D.B. & Feldman, M.P. 1997, *Innovative Clusters and the Industry Life Cycle*, C.E.P. R. Discussion Papers 1161, Centre for Economic Policy Research, London.

Australia Council 1989a, *The Arts: Some Australian Data*, 3rd edn, Australia Council, Sydney.

— 1989b, *Annual Report 1988–89*, Australia Council, Sydney.

— 1990a, *Museums, Arts Museums and Public Galleries: Report of a Survey, 1988–89*, Research Paper No. 3, Policy & Research, Strategic Development Unit, Australia Council, Redfern.

— 1990b, *International Visitors and Aboriginal Arts*, Research Paper No. 4, Policy and Research, Strategic Development Unit, Australia Council, Redfern.

— 1990c, *Arts Participation by International Visitors*, Research Paper No. 2, Policy and Research, Strategic Development Unit, Australia Council, Redfern.

— 1991, *Arts Participation by International Visitors*, Research Paper No. 5, Policy and Research, Strategic Development Unit, Australia Council, Redfern.

— 1992, *Arts Attendance by International Visitors*, Research Paper No. 8, Policy and Research, Strategic Development Unit, Australia Council, Redfern.

— 1993, *International Visitors and Aboriginal Arts*, Australia Council, Redfern.

— 2000a, *Australians and the Arts*, Australia Council for the Arts & Saatchi and Saatchi, Surry Hills.

— 2000b, *The Arts in Australia—Some Statistics*, Australia Council for the Arts, Surry Hills, **http://www.ozco.gov.au/resources/snapshots/statistics.html**

The Australian, 14 December 1989.

— 3 July 1990.

Australian Bureau of Statistics (ABS) 1986a, *1984 Household Expenditure Survey, Australia: Detailed Expenditure Items*, ABS, Canberra.

— 1986b, *1984 Household Expenditure Survey, Australia: Summary of Results*, ABS, Canberra.

— 2000, Catalogue No. 8142.0—Business Operations and Industry Performance, 1999–2000, ABS, Canberra.

— 2000, Catalogue No. 5204.0—Australian System of National Accounts, 1999–2000, ABS, Canberra.

— 2001, Catalogue No. 5625.0—Private New Capital Expenditure and Expected Expenditure to June 2002, ABS, Canberra.

Australian Capital Territory Tourism Commission 1993, *1992–93 Annual Report*, Chief Minister's Department, Canberra.

Australian Embassy to Turkey 2001, *Anzac Day*, **http://www.embaustralia. org.tr/anzac/anzacdayatgallipoli.htm**

Australian Farm and Country Tourism (AFACT) 1997, *Australian Farm and Country Tourism Inc.*, **http://www.farmwide.com.au/nff/afact/AFACTJUN.pub** (accessed 31/12/97).

Australian Federal Police 1986, *Australian Federal Police Annual Report 1985–86*, Parliamentary Paper No. 416/1986, Australian Government Publishing Service, Canberra.

Australian Government Committee of Inquiry into Tourism 1987a, *Report of the Australian Government Committee of Inquiry into Tourism*, vol. 1, Australian Government Publishing Service, Canberra.

— 1987b, *Report of the Australian Government Committee of Inquiry into Tourism*, vol. 2 (Consultants' Reports), Australian Government Publishing Service, Canberra.

Australian Labor Party 1979, *Australian Labor Party Seminar on Tourism*, Townsville, 22 June.

Australasian Leisure Management 2002, 'Yes minister: Tourism', *Australasian Leisure Management*, no. 31, February/March pp. 38, 40.

Australian National Travel Association 1973, *Policy Considerations Affecting the Promotion and Development of Travel, Tourism and Recreation*, Australian National Travel Association, Canberra.

Australian Tourism Industry Association (ATIA) 1988, *ATIA Careers Report*, ATIA, Canberra, June.

— 1989a, *An Environmental Code of Practice for the Tourism Industry Background, Second Draft*, ATIA, Canberra.

— 1989b, *Environmental Guidelines for Tourist Developments, Second Discussion Draft*, ATIA, Sydney.

— 1990a, *ATIA Now*, ATIA, Canberra, April.

— 1990b, *Tourism Setting the Agenda*, Old Parliament House, Canberra, 3 May 1990 (draft), ATIA, Canberra.

— 1990c, *Development of Farm and Country Holidays in Australia (An assessment of the potential for the accelerated development of farm and country holidays in Australia)*, ATIA, Canberra.

— 1990d, *Code of Environmental Practice*, ATIA, Canberra.

ATIA & Australian Tourist Commission 1994, *1994 National Tourism Seminar Program*, ATIA & Australian Tourist Commission.

Australian Tourism Monitor 1993, 'Battle of Byron Bay', *Australian Tourism Monitor*, vol. 7, no. 3, p. 31.

Australian Tourist Commission (ATC) 1987, *Tourism Update*, March 1987, Market Research Division, Australian Tourist Commission, Melbourne.

— 1993a, *1993 Annual Report*, Australian Tourist Commission, Sydney.

— 1993b, *Tourism Market Potential: Targets 1993–2003*, Australian Tourist Commission, Sydney.

— 1994, *Natural Holiday Guide* (promotional guide), Australian Tourist Commission, Sydney.

— 1995, *Partnership Australia: Information for Australian Tourism Operators*, Australian Tourist Commission, Sydney.

— 2001a, *Brand Australia*. http://www.atc.net.au/brand/campaigns/brand/brand.htm (accessed 6 May 2001).

— 2001b, *Corporate Plan 2001/2002–2005/2006*, http://atc.australia.com/aboutus.asp?art=1032#obs (accessed 9 March 2002).

— 2001c, *Tourism Reaps Rewards of the Games*. http://www.atc.net.au/news/olympic/olympic2.htm (accessed 6 May 2001).

— 2002a, *Preliminary Arrivals Year ending December 2001*, ATC Online, http://www.atc.net.au/research.asp?art=1747

Australian Travel Industry Association 1982, *Australia Tourism in the 80s. A National Tourism Strategy*, Australian Travel Industry Association, September.

Australian Wine Foundation 1996, *Strategy 2025: The Australian Wine Industry*, Winemakers' Federation of Australia, Adelaide.

Back, L. 1995, '"The bronzed Aussie" (collection notes: art)', *Journal of the Australian War Memorial*, vol. 27, p. 26.

Backas, J. 1983, *The Hotel Tax and the Arts*, National Endowment for the Arts, Washington D.C.

Bailie, J.G. 1980, 'Recent international travel trends in Canada', *Canadian Geographer*, vol. 24, no. 1, pp. 13–21.

Baldassar, L. 1995, 'Migration as transnational interaction: Italy re-visited', *Con Vivio*, vol. 1, no. 2, pp. 114–26.

— 1997, 'Home and away: migration, the return visit and "transnational identity"', pp. 69–94 in *Communal Plural: Home, Displacement, Belonging*, eds I. Ang & M. Symonds, RCIS, Sydney.

— 1998, 'The return visit as pilgrimage: secular redemption and cultural renewal in the migration process', pp. 127–56 in *The Australian Immigrant in the 20th Century: Searching Neglected Sources*, eds E. Richards & J. Templeton, Division of Historical Studies, Research School of the Social Sciences, Australian National University, Canberra.

Baloglu, S. & McCleary, K. 1999, 'A model of destination image formation', *Annals of Tourism Research*, vol. 26, no. 1, pp. 868–97.

Baloglu, S. & Mangaloglu, M. 2001, 'Tourism destination images of Turkey, Egypt, Greece, and Italy as perceived by US-based tour operators and travel agents', *Tourism Management*, vol. 22, pp. 1–9.

Barbier, E.B. 1987, 'The concept of sustainable economic development', *Environmental Conservation*, vol. 14, no. 2, pp. 101–10.

Bardwell, S. 1979, 'National parks for all—a New South Wales interlude', *Parkwatch*, no. 118, pp. 16–20.

Baretje, R. 1982, 'Tourism's external account and the balance of payments', *Annals of Tourism Research*, vol. 9, pp. 57–67.

Barge, P. 1988, 'Employment opportunities and needs in tourism', pp. 7–13 in *Education for Tourism*, ed. D. McSwan, Seminar Series: No. 2, Centre for Studies in Travel and Tourism, James Cook University, Townsville.

Barich, H. & Kotler, P. 1991, 'A framework for marketing image management', *Sloan Management Review*, vol. 32, no. 2, pp. 94–104.

Barker, M.L. 1982, 'Traditional landscape and mass tourism in the Alps', *Geographical Review*, vol. 72, pp. 395–415.

Barnes, C. 1988, 'Bureaux—the marketing professionals', pp. 245–50 in *The Tourism and Hospitality Industry*, ed. J. Blackwell, International Magazine Services, Sydney.

Barnes, J. 1966, 'economic characteristics of the demand for wildlife viewing tourism in Botswana', *Development Southern Africa*, vol. 13, pp. 377–97.

Barr, T. 1989, 'Looking back: Lindeman Island before World War II', *At the Centre*, vol. 1, no. 4, p. 8.

— 1990a, 'From quirky islanders to entrepreneurial magnates: The transition of the Whitsundays', *Journal of Tourism Studies*, vol. 1, no. 2, pp. 26–32.

— 1990b, *No Swank Here? The Development of the Whitsundays as Tourist Destination to the Early 1970s*, Studies in North Queensland History, No. 15, Department of History and Politics in conjunction with Department of Tourism, James Cook University of North Queensland, Townsville.

Barstow, R. 1986, 'Non-consumptive utilization of whales', *Ambio*, vol. 15, no. 3, pp. 155–63.

Bates, J. 1989, *Planning for Tourism and Major Tourism Developments: Issues Affecting Local Government*, Tourism Information Paper No. 1, NSW Tourism Commission, Sydney.

Baud-Bovy, M. & Lawson, F. 1977, *Tourism and Recreational Development*, The Architectural Press, London.

Baudrillard, J. 1983, *Simulations*, Semiotext, New York.

Baum, E.L. & Moore, E.J. 1966, 'Some economic opportunities and limitations of outdoor recreation enterprises', pp. 52–64 in *Guidelines to the Planning, Developing, and Managing of Rural Recreation Enterprises*, eds G.W. Cornwall and C.J. Holcomb, Bulletin 301, Cooperative Extension Service, Virginia Polytechnic Institute, Blacksburg.

Bauman, Z. 1998, *Globalization: The Human Consequences*, Polity Press, London.

Beasley, I. 1992, *Marine Mammal Tourism: Educational Implications and Legislation*, University of Otago Wildlife Management Report Number 78, University of Otago, Dunedin.

Beattie, N. 1987, 'Observation on cyclical events and seasonal population changes in small towns', in *Conference on People and Physical Environment Research*, Centre for Urban Research, University of Western Australia, Nedlands.

Beaumont, C. 1980, *Local History in Victoria: An Annotated Bibliography and Victorian Directories 1836–1974*, La Trobe University, Bundoora.

Beaumont, N. 1997, 'Perceived crowding as an evaluative standard for determining social carrying capacity in tourist recreation areas: The case of Green Island, north Queensland', pp. 168–80 in *Tourism Planning and Policy in Australia and New Zealand: Cases, Issues and Practice*, eds C.M. Hall, J. Jenkins & G. Kearsley, Irwin Publishers, Sydney.

Beeton, S. 1997, 'Hoof prints on the mind . . . an exploration of attitudinal relationships between bushwalkers and commercial horseback tours', pp. 1–14 in *Trails, Tourism and Regional Development*, eds J. Higham & G. Kearsley, Centre for Tourism, University of Otago, Dunedin.

Belch, G.E. & Belch, M.A. 1998, *Advertising and Promotion: An Integrated Marketing Communications Perspective: International Edition*, 4th edn McGraw Hill, Boston.

Bell, D. 1974, *The Coming of the Post-Industrial Society—a Venture in Social Forecasting*, Heinemann, London.

Bell, M. 2001, 'Understanding circulation in Australia', *Journal of Population Research*, vol. 18, no. 1.

Bell, M. & Ward, G. 2000, 'Comparing temporary mobility with permanent migration', *Tourism Geographies*, vol. 2, no. 1, pp. 87–107.

Bennett, T. & Frow, J. 1991, *Art Galleries: Who Goes?: A Study of Visitors to Three Australian Art Galleries, with International Comparisons*, Australia Council, Redfern.

Benns, M. 2002, 'Shrewd Branson plots his next move', *The Sunday Age*, 3 March.

Bentick, B.L. 1986, 'The role of the Grand Prix in promoting South Australian entrepreneurship; exports and the terms of trade', pp. 169–85 in *The Adelaide Grand Prix: The Impact of a Special Event*, eds J.P. A. Burns, J.H. Hatch & T.J. Mules, The Centre for South Australian Economic Studies, Adelaide.

Bergman, E.M., Maier, G. & Tödtling, F. 1991, *Regions Reconsidered: Economic Networks, Innovation and Local Development in Industrialized Countries*, Mansell, London.

Berle, P.A. 1990, 'Two faces of Ecotourism', *Audobon*, vol. 92, no. 2, p. 6.

Berry, C. 1986, 'The York–Avon Valley: A cultural landscape', *Heritage Australia*, vol. 5, no. 1, pp. 19–22.

Best, L. 1968, 'A model of pure plantation economy', *Social and Economic Studies*, vol. 17, no. 3, pp. 283–326.

Bianchini, F. & Parkinson, M. (eds) 1993, *Cultural Policy and Urban Regeneration: The West European Experience*, Manchester University Press, Manchester.

Bigsby, H., Trought, M., Lambie, R. & Bicknell, K. 1998, *An Economic Analysis of the Wine Industry in Marlborough*, A Report to The Marlborough Winemakers, The Marlborough Grape Growers Association, The Wine Institute of New Zealand and The Marlborough District Council, Agribusiness and Economics Research Unit, Canterbury.

Bingham, M. 1994, 'Seeing the forest beyond the trees', *The Saturday Mercury*, 12 March, p. 35.

Bird, E. 1988, 'The future of the beaches', pp. 163–77 in *The Australian Experience Essays in Australian Land Settlement and Resource Management*, ed. R.L. Heathcote, Longman Cheshire, Melbourne.

Bishop, R. & Robinson, L.S. 1998, *Night Market: Sexual Cultures and the Thai Economic Miracle*, Routledge, London.

Blackwell, J. (ed.) 1988, *The Tourism & Hospitality Industry*, Australian–International Magazine Services, Chatswood.

Blackwell, J. & Stear, L. (eds) 1989, *Case Histories of Tourism & Hospitality*, Australian–International Magazine Services, Chatswood.

Blainey, G. 1983, *The Tyranny of Distance: How Distance Shaped Australia's History*, Rev. edn, Sun Books, South Melbourne.

— 1985, 'Foreword', pp. v–xi in Froude, J.A. 1985 (1886) *Oceana: or the tempestuous voyage of J.A. Froude 1885*, ed. G. Blainey, Methuen Haynes, North Ryde.

Blamey, R. 1995, *The Nature of Ecotourism*, Occasional Paper No. 21, Bureau of Tourism Research, Canberra.

Blandy, R. 2000, *Industry Clusters Program: A Review*, South Australian Business Vision 2010, Government of South Australia, Adelaide.

Blane, J.M. & Jackson, R. 1994, 'Impact of ecotourism boats on the St. Lawrence beluga whales', *Environmental Conservation*, vol. 21, no. 3, pp. 267–69.

Blanton, D. 1981, 'Tourism training in developing countries: The social and cultural dimension', *Annals of Tourism Research*, vol. 8, pp. 116–33.

Blowers, A. 1997, 'Environmental planning for sustainable development: the international context', pp. 34–53 in *Town Planning Into the 21st Century*, eds A. Blowers & B. Evans, Routledge, London.

Blunn, A.S. 1988, 'The roles of government: A government point of view', pp. 43–52 in *The Roles of Government in the Development of Tourism as an Economic Resource*, ed. D. McSwan, Seminar Series No. 1, Centre for Studies in Travel and Tourism, James Cook University, Townsville.

Blunn, T. 1988, 'Goals and objectives for Australian tourism: A government view', pp. 9–16 in *Frontiers in Australian Tourism: The Search for New Perspectives in Policy Development and Research*, eds B. Faulkner & M. Fagence, Bureau of Tourism Research, Canberra.

Bodewes, T. 1981, 'Development of advanced tourism studies in Holland', *Annals of Tourism Research*, vol. 8, pp. 35–51.

Boele, N. 1996, *Tourism Switched: Sustainable Energy Technologies for the Australian Tourism Industry*, A guide presented by Tourism Council Australia and the World Travel & Tourism Environment Research Centre in association with the ONT, ONT, Canberra.

Boland, M. 1988, 'Perspectives on tourism development—a union view', pp. 57–72 in *Frontiers in Australian Tourism: The Search for New Perspectives in Policy Development and Research*, eds B. Faulkner & M. Fagence, Bureau of Tourism Research, Canberra.

Boniface, P. 1995, *Managing Quality Cultural Tourism*, Routledge, London and New York.

Boo, E. 1990, *Ecotourism: The Potentials and Pitfalls*, 2 Vols., World Wildlife Fund, Washington D.C.

Boorstin, D.J. 1973, *The Image: a Guide to Pseudo-Events in America*, Atheneum, New York.

Booth, D. 2001, *Australian Beach Cultures: The History of Sun, Sand, and Surf*, Sport in the Global Society, vol. 28, Frank Cass & Co.

Bosselman, F. 1978, *In the Wake of the The Tourist: Managing Special Places in Eight Countries*, The Conservation Foundation, Washington D.C.

Botterill, T.D. 1991, 'A new social movement: Tourism concern, the first two years', *Leisure Studies*, vol. 10, no. 3, pp. 203–17.

Bouquet, M. & Winter, M. 1987, 'Introduction: Tourism politics and practice', pp. 1–8 in *Who from their Labours Rest? Conflict and Practice in Rural Tourism*, eds M. Bouquet & M. Winter, Avebury, Aldershot.

Boyd, S. & Timothy, D. 2002, *Heritage Tourism*, Prentice-Hall, Harlow.

Boyden, S.V. & Harris, J.A. 1978, 'Contribution of the wilderness to health and wellbeing', pp. 34–47 in *Australia's Wilderness: Conservation Progress and Plans, Proceedings of the First National Wilderness Conference*, ed. G. Mosley, Australian Conservation Foundation, Hawthorn.

Boyer, P. 1984, 'Tourism and the Port Arthur historic site', pp. 134–8 in *Parks, Recreation and Tourism, Papers of the 57th National Conference of the Royal Australian Institute of Parks and Recreation*, ed. M. Wells, Royal Australian Institute of Parks and Recreation, Belconnen.

Bradley, R. 1982, *The Small Wineries of Australia: A Guide to the Best Winemakers*, McMillan, South Melbourne.

Bramham, P., Henry, I., Mommaas, H. & van der Poel, H. (eds) 1989a, *Leisure and Urban Processes: Critical Studies of Leisure Policy in Western European Cities*, Routledge, London and New York.

— 1989b, 'Introduction', pp. 1–13 in *Leisure and Urban Processes: Critical Studies of Leisure Policy in Western European Cities*, eds P. Bramham, I. Henry, H. Mommaas & H. van der Poel. Routledge, London and New York.

Bramwell, B. 1994, 'Rural tourism and sustainable rural tourism', *Journal of Sustainable Tourism*, vol. 2, pp. 1–6.

Bramwell, B. & Lane, B. 1993, 'Sustainable tourism: An evolving global approach', *Journal of Sustainable Tourism*, vol. 1, no. 1, pp. 6–16.

Bramwell, B. & Rawding, L. 1996, 'Tourism marketing images of industrial cities', *Annals of Tourism Research*, vol. 23, pp. 201–21.

British Tourism Authority 1999.

Britton, R. 1979a, 'Some notes on the geography of tourism', *The Canadian Geographer*, vol. 23, no. 3, pp. 6–16.

— 1979b, 'The image of the third world in tourism marketing', *Annals of Tourism Research*, vol. 6, no. 3, pp. 318–29.

Britton, S.G. 1991, 'Tourism, capital and place: Towards a critical geography of tourism', *Environment and Planning D: Society and Space*, vol. 9, no. 4, pp. 451–78.

Brokensha, P. & Guldberg, H. 1992, *Cultural Tourism in Australia*, A Study Commissioned by the Department of the Arts, Sport, the Environment and Territories, Australian Government Publishing Service, Canberra.

Brokensha, P. & Tonks, A. 1985, *An Interim Report on the Economic Impact of the 1984 Adelaide Festival of Arts*, a report prepared for the South Australian Department for the Arts by the Graduate Studies Centre, Elton Mayo School of Management, South Australian Institute of Technology, Adelaide.

Brook, A.J. 1957, 'Water blooms', *New Biologist*, vol. 23, pp. 86–101.

Brookfield, H. 1988, 'Sustainable development and the environment', *Journal of Development Studies*, vol. 25, no. 1, pp. 126–35.

— 1991, 'Environmental sustainability with development: What prospects for a research agenda?', pp. 42–66 in *Sustainable Development*, ed. O. Stokke, Frank Cass, London.

Brown, C. 2000, 'One voice, one message, our best bet', *Tourism Queensland News*, no. 3, **http://www.qttc.com.au/tqnews/issue03/3comment/c04.htm**

Brown, G. 1985, 'The tourism industry in Australia', pp. 8–11 in *Tourist Development in Australia*, eds J. Dean & B. Judd, Royal Australian Institute of Architects Education Division, Canberra.

Brown, G., Chalip, L., Jago, L. & Mules, T. 2002, 'The Sydney Olympics and brand Australia', pp. 163–86 in *Destination Branding: Creating the Unique Destination*

Proposition, eds N. Morgan, A. Pritchard & N. Pride, Butterworth-Heinemann, Oxford.

Brown, G. & Giles, R. 1994, 'Coping with tourism: An examination of resident responses to the social impact of tourism', pp. 755–63 in *Tourism: The State of the Art*, eds T. Seaton, C.L. Jenkins, R.C. Wood, P.U.C. Dieke, M.M. Bennett, L.R. MacLellan & R. Smith, John Wiley, Chichester.

Bryant, B.E. & Morrison, A.J. 1980, 'Travel market segmentation and the implementation of market strategies', *Journal of Travel Research*, Winter, pp. 2–8.

Buck, R. 1977, 'The ubiquitous tourist brochure: Explorations in its intended and unintended use', *Annals of Tourism Research*, vol. 4, pp. 192–207.

— 1978, 'Towards a synthesis in tourism theory', *Annals of Tourism Research*, vol. 5, pp. 100–11.

Buckley, R. & Pannell, J. 1990, 'Environmental impacts of tourism and recreation in national parks and conservation reserves', *Journal of Tourism Studies*, vol. 1, no. 1, pp. 24–32.

Budowski, G. 1976, 'Tourism and conservation: Conflict, coexistence or symbiosis', *Environmental Conservation*, vol. 3, no. 1, pp. 27–31.

Buhalis, D. 2000, 'Marketing the competitive destination of the future', *Tourism Management*, vol. 21, pp. 97–116.

Bull, A. 1988, 'An evaluation of direct foreign investment in the Australian tourism industry', pp. 103–13 in *Frontiers in Australian Tourism: The Search for New Perspectives in Policy Development and Research*, eds B. Faulkner & M. Fagence, Bureau of Tourism Research, Canberra.

— 1990, 'Australian tourism: Effects of foreign investment', *Tourism Management*, December, pp. 325–31.

— 1991, *The Economics of Travel and Tourism*, Longman Cheshire, South Melbourne.

— 1994, *The Economics of Travel and Tourism*, 2nd edn Longman Australia, South Melbourne.

Bureau of East Asian and Pacific Affairs 1996, *Fact Sheet: Asia–Pacific Economic Cooperation*, Bureau of Public Affairs, Washington.

Bureau of Industry Economics 1984, *Tourist Expenditure in Australia*, Research Report 16, Australian Government Publishing Service, Canberra.

Bureau of Tourism Research (BTR) 1988, *BTR Tourism Update*, vol. 1, no. 1.

— 1989a, *Hospitality Industry Labour Force Survey 1988 Preliminary Results*, BTR, Canberra.

— 1989b, *Tourism Update*, vol. 2, no. 2.

— 1989c, *Australian Tourism Data Card*, BTR, Canberra.

— 1989d, *International Visitor Survey 1988*, BTR, Canberra.

— 1990a, *Australian Tourism Trends 1990*, BTR, Canberra.

— 1990b, *Australian Tourism Outlook Forum 1990*, BTR/Australian Tourism Research Institute, Canberra.

— 1990c, *Australian Tourism Data Card*, BTR, Canberra.

— 1991a, *Australian Tourism Data Card 1991*, BTR, Canberra.

— 1991b, *Domestic Tourism Monitor Annual Summary 1989/90*, BTR, Canberra.

— 1992a, *Australian Tourism Data Card, Autumn 1992*, BTR, Canberra.

— 1992b, *Australian Tourism Data Card, Spring 1992*, BTR, Canberra.

— 1992c, *Annual Report 1991–92*, BTR, Canberra.

— 1993a, *Australian Tourism Data Card, Autumn 1993*, BTR, Canberra.

— 1993b, *Domestic Tourism Expenditure 1992; Survey Results Summary*, BTR, Canberra.

— 1994, *Domestic Tourism Monitor Annual Summary 1992/93*, BTR, Canberra.

— 1996, *International Visitor Survey*, BTR, Canberra.

— 1997, *Australian Tourism Data Card*, BTR, Canberra.

— 1998a, *The Australian MICE Sector*, BTR, Canberra.

— 1998b, *Australian Tourism Data Card*, BTR, Canberra.

— 2000, *Tourism Trends in New South Wales: New South Wales State Profile: Year End December 1999*, produced for Tourism New South Wales, TNSW, Sydney.

Bureau of Transport Economics 1985, *Reference Paper: Australian Long Distance Coach Industry*, Bureau of Transport Economics, Canberra.

Burkart, A.J. & Medlik, S. 1974, *Tourism Past, Present and Future*, Heinemann, London.

— 1981, *Tourism Past, Present and Future*, 2nd edn, Heinemann, London.

Burke, A. 1981, Images of popular leisure in the Blue Mountains, unpublished honours thesis, Department of Fine Arts, University of Sydney.

— 1988, 'Awesome cliffs, fairy dells and lovers silhouetted in the sunset—a recreation history of the Blue Mountains', pp. 99–117 in *The Blue Mountains Grand Adventure for All*, 2nd edn, ed. P. Stanbury, The Macleay Museum/Second Back Row Press, Leura.

Burke, B. 1985, 'The Tourism industry in Australia', pp. 18–20 in *Tourist Developments in Australia*, eds J. Dean & B. Judd, Royal Australian Institute of Architects Education Division, Canberra.

Burns, J.P.A., Hatch, J.H. & Mules, F.J. (eds) 1986, *The Adelaide Grand Prix: The Impact of a Special Event*, The Centre for South Australian Economic Studies, Adelaide.

Burns, J.P.A. & Mules, T.L. 1986, 'A framework for the analysis of major special events', pp. 5–38 in *The Adelaide Grand Prix: The Impact of a Special Event*, eds J.P.A. Burns, J.H. Hatch & T.L. Mules, The Centre for South Australian Economic Studies, Adelaide.

Burns, M. 1989, *The Environmental Impacts of Travel and Tourism*, Discussion Paper No. 1, Industries Assistance Commission Inquiry into Travel and Tourism, AGPS, Canberra.

Burrell, J. 1986, 'Beaches as a tourism resource', pp. 375–82 in *Proceedings, Australian Environmental Council Coastal Management Conference*, Australian Environmental Council.

Burtenshaw, D., Bateman, M. & Ashworth, G.J. 1991, *The European City*, David Fulton Publishers, London.

Busby, G. & Klug, J. 2001, 'Movie-induced tourism: The challenge of measurement and other issues', *Journal of Vacation Marketing*, vol. 7, no. 4, pp. 316–32.

Bussey, K. 1987, 'Leisure + Shopping = ?', *Leisure Management*, vol. 7, no. 9, pp. 22–4.

Butler, R.W. 1980, 'The concept of a tourist area cycle of evolution, implications for management of resources', *Canadian Geographer*, vol. 24, no. 1, pp. 5–12.

— 1990, 'Alternative tourism: Pious hope or trojan horse', *Journal of Travel Research*, vol. 28, no. 3, pp. 40–5.

— 1990b, 'The influence of the media in shaping international tourist patterns', *Tourism Recreation Research*, vol. 15, no. 2, pp. 46–53.

— 1991, 'Tourism, environment, and sustainable development', *Environmental Conservation*, vol. 18, no. 3, pp. 201–9.

— 1992, 'Alternative tourism: The thin edge of the wedge', pp. 31–46 in *Tourism Alternatives: Potentials and Problems in the Development of Tourism*, eds V.L. Smith & W.R. Eadington, University of Pennsylvania Press, Philadelphia.

— 1998, 'Sustainable tourism—looking backwards in order to progress?', in *Sustainable Tourism Development: A Geographical Perspective*, eds C.M. Hall & A. Lew, Addison Wesley Longman, London.

Butler, R.W., Hall, C.M. & Jenkins, J. (eds) 1998, *Tourism and Recreation in Rural Areas*, John Wiley, Chichester.

Butler, R.W. & Wall, G. 1985, 'Introduction: Themes in research on the evolution of tourism', *Annals of Tourism Research*, vol. 12, pp. 287–96.

Byrne, J.H. 1977, *Study of the Economic Effects of Tourism on the Gosford–Wyong Sub-Region*, P. A. Consulting Services, Planning and Environment Commission New South Wales, Sydney.

Bywater, M. 1993, 'Market segments in the youth and student travel market', *EIU Travel and Tourism Analyst*, vol. 3, pp. 35–50.

Calais, S.S. & Kirkpatrick, J.B. 1986, 'The impact of trampling on the natural eco-systems of the Cradle Mt.–Lake St. Claire National Park', *Australian Geographer*, vol. 17, pp. 6–15.

Calantone, R.J., di Benedito, A. & Bojanic, D. 1987, 'A comprehensive review of tourism forecasting literature', *Journal of Travel Research*, Fall, pp. 28–39.

Calantone, R., di Benedetto, C., Hakam A. & Bojanic, D.C. 1989, 'Multiple multi-national tourism positioning using correspondence analysis', *Journal of Travel Research*, vol. 28, no. 2, pp. 25–32.

Cambourne, B., Hall, C.M., Johnson, G., Macionis, N., Mitchell, R. & Sharples, L. 2000, 'The future of wine tourism', pp. 297–320 in *Wine Tourism Around the World: Development, Management and Markets*, eds C.M. Hall, E. Sharples, B. Cambourne & N. Macionis, Butterworth-Heinemann, Oxford.

Cameron, C. 1989, 'Cultural tourism and urban revitalization', *Tourism Recreation Research*, vol. 14, no. 1, pp. 23–32.

Cameron, F. 1991, 'Foreigners aim at upper end of tourism market', *The Australian*, 24 April, p. 29.

Cameron McNamara 1986, *Cairns Region Joint Research Study*, Cairns City and Mulgrave Shire Councils, Cairns.

Campbell, G. 2001a, 'Absolutely, positively Middle Earth', *Listener*, 3rd February, pp. 33–4.

— 2001b, 'Planet Middle Earth', *Listener*, 15th December, pp. 16–24.

Canadian Council on Rural Development 1975, *Economic Significance of Tourism and Outdoor Recreation for Rural Development*, Working paper, Canadian Council on Rural Development, Ottawa.

Canberra Development Board 1988, *The Canberra Tourism Strategy*, Canberra Development Board, Canberra.

Canberra Tourism 1997, *Target Tourism*, Winter.

Canberra Tourism & Events Corporation (CTEC) 2000a, *Marketing Strategy 1999–2000*, CTEC, Canberra.

— 2000b, Canberra Tourism & Events Corporation *Annual Report 1999–2000*, CTEC, Canberra.

Canberra Tourism & Events Corporation & Tourism Industry Council (CTEC & TIC) 2001, *ACT Tourism Masterplan*, CTEC & TIC, Canberra.

Canberra Tourism Development Bureau 1989, *1989/90 Marketing Strategy*, Canberra Tourism Development Bureau, Canberra.

Capello, R. & Gillespie, A. 1994, 'Communication infrastructure and possible future spatial scenarios', pp. 167–91 in *Moving Frontiers: Economic Restructuring, Regional Development and Emerging Networks*, eds J.R. Cuadrado-Roura, P. Nijkamp & P. Salva, Avebury, Aldershot.

Carlin, M. 1987, *An Analysis of the Farm Holidays in the Central Tablelands*, unpublished thesis, Hawkesbury Agricultural College, Richmond.

Carmody, G. 1994, *Economic Recovery and Its Implications for Australia's Tourism Industry: Will a Strong Australian Dollar Undermine the Benefits of Recovery for Tourism Industry Yield*, paper presented at the 1994 ATIA/ATC National Tourism Seminar Program: 'Sharing in Tourism Recovery', Access Economics, Canberra.

Carroll, P. 1991, 'The federal government and tourism, 1945–1990', pp. 68–81 in *Tourism in Australia*, eds P. Carroll, K. Donohue, M. McGovern & J. McMillen, Harcourt Brace Jovanovich, Marrickville.

Carter, J., Jolliffe, L. & Baum, T. 2001, 'Heritage tourism and World Heritage sites: the case of Newfoundland', *Tourism Recreation Research*, vol. 26, no. 1, pp. 113–16.

Castells, M. 1996, 'The net and the self', *Critique of Anthropology*, vol. 16, no. 1, pp. 9–38.

Cater, E.A. 1993, 'Ecotourism in the third world: Problems for sustainable development', *Tourism Management*, vol. 14, no. 2, pp. 85–90.

Cater, E.A. & Lowman, G. (eds) 1994, *Ecotourism: A Sustainable Option?* Wiley, Chichester.

Cathie, I. 1984, *Victorian Tourism Strategy: Statement by the Hon. Ian Cathie, M.P. Minister Responsible for Tourism*, Economic Strategy for Victoria Statement No. 4, August.

Cato, N. 1982, *The Noosa Story: A Study in Unplanned Development*, 2nd edn, The Jacaranda Press, Milton.

Cato, N. 1989, *The Noosa Story: A Study in Unplanned Development*, 3rd edn, The Jacaranda Press, Milton.

Ceballos-Lacuarain, H. 1996, *Tourism, Ecotourism and Protected Areas: The State of Nature Based Tourism Around the World and Guidelines for its Development*, IUCN, Gland.

Centre for Applied and Business Research 1987, *America's Cup Defence Series, 1986/87, Impact on the Community*, Centre for Applied and Business Research, University of Western Australia, Nedlands.

Centre for Regional Economic Analysis 1988, *The Contribution of Tourism to the Tasmanian Economy in 1986: A Report Prepared for the Department of Tourism*, Centre for Regional Economic Analysis, University of Tasmania, Hobart.

Centre for Studies in Travel and Tourism 1988, *The Queensland Recreational Scuba Diving Industry Study Report 1988*, Centre for Studies in Travel and Tourism, James Cook University of North Queensland, Townsville.

Chadee, D. & Cutler, J. 1996, 'Insights into international travel by students', *Journal of Travel Research*, vol. 22, no. 1, pp. 75–80.

Chadwick, R. 1994, 'Concepts, definitions and measures used in travel and tourism research', in *Travel, Tourism and Hospitality Research: A Handbook for Managers and Researchers*, eds J.R.B. Ritchie & C. Goeldner, 2nd edn, Wiley, New York.

Chaffee, E.E. 1985, 'Three models of strategy', *Academy of Management Review*, vol. 10, no. 1, pp. 89–96.

Chape, S. & Chalmers, C. 1984, 'Tourism and the role of coastal management planning in Western Australia', *Australian Ranger Bulletin*, vol. 2, no. 4, pp. 5–6.

Chapman, R.J.K. & Wood, M. 1984, *Australian Local Government: The Federal Dimension*, George Allen and Unwin, Sydney.

Chen, J. & Hsu, C. 2000, 'Measurement of Korean tourists' perceived images of overseas destinations', *Journal of Travel Research*, vol. 38, pp. 411–16.

Chenoweth, N. 1991, 'Casino boom: You can bet on it', *Australian Business*, 29 May, pp. 14–18.

Chesney-Lind, M. & Lind, I.Y. 1986, 'Visitors as victims: Crimes against tourists in Hawaii', *Annals of Tourism Research*, vol. 13, pp. 167–91.

Chester, G. & Roberts, G. 1992, 'The Wet Tropics of Queensland World Heritage Area: The planning challenge', pp. 177–94 in *Heritage Management: Parks, Heritage and Tourism, Conference Proceedings*, Royal Australian Institute of Parks and Recreation, Hobart.

Chief Minister's Department 1993, *Canberra Visitors Survey: A Summary of the Main Findings for 1992/93*, Strategic Research Section, Chief Minister's Department, Canberra.

Chon, K.S. 1991, 'Tourism destination image modification process: Marketing implications', *Tourism Management*, March, pp. 68–72.

Christaller, W. 1963, 'Some considerations of tourism location in Europe: The peripheral regions—underdeveloped countries—recreation areas', *Regional Science Association Papers*, vol. 12, pp. 95–105.

Chu Te, G. 1993, 'Airline deregulation and domestic tourism', *Papers of the Australasian Transport Reseach Forum*, vol. 18, no. 1, pp. 259–75.

Cicin-Sain, B. & Knecht, R.W. 1998, *Integrated Coastal and Ocean Management: Concepts and Experiences*, Island Press, Washington, D.C.

Claringbold, R., Deakin, J. & Foster, P. 1984, *Data Review of Reef Related Tourism 1946–1980*, Great Barrier Reef Marine Park Authority, Townsville.

Clark, L. 1988, 'Planning for tourism in far north Queensland: a local government response', pp. 77–88 in *Frontiers in Australian Tourism: The Search for New Perspectives in Policy Development and Research*, eds B. Faulkner & M. Fagance, Bureau of Tourism Research, Canberra.

Clarke, J. 1990, 'Pessimism versus populism: The problematic politics of popular culture', pp. 28–44 in *For Fun and Profit: The Transformation of Leisure into Consumption*, ed. R. Butsch, Temple University Press, Philadelphia.

Clary, D. 1984, 'The impact of social change on a leisure region, 1960–1982: A study of Nord Pays D'Auge', pp. 51–6 in *Leisure, Tourism and Social Change*, eds J. Long & R. Hecock, Centre for Leisure Research, Dunfermline College of Physical Education, Dunfermline.

Clawson, M. & Knetsch, J. 1966, *The Economics of Outdoor Recreation*, John Hopkins University Press, Baltimore.

Clement, H.G. 1961, *The Future of Tourism in the Pacific and Far East*, United States Government Printing Office, Washington D.C.

— 1967, 'The impact of tourist expenditures', *Development Digest*, vol. 5, pp. 70–81.

Clout, H.D. 1972, *Rural Geography: An Introductory Survey*. Pergammon Press, Oxford.

Cohen, E. 1974, 'Who is a tourist? A conceptual clarification', *Sociological Review*, vol. 22, no. 4, pp. 527–55.

— 1978, 'The impact of tourism on the physical environment', *Annals of Tourism Research*, vol. 5, pp. 215–37.

— 1979, 'Rethinking the sociology of tourism', *Annals of Tourism Research*, vol. 6, pp. 18–35.

— 1982, 'Thai girls and farang men: the edge of ambiguity', *Annals of Tourism Research*, vol. 9, pp. 403–28.

Cole, D.N. 1978, 'Estimating the susceptibility of wildland vegetation to trailside alteration', *Journal of Applied Ecology*, vol. 15, pp. 281–6.

Coltman, M.M. 1989, *Tourism Marketing*, Van Nostrand Reinhold, New York.

Commission of the European Communities 1982, *A Community Policy on Tourism*, Commission of the European Communities, Brussels.

Committee of Inquiry into the National Estate 1975, *Report of the Committee of Inquiry into the National Estate*, Parliamentary Paper No. 195, 1974, The Government Printer of Australia, Canberra.

Commonwealth of Australia 1991, *The Royal Commission into Aboriginal Deaths in Custody*, 5 vols., Australian Government Publishing Service, Canberra.

Commonwealth of Australia and Government of New Zealand 1991, *Costs and Benefits of a Single Australasian Aviation Market*, prepared by a Joint Australia–New Zealand study team consisting of the Bureau of Transport and Communications Economics and Jarden Morgan NZ Limited (now CS First Boston New Zealand Limited), Australian Government Publishing Service, Canberra.

Constantine, R. 1999, *Effects of Tourism on Marine Mammals in New Zealand*, Science for Conservation 106, Department of Conservation, Wellington.

Cook, C. 1985, 'Tourist boats erode banks of Gordon River', *Australian Ranger Bulletin*, vol. 3, no. 3, pp. 26–7.

Cooke, K. 1982, 'Guidelines for socially appropriate tourism development in British Columbia', *Journal of Travel Research*, vol. 21, no. 1, pp. 22–8.

Cooks' Excursionist and Tourist Advertiser, 24 June, 1872, p. 9.

Cooper, C.P. 1990, 'Resorts in decline: The management response', *Tourism Management*, vol. 11, pp. 63–7.

— 1992, 'The life cycle concept and tourism', pp. 145–60 in *Choice and Demand in Tourism*, eds P. Johnson & B. Thomas, Mansell, London.

— 1994, 'Product lifecycle', pp. 145–60 in *Tourism Marketing and Management Handbook*, eds S.F. Witt & L. Moutinho, Prentice Hall, Englewood Cliffs.

Cooper, C.P. & Jackson, S. 1989, 'Destination life cycle: the Island of Man case study', *Annals of Tourism Research*, vol. 16, pp. 377–98.

Cooper, D.E. 1993, 'Human sentiment and the future of wildlife', *Environmental Values*, vol. 2, no. 4, pp. 335–46.

Cooper, M.J. 2002, 'Flexible labour markets, ethnicity and tourism-related migration in Australia and New Zealand', in *Tourism and Migration: New Relationships Between Consumption and Production*, eds. C.M. Hall & A.M. Williams, Kluwer, Dortrecht.

Cooper, M.J. & Pigram, J.J. 1984, 'Tourism and the Australian economy', *Tourism Management*, vol. 5, no. 1, pp. 2–12.

Coppock, J.T. 1977, 'Tourism as a tool for regional development', pp. 1.1–1.15 in *Tourism: A Tool for Regional Development*, ed. B.S. Duffield, Tourism and Recreation Research Unit, University of Edinburgh, Edinburgh.

Corbin, A. 1995, *The Lure of the Sea*, Penguin, London.

Corner, J. & Harvey, S. (eds) 1991, *Enterprise and Heritage: Crosscurrents of National Culture*, Routledge, London and New York.

Corporation of the City of Melbourne 1989, *Tourism Development Plan*, Part 1, Corporation of the City of Melbourne, Melbourne.

Coshall, J. 2000, 'Measurement of tourists' images: the repertory grid approach', *Journal of Travel Research*, vol. 39, pp. 85–9.

Cossons, N. 1989, 'Heritage tourism—trends and tribulations', *Tourism Management*, vol. 10, no. 3, pp. 192–4.

Cotterill, D. 1996, 'Developing a sustainable tourism business', in *Proceedings of the 1995 Ecotourism Association of Australia Conference*, eds H. Richins, A. Crabbe & J. Richardson, Ecotourism Association of Australia.

Council of Nature Conservation Ministers (CONCOM) Working Group for the Management of National Parks 1986, *Guidelines for Reservation and Management of Wilderness Areas in Australia*, A Report by the CONCOM Working Group on Management of National Parks, Council of Nature Conservation Ministers, Canberra.

Country Victoria Tourism Council 1997, *Local Government and Tourism: The Partnerships*, Country Victoria Tourism Council & Tourism Victoria, Melbourne.

Courtney, B. 1995, 'Venue lack costs $ million', *Dominion*, 21 May, p. 9.

Coventry, N. 1990, NZ/Australia tourism members press for one-entry concept', *Asia Travel Trade*, vol. 22, October, pp. 6–8.

Cowell, D.W. 1984, *The Marketing of Services*, Heinemann, Oxford.

Cowie, I. 1985, 'Housing policy options in relation to the America's Cup', *Urban Policy and Research*, vol. 3, pp. 40–1.

Cox, P. 1985, 'The architecture & non-architecture of tourism developments', pp. 46–51 in *Tourist Developments in Australia*, eds J. Dean & B. Judd, Royal Australian Institute of Architects Education Division, Canberra.

Craig-Smith, S. & French, C. 1994, *Learning to Live with Tourism*, Longman Australia, South Melbourne.

Craik, J. 1987, 'A crown of thorns in paradise: Tourism on Queensland's Great Barrier Reef', pp. 135–58 in *Who From Their Labours Rest? Conflict and Practice in Rural Tourism*, eds M. Bouquet & M. Winter, Avebury, Aldershot.

— 1988a, 'The social impacts of tourism', pp. 17–31 in *Frontiers in Australian Tourism: The Search for New Perspectives in Policy Development and Research*, Canberra, eds B. Faulkner & M. Fagence, Bureau of Tourism Research.

— 1988b, Showing the world: The politics of Expo 88, paper presented at the Australasian Political Studies Association Conference, University of New England, Armidale, August.

— 1989, 'The Expo experience: The politics of expositions', *Australian–Canadian Studies*, vol. 7, nos.1–2, pp. 95–112.

— 1990, 'A classic case of clientelism: The Industries Assistance Commission Inquiry into Travel and Tourism', *Culture and Policy*, vol. 2, no. 1, pp. 29–45.

— 1991a, *Resorting to Tourism: Cultural Policies for Tourist Development in Australia*, Allen & Unwin, St. Leonards.

— 1991b, *Government Promotion of Tourism: The Role of the Queensland Tourist and Travel Corporation*, The Centre for Australian Public Sector Management, Griffith University, Brisbane.

Crick, M. 1989, 'Representations of international tourism in the social sciences: Sun, sex, sights, savings, and servility', *Annual Review of Anthropology*, vol. 18, pp. 307–44.

Crockett, S.R. & Wood, L.J. 1999, 'Brand Western Australia: a totally integrated approach to destination branding', *Journal of Vacation Marketing*, vol. 5, no. 3, pp. 276–89.

— 2002, 'Brand Western Australia: "Holidays of an entirely different nature"', pp. 124–47 in *Destination Branding: Creating the Unique Destination Proposition*, eds N. Morgan, A. Pritchard & N. Pride, Butterworth-Heinemann, Oxford.

Crompton, J.L. 1979a, 'Motivations for pleasure vacation', *Annals of Tourism Research*, vol. 6, pp. 408–24.

— 1979b, 'An assessment of the image of Mexico as a vacation destination and the influence of geographical location upon that image', *Journal of Travel Research*, vol. 17, no. 4, pp. 18–23.

Crompton, J.L. & Richardson, S.L. 1986, 'The tourism connection where public and private leisure services merge', *Parks and Recreation*, October, pp. 38–44, 67.

Cronin, L. 1990, 'Sustainable development and tourism', in Environment, Tourism and Development: An Agenda for action? A Workshop to Consider Strategies for Sustainable Tourism Development, 4–10 March 1990, Valletta, Malta, Centre for Environmental Management and Planning, Old Aberdeen.

Crossette, B. 1999, *The Great Hill Stations of Asia*, Basic Books, New York.

Crouch, D. 1999a, 'Introduction: encounters in leisure/tourism', pp. 1–16 in *Leisure/Tourism Geographies: Practices and Geographical Knowledge*, ed. D. Crouch, Routledge, London.

— (ed.) 1999b, *Leisure/Tourism Geographies: Practices and Geographical Knowledge*, Routledge, London.

Crouch, G.I. 1993, 'Currency exchange rates and the demand for international tourism', *Journal of Tourism Studies*, vol. 4, no. 2, pp. 45–53.

— 2001, Researching the space tourism market. Paper presented at the XX Annual Conference of the Travel and Tourism Research Association, June 2001, Ft. Meyers, Florida.

Crouch, G.I., Schultz, L. & Valerio, P. 1992, 'Marketing international tourism to Australia: A regression analysis', *Tourism Management*, vol. 13, no. 2, pp. 196–208.

Crowley, F. 1973a, *Modern Australia in Documents 1901–1939*, vol. 1, Wren Publishing, Melbourne.

— 1973b, *Modern Australia in Documents 1939–1970*, vol. 2, Wren Publishing, Melbourne.

— 1980a, *Colonial Australia 1841–1874*, vol. 1, Thomas Nelson Australia, West Melbourne.

— 1980b, *Colonial Australia 1875–1900*, vol. 2, Thomas Nelson Australia, West Melbourne.

Croy, W.G. 2001, 'The ideal spot: the appraisive component of destination image', in *2001: Geography, a Spatial Odyssey*, Otago Branch of the New Zealand Geographical Society, Dunedin.

Cubit, S. 1990, 'Horse riding in national parks: Some critical issues', *Australian Parks and Recreation*, vol. 26, no. 4, pp. 39–40.

Curr, E. 1824, *An Account of the Colony of Van Diemen's Land principally designed for the use of emigrants*, George Cowie, London; facsimile, 1967, Platypus Productions, Hobart.

D'Amore, L. 1983, 'Guidelines to planning harmony with the host community', pp. 135–59 in *Tourism in Canada: Selected Issues and Options*, ed. P.E. Murphy, Western Geographical Series 21, University of Victoria, Victoria.

Da Costa, G. 1988, *Car Tourism and Bushwalking in East Gippsland Victoria's Wilderness Corner*, Australian Conservation Foundation, Hawthorn.

Daly, M.T. & Stimson, R.J. 1993, Dependency in the Modern Global Economy: Australia and the Changing Face of Asian Finance, paper presented at the Institute of Australian Geographer's Conference, Monash University, Clayton, September.

Damette, F. 1980, 'The regional framework of monopoly exploitation: New problems and trends', in *Regions in Crisis*, eds J. Carney, R. Hudson & J.R. Lewis, Croom Helm, London.

Dann, G.M.S. 1976, 'The holiday was simply fantastic', *Tourist Review*, vol. 31, no. 3, pp. 19–23.

— 1977, 'Anomie, ego–enhancement and tourism', *Annals of Tourism Research*, vol. 4, pp. 184–94.

— 1981, 'Tourism motivation: An appraisal', *Annals of Tourism Research*, vol. 8, pp. 187–219.

Dasmann, R.F. 1985, 'Achieving the sustainable use of species and ecosystems', *Landscape Planning*, vol. 12, pp. 211–19.

Dasmann, R.F., Milton, J.P. & Freeman, P.H. 1973, *Ecological Principles of Economic Development*, John Wiley and Sons, London.

David, A. & Wheelwright, T. 1989, *The Third Wave: Australia and Asian Capitalism*, Left Book Club Co-operative, Sutherland.

Davidson, J. 1996, 'The gallop towards the sea', *Eureka Street*, vol. 6, no. 1, pp. 34–7.

Davidson, R. & Maitland, R. 1997, *Tourism Destinations*, Hodder and Stroughton, London.

Davies, E. 1987, 'Shaping tourism trends: the commercial perspective', *Tourism Management*, vol. 8, no. 2, pp. 102–4.

Davis, D. 1993, 'SCUBA diving: Conflicts in marine protected areas', *Leisure Options: Australian Journal of Leisure and Recreation*, vol. 3, no. 4, pp. 30–6.

Davis, D., Banks, S., Birtles, A., Valentine, P. & Cuthill, M. 1997, 'Whale sharks in Ningaloo Marine Park: Managing tourism in an Australian protected area', *Tourism Management*, vol. 18, no. 5, pp. 259–71.

Davis, D. & Weiler, B. 1992, 'Kakadu National Park—conflicts in a World Heritage Area', *Tourism Management*, vol. 13, no. 3, pp. 313–20.

Davis, G., Wanna, J., Warhurst, J. & Weller, P. 1993, *Public Policy in Australia*, 2nd edn, Allen & Unwin, St Leonards.

Dawkins, J.S. 1988, 'Opening address', pp. 3–6 in *Education for Tourism*, ed. D. McSwan, Seminar Series No. 2, Centre for Studies in Travel and Tourism, James Cook University, Townsville.

de Kadt, E. (ed.) 1979, *Tourism: Passport to Development?*, Oxford University Press, Oxford.

— 1990, 'Making the alternative sustainable: Lessons from development for tourism', in *Environment, Tourism and Development: An Agenda for action? A Workshop to*

Consider Strategies for Sustainable Tourism Development, 4–10 March 1990, Valletta, Malta, Centre for Environmental Management and Planning, Old Aberdeen.

Dean, J. & Judd, B. 1985, 'Introduction', p. 5 in *Tourist Developments in Australia*, eds J. Dean & B. Judd, Royal Australian Institute of Architects Education Division, Canberra.

Delaney, C. 1990, 'The Hajj: sacred and secular', *American Ethnologist*, vol. 17, pp. 513–30.

Delaney-Smith, P. 1987, 'The tour operator—new and maturing business', pp. 94–106 in *The Travel and Tourism Industry: Strategies For The Future*, ed. A. Hodgson, Pergamon Press, Oxford.

Delforce, R.J., Sinden, J.A. & Young, M.D. 1986, *An Economic Analysis of Relationships between Pastoralism and Tourism in the Flinders Ranges of South Australia*, Project Report No. 1, CSIRO Division of Wildlife and Rangelands Research, Melbourne.

Department for the Arts 1989, *Annual Report 1988–89*, South Australian Department for the Arts, Adelaide.

Department of the Arts, Sport, Entertainment, Tourism and Territories (DASETT) 1988a, *Directions for Tourism—A Discussion Paper*, DASETT, Canberra.

— 1988b, *Tourism Shopping in Australia*, *Report of the Committee of Inquiry*, Australian Government Publishing Service, Canberra.

— 1988c, *The Tourism Training Challenge*, DASETT, Canberra.

— 1988d, *The Economic Impact of Sport and Recreation—Household Expenditure*, Technical Paper No. 1, DASETT, Australian Government Publishing Service, Canberra.

— 1989a, *Tourism Infrastructure Developments, September Quarter 1989*, DASETT, Canberra.

— 1989b, *Tourism Facts Sheet*, August 1989, DASETT, Canberra.

— 1990, *Tourism Shopping in the Nineties: Report of the Tourism Shopping Implementation Committee*, DASETT, Canberra.

Department of Communication and the Arts 1996, *Cultural Tourism in Australia*, prepared by the Bureau of Tourism Research, Department of Communication and the Arts, Canberra.

Department of Communications, Information Technology and the Arts (DOCITA) 1999, *Australia's E-commerce Report Card*, DOCITA, Canberra.

Department of Conservation and the Environment 1992a, *Ecotourism Victoria Australia*, Department of Conservation and the Environment, Melbourne.

— 1992b, *Ecotourism a Natural Strength for Victoria—Australia*, Department of Conservation and the Environment, Melbourne.

Department of Employment, Education and Training (DEET) 1988, *Training for the Hospitality Sector of the Tourism Industry*, DEET, Canberra.

— 1989, *Report on the National Hospitality Training Conference*, DEET, Canberra.

— 1997b, *Review of Business Programs, Going For Growth—Business Programs for Investment, Innovation and Export (The Mortimer Report)*, DIST, Canberra.

Department of Industry, Science and Resources (DISR) 2000a, *Industry Science Resources: Sport & Tourism, Strong Outlook for Inbound Tourism: 1999–2001*, DISR, Canberra. **http://www.sport.gov.au/forecasts/inbound/** (accessed 4 April 2001).

— 2000b, *Industry Science Resources: Sport & Tourism. 2000, Steady Rise in Outbound*

Travel: 1999–2010, DISR, Canberra, **http://www.sport.gov.au/Forecasts/outbound/index.html** (accessed 24 May 2001).

— 2000c, *Industry Science Resources: Sport & Tourism. 2000. Positive Long-Term Outlook For Domestic Tourism: 1999–2010*, DISR, Canberra. **http://www.sport.gov.au/Forecasts/domestic/index.html** (accessed 24 May 2001).

— 2000d, *Australia's Tourism Satellite Account*, DISR, Canberra, July.

Department of Industry, Science and Tourism (DIST) 1997a, *Annual Report 1996–97*, Department of Industry, Science and Tourism, Canberra (also available at **http://www.dist.gov.au/pubs/reports/annual97/index.html**).

Department of Industry, Tourism and Resources (DITR) 2002a, *Tourism*, DITR, Canberra. **http://www.industry.gov.au/content/root.cfm?objectid=1C66D24D-C9B8-4439-B3F3BA20F6C65C87** (accessed 8 March 2002).

— 2002b, *Tourism Strategy*, DITR, Canberra, **http://www.industry.gov.au/content/controlfiles/display_details.cfm?objectid=6CAA3E62-D2DF-4340-9 F4AA9CC6563504C** (accessed 8 March 2002).

— 2002c, *Impact*, February 2002.

— 2002d, Tourism Forecasting Council: Tourism Accommodation Development Survey: State Analysis, DITR, Canberra, **http://www.industry.gov.au/content/controlfiles/display_details.cfm?objectid=370D3075-ED49-496C-867E5454342A7F76** (accessed 10 March 2002).

— 2002e, Tourism Forecasting Council: Tourism Accommodation Development Survey, DITR, Canberra, **http://www.industry.gov.au/content/controlfiles/display_details.cfm?ObjectID=CA6E07E1-5571-44C9-86BC804C 681243E1** (accessed 10 March 2002).

— 2002f, *Research Report Number 4: Tourism Workforce and Training*, DITR, Canberra.

— 2002g, *Research Report Number 1: The Australian Tourism Satellite Account*, DITR, Canberra.

— 2002h, *Ten Year Plan for Tourism, A Discussion Paper*, DITR, Canberra.

— 2002i, *Research Report Number 2: Tourism Productivity and Profitability*, DITR, Canberra.

— 2002j, *Research Report Number 3: Tourism Investment*, DITR, Canberra.

Department of Sport, Recreation and Tourism (DSRT) 1985, *Tourism Training in Australia*, Report of the Tourism Training Review Group, DSRT, Canberra.

— 1986, *Department of Sport, Recreation and Tourism Annual Report 1985–86*, Parliamentary Paper No. 413/1986, Australian Government Publishing Service, Canberra.

Department of Tourism (DOT) (Cwlth) 1992, *Tourism Australia's Passport to Growth A National Tourism Strategy*, Commonwealth Department of Tourism, Canberra.

— 1993a, *Annual Report 1992–93*, Commonwealth Department of Tourism, Canberra.

— 1993b, *Tourism Australia's Passport to Growth A National Tourism Strategy: Implementation Progress Report No. 1*, Commonwealth Department of Tourism, Canberra.

— 1993c, *Rural Tourism, Tourism Discussion Paper No. 1*, Commonwealth Department of Tourism, Canberra.

— 1994a, *National Ecotourism Strategy*, Commonwealth Department of Tourism, Canberra.

— 1994b, *National Rural Tourism Strategy*, Commonwealth Department of Tourism, Canberra.

— 1995a, *The Yield from Inbound Tourism*, Occasional Paper No. 3, Commonwealth Department of Tourism, Canberra.

— 1995b, *How Tourism Labour Markets Work*, Research Paper No. 1, Commonwealth Department of Tourism, Canberra.

Department of Tourism (Tasmania) 1987, *Department of Tourism Report for the Year 1986–87*, Government Printer, Hobart.

Department of Tourism and Recreation (Cwlth) 1975, *Development of Tourism In Australia*, Australian Government Publishing Service, Canberra.

Department of Tourism and Recreation Cities Commission 1975, *Holiday and Leisure Patterns and Attitudes to Growth Centres*, PA Management Consultants, Department of Tourism and Recreation Cities Commission, Canberra.

Department of Tourism, Sport and Recreation 1992, *Annual Report for 1991–92*, Department of Tourism, Sport and Recreation, Hobart.

Department of the Treasury 1993, *Foreign Investment Review Board Report 1991/92*, Australian Government Publishing Service, Canberra.

Department of Veterans Affairs 2001, Visit Gallipoli, http://www.anzacsite.gov.au/

Dernoi, L.A. 1983, 'Farm tourism in Europe', *Tourism Management*, vol. 4, pp. 155–66.

Derrett, R. 2001, 'Special interest tourism: starting with the individual', pp. 1–24 in *Special Interest Tourism*, eds N. Douglas, N. Douglas & R. Derrett, Wiley, Brisbane.

Desmond, J.C. 1999, *Staging Tourism: Bodies on Display From Waikiki to Sea World*, University of Chicago Press, Chicago.

Deutsch, K. 1970, *Politics and Government: How People Decide Their Fate*, Houghton Mifflin, Boston.

Dickman, S. 1989, *Tourism: An Introductory Text*, Edward Arnold, Caulfield East.

Dilley, R.S. 1986, 'Tourist brochures and tourist images', *The Canadian Geographer*, vol. 30, no. 1, pp. 59–65.

Dillon, M.C. 1987, *Aborigines and Tourism in North Australia: Some Suggested Research Approaches*, East Kimberley Working Paper No. 14, Centre for Resource and Environmental Studies, Australian National University, Canberra.

Ding, P. & Pigram, J. 1995, 'Environmental audits: an emerging concept for sustainable tourism development', *Journal of Tourism Studies*, vol. 2, pp. 2–10.

Dodd, T. 1995, 'Opportunities and pitfalls of tourism in a developing wine industry', *International Journal of Wine Marketing*, vol. 7, pp. 5–16.

Donovan, P. 1988, 'Protecting the geese that lay the golden eggs', pp. 189–97 in *Frontiers of Australian Tourism. The Search for New Perspectives in Policy Development and Research*, eds B. Faulkner & M. Fagence, Bureau of Tourism Research, Canberra.

Douglas, N. & Douglas, N. 2000, 'Tourism in South and South-east Asia: historical dimensions', pp. 29–44 in *Tourism in South and South East Asia: Issues and Cases*, eds C.M. Hall & S.J. Page, Butterworth Heinemann, Oxford.

Douglas, N., Douglas, N., & Derrett, R. (eds) 2001, *Special Interest Tourism*, Wiley, Brisbane.

Douglas Shire's Wilderness Action Group 1984, *The Trials of Tribulation*, The Douglas Shire's Wilderness Action Group, Port Douglas.

Dovey, K. 1989, 'Old scabs/new scars: The hallmark event and the everyday environment', pp. 73–80 in *The Planning and Evaluation of Hallmark Events*, eds G.J. Syme, B.J. Shaw, D.M. Fenton, & W.S. Mueller, Avebury, Aldershot.

Dowling, R.K. 1991, The Ecoethics of Tourism: Guidelines for Developers, Operators and Tourists, paper presented at the International Ecotourism Symposium, University of Queensland, Brisbane, September.

— 1993a, 'Tourism planning, people and the environment in Western Australia', *Journal of Travel Research*, vol. 31, no. 4, pp. 52–8.

— 1993b, 'Tourist and resident perceptions of the environment–tourist relationship in the Gascoyne region, Western Australia', *Geojournal*, vol. 29, no. 3, pp. 243–51.

— 1997, 'Plans for the development of regional ecotourism: Theory and practice', pp. 110–26 in *Tourism Planning and Policy in Australia and New Zealand: Cases, Issues and Practice*, eds C.M. Hall, J. Jenkins & G. Kearsley, Irwin Publishers, Sydney.

Down Under Travel Agency 2001, http://www.downundergallipoli.com/14dayitinad.shtml

Doxey, G.V. 1975, 'A causation theory of visitor–resident irritants: Methodology and research inferences', pp. 195–8 in *Proceedings of the Travel Research Association 6th Annual Conference*, Travel Research Association, San Diego.

Drakeford, A.S. 1949, Minister for Aviation, House of Representatives *Hansard*, 11 June, vol. 197, pp. 1926–8.

Dredge, D. & Moore, S. 1992, 'A methodology for the integration of tourism in town planning', *Journal of Tourism Studies*, vol. 3, no. 1, pp. 8–21.

Driml, S. & Common, M. 1995, 'Economic and financial benefits of tourism in major protected areas', *Australian Journal of Environmental Management*, vol. 2, no. 1, pp. 19–29.

Drost, A. 1996, 'Developing sustainable tourism for World Heritage sites', *Annals of Tourism Research*, vol. 23, pp. 479–92.

Dubecki, L. 2002, 'Ferrari fever keeps numbers up', *The Age*, 4 March.

Duffield, B.S. & Long, J. 1981, 'Tourism in the highlands and islands of Scotland: Rewards and conflicts', *Annals of Tourism Research*, vol. 8, pp. 403–31.

Duffus, D. 1996, 'The recreational use of grey whales in the southern Clayquot Sound, Canada', *Applied Geography*, vol. 16, no. 3, pp. 179–90.

Duffus, D. & Dearden, P. 1990, Non-consumptive wildlife-oriented recreation: a conceptual framework', *Biological Conservation*, vol. 53, pp. 213–31.

— 1993, 'Recreational use, valuation and management of Killer Whales (*orcinus orca*) on Canada's Pacific coast', *Environmental Conservation*, vol. 20, no. 2, pp. 149–56.

Durst, P. B. & Ingram, C.D. 1988, 'Nature-oriented tourism promotion by developing countries', *Tourism Management*, vol. 9, no. 1, pp. 39–43.

Dutton, G. 1985, *Sun, Sea, Surf and Sand—the Myth of the Beach*, Oxford University Press, Melbourne.

Dutton, I.M., Derret, R., Luckie, K., Boyd, W.E. & Know, S. 1994, *Images From the Edge—Landscape and Lifestyle Choices for the Northern Rivers Region of NSW, Report to Australia Council*, Australian Heritage Commission and Australian Conservation Foundation, Southern Cross University, Lismore.

Dutton, I. & Hall, C.M. 1989, 'Making tourism sustainable: The policy/practice conundrum', *Proceedings of the Environment Institute of Australia Second National Conference*, Melbourne, 9–11 October.

Dwyer L., Burnley I., Forsyth P. & Murphy P. 1993, *Tourism-Immigration Inter-relationships*, Bureau of Immigration and Population Research, AGPS, Canberra.

Dwyer, L., Bushell, R. & Knowd, I. 1997, 'A theme-driven approach to sustainable tourism development: Tourism action plan for greater Western Sydney', pp. 227–40 in *Tourism Planning and Policy in Australia and New Zealand: Cases, Issues and Practice*, eds C.M. Hall, J. Jenkins & G. Kearsley, Irwin Publishers, Sydney.

Dwyer, L., Findlay, C. & Forsyth, P. 1990, *Foreign Investment in Australian Tourism*, Occasional Paper No. 6, Bureau of Tourism Research, Canberra.

— 1996, 'Economic impacts of cruise tourism in Australia', *Journal of Tourism Studies*, vol. 7, no. 2, pp. 36–43.

— 1998, 'Economic significance of cruise tourism', *Annals of Tourism Research*, vol. 25, pp. 393–415.

Dwyer, L., Forsyth, P. & Findlay, C. 1990, Japanese investment in the Australian tourism industry: Rationales and consequences, paper presented at the Asian Studies Association of Australia 8th Annual Conference, Griffith University, Nathan, July.

Dye, T. 1992, *Understanding Public Policy*, 7th edn, Prentice Hall, Englewood Cliffs.

Eagles, P. 1999, 'Nature-based tourism in terrestrial protected areas', pp. 144–52 in *Partnerships for Protection: New Strategies for Planning and Management for Protected Areas*, eds. S. Bolton & N. Dudley, Earthscan, London.

Echtner, C.M. & Ritchie, J.R.B. 1993, 'The measurement of destination image: An empirical assessment', *Journal of Travel Research*, vol. 31, no. 4, pp. 3–13.

Ecologically Sustainable Development Working Groups 1991, *Final Report—Tourism*, Australian Government Publishing Service, Canberra.

Economic Commission for Europe 1976, *Planning and Development of the Tourist Industry in the ECE Region*, Economic Commission for Europe, United Nations, New York.

Economists At Large 1997, *Grand Prixtensions: The Economics of the Magic Pudding*, prepared for the Save Albert Park Group, Economists At Large, Melbourne.

Ecotourism Association of Australia 1993, *Membership Brochure*, Ecotourism Association of Australia, Brisbane.

Edgell, D. 1978, 'International tourism and travel', pp. 171–3 in *International Business Prospects, 1977–1999*, ed. H.F. Van Zandt, Bobbs-Merrill, Indianapolis.

Edgell, D.L. 1990, *International Tourism Policy*, Van Nostrand Reinhold, New York.

Edington, J.M. & Edington, M.A. 1986, *Ecology, Recreation & Tourism*, Cambridge University Press, Cambridge.

Edwards, I.J. 1977, 'The ecological impact of pedestrian traffic on alpine vegetation in Kosciusko National Park', *Australian Forestry*, vol. 40, pp. 108–20.

Egloff, B.J. 1982, 'Port Arthur historic site', *Heritage Australia*, vol. 1, no. 2, pp. 2–6.

Elkington, J. & Hailes, J. 1992, *Holidays That Don't Cost the Earth*, Victor Gollancz, London.

Elliot, J. 1997, *Tourism: Politics and Public Sector Management*, Routledge, London.

Elwell, T.D. 1893,*Official Guide to the National Park of New South Wales*, Government Printer, Sydney.

Embacher, H. 1994, 'Marketing for agri-tourism in Austria: Strategy and realisation in a highly developed tourist destination', *Journal of Sustainable Tourism*, vol. 2, pp. 61–76.

Embacher, J. & Buttle, F. 1989, 'A repertory grid analysis of Austria's image as a summer vacation destination', *Journal of Travel Research*, vol. 27, no. 3, pp. 3–7.

English Tourist Board/Department of Employment 1991, *Tourism and the Environment: Maintaining the Balance*, English Tourist Board, London.

Enright, M.J. & Roberts, B.H. 2001, 'Regional clustering in Australia', *Australian Journal of Management*, vol. 26, August, **http://www.agsm.unsw.edu.au/eajm/index.html**

Environment Australia 2001, *Implications of World Heritage Listing*, Canberra: Environment Australia, **http://www.ea.gov.au/heritage/awh/worldheritage/implications.html**

Eurobarometer 2000, *European Travel and the Internet*, Eurobarometer, London.

European Commission 2001a, *The Introduction of Third Generation Mobile Communications in the European Union: State of Play and the Way Forward*, Communication from the Commission to the Council, the European Parliament, The Economic and Social Committee and the Committee of the Regions. Brussels, 20.3.2001. COM(2001) 141 final.

— 2001b, *eEurope 2002, Impact and Priorities Communication from the Commission to the Council and the European Parliament*, A communication to the Spring European Council in Stockholm, 23–24 March 2001, **http://europa.eu.int/comm/information_society/eeurope/documentation/impact/index_en.htm**

Evans, M. 1997, 'Plugging into TV tourism', *Insights*, March, pp. D35–D38.

Fair, L. 1985, 'Feasibility studies', pp. 22–30 in *Tourist Developments in Australia*, eds J. Dean & B. Judd, Royal Australian Institute of Architects Education Division, Canberra.

Farrell, B.H. 1977, 'Breaking down the paradigms: The realities of tourism', pp. 1–6 in *The Social and Economic Impact of Tourism on Pacific Communities*, ed. B.H. Farrell, Centre for South Pacific Studies, University of California, Santa Cruz.

Faulkner, B. 1990, 'Tourism trends', paper presented at Tourism: The Way Ahead, Australian Tourism Research Institute & BTR, Sydney.

— 1994, 'The future ain't what it used to be: Reflections on the nature and role of tourism forecasting in Australia', in *Tourism Forecasting, Proceedings of the 1993 Australian Tourism Research Workshop*, BTR, Canberra.

— 2001, 'Towards a framework for tourism disaster management', *Tourism Management*, vol. 22, no. 2, pp. 135–48.

Faulkner, B. & Fagence, M. (eds) 1988, *Frontiers in Australian Tourism: The Search for New Perspectives in Policy Development and Research*, BTR, Canberra.

Faulkner, B., Pearce, P., Shaw, R. & Weiler, B. 1994, 'Tourism research in Australia: Confronting the challenges of the 1990's and beyond', in *National Tourism Research Conference Proceedings*, BTR, Canberra.

Faulkner, B. & Poole, M. 1989, *Impacts on Tourism of the Disruption to Domestic Airline Services*, BTR Occasional paper No. 5, BTR, Canberra.

Faulkner, B. & Tideswell, C. 1996, Gold Coast resident attitudes toward tourism: The influence of involvement in tourism, residential proximity, and period of residence, in *Tourism and Hospitality Research: Australian and International Perspectives*, ed. G. Prosser, BTR, Canberra.

Faulkner, B. & Vikulov, S. 2001, 'Katherine, washed out one day, back on track the next: A post-mortem of a tourist disaster', *Tourism Management*, vol. 22, pp. 331–4.

Faulkner, H.W. 1991, 'Editorial: The role of research in tourism development', *BTR Tourism Update*, September quarter, pp. 2–3.

Faulkner, H.W. & Walmsley, D.J. 1998, 'Globalisation and the pattern of inbound tourism in Australia', *Australian Geographer*, vol. 29, no. 1, pp. 91–105.

Federal Bureau of Transport Economics 1987, *Intrastate Bus Services in New South Wales: Trial Entry Liberalisation*, Occasional Paper 85, Australian Government Publishing Service, Canberra.

Fedler, A. 1987, 'Introduction: Are leisure, recreation and tourism interrelated?', *Annals of Tourism Research*, vol. 14, pp. 311–13.

Feifer, M. 1985, *Tourism in History From Imperial Rome to the Present*, Stein & Day, New York.

Fennell, D. 1999, *Ecotourism: An Introduction*, Routledge, London.

— 2000, 'What's in a name? Conceptualising natural resource-based tourism', *Tourism Recreation Research*, vol. 25, no. 1, pp. 97–100.

Film New Zealand 2000, *Film NZ Strategic Plan*, Film New Zealand, Wellington.

Finlayson, J. 1991, *Australian Aborigines and Cultural Tourism: Case Studies of Aboriginal Involvement in the Tourist Industry*, Working Papers on Multiculturalism No. 15, Centre for Multicultural Studies, University of Wollongong, Wollongong.

Finlayson, J. & Madden, R. 1994, 'Regional tourism case studies: Indigenous participation in tourism in Victoria', in *National Tourism Research Conference Proceedings*, Bureau of Tourism Research, Canberra.

First 48 Tours 2001, **http://www.first48.com/tours/turkey/anzac2001.phtml**

Fischer, A., Hatch, J. & Paix, B. 1986, 'Road accidents and the Grand Prix', pp. 151–68 in *The Adelaide Grand Prix: The Impact of a Special Event*, eds J.P.A. Burns, J.H. Hatch & T.J. Mules, The Centre for South Australian Economic Studies, Adelaide.

Fisher, D.E. 1980, *Environmental Law in Australia: An Introduction*, University of Queensland Press, St. Lucia.

Fishman, R. 1989, 'Adventure tours come of age', *Australian Financial Review*, April 18.

Fiske, J., Hodge, B. & Turner, G. 1987, *Myths of Oz: Reading Australian Popular Culture*, Allen & Unwin, Sydney.

Fitzgerald, R. 1984, *A History of Queensland from 1915 to the 1980s*, University of Queensland Press, St. Lucia.

Fodness, D. & Murray, B. 1999, 'A model of tourist information search behaviour', *Journal of Travel Research*, vol. 37, pp. 220–30.

Foo, L.M. 1999, 'A profile of international visitors to Australian wineries', *Bureau of Tourism Research Report*, vol. 1, no. 1, August.

Forsyth, P. & Dwyer, L. 1993, 'Foreign investment in Australian tourism: A framework for analysis', *Journal of Tourism Studies*, vol. 4, no. 1, pp. 26–37.

Fowler, R.J. 1984, 'Environmental law and its administration in Australia', *Environmental Planning and Law Journal*, April, pp. 10–49.

France, L. (ed.) 1997, *The Earthscan Reader in Sustainable Tourism*, Earthscan Publications, London.

Franklin, T. 1996, 'Research priorities for whale watching from an industry viewpoint', pp. 199–212 in *Encounters With Whales*, eds K. Colgan, S. Prasser & A. Jeffery, Australian National Conservation Agency, Canberra.

REFERENCES

Frater, J.M. 1983, 'Farm tourism in England: Planning, funding, promotion and some lessons from Europe', *Tourism Management*, vol. 4, pp. 167–79.

Frechtling, D.C. 1987, 'Assessing the impacts of travel and tourism—introduction to travel impact estimation', pp. 325–31 in *Travel, Tourism and Hospitality Research A Handbook for Managers and Researchers*, eds J.R.B. Ritchie & C.R. Goeldner, John Wiley & Sons, New York.

— 1999, 'The tourism satellite account: foundations, progress and issues', *Tourism Management*, vol. 20, pp. 163–70.

Fredline, E. 1996, Resident Perceptions of the Gold Coast Indy: An Exploratory Study, unpublished honours thesis, Griffith University, Gold Coast.

— 1998, 'Resident reactions to a major tourist event: The Gold Coast Indy Car Race', *Festival Management and Event Tourism*, vol. 5, pp. 185–205.

Fredline, E. & Faulkner, B. 2000, 'Host community reactions: a cluster analysis', *Annals of Tourism Research*, vol. 27, pp. 764–85.

French, C., Craig-Smith, S. & Collier, A. 1995, *Principles of Tourism*, Addison Wesley Longman, South Melbourne.

Frew, W. 1989, 'On the trail of adventure travel', *Australian Financial Review*, 17 May.

Fridgen, J.D. 1984, Environmental psychology and tourism, *Annals of Tourism Research*, vol. 11, pp. 19–40.

Friedmann, J. 1980, 'An alternative development?', pp. 4–1 in *Development Strategies in the Eighties*, eds J. Friedmann, T. Wheelwright & J. Connell, Monograph No. 1, Development Studies Colloquim, Department of Town and Country Planning, University of Sydney, Sydney.

Frost, J. 1988, 'Catering in Australia', pp. 208–13 in *The Tourism and Hospitality Industry*, ed. J. Blackwell, International Magazine Services, Sydney.

Frost, W. 2001, 'Golden anniversaries: festival tourism and the 150th anniversary of the gold rushes in California and Victoria', *Pacific Tourism Review*, vol. 3, no. 3/4, pp. 149–58.

Froude, J.A. 1985 (1886), *Oceana: or the tempestuous voyage of J.A. Froude 1885*, ed. G. Blainey, Methuen Haynes, North Ryde.

Fry, P. 1984, *Farm Tourism in Western Australia: Report of a Pilot Study*, Rural and Allied Industries Council, Perth.

Fujii, E.T. & Mak, J. 1980, 'Tourism and crime: Implication for regional development policy', *Regional Studies*, vol. 14, pp. 27–36.

Fuller, P. 1997, 'Value adding the regional wine experience', *The Australian and New Zealand Wine Industry Journal*, vol. 12, no. 1, pp. 35–9.

Gale, F. & Jacobs, J.M. 1987, *Tourists and the National Estate Procedures to Protect Australia's Heritage*, Australian Heritage Commission Special Australian Heritage Publication Series No. 6, Australian Government Publishing Service, Canberra.

Gammage, B., Williamson, D. & Weir, P. 1994, *The Story of Gallipoli—The Film about the Men who Made a Legend*, University of Queensland Press, St. Lucia.

Gardner, T. & McArthur, S. 1994, *Nature-based Tourism in Tasmania's Forests: Trends, Constraints and the Future*, Forestry Commission Tasmania, Hobart.

Garratt, B. 1987, *The Learning Organisation*, Fontana, London.

Gartner, W.C. 1993, 'Image formation process', *Journal of Travel and Tourism Marketing*, vol. 2, pp. 191–215.

Geale, P. 1985, *Farm Tourism*, Queensland Tourist and Travel Corporation, Brisbane.

George, M. 1987, 'Tourist related development—getting projects through the system', pp. 89–92 in *Tourist Resort Development: Markets, Plans and Impacts*, ed. K. Hollinshead, 2nd edn, The Centre for Leisure and Tourism Studies, Kuring-gai College of Advanced Education.

Gershuny, J. & Miles, I. 1983, *The New Service Economy: The Transformation of Employment in Industrial Societies*, Frances Pinter, London.

Gessel, P.V. 2000, 'Events: outstanding means for joint promotion', *Event Management*, vol. 6, pp. 111–16.

Gethin, C.J.F. 1970, An approach to planning for historic places as tourist attractions, unpublished Master of Town and Country Planning thesis, University of Sydney, Sydney.

Getz, D. 1986, 'Models in tourism planning towards integration of theory and practice', *Tourism Management*, vol. 7, no. 1, pp. 21–32.

— 1987, Tourism Planning and Research: Traditions, Models and Futures, paper presented at The Australian Travel Research Workshop, Bunbury, Western Australia, November 5–6.

— 1991a, *Festivals, Special Events, and Tourism*, Van Nostrand Reinhold, New York.

— 1991b, 'Assessing the economic impacts of festivals and events: Research issues', *Journal of Applied Recreation Research*, vol. 16, no. 1, pp. 61–77.

— 1992, 'Tourism planning and destination life cycle', *Annals of Tourism Research*, vol. 19, pp. 752–70.

— 1993a, 'Tourist shopping villages: Development and planning strategies', *Tourism Management*, vol. 14, no. 1, pp. 15–26.

— 1993b, 'Planning for tourism business districts', *Annals of Tourism Research*, vol. 20, pp. 583–600.

— 1997, *Event Management & Event Tourism*, Cognizant Communication Corporation, New York.

Gibson, N. 1984, 'Impact of trampling on bolster heath communities of Mt. Field National Park, Tasmania', *Papers and Proceedings of the Royal Society of Tasmania*, vol. 121, pp. 93–100.

Gill, A. & Williams, P.W. 1994, 'Managing growth in mountain tourism communities', *Tourism Management*, vol. 15, no. 3, pp. 212–20.

Gillespie, D. 1988, 'Tourism in Kakadu National Park', pp. 224–50 in *Contemporary Issues in Development, Northern Australia: Progress and Prospects*, vol. 1, eds D. Wade-Marshall & P. Loveday, North Australian Research Unit, Darwin.

Glasson, J., Godfrey, K. & Goodey, B. with Absalom, H. & Van Der Borg, J. 1995, *Towards Visitor Impact Management: Visitor Impacts, Carrying Capacity and Management Responses in Europe's Historic Towns and Cities*, Avebury, Aldershot.

Gold, J. and Ward, S. (eds) 1994, *Place Promotion: The Use of Publicity and Public Relations to Sell Places*, Belhaven, London.

Goldblatt, J. 1997, *Special Events: Best Practice in Modern Event Management*, Van Nostrand Reinhold, New York.

Golledge, S. & Maddern, C. 1994, *A Survey of Tourism Activity at Victorian Wineries*, Victorian Wineries Tourism Council, Melbourne.

Goodall, B. 1988, 'How tourists choose their holidays: An analytical framework', pp. 1–17 in *Marketing in the Tourism Industry: The Promotion of Destination Regions*, eds B. Goodall & G. Ashworth, Routledge, London.

REFERENCES

465

Goodall, B. & Ashworth, G. (eds) 1988, *Marketing in the Tourism Industry: The Promotion of Destination Regions*, Routledge, London.

Goodhead, T. & Johnson, D. (eds) 1996, *Coastal Recreation Management: The Sustainable Development of Maritime Leisure*, E & FN Spon, London.

Goodrich, J.N. 1994, Health tourism: A new positioning strategy for tourist destinations, *Journal of International Consumer Marketing*, vol. 6, no. 3/4, pp. 227–37.

Gorman, A. 1988, 'Tourism: Trojan horse or white knight? The role of social impact analysis', pp. 199–209 in *Frontiers in Australian Tourism: The Search for New Perspectives in Policy Development and Research*, eds B. Faulkner & M. Fagence, Bureau of Tourism Research, Canberra.

Government of Victoria 1987, *Victoria the Next Decade: Leading Australia Into The Next Decade*, Government of Victoria, Melbourne.

Graber, K. 1997, 'Cities and the destination life cycle', pp. 39–53 in *International City Tourism: Analysis and Strategy*, ed. J.A. Mazanec, Pinter, London.

Graburn, N. 1983, 'The anthropology of tourism', *Annals of Tourism Research*, vol. 10, pp. 9–33.

— 1983, 'Tourism and prostitution', *Annals of Tourism Research*, vol. 10, pp. 437–43.

Graefe, A.R. & Vaske, J.J. 1987, 'A framework for managing quality in the tourist experience', *Annals of Tourism Research*, vol. 14, pp. 390–404.

Graham, D. 1988, The impact of Expo '88 on rental housing in Highgate Hill, South Brisbane and West End, unpublished Dip. Urb.Reg.Plan. thesis, Department of Geography and Planning, University of New England, Armidale.

Graham, P. (ed.) 1988, *Readings and Cases in Marketing*, Prentice Hall, Sydney.

Grattan, M. 2000, 'Emotional dawn for pilgrims at Gallipoli', *Sydney Morning Herald*, 26 April, p. 1.

Gratton, C. & Taylor, P. 1987, 'Leisure and shopping', *Leisure Management*, vol. 7, no. 3, pp. 29–30.

Gray, H.P. 1970, *International Travel–International Trade*, Heath Lexington, Lexington.

— 1974, 'Toward an economic analysis of tourism policy', *Social and Economic Studies*, vol. 23, no. 3, pp. 386–97.

Green, J., Tonge, R. & Sceats, D. 1980, *Tourist Associations and Regional Promotion Committees 1980 National Survey of Finance and Funding*, Rob Tonge and Associates, Maroochydore.

Greene, J. 1995, Challenges in the Regional Market place, paper presented at the Australian Institute of Travel and Tourism 11th Annual Conference, Hyatt Hotel, Canberra.

Grimwood, A.C. 1982, The social impact of tourist development: A study on the NSW coastal resort of Yamba–Angourie, unpublished thesis, School of Geography, University of New South Wales, Kensington.

Groome, D. 1993, *Planning and Rural Recreation in Britain*, Avebury, Aldershot.

The Guardian (2002) 'What is ecotourism?', Guardian Travel special on ecotourism, **http://travel.guardian.co.uk/ecotourism/0,8944,431437,00.html** (accessed 10 March 2002).

Guldberg, H.H. & Prosser, J.R. 1974, *The Role of Tourism and Recreation in the Albury–Wodonga Growth Centre*, P. A. Management Consultants, Department of Tourism and Recreation, Canberra.

Gunn, C.A. 1977, 'Industry pragmatism vs tourism planning', *Leisure Sciences*, vol. 1, no. 1, pp. 85–94.

— 1979, *Tourism Planning*, Crane Russak, New York.

— 1988, *Tourism Planning*, 2nd edn, Taylor & Francis, New York.

— 1994, *Tourism Planning*, 3rd edn, Taylor & Francis, Washington.

Hagan, J. & Patterson, E. 1991, *'Oars Aweigh': Assessing the Impact of the 1990 World Rowing Championships on Tasmania*, Australian Sport and Recreation Facilities Advisory Committee, Department of Tourism, Sport and Recreation, Hobart.

Hage, G. 1997, 'At home in the entrails of the west: multiculturalism, 'ethnic food' and migrant home building', pp. 99–153 in *home/world: space, community and marginality in Sydney's west*, eds H. Grace, G. Hage, L. Johnson, J. Langsworth & M. Symonds, Pluto Press, Annandale.

Haigh, R. 1994, *Holidays in Store: Shopping Patterns of International Tourists*, Occasional Paper No. 14, Bureau of Tourism Research, Canberra.

Haigh, R. & Rieder, L. 1989, 'Report on the economic impacts of tourism in New South Wales and Australia input–output analysis component', pp. 1–54 in *The Economic Impacts of Tourism*, New South Wales Tourism Commission, Sydney.

Hall, C.M. 1985, 'Outdoor recreation and national identity: A comparative study of Australia and Canada', *Journal of Canadian Culture*, vol. 2, no. 2, pp. 25–39.

— 1988a, 'Broadening the scope of tourism research in Australia', pp. 329–40 in *Frontiers in Australian Tourism: The Search for New Perspectives in Policy Development and Research*, eds B. Faulkner & M. Fagence, Bureau of Tourism Research, Canberra.

— 1988b, 'The future of tourism in Australia: Counting the pennies without counting the cost', *Recreation Australia*, vol. 7, no. 4, pp. 2–11, 20.

— 1988c, The geography of hope: The history, identification and preservation of wilderness in Australia, unpublished Ph.D. thesis, Department of Geography, University of Western Australia, Nedlands.

— 1988d, Expo 86 and Expo 88: Some comparisons, World Expo 88 Seminar, School of Management, Queensland Institute of Technology, Brisbane, October.

— 1989a, 'The worthless lands hypothesis and Australia's national parks and reserves', pp. 441–56 in *Australia's Ever Changing Forests*, eds K. Frawley & N. Semple, Department of Geography Monograph Series, Australian Defence Force Academy, Canberra.

— 1989b, 'Special interest tourism: A prime force in the development of tourism?', pp. 81–9 in *Geography in Action*, ed. R. Welch, Department of Geography, University of Otago, Dunedin.

— 1989c, 'Hallmark tourist events: Analysis, definition, methodology and review', pp. 3–19 in *The Planning and Evaluation of Hallmark Events*, eds G.J. Syme, B.J. Shaw, D.M. Fenton & W.S. Mueller, Avebury, Aldershot.

— 1989d, 'The impacts of the 1987 America's Cup on Fremantle, Western Australia: Implications for the hosting of hallmark events, pp. 74–80 in *Geography in Action*, ed. R. Welch, Department of Geography, University of Otago, Dunedin.

— 1989e, 'The definition and analysis of hallmark tourist events', *GeoJournal*, vol. 19, no. 3, pp. 263–8.

— 1989f, 'The politics of hallmark events', pp. 219–41 in *The Planning and Evaluation of Hallmark Events*, eds G.J. Syme, B.J. Shaw, D.M. Fenton & W.S Mueller, Avebury, Aldershot.

— 1989g, 'Hallmark events and the planning process', pp. 20–39 in *The Planning and Evaluation of Hallmark Events*, eds G.J. Syme, B.J. Shaw, D.M. Fenton, & W.S. Mueller, Avebury, Aldershot.

— 1990, 'From cottage to condominium: Recreation, tourism and regional development in northern New South Wales', pp. 85–99 in *Change and Adjustment in Northern New South Wales*, ed. D.J. Walmsley, Department of Geography and Planning, University of New England, Armidale.

— 1992a, *Wasteland to World Heritage: Preserving Australia's Wilderness*, Melbourne University Press, Carlton.

— 1992b, *Hallmark Tourist Events: Impacts, Management and Planning*, Belhaven, London.

— 1992c, 'Issues in ecotourism: From susceptible to sustainable development', pp. 152–8 in *Heritage Management: Parks, Heritage and Tourism*, Royal Australian Institute of Parks and Recreation, Hobart.

— 1992d, 'Adventure, sport and health tourism', pp. 141–58 in *Special Interest Tourism*, eds B. Weiler & C.M. Hall, Belhaven Press, London.

— 1993a, 'John Muir's travels in Australasia, 1903–1904: Their significance for conservation and environmental thought', pp. 286–308 in *John Muir: Life and Work*, ed. S.M. Miller, University of New Mexico Press, Albuquerque.

— 1993b, 'Ecotourism in Australia, New Zealand and the South Pacific: Appropriate tourism or a new form of ecological imperialism?', in *Ecotourism: A Sustainable Option*, eds E.A. Cater & G.A. Bowman, Belhaven and Royal Geographical Society, London.

— 1994a, *Tourism and Politics: Policy, Power and Place*, John Wiley & Sons, Chichester.

— 1994b, *Tourism in the Pacific Rim: Development, Impacts and Markets*, Longman Cheshire, South Melbourne.

— 1996a, 'Wine tourism in New Zealand', pp. 109–19 in *Tourism Down Under II, Towards a More Sustainable Tourism, Conference Proceedings*, ed. G. Kearsley, Centre for Tourism, University of Otago, Dunedin.

— 1996b, 'Environmental impact of tourism in the Pacific', in *Tourism in the Pacific: Issues and Cases*, eds C.M. Hall & S.J. Page, International Thomson Business Press, London.

— 1996c, 'Communication from the guest editor', *Festival Management & Event Tourism*, vol. 4, no. 1/2, pp. 1–2.

— 1997a, 'The politics of heritage tourism: Place, power and the representation of values in an urban context', pp. 91–101 in *Quality Management in Urban Tourism*, ed. P. Murphy, John Wiley & Sons, Chichester.

— 1997b, *Tourism in the Pacific Rim: Development, Impacts and Markets*, 2nd edn, Addison Wesley Longman, South Melbourne.

— 1997c, 'Cultural tourism and urban imaging strategies in Canada', pp. 287–304 in *Canada–Australia: Towards a Second Century of Partnership*, eds K. Burridge, L. Foster & G. Turcotte, International Council of Canadian Studies and Carleton University Press, Ottawa.

— 1997d, 'Blazing Trails: Myles Dunphy, the bushwalking movement and the creation of national parks and primitive areas in Australia in the inter-war period', pp. 65–72 in *Trails in the Third Millenium, Conference Proceedings*, eds. J. Higham & G. Kearsley, Centre for Tourism, University of Otago, Dunedin.

— 1998a, 'Historical antecedents of sustainable development and ecotourism: New labels on old bottles?', in *Sustainable Tourism Development: A Geographical Perspective*, eds C.M. Hall & A. Lew, Addison Wesley Longman, London.

— 1998b, 'The politics of decision making and top-down planning: Darling Harbour, Sydney', pp. 9–24 in *Tourism Management in Cities: Policy, Process and Practice*, eds. D. Tyler, M. Robertson & Y. Guerrier, John Wiley & Sons, Chichester.

— 1998c, 'The legal and political dimensions of sex tourism: the case of Australia's child sex tourism legislation', pp. 87–96 in *Sex Tourism and Prostitution: Aspects of Leisure, Recreation, and Work*, ed. M. Oppermann, Cognizant Communication Corporation, New York.

— 1999, 'Rethinking collaboration and partnership: A public policy perspective', *Journal of Sustainable Tourism*, vol. 7, no. 3/4, 274–89.

— 2000a, *Tourism Planning*, Prentice Hall, Harlow.

— 2000b, 'Tourism and the establishment of national parks in Australia', pp. 29–38 in *Tourism and National Parks*, eds R.W. Butler & S.W. Boyd, John Wiley, Chichester.

— 2000c, 'The future of tourism: a personal speculation', *Tourism Recreation Research*, vol. 25, pp. 85–95.

— 2000d, 'Tourism in Indonesia: The end of the New Order', pp. 157–66 in *Tourism in South and South-East Asia: Critical Perspectives*, eds C.M. Hall & S.J. Page, Butterworth-Heinemann, Oxford.

— 2000e, 'Tourism, national parks and aboriginal populations', pp. 55–71 in *Tourism and National Parks*, eds R. Butler & S. Boyd, John Wiley, Chichester.

— 2001a, 'Territorial economic integration and globalisation', pp. 22–44 in *Tourism in the Age of Globalisation*, eds C. Cooper & S. Wahab, Routledge, London.

— 2001b, 'Tourism and political relationships in South East Asia', pp. 13–26 in *Interconnected Worlds: Tourism in South East Asia*, ed. P. Teo, Elsevier, Oxford.

— 2001c, 'Trends in coastal and marine tourism: impacts, strategies and sustainability', *Ocean and Coastal Management*, vol. 44, no. 9–10, pp. 601–18.

— 2001d, 'Japan and tourism in the Pacific Rim: Locating a sphere of influence in the global economy', pp. 121–36 in *Tourism and the Less Developed Countries*, ed. D. Harrison, CAB International, Wallingford.

— 2001e, 'Tourism as a mechanism for regional development in rural Australia and New Zealand: The Creation of food and wine tourism networks', in *Creating and Managing Growth in Travel and Tourism*, 3rd TTRA European Chapter Conference, Sweden, April 22–25, 2001, ed. M. Bohlin, TTRA (CD).

— 2001f, 'The development of rural wine and food tourism networks: factors and issues', in *New Directions in Managing Rural Tourism and Leisure: Local Impacts, Global Trends*, Scottish Agricultural College, Auchenvyre (CD).

— 2002a, 'Anzac Day and secular pilgrimage', *Tourism Recreation Research*, in press.

— 2002b, 'Seducing global capital: reimaging and the creation of seductive space in Melbourne and Sydney', in *Seductions of Place: Geographies of Touristed Landscapes*, eds C. Cartier & A. Lew, Routledge, New York, in press.

Hall, C.M. & Butler, D. 1995, 'In search of common ground: Reflections on sustainability, complexity and process in the tourism system', *Journal of Sustainable Tourism*, vol. 3, no. 2, pp. 99–105.

Hall, C.M., Cambourne, B., Macionis, N. & Johnson, G. 1998, 'Wine tourism and network development in Australia and New Zealand: review, establishment and prospects', *International Journal of Wine Marketing*, vol. 9, no. 2/3, pp. 5–31.

Hall, C.M. & Hamon, C. 1996, 'Casinos and urban redevelopment in Australia', *Journal of Travel Research*, vol. 34, no. 3, pp. 30–6.

Hall, C.M. & Hodges, J. 1996, 'The party's great, but what about the hangover? The housing and social impacts of mega-events with special reference to the Sydney 2000 Olympics', *Festival Management & Event Tourism*, vol. 4, no. 1/2, pp. 13–20.

Hall, C.M. & Jenkins, J. 1989, 'Frontiers in Australian tourism', *Annals of Tourism Research*, vol. 16, pp. 122–3.

— 1995, *Tourism and Public Policy*, Routledge, London.

— 1998, 'Rural tourism and recreation policy dimensions', in *Tourism and Recreation in Rural Areas*, eds R.W. Butler, C.M. Hall & J. Jenkins, John Wiley, Chichester.

Hall, C.M., Jenkins, J. & Kearsley, G. (eds) 1997a, *Tourism Planning and Policy in Australia and New Zealand: Cases, Issues and Practice*, Irwin Publishers, Sydney.

— 1997b, 'Introduction: Issues in tourism planning and policy in Australia and New Zealand', pp. 16–36 in *Tourism Planning and Policy in Australia and New Zealand: Cases, Issues and Practice*, eds C.M. Hall, J. Jenkins & G. Kearsley, Irwin Publishers, Sydney.

Hall, C.M. & Johnson, G. 1997, 'Wine tourism in New Zealand: Alliances and relationships', in *Trails, Tourism and Regional Development*, eds G. Kearsley & J. Higham, Centre for Tourism, University of Otago, Dunedin.

Hall, C.M., Johnson, G. & Mitchell, R. 2000, 'Wine tourism and regional development', pp. 196–225 in *Wine Tourism Around the World: Development, Management and Markets*, eds C.M. Hall, E. Sharples, B. Cambourne & N. Macionis, Butterworth-Heinemann, Oxford.

Hall, C.M. & Kearsley, G.K. 2001, *Introduction to Tourism in New Zealand*, Oxford University Press, Melbourne.

Hall, C.M. & Lew, A. (eds) 1998, *Sustainable Tourism Development: A Geographical Perspective*, Addison Wesley Longman, London.

Hall, C.M. & McArthur, S. 1991a, 'Commercial whitewater rafting in Australia: History, development and profile', *Leisure Options: Australian Journal of Leisure and Recreation*, vol. 1, no. 2, pp. 25–30, 44.

— 1991b, 'Commercial whitewater rafting in Australia: Motivations and expectations of the participant and the relevance of group size for the rafting experience', *Leisure Options: Australian Journal of Leisure and Recreation*, vol. 1, no. 4, pp. 25–31, 41.

— (eds) 1993, *Heritage Management in New Zealand and Australia: Interpretation, Marketing and Visitor Management*, Oxford University Press, Auckland.

— (eds) 1996, *Heritage Management in Australia and New Zealand: The Human Dimension*, Oxford University Press, Melbourne.

— 1998, *Integrated Heritage Management*, Stationery Office, London.

Hall, C.M. & Macionis, N. 1998, 'Wine tourism in Australia and New Zealand', in *Tourism and Recreation in Rural Areas*, eds R.W. Butler, C.M. Hall & J. Jenkins, John Wiley, Chichester.

Hall, C.M. & Mitchell, R. 1998, 'We are, what we eat: food, tourism and globalisation', paper presented at Innovative Approaches to Culture and Tourism, ATLAS

Conference, 22–24 October 1998, Rethymnon, Crete.

Hall, C.M. & Page, S. (eds) 2000, *Tourism in South and South-East Asia: Issues and Cases*, Butterworth-Heinemann, Oxford.

— 2002, *The Geography of Tourism and Recreation*, 2nd edn, Routledge, London.

Hall, C.M. & Piggin, R. 2001, 'Tourism and World Heritage in OECD countries', *Tourism Recreation Research*, vol. 26, no. 1, pp. 103–5.

Hall, C.M. & Samways, R. 1997, 'Tourism and regionalism in the Pacific Rim: An overview', pp. 31–44 in *Pacific Rim Tourism*, ed. M. Oppermann, CAB International, Wallingford.

Hall, C.M. & Selwood, H.J. 1987, 'Cup gained, paradise lost? A case study of the 1987 America's Cup as a hallmark event', pp. 267–74 in *Geography and Society in a Global Context*, eds R. Le Heron, M. Roche & M. Shepherd, Department of Geography, Massey University, Palmerston North.

— 1989, 'America's Cup lost, paradise retained? The dynamics of a hallmark tourist event', in *The Planning and Evaluation of Hallmark Events*, eds G.J. Syme, B.J. Shaw, D.M. Fenton & W.S Mueller, Avebury, Aldershot.

Hall, C.M., Selwood, J. & McKewon, E. 1995, 'Hedonists, ladies and larrikins: Crime, prostitution and the 1987 America's Cup', *Visions in Leisure and Business*, vol. 14, no. 3, pp. 28–51.

Hall, C.M., Sharples, E., Cambourne, B. & Macionis, N. (eds) 2000, *Wine Tourism Around the World: Development, Management and Markets*, Butterworth-Heinemann, Oxford.

Hall, C.M., Springett, D. & Springett, B. 1993, 'The development of an environmental education tourist product: a case study of the New Zealand Natural Heritage Foundation's Nature of New Zealand Programme', *Journal of Sustainable Tourism*, vol. 1, no. 2, pp. 130–6.

Hall, C.M. & Weiler, B. 1989, *Trends and Issues in Australian Tertiary Tourism Education*, Occasional Paper No. 1, Australian Institute of Tourism Industry Management, University of New England, Northern Rivers, Lismore.

— 1992, 'What's so special about special interest tourism?', in *Special Interest Tourism*, eds B. Weiler & C.M. Hall, Belhaven Press, London.

Hall, C.M. & Williams, A.M. (eds) 2002, *Tourism and Migration: New Relationships Between Consumption and Production*, Kluwer, Dortrecht.

Hall, C.M. & Wouters, M. 1994, 'Managing nature tourism in the sub-Antarctic', *Annals of Tourism Research*, vol. 21, pp. 355–74.

Hall, C.M. & Zeppel, H. 1990, 'Cultural and heritage tourism: The new grand tour?', *Historic Environment*, vol. 7, no. 3–4, pp. 86–98.

Hall, D. 1984, 'Conservation by ecotourism', *New Scientist*, No. 1399, pp. 38–9.

— 1999, 'Destination branding, niche marketing and national image projection in Central and Eastern Europe', *Journal of Vacation Marketing*, vol. 5, no. 3, pp. 227–37.

Hall, D. & Brown, F. 1996, 'Towards a welfare focus for tourism research', *Progress in Tourism and Hospitality Research*, vol. 2, pp. 41–57.

Halstrup, K. & Olwig, K.F. 1997, 'Introduction', in *Saving Culture: The Shifting Anthropological Object*, eds K.F. Olwig & K. Halstrup, Routledge, London.

Haraven, T.K. & Langenbach, R. 1981, 'Living places, work places and historical identity', pp. 109–23 in *Our Past Before Us Why Do We Save It?*, ed. D. Lowenthal & M. Binney, Temple Smith, London.

Harris, C.C., McLaughlin, W.J. & Ham, S.H. 1987, 'Integration of recreation and tourism in Idaho', *Annals of Tourism Research*, vol. 14, pp. 405–19.

Harris, Kerr, Forster & Co., Stanton Robbins & Co. 1966, *Australia's Travel and Tourism Industry 1965*, Australian National Travel Association, Sydney.

Harris, R. & Leiper, N. 1995, *Sustainable Tourism: An Australian Perspective*, Butterworth-Heinemann, Sydney.

Harrison, D. (ed.) 1992, *Tourism and the Less Developed Countries*, Belhaven, London.

— 2001, *Tourism and the Less Developed Countries*, CAB International, Wallingford.

Harrison, J. 1997, 'Museum and touristic expectations,' *Annals of Tourism Research*, vol. 24, pp. 23–40.

Harrison, R. (ed.) 1994, *Manual of Heritage Management*, Butterworth-Heinemann, Oxford.

Harron, S. & Weiler, B. 1992, 'Ethnic tourism', pp. 83–94 in *Special Interest Tourism*, eds B. Weiler & C.M. Hall, Belhaven, London.

Hart, W. 1966, *A Systems Approach to Park Planning*, International Union for the Conservation of Nature, Morges.

Harvest Pilgrimages 2000, *2000–2001, Official Tour Operator for the Great Jubilee*, Harvest Pilgrimages Australia, Sydney.

Harvey, D. 1988, 'Voodoo cities', *New Statesman and Society*, 30 September: 33–35.

— 1989, *The Condition of Postmodernity An Enquiry into the Origins of Cultural Change*, Basil Blackwell, Oxford.

— 1993, 'From space to place and back again: reflections on the condition of postmodernity', pp. 3–29 in *Mapping the Futures: Local Cultures, Global Change*, eds J. Bird, B. Curtis, T. Putnam, G. Robertson & L. Tickner, Routledge, London and New York.

— 1996, *Justice, Nature and the Geography of Difference*, Blackwell, London.

— 2000, *Spaces of Hope*, University of California Press, Berkeley.

Haulot, A. 1981, 'Social tourism: Current dimensions and future developments', *Tourism Management*, vol. 2, pp. 207–12.

Hay, J.E. (ed.) 1992, *Ecotourism Business in the Pacific: Promoting a Sustainable Experience, Conference Proceedings*, Environmental Science, University of Auckland, Auckland.

Haywood, K.M. 1986, 'Can the tourist–area life cycle be made operational?', *Tourism Management*, vol. 7, no. 3, pp. 154–67.

— 1988, 'Responsible and responsive tourism planning in the community', *Tourism Management*, vol. 9, no. 2, pp. 105–18.

Healy, R. 1994, 'Tourist merchandise as a means of generating local benefits from ecotourism', *Journal of Sustainable Tourism*, vol. 2, no. 3, pp. 137–51.

Heath, E. & Wall, G. 1992, *Marketing Tourism Destinations: A Strategic Planning Approach*, John Wiley & Sons, New York.

Heathcote, R.L. 1975, *Australia*, Longman, Harlow.

Heeley, J. 1981, 'Planning for tourism in Britain', *Town Planning Review*, vol. 52, pp. 61–79.

Heenan, D. 1978, 'Tourism and the community, a drama in three acts', *Journal of Travel Research*, vol. 16, no. 4, pp. 30–2.

Heeringa, V. 1996, 'Conventions, niche convention business helps grow tourism pie', *The Independent*, 14 February, pp. 30–1.

Helber, L. 1985, 'The resort development planning process', pp. 37–45 in *Tourist Developments in Australia*, eds J. Dean & B. Judd, Royal Australian Institute of Architects Education Division, Canberra.

Helber, L.E. 1988, 'The roles of government in planning in tourism with special regard for the cultural and environmental impact of tourism', pp. 17–23 in *The Roles of Government in the Development of Tourism as an Economic Resource*, ed. D. McSwan, Seminar Series No. 1, Centre for Studies in Travel and Tourism, James Cook University, Townsville.

Helburn, N. 1977, 'The wilderness continuum', *Professional Geographer*, vol. 29, pp. 337–47.

Helu-Thaman, K. 1992, 'Ecocultural tourism: A personal view for maintaining cultural integrity in ecotourism development', pp. 4–9 in *Ecotourism Business in the Pacific: Promoting a Sustainable Experience, Conference Proceedings*, ed. J.E. Hay, Environmental Science, University of Auckland, Auckland.

Hensher, D.A. 1989, *A Methodology for Investigating the Passenger Demand for High Speed Rail*, Working Paper No. 51, Transport Research Group, Macquarie University, Sydney.

Hewison, R. 1987, *The Heritage Industry: Britain in a Climate of Decline*, Methuen, London.

— 1988, 'Great expectations–hyping heritage', *Tourism Management*, vol. 9, no. 3, pp. 239–40.

— 1991, 'Commerce and culture', pp. 162–77 in *Enterprise and Heritage: Cross-currents of National Culture*, eds J. Corner & S. Harvey, Routledge, London and New York.

Heywood, P. 1990, 'Truth and beauty in landscape—trends in landscape and leisure', *Landscape Australia*, vol. 12, no. 1, pp. 43–7.

Higgins, E. 1993, 'Japanese funds dry up for new tourist projects', *The Australian*, 13 November.

Hill, G., Koslowski, J. & Rosier, J. 1985, 'A threshold-based reply to tourist development', *Queensland Planner*, vol. 26, no. 1, pp. 10–15.

Hill, G. & Rosier, J. 1989, 'Seabird ecology and resort development on Heron Island', *Journal of Environmental Management*, vol. 27, pp. 107–14.

Hill, K. 2000, 'We will remember them: a legend reborn', *Sydney Morning Herald*, 26 April, p. 1.

Hiller, H.H. 1995, 'Conventions as mega-events: A new model for convention—host city relationships', *Tourism Management*, vol. 16, no. 5, pp. 375–81.

Hinch, T.D. 1996, 'Urban tourism: perspectives on sustainability', *Journal of Sustainable Tourism*, vol. 4, no. 2, pp. 95–110.

Hogh, L. 2001, '"Farming the tourist": The social benefits of farm tourism in Southland, New Zealand', *Pacific Tourism Review*, vol. 4, no. 4, pp. 171–8.

Hogwood, B. & Gunn, L. 1984, *Policy Analysis for the Real World*, Oxford University Press, New York.

Holden, A. 2000, *Environment and Tourism*, Routledge, London.

Holding, C. (Minister for the Arts, Tourism and Territories) 1989, Address to the annual general meeting of the Australian Federation of Friends of Galleries and Museums, The Australian National Library, Canberra, 14 September.

Hollander, G., Threlfall, P. & Tucker, K.A. 1982, *Energy and the Australian Tourism Industry*, Working Paper, Bureau of Industry Economics, Canberra.

Hollinshead, K. 1988, 'First-blush of the longtime: The market development of Australia's living Aboriginal heritage', pp. 183–98 in *Tourism Research: Expanding Boundaries, The Travel and Tourism Research Association 19th Annual Conference Proceedings*, Bureau of Economic and Business Research, Graduate School of Business, University of Utah, Salt Lake City.

— 1990, 'The powers behind play: The political environments for recreation and tourism in Australia', *Journal of Park and Recreation Administration*, vol. 8, no. 1, pp. 35–50.

Holloway, J.C. 1985, *The Business of Tourism*, 2nd edn, MacDonald & Evans, Plymouth.

Holloway, J.C. & Plant, R.V. 1988, *Marketing for Tourism*, Pitman, London.

— 1992, *Marketing for Tourism*, 2nd edn, Pitman, London.

Hooper-Greenhill, E. 1992, *Museums and the Shaping of Knowledge*, Routledge, London.

Hopper, M. 1984, 'Australian resort timesharing', *International Journal of Hospitality Management*, vol. 3, no. 1, pp. 3–10.

Horne, D. 1984, *The Great Museum: The Re-presentation of History*, Pluto Press, London.

— 1991, 'Visitors in our own lives', *Australian Cultural History*, no. 10, pp. 1–5.

Horne, J. 1991, 'Travelling through the romantic landscapes of the Blue Mountains', *Australian Cultural History*, no. 10, pp. 84–98.

Horne, J. & Walker, D. 1991, *Travellers, Journeys, Tourists*, special edition of *Australian Cultural History*, no. 10, School of History, University of New South Wales, Kensington.

Horne, W.R. 2000, 'Municipal economic development via hallmark tourist events', *The Journal of Tourism Studies*, vol. 11, no. 1, pp. 30–5.

House of Representatives Select Committee on Tourism 1977, *Interim Report of the House of Representatives Select Committee on Tourism*, Australian Government Publishing Service, Canberra.

— 1978, *House of Representatives Select Committee on Tourism Final Report*, Australian Government Publishing Service, Canberra.

House of Representatives Standing Committee on Environment and Conservation 1984, *Protection of the Greater Daintree*, Australian Government Publishing Service, Canberra.

House of Representatives Standing Committee on Environment, Recreation and the Arts 1989, *Tourism in Antarctica*, Report of the House of Representatives Standing Committee on Environment, Recreation and the Arts, Australian Government Publishing Service, Canberra.

— 1990, *Tourism in the Indian Ocean Territories*, Report of the House of Representatives Standing Committee on Environment, Recreation and the Arts, Australian Government Publishing Service, Canberra.

Hovinen, G. 1981, 'A tourist cycle in Lancaster County, Pennsylvania', *Canadian Geographer*, vol. 25, no. 3, pp. 283–6.

— 1982, 'Visitor cycles outlook for tourism in Lancaster County, Pennsylvania', *Annals of Tourism Research*, vol. 9, pp. 563–83.

Howard, J. 1997, Address at the Tourism Council Australia Lunch, Regent Hotel, Sydney, 29 August, **http://www.pm.gov.au/media/pressrel/speech/1997/touris.html** (accessed 6/11/97).

Hoyt, E. 1995, *The Worldwide Value and Extent of Whale Watching 1995*, Whale and Dolphin Conservation Society, Bath.

Hu, Y. & Ritchie, J.R.B. 1993, 'Measuring destination attractiveness: a contextual approach', *Journal of Travel Research*, vol. 32, no. 2, pp. 25–34.

Hudson, K. 1987, *Museums of Influence*, Cambridge University Press, Cambridge.

Hudson, P. 1990a, Stresses in small towns in north-western Australia: The impact of tourism and development, paper presented at the 24th Institute of Australian Geographers Conference, University of New England, Armidale, September.

— 1990b, Structural changes in three small north Western Australian communities: The relationship between development and local quality of life, paper presented at Annual Conference of Regional Science Association, Australian and New Zealand section, Perth, December.

Hudson, R. & Townsend, A. 1992, 'Tourism employment and policy choices for local government', pp. 49–68 in *Perspectives on Tourism Policy*, eds P. Johnson & B. Thomas, Mansell, London.

Hughes, C.G. 1982, 'The employment and economic effects of tourism reappraised', *Tourism Management*, vol. 3, no. 3, pp. 167–76.

Hughes, G. 2002, 'Ansett's death spiral started decades ago', *The Sunday Age*, 3 March.

Hughes, H.L. 1984, 'Government support for tourism in the UK: A different perspective', *Tourism Management*, vol. 5, no. 1, pp. 13–19.

— 1987, 'Culture as a tourist resource—a theoretical consideration', *Tourism Management*, vol. 8, no. 3, pp. 205–16.

— 1989, 'Tourism and the arts. A potentially destructive relationship?', *Tourism Management*, vol. 10, no. 2, pp. 97–9.

— 1997, 'Urban tourism and the performing arts', pp. 103–13 in *Quality Management in Urban Tourism*, ed. P. Murphy, John Wiley & Sons, Chichester.

Hughes, P. 2001, 'animals, values and tourism—structural shifts in UK dolphin tourism provision', *Tourism Management*, vol. 22, pp. 321–9.

Hughes, R. 1987, *The Fatal Shore: A History of the Transportation of Convicts to Australia, 1787–1868*, Collins Harvill, London.

Huie, J. 1993, 'Trends in tourism today: Their relevance to parks and heritage', *Australian Parks & Recreation*, vol. 29, no. 1, pp. 26–9.

Hultkrantz, L. 2002, 'Will there be a unified wireless marketplace for tourism?', *Current Issues in Tourism*, in press.

Hundloe, T. 1990, 'Measuring the value of the Great Barrier Reef', *Australian Parks & Recreation*, vol. 26, no. 3, pp. 11–15.

Hunt, J.D. 1975, 'Image as a factor in tourist development', *Journal of Travel Research*, vol. 13, no. 3, pp. 1–7.

Hunter, C. 1995, 'On the need to re-conceptualise sustainable tourism development', *Journal of Sustainable Tourism*, vol. 3, no. 3, pp. 155–65.

Hunter, C. & Green, H. 1995, *Tourism and the Environment: A Sustainable Relationship?*, Routledge, London.

ICTurkey 2001, Anzac Day London: icTurkey, **http://www.anzactours.co.uk/**

Images 1988, *Images: A Quarterly Report on Cultural & Heritage Matters from the Department of the Arts, Sport, Environment, Tourism and Territories*, vol. 4, no. 2.

Industries Assistance Commission 1989, *Travel and Tourism*, Report No. 423, Australian Government Publishing Service, Canberra.

Industry Commission (IC) 1995, Tourism Accommmodation and Training, IC, Melbourne.

Inskeep, E. 1987, 'Environmental planning for tourism', *Annals of Tourism Research*, vol. 14, pp. 118–35.

— 1991, *Tourism Planning: An Integrated and Sustainable Development Approach*, Van Nostrand Reinhold, New York.

International Trade Administration 2001, *The Migration of U.S. Film and Television Production: Impact of "Runaways" on Workers and Small Business in the U.S. Film Industry*, United States Department of Commerce, Washington DC.

International Union for the Conservation of Nature and Natural Resources (IUCN) 1980, *World Conservation Strategy*, The IUCN with the advice, cooperation and financial assistance of the United Nations Environment Education Program and the World Wildlife Fund and in collaboration with the Food and Agricultural Organization of the United Nations and the United Nations Educational, Scientific and Cultural Organization, IUCN, Morges.

International Union of Tourism Organizations (IUOTO) 1974, 'The role of the state in tourism', *Annals of Tourism Research*, vol. 1, pp. 66–72.

Ioannides, D. 1992, 'Tourism development agents: The Cypriot resort cycle', *Annals of Tourism Research*, vol. 19, pp. 711–31.

Iso-Ahola, S.E. 1980, *The Social Psychology of Leisure and Recreation*, Wm. C. Brown, Dubuque.

— 1982, 'Toward a social psychological theory of tourist motivation: A rejoinder', *Annals of Tourism Research*, vol. 9, pp. 256–61.

— 1983, 'Toward a social psychology of recreational travel', *Leisure Studies*, vol. 2, pp. 45–56.

Israel, P. 1985, 'Whatever happened to the sojourn to paradise', pp. 61–2 in *Tourist Developments in Australia*, eds J. Dean & B. Judd, Royal Australian Institute of Architects Education Division, Canberra.

Jaakson, R. 1986, 'Second-home domestic tourism', *Annals of Tourism Research*, vol. 13, pp. 367–91.

Jackson, R.T. 1990, 'VFR tourism: Is it underestimated?', *Journal of Tourism Studies*, vol. 1, no. 2, pp. 10–17.

Jafari, J. 1977, 'Editor's page', *Annals of Tourism Research*, vol. 5, pp. 11.

— 1988, 'Tourism mega-events', *Annals of Tourism Research*, vol. 15, pp. 272–3.

Jafari, J. & Ritchie, J.R.B. 1981, 'Toward a framework for tourism education problems and prospects', *Annals of Tourism Research*, vol. 8, pp. 13–34.

Jamal, T.B. & Getz, D. 1995, 'Collaboration theory and community tourism planning', *Annals of Tourism Reseach*, vol. 22, pp. 186–204.

James, J. 1988, 'Tourism training: An issue now and for the future', pp. 123–32 in *Frontiers in Australian Tourism: The Search for New Perspectives in Policy Development and Research*, eds B. Faulkner & M. Fagence, Bureau of Tourism Research, Canberra.

Jamieson, K. 1996, Been There, Done That. Identity and the Overseas Experiences of Young Pakeha New Zealanders, unpublished MA dissertation, Massey University, Palmerston North.

Jansen-Verbeke, M. 1986, 'Inner-city tourism: Resources, tourists and promoters', *Annals of Tourism Research*, vol. 13, pp. 79–100.

— 1989, 'Inner cities and urban tourism in the Netherlands: New challenges for local authorities', pp. 233–53 in *Leisure and Urban Processes: Critical Studies of Leisure Policy in Western European Cities*, eds P. Bramham, I. Henry, H. Mommaas & H. van der Poel, Routledge, London and New York.

— 1990, 'Leisure + shopping = tourism product mix', pp. 128–37 in *Marketing Tourism Places*, eds G. Ashworth & B. Goodall, Routledge, London.

— 1991, 'Leisure shopping: A magic concept for the tourism industry?' *Tourism Management*, vol. 11, no. 1, pp. 9–14.

Januarius, M. 1993, 'Challenges and Choices', *Leisure Management*, vol. 13, no. 2, pp. 28–30.

Japan Travel Bureau 1991, *JTB Report '91: All About Japanese Overseas Travelers*, Japan Travel Bureau, Tokyo.

Jeffreys, A. 1987, 'A draft policy for a conservation council', pp. 2–11 in *Tourism and the Conservation Movement*, ed. J. Corkhill, North Coast Environment Council, Lismore.

Jeffries, D. 1989, 'Selling Britain—a case for privatisation?', *Travel and Tourism Analyst*, vol. 1, pp. 69–81.

Jenkins, J. 1988, Issues in the development of fossicking as a recreational activity and tourist attraction in the New England Region, unpublished honours thesis, Department of Geography and Planning, University of New England, Armidale.

— 1993, 'Tourism policy in rural New South Wales—policy and research priorities', *Geojournal*, vol. 29, no. 3, pp. 281–90.

— 1997, 'The role of the Commonwealth Government in rural tourism and regional development in Australia', pp. 181–90 in *Tourism Planning and Policy in Australia and New Zealand: Cases, Issues and Practice*, eds C.M. Hall, J. Jenkins & G. Kearsley, Irwin Publishers, Sydney.

— 2001, 'Statutory authorities in whose interests? The case of Tourism New South Wales, the bed tax, and "the Games"', *Pacific Tourism Review*, vol. 4, no. 4, pp. 201–18.

Jenkins, J., Hall, C.M. & Troughton, M. 1998, 'The restructuring of rural economies: Rural tourism and recreation as a government response', in *Tourism and Recreation in Rural Areas*, eds R.W. Butler, C.M. Hall & J. Jenkins, John Wiley, Chichester.

Jessop, B. 1999, 'Reflections on globalisation and its (il)logic(s)', pp. 19–38 in *Globalisation and the Asia–Pacific: Contested Territories*, Warwickshire Studies in Globalisation Series, eds K. Olds, P. Dicken, P. F. Kelly, L. Kong & H.W. Yeung, Routledge, London.

Johnston, R.J. 1991, *Geography and Geographers: Anglo-American Human Geography Since 1945*, 4th edn, Edward Arnold, London.

Johnston, W.R. 1981, *A Bibliography of Queensland History*, Library Board of Queensland, Brisbane.

Johnston, W.R. & Zerner, M. 1985, *A Guide to the History of Queensland: A Bibliographic Survey of Selected Resources in Queensland History*, Library Board of Queensland, Brisbane.

Joint Committee on the Australian Capital Territory (JCACT) 1961, *Report on the Australian Capital Territory Tourist Industry*, Parliament of the Commonwealth of Australia, Canberra.

— 1972, *Report of the Joint Committee on the Australian Capital Territory on Employment Opportunities in the A.C.T.*, Parliament of the Commonwealth of Australia, Canberra.

— 1980, *Tourism in the A.C.T.*, *Report of the Joint Committee on the Australian Capital Territory Tourist Industry*, Australian Government Publishing Service, Canberra.

— 1986, *Hospitality in the ACT*, *Report of the Joint Committee on the Australian Capital Territory*, Commonwealth of Australia, Canberra.

Jones, M. 1977, *Organisational and Social Planning in Australian Local Government*, Heinemann Educational, Richmond.

— 1986, *A Sunny Place for Shady People: The Real Gold Coast Story*, Allen and Unwin, Sydney.

Joppe, M., Martin, D.W. & Waalen, J. 2001, 'Toronto's image as a destination: A comparative importance-satisfaction analysis by origin of visitor', *Journal of Travel Research*, vol. 39, February, pp. 252–60.

Kang, S. & Page, S.J. 2000, 'Tourism, migration and emigration: travel patterns of Korean-New Zealanders in the 1990s', *Tourism Geographies: International Journal of Place, Space and the Environment*, vol. 2, no. 3, pp. 50–65.

Kariel, H.G. 1989, 'Tourism and development: Perplexity or panacea?', *Journal of Travel Research*, vol. 28, no. 1, pp. 2–6.

Karn, V.A. 1977, *Retiring to the Seaside*, Routledge and Kegan Paul, London.

Kavass, I.I. 1960, 'Adelaide Festival of Arts', *Australian Quarterly*, vol. 32, no. 2, pp. 7–10, 16.

Kaza, S. 1982, 'Recreational whalewatching in California: A profile', *Whalewatcher*, vol. 16, no. 1, pp. 6–8.

Keane, P.A., Wild, A.E.R., & Rogers, J.H. 1979, 'Trampling and erosion in alpine country', *Journal of the Soil Conservation Service of New South Wales*, vol. 35, pp. 7–12.

Kearns, G. & Philo, C. (eds) 1993, *Selling Places: The City as Cultural Capital, Past and Present*, Pergamon Press, Oxford.

Kearsley, G. 1997a, 'Managing the consequences of over-use by tourists of New Zealand's conservation estate', pp. 87–98 in *Tourism Planning and Policy in Australia and New Zealand: Cases, Issues and Practice*, eds C.M. Hall, J. Jenkins & G. Kearsley, Irwin Publishers, Sydney.

— 1997b, 'Public acceptance of heritage tourism as an instrument of urban restructuring', pp. 241–51 in *Tourism Planning and Policy in Australia and New Zealand: Cases, Issues and Practice*, eds C.M. Hall, J. Jenkins & G. Kearsley, Irwin Publishers, Sydney.

Kearsley, G., Hall, C.M. & Jenkins, J.M. 1997, 'Tourism planning and policy in natural areas: Introductory comments', pp. 66–74 in *Tourism Planning and Policy in Australia and New Zealand: Cases, Issues and Practice*, eds C.M. Hall, J. Jenkins & G. Kearsley, Irwin Publishers, Sydney.

Kelly, I. 1993, 'Tourist destination crime rates: An examination of Cairns and the Gold Coast, Australia', *Journal of Tourism Studies*, vol. 4, no. 2, pp. 2–11.

Kelly, M. & McConvill, C. 1991, 'Down by the docks', in Davidson, G. and McConvill, C. (eds) *A Heritage Handbook*, Allen & Unwin, North Sydney, pp. 91–114.

Kelly, P. F. & Olds, K. 1999, 'Questions in a crisis: the contested meanings of globalisation in the Asia–Pacific', pp. 1–15 in *Globalisation and the Asia–Pacific: Contested Territories*, Warwickshire Studies in Globalisation Series, eds K. Olds, P. Dicken, P. F. Kelly, L. Kong & H.W. Yeung, Routledge, London.

Kendziorek, M. 1994, 'Making your tasting room profitable, Part I, ten commandments of the tasting room', *Wine Marketing PWV*, July/August, pp. 75–6.

Kent, W., Schock, P. & Snow, R. 1983, 'Shopping: Tourism's unsung hero(ine)', *Journal of Travel Research*, vol. 21, no. 4, pp. 2–4.

Kerr, J.H. 1872, *Glimpses of Life in Victoria by a Resident*, Edinburgh.

Kesteven, S. 1987, *Aborigines in the Tourist Industry*, East Kimberley Working Paper No. 14, Centre for Resource and Environmental Studies, Australian National University, Canberra.

King, B. 1994, 'What is ethnic tourism? An Australian perspective', *Tourism Management*, vol. 15, no. 3, pp. 173–6.

King B. & Gamage M. 1994, 'Measuring the value of the ethnic connection: expatriate travelers from Australia to Sri Lanka', *Journal of Travel Research*, Fall, pp. 46–50.

King, B. & Hyde, G. (eds) 1989, *Tourism Marketing in Australia*, Hospitality Press, Melbourne.

King, B., Pizam, A. & Milman, A. 1993, 'Social impacts of tourism: Host perceptions', *Annals of Tourism Research*, vol. 20, pp. 650–65.

King, R.L. 1988, Coach transport to the year 2000, paper presented at the *Frontiers in Australian Tourism Conference*, University House, Australian National University, Canberra.

Kingston, M. 1987, 'Llew's Expo auction: Eight bid for Brisbane's heart', *Times on Sunday*, 19 July, pp. 1, 3.

Kinkade, D. & Woodward, G. 2001, 'Shopping for souvenir clothing', *Pacific Tourism Review*, vol. 5, pp. 159–65.

Kirkpatrick, J. 1980 'Hydro-Electric development and wilderness: report to the Department of the Environment', attachment to *Department of the Environment (Tas.), Assessment of the HEC Report on the Lower Gordon River Development Stage Two*, Department of the Environment, Hobart.

Kirkpatrick, J.B. & Haney, R.A. 1980, 'The quantification of developmental wilderness loss: the case of forestry in Tasmania', *Search*, vol. 11, no. 10, pp. 331–5.

Knapman, B. 1991, 'Tourism in the Northern Territory economy', pp. 240–58 in *Tourism in Australia*, eds P. Carroll, K. Donohue, M. McGovern & J. McMillen, Harcourt Brace Jovanovich, Marrickville.

Konrad, V.A. 1982, 'Historical artifacts as recreational resources', pp. 393–416 in *Recreational Land Use: Perspectives on its evolution in Canada*, eds G. Wall & J. Marsh, Carleton University Press, Ottawa.

Koslowski, J., Rosier, J. & Hill, G. 1988, 'Ultimate environmental threshold (UET) method in a marine environment', *Landscape and Urban Planning*, vol. 15, pp. 327–36.

Kotler, P. , Haider, D.H. & Rein, I. 1997, *Marketing Places: Attracting Investment, Industry, and Tourism to Cities, States, and Nations*, Macmillan, New York.

KPMG Peat Marwick Management Consultants 1991, *The Tourism Labour Market: Constraints and Attitudes*, Report for Tourism Training Australia, KPMG Peat Marwick Management Consultants, Sydney.

Krippendorf, J. 1982, 'Towards new tourism policies: The importance of environmental and sociocultural factors', *Tourism Management*, vol. 3, no. 3, pp. 135–48.

— 1986a, 'The new tourist—turning point for leisure and travel', *Tourism Management*, vol. 7, pp. 131–5.

— 1986b, 'Tourism in the system of industrial society', *Annals of Tourism Research*, vol. 13, pp. 517–32.

— 1987, *The Holiday Makers: Understanding the Impact of Leisure and Travel*, Heinemann Professional Publishing, Oxford.

Lamb, A.N. 1988, 'Tourism development and planning in Australia—the need for a national strategy', *International Journal of Hospitality Management*, vol. 7, no. 4, pp. 353–61.

Lane, B. 1994, 'What is rural tourism?', *Journal of Sustainable Tourism*, vol. 2, no. 1/2, pp. 7–21.

Lang, R. 1986, 'Achieving integration in resource planning', pp. 27–50 in *Integrated Approaches to Resource Planning and Management*, ed. R. Lang, University of Calgary Press, Calgary.

Lankford, S.V. & Howard, D.R. 1994, 'Developing a tourism impact attitude scale', *Annals of Tourism Research*, vol. 21, pp. 121–39.

Lansbury, C. 1970, *Arcady in Australia: The Evocation of Australia in Nineteenth-Century English Literature*, Melbourne University Press, Melbourne.

Law, C. 1985, *Urban Tourism: Selected British Case Studies*, Working Paper, Department of Geography, University of Salford, Salford.

— 1987, 'Conference and exhibition tourism', *Built Environment*, vol. 13, no. 2, pp. 85–95.

— 1993, *Urban Tourism: Attracting Visitors to Large Cities*, Mansell, London.

Lawrence, G. 1987, *Capitalism and the Countryside*, Pluto Press, Sydney.

Laws, E. 1991, *Tourism Marketing*, Stanley Thomas, Cheltenham.

Laws, E., Faulkner, B. & Moscardo, G. (eds) 1998, *Embracing and Managing Change in Tourism: International Case Studies*, Routledge, London.

Lawson, F. & Baud-Bovy, M. 1977, *Tourism and Recreation Development: A Handbook of Physical Planning*, The Architectural Press, London.

Lee, M. 1994, *Meetings Industry a Big Export Earner*, news release from the office of the Minister for Tourism, Parliament House, Canberra, 22 March.

Leiper, N. 1979, 'The framework of tourism: Towards a definition of tourism, tourist, and the tourist industry', *Annals of Tourism Research*, vol. 6, pp. 390–407.

— 1980, An interdisciplinary study of Australian tourism: Its scope, characteristics and consequences, with particular reference to governmental policies since 1965, unpublished Master of General Studies Thesis, University of New South Wales, Kensington.

— 1981, 'Towards a cohesive curriculum in tourism: The case for a distinct discipline', *Annals of Tourism Research*, vol. 8, pp. 69–74.

— 1983, 'An etymology of "tourism"', *Annals of Tourism Research*, vol. 10, pp. 277–81.

— 1984, 'Tourism and leisure: The significance of tourism in the leisure spectrum', pp. 249–53 in *Proceedings 12th New Zealand Geography Conference*, New Zealand Geography Society, Christchurch.

— 1989, *Tourism and Tourism Systems*, Occasional Paper No. 1, Department of Management Systems, Massey University, Palmerston North.

— 1990a, *Tourism Systems: An Interdisciplinary Perspective*, Occasional Papers No. 2, Department of Management Systems, Business Studies Faculty, Massey University, Palmerston.

— 1990b, 'Partial industrialization of tourism systems', *Annals of Tourism Research*, vol. 17, pp. 600–5.

— 1993, 'Industrial entrophy in tourism systems', *Annals of Tourism Research*, vol. 20, pp. 221–26.

— 1995, *Tourism Management*, RMIT Press, Melbourne.

— 1999, 'A conceptual analysis of tourism-supported employment which reduces the incidence of exaggerated, misleading statistics about jobs', *Tourism Management*, vol. 20, pp. 605–13.

— 2002, 'Ansett's collapse: An explanation of why the airline failed and how to prevent it happening again', *Current Issues in Tourism*, in press.

Leiper, N. & Hall, C.M. 1993, *The 2000 Olympics and Australia's Tourism Industries*, submission to House of Representatives' Standing Committee on Industry, Science and Technology Inquiry into Implications for Australian Industry Arising from the Year 2000 Olympics, Southern Cross University/University of Canberra, Lismore/Canberra.

Lengyel, P. 1975, 'A rejoinder', *International Social Science Journal*, vol. 27, no. 4, pp. 753–57.

Lesslie, R. 1991, 'Wilderness survey and evaluation in Australia', *Australian Geographer*, vol. 22, pp. 35–43.

Lesslie, R.G., Mackey, B.G. & Preece, K.M. 1988, 'A computer-based method for the evaluation of wilderness', *Environmental Conservation*, vol. 15, no. 3, pp. 225–32.

Lesslie, R.G. & Taylor, S.G. 1983, *Wilderness in South Australia: An Inventory of the State's Relatively High Quality Wilderness Areas*, Occasional Paper No. 1, Centre for Environmental Studies, University of Adelaide, Adelaide.

— 1985, 'The wilderness continuum concept and its implications for Australian wilderness preservation policy', *Biological Conservation*, vol. 32, pp. 309–33.

Letcher, G. 1981, *Local Histories of South Australia: A Selected Bibliography 1976–Feb. 1981*, School of Architecture and Building Library, South Australian Institute of Technology, Adelaide.

Lew, A.A. 1985, 'Bringing tourists to town', *Small Town*, vol. 16, pp. 4–10.

— 1989, 'Authenticity and sense of place in the tourism development experience of older retail districts', *Journal of Travel Research*, vol. 27, no. 4, pp. 15–22.

Lew, A.A. & Hall, C.M. 1998, 'The Geography of Sustainable Tourism: Lessons and Prospects', in *Sustainable Tourism Development: A Geographical Perspective*, eds C.M. Hall & A. Lew, Addison Wesley Longman, London.

Liberal Party-National Party 1993, *Tourism Policy*, Office of David Jull, Shadow Minister for Tourism and Aviation, Upper Mt Gravatt, Queensland, February.

— 1996, *Destination Australia: The Coalition's Policy On Tourism "A National Priority"*, Office of Senator Warwick Parer, Shadow Minister for Tourism, Aviation and Customs, 13 February 1996, Parliament House, Canberra.

Lickorish, L.J. & Jenkins, C.L. 1997, *An Introduction to Tourism*, Butterworth-Heinemann, Oxford.

Lickorish, L.J., Jefferson, A., Bodlender, J. & Jenkins, C.L. 1991, *Developing Tourism Destinations: Policies and Perspectives*, Longman, Harlow.

Lindberg, K. & McKercher, B. 1997, 'Ecotourism: A critical overview', *Pacific Tourism Review*, vol. 1, pp. 65–79.

Lines, W.J. 1991, *Taming the Great South Land*, University of California Press, Berkeley.

Lloyd, T. 1989, 'The Adelaide Festival: SA reaps the economic benefits', *The Advertiser*, 24 March.

Local Government & Shires Association of New South Wales 1988, *Tourism and Local Government*, Local Government & Shires Association of New South Wales, Sydney.

Loh, D. 1989, 'Sovereign Hill', pp. 170–1 in *Melbourne, Insight City Guides*, eds J. Borthwick & D. McGonigal, APA Publications/Victorian Tourism Commission, Melbourne.

Long, P. T. & Nuckolls, J.S. 1994, 'Organising resources for rural tourism development: the importance of leadership, planning and technical assistance', *Tourism Recreation Research*, vol. 19, no. 2, pp. 19–34.

Lonsdale, W. & Lane, A. 1994, 'Tourist vehicles as vectors of weed seeds in Kakadu National Park, Northern Australia', *Biological Conservation*, vol. 69, pp. 277–83.

Lord Parry 1988, 'The nature of tourism as an economic resource', pp. 5–15 in *The Roles of Government in the Development of Tourism as an Economic Resource*, ed. D. McSwan, Seminar Series No. 1, Centre for Studies in Travel and Tourism, James Cook University, Townsville.

Lowenthal, D. 1981, 'Conclusion: Dilemmas of preservation', pp. 213–37 in *Our Past Before Us, Why do we save it?*, eds M. Binney & D. Lowenthal, Temple Smith, London.

Lucas, R.C. 1964, 'Wilderness perception and use: The example of the Boundary Waters Canoe Area', *Natural Resources Journal*, vol. 3, no. 3, pp. 394–411.

Lundgren, J.O.J. 1982, 'The tourist frontier of Nouveau Quebec: Functions and regional linkages', *Tourist Review*, vol. 37, no. 2, pp. 10–16.

Lynch, P.G. & Jensen, R.C. 1984, 'The economic impact of the XII Commonwealth Games on the Brisbane region', *Urban Policy and Planning*, vol. 2, no. 3, pp. 11–14.

Lynch, R. & Veal, A.J. 1996, *Australian Leisure*, Longman Australia, South Melbourne.

— 1998, 'The casino in the post-industrial city: the social and economic impact of the Sydney casino', pp. 181–96 in *Leisure Management: Issues and Applications*, eds M.F. Collins & I.S. Cooper, CAB International, Wallingford.

Mabogunje, A.L. 1980, *The Development Process: A Spatial Perspective*, Hutchinson, London.

McArthur, S. 1989, Working hard to be a solo man: An investigation into the facets and ramifications of group size, as it relates to adventure tourism in white water rafting, unpublished integrated project, University of New England, Northern Rivers, Lismore.

— 1996, 'Beyond the limits of acceptable change—developing a model to monitor and manage tourism in remote areas', in *Tourism Down Under: 1996 Tourism Conference Proceedings*, Centre for Tourism, University of Otago, Dunedin.

— 2000a, Visitor Management in Action: An Analysis of the Development and Implementation of Visitor Management Models at Jenolan Caves and Kangaroo Island, unpublished PhD thesis, University of Canberra, Belconnen.

— 2000b, 'Beyond carrying capacity: Introducing a model to monitor and manage visitor activity in forests', pp. 259–78 in *Forest Tourism and Recreation: Case Studies in Environmental Management*, eds X. Font & J. Tribe CABI, Wallingford.

McArthur, S. & Hall, C.M. 1993, 'Strategic planning for visitor heritage management: Integrating people and places through participation', in *Heritage Management in New Zealand and Australia: Interpretation, Marketing and Visitor Management*, eds C.M. Hall & S. McArthur, Oxford University Press, Auckland.

Macbeth, J. 1997, 'Planning in action: A report and reflections on sustainable tourism in the ex-Shire of Omeo', pp. 145–53 in *Tourism Planning and Policy in Australia and New Zealand: Cases, Issues and Practice*, eds C.M. Hall, J. Jenkins & G. Kearsley, Irwin Publishers, Sydney.

McCann, C. & Thompson, G. 1992, 'An economic analysis of the first Western Australian state masters games', *Journal of Tourism Studies*, vol. 3, no. 1, pp. 28–34.

MacCannell, D. 1973, 'Staged authenticity: Arrangements of social space in tourist settings', *American Journal of Sociology*, vol. 79, no. 3, pp. 357–61.

— 1976, *The Tourist: A New Theory of the Leisure Class*, Schocken Books, New York.

MacDermott, K. 1992, 'Australia "lagging" in development incentives', *Australian Financial Review*, 17 March, p. 38.

McDermott Miller Group 1991, 'Destination South West Pacific', *Tourism FX: A Quarterly Analysis of New Zealand Tourism*, July.

McDonald, S. 1988, *The 1988 Adelaide Festival: An Economic Impact Study*, Centre for South Australian Economic Studies, University of Adelaide, Adelaide.

McDonnell, I., Allen, J. & O'Toole, W. 1999, *Festival and Special Event Management*, Wiley, Brisbane.

McGinnity, B.C. & Jackson, L.A. 1986, 'Coastal management and the Gold Coast', pp. 213–17 in *Proceedings, Australian Environmental Council Coastal Management Conference*, Australian Environmental Council.

McGregor, C. 1966, *Profile of Australia*, Penguin, Ringwood.

McHugh, E. 1995, 'Lucky breaks', *The Australian Magazine*, 1–2 April, pp. 41–50.

McIntosh, R.W. & Goeldner, C.R. 1986, *Tourism: Principles, Practices, Philosophies*, 5th edn, John Wiley & Sons, New York.

— 1990, *Tourism Principles, Practices, Philosophies*, 6th edn, John Wiley & Sons, New York.

Macionis, N. 1996, 'Wine tourism in Australia', pp. 264–86 in *Proceedings of Tourism Down Under II: A Tourism Research Conference*, University of Otago, Dunedin.

— 1997, Wine tourism in Australia: Emergence, development and critical issues, unpublished Masters thesis, University of Canberra, Canberra.

Macionis, N. & Cambourne, B. 1994, *Marketing the Canberra District Wineries*, unpublished research report, National Capital Wine Tours, Canberra.

McKanna, G. 1989, 'How tourist dollars leak away', *Australian Financial Review*, 29 August, pp. 1, 2.

Mackay, J. & Virtanen, S. 1992, 'Tourism and the Australian Alps', pp. 159–65 in *Heritage Management: Parks, Heritage and Tourism, Conference Proceedings*, Royal Australian Institute of Parks and Recreation, Hobart.

Mackay, K. & Fesenmaier, D. 1997, 'Pictorial element of destination image formation', *Annals of Tourism Research*, vol. 24, pp. 537–65.

— 2000, 'An exploration of cross-cultural destination image assessment', *Journal of Travel Research*, vol. 38, pp. 417–23.

McKenry, K. 1977, 'Value Analysis of Wilderness Areas', pp. 209–21 in *Leisure and Recreation in Australia*, D. Mercer (ed.), Sorrett Publishing, Malvern.

McKercher, B. 1993a, 'Some fundamental truths about tourism: Understanding tourism's social and environmental impacts', *Journal of Sustainable Tourism*, vol. 1, no. 1, pp. 6–16.

— 1993b, 'The unrecognized threat to tourism: Can tourism survive sustainability', *Tourism Management*, vol. 14, no. 2, pp. 131–6.

— 1993c, 'Australian conservation organisations' perspectives on tourism in National Parks: A critique', *Geojournal*, vol. 29, no. 3, pp. 307–13.

— 1997, 'Benefits and costs of tourism in Victoria's Alpine National Park: Comparing attitudes of tour operators, management staff and public interest group leaders', pp. 99–110 in *Tourism Planning and Policy in Australia and New Zealand: Cases, Issues and Practice*, eds C.M. Hall, J. Jenkins & G. Kearsley, Irwin Publishers, Sydney.

McKercher, B. & Davidson, P. 1995, 'Women and commercial adventure tourism: Does the industry understand its dominant market?', pp. 129–40 in *Tourism Research and Education in Australia*, eds B. Faulkner, M. Fagence, M. Davidson & S. Craig-Smith, Bureau of Tourism Research, Canberra.

McMillen, J. 1991a, 'The politics of Queensland tourism', pp. 97–113 in *Tourism in Australia*, eds P. Carroll, K. Donohue, M. McGovern & J. McMillen, Harcourt Brace Jovanovich, Marrickville.

— 1991b, 'Casinos and tourism: What's the big attraction?', pp. 153–72 in *Tourism in Australia*, eds P. Carroll, K. Donohue, M. McGovern & J. McMillen, Harcourt Brace Jovanovich, Marrickville.

McMillen, J. & Lafferty, G. 1991, 'The tourism workforce: Service or servility', pp. 82–96 in *Tourism in Australia*, eds P. Carroll, K. Donohue, M. McGovern & J. McMillen, Harcourt Brace Jovanovich, Marrickville.

McMullan, J. 1988, 'Opening address: Frontiers of Australian tourism', pp. 3–6 in *Frontiers of Australian Tourism: The Search for New Perspectives in Policy Development and Research*, eds B. Faulkner & M. Fagence, Bureau of Tourism Research, Canberra.

Macquarie Bank's Tourism and Leisure Investment Banking Group 1995, *Perspectives on Tourism Investment: A study of the attitudes of institutional investors*, Macquarie Bank, Sydney.

McVey, M. & King, B. 1989, 'Hotels/accommodation: Hotels in Australia', *EIU Travel and Tourism Analyst*, no. 4, pp. 16–37.

Maddern, C. & Golledge, S. 1996, *Victorian Wineries Tourism Council Cellar Door Survey*, Victorian Wineries Tourism Council, Melbourne.

Maier, G. & Kaufmann, A. 1997, 'Business use of the internet in Austria: Types of use and barriers to adoption', paper presented at *Regional Science Association 37th European Congress Rome, Italy 26–29 August*, Regional Science Association, Rome.

Malloy, D.C. & Fennell, D. 1998, 'Codes of ethics and tourism: an exploratory content analysis', *Tourism Management*, vol. 19, no. 5, pp. 453–61.

Manidis Roberts Consultants 1996, *Tourism Optimisation Management Model for Kangaroo Island*, Working Draft, SATC, Adelaide.

Marconi, J. 1997, *Image Marketing: Using Public Perceptions to Attain Business Objectives*, NTC Business Books, Chicago.

Marsden, T., Lowe, P. & Whatmore, S. (eds) 1993, *Rural Restructuring: Global Processes and Their Response*, David Fulton Publishers, London.

Marsh, I. & Greenfield, J. 1993, *Sydney Gay & Lesbian Mardi Gras: An Evaluation of its Economic Impact*, Australian Graduate School of Management, Sydney.

Marsh, I. & Shaw, B. 2000, *Australia's Wine Industry, Collaboration and Learning as Causes of Competitive Success*, Australian Business Foundation, North Sydney.

Marsh, J. 1986, 'Wilderness tourism', pp. 47–59 in *Tourism and the Environment: Conflict or Harmony*, Canadian Society of Environmental Biologists—Alberta Chapter, Edmonton.

Marsh., J. & Staple, S. 1995, 'Cruise tourism in the Canadian Arctic and its implications', pp. 63–72 in *Polar Tourism: Tourism in the Arctic and Antarctic regions*, eds C.M. Hall & M. Johnston, John Wiley & Sons, Chichester.

Martyn, H. 1970, 'International tourism: Public attitudes and government policies', *Dalhousie Review*, vol. 50, pp. 40–54.

Mason, P. 2000, 'Zoo tourism: the need for more research', *Journal of Sustainable Tourism*, vol. 8, no. 4, pp. 333–9.

— 2002, 'The Big OE: New Zealanders' overseas experience in Britain', in *Tourism and Migration: New Relationships Between Consumption and Production*, eds C.M. Hall & A.M. Williams, Kluwer, Dortrecht.

Mason, P. & Legg, S. 1999, 'Antarctic Tourism: activities, impacts, management issues and a proposed research agenda', *Pacific Tourism Review*, vol. 3, no. 1, pp. 71–84.

Mason, P. & Mowforth, M. 1996, 'Codes of conduct in tourism', *Progress in Tourism and Hospitality Research*, vol. 2, no. 2, pp. 151–67.

Mathieson, A. & Wall, G. 1982, *Tourism: Economic, Physical and Social Impacts*, Longman, London.

Matthews, H.G. 1978, *International Tourism a Political and Social Analysis*, Schenkman Publishing Company, Cambridge.

Meethan, K. 1996, 'Consumed (in) in civilised city', *Annals of Tourism Research*, vol. 32, pp. 322–40.

— 2001, *Tourism in Global Society: Place, Culture and Consumption*, Palgrave, London.

Mercer, D. (ed.) 1981, *Outdoor Recreation: Australian Perspectives*, Sorrett Publishing, Malvern.

— 1994, 'Native peoples and tourism: Conflict and compromise', in *Global Tourism: The Next Decade*, ed. W.F. Theobald, Heinemann, Boston, pp. 124–5.

— 2000, *A Question of Balance: Natural Resources Conflict Issues in Australia*, 3rd edn, Federation Press, Leichardt.

The Mercury, 29 October 1968.

Merrett, D. & Whitwell, G. 1994, 'The empire strikes back: Marketing Australian beer and wine in the United Kingdom', pp. 162–88 in *Adding Value: Brands and Marketing in Food and Drink*, eds G. Jones & N.J. Morgan, Routledge, London and New York.

Messer, J. & Mosley, G. (eds) 1983, *What Future for Australia's Arid Lands*, Australian Conservation Foundation, Hawthorn.

Middleton, V. 1988, *Marketing in Travel and Tourism*, Heinemann, Oxford.

— 1994, 'Vision, strategy and corporate planning: An overview', in *Manual of Heritage Management*, ed. R. Harrison, Butterworth-Heinemann, Oxford.

Mieczkowski, Z. 1995, *Environmental Issues of Tourism and Recreation*, University Press of America, Lanham.

Mill, R.C. & Morrison, A.M. 1985, *The Tourism System: An Introductory Text*, Prentice-Hall International, Englewood Cliffs.

Millar, C. & Aiken, D. 1995, 'Conflict resolution in aquaculture: a matter of trust', pp. 617–45 in *Coldwater Aquaculture in Atlantic Canada*, 2nd edn, ed. A. Boghen, Canadian Institute for Research on Regional Development, Moncton.

Millar, S. 1989, 'Heritage management for heritage tourism', *Tourism Management*, vol. 10, no. 3, pp. 9–14.

Miller, G. 2001, 'The development of indicators for sustainable tourism', *Tourism Management*, vol. 22, no. 4, pp. 351–62.

Miller, M. 1993, 'The rise of coastal and marine tourism', *Ocean and Coastal Management*, vol. 21, pp. 183–99.

Miller, M.L. & Auyong, J. 1991, 'Coastal zone tourism: a potent force affecting environment and society', *Marine Policy*, vol. 15, no. 2, pp. 75–99.

Mills, E.D. 1983, *Design for Holidays and Tourism*, Butterworths, London.

Minerbi, L. 1992, *Impacts of Tourism Development in Pacific Islands*, Greenpeace Pacific Campaign, San Francisco.

Ministry of Economic Development 2001, Enhancing Economic Transformation and Growth. Industry and Regional Development. **http://www.med.govt.nz/ irdev/asst_prog/budget2001/enhancing.html**. (24th May).

Ministry of Tourism 1999. *Bulletin of Accommodation Statistics 1998*, Ministry of Tourism, Ankara.

Minnikin, R.N. 1987, 'World Expo 88—an economic impact study', in *The Effects of Hallmark Events on Cities*, Centre for Urban Research, University of Western Australia, Nedlands.

Mitchell, B. 1989, *Geography and Resource Analysis*, 2nd edn, Longmans, London.

Mitchell, R. & Hall, C.M. 2001, 'The winery consumer: A New Zealand perspective', *Tourism Recreation Research*, vol. 26, no. 2, pp. 63–75.

Mitchell, R., Hall, C.M. & McIntosh, A. 2000, 'Wine tourism and consumer behaviour', pp. 115–35 in *Wine Tourism Around the World: Development, Management and Markets*, eds C.M. Hall, E. Sharples, B. Cambourne & N. Macionis, Butterworth-Heinemann, Oxford.

Moffat, K.P., Tselpi, N.N. & Mayo, T.S. 1973, *Tourism in the Snowy Mountains, New South Wales, Australia*, New South Wales Department of Tourism, Sydney.

Moldan, B. & Bilharz, S. (eds) 1997, *Sustainability Indicators: Report of the Project on Indicators of Sustainable Development*, John Wiley & Sons, Chichester.

Mommaas, H. & van der Poel, H. 1989, 'Changes in economy, politics and lifestyles: An essay on the restructuring of urban leisure', pp. 254–76 in *Leisure and Urban Processes: Critical Studies of Leisure Policy in Western European Cities*, eds P. Bramham, I. Henry, H. Mommaas & H. van der Poel, Routledge, London and New York.

Montgomery, R.J. & Strick, S.K. 1995, *Meetings, Conventions, and Expositions: An Introduction to the Industry*, Van Nostrand Reinhold, New York.

Moore, K., Cushman, G. & Simmons, D. 1995, 'Behavioural conceptualisation of tourism and leisure', *Annals of Tourism Research*, vol. 22, pp. 67–85.

Morgan, N. & Pritchard, A. 1998, *Tourism Promotion and Power—Creating Images, Creating Identities*, John Wiley & Sons, Chichester.

— 1999, 'Building destination brands: the cases of Wales and Australia', *Journal of Brand Management*, vol. 7, no. 2, pp. 102–19.

— 2000, *Advertising in Tourism and Leisure*, Butterworth-Heinemann, Oxford.

— 2002, 'Contextualising destination branding', pp. 11–41 in *Destination Branding: Creating the Unique Destination Proposition*, eds N. Morgan, A. Pritchard & N. Pride, Butterworth-Heinemann, Oxford.

Morgan, N., Pritchard, A. & Pride, N. (eds) 2002, *Destination Branding: Creating the Unique Destination Proposition*, Butterworth-Heinemann, Oxford.

Morinis, E.A. 1992, 'Introduction,' pp. 1–17 in *Sacred Journeys: The Anthropology of Pilgrimage*, ed. E.A. Morinis, Greenwood Press, Westport.

Morrison, A.M. 1989, *Hospitality and Travel Marketing*, Delmar Publishers, Albany.

Morse, J. 2001, The Sydney 2000 Olympic Games: how the Australian Tourist Commission leveraged the games for tourism', *Journal of Vacation Marketing*, vol. 7, no. 2, pp. 101–9.

Moscardo, G.M. & Pearce, P. L. 1986, 'Historic theme parks: an Australian experience in authenticity', *Annals of Tourism Research*, vol. 13, pp. 467–79.

Mosley, J.G. 1963, Aspects of the geography of recreation in Tasmania, unpublished Ph.D. Thesis, Australian National University, Canberra.

Moutinho, L. 1987, 'Consumer behaviour in tourism', *European Journal of Marketing*, vol. 21, no. 10, pp. 3–44.

Mowforth, M. & Munt, I. 1998, *Tourism and Sustainability: New Tourism in the Third World*, Routledge, London.

Mowlana, H. & Smith, G. 1990, 'Tourism, telecommunications and transnational banking: A framework for policy analysis', *Tourism Management*, vol. 11, no. 4, pp. 315–24.

Moynahan, B. 1985, *The Tourist Trap*, Pan Books, London.

Mucciaroni, G. 1991, 'Unclogging the arteries: the defeat of client politics and the logic of collective action', *Policy Studies Journal*, vol. 19, nos. 3–4, pp. 474–94.

Muir, F. & Chester, G. 1993, 'Managing tourism to a seabird nesting island', *Tourism Management*, vol. 14, no. 2, pp. 99–105.

Mullins, P. 1984, 'Hedonism and real estate: Resort tourism and Gold Coast development', pp. 31–50 in *Conflict and Development*, ed. P. Williams, Allen & Unwin, Sydney.

— 1990, 'Tourist cities as new cities: Australia's Gold Coast and Sunshine Coast', *Australian Planner*, vol. 28, no. 3, pp. 37–41.

— 1994, 'Class relations and tourism urbanisation: The regeneration of the petite bourgeoisie and the emergence of a new urban form', *International Journal of Urban and Regional Research*, vol. 18, no. 4, pp. 591–607.

Muloin, S. 1998, 'Psychological benefits of whale watching', *Pacific Tourism Review*, vol. 2, pp. 199–213.

Murdoch, W. 1939, *Collected Essays of Walter Murdoch*, Angus and Robertson, Sydney.

Murphy, D. & Reid, B. 1992, 'A Tasman marriage of convenience', *Time International*, vol. 7, no. 37, 14 September, pp. 18–23.

Murphy, P. & Watson, S. 1997, *Surface City: Sydney at the Millennium*, Pluto Press Australia, Annandale.

Murphy, P. A. 1981, 'Patterns of coastal retirement migration', pp. 301–14 in *Towards an Older Australia*, ed. A. Howe, University of Queensland Press, St. Lucia.

Murphy, P. E. 1981, 'Tourism course proposal for a social science curriculum', *Annals of Tourism Research*, vol. 8, pp. 96–105.

— 1983, 'Perceptions and attitudes of decision-making groups in tourism centers', *Journal of Travel Research*, vol. 21, pp. 8–12.

— 1985, *Tourism: A Community Approach*, Methuen, New York.

— 1988, 'Community driven tourism planning', *Tourism Management*, vol. 9, no. 2, pp. 96–104.

— 1994, 'Tourism and sustainable development', pp. 274–90 in *Global Tourism: The Next Decade*, ed. W. Theobold, Butterworth-Heinemann, Oxford.

— (ed.) 1997, *Quality Management in Urban Tourism*, International Western Geographical Series, John Wiley & Sons, Chichester.

Murray, M. & Sproats, J. 1990, 'The disabled traveller: tourism and disability in Australia', *The Journal of Tourism Studies*, vol. 1, no. 1, pp. 9–14.

Narayana, C.L. & Markin, R.J. 1975, 'Consumer behaviour and product performance: an alternative conceptualization', *Journal of Marketing*, vol. 39, pp. 1–6.

National Capital Development Committee 1981, *Assessment of ACT Tourist Industry Structure*, National Capital Development Commission, Canberra.

National Capital Planning Authority 1991, *National Capital Plan, Amendment no. 2*, AGPS, Canberra.

National Centre for Studies in Travel and Tourism 1989, *Expo 88 Impact The Impact of World Expo 88 on Queensland's Tourism Industry*, prepared by the National Centre for Studies in Travel and Tourism for the Queensland Tourist and Travel Corporation, James Cook University, Townsville.

National Oceanic and Atmospheric Administration (NOAA) 1997, *1998 Year of the Ocean—Coastal Tourism and Recreation* (Discussion paper), **http://www.yoto98. noaa.gov/yoto/meeting/tour_rec_316.html**

National Parks and Primitive Areas Council 1934, Blue Mountains National Park Special Supplement, *Katoomba Daily*, 24 August.

National Tourism Committee 1988, *Tourism*, produced by the Australian Tourism Commission on behalf of the National Tourism Committee, Canberra.

Nature Conservation Council of NSW 1988, *Policy on Tourism*, Nature Conservation Council of NSW, Sydney.

Negroponte, N. 1995, *Being Digital*, Knopf, New York.

Neville, N. 1986, *Local History in Victoria: An Update of Carole Beaumont's 1980 Bibliography*, State Library of Victoria, Melbourne.

New South Wales Film and Tourism Office 1998, *Everything You Need to Know About Developing Model Film Policy*, New South Wales Film and Tourism Office, Sydney, **http://www.ftosyd.nsw.gov.au/TEXTONLY/ftohome.htm** (14/02/02).

— 2002, *Production Updates*, New South Wales Film and Television Office, Sydney

New South Wales Government 1990, *The New South Wales Coast Government Policy*, New South Wales Government, Sydney.

New South Wales Tourism Commission 1989a, *Tourism Trends in New South Wales*, Prepared by Bureau of Tourism Research, Canberra, for Policy and Research Branch, NSW Tourism Commission, Sydney.

— 1989b, *The Social, Cultural and Environmental Impacts of Tourism*, New South Wales Tourism Commission, Sydney.

— 1990, *New South Wales Tourist Development Strategy—A Plan for the Future*, New South Wales Tourism Commission, Sydney.

— 1993, *Annual Report 1992–93*, New South Wales Tourism Commission, Sydney.

New Zealand Film Commission 2000, *About Us*, New Zealand Film Commission, Wellington, **http://www.nzfilm.co.nz/frame4aboutus.html** (assessed 9th June).

New Zealand Parliamentary Commission for the Environment 1997, *Report on Tourism's Impact on the Environment*, Parliamentary Commission for the Environment, Wellington.

Newsome, D., Moore, S. & Dowling, R. 2001, *Natural Area Tourism: Ecology, Impacts and Management*, Channelview Publications, Clevedon.

NZ History Net 2000, *Anzac Day*, An essay from the Oxford Companion to New Zealand Military History, edited by Ian McGibbon with the assistance of

Paul Goldstone. Published by Oxford University Press in September 2000, **http://www.nzhistory.net.nz/Gallery/Anzac/Anzacday.htm**

Ng, S. & Hall, C.M. 1997, 'Internet use by the New Zealand tourism industry: Adoption, attitudes and use', in *Trails, Tourism and Regional Development*, eds J.Higham & G. Kearsley, Centre for Tourism, Dunedin.

Nguyen, T.H. & King, B.E.M. 2001, 'Migrant communities and tourism consumption: The case of the Vietnamese in Australia,' in *Tourism and Migration: New Relationships Between Consumption and Production*, eds. C.M. Hall & A.M. Williams, Kluwer, Dortrecht.

Nichols, L.L. 1976, 'Tourism and crime', *Annals of Tourism Research*, vol. 3, pp. 176–81.

Norkunas, M.K. 1993, *The Politics of Memory: Tourism, History and Ethnicity in Monterey, California*, State University of New York Press, Albany.

North Coast Environment Council 1987, *Tourism and the Environment, A Position Paper on Tourism Development by the North Coast Environment Council*, North Coast Environment Council, Lismore.

Northern Australia Development Council 1980, *Trade and Tourism in the 80's, Seminar Proceedings*, vol. 2, Northern Australia Development Council, Cairns.

Northern Territory Tourism Commission (NTTC) 1993a, *Corporate Plan 1993/4–1997/98*, NTTC, Darwin.

— 1993b, *Annual Report 1992/93*, NTTC, Darwin.

— 1994, *Northern Territory Tourism Master Plan*, NTTC, Darwin.

— 1996a, *Annual Report 1995/96*, NTTC, Darwin.

— 1996b, *Tennant Creek Regional Tourism Development Plan: 'A commitment to growth'*, NTTC, Darwin.

— 1996c, *Katherine Regional Tourism Development Plan: 'A commitment to growth'*, NTTC, Darwin.

— 1996d, *Top End Regional Tourism Development Plan: 'A commitment to growth'*, NTTC, Darwin.

— 1997a, *Australia's Northern Territory Selected Statistics 1996/97*, NTTC, Darwin.

— 1997b, *Northern Territory Tourist Commission Corporate Plan 1997/98*, NTTC, Darwin.

— 1997c, *Central Australian Regional Tourism Development Plan: 'A commitment to growth'*, NTTC, Darwin.

— 2000, *Territory Tourism Selected Statistics 1999/2000*, NTTC, Darwin, **http://www.nttc.com.au/statistics/pdf/Selected_Stats_99-00.pdf** (accessed 18 June 2001).

— 2001a, 2000–2005 Tourism Development Masterplan, NTTC, Darwin, **http://www.nttc.com.au/IndustryDevelopment/masterplan.asp** (accessed 10 March 2002).

— 2001b, *Annual Report 2000–2001*, NTTC, Darwin.

— 2002a, *Introduction to the NTTC*, NTTC Darwin, **http://www.nttc.com.au/About/Overview.asp** (accessed 10 March 2002).

Norval, A.J. 1936, *The Tourist Industry: A National and International Survey*, Sir Isacc Pitman & Sons, London.

Nuñez, T. 1989, 'Touristic studies in anthropological perspective', pp. 265–74 in *Hosts and Guests: The Anthropology of Tourism*, 2nd edn, ed. V. Smith, University of Pennsylvania Press, Philadelphia.

O'Brien B.J. and Associates 1988, *Draft Environmental Guidelines for Tourist Developments*, Report to West Australian Environmental Protection Authority and the West Australian Tourism Commission, Perth.

O'Clery, P. 1988, 'Private enterprise leadership from the ATIA', pp. 131–5 in *The Tourism and Hospitality Industry*, ed. J. Blackwell, International Magazine Services, Sydney.

— 1990a, 'There is a way: Tourism earnings could be the answer to our overseas debt problem', *Tourism Travel and Management*, April, p. 39.

— 1990b, 'Clear strategies essential', *Tourism Travel and Management*, November, p. 30.

Odum, W.E. 1976, *Ecological Guidelines for Tropical Coastal Development*, International Union for Conservation of Nature and Natural Resources, Morges.

— 1982, 'Environmental degradation and the tyranny of the small decision', *Bioscience*, vol. 32, p. 728.

Office of Local Government 1987, *Tourism Research Study Cairns–Mulgrave*, prepared by Cameron McNamara for the Cairns City Council and Mulgrave Shire Council, Office of Local Government, Department of Local Government and Administration, Australian Government Publishing Service, Canberra.

Office of National Tourism (ONT) 1997a, *Australian Tourism Investment Incentives*, Tourism Facts No 9, May, **http://www.tourism.gov.au/new/cfa/cfa_fs9.html** (accessed 31/12/97).

— 1997b, *Meetings, Incentives, Conventions & Exhibitions*, Tourism Facts No 4, May, **http://www.tourism.gov.au/new/cfa/cfa_fs4.html** (accessed 31/12/97).

— 1997c, *Cultural Tourism*, Tourism Facts No 10, May, **http://www.tourism.gov.au/new/cfa/cfa_fs10.html** (accessed 31/12/97).

— 1997d, *Aboriginal and Torres Strait Islander Tourism*, Tourism Facts No 11, May, **http://www.tourism.gov.au/new/cfa/cfa_fs11.html** (accessed 31/12/97).

— 1997e, *Ecotourism*, Tourism Facts No 16, May, **http://www.tourism.gov.au/new/cfa/cfa_fs16.html** (accesssed 31/12/97).

— 1997f, *Towards a National Tourism Plan: A Discussion Paper*, Office of National Tourism, Canberra, **http://www.tourism.gov.au/publications/tourplan/discussion.html** (accessed 6/1/98).

— 1997g, *Getting it Right for the Millenium*, report by Jon Hutchison to the Minister for Industry, Science and Tourism, Office of National Tourism, Canberra.

— 1997h, *Impact*, November.

— 1997i, *The Backpacker Market*, Tourism Facts No 15, May, **http://www.tourism.gov.au/new/cfa/cfa_fs15.html** (accesssed 31/12/97).

— 1998, *Impact*, February.

Office of Tourism Industry Development 1993, *Business Statement*, Office of Tourism Industry Development, Adelaide.

Olds, K. 1988, Planning for the housing impacts of a hallmark event: A case study of Expo 86, Unpublished M.A. Thesis, School of Community and Regional Planning, University of British Columbia, Vancouver.

— 1998, 'The housing impacts of mega-events', *Current Issues in Tourism*, vol. 1, no. 1, forthcoming.

Oppermann, M. 1998, 'Farm tourism in New Zealand', in *Tourism and Recreation in Rural Areas*, eds R.W. Butler, C.M. Hall & J. Jenkins, John Wiley, Chichester.

— 1999, 'databased marketing in travel agencies', *Journal of Travel Research*, vol. 37, pp. 231–7.

Oppermann, M., McKinley, S. & Chon, K-S. 1998, 'Marketing sex and tourism destinations', pp. 20–9 in *Sex Tourism and Prostitution: Aspects of Leisure, Recreation and Work*, ed. M. Oppermann, Cognizant Communication Corporation, New York.

Orams, M.B. 1995, 'Towards a more desirable form of ectourism', *Tourism Management*, vol. 16, no. 1, pp. 3–8.

— 1996, 'A conceptual model of tourist-wildlife interaction: the case for education as a management strategy', *Australian Geographer*, vol. 27, no. 1, pp. 39–51.

— 1997, 'Historical accounts of human–dolphin interaction and recent developments in wild dolphin based tourism in Australasia', *Tourism Management*, vol. 18, no. 5, pp. 317–26.

— 1999, *Marine Tourism: Development, Impacts and Management*, Routledge, London.

O'Regan, T. 1988, 'Fair dinkum fillums: the *Crocodile Dundee* phenomenon', pp. 155–75 in *The Imaginary Industry: Australian Film in the Late '80*, eds E. Jacka & S. Dermody, Australian Film Television and Radio School and Media Information Australia, Sydney.

O'Riordan, T. & Turner, R.K. (eds) 1983, *An Annotated Reader in Environmental Planning and Management*, Pergamon Press, Oxford.

Organization for Economic Co-operation and Development (OECD) 1974, *Government Policy in the Development of Tourism*, OECD, Paris.

Ovington, J.D. & Fox, A.M. 1980, 'Wilderness—a natural asset', *Parks*, vol. 5, no. 3, pp. 1–4.

Pacific Asia Tourism Association (PATA) 1998, 'The Asian financial market crisis: Possible impacts on Australian tourism performance', *Issues and Trends, Pacific Asia Travel*, January.

Page, S. 1995, *Urban Tourism*, Routledge, London.

— 1996, 'Urban heritage tourism in New Zealand: The Wellington waterfront development', pp. 281–94 in *Heritage Management in Australia and New Zealand: The Human Dimension*, eds C.M. Hall & S. McArthur, Oxford University Press, Melbourne.

Page, S.J. & Getz, D. (eds) 1997, *The Business of Rural Tourism*, Routledge, London.

Page, S.J. & Hall, C.M. 2003, *Managing Urban Tourism*, Prentice-Hall, Harlow.

Page, S. & Lawton, G. 1997, 'The impact of urban tourism on destination communities: Implications for community tourism planning in Auckland', pp. 209–26 in *Tourism Planning and Policy in Australia and New Zealand: Cases, Issues and Practice*, eds C.M. Hall, J. Jenkins & G. Kearsley, Irwin Publishers, Sydney.

Page, S.J. & Thorn, K. 1997, 'Towards sustainable tourism planning in New Zealand: Public sector planning responses', *Journal of Sustainable Tourism*, vol. 5, no. 1, pp. 59–78.

Palmer, I. 1989, 'Images of regulation: Travel agent legislation and the deregulation debate', *Politics*, vol. 24, no. 2, pp. 13–22.

Palmer, K. (ed.) 1985, *Aborigines and Tourism: A Study of the Impact of Tourism on Aborigines in the Kakadu Region, Northern Territory*, Northern Land Council, Darwin.

Park, D. & Feros, V. 1985, 'Planning for World Expo 88', *Australian Planner*, June, pp. 11–15.

Parker, R.S. 1978, *The Government of New South Wales*, University of Queensland Press, St. Lucia.

Parliamentary Commissioner for the Environment 1997, *Management of the Environmental Effects Associated With the Tourism Sector*, Office of the Parliamentary Commissioner for the Environment, Wellington.

Parsons, M. 1991, 'Altman's tourism dilemmas', *Annals of Tourism Research*, vol. 18, pp. 315–17.

Patmore, J.A. 1983, *Recreation and Resources: Leisure Patterns and Leisure Places*, Blackwell, Oxford.

Patterson, E. & Hagan, J. 1988, *First Australian Masters Games: Analysis Appraisal*, Tasmanian Department of Sport and Recreation, Hobart.

Pawson, E. & Le Heron, R. 1995, *Changing Places: A Geography of Restructuring in New Zealand*, 2nd edn, Longman Paul, Auckland.

Pawson, E. & Scott, G. 1992, 'The regional consequences of economic restructuring: The West Coast, New Zealand (1984–1991)', *Journal of Rural Studies*, vol. 8, no. 4, pp. 373–86.

Pearce, D.G. 1985, 'Tourism and environmental research: A review', *International Journal of Environmental Studies*, vol. 25, pp. 247–55.

— 1987, *Tourism Today: A Geographical Analysis*, Longman Scientific and Technical, Harlow.

— 1989, *Tourism Development*, 2nd edn, Longman Scientific and Technical, Harlow.

— 1992, *Tourist Organizations*, Longman Scientific and Technical, Harlow.

— 1993, 'Domestic tourist travel patterns in New Zealand', *Geojournal*, vol. 29, no. 3, pp. 225–32.

— 1995, *Tourism Today: A Geographical Analysis*, 2nd edn, Longman Scientific and Technical, Harlow.

Pearce, D.W., Barbier, E.B. & Markandya, A. 1986, *Sustainable Development and Cost–Benefit Analysis*, IIED/UCL London Environment Economics Centre, LEEC Paper 88-03.

Pearce, J.A. II 1980, 'Host community acceptance of foreign tourists strategic considerations', *Annals of Tourism Research*, vol. 7, pp. 224–33.

Pearce, P. L. 1982a, *The Social Psychology of Tourist Behaviour*, Pergamon, Oxford.

— 1982b, 'Perceived changes in holiday destinations', *Annals of Tourism Research*, vol. 9, no. 2, pp. 145–64.

— 1988, *The Ulysses Factor: Evaluating Visitors in Tourist Settings*, Springer-Verlag, New York.

— 1990, 'Farm tourism in New Zealand: A social situation analysis', *Annals of Tourism Research*, vol. 17, pp. 337–52.

Pearce, P. L. & Moscardo, G.M. 1985, 'Tourist theme parks: Research practices and possibilities', *Australian Psychologist*, vol. 20, no. 3, pp. 303–12.

— 1986, 'The concept of authenticity in tourist experiences', *Australian and New Zealand Journal of Sociology*, vol. 22, no. 1, pp. 121–32.

Pearson, A. & McKanna, G. 1988, 'The corporate meeting industry', pp. 303–9 in *The Tourism and Hospitality Industry*, ed. J. Blackwell, International Magazine Services, Sydney.

Peters, M. 1969, *International Tourism: The Economics and Development of the International Tourist Trade*, Hutchinson, London.

Phillips, J. 1999, 'Unforgettable war memorials', *New Zealand Defence Quarterly*, vol. 24, pp. 27–31.

Piesse, R.D. 1966, *Travel and Tourism in Australia: An Outline of its History and Growth, Organizational Structure, Development of Facilities, Volume and Value, Research and Survey Aspects*, reprinted for the Official Year Book of the Commonwealth of Australia, No. 52, 1966, Australian National Travel Association, Melbourne.

— 1970, 'Tourism, Aboriginal antiquities and public education', pp. 177–88 in *Aboriginal Antiquities in Australia: Their Nature and Preservation*, ed. F.D. McCarthy, Australian Aboriginal Studies No. 22, Australian Institute of Aboriginal Studies, Canberra.

Pigram, J.J. 1980, 'Environmental implications of tourism development', *Annals of Tourism Research*, vol. 7, pp. 554–83.

— 1985, *Outdoor Recreation and Resource Management*, 2nd edn, Croom Helm, London.

— 1986, Submission to the Australian Government Inquiry into Tourism, unpublished paper, University of New England, Armidale, March.

— 1987, *Tourism in Coffs Harbour: Attitudes, Perceptions and Implications*, North Coast Regional Office, Department of Continuing Education, University of New England, Coffs Harbour.

— 1990, 'Sustainable tourism: Policy considerations', *Journal of Tourism Studies*, vol. 1, no. 2, pp. 2–9.

Pigram, J.J. & Jenkins, J. 1999, *Outdoor Recreation Management*, Routledge, London.

Pizam, A. 1978, 'Tourism's impacts: The social costs to the destination community as perceived by its residents', *Journal of Travel Research*, vol. 16, no. 4, pp. 8–12.

Pizam, A. & Mansfield, Y. (eds) 1996, *Tourism, Crime and International Security Issues*, John Wiley & Sons, Chichester.

Pizam, A. & Pokela, J. 1980, 'The vacation farm: A new form of tourism destination', pp. 203–16 in *Tourism Marketing and Management Issues*, eds D.E. Hawkins, E.L. Shafer & J.M. Rovelstad, George Washington University, Washington, D.C.

Planning Workshop Pty Ltd 1977, *Broken Hill Region Tourist Study*, prepared for NSW Department of Tourism, Planning Workshop, North Sydney.

Plog, S.C. 1974, 'Why destination areas rise and fall in popularity', *The Cornell Hotel and Restaurant Administration Quarterly*, vol. 15, November, pp. 13–16.

Poole, E. 1983, 'Tourism', pp. 82–3 in *What Future for Australia's Arid Lands?*, eds J. Messer & G. Mosley, Australian Conservation Foundation, Hawthorn.

Poon, A. 1997, 'Global transformation: new tourism defined', pp. 47–53 in *The Earthscan Reader in Sustainable Tourism*, ed. L. France, Earthscan Publications, London.

Porter, M. 1990, *The Competitive Advantage of Nations*, Macmillan, London.

Powell, J.M. 1972, *Images of Australia 1788–1914*, Monash Publications in Geography, No. 3, Department of Geography, Monash University, Melbourne.

— 1976, *Conservation and Resource Management in Australia 1788–1914, Guardians, Improvers and Profit: An Introductory Survey*, Oxford University Press, Melbourne.

— 1977, *Mirrors of the New World Images and Image-makers in the Settlement Process*, Dawson/Archon Books, Folkestone/Hamden.

Powell, R., Davidson, B., Hunter, J., Lynn, F., McGovern, M. & Westmore, A. 1987,

The Impact of Tourism Demand on the Coffs Harbour Local Government Area in 1984–85, North Coast Regional Office, Department of Continuing Education, University of New England, Coffs Harbour.

PPK Planning 1993a, *Victor Harbor Tourism Strategy*, PPK Planning in association with Graham Gaston & Associates and Hannaford Benson Ainslie on behalf of Tourism SA and the District Council of Victor Harbor, Adelaide.

— 1993b, *Lower Mid North Region (Clare–Burra) Tourism Strategy*, PPK Planning in association with Hannaford Benson Ainslie on behalf of Tourism SA, the District Councils of Burra Burra, Clare, Riverton and Saddleworth and Auburn, and the Mid North Region Regional Development Board, Adelaide.

Preston, J. A. C. 2000, The touristic implications of film: an examination of the intersection of film and place promotion, unpublished Master of Applied Science thesis, Lincoln University, Christchurch.

Prideaux, B. 1993, 'Possible effects of new transport technologies on the tourism industry in the 21st century', *Papers of the Australasian Transport Research Forum*, vol. 18, no. 1, pp. 245–57.

— 1996, 'The tourism crime cycle: A beach destination case study', pp. 59–75 in *Tourism, Crime and International Security Issues*, eds A. Pizam & Y. Mansfield, John Wiley & Sons, Chichester.

Priskin, J. 2001, 'Assessment of natural resources for nature-based tourism: The case of the Central Coast Region of Western Australia', *Tourism Management*, vol. 22, pp. 637–48.

Prosser, G. 1986, 'The limits of acceptable change: An introduction to a framework for natural area planning', *Australian Parks and Recreation*, vol. 22, no. 2, pp. 5–10.

Proudfoot, P.R. 1986, 'Arcadia and the idea of amenity', *Journal of the Royal Australian Historical Society*, vol. 72, no. 1, pp. 3–18.

Puddicombe, R.A. 1986, 'Australian marine mammals', pp. 255–60 in *Proceedings*, *Australian Environmental Council Coastal Management Conference*, Australian Environmental Council.

Queensland Department of Local Government and Planning (QDLGP) 1997, *Steering Committee Report on Economic Development*, Department of Local Government and Planning, Cairns.

Queensland Tourist and Travel Corporation (QTTC) 1988a, *Annual Report of the Queensland Tourist and Travel Corporation for the Year ended 30 June, 1988*, Parliament of Queensland, Brisbane.

— 1988b, *Queensland Tourism: A Business Perspective*, QTTC, Brisbane.

— 1993, *Annual Report 1993*, QTTC, Brisbane.

— 1997a, *Annual Report 1997*, QTTC, Brisbane.

— 1997b, 'Trends in Queensland's commercial accommodation market', *Trends*, no. 11, p. 2.

— 1997c, *Snapshots*, No. 215/3, March.

— 1997d, 'International tourism trends', *Trends*, no. 11, p. 5.

— 1997e, *Queensland Tourism: A Framework for the Future*, QTTC, Brisbane.

— 1997f, *Queensland Tourist and Travel Corporation: Corporate Plan*, QTTC, Brisbane.

Queenstown-Lakes District Council 2000, *Queenstown Film Friendly*, Queenstown-Lakes District Council, Queenstown.

Randall, G. 1997, *Branding*, Kogan Page, London.

Randall, S. 1999, 'Television representations of food: a case study of "Rick Stein's Taste of the Sea"', *International Tourism and Hospitality Research Journal: The Surrey Quarterly Review*, vol. 1, no. 1, pp. 41–54.

— 2000 'How does the media influence public taste for food and beverage?,' in Wood, R. (ed.) *Strategic Questions in Food and Beverage Management*, Butterworth-Heinemann, Oxford.

Rann, M. 1993, *Marketing Directions for South Australia: A Statement from the Minister of Tourism, Mike Rann*, Office of the Minister of Tourism, Parliament House, Adelaide.

Read, S.E. 1980, 'A prime force in the expansion of tourism in the next decade: Special interest travel', pp. 193–202 in *Tourism Marketing and Management Issues*, eds D.E. Hawkins, E.L. Shafer & J.M. Rovelstad, George Washington University, Washington D.C.

Redclift, M. 1987, *Sustainable Development: Exploring the Contradictions*, Methuen, London.

Rees, W.E. 1989, 'Defining sustainable development', *CHS Research Bulletin*, May, p. 3.

Reid, R. 1995. '"Up North": the *Australia Remembers* veterans' pilgrimage to Papua New Guinea, 29 June to 13 July 1995 (Reflections)', *Journal of the Australian War Memorial*, vol. 27, p. 27.

Reilly, M. 1990, 'Free elicitation of descriptive adjectives for tourism image assessment', *Journal of Travel Research*, vol. 28, no. 4, pp. 21–6.

Relph, E. 1976, *Place and Placelessness*, Pion, London.

Research and Planning Division West Australian Tourism Commission 1986, 'Tourism as a sustainable use of natural resources', pp. 43–52 in *Towards a State Conservation Strategy: Invited Review Papers*, ed. C. McDavitt, Bulletin 251, Department of Conservation and Environment, Perth.

Resource Assessment Commission (RAC)1992a, *Coastal Zone Inquiry: Government Approaches to Coastal Zone Resource Management*, Information Paper No. 1, RAC, Canberra.

— 1992b, *Coastal Zone Inquiry*, Background Paper, RAC, Canberra.

— 1992c, *Coastal Zone Inquiry: Draft Report*, RAC, Canberra.

Rethinking Tourism Project 2000, 'EPA solicits public input on cruise ship discharges—EPA Water News', *RTP Electronic Newsletter*, August 29.

Reynolds, A. 1989, The social, environmental and economic impacts of tourism on the North Coast of New South Wales (as perceived by its residents), unpublished integrated project, School of Resource Science and Management, University of New England, Northern Rivers, Lismore.

Reynolds, G. 1988, The Expo–West End conflicts: Neighbourhood resistance and the politics of urban land use change, unpublished honours thesis, Department of Geography and Oceanography, Australian Defence Force Academy, University of New South Wales, Duntroon.

Reynolds, M. 1988, 'The roles of government in the development of tourism as an economic resource', pp. 65–7 in *The Roles of Government in the Development of Tourism as an Economic Resource*, ed. D. McSwan, Seminar Series No. 1, Centre for Studies in Travel and Tourism, James Cook University, Townsville.

Reynolds, P. & Braithwaite, D. 2001, 'Towards a conceptual framework for wildlife tourism', *Tourism Management*, vol. 22, no.1, pp. 31–42.

Richards, G. (ed.) 1996a, *Cultural Tourism in Europe*, CAB International, Walling-ford.

— 1996b, 'The scope and significance of cultural tourism', pp. 19–45 in *Cultural Tourism in Europe*, ed. G. Richards, CAB International, Wallingford.

Richardson, B. & Richardson, R. 1989, *Business Planning: An Approach to Strategic Management*, Pitman, London.

Richardson, J. 1999, *A History of Australian Travel and Tourism*, Hospitality Press, Melbourne.

Richins, H. & Pearce, P. 2000, 'Influences on tourism development decision making: Coastal local government areas in Eastern Australia', *Journal of Sustainable Tourism*, vol. 8, no. 3, pp. 207–32.

Richter, L.K. 1983, 'Tourism politics and political science—a case of not so benign neglect', *Annals of Tourism Research*, vol. 10, pp. 313–35.

— 1985a, 'Fragmented politics of US tourism', *Tourism Management*, September, pp. 162–73.

— 1985b, 'State-sponsored tourism: A growth field for public administration', *Public Administration Review*, vol. 45, no. 6, pp. 832–9.

— 1987, 'The political dimensions of tourism', pp. 215–27 in *Travel, Tourism and Hospitality Research: A Handbook for Managers and Researchers*, eds J.R.B. Ritchie & C.R. Goeldner, John Wiley & Sons, New York.

— 1989, *The Politics of Tourism in Asia*, University of Hawaii Press, Honolulu.

Richter, L.K. & Richter, W.L. 1985, 'Policy choices in South Asian tourism development', *Annals of Tourism Research*, vol. 12, pp. 201–17.

Riley, R. 1994, 'Movie induced tourism', pp. 453–8 in *Tourism: The Start of the Art*, ed. A. Seaton, John Wiley and Sons, Chichester.

Riley, R., Baker, D. & Van Doren, C.S. 1998, 'Movie induced tourism', *Annals of Tourism Research*, vol. 25, no. 4, pp. 919–35.

Riley, R. & Van Doren, C. 1992, 'Movies as tourism promotion: a "pull" factor in a "push" location', *Tourism Management*, vol. 13, no. 3, pp. 267–74.

Ritchie, J.B.R. 1984, 'Assessing the impact of hallmark events: Conceptual and research issues', *Journal of Travel Research*, vol. 23, no. 1, pp. 2–11.

Ritchie, J.B.R. & Beliveau, D. 1974, 'Hallmark events: An evaluation of a strategic response to seasonality in the travel market', *Journal of Travel Research*, vol. 14 (Fall), pp. 14–20.

Ritchie, J.B.R. & Yangzhou, H. 1987, The role and impact of mega-events and attractions on national and regional tourism: A conceptual and methodological overview, Paper prepared for presentation at the 37th Annual Congress of the International Association of Scientific Experts in Tourism (AIEST), Calgary, Canada.

Ritchie, J.B.R. & Zins, M. 1978, 'Culture as a determinant of the attractiveness of a tourist region', *Annals of Tourism Research*, vol. 5, pp. 252–67.

Ritter, W. & Schafer, C. 1998, 'Cruise-tourism: A chance of sustainability', *Tourism Recreation Research*, vol. 23, no. 1, pp. 65–71.

Ritzer, D. 1996, *The McDonaldisation of Society*. Revised edition, Thousand Oaks, Pine Forge.

Robe Tourism Working Party 1990, *Robe Tourism Strategy*, Tourism South Australia Planning and Development Division, Adelaide.

Roberts, J. 1987, 'Buying leisure', *Leisure Studies*, vol. 6, no. 1, pp. 87–91.

Robinson, J. 1994, 'Tourism', pp. 980–1 in *The Oxford Companion to Wine*, ed. J. Robinson, Oxford University Press, Oxford.

Robinson, O. & Wallace, J. 1984, 'Earnings in hotel and catering industry in Great Britain', *Service Industries Journal*, vol. 4, pp. 143–60.

Roche, M. 1992, 'Mega-events and micro-modernization: On the sociology of the new urban tourism', *British Journal of Sociology*, vol. 43, no. 4, pp. 563–600.

Rockel, I. 1986, *Taking the Waters: Early Spas in New Zealand*, Government Printing Office, Wellington.

Roe, D., Leader-Williams, N. & Dalal-Clayton, B. 1997, *Take Only Photographs, Leave Only Footprints: The Environmental Impacts of Wildlife Tourism*, IIED Wildlife and Development Series No. 10, International Institute for Environment and Development, London.

Romeril, M. 1989, 'Tourism: The environmental dimension', pp. 103–13 in *Progress in Tourism, Recreation and Hospitality Management*, ed. C.P. Cooper, Belhaven Press, London.

Ross, G. 1991a, 'The impact of tourism on regional Australian communities', *Regional Journal of Social Issues*, no. 25, pp. 15–21.

— 1991b, 'Tourist destination images of the Wet Tropical rainforests of North Queensland', *Australian Psychologist*, vol. 26, no. 3, pp. 153–7.

— 1992a, 'Community impacts of tourism among older and long-term residents', *Australian Journal on Ageing*, vol. 10, no. 4, pp. 17–24.

— 1992b, 'Resident perceptions of the impact of tourism on an Australian city', *Journal of Travel Research*, vol. 30, no. 3, pp. 13–17.

Ross, H. 1991, 'Controlling access to environment and self: Aboriginal perspectives on tourism', *Australian Psychologist*, vol. 26, no. 3, pp. 176–82.

Ross, S. & Wall, G. 1999, 'Ecotourism: towards congruence between theory and practice', *Tourism Management*, vol. 20, pp. 123–32.

Rothman, R.A. 1978, 'Residents and transients: Community reaction to seasonal visitors', *Journal of Travel Research*, vol. 16, no. 3, pp. 8–13.

Rothman, R.A., Donnelly, P.G. & Tower, J.K. 1979, 'Police departments in resort communities: Organizational adjustments to population undulation', *Leisure Sciences*, vol. 2, no. 2, pp. 105–18.

Roux, S. 1987, *Up Market with the Arts*, Policy and Planning Division, Australia Council, Sydney.

Rowe, J. 1993, 'Leisure, tourism and "Australianness"', pp. 370–4 in *Leisure and Tourism: Social and Environmental Change*, eds A.J. Veal, P. Jonson & G. Cushman, Centre for Leisure and Tourism Studies, University of Technology, Sydney.

Royal British Legion 2001, *Commonwealth War Cemetery Visits*, The Pilgrimage Department, Royal British Legion Village, Aylesford.

Ruberto, A. 1996, 'Visitors to wine regions', *BTR Tourism Update*, Summer, p. 4.

Runte, A. 1987, *National Parks: The American Experience*, 2nd edn, University of Nebraska Press, Lincoln.

Ryan, C. 1991, *Recreational Tourism: A Social Science Perspective*, Routledge, London.

— 1995, *Researching Tourist Satisfaction: Issues, Concepts, Problems*, Routledge, London.

— 1997, 'Tourism—a mature subject discipline?', *Pacific Tourism Review*, vol. 1, pp. 3–5.

— 2001, 'Academia-industry tourism research links: states of confusion', *Pacific Tourism Review*, vol. 5, no. 3/4, pp. 83–96.

Ryan, C. & Hall, C.M. 2001, *Sex Tourism: Marginal People*, Routledge, London.

Ryan, C., Hughes, K. & Chirgwin, S. 1999, 'The gaze, spectacle and ecotourism', *Annals of Tourism Research*, vol. 27, no. 1, pp. 148–67.

Ryan, C. & Huyton, J. 2000, 'Who is interested in Aboriginal tourism in the Northern Territory, Australia? A cluster analysis', *Journal of Sustainable Tourism*, vol. 8, no. 1, pp. 53–88.

Ryan, C. & Kinder, R. 1996, 'The deviant tourist and the crimogenic place', pp. 23–36 in *Tourism Crime and International Security Issues*, eds A. Pizam & Y. Mansfield, Wiley, Chichester.

Ryan, C., Murphy, H. & Kinder, R. 1998, 'The New Zealand sex industry and tourist demand: illuminating liminalities', *Pacific Tourism Review*, vol. 1, no. 4, pp. 313–28.

Sadler, B. 1990, 'Sustainable development, northern realities and the design and implementation of regional conservation strategies', pp. 3–31 in *Achieving Sustainable Development Through Northern Conservation Strategies*, University of Calgary Press, Calgary.

Sandy, G.A. 1983, *Visitor Industry Report: North West region of Victoria*, Volume Two: Host Community Attitudes to the Visitors, a project financed by the North West Regional Tourist Authority, Footscray Institute of Technology, Footscray.

Sargeant, D. 1988, 'Perspectives on tourism development—industry panel division', pp. 53–6 in *Frontiers of Australian Tourism: The Search for New Perspectives in Policy Development and Research*, eds B. Faulkner & M. Fagence, Bureau of Tourism Research, Canberra.

Saville, B. 1994, 'The development of new hotel projects', *Australian Journal of Hospitality Management*, vol. 1, no. 1, pp. 27–30.

Schiller, N.G., Basch, L., & Blanc-Szanton, C. 1992, 'Transnationalism: a new analytic framework for understanding migration', *Annals New York Academy of Sciences*, vol. 645, pp. 1–24.

Schofield, P. 1996, 'Cinematographic images of a city: alternative heritage tourism in Manchester,' *Tourism Management*, vol. 17, no. 5, pp. 333–40.

Seebohm, K. 1990, A semiotic analysis of the 1990 Sydney Gay and Lesbian Mardi Gras, paper presented at the Institute of Australian Geographers Conference, University of New England, Armidale, September.

Selin, S. 1993, 'Collaborative alliances: new interorganizational forms in tourism', *Journal of Travel and Tourism Marketing*, vol. 2, no. 2/3, pp. 217–27.

— 1998, 'The promise and pitfalls of collaborating', *Trends*, vol. 35, no. 1, pp. 9–13.

Selin, S. & Chavez, D. 1995, 'Developing a collaborative model for environmental planning and management', *Environmental Management*, vol. 19, no. 2, pp. 189–96.

Selin, S. & Myers, N. 1998, 'Tourism marketing alliances: member satisfaction and effectiveness attributes of a regional initiative', *Journal of Travel and Tourism Marketing*, vol. 7, no. 3, pp. 79–94.

Selwood, H.J. & Hall, C.M. 1988, The hidden underbelly: Some observations on the unpublicized impacts of the America's Cup, paper presented to the Canadian Association of Geographers Annual Conference, St. Mary's University, Halifax.

Selwood, H.J. & Jones, R. 1993, 'The America's Cup in retrospect: The aftershock in Fremantle', pp. 656–60 in *Leisure and Tourism: Social and Environ-*

mental Change, eds A.J. Veal, P. Jonson & G. Cushman, Centre for Leisure and Tourism Studies, University of Technology, Sydney.

Selwyn, T. 1994, 'The anthropology of tourism: Reflections on the state of the art', pp. 729–36 in *Tourism: The State of the Art*, eds T. Seaton, C.L. Jenkins, R.C. Wood, P.U.C. Dieke, M.M. Bennett, L.R. MacLellan, & R. Smith, John Wiley, Chichester.

Senate Standing Committee on Environment, Recreation and the Arts 1988, *The Potential of the Kakadu National Park Region*, Senate Standing Committee on Environment, Recreation and the Arts, The Parliament of the Commonwealth of Australia, AGPS, Canberra.

— 1992, *The Australian Environment and Tourism Report*, Senate Standing Committee on Environment, Recreation and the Arts, The Parliament of the Commonwealth of Australia, AGPS, Canberra.

Shackley, M. 1995, 'The future of gorilla tourism in Rwanda', *Journal of Sustainable Tourism*, vol. 3, pp. 61–72.

— 1996, *Wildlife Tourism*, International Thomson Business Press, London.

— (ed.) 1998, *Visitor Management: Case Studies from World Heritage Sites*, Butterworth-Heinemann, Oxford.

Sharp, J. 1988, 'National tourism strategy needed', pp. 73–6 in *Frontiers of Australian Tourism: The Search for New Perspectives in Policy Development and Research*, eds B. Faulkner & M. Fagence, Bureau of Tourism Research, Canberra.

Shaw, B.J. 1985, 'Fremantle and the America's Cup… the spectre of development?', *Urban Policy and Research*, vol. 3, pp. 38–40.

— 1986, *Fremantle W.A. and the America's Cup The Impact of a Hallmark Event*, Australian Studies Centre, University of London.

Shelley, P. 2001, 'Tourism represents one million votes', *Tourism and Hospitality Review*, http://www.tourismreview.com.au/

Shoalhaven City Council 1988, *Tourism in the Shoalhaven: A Profile and Statement of Economic Impact for 1987*, Shoalhaven City Council, Nowra.

Shumway, J.M. & Otterstrom, S.M. 2001, 'Spatial patterns of migration and income change in the Mountain West: The dominance of service-based, amenity rich counties', *Professional Geographer*, vol. 53, no. 4, pp. 492–502.

Simmons, M. 2000, 'Aboriginal heritage art and moral rights', *Annals of Tourism Research*, vol. 2, no. 2, pp. 412–31.

Sindiga, I. 1996, 'Domestic tourism in Kenya', *Annals of Tourism Research*, vol. 23, pp. 19–31.

— 2000, 'Tourism development in Kenya', pp. 129–53 in *The Political Economy of Tourism Development in Africa*, ed. P. Diecke, Cognizant Communications, New York.

Sirgy, M. & Chenting, S. 2000, 'Destination image, self-congruity, and travel behaviour: toward an integrative model', *Journal of Travel Research*, vol. 38, no. 4, pp. 340–52.

Skene, J. 1996, *Estimating Tourism's Economic Contribution*, Research Paper No. 2, Bureau of Tourism Research, Canberra.

Slatyer, R. 1983, 'The origin and evolution of the World Heritage Convention', *Ambio*, vol. 12, nos 3–4, pp. 138–45.

Smith, D. 1977, *Human Geography: A Welfare Approach*, Edward Arnold, London.

Smith, F. 1993, 'Gambling on casinos: Rejuvenated market opens competition', *Weekend Australian*, 27–28 March.

Smith, L.G. 1992, 'From condescension to conflict resolution: adjusting to the changing role of the public in impact assessment', pp. 96–101 in *Proceedings of an International Symposium on Hazardous Materials/Waste: Social Aspects of Facility Planning and Management*, Institute for Social Impact Assessment, Toronto.

Smith, J. 1984, *From Katoomba to Jenolan Caves The Six-Foot Track 1884–1984*, a Megalong Book, Second Back Row Press, Katoomba.

Smith, R. 1989, Farm tourism: Fact or fiction, paper presented at The North Coast Outlook Conference: The Regional Rural Economy, The University of New England and the Department of Agriculture N.S.W., Lismore, 8 August.

Smith, S.L.J. 1988, 'Defining tourism: A supply-side view', *Annals of Tourism Research*, vol. 15, pp. 179–90.

— 1989, *Tourism Analysis A Handbook*, Longman Scientific & Technical, Harlow.

— 1991, 'The supply-side definition of tourism: Reply to Leiper', *Annals of Tourism Research*, vol. 18, pp. 312–18.

— 1993, 'Return to the supply side', *Annals of Tourism Research*, vol. 20, pp. 226–29.

— 1995, *Tourism Analysis: A Handbook*, 2nd edn, Longman, Harlow.

Smith, S.J. & Wilton, D. 1997, 'TSAs and the WTTC/WEFA methodology: different satellites or different planets', *Tourism Economics*, vol. 3, no. 3, pp. 249–65.

Smith, T. 1988, 'Hotel investors/operators—Australia', pp. 182–8 in *The Tourism and Hospitality Industry*, ed. J. Blackwell, International Magazine Services, Sydney.

Smith, V. 1985, 'The Tourism Industry in NSW', pp. 12–15 in *Tourist Developments in Australia*, eds J. Dean & B. Judd, Royal Australian Institute of Architects Education Division, Canberra.

Smith, V.L. 1979, 'Women the taste-makers in tourism', *Annals of Tourism Research*, vol. 6, pp. 49–60.

— (ed.) 1989a, *Hosts and Guests: The Anthropology of Tourism*, 2nd edn, University of Pennsylvania Press, Pennsylvania.

— 1989b, 'Preface', pp. ix–xi in *Hosts and Guests: The Anthropology of Tourism*, 2nd edn, ed. V. Smith, University of Pennsylvania Press, Philadelphia.

Smith, V.L. & Eadington, W.R. (eds) 1992, *Tourism Alternatives: Potentials and Problems in the Development of Tourism*, 2nd edn, University of Pennsylvania Press, Pennsylvania.

Smith, V.L., Hetherington, A. & Brumbaugh, M.D.D. 1986, 'California's Highway 89: A regional tourism model', *Annals of Tourism Research*, vol. 13, pp. 415–423.

Snepenger, D. 1987, 'Segmenting the vacation market by novelty-seeking role', *Journal of Travel Research*, vol. 27, no. 2, pp. 8–14.

Solomon, D. 1990, 'Greens "leaving little chance for consensus"', *The Australian*, 27 August, p. 5.

Sorensen, A.D. & Epps, R. (eds), 1993, *Prospects and Policies for Rural Australia*, Longman Cheshire, South Melbourne.

Sorkin, M. 1992, 'Introduction: variations on a theme park', pp. xi–xv in *Variations on a Theme Park: The New American City and the End of Public Space*, ed. M. Sorkin, Hill and Wang, New York.

Soutar, G.N. & McLeod, P.B. 1993, 'Resident perceptions on impacts of the America's Cup', *Annals of Tourism Research*, vol. 20, pp. 571–82.

South Australian Government 1988, *Tourism in South Australia—Invest in Success*, The Government of South Australia, Adelaide.

South Australian Tourism Commission Act 1993.

South Australian Tourism Commission (SATC) 1996a, *Annual Report 1995–96*, SATC, Adelaide.

— 1996b, *South Australian Tourism Plan 1996–2001*, SATC, Adelaide.

— 1997, *Visitation to Major Attractions and Attendance at Major Events, South Australia* **http://www.tourism.sa.gov.au/visitors.htm** (accessed 20 May 1997).

— 2000, *Visitation to Major Attractions and Major Events in South Australia 1999/2000*, Strategic Services Group. SATC, Adelaide.

— 2001a, *Wine Tourism Market Research*, Research Group. SATC, Adelaide.

— 2001b, *Review of the State Tourism Plan 2001–2006* (Information Sheet), SATC, Adelaide.

— 2002a, *South Australian Tourism Commission*, **http://www.tourism.sa.gov.au/about/default.asp** (accessed 10 March 2002).

— 2002b, *Tourism Policy and Planning*, **http://www.tourism.sa.gov.au/tourism/default.asp** (accessed 10 March 2002).

— 2002c, *SATC Corporate Plan*, SATC, Adelaide.

— 2002d, *South Australian Tourism Indicators*, SATC, Adelaide, **http://www.tourism. sa.gov.au/publications/pubs.asp?archive=0&Pub CatID=1** (accessed 10 march 2002).

South Australian Tourism Development Board 1987a, *Tourism in South Australia. The Strategic Plan. The South Australian Tourism Plan 1987–89*, National Library of Australia, Canberra.

— 1987b, *Tourism in South Australia. The Trends. The Challenge. The Future. A Summary of the South Australian Tourism Plan 1987–89*, National Library of Australia, Canberra.

Spann, R.N. 1979, *Government Administration in Australia*, George Allen and Unwin, Sydney.

Spearitt, P. 1987, 'City and region', pp. 131–9 in *Australians: A Guide to Sources*, eds D.H. Borchardt & V. Crittenden, Australians: A Historical Library, vol. 7, Fairfax, Syme & Weldon, Broadway.

— 1990, 'How we've sold images of Australia', *Australian Society*, vol. 9, no. 11.

Spiegler, A. 1990, 'Sustainable tourism', in *Environment, Tourism and Development: An Agenda for action? A Workshop to Consider Strategies for Sustainable Tourism Development*, 4–10 March 1990, Valletta, Malta, Centre for Environmental Management and Planning, Old Aberdeen.

Sport and Tourism Division, Department of Industry, Science and Resources (DISR) 2001, *Business Plan 2001–2*, DISR, Canberra.

Spring, J. 1988, 'Arts and entertainment in tourism', pp. 349–54 in *Frontiers of Australian Tourism. The Search for New Perspectives in Policy Development and Research*, eds B. Faulkner & M. Fagence, Bureau of Tourism Research, Canberra.

Stabler, M.J. (ed.) 1997, *Tourism and Sustainability: Principles to Practice*, CAB International, Wallingford.

Stanbury, P. (ed.) 1988, *The Blue Mountains Grand Adventure for All*, 2nd edn, The Macleay Museum/Second Back Row Press, Leura.

Standing Committee on State Development 1989, *Coastal Development in New South Wales: Public Concerns and Government Processes*, Discussion Paper No. 2, Legislative Council Standing Committee on State Development, Sydney.

Standing Committee on Tourism and ACT Promotion 1993, *ACT and Region Tourism*, Legislative Assembly for the Australian Capital Territory, The Standing Committee on Tourism and ACT Promotion, Canberra.

Stankey, G.H. 1982, 'Carrying capacity, impact management and the recreation opportunity spectrum', *Australian Parks and Recreation*, May, pp. 24–30.

Stanner, W.E.H. 1965, 'Aboriginal territorial organization, estate, range, domain and regime', *Oceania*, vol. 36, no. 1, pp. 1–26.

Stansfield, C. 1978, 'Atlantic City and the resort cycle: Background to the legalization of gambling', *Annals of Tourism Research*, vol. 5, pp. 238–51.

Stansfield, C.A. Jr. & Rickert, J.F. 1970, 'The recreational business district', *Journal of Leisure Research*, vol. 2, pp. 209–25.

Stanton, J. & Aislabie, C. 1992a, 'Local government regulation and the economics of tourist resort development: An Australian case study', *Journal of Tourism Studies*, vol. 3, no. 2, pp. 20–31.

— 1992b, 'Up-market integrated resorts in Australia', *Annals of Tourism Research*, vol. 19, pp. 435–49.

Statistics Working Group of the Cultural Ministers Council 1996, *Australia's Balance of Trade in Culture*, Department of Communication and the Arts, Canberra.

Stear, L. 1981, 'Design of a curriculum for destination studies', *Annals of Tourism Research*, vol. 8, no. 1, pp. 85–95.

Stehlik, D. & Jennings, G. 1999, 'gendered places and touristic spaces: the case of farm tourism', paper presented to the *Sustaining Rural Environments Conference, Issues in Globalization, Migration and Tourism, 20–23 October, 1999*, University of Northern Arizona, Flagstaff.

Strehlow, T.G.H. 1947, *Aranda Traditions*, Melbourne University Press, Melbourne.

The Sun (Sydney), 14 August 1911.

Swinglehurst, E. 1982, *Cook's Tours: The Story of Popular Travel*, Blandford Press, Poole.

The Sydney Herald, 10 March 1842.

The Sydney Morning Herald, 29 May 1879.

— 17 September 1879.

— 3 October 1888.

Tabata, R.S., Yamashiro, J. & Cherem, G. 1992, *Joining Hands for Quality Tourism: Interpretation, Preservation and the Travel Industry*, Proceedings of the Heritage Interpretation International Third Global Congress, 3–8 November, 1991, Honolulu, Hawaii. University of Hawaii, Sea Grant Extension, Honolulu.

Tallantire, J. 1993, 'Adventure tourism in remote places', pp. 279–94 in *Leisure and the Environment. Essays in Honour of Professor J.A. Patmore*, ed. S. Glyptis, Belhaven Press, New York.

Tapachai, N. & Waryszak, R. 2000, 'An examination of the role of beneficial image in tourist destination selection', *Journal of Travel Research*, vol. 39, pp. 37–44.

Tasmanian Gaming Commission 2001, *Australian Gambling Statistics*, Tasmanian Gaming Commission, Hobart.

Taylor, J. & Bell, M. 1996, 'Population mobility and indigenous peoples: the view from Australia', *International Journal of Population Geography*, vol. 2, pp. 153–69.

Taylor, L. 1990, 'Kelly's tirade prompts talks walkout threat', *The Australian*, 30 August, p. 4.

Taylor, P. & Cupper, P. 1997. *Gallipoli: A Battlefield Guide*, 2nd edn, Kangaroo Press, Sydney.

Tayt, A. 1988, 'Exhibitions', pp. 298–302 in *The Tourism and Hospitality Industry*, ed. J. Blackwell, International Magazine Services, Sydney.

Teleisman-Kosuta, N. 1989, 'Tourism destination image', pp. 557–61 in *Tourism Marketing and Management Handbook*, eds S. Witt & L. Moutinho, New Jersey, Prentice Hall.

Telfer, D.J. 2000, 'Tastes of Niagara: Building strategic alliances between tourism and agriculture', *International Journal of Hospitality and Tourism*, vol. 1, no. 1, pp. 71–88.

— 2001, 'Strategic alliances along the Niagara wine route', *Tourism Management*, vol. 22, no. 1, pp. 21–30.

Telfer, D.J. & Wall, G. 1996, 'Linkages between tourism and food production', *Annals of Tourism Research*, vol. 23, pp. 635–53.

Testoni, L. 2001, 'Planning for sustainable tourism', *Pacific Tourism Review*, vol. 4, pp. 191–9.

The Numbers 2000, 'All time top 20 movies at the box office', *The Numbers—Box Office Data, Movie Stars, Idle Speculation*. **http://www.the-numbers.com/ movies/records/index.htm** (accessed 7th June 2001).

Thirlwell, T. 1997, 'Atlanta revisited', *Tourism Now*, no. 25, April, p. 5.

Thomas Cook and Son 1889, *Memoranda for Travellers to Australasia and Useful Hints*, Thomas Cook and Son, London.

Thomas, I. 1998, 'Chiefs' tour down lobby lane', *Australian Financial Review*, 13 March, p. 24.

Thorne, R. & Munro-Clark, M. 1989, 'Hallmark events as an excuse for autocracy in urban planning: A case history', pp. 154–72 in *The Planning and Evaluation of Hallmark Events*, eds G.J. Syme, B.J. Shaw, D.M. Fenton & W.S. Mueller, Avebury, Aldershot.

Thorne, R., Munro-Clark, M. & Boers, J. 1987, 'Hallmark events as an excuse for autocracy in urban planning: A case history', in *The Effects of Hallmark Events on Cities*, Centre for Urban Research, University of Western Australia, Nedlands.

Thorsell, J. & Sigaty, T. 2001, 'Human use in World Heritage natural sites: a global inventory', *Tourism Recreation Research*, vol. 26, no. 1, pp. 85–101.

Tighe, A.J. 1985, 'Cultural tourism in the U.S.A.', *Tourism Management*, vol. 6, no. 4, pp. 234–51.

— 1986, 'The arts/tourism partnership', *Journal of Travel Research*, vol. 24, no. 3, pp. 2–5.

Tilt, W.C. 1985, 'From whaling to whale watching', *Transactions of the 52nd National American Wildlife and Natural Resources Conference*, vol. 2, no. 1, pp. 34–6.

Timo, N. 1994, 'Enterprise bargaining in the Australian hospitality industry', *Australian Journal of Hospitality Management*, vol. 1, no. 1, pp. 31–6.

Tolhurst, C. 1990, 'Eye on the environment', *Tourism Travel and Management*, April, pp. 8–11.

— 1994, 'Tourism industry worried about training resources', *Australian Financial Review*, 29 March, p. 40.

Tomlinson, J. 1991, *Cultural Imperialism: A Critical Introduction*, John Hopkins Press, Baltimore.

Tooke, N. & Baker, M. 1996, 'Seeing is believing: the effect of film on visitor numbers to screened locations', *Tourism Management*, vol. 17, no. 2, pp. 87–94.

Tourism Commission of New South Wales 1985, *Annual Report February–June 1985*, Tourism Commission of New South Wales, Sydney.

— 1987a, *North Coast Region Tourism Development Strategy*, Tourism Commission of New South Wales on behalf of the North Coast Advisory Committee, Tourism Commission of New South Wales, Sydney.

— 1987b, *Tourism Development Strategy for New South Wales*, Tourism Commission of New South Wales, Sydney.

— 1988, *Annual Report 1987–1988*, Tourism Commission of New South Wales, Sydney.

— 1991, *Annual Report 1990–1991*, Tourism Commission of New South Wales, Sydney.

Tourism Forecasting Council (TFC) 1995, 'An encouraging but patchy recovery for hotels and motels', *Forecast*, The Second Report of the Forecasting Council, April, pp. 24–6.

— 1997a, 'A healthy outlook for inbound tourism', *Forecast*, The Sixth Report of the Forecasting Council, vol. 3, no. 2, pp. 5–15.

— 1997b, 'Accommodation still strong but challenges ahead', *Forecast*, The Sixth Report of the Forecasting Council, vol. 3, no. 2, pp. 16–22.

— 1997c, *Short, Sharp Shock Or Lower Growth Outlook?*, Special Report No. 1, Tourism Forecasting Council, Canberra.

— 1997d, 'Compendium', *Forecast*, The Sixth Report of the Forecasting Council, vol. 3, no. 2, pp. 32–7.

Tourism Industry Association of New Zealand (TIA) 2002, *T-mail* (e-newsletter), 15 February.

Tourism Industry Working Group 2001, *Bulletin*, report No. 4, 4 October.

Tourism New Zouth Wales (TNSW) 1996a, *New South Wales Tourism Masterplan*, TNSW, Sydney.

— 1996b, *Food & Wine in Tourism: A Plan*, TNSW, Sydney.

— 1997a, *Corporate Plan and 1997/1998 Operational Plan*, TNSW, Sydney.

— 1997b, *Working With You: A Guide to Our Programs and Services for 1997/98*, TNSW, Sydney.

— 1997c, *New South Wales Tourism Masterplan: Fact Sheet*, TNSW, Sydney.

— 1997d, *Annual Report 1996/97*, TNSW, Sydney.

— 1997e, 'Sydney's brand new image', *News*, Spring, p. 1.

— 1997f, *Sydney 2000: Tourism and the 2000 Games Fact Sheet*, TNSW, Sydney.

— 1997g, 'Olympic visitor boost', *News*, Spring, p. 9.

— 2000, *Tourism New South Wales Annual Report 1999–2000*, TNSW, Sydney, **http://www.tourism.nsw.gov.au/corporate/downloads/Annualreport.pdf** (accessed 15 June 2001).

— 2001, *Tourism New South Wales Annual Report 2000–2001*, TNSW, Sydney.

— 2002, Brand New South Wales—'Feel free', TNSW, Sydney, **http://www.tourism. nsw.gov.au/corporate/branding/feelfree.asp** (accessed 10 March 2002).

Tourism Queensland (TQ) 2000a, *Fact Sheet—Queensland*. Tourism Queensland, Brisbane.

— 2001a, *Domestic Marketing*, **www.tq.com.au.hwchy.dommkt.html** (accessed 5 May 2001).

— 2001b, *Annual Report 2000–2001*, Tourism Queensland, Brisbane.

Tourism South Australia 1988, *Annual Report 1987/1988*, Tourism South Australia, Adelaide.

— 1989a, *South Australian Tourism Product Strategy*, Tourism South Australia, Adelaide.

— 1989b, *Tourism South Australia: Environmental Code of Practice*, Tourism South Australia, Adelaide.

— 1990, *Planning for Tourism: A Handbook for South Australia*, Tourism South Australia, Adelaide.

— 1991, *Making South Australia Special: South Australian Tourism Plan 1991–1993*, Tourism South Australia, Adelaide.

— 1992, *Cultural Tourism: The Rewarding Experience*, Cultural Tourism Committee, Tourism South Australia, Adelaide.

Tourism Tasmania (TT) 1997a, *1996/97 Annual Report*, Tourism Tasmania, Hobart.

— 1997b, *Tasmania Visitor Survey Bulletin 1996/97*, Tourism Tasmania, Hobart.

— 2000, *Tourism Tasmania: Tasmanian Visitor Survey 1999/2000*, Tourism Tasmania, Hobart, **http://www.tourismtasmania.com.au/pdf/tvs99_2000. pdf** (accessed 7 May 2001).

— 2002a, *About Tourism Tasmania*, **http://www.tourismtasmania.com.au/org/ org_units/theorg.html** (accessed 10 March 2002).

— 2002b, *Corporate Plan*, **http://www.tourismtasmania.com.au/org/ corp_plan/2001_plan.html** (accessed 10 March 2002).

— 2002c, *The Contribution of Tourism to the Tasmanian Economy in 1998*, **http://www.tourismtasmania.com.au/corp/research/Crea98.html** (accessed 10 March 2002).

Tourism Training Review Group 1986, *Tourism Training in Australia: Future Needs, Report to the Minister for Sport, Recreation and Tourism*, prepared by the Tourism Training Committee, Department of Sport, Recreation and Tourism, Canberra.

Tourism Victoria 1993, *Annual Report 1992–93*, Tourism Victoria, Melbourne.

— 1995, *Building Tourism: Guidelines for Tourism Development in Victoria*, Tourism Victoria, Melbourne.

— 1997a, *Annual Report 1996–97*, Tourism Victoria, Melbourne.

— 1997b, *Strategic Business Plan 1997–2001: Building Partnerships*, Tourism Victoria, Melbourne.

— 1997c, *Planning Tourism Taking a Concept to Reality: Planning Guidelines for Local Councils and Developers*, Tourism Victoria, Melbourne.

— 2000, *Tourism Victoria Annual Report 1999–2000*. Tourism Victoria, Melbourne, **http://www.tourismvictoria.com.au/HTML_Documents/about_tv/Annual Report.pdf** (accessed 7 May 2001).

— 2000b, *International Travel to Victoria: Summary Results 1998*, **http://www.tourismvictoria.com.au/HTML_Documents/research/research _kit/int_travel_victoria.pdf** (accessed 7 May 2001).

— 2001, *Tourism Victoria Strategic Business Plan 1997–2001*, **http://www.tourism victoria.com.au/HTML_Documents/about_tv/business_plan_home.htm** (accessed 7 May 2001).

— 2002a, *Tourism Victoria Strategic Plan 2002–2006, Fact Sheet No. 1, Strategic Plan Overview*, Tourism Victoria, Melbourne, **http://www.tourismvictoria. com.au/strategic_plan/index.htm** (accessed 10 March 2002).

— 2002b, *Mission Statement*, Tourism Victoria, Melbourne, **http://www.tourism victoria.com.au/documents/about_tv/mission_statement.htm** (accessed 10 March 2002).

Town Planning Department, City of Wollongong 1983, *Tourism and Wollongong A Report on the Prospects for the Development of Tourism in the Wollongong Area*, Town Planning department, City of Wollongong, Wollongong.

Towner, J. 1996, *An Historical Geography of Recreation and Tourism in the Western World 1540–1940*, John Wiley, Chichester.

Travelstrength Limited 1988, *Travelling*, Travelstrength Limited, Sydney.

Travelweek Australia 1994, 'Monitor', *Travelweek Australia*, no. 815, 16 March, p. 2.

Tribe, J. 1997, 'The indiscipline of tourism', *Annals of Tourism Research*, vol. 24, pp. 638–57.

Tuan, Y–F. 1974, 'Space and place: Humanistic perspectives', *Progress in Geography*, vol. 6, pp. 211–52.

Tucker, R., Green, P. & Lewis, S. 1986, 'Offroad recreational vehicles in South Australia', pp. 325–31 in *Proceedings, Australian Environmental Council Coastal Management Conference*, Australian Environmental Council.

Tunbridge, J.E. & Ashworth, G.J. 1996, *Dissonant Heritage: The Management of the Past as a Resource in Conflict*, John Wiley & Sons, Chichester.

Turner, C. & Manning, P. 1988, 'Placing authenticity—on being a tourist: A reply to Pearce and Moscardo', *Australian and New Zealand Journal of Sociology*, vol. 24, no. 1, pp. 136–9.

Turner, L. & Ash, J. 1975, *The Golden Hordes: International Tourism and the Pleasure Periphery*, Constable, London.

Turner, V. 1969, *The Ritual Process—Structure and Anti-structure*, Routledge and Kegan Paul, London.

— 1973, 'The centre out there; the pilgrim's goal', *History of Religions*, vol. 12, no. 3, pp. 191–230.

— 1974, 'Liminal to liminoid in play, flow and ritual; an essay in comparative symbology', *Rice Universities Studies*, vol. 60, pp. 53–92.

— 1982, *From Ritual to Theater: The Human Seriousness of Play*, PAJ Publications, New York.

Turner, V. & Turner, E. 1978, *Image and Pilgrimage in Christian Culture*, Columbia University Press, New York.

Tweed, D.M. & Hall, C.M. 1991, 'The management of quality in the service sector: An end in itself or a means to an end?', in *Australian and New Zealand Association of Management Educators Conference Proceedings*, Bond University, Queensland.

United Nations 1994, *Recommendations on Tourism Statistics*, United Nations, New York.

United Nations Centre on Transnational Corporations 1982, *Transnational Corporations in International Tourism*, United Nations Centre on Transnational Corporations, New York.

United Nations Educational, Scientific and Cultural Organisation Intergovernmental Committee for the Protection of the Worlds Cultural and Natural Heritage 1999, *Operational Guidelines for the Implementation of the World Heritage Convention*, UNESCO, Paris. **http://www.unesco.org/whc/toc/mainf8.htm**

United Nations Environment Programme (UNEP) 1995, *Environmental Codes of Conduct for Tourism*, United Nations Environment Programme—Industry and Environment, Paris.

Upper Yarra Valley and Dandenong Ranges Authority 1988, *Draft Tourism Strategy for the Upper Yarra Valley and Dandenong Ranges Region*, Upper Yarra Valley and Dandenong Ranges Authority, Lilydale.

Urdde, M. 1999, 'Brand orientation: a mindset for building brands into strategic resources', Journal of Marketing Management, vol. 15, nos. 1–3, pp. 117–33.

Urry, J. 1987, 'Some social and spatial aspects of services', *Environment and Planning D: Society and Space*, vol. 5, pp. 5–26.

— 1990, *The Tourist Gaze: Leisure and Travel in Contemporary Societies*, Sage Publications, London.

— 2000, *Sociology Beyond Societies: Mobilities for the Twenty-First Century*, Routledge, London.

Uysal, M. & Crompton, J.L. 1985, 'An overview of approaches used to forecast tourism demand', *Journal of Travel Research*, Spring, pp. 7–15.

Vader, J. & Lang, F. 1980, *The Gold Coast: An Illustrated History*, The Jacaranda Press, Milton.

Valentine, P. 1984, 'Wildlife and tourism: Some ideas on potential and conflict', pp. 29–54 in *Contemporary Issues in Australian Tourism*, 19th Institute of Australian Geographer's Conference and International Geographical Union Sub-Commission on Tourism in the South West Pacific, ed. B. O'Rourke, Department of Geography, University of Sydney, Sydney.

— 1992, 'Review. Nature-based tourism', in *Special Interest Tourism*, eds B. Weiler & C.M. Hall, Belhaven Press, London.

Van Der Lee, P. 1990, 'The domestic market under the microscope', paper presented at *Tourism: The Way Ahead*, Australian Tourism Research Institute & Bureau of Tourism Research, Sydney.

Van Der Lee, P. & Williams, J. 1986, 'The Grand Prix and tourism', pp. 124–50 in *The Adelaide Grand Prix: The Impact of a Special Event*, eds J.P.A. Mules, J.H. Hatch & T.L. Mules, The Centre for South Australian Economic Studies, Adelaide.

Vas, A.C. 1999, 'Jobs follow people in the rural rocky Mountain West', *Rural Development Perspectives*, vol. 14, no. 2, pp. 14–23.

Victoria 1988, *A Coastal Policy for Victoria, Victoria—Protecting Our Environment A State Conservation Strategy Initiative*, Government Printer, Melbourne.

Victorian Parliament Economic Budget Review Committee 1985, *Report on the Wine Industry in Victoria*, Parliament of Victoria, Melbourne.

Victorian Tourism Commission (VTC) 1984, *Regional Tourism Policy*, VTC, Melbourne.

— 1988, *Victorian Tourism Commission Annual Report 1986–87*, VTC, Melbourne.

Vukonic, B. 1997, 'Selective tourism growth: targeted tourism destinations', pp. 95–108 in *Tourism, Development and Growth: The Challenge of Sustainability*, eds S. Wahab & J. Pigrim, Routledge, London.

Waits, M.J. 2000, 'The added value of the industry cluster approach to economic analysis, strategy development, and service delivery', *Economic Development Quarterly*, vol. 14, pp. 35–50.

Waitt, G. 1999, 'Playing games with Sydney: marketing Sydney for the 2000 Olympics', *Urban Studies*, vol. 36, no. 7, pp. 1055–77.

Wales, K.A. 1976, Tourism and the economy of Richmond-Tweed, unpublished B.A. honours thesis, Department of Geography, Monash University, Clayton.

Walkley, P. 1993, 'Why casinos may not be the best bet', *Australian Financial Review*, 29 April, p. 40.

Wall, G. 1994, 'Ecotourism: Old wine in new bottles?', *Trends*, vol. 31, no. 2, pp. 4–9.

— 1997, 'Is ecotourism sustainable?', *Environmental Management*, vol. 21, no. 4, pp. 483–91.

Wall, G. & Wright, C. 1977, *The Environmental Impact of Outdoor Recreation*, Publication Series No. 11, Department of Geography, University of Waterloo.

Walmsley, D.J., Boskovic, R.M. & Pigram, J.J. 1981, *Tourism and Crime*, Report undertaken through a Criminology Research Council Grant, Department of Geography, University of New England, Armidale.

— 1983, 'Tourism and crime: An Australian perspective', *Journal of Leisure Research*, vol. 15, pp. 136–55.

Walmsley, D.J. & Jenkins. J.M. 1993, 'Appraisive images of tourist areas: application of personal constructs', *Australian Geographer*, vol. 24, no. 2, pp. 1–13.

Walmsley, D.J. & Young, M. 1998, 'Evaluative images and tourism: the use of personal constructs to describe the structure of destination images', *Journal of Travel Research*, vol. 36, pp. 65–9.

Walton, J. 1983, *The English Seaside Resort: A Social History 1750–1914*, Leicester University Press, Leicester.

Walton, T., Ward, T., McInerney, J. & Sparks, B. 2000, 'The future of tourism—an online debate by experts in the field', *Tourism and Hospitality Research*, vol. 2, no. 4, pp. 378–82.

Wanhill, S.R.C. 1987, 'UK—politics and tourism', *Tourism Management*, vol. 8, no. 1, pp. 54–8.

Warnken, J. & Buckley, R. 1995, 'Triggering EIA in Queensland—a decade of tourism development', *Environmental Policy and Law*, vol. 25, no. 6, pp. 340–7.

— 2000, 'Monitoring diffuse impacts: Australian tourism developments', *Environmental Management*, vol. 25, no. 4, pp. 453–61.

Waters, M. 1995, *Globalization*, Routledge, London.

Waters, S.R. 1967, 'Trends in international tourism', *Development Digest*, vol. 5, pp. 57–62.

Waterways Commission 1982, *Managing an Estuary: An Overview of a Management Programme for the Peel Inlet and Harvey Estuary and their Environs*, Waterways Commission/Peel Inlet Management Authority, Perth.

Watson, S. 1991, 'Gilding the smokestacks: The new symbolic representation of deindustrialised regions', *Environment and Planning D: Society and Space*, vol. 9, pp. 59–70.

Wearing, R.J. 1981, *Tourism: Blessing for Bright*, Australian Institute for Urban Studies, Canberra.

Weaver, D. 2001, *Ecotourism*, John Wiley & Sons Australia, Brisbane.

Weaver, D.B. & Lawton, L.J. 2001, 'Resident perceptions in the urban-rural fringe', *Annals of Tourism Research*, vol. 28, no. 2, pp. 439–58.

Weaver, T. & Dale, D. 1978, 'Trampling effects of hikers, motorcycles and horses in meadows and forests', *Journal of Applied Ecology*, vol. 15, pp. 451–57.

Webb, R. 2002, 'How will Victoria fare post-Ansett?' *The Sunday Age*, 3 March.

Weigh, J. 1988, 'The role of government in tourism research', pp. 37–40 in *The Roles of Government in the Development of Tourism as an Economic Resource*, ed. D. McSwan, Seminar Series No. 1, Centre for Studies in Travel and Tourism, James Cook University, Townsville.

Weiler, B. (ed.) 1992, *Ecotourism Incorporating The Global Classroom, 1991 International Conference Papers*, Bureau of Tourism Research, Canberra.

Weiler, B. & Hall, C.M. (eds) 1992, *Special Interest Tourism*, Belhaven Press, London.

Wells, J. 1996, 'Marketing indigenous heritage: A case study of Uluru National Park', pp. 220–30 in *Heritage Management in Australia and New Zealand: The Human Dimension*, eds C.M. Hall & S. McArthur, Oxford University Press, Melbourne.

Wells, L. 1982, *Sunny Memories: Australians at the Seaside*, Greenhouse Publications, Richmond.

Wentworth, W. C. 1873, *Australasia: A Poem*, Whittaker and Co., London.

West, G. 1989, 'Tapping into tourism', *Another World*, vol. 1, pp. 1, 4.

West, G.R. 1993, 'Economic significance of tourism in Queensland', *Annals of Tourism Research*, vol. 20, pp. 490–504.

The *West Australian*, 22 November 1962.

West Australian Tourism Commission (WATC) 1991, *1991 Annual Report*, WATC, Perth.

— 1992, *1992 Annual Report*, WATC, Perth.

— 1996, *Partnership Western Australia Developing Brand Western Australia: Summary of Market Research in Key South East Asian and Australian Markets*, WATC, Perth.

— 1997a, *Nature Based Tourism Strategy for Western Australia, Report by the Nature Based Tourism Advisory Committee*, WATC, Perth.

— 1997b, *1997 Annual Report*, WATC, Perth.

— 1997c, *Corporate Plan 1997–2001*, WATC, Perth.

— 1997d, *Research Brief on Tourism June 1997*, WATC, Perth.

— 1997e, *Tourism Research Brief on Daytripping*, WATC, Perth.

— 2000a, *Annual Report 1999–2000*, WATC, Perth.

— 2000b, *Partnership 21: 2001–2005 Tourism Industry Plan: A Working Strategy Reviewed Annually*, http://www.tourism.wa.gov.au//pdfs/p21master.pdf (accessed 24 May 2001).

— 2001, *Research Brief on Tourism*. http://www.tourism.wa.gov.au/pdf/RBTFeb2001.pdf (accessed 5 May 2001).

Westcott, R.L. 1988, 'Establishing an exhibition centre', pp. 251–4 in *The Tourism and Hospitality Industry*, ed. J. Blackwell, International Magazine Services, Sydney.

Western Australian Police Department 1986, *America's Cup Defence Operational Orders*, America's Cup Division, Western Australian Police Department, Perth.

— 1987, *America's Cup Division De-Briefing Report*, America's Cup Division, Western Australian Police Department, Perth.

Westwood, S., Morgan, N., Pritchard, A. & Ineson, E. 1999, 'Branding the package holiday: the role and significance of brands for UK air tour operators', *Journal of Vacation Marketing*, vol. 5, no. 3, pp. 238–52.

Wet Tropics Management Authority 1992, *Wet Tropics Plan: Strategic Directions*, Wet Tropics Management Authority, Cairns.

— 1994, 'Community Attitudes Survey 1993', *Wet Tropics Update: Wet Tropics World Heritage Area Newsletter*, no. 5, January, pp. 2–4.

— 1995, *Draft Wet Tropics Plan: Protection Through Partnerships*, Wet Tropics Management Authority, Cairns.

— 1997, *Protection Through Partnerships, Policies for Implementation of the Wet Tropics Plan*, Wet Tropics Management Authority, Cairns.

Wheeler, B. 1994, 'Ecotourism, sustainable tourism and the environment—a symbiotic, symbolic or shambolic relationship?', pp. 655–64 in *Tourism: The State of the Art*, eds A.V. Seaton, C.L. Jenkins, R.C. Wood, P.U.C. Dieke, M.M. Bennett, L.R. MacLellan & R. Smith, John Wiley, Chichester.

Wickens, E. 1994, 'Consumption of the authentic: the hedonistic tourist in Greece', pp. 818–25 in *Tourism: The State of the Art*, eds A.V. Seaton, C.L. Jenkins, R.C. Wood, P.U.C. Dieke, M.M. Bennett, L.R. MacLellan & R. Smith, John Wiley, Chichester.

Wight, P. A. 1993, 'Sustainable ecotourism: Balancing economic, environmental and social goals within an ethical framework', *Journal of Tourism Studies*, vol. 4, no. 2, pp. 54–66.

— 1998, 'Tools for sustainability analysis in planning and managing tourism and recreation in the destination', in *Sustainable Tourism Development: A Geographical Perspective*, eds C.M. Hall & A. Lew, Addison Wesley Longman, London.

Wilderness News 1988, 'Tourism and wilderness—a natural combination?', *Wilderness News*, vol. 9, no. 4, pp. 12–13.

Wilderness Society 1988, *Submission to the Industries Assistance Commission Inquiry into Travel and Tourism*, The Wilderness Society, Hobart.

Wilks, J., Watson, B. & Faulks, I.J. 1999, 'International tourists and road safety in Australia: developing a national research and management programme [work in progress],' *Tourism Management*, vol. 20, no. 5, pp. 645–54.

Williams, A.M. & Hall, C.M. 2000, 'Tourism and migration: new relationships between production and consumption', *Tourism Geographies*, vol. 2, no. 1, pp. 5–27.

— 2002, 'Tourism, migration, circulation and mobility: The contingencies of time and place', in *Tourism and Migration: New Relationships Between Consumption and Production*, eds C.M. Hall & A.M. Williams, Kluwer, Dortrecht.

Williams, A.M., King, R., Warnes, A. & Patterson, G. 2000, 'Tourism and international retirement migration: new forms of an old relationship in southern Europe', *Tourism Geographies*, vol. 2, pp. 28–49.

Williams, A.M. & Shaw, G. 1988a, 'Tourism and development: Introduction', pp. 1–11 in *Tourism and Economic Development: Western European Experiences*, eds A.M. Williams & G. Shaw, Belhaven Press, London.

— 1988b, 'Western European tourism in perspective', pp. 12–38 in *Tourism and Economic Development: Western European Experiences*, eds A.M. Williams & G. Shaw, Belhaven Press, London.

— 1988c, 'Tourism policies in a changing economic environment', pp. 230–9 in *Tourism and Economic Development: Western European Experiences*, eds A.M. Williams & G. Shaw, Belhaven Press, London.

— 1998, 'Tourism and the environment: sustainability and economic restructuring,' pp. 45–59 in *Sustainable Tourism Development: Geographical Perspectives*, eds C.M. Hall & A.A. Lew, Addison Wesley Longman, Harlow.

Williams, D.R. & Kaltenborn, B.P. 1999, 'Leisure places and modernity: the use and meaning of recreational cottages in Norway and the USA', pp. 214–30 in *leisure/tourism geographies: practices and geographical knowledge*, ed. D. Crouch, Routledge, London.

Williams, P. W. 1987, 'Evaluating environmental impact and physical carrying capacity in tourism', pp. 385–97 in *Travel, Tourism, and Hospitality Research A Handbook for Managers and Researchers*, eds B. Ritchie & C. Goeldner, John Wiley & Sons, New York.

Williams, R.J. & Smith, R.J. 1986, 'Tourism in estauries', pp. 349–51 in *Proceedings, Australian Environmental Council Coastal Management Conference*, Australian Environmental Council.

Williams, S. 1998, *Tourism Geography*, Routledge, London.

Wilson, C. 1996, Landscapes in the Living Room: Heartland Documentaries and the Construction of Place, Unpublished MSocSc. Thesis, University of Waikato, Hamilton.

Wilson, C. & Tisdell, C. 2001, 'Sea-turtles as a non-consumptive tourism resource especially in Australia', *Tourism Management*, vol. 22, no. 3, pp. 279–88.

Winter, D. 1994, *25 April 1915—The Inevitable Tragedy*, University of Queensland Press, St. Lucia.

Witt, S.F. & Martin, C.A. 1988, 'Forecasting performance', *Tourism Management*, vol. 9, no. 4, pp. 326–9.

Witt, S.F. & Witt, C.A. 1992, *Modelling and Forecasting Demand in Tourism*, Academic Press, London.

Wood, J.T.D. 1982, 'Along the Ghan Track', *Heritage Australia*, vol. 1, no. 1, pp. 56–63.

Wood, K. & House, S.L. 1991, *The Good Tourist*, Mandarin, London.

Wood, R.E. 2000, 'Caribbean cruise tourism: globalization at sea', *Annals of Tourism Research*, vol. 27, no. 2, pp. 345–70.

Woods, L.E. 1983, *Land Degradation in Australia*, Australian Government Publishing Service, Canberra.

Woodside, A.G. & Sherrell, D. 1977, 'Traveler evoked, inept, and inert sets of vacation destinations', *Journal of Travel Research*, vol. 16, no. 1, pp. 14–18.

Woodward, I. 2000, *Why Should The UK's Tourism Industry Be Interested in 'Bollywood' Films?* Tourism Intelligence Papers. British Tourism Authority. London, July.

Wootton, G. & Stevens, T. 1995, 'Business tourism: A study of the market for hotel-based meetings and its contribution to Wales's tourism', *Tourism Management*, vol. 16, no. 4, pp. 305–15.

Worland, D. & Wilson, K. 1988, 'Employment and labour costs in the hospitality industry: Evidence from Victoria, Australia', *International Journal of Hospitality Management*, vol. 7, no. 4, pp. 363–77.

World Commission on Environment and Development (the Brundtland Report) 1987, *Our Common Future*, Oxford University Press, London.

World Tourism Organization (WTO) 1976, *Economic Review of World Tourism*, WTO, Madrid.

— 1980, *Physical Planning and Area Development for Tourism*, WTO, Madrid.

— 1981, *Technical Handbook on the Collection and Presentation of Domestic and International Tourist Statistics*, WTO, Madrid.

— 1984, *Economic Review of World Tourism*, WTO, Madrid.

— 1985, *The state's role in protecting and promoting culture as a factor of tourism development and the proper use and exploitation of national cultural heritage of sites and movements for tourism*, WTO, Madrid, 28 June.

— 1986, *The Role of Recreation Management in the Development of Active Holidays and Special Interest Tourism and the Consequent Enrichment of the Holiday Experience*, WTO, Madrid.

— 1991, *Resolutions of International Conference on Travel and Tourism, Ottawa, Canada*, WTO, Madrid.

— 1998, *WTO Revises Forecasts for Asian Tourism*, Press Release 27/1/98, WTO, Madrid.

— 2001a, *Approval of the Global Code of Ethics for Tourism*, WTO, Madrid, **http://www.world.org/projects/ethics/preamble.htm**

— 2001b, *Tourism 2020 Vision*, WTO, Madrid.

— 2002a, 'World tourism stalls in 2001', WTO Press release, WTO, Madrid, 29 January.

WTO & United Nations Environment Program 1982, *Joint Declaration Between World Tourism Organization and the United Nations Environment Program*, WTO, Madrid.

World Travel and Tourism Council 1996, *Australia Travel & Tourism: Millennium Vision*, World Travel and Tourism Council, Brussels.

— 1997, 'Rejoinder: from the World Travel and Tourism Council', *Tourism Economics*, vol. 3, no. 3, pp. 282–8.

Wright, B. 1988, 'The co-ordinating, legislative and regulatory roles of government', pp. 29–33 in *The Roles of Government in the Development of Tourism as an Economic Resource*, ed. D. McSwan, Seminar Series No. 1, Centre for Studies in Travel and Tourism, James Cook University, Townsville.

Wright, B. & King, B. 1983, 'Tourism', pp. 169–70 in *What Future for Australia's Arid Lands*, eds J. Messer & G. Mosley, Australian Conservation Foundation, Hawthorn.

Yabsley, M. 1991, 'NSW Committed to Research', *Australian Financial Review*, 5 November.

Yapp, G. 1986, 'Aspects of population, recreation and management of the Australian coastal zone', *Coastal Management*, vol. 14, pp. 47–66.

Yencken, D. 1985, *Australia's National Estate: The Role of the Commonwealth*, Australian Heritage Commission, Special Australian Heritage Publication Series No. 1, Australian Government Publishing Service, Canberra.

Young, G. 1973, *Tourism: Blessing or Blight?*, Penguin, Harmondsworth.

Younger, S. 1988, Planning for vacation farms in Bellingen Shire, unpublished Bachelor of Urban and Regional Planning dissertation, Department of Urban and Regional Planning, University of New England, Armidale.

Yuan T., Fridgen J., Hsieh S. & O'Leary J. 1995, 'Visiting friends and relatives travel market: the Dutch case', *Journal of Tourism Studies*, vol. 6, no. 1, pp. 19–26.

Zeppel, H. & Hall, C.M. 1992, 'Review: Arts and heritage tourism', pp. 47–68 in *Special Interest Tourism*, eds B. Weiler & C.M. Hall, Belhaven Press, London.

Zukin, S. 1991, *Landscapes of Power: From Detroit to Disney World*, University of California Press, Berkeley.

INDEX

INTRODUCTION TO TOURISM